$9-
8193

THE SPIRIT OF
WESTERN PHILOSOPHY

THE SPIRIT OF
Western Philosophy

A Historical Interpretation
Including Selections
from the
Major European Philosophers

->>>-<<<-

NEWTON P. STALLKNECHT
Indiana University

ROBERT S. BRUMBAUGH
Indiana University

LONGMANS, GREEN and Co.
NEW YORK · LONDON · TORONTO
1950

LONGMANS, GREEN AND CO., INC.
55 FIFTH AVENUE, NEW YORK 3

LONGMANS, GREEN AND CO. Ltd.
6 & 7 CLIFFORD STREET, LONDON W 1

LONGMANS, GREEN AND CO.
215 VICTORIA STREET, TORONTO 1

THE SPIRIT OF WESTERN PHILOSOPHY

FIRST EDITION

Printed in the United States of America
VAN REES PRESS • NEW YORK

Preface

The authors of this book have proceeded on the working hypothesis that the study of philosophy is best pursued, especially by the beginner, along historical lines. While not, to be sure, accepting Benedetto Croce's extreme view that ultimately philosophy and the history of ideas are identical subjects, we feel that the easiest and the most fruitful way of comprehending the persistent problems and the typical hypotheses current today in philosophical discussion is to share, through an effort of imagination, in their origin and development. To do this requires a survey of ancient and medieval as well as of modern philosophy. It is not necessary to become intimately acquainted with the host of lesser thinkers that surround the masters in each great period, but it is worth while to have faced the great problems from the standpoint of a Plato, an Aristotle, a Descartes, or a Kant.

The late Professor Alfred North Whitehead was hardly exaggerating when he said that the development of Western philosophy has been largely a matter of adding footnotes to Plato. At any rate, his famous remark very properly emphasizes the continuity of ideas —we might almost say, the continuity of question and answer—that has characterized twenty-five centuries of almost unbroken philosophical conversation. This conversation is a historical ingredient of our modern intellectual life, and its study is indispensable to an understanding of modern philosophical endeavor. Without it we are newcomers upon the scene, overhearing a conversation in which we can hardly participate, only partially aware of the issues at stake and the strategy employed.

We have tried to emphasize the solidarity of past and present, and accordingly have carried our survey through modern times.

Of course, in commenting upon contemporary or recent thinkers, it is often impossible to achieve as mature and as rounded an estimate as in the case of their predecessors. But we might almost argue that the presence of recent thinkers is necessary for this very reason. It is, after all, not ready-made philosophy but a philosophical life of confused curiosity and gradual enlightenment that we wish to share with our readers.

It is with some hesitation that the authors offer this historical introduction under the title *The Spirit of Western Philosophy,* thereby inviting comparison with two outstanding, almost classical studies, Josiah Royce's *The Spirit of Modern Philosophy* and Etienne Gilson's more recent *The Spirit of Medieval Philosophy.* Both of these works, the outcome of wide scholarship and most mature insight, occupy a position to which the present introductory study can make no pretensions. However, the two classics mentioned have served as models of interpretation and the authors have tried to imitate them on a more elementary level in this volume. Furthermore, as regards a work so largely composed of selections quoted from thinkers of the first rank, it is seemly that the authors consider its merits with fewer reservations than would be in order were the whole text of their own composition. However that may be, the title seems an excellent one under which to declare the scope of the present volume. The purpose has been to outline the central argument of ancient, medieval, and modern philosophy, and to follow the growth of the presiding themes and concepts without confusing the reader by including too many historical details or relying too heavily upon a technical vocabulary. Nevertheless, it is hoped that sufficient material of a dialectical sort has been introduced to guard against the impression that philosophy advances in a series of gratuitous hypotheses. At this date, it would be worse than futile to attempt to map another royal road to universal wisdom.

In choosing passages to illustrate the development of philosophical ideas, the authors have kept in mind the needs and the limitations of the average undergraduate reader. Thus in a few cases they have selected translations and arrangements for their attractiveness or general intelligibility rather than for any stricter accuracy. In this matter, they feel justified in requesting the indulgence of the specialist, who in more advanced instruction is well advised to emphasize the letter as well as the spirit of the philosophy he teaches.

The authors wish especially to thank Professor M. Phillips Mason of Bowdoin College for many helpful suggestions and comments. Professor Reinhart L. Korgen of the Department of Mathematics of Bowdoin College read the manuscript of the section treating contemporary logic and offered many valuable suggestions, a courtesy we particularly appreciated, since our position differs radically from Professor Korgen's own. This section has also been read by Professor Lawrence Hall and Mr. William Leue, of Bowdoin College, both of whom offered many suggestions for improvements that have been incorporated.

N. P. S.
R. S. B.

Bloomington, Indiana
June, 1950

Contents

Introduction: The Philosophical Enterprise

PHILOSOPHY AS ANALYSIS AND SPECULATION

The French thinker Pascal has insisted that to criticize philosophy is to philosophize, and it is certainly true that to define philosophy is actually to practice philosophical reflection—to practice a very difficult reflection in which the eye of the philosopher must be turned upon his own intellectual activity. Therefore we shall not attempt to construct a comprehensive definition of our subject. Such an exercise, as a matter of fact, would constitute an admirable conclusion for a course of study such as this. Nonetheless, we must frame some sort of working definition as a point of departure or we shall leave the student wholly in the dark about our intentions in this work, and so we offer the following as a preliminary guide.

Philosophy is the pursuit of wisdom. Accordingly, in the discussion of matters scientific, artistic, and ethical, the philosopher is the man who persistently tries, not always with complete success, to have the last word. By this we do not mean that the philosopher hopes to utter pronouncements that will never be superseded. He is as aware of the instability of human knowledge, as is any other student. What the philosopher proposes is to push his inquiry beyond the limits which for example, the specialist, the natural scientist, the art critic, or the historian of morals recognizes. Only thus can knowledge be transformed into wisdom.

The philosopher does this in two ways. He presses *analysis* of the meaning of words and of phrases beyond the limit usually recognized in science and elsewhere, and he carries his *synthesis* of such concepts far beyond the scope of any specialized study, being eager to sketch in outline a map of the universe to include, or perhaps to exclude, such entities as God, the human soul, truth, beauty, and goodness, in order to show how these much-talked-of things depend upon or are related to one another. A man's philosophy of life, his conception of the world and of his own place in it, is the outcome of such a synthesis more or less clearly and distinctly grasped in its broader outlines. The attempt to construct such a picture is called *speculation*. Thus when we tell one another that there is a God who created heaven and earth and fashioned man in his image, we are advancing what is for philosophy a speculative doctrine. The same is true when we insist that there is "no point in worrying," since all things happen as they must, that everything is in the hands of fate. The speculative philosopher tries to comprehend the world as a whole and to interpret human life against this background. Thus he has something in common with the great poet and the religious teacher.

Speculation can proceed but a little way without analysis. The latter is a persistent effort to determine just what we mean by certain key words and phrases toward which our thinking and our experience is oriented. Analysis must discover to what propositions or statements we commit ourselves when we accept the many plausible assumptions that guide our thinking; for instance, that every event must have a cause, that every body must be somewhere in space, that human beings are born with equal, inalienable rights, and so on. The reader only need attempt to frame definitions of the things just mentioned and compare his results with those of others in order to recognize the difficulties that surround the simplest form of analysis. The author recalls reading reports of an official inquiry into a steamship disaster some years ago, in which the hearings were sadly confused by the inability or the unwillingness of the participants to agree upon the meaning of the word "cause." Those who were on the defensive always treated the term as if it meant "necessary and sufficient" cause. Thus they would recognize A as a cause of B only if A is always followed by B and B is always preceded by A. On the other hand, the investigators continued to search for avoidable conditions that might have *contributed* to the disaster without being its "necessary and sufficient" cause. The quibbling that followed, owing to lack of explicit analysis of terms, tended to obscure the whole investigation.

One who attempts to speculate without preliminary analysis is attempting to piece together a picture puzzle before he can discern clearly the shape of the pieces with which he has to work. Even so, philosophy begins, both in the history of the race and in the life of the individual, as primarily speculative, and is forced into analysis only by the obvious failure of early speculation, which tends, as we shall soon see, to contradict itself and, once it is given a free rein, to produce the most painful confusion.

The earliest utterances of philosophical importance seem to involve recognition of only one problem. In other words, there seems to be for the earliest philosophers only one question to be answered. Put very crudely, this question is simply: "What is the world made of? What single stuff or material underlies the varied surface of things, the forms of earth, air, fire, and water that we behold?" This question is no doubt naïve. For instance, it takes for granted, on intuition and quite without explicit consideration, that all things are actually made of the same stuff. (And certainly before we undertake to answer such a problem as this we should try to clarify our ideas concerning its meaning. Just what, for instance, do we mean by "stuff" or its philosophical synonym "matter"?) But nevertheless this problem is important historically, because it reveals a definite attitude toward the world on the part of the questioner. What we see and experience about us we recognize as being only an *appearance*. The true nature of things does not lie on the surface for all to see. The surface is a forever changing appearance that is open to the awareness of the most unreflective person. But we may correctly interpret this appearance and penetrate to its *reality* only if we proceed with the utmost care and ingenuity. Speculative philosophy put the question What is reality? at the very beginning of its course; the many conflicting answers received slowly taught philosophers to be cautious and self-disciplined.

This attempt to distinguish reality from appearance is an inevitable outcome of the emergence of human consciousness. In fact, a human being who completely lacked this type of curiosity would hardly be human at all. The late Professor A. E. Taylor commented upon this important distinction as follows: [1]

The course of our ordinary experience, as well as our education in the rudiments of the sciences, has made us all familiar with the distinction between what really *is* or *exists* and what merely *appears* to be. There is no opposition more thoroughly enshrined in the language and literature of civilised races than the contrast of *seeming* with *reality,* or *substance* with *show*. We come upon it alike in our study of the processes of nature and our experience of human character and purpose.... So long as our various direct perceptions are not felt to conflict with one another, we readily accept them all as equally real and valid, and no question arises as to their relative truth or falsehood. Were all our perceptions of this kind, there would be no need for the correction, by subsequent reflection, of our first immediate impressions about the nature of ourselves and the world; error would be a term of no meaning for us, and science would have no existence. But when two immediate perceptions, both apparently equally authenticated by our senses, stand in direct conflict with one another, we cannot, without doing violence to the fundamental law of rational thinking, regard both as equally and in the same sense true. Unless we abandon once for all the attempt to reconcile the course of our experience with the demand of our intellect for consistency in thinking, we are driven to make a momentous distinction. We have to recognise that things are not always what they seem to be; what appears to us is, sometimes at any rate, not real, and what really is does not always appear. Of our two conflicting perceptions, only one at best can be a correct representation of the real course of things; one of them at least, and possibly both, must be mere seeming or appearance, and we are thus cast upon the problem which every science tries, in its own sphere and its own way, to solve: what part of our conceptions about the world gives us reality and what part only appearance? It is because of the importance of these puzzles of immediate perception as stimulating to such scientific reflection that Plato and Aristotle called philosophy the child of Wonder.

In time this question—What is the real?—forces upon us a more strictly analytical problem, which may not at first seem closely

[1] A. E. Taylor, *The Elements of Metaphysics,* pp. 2-3. Methuen & Co., London. 7th ed., 1924. Reprinted by permission of the publisher.

related to the original query. The new formulation runs as follows: What meanings may be attached to the verb "to be," in particular to the third person singular of the present indicative? What do we mean by "is" when we say:

The book *is* red.	Here *is* means *is qualified by*.
Two *is* half of four.	Here *is* means *is equal to*.
Albany *is* north of New York.	Here *is* means *is situated*.
That man *is* the President.	Here *is* means *is identical with*.
Is there a God?	Here *is* means simply *exists*.

In what way do these various uses of the verb "to be" differ from one another? What different modes of being or types of reality do they reveal? This study in all its ramifications constitutes the foundation of philosophical inquiry. It is frequently called *ontology,* or the study of being, or "isness" as such. The philosopher is likely to be especially interested in the last of the sentences quoted above, not primarily because it asks a question concerning the deity, but because it presents a philosophically indispensable use of the verb "to be," since it indicates sheer existence. God exists or he does not exist. What in this case is the meaning of "exist"?

Ontology, the examination of the nature of existence, was called by Aristotle "first philosophy," the knowledge of *being* as *being;* that is, as distinguished from the knowledge of the mathematician and of the physicist, who according to Aristotle consider the real *only insofar as* it exhibits number and magnitude or observable motion and some form of change. Ontology is an analytical study. It invites us to concentrate our attention upon the meaning of certain words that are used so frequently that we often fail to ponder their significance attentively, considering them too common-place to be important.

Such an analysis does more than fix the meaning of the terms used. By clarifying the full meaning that certain words have taken on as we use them, we come to understand more fully their reference to things, and thereby we actually increase and sharpen our comprehension of the situation in which we find ourselves. We do not arbitrarily fix the meaning of these words. Through analysis of the use to which we put them, we *recognize* the meanings or power of reference that they have gradually acquired. Furthermore, in ontological analysis we study not only the language we employ but also the effectiveness of that language in rendering consistent account of objective situations. To be sure, in recent years some writers have tried to develop an analytical study of language independent of such objective reference. These philosophers, who are known as Positivists, are committed to constructing a philosophy without an ontology. But this group, although distinguished by the ingenuity and resourcefulness of its leaders, is still a minority one.

Philosophers do not confine themselves to analytical operations. The speculative philosopher, as we have seen, undertakes to draw an outline map of the world with particular reference to the place occupied therein by human life and human consciousness. He will not content himself with trying to answer such questions as "What do we mean by "reality," or "beauty," or "justice"?" But he undertakes to arrange the broader outlines of human knowledge in a more or less consistent scheme. This undertaking is called *philosophical cosmology*. Such a cosmology or world view is the ultimate conclusion toward which the majority of philosophers have felt themselves to be working. Most of them, however, are willing to admit that this vast task is never complete and that at best we can only hope to approximate the truths of cosmology. Indeed, today some philosophers have quite despaired of framing a consistent and adequate cosmology and advise us to turn our attention wholly to problems of analysis.

THE DEPARTMENTS OR DIVISIONS OF PHILOSOPHY

Besides *ontology*, analytic philosophy contains the following subdivisions: *logic* and *epistemology*, that is, the philosophy of reasoning and of science respectively; *aesthetics*, or the philosophy of art and beauty; *ethics*, or the philosophy of conduct and of moral value; and the *philosophy of religion*, which comprises an analysis of such concepts as holiness and investigates the full meaning of prayer and other forms of religious practice. *Cosmology* as described above is the central study of speculative philosophy.

The term *metaphysics* may be employed to include ontology, cosmology, and epistemology. Metaphysics may be said to involve discussion of what exists as distinct from what ought to be or what is thought to be valuable. On the other hand, aesthetics, ethics, logic, and the philosophy of religion are sometimes described as *normative* or value studies in that they have to do with such subject matter as the beautiful, the good, the true, and the holy. Philosophical literature does not confine itself rigorously to this or that division of the subject. Thus one volume may treat of several departments of philosophy. This is especially true of early literature.

Analytic Philosophy	*Speculative Philosophy*
Ontology	Cosmology
Logic	
Epistemology	
Ethics	
Aesthetics	
Philosophy of Religion	

Metaphysics	*Normative Philosophy* (*Axiology*)
Ontology	Logic
Epistemology	Ethics
Cosmology	Aesthetics
	Philosophy of Religion

THE RELATION OF PHILOSOPHY TO OTHER SUBJECTS OF STUDY

It should be clear that philosophical knowledge is in one sense the most comprehensive knowledge we can possess. Thus ontology especially is comprehensive in that it includes the foundation of all further knowledge concerning existing things. We might, then, suppose that such philosophy must be perfected before the other sciences can advance safely. This would, perhaps, constitute an ideal development. But historically, philosophy has never been able to assume so authoritative a position. Philosophy actually develops much more slowly than, say, mathematics or physics, and is continually having to retrace its steps. Accordingly, the special sciences can hardly look to philosophy for final and authoritative guidance, even in their first steps and their presuppositions. Nonetheless, it is interesting to observe that although philosophy can maintain no clearly defined jurisdiction over the sciences, the special sciences do actually spring from philosophy. since in the earliest period of their history they were, each one of them, actually maintained by philosophers. The sciences have, so to speak, separated off from a common nucleus of philosophy. Thus psychology has emerged as a distinct study only within the last half century, physics within the last three centuries.

It is also true that many statements often attributed to the authority of common sense are nothing more than the echoes of some half-forgotten philosophy. Thus "Seeing is believing," "All's well that ends well," are utterances pregnant with philosophy. But since no one system of philosophical wisdom has ever been successfully established as *the* official and authoritative philosophy, we cannot speak of science and common sense as applied philosophy in the way that we might speak of engineering as applied physics. The following quotation from an English writer, the late Professor R. G. Collingwood, indicates as clearly as is possible the historical relation between philosophy and the development of other studies, such as the natural and social sciences, and further the relation between philosophy and the practice of affairs in statecraft or in social organization.[2]

[Philosophy] cannot descend like a *deus ex machina* upon the stage of practical life and, out of its superior insight into the nature of things, dictate the correct solution for this or that problem in morals, economic organization, or international politics. There is nothing in a philosopher's special work qualifying him to pilot a perplexed generation through those rocks and shoals. If a mariner finds himself at sea without navigator, chart, or compass, the Astronomer Royal himself, discovered among the passengers, could do little for him; he would be wiser to hail some coastwise fisherman....
Christian theology holds that the faith of a simple peasant, without any tincture of theological learning, is sufficient for salvation;

[2] R. G. Collingwood, "The Present Need of a Philosophy," in *Philosophy*, Vol. IX (1934), pp. 262-64. Reprinted by permission of the editor. The italics in paragraph 4 are added.

modern philosophy of whatever school, follows its example in holding that non-philosophical thought in all its forms—moral and political, scientific, religious, or artistic—is able to do its work without asking philosophy's help and to justify itself without awaiting philosophy's verdict.

In this opinion there lurks an opposite danger. It may seem that philosophy's only task is to analyse knowledge we already possess, and theorize about activities we are already able to perform; that it is no more able to influence the processes which it describes than astronomy can influence the movements of the stars; that the only motive to pursue it is a pure disinterested curiosity, the only good to be gained from it, pure theoretical knowledge; and that Plato, Spinoza, and all others who have thought this knowledge somehow serviceable to our well-being were victims of a gigantic and inexplicable illusion.

The truth seems to me to lie somewhere between these two extremes. If the philosopher is no pilot, neither is he a mere spectator, watching the ship from his study window. He is one of the crew; but what, as such, is his function? In order to find an answer to this question, I suggest that we should look back three hundred years or more, to the infancy of modern science. At the beginning of the seventeenth century no one could foresee the triumphs which science was one day to achieve. It was not, therefore, a foreknowledge of these triumphs that encouraged innumerable men to persevere in almost incredibly detailed inquiries concerning the laws of nature, in a corporate effort shared by all parts of the civilized world and extending over many generations. The will to pursue those inquiries was not based on any conception of their future outcome, but it was based on something: it was based on the belief that nature is a single system of things, controlled throughout its extent by a single system of laws. *In adopting this idea, civilized man was setting aside his immemorial belief in demonic agencies, magical influences, and the inscrutable caprices of individual things, and accepting a new view of the world, not received on faith, and not arrived at by scientific induction, but thought out and stated in a systematic form by the philosophers of the sixteenth century.*

The notion of a uniformly law-abiding natural world is so familiar to ourselves that we are apt to forget how recent a thing it is in the history of thought, how hardly it was won by Renaissance thinkers...and how dramatic was its verification by one scientific discovery after another. This philosophical conception of nature has played the part, in relation to scientific research, of a constant stimulus to effort, a reasoned refutation of defeatism, a promise that all scientific problems are in principle soluble.

[The same argument applies to the social problems of today.]

There is a certain analogy between the state of things at the beginning of the seventeenth century, when the special problems of civilized life were concerned with man's control over nature, and the state of things in the modern world, whose special problems are concerned with human relations. Sir Herbert Samuel justly enumerates them: "personal and social morality, economic organization, international relationship." These problems, like the problems of natural science, can be solved only by detailed and patient investigation, exhaustive inquiry, skilful experiment. But this arduous and slow labour, if it is to be undertaken at all, must rest on two things: a conviction that the problems can be solved, and a determination that they shall be solved. Of these two, the first is, I think, capable of being provided, in a reasoned form, by philosophy. Apart from such a reasoned conviction, the will to solve them is so handicapped by doubts within and opposition without, that its chance of success dwindles to the vanishing-point. There is always a vast mass of opinion (and very respectable opinion) in favour of allowing established institutions to stand firm for fear of worse to follow; there is always a dead weight of inclination, however bad things may be, to enjoy what good we can snatch for the short time allowed us; but, more dangerous than either of these, there is the defeatist spirit which fears that what we are aiming at is no more than a Utopian dream. And this fear becomes paralysing when, not content with the status of a natural timidity or temporary loss of nerve, it calls in the help of philosophical ideas, and argues that the evils admittedly belonging to our moral, social, and political life are essential elements in all human life, or in all civilization, so that the special problems of the modern world are inherently insoluble. The philosophical ideas underlying this argument are connected with certain aspects of the idea of progress; especially the false conception of progress as due to a cosmic force which can be trusted to advance human life automatically, without the active co-operation of human beings, and (the natural reaction from this) an equally false denial that progress is possible at all.

Thus, according to Collingwood, whose interpretation is both sober and historically well informed, philosophy often stands as a starting point from which special sciences derive their initial direction, and sometimes also the assurance needed to carry them through the earlier stages of their development. At later periods in the development of science, philosophical analysis may aid in clarifying certain terms and concepts that have for too long been taken for granted by specialists. Even so, the relation of philosophy to the sciences is a two-way affair, a reciprocal giving and taking of criticism and assistance.

In general, then, we may say that philosophy presides over the first emergence of an idea and—sometimes centuries later—over its final formulation. At the very start an idea, unfamiliar and disturbing, is likely to appear as a remote hypothesis of interest only to the philosopher, who is therefore sometimes considered a visionary crank. In its final formulation the idea, now become commonplace, appeals again to the philosopher, who tries hard to sharpen its meaning and to clarify its usage. When so employed, the philosopher is often considered a hair-splitting pedant. A study of the history of philosophy in its relation to the history of natural and social science, and to that of social and political practice, should help us to recognize how much civilization owes to the "crank" and the "pedant." Without speculative vision and analytical criticism, civilization as a conscious human enterprise would be well-nigh impossible.

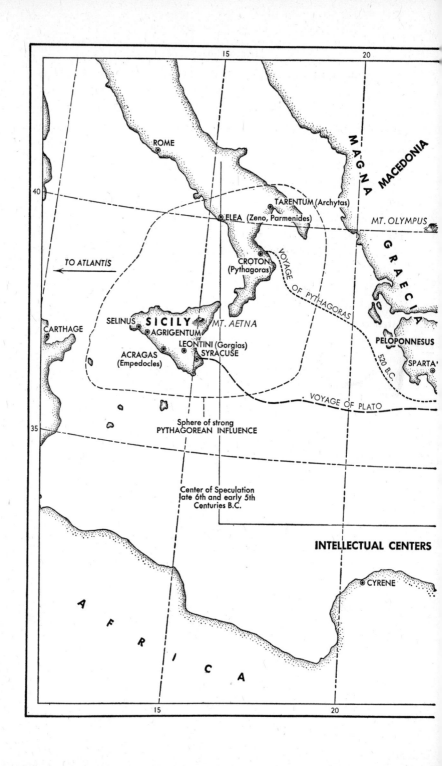

INTELLECTUAL CENTERS

Center of Speculation
late 6th and early 5th
Centuries B.C.

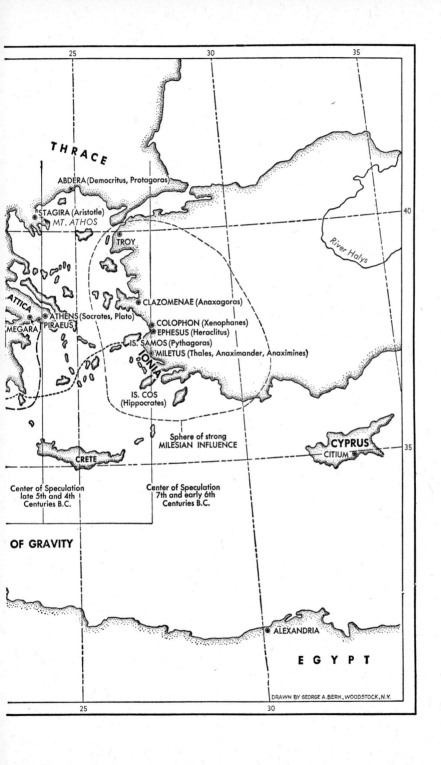

THRACE

ABDERA (Democritus, Protagoras)

STAGIRA (Aristotle)
MT. ATHOS

TROY

CLAZOMENAE (Anaxagoras)

ATTICA

ATHENS (Socrates, Plato)
MEGARA   PIRAEUS

COLOPHON (Xenophanes)
EPHESUS (Heraclitus)
IS. SAMOS (Pythagoras)
IONIA
MILETUS (Thales, Anaximander, Anaximines)

IS. COS
(Hippocrates)

Sphere of strong
MILESIAN INFLUENCE

CRETE

River Halys

CYPRUS
CITIUM

Center of Speculation
late 5th and 4th
Centuries B.C.

Center of Speculation
7th and early 6th
Centuries B.C.

OF GRAVITY

ALEXANDRIA

E G Y P T

DRAWN BY GEORGE A. BERK, WOODSTOCK, N.Y.

CHAPTER I

The Beginnings of European Philosophy

PRE-SOCRATIC SPECULATION

The earliest European philosophy was a product of ancient Greek civilization. The speculative picture painted by the first Greek philosophers is today fresh and memorable for its broad simplicity, but it is logically unstable, and lacking in conviction. This is because the early thinkers proceeded upon a minimum of reflective analysis and, to put the matter bluntly, hardly knew what it was that they were talking about. It was the achievement of the Athenian philosopher Socrates to make clear the need of thoroughgoing analysis of the terms used so freely in popular discussion and in philosophical speculation. Hence it is in the person of Socrates that philosophy may be said to reach its first maturity in the proper use of both analysis and speculation. But in order to understand the contribution of this great thinker, we must survey as swiftly as we can the rudimentary philosophy that preceded him.

The men who produced this earliest philosophy are usually called *Pre-Socratics,* perhaps to indicate that their work was extremely incomplete, and important only because it served as a background for the thinking of Socrates and his followers. This early philosophy was unique not only in that it lacked overt and explicit analysis, but also in that, unlike recent philosophy, it was not aided by the conclusions of well-grounded special sciences, such as physics or biology. At this early date not even geometry existed in any strictly systematic form. Astronomy was in its infancy and geometry itself was little in advance of philosophy, although, as we shall see, it sometimes served as an inspiration to the latter. The philosophers of this period were usually astronomers and mathematicians as well. In fact, the early Greek thinkers are the forebears both of modern philosophy and of the modern sciences in that they are the first to exhibit a genuine curiosity concerning the goings-on of nature, free from purely practical considerations on the one hand, and from the imaginative moralizing of ancient mythology on the other.

In Hebrew the word "prophet" signifies "one who bursts forth," one who, overcome by inspiration, seeks memorable utterance for the enthusiasm that possesses him. The prophet is hardly a philosopher, for he is not bound to exhibit the steps of his argument. As the nineteenth-century prophet Nietzsche insisted, he has "forgotten his reasons," or perhaps never clearly singled them out in his attention. The first Greek philosophers have a prophetic strain in their utterances. We find conclusions, often in epigrammatic form, with no premises explicitly stated. Nonetheless, despite their intuitive and unsystematic way of thought, these thinkers seek to describe the world as they see it, and they are no longer satisfied with mythology as an explanation of nature. The earlier tendency to account for natural phenomena as the expression of benevolent or mischievous personalities resident in nature is being overcome, if slowly and only in part. Nature appears too uniform and steady in her processes to be the outcome of the whims and caprices of gods such as those described by the Greek poets. Men who have heard their most brilliant colleague, Thales,[1] successfully predict an eclipse of the sun are hardly prone to accept, say, the story of the sun god Helios and his unruly offspring Phaëton. Here we are told that Phaëton had once presumed to drive the chariot of the sun around its daily course, when the horses broke away from him. The barren sands of the Sahara were said to be the disastrous result

---

[1] Thales (flourished 580 B.C.), a native of Miletus, merchant, statesman, mathematician, astronomer, and philosopher. The first of the Pre-Socratic thinkers, he considered the primitive elements of Greek science—earth, air, fire, and water—and decided that the first three sprang from water, perhaps because we can observe the passage of water into solid and gaseous forms, and certainly because water is an essential of life.

produced when the sun chariot swung too close to the earth during the mad ride that followed.

The decline of such mythological thinking is only possible insofar as some other mode of explanation arises to take its place. Thus Greek science and Greek philosophy begin with a primitive theory of nature, which replaces the ancient mythology. This occurs as more or less responsible guesswork takes the place of fantasy. In the new philosophy we hear little about the gods, while attention turns to the material world. The first Greek philosophers lived along the Ionian seaboard of Asia Minor. Some of them served as engineers in the Persian army; they were interested in the construction of fortifications, bridges, canals, and even tunnels. They became familiar with objects of complex design. This familiarity reflects itself in their ingenious astronomical theories, according to which the celestial motions are represented as the operations of a complex machine.[2]

NATURE AND THE FOUR ELEMENTS

In Ionian speculation four elements or types of physical being were recognized: earth, air, fire, and water. All things that exist were thought to be composed of these elementary forms in some combination or blend. The living human body contains them all. Sky, sea, and land each indicate the dominance of one of the elements, and fire is always present in the sun, the stars, and the thunderbolts. Each element is characterized by certain qualities of its own. Thus fire is dry and hot, water moist and cool. Water is always thought of as liquid, air as vaporous, earth as solid. Fire, as essentially light and active, tends to rise; earth, to fall. Thus earth stands at the center, fire at the outer frontier, of the world.

[2] Thus one of these philosophers describes the mechanism of the celestial motions as follows:..."the sun was a wheel 28 times the size of the earth, like a chariot-wheel with the rim hollow, full of fire, showing the fire at a certain point through an orifice, as through the nozzle of a pair of bellows." The sun was eclipsed when the orifice of the wheel was stopped.—John Burnet, *Early Greek Philosophy*, p. 67 A. & C. Black, London, 4th ed., 1930. This passage illustrates the use of technological, mechanical analogies in Milesian speculation; the chariot wheel and bellows nozzle suggest a mechanism that may explain the behavior of the heavenly bodies.

The goings-on of nature involve an interplay—combination, separation, and recombination of the elements. Furthermore, unlike the elements of modern chemical theory, the earth, air, fire, and water of the earliest Greek thinkers are subject to transformation or transmutation one into another. This introduces the first problem, scientific or philosophical, that occupied the Greek thinkers. Which one of the four elements may be considered the basic or primary material from which the others spring? Has the earth risen from the waters, precipitated out of solution, so to speak, according to some obscure rhythm or cycle of cosmic change?

After all, water is very possibly the *archē,* or basic material, out of which the other elements emerge. Does it not change readily from its proper liquid state into a solid earthlike form? Are there not some who believe that the waters of the river Nile are actually producing the earth deposited in the mud flats of the Delta? Again, does water not transform itself into an airlike vapor in the presence of fire? And is water not indispensable to the growth of all living things, thus revealing an extraordinary power to initiate growth and change?

But there are other possibilities. Have the land and the sea perhaps come into existence by condensation, separating out from the vast reservoir of atmosphere that still surrounds them? And again, all four elements may perhaps rise from or be special forms of some fifth material. This material would contain as latent powers all the properties that appear overtly in the four elements. For this reason, such a basic material might be described as the "indefinite," the "boundless," or the "unlimited," since it contains within itself as a matrix the latent possibilities of incompatible qualities—for instance, of both hot and cold, moist and dry. Such a "boundless" must enjoy a curious form of existence. Since it is not definitely this or that, we can hardly say that *it is* at all. And it certainly cannot be observed. The "boundless" presents itself to the early philosophers as a primordial chaos, a plenitude of confused fertility out of which orderly existence somehow emerges.

HERACLITUS AND THE PHILOSOPHY OF CHANGE

Whatever the speculative interpretation they put upon their beliefs, the earliest Greek philosophers tended to agree with one another in many ways. Their thinking tended to interpret nature, whatever its origin, as a system of cyclic change, in broad outline suggested by the order of the seasons. This process was often thought of as a battle of opposites or of incompatible qualities, struggling to succeed one another in the actual world. Thus hot and cold, dry and moist—sometimes even conceived as active powers, like gods or demons—struggled to dominate the course of events. The elements themselves may even be thought of as the outcome of this interplay of powers. But there is also a cosmic justice or balance that prevents any one quality from gaining a complete victory, and which banishes such a quality from the world when it has overstepped itself. Thus there is in the order of things nothing fixed or permanent, but rather a constant struggle in which nature vacillates between incompatible extremes. In this vacillation nature is never at rest and never quite the same.

This latter notion was expressed with great energy and wit, if with but little logic, by the philosopher Heraclitus of Ephesus.[3] Heraclitus chooses fire as the prototype of the ever changing reality. Perhaps at first he thought of fire in the manner of his predecessors as the *archē,* the basic stuff from which earth, air, water, and their innumerable combinations arise. But he seems to have gone further and to have used the word "fire" as an image or symbol of the incessant transformation, which he recognized as a fundamental condition of all things. Fire itself is always mobile, and in its presence nothing remains unchanged. Again, heat is indispensable to animal life. Thus by "fire" Heraclitus seems to have understood at once the restless course of nature and the productivity of life.

---

[3] Heraclitus of Ephesus (flourished 504 B.C.) came of an aristocratic family and harbored a haughty scorn for all democratic ideas. He is sometimes spoken of as Heraclitus the Dark, because of the obscurity of his teaching. It was said among the ancients that "Heraclitus weeps and Democritus laughs at all things."

A few fragments from Heraclitus' writings follow: [4]

o. All things flow; nothing abides.

91. One cannot step twice into the same river.

(81. Bywater). Into the same rivers we step and we do not step; we are and we are not.

94. The sun will not overstep his measures, else would the Erinnyes, the handmaids of justice, find him out.

30. This universe, the same for all, no one, either god or man, has made; but it always was, and is, and ever shall be an ever-living fire, fixed measures kindling and fixed measures dying out.

8. Opposition brings men together, and out of discord comes the fairest harmony, and all things have their birth in strife.

51. Men do not understand how that which is torn in different directions comes into accord with itself—harmony in contrariety, as in the case of the bow and the lyre.

126. It is the cold things that become warm, the warm that become cold, the moist that become dry, and the dry that become moist.

For Heraclitus, change is considered in terms of the alternation of contrasted or opposite qualities. He is much impressed by the fact that a quality is usually doomed to beget its opposite, or at least to yield place to it, and that no qualitative state endures permanently. It is only our lack of observation and of proper understanding that allow us to think of any object or condition as exempt from change. Indeed nothing can be properly understood unless we see it in connection with the opposites from which it springs and toward which it moves. Nothing ever simply *is* this or that. Everything is always on the move, passing from one form of being to another. Water, for instance, is never hot or cold—it is always cooling off or warming up. Things do not retain their properties by a sort of marking time. They come to be and pass away. Their very existence is a becoming.

[4] Heraclitus, fragments from Diels and one from Bywater, in Charles M. Bakewell, *Source Book of Ancient Philosophy*, pp. 28-35. Charles Scribner's Sons, New York rev. ed., 1939. This and later quotations are reprinted by permission of the publisher.

For Heraclitus, this firelike becoming is the substance of things. For him, although not always for Greek common sense, the opposites that struggle for supremacy are really only manifestations of the one all-pervading flux. They are like waves in a stream of fire that knows no stay or permanence, transforming everything it touches, changing "all things into all things." This flux is guided in some way—Heraclitus does not tell us exactly how—by a thought or *logos* that is the indwelling spirit of the world. This last doctrine is a prophetic intuition. Thus the sequence of the seasons, the growth and decay of all living things, the instabilities of social existence, all indicate that our world is a transitory one. But throughout there is apparent a certain restraint or measure. The movements of the heavenly bodies, the comparative regularity of the seasons, the fact of heredity in the generation of living things, all indicate the presence of a rhythm or measure that distinguishes our world from chaos.

Heraclitus' philosophy is the more easily understood by those who remember that much early Greek speculation is justly termed *hylozoist*. By this we mean that no very sharp boundary is drawn between the living and the nonliving. The primitive attitude that finds no difficulties in attributing natural phenomena to spiritual forces is still strong enough among the Pre-Socratics to support the nature mysticism of Heraclitus. As we have seen, it is likely that Heraclitus chose fire as the prototype of the flux because he believed heat to be indispensable to animal life, just as Thales had chosen water for a similar reason. For both Thales and Heraclitus all nature is alive. It was Thales who insisted that "even a magnetic stone has life [soul], because it moves iron," and who believed that "all things are full of divine [creative] living powers."

This philosophy of flux developed upon the eastern edge of the Greek world among the trading cities of Ionian Asia Minor, such as Miletus and Ephesus. Two rival philosophies appeared in southern Italy, which was then the western limit of Greek civilization. It is interesting to notice in passing that philosophical ideas first appear not in Athens or Corinth, but upon the frontiers of trade. Perhaps this is owing to the stimulating contacts with foreign

7

ideas and points of view. Philosophy seems to require a cosmopolitan background, at least in the beginning. It has also been suggested—for instance, by the brilliant historian of Greek philosophy Theodor Gomperz—that the conditions of colonial life aroused the individual's sense of his own independence and that this sense of freedom penetrated the intellectual and religious life of the people. Certainly, the first out-and-out condemnation of the established Greek religion as a guide of life came from Asia Minor.

PYTHAGORAS AND THE PHILOSOPHY OF MEASURE

The earliest Greek philosophers had a curious way of summarizing their speculative contributions. These summaries were often reduced each to a single sentence. Each sentence identified the world in all its diversified complexities with the *archē* or basic stuff from which it was thought to have arisen. Thus we hear:

> All things are water.
> All things are air.
> All things are the boundless.
> All things are fire (= the flux).

Here the verb "to be" has a special significance, which the early thinkers, being careless analysts, probably did not clearly distinguish from other meanings. In the above formulas, the word "are" is difficult to paraphrase. The phrases "are composed of," "spring from," "are caused by," may help us catch the meaning that the early thinkers attached to the verb "to be" in these statements.

This problem of interpretation is rendered even more difficult when we consider the work of another school of philosophers, the so-called Pythagoreans, or followers of Pythagoras.[5] These phi-

---

[5] Pythagoras (died 504 B.C.) came to Italy from Asia Minor. He was the founder of a religious body of strongly mystical tendencies, which attempted to dominate the political and religious life of southern Italy. By Plato's time, however, the school had lost its political power, and there was little likelihood of its dominating the religious life of the Greek world. It has been pointed out that this was probably fortunate, as the mystical teachings of the early Pythagorean religious reformers might well have plunged the Greek world into an abyss of irrationalism. Many members of the school, however, emphasized the "number philosophy" described below, and were less inclined toward religious reform.

iosophers were active in southern Italy from the sixth century B.C. The Pythagoreans issued a new formula, outwardly similar to those current in Asia Minor: "All things are number." A modern student will have to interpret this statement as an epigrammatic oversimplification, the meaning of which is not at once obvious. Surely all things cannot *be* number in quite the same sense that they might *be* water or even the firelike flux.

For the Pythagorean, number seems to have connoted measure or proportion. For him, the world is systematic and measurable throughout. Such a universe he describes as a *cosmos,* or ordered whole, whose intricate yet unified structure is a source of man's intellectual admiration and religious awe.

This doctrine of number as the essence of all things springs from two sources, the Pythagorean's interest in geometry and his interest in music. Pythagoras, or at any rate one of his early followers, is supposed to have demonstrated the theorem that the sum of the squares on the arms of a right triangle is equal to the square on the hypotenuse or greatest side. The Pythagoreans also prepared a list of whole numbers, the so-called Pythagorean numbers, which if applied to the sides of a triangle will yield a right angle opposite the hypotenuse. The integers 3, 4, and 5 constitute the first of these triads. Thus the Pythagoreans noted that a spatial pattern, a right angle, may be said to depend for its existence upon the presence of a given numerical ratio. Space, they thought, is accordingly dominated by number. Or to put it in another way, number itself may be described as spatial, as when we speak of *square* or *cubic* numbers.

The Pythagoreans were shocked and puzzled when they discovered that their theorem involves the admission of incommensurables. Consider the case of the diagonal of a square of unit side. The diagonal must have a length equivalent to the square root of 2. But the Pythagoreans, unlike modern mathematicians, were not prepared to admit that there is a number equivalent to the square root of 2. They were bitterly disappointed to have to recognize a right triangle the length of one of whose sides is not a genuine number, and which accordingly cannot be measured in terms of the other side. But they did not allow this difficulty to dampen their enthusiasm, which was religious as well as scientific in nature, and they clung to their belief that space is dominated by what we call rational numbers, the whole numbers and the fractions. Not only space but natural process, the behavior of bodies in motion, and the growth of living things was thought to be dominated by numerical ratios.

This was, of course, a bit of sheer speculative intuition on the part of the Pythagoreans. They possessed only a small fraction of the evidence necessary to establish such a sweeping and all-inclusive hypothesis. To be sure, astronomy helped to strengthen this belief, and the Pythagoreans found another and quite unexpected type of evidence in their analysis of the musical scale. Scholars surmise that this discovery was made by measuring, on a monochord with a movable bridge, the lengths of string required to yield the several notes forming the perfect intervals. The ratio of the octave is 2:1, the ratio of the fifth is 3:2, of the fourth, 4:3. Thus sound, like space, seems to be dominated by number.

The Pythagorean speculation is summarized happily by Professor Cornford in his instructive study *Before and after Socrates.*[6]

If you run your finger up or down the string of a violin, it will yield a continuous range of rising or falling sound, extending vaguely in both directions. If you stop the string at the right points, determined by these numerical ratios, it will yield a concord of sounds, the structure of a limited and harmonious order. That structure, constant through all the variety of musical scales, is the key to the whole architecture of music, opening a world not only of order but of beauty, a cosmos.... For if the chaotic welter of sounds that besiege our hearing can be reduced, by the simple principle of limiting measure, to the harmonious order of art and finally to proportions of number, might not the whole order of Nature, with its acknowledged beauty, be framed on a principle analogous or even identical? If this thought is pursued in the physical direction, it leads to the Pythagorean doctrine that the reality of things lies, not in the unordered and indefinite principle of matter (the Unlimited), but in the opposite limiting principle of

[6] Francis M. Cornford, *Before and after Socrates*, pp. 67-69. Cambridge University Press, Cambridge, 1932. Reprinted by permission of the publisher.

form and measure, proportion and number. All things we see and touch represent or embody number. Under this aspect of measurable quantity, the world of Nature can be known and understood. In astronomy, the speeds and distances of the heavenly bodies are ruled by the proportions of a harmony ... of the spheres. The forms or surfaces which limit tangible bodies represent the perfect figures of geometry; and the laws of these figures can be finally reduced to relations of number. This discovery—that the key to physical science lies in mathematics—is one of those intuitions of genius which date from the childhood of philosophic speculation and still serve as guiding principles to science. The physicists of this generation tell us that the laws of material substance are to be expressed in mathematical equations.

Next, turning from the macrocosm of Nature to the microcosm of man's soul and body, Pythagoras saw that the perfection of the body—its beauty, strength, and health—depends upon a harmony of material elements; and from his time onwards the theory and practice of Greek medicine were in large part governed by the principle that healing is the restoration of a balance or proportion dislocated by disease.[7] The same principle was applied to the goodness or 'virtue' of the soul, whose health is disordered by vices of excess and defect. The perfecting of the soul is the restoration of harmony in the human cosmos. The disorderly motions of passion and bodily desire need to be controlled and attuned in *Sophrosyne*—temperance, self-control, right-mindedness, wisdom.

It is not enough, however, simply to say *that* things are numbers, without giving an explanation of *how* they are. As critics of the Pythagoreans pointed out, mathematics can give essential information only about things which themselves are essentially quantitative. Thus there are seven stars in the Pleiades, and seven strings on a Greek lyre, but this arithmetical property of "seven-ness" gives no real insight into the nature of a Pleiad or of a lyre string. The observation that certain relations, such as position and pitch, are essentially quantitative does not in itself justify the inference that mathematics is a suitable tool for describing the objects that are thus related.

But an exciting sequence of successes marked the Pythagorean

---

[7] Thus disease is an instance of the human organism's failing to maintain its proper internal and external adjustments, being, so to speak, out of tune.

attempts to apply mathematics to science. Music, astronomy, politics, and medicine yielded new discoveries when their problems were analyzed mathematically. The explanation seemed to the Pythagoreans to be that reality is essentially quantitative. Thus in their speculation they pictured the physical world as made up of sets of unchanging mathematical points, which combined together in patterns to form the objects that we experience. The fact that numbers are also classes or sets of "units," exactly like "points" except that they lack position, explains why things behave like geometrical figures, and why the application of mathematical speculation had been able so to enrich contemporary science.

PARMENIDES AND THE PHILOSOPHY OF
THE CHANGELESS [8]

Another Graeco-Italian philosophy originated in the city of Elea, and its champions are known as Eleatics. These thinkers broke sharply and dogmatically with the tradition of earlier Greek philosophy. They formulated the startling doctrine that nothing real can change, thus striking directly at Heraclitus and the philosophy of Asia Minor, and at the same time repudiating the evidence of daily experience and of what we nowadays call common sense. The Eleatics are the first European philosophers to hold that things are really wholly different from what they seem. As Parmenides insisted, according to reason "all things," so called, are one and this one does not change, so that all change or movement is a distortion of reality brought upon us somehow by the weakness of our organs of experience, which must be corrected by pure reason itself.[9] Parmenides' argument is difficult to extract from the dark reasoning of his poem *On Nature,* which unfortunately does not exist today

---

[8] Parmenides (born c. 516 B.C.) was active in the political affairs of his native city of Elea. His ideas are broadly similar to the thinking of Xenophanes, a native of Colophon in Asia Minor, who fled to Italy when his home was conquered by the Persians.

[9] This is expressed in Parmenides' dictum "One thing are thinking and being." Here "thinking" stands for reason or theory as opposed to experience and common sense.

in its entirety. Let us quote a passage that seems to contain the core of the argument. Parmenides tells us:[10]

... That Being doth be—and on *it* there are tokens
Many and many to show that what is is birthless and deathless ...
Never it was or shall be; but the ALL simultaneously now is,
One continuous one; for of it what birth shalt thou search for?
How and whence it hath sprung? I shall not permit thee to tell me,
Neither to think: 'Of what is not,' for none can say or imagine
How Not-Is becomes Is; or else what need should have stirred it,
After or yet before its beginning, to issue from nothing?

The argument here seems to be a form of reductio ad absurdum, whereby a theorem is disproved when we indicate that a supposedly impossible state of affairs—one that we cannot describe without contradicting ourselves—may be said to follow from it. Thus suppose "A changes into B," as an example of any process of change:

$$A \rightarrow B \qquad A \rightarrow B \qquad A \rightarrow B$$
$$\searrow \qquad \searrow \; \nearrow$$
$$a \; ? \qquad a?b$$

A loses something as it becomes *B*. This is a characteristic or criterion whereby *A* differed from *B*. Let us call this *a*. Also, as *A* becomes *B* it gains something that it has lacked; namely, the individuality of *B*, which was not at first present. Let us call this *b*. Thus when *A* changes into *B*, *a* must depart from the actual scene and *b* must enter it. Where does *a* go? And where does *b* come from? (As the log on my fireplace burns to ashes, what becomes of the *red* flame and the *warm* glow? and where does the *gray* of the ash originate?)

Shall we say with Anaximander that *a* retreats into the "boundless,"[11] the neutral reservoir of "rejected" qualities that have lost their grip upon actuality, and that *b* in turn springs from or is produced by the boundless?—No, says Parmenides. The boundless

---

[10] Parmenides, *On Nature*, fragments trans. by Thomas Davidson in *Journal of Speculative Philosophy*, quoted in Bakewell, *op. cit.*, p. 15.

[11] Anaximander (flourished about 570 B.C.) was a native of Miletus, like his master Thales.

reservoir of nonactual entities, even if pictured as the infinite sea
of atmosphere surrounding the earth, is just another word for sheer
emptiness—nothing at all. Thus Anaximander would be saying *a*
"goes nowhere," which is equivalent to saying that *a* does not move.
In the same way *b* "comes from nowhere," or *b* does not come at
all. Shall we say that *a* passes into *B*?—No, says Parmenides, for
then *B* would not differ from *A*. Just so, we cannot say that *A*
contains *b* in the first place, for then *A* would not differ from *B*.
Hence, since *A* cannot lose *a* or gain *b*, *A* cannot become *B*. But
"*A* changes into *B*" represented any process or change. Therefore
change is impossible.

At this point Heraclitus might answer: Change is not impossible
because all things are really one, the ever restless fire itself: [12]

88. One and the same thing are the living and the dead, the
waking and the sleeping, the young and the old; the former change
and are the latter, the latter change in turn and are the former.

90. All things are exchanged for fire and fire for all things, just
as wares are exchanged for gold and gold for wares.

Thus *A* and *a*, *B* and *b*, are all one and the same flux. *A* exists
only as a pulse of change; so does *B*. Let us return to our diagram:

$$A \rightarrow B \text{ yields } \overset{\frown}{AB}$$

We can imagine Heraclitus pointing out that Parmenides is
beginning with two static entities, *A* and *B*, and then trying to
describe change as that which connects them, whereas *A* itself is a
process, and so is *B*. Suppose, we might add, that *A* stands for the
Middle Ages and *B* for the Renaissance. It is obvious that neither
A nor *B* can be conceived as being static in nature. There is not
only historical passage and transition between *A* and *B* but passage
and transition internal to both of them. Change is prior to permanence, motion to rest. But does this mean that *A* is *identical* with *B*?
Here, perhaps, Heraclitus has overstepped himself. *A* and *B* are
ways of considering earlier and later phases of one and the same

---

[12] Heraclitus, in Bakewell, *op. cit.*, p. 33.

process, but they are hardly identical. We must remember that for Parmenides also all things are one, but that this "one" has nothing to do with change. After all, we may ask of Heraclitus, if there are *no* differences between opposites, how can one thing *change* into another?

At this point Greek philosophy stands in great need of a clear analysis of change, carried out with a minimum of speculative bias. Such an analysis was at last offered by Plato, as we shall learn presently. Plato followed the lead of Socrates in this matter, combining speculation and analysis in a brilliant fashion. But in Parmenides' day no such treatment of the problem was forthcoming, and he remained unanswered and unrefuted, although by no means universally accepted.

Although we have traced many of the shortcomings of these early philosophies to an absence of adequate analysis, in the work of Parmenides and Zeno [13] we find evidence that the need for analytic techniques was beginning to be felt. In particular, the term "being" as it was used by the Ionians and Pythagoreans is treated with some analytic criticism. If we assume that all things are really different modifications of fire or water—that is, of some underlying stuff called "being"—then it is hard to see how we can explain the meaning of "change" without self-contradiction. For the log in my fireplace is *really* some form of water, on this theory, and so are the gases and the ashes that result from its burning. It seems, then, since what remains after the change is the same as what we started with, that there *really* has been no change at all. Or if, with the Pythagoreans, we assume that before and after the change, the changed object is really just a collection of mathematical points, it is hard to see that it has been really changed.

Zeno and Parmenides examine what these other philosophers have meant by "change," and find that they have meant "coming into and passing out of being"; but since on these older theories the basic reality is always the same and indestructible, this results in a self-contradiction. Parmenides' speculation is colored through-

---

[13] Zeno (about 490-430 B.C.) was, like Parmenides, a native of Elea in southern Italy, which was also the home territory of the Pythagoreans.

out by this analytic problem: How can we understand change, if we accept the meanings of "change" and "being" that are commonly understood at this time? It is a head-on contradiction, and Parmenides chooses to preserve consistency by denying the reality of change. Nothing *really* changes its basic substantiality; the changes we observe are only apparent, not real. Zeno centers his attack more specifically on the contradictions that result if we assume things to be built up out of an infinite number of discrete, unchanging mathematical points. His analysis of the significance of such a building-up is so acute that it has forced mathematicians to re-analyze their definitions of "point," "infinitesimal," and "limit," even in our own period.

By another argument equally dark as it stands in his own language, Parmenides urges upon us the unity of reality that possesses throughout but one characteristic or set of characters. Reality is not only nontemporal or changeless, but nonspatial or indivisible, even in theory. Thus we may not attribute a character to a part of reality and not to the whole, nor can we speak of one phase or aspect of reality as distinct from another. Here Parmenides insists that reality is compact, for he has denied the "boundless" or "emptiness" that might be thought to separate one "thing" from another.[14]

Nor is there aught of distinct; for the All is self-similar alway.
Nor is there anywhere more to debar it from being unbroken;
Nor is there anywhere less, for the All is sated with Being;
Wherefore the All is unbroken, and Being approacheth to Being....
Wherefore that that which IS should be infinite is not permitted;
For it is lacking in naught, or else it were lacking in all things.

If reality or any aspect or part of reality lacks a characteristic, then that characteristic is unreal. And it seems clear to Parmenides that what is once called unreal in this way cannot be real at all. Hence reality as a whole possesses any mentioned characteristic or it does not; there is no middle path. Here the naïveté of Pre-

[14] Parmenides, in Bakewell, *op. cit.,* p. 16. The first four lines may be read as denying the possibility of empty space. Contrast this with the doctrine of Leucippus given below, page 20.

Socratic philosophy is obvious. A little analysis of the terms "real" and "unreal" would have saved Greek thought from whole decades of spectacular and disheartening paradox. It would have shown that these words are used in several senses and in several connections. Thus when we are discussing thought, we must admit that thinking lacks weight, and that thought is real. But it does not follow that weight is unreal, in the sense that mermaids or centaurs are unreal. Weight is simply irrelevant to thought, just as death is irrelevant to the square root of 2. But we must not be impatient with these sages of the past, upon whose shoulders we stand today. Our purpose here is to comprehend rather than to judge.

Parmenides' conclusions were supported by the subtle, if fallacious, reasoning of his mathematical-minded pupil Zeno. He directed his attention toward motion or change of place, and seconded Parmenides' argument by showing that motion is impossible. His argument takes the general form: If a thing moves, it must move either in the place where it is or in the place where it is not. But a thing cannot move in the place where it is, since that would be equivalent to being at rest there, and it cannot move where it is not, since nothing under any circumstances can be where it is not.

Here obviously analysis of the verb "to be" is called for. Does "to be here" mean "to be at rest here"? And can anyone insist that it *must* mean this? This same lack of analysis appears in another form of the argument against motion. An arrow cannot pass from any point, A, to another, B, since before it can reach B it must reach B_1, which is, say, halfway between A and B. Before it can reach B_1 it must reach B_2, halfway between A and B_1, and so on indefinitely. Thus before the arrow reaches B it must have occupied an infinite number of points or positions. This is clearly impossible in a finite time. But A and B stand for any two points. Therefore the arrow can never accomplish the passing of any distance, no matter how great or small.

$$\rightarrow A \overset{B_3}{\underset{|}{\rule{0pt}{0pt}}}\overset{B_2}{\underset{|}{\rule{0pt}{0pt}}}\overset{B_1}{\underset{|}{\rule{0pt}{0pt}}}\underline{\hspace{3cm}}B$$

If we suppose that when the tip of the arrow reaches B_1, it is there for a moment *as if at rest*, then Zeno is right, the motion of the arrow from A to B is impossible in a finite time. But suppose that while the arrow is moving, there is no moment when the tip of the arrow is *as if at rest* at B_1. In other words, suppose that moving is not composed of a series of rests. Clearly, Zeno has rushed hastily to defend the speculative dogma "There is no motion," whereas he should have started upon the more difficult but more rewarding path of determining what we mean by motion from A to B. The early philosophers paid dearly for their lack of interest in determining just what it was that they were talking about. As we shall see, it was Socrates who discovered this widespread failing and took steps to correct it.

DEADLOCK AND RECONSTRUCTION

Greek philosophy was rent asunder by the diametric opposition and flat contradiction that Asia Minor offered to Italy, Ephesus to Elea. Untrained as they were in analysis of concepts, the Greek thinkers found themselves in a cruel impasse. Clearly, philosophy had gone too far in its first great outburst, magnificent but wholly confusing as it was. Some sort of reconstruction was called for, some way of man's convincing himself that his world is not shot through and through with unreasonable paradoxes, that the near and familiar aspect of things, the very fact of motion itself, so dear to common sense and to Heraclitus, is not logically an utter scandal.

There are three types of reconstruction offered: the skeptical—that of the Sophists; the materialistic—that of the Atomists; and the critical—that of Socrates. The Sophists may be called rebels against speculative philosophy, but they desired to find no new type of philosophy to put in its place. Leucippus, the Atomist, chose to give speculation one last chance. Socrates, subtlest of them all, sought a new method entirely.

The Sophists

The skeptical restatement of the Sophists is a simple one. Philosophy has had its chance and has failed. The implication is clear; the human mind is not equipped to mirror the universe. Pure science, pure contemplation, is not a human faculty, and man will reap nothing but confusion if he attempts presumptuously to describe the universe. However, it does not follow that mind is out of place or useless in human life. On the contrary, reflection is a most valuable activity if it is applied to practical affairs. Let the young men study the arts of politics and public speaking and they will profit greatly by their efforts. They will gain wealth and power, even if they cannot grasp "the scheme of things entire." Therefore let them forget philosophy, which is after all a childish pursuit, unbecoming a mature man with important practical problems before him. If "divine philosophy" prove a temptation, let the student rehearse the paradoxes of Zeno, and the deadlock between the philosophy of Parmenides on the one hand and the teachings of Heraclitus and the wisdom of ordinary experience upon the other. One Sophist, Gorgias of Leontini by name,[15] perfected an exposition of Eleatic doctrine with the apparent intention of frightening his hearers away from philosophy. In its place he wanted to teach them the art of rhetorical persuasion.

Unhappily, the Sophists did not rest in this cautious, if somewhat narrow, position. They turned their skepticism into something positive and militant. If man is quite unable to describe the absolute nature of reality, is he not also unable to grasp any absolute and fundamental principles of justice and loyalty? The Sophists, always interested in preparing powerful instruments for successful practice rather than in cultivating nice distinctions and in pondering matters of theory, were eager to answer this question in the negative. After all, there is no theory of justice, no absolute norm or criterion, that we must feel obliged to respect. There is indeed no clear theory of anything. We can describe only what we find. So we soon come upon Thrasymachus insisting that justice is after all only the interest of the stronger or the cleverer man who is able to force or cajole other people into "respecting his rights."[16] This is,

---

[15] Gorgias of Leontini in Sicily (about 483-375, B.C.), a diplomat and writer of considerable literary power. He once represented his native town before the Athenians.

[16] Thrasymachus of Chalcedon (flourished 400 B.C.), one of the later Sophists, figures prominently in Plato's dialogue *The Republic*.

to be sure, a point of view for which a disillusioned and realistic student of history will find much to be said, and, as we shall soon learn, it presented a grave problem to Socrates himself.

The Atomists

Under Leucippus and Democritus arises a school of speculation that attempts to translate the problems of Elea into the language of Materialism, and there to find an answer.[17] As one student has put it, Leucippus and Democritus are Eleatic "heretics," deserting the orthodox doctrine of Parmenides and Zeno without wholly repudiating their logic. We have seen that Parmenides repudiates change because it seems to involve acceptance of a nonactual reservoir or receptacle for entities that have been driven from the actual world. To believe in change is to believe that there is a *nothing,* and this is too strange an idea for Parmenides to tolerate. Anaxagoras,[18] of whom we shall hear more presently in connection with Socrates, tried to avoid the concept of passage into nothing as follows:[19]

We Greeks are wrong in using the expressions "to come into being" and "to be destroyed," for no thing comes into being or is destroyed. Rather, a thing is mixed with or separated from already existing things. And so it would be more accurate to say, instead of origin, commingling; instead of destruction, dissolution.

Leucippus, on the other hand, boldly admits *nothing* into the household of philosophy, although he dignifies it with the title of *the void* or empty space. All change is thought of as change of place, as the motion of material particles through the void. The particles, the indivisible nuggets, are real. They constitute being. The void is nonbeing or *nothing.* Together these two orders make up the world of change that is open to sense experience. To be sure, our senses

[17] Leucippus (flourished about 420 B.C.). Little is known of his life. It is thought that he visited Elea and later settled in Abdera in Thrace, home of Democritus (460-370 B.C.), who learned much from the school of Leucippus.

[18] Anaxagoras of Clazomenae (500-427 B.C.) lived for a time in Athens, where he enjoyed the friendship of Pericles. He may be said to have introduced philosophy into Athens. Until his day philosophy dwelt on the frontiers of the Greek world rather than at the center.

[19] Fragment from Diels, in Bakewell, *op. cit.,* p. 50.

cannot perceive the single atoms. Only groups of many atoms are visible or in any way perceptible, but the theory "saves the appearances" in that it purports to recognize change as a logically respectable entity. When atoms combine, a new physical thing arises; when the atoms separate, the thing passes away, "is lost in the void," so to speak.

The atoms possess the properties attributed by Parmenides to the one reality of his own theory. They are indivisible and changeless (except for the fact that they can move in empty space).[20]

An atom is an eternal unity. The fact that reality is composed of many atoms, each possessing a form or shape of its own, does not trouble Leucippus, and he offers two reasons. Why, he asks, should the atom possess one form rather than another? No reason can be assigned, and therefore we have a right to expect all possible forms or shapes, an infinity of unique atoms. Furthermore, the inexhaustible variety of birth and decay, the coming-to-be and passing-away of observable entities, indicates an unlimited range of material from which these spring.[21]

Democritus follows Leucippus, but adds some interesting and important details to the atomic theory.[22]

[20] The reader should avoid too hurried acceptance of this notion of an empty space in which change "takes place." The theory has been kept alive for centuries, despite its very grave philosophical difficulties, by the fact that in the earlier stages of modern physics theories were advanced which made this ancient concept of the void continue to be plausible. Today physical theory has deserted it. Philosophers were rarely much impressed with the idea; even some of the Atomists tried to avoid it. Can an event "take place" in the void? In other words, can atoms swim in the void as a fish swims in the sea? The void as such can have no limits, for every part of it must be the same as every other. How then do we conceive of motion in such a space? When we move, do we approach anything? Do we have any velocity? These terms have nothing to do with the void, but refer to relations between a moving body and another actual body. The void itself seems to offer very little help. After all, the void is *nothing,* to which is surreptitiously added the power of containing motion. And Parmenides might well ask: "If you believe that motion can take place only in *nothing,* are you not admitting that motion can take place nowhere?" At this juncture, philosophy still stands sorely in need of a more thoroughgoing analysis of change.

[21] The reader will do well to examine these two arguments of Leucippus as an exercise in what we might call philosophical or logical resistance. What assumptions does Leucippus seem to be making?

[22] Democritus, fragment from Sextus Empiricus (Diels), in Bakewell, *op. cit.,* p. 60.

o. By convention sweet is sweet, by convention bitter is bitter, by convention hot is hot, by convention cold is cold, by convention color is color. But in reality there are atoms and the void. That is, the objects of sense are supposed to be real and it is customary to regard them as such, but in truth they are not. Only the atoms and the void are real.

Taste, temperature, and color are appearances, not realities. They constitute our way of apprehending what is really only a "concourse" or combination of atoms. Thus sheer quality of color, taste, and so on is substituted in the mind for the extremely complicated patterns of atomic arrangement. This theory is the most durable contribution made by the Atomist, being held in modern form by many competent thinkers today. But it is, nonetheless, one of the strangest of their teachings. This becomes particularly clear when we recognize that the mind itself is for Democritus a concourse of spherical, fiery atoms, capable of very fast motion one against another. Atoms, then, mind atoms and less mobile atoms, together produce something quite unatomic—namely, a stab of pain or a musical note. Is this consistent with the doctrine that nothing exists but atoms and the void? After all, to call quality a matter of convention does not alter the fact that its perception exists. And a perception of quality is neither an atom nor a group of atoms, however fiery or "subtle" we may think them.

But despite many such difficulties of detail, the atomic theory of the universe is an impressive doctrine. Leucippus and Democritus touch the very core of the problem that haunts all Pre-Socratic philosophy: How can nature change in detail and still possess an essential permanence? They are learning the great truth, so simple that it often appears trivial, that only the permanent can change. For Parmenides this can only seem paradoxical, and he accordingly repudiates the very idea of change. The Atomists, on the other hand, recognize the possibility of a permanent something—in their case, the infinite variety of the actual atomic shapes—that supplies the foundation for all change. Without some such permanence, natural process might be said to begin anew at every instant, and all continuity between past, present, and future would be lost. There would be no recognizable change because there would be "nothing to change," no body of permanence taking on new aspects or new configurations. There are many great differences between ancient atomism and the world picture of modern science, but there is one theme that the two include, and that is the notion of some sort of quantitative permanence underlying physical change. Modern physics expresses this idea in the great law of the conservation of energy.

We shall find Socrates looking with considerable distrust upon the teachings of these Materialists. They may indeed reduce the philosophy of change to a reasonable formula, but they see fit to leave out of their world picture a very familiar fact—that of purpose. The atoms influence one another's course only by the shock of collision, which their constant motion renders frequent, and there is no original ordering of these atoms according to any plan. The atoms vary in weight, as in size and shape, and the heavier atoms are thought of as forming the centers of the many vortices the shock of collision is said to produce. The lighter atoms, such as those of fire, are driven to the outer layers of these vortices. Thus a world like our own—for Democritus there are many worlds—is built upon chance and necessity. Chance collision combines with the mechanical necessity whereby heavier and lighter atoms find their places. How then explain the amazing nicety with which animals seem built to fit their environment, the innumerable adaptations of life to the world? This seems too delicate an adjustment to leave to chance. More difficult still, how explain human will and purpose? On the Atomist theory, nothing ever happens for the sake of any end or value to be realized in the future. All events flow without reason, by chance and necessity, as combination after combination of atoms occurs. Accordingly my acts of purpose when, for the sake of something to be gained in the future, I expend present effort or exercise restraint, are as out of place in the world of the Atomist as are the perceptible qualities of color or temperature. This Socrates felt, and he argued vehemently against the Materialists' denial of purpose.

CHAPTER II

Analysis and Speculation in Socrates

Socrates' philosophy may be described as a well-considered attack upon both the Sophists and the Materialists. Socrates refuses to admit that we must renounce the pursuit of truth because of the confusion earlier thinkers have evoked. Nor will he accept the theory of Materialism as an answer to the problems of philosophy. In defending these tenets Socrates is forced to construct a new method of thought—two new methods, to be exact, one of analysis and the other of speculation. His method of analysis is founded upon his theory of *definition,* and his method of speculation upon a theory of *hypothesis.* It is the first of these to which we nearly always refer when we speak of the "Socratic method."

SOCRATES' METHOD OF ANALYSIS

Aristotle calls Socratic analysis *inductive definition,* and he points out that it involves the discovery of the concept. We are all familiar with the word "courage," but how many of us are ready to say just what it includes and does not include? Until we can do so we have no clear *concept* of courage. We may determine and exhibit concepts in Socratic fashion by defining the terms already in popular or at least in current usage. By this procedure we seek a definition that will include all the uses to which a given term is put. This we do by eliminating any definition suggested that will not fit instances of usage which can be cited. In this way we refer to the actual facts of the widespread usage of words. This justifies Aristotle's phrase *inductive definition.* Induction must always have reference to fact

---

[1] Socrates (469-399 B.C.), an Athenian, was outwardly to be distinguished from the Sophists primarily because he refused to take payment for his teaching. Some account of his activities and of the manner of his death appears in the text.

of some sort. (It may of course be necessary to indicate that the term has more than one consistent use, and to distinguish between them. This is perhaps truer today than it was in the time of Socrates. Our language, being a composite of many earlier tongues, is much more complex in vocabulary than was the Greek language of the fifth century B.C.) Socrates believes that if we practice such analysis so that we learn to know just what we mean when we say—for instance, "Aristogeiton was a brave man"—in other words, if we have a clear concept of our topic, we will avoid that most frequent type of human error which arises when we fall unconsciously into using a word in more than one sense. If all men practiced such logical discretion and used terms only after "purifying" them by analysis, the deadlocks of philosophy would be avoided, and the Sophistic suspicion of pure theory would be shown to be unfounded. It is true that Socrates himself usually employed this method in purely *ethical* discussions against the Sophists rather than in the framing of a philosophy of man and of the world. His greatest pupil, Plato, extended the scope of the method and employed it with marked success to meet the problems that he inherited from the times of Heraclitus and Parmenides. But we must not anticipate Plato's thought at this point.

The following excerpt from Plato's dialogue *Laches* affords an excellent example of the Socratic method in operation.[2] Notice that Socrates does not himself advance definitions, but puts to the test the definition suggested by his companions. Socrates boasted that he was not himself the author of any theory, but that by his questioning he helped others to "give birth to" clear ideas. He called himself an intellectual midwife.

Laches is a bluff old campaigner; Nicias, although not without a military background, has studied philosophy and engaged in political and diplomatic undertakings. The subject of the discussion is courage.[3]

---

[2] In this dialogue Plato presents what is, almost without question, Socrates' own point of view. As we shall see later, he does not always do this, even when he puts definite conclusions into Socrates' mouth.

[3] Plato, *Laches*, in *Dialogues*, trans. by Benjamin Jowett, Vol. I, pp. 98-110. The Clarendon Press. Oxford, 5 vols., 3d ed. This and later quotations from the *Dialogues* in this edition are reprinted by permission of the publisher.

Soc[rates]. Then, Laches, suppose that we first set about determining the nature of courage. . . . Tell me, if you can, what is courage.

La[ches]. Indeed, Socrates, I see no difficulty in answering; he is a man of courage who does not run away, but remains at his post and fights against the enemy; there can be no mistake about that.

Soc. Very good, Laches; and yet I fear that I did not express myself clearly; and therefore you have answered not the question which I intended to ask, but another.

La. What do you mean, Socrates?

Soc. I will endeavour to explain; you would call a man courageous who remains at his post, and fights with the enemy?

La. Certainly I should.

Soc. And so should I; but what would you say of another man, who fights flying, instead of remaining?

La. How flying?

Soc. Why, as the Scythians are said to fight, flying as well pursuing; and as Homer says in praise of the horses of Aeneas, that they knew 'how to pursue, and fly quickly hither and thither'; and he passes an encomium on Aeneas himself, as having a knowledge of fear or flight, and calls him 'an author of fear or flight.'

La. Yes, Socrates, and there Homer is right: for he was speaking of chariots, as you were speaking of the Scythian cavalry, who have that way of fighting; but the heavy-armed Greek fights, as I say, remaining in his rank.

Soc. And yet, Laches, you must except the Lacedaemonians at Plataea, who, when they came upon the light shields of the Persians, are said not to have been willing to stand and fight, and to have fled; but when the ranks of the Persians were broken, they turned upon them like cavalry, and won the battle of Plataea.

La. That is true.

Soc. That was my meaning when I said that I was to blame in having put my question badly, and that this was the reason of your answering badly. For I meant to ask you not only about the courage of heavy-armed soldiers, but about the courage of cavalry and every other style of soldier; and not only who are courageous in war, but who are courageous in perils by sea, and who in disease, or in poverty, or again in politics, are courageous; and not only who are courageous against pain or fear, but mighty to contend against desires and pleasures, either fixed in their rank or turning upon their enemy. There is this sort of courage —is there not, Laches?

La. Certainly, Socrates.

26

Soc. And all these are courageous, but some have courage in pleasures, and some in pains: some in desires, and some in fears, and some are cowards under the same conditions, as I should imagine.

La. Very true.

Soc. Now I was asking about courage and cowardice in general. And I will begin with courage, and once more ask, What is that common quality, which is the same in all these cases, and which is called courage? Do you now understand what I mean?

La. Not over well.

Soc. I mean this: As I might ask what is that quality which is called quickness, and which is found in running, in playing the lyre, in speaking, in learning, and in many other similar actions, or rather which we possess in nearly every action that is worth mentioning of arms, legs, mouth, voice, mind;—would you not apply the term quickness to all of them?

La. Quite true.

Soc. And suppose I were to be asked by some one: What is that common quality, Socrates, which, in all these uses of the word, you call quickness? I should say the quality which accomplishes much in a little time—whether in running, speaking, or in any other sort of action.

La. You would be quite correct.

Soc. And now, Laches, do you try and tell me in like manner, What is that common quality which is called courage, and which includes all the various uses of the term when applied both to pleasure and pain, and in all the cases to which I was just now referring?

La. I should say that courage is a sort of endurance of the soul, if I am to speak of the universal nature which pervades them all.

Soc. But that it what we must do if we are to answer the question. And yet I cannot say that every kind of endurance is, in my opinion, to be deemed courage. Hear my reason: I am sure, Laches, that you would consider courage to be a very noble quality.

La. Most noble, certainly.

Soc. And you would say that a wise endurance is also good and noble?

La. Very noble.

Soc. But what would you say of a foolish endurance? Is not that, on the other hand, to be regarded as evil and hurtful?

La. True.

Soc. And is anything noble which is evil and hurtful?

La. I ought not to say that, Socrates.

Soc. Then you would not admit that sort of endurance to be cour-age—for it is not noble, but courage is noble?

La. You are right.

Soc. Then, according to you, only the wise endurance is courage?

La. True.

Soc. But as to the epithet 'wise,'—wise in what? In all things small as well as great? For example, if a man shows the quality of en-durance in spending his money wisely, knowing that by spending he will acquire more in the end, do you call him courageous?

La. Assuredly not.

Soc. Or, for example, if a man is a physician, and his son, or some patient of his, has inflammation of the lungs, and begs that he may be allowed to eat or drink something, and the other is firm and refuses; is that courage?

La. No; that is not courage at all, any more than the last.

Soc. Again, take the case of one who endures in war, and is willing to fight, and wisely calculates and knows that others will help him, and that there will be fewer and inferior men against him than there are with him; and suppose that he has also advan-tages of position;—would you say of such a one who endures with all this wisdom and preparation, that he, or some man in the opposing army who is in the opposite circumstances to these and yet endures and remains at his post, is the braver?

La. I should say that the latter, Socrates, was the braver.

Soc. But, surely, this is a foolish endurance in comparison with the other?

La. That is true.

Soc. Then you would say that he who in an engagement of cavalry endures, having the knowledge of horsemanship, is not so coura-geous as he who endures, having no such knowledge?

La. So I should say.

Soc. And he who endures, having a knowledge of the use of the sling, or the bow, or of any other art, is not so courageous as he who endures, not having such a knowledge?

La. True.

Soc. And he who descends into a well, and dives, and holds out in this or any similar action, having no knowledge of diving, or the like, is, as you would say, more courageous than those who have this knowledge?

La. Why, Socrates, what else can a man say?

Soc. Nothing, if that be what he thinks.

La. But that is what I do think.

Soc. And yet men who thus run risks and endure are foolish, Laches, in comparison of those who do the same things, having the skill to do them.

La. That is true.

Soc. But foolish boldness and endurance appeared before to be base and hurtful to us.

La. Quite true.

Soc. Whereas courage was acknowledged to be a noble quality.

La. True.

Soc. And now on the contrary we are saying that the foolish endurance, which was before held in dishonour, is courage.

La. Very true.

Soc. And are we right in saying so?

La. Indeed, Socrates, I am sure that we are not right.

Soc. Then according to your statement, you and I, Laches, are not attuned to the Dorian mode, which is a harmony of words and deeds; for our deeds are not in accordance with our words. Any one would say that we had courage who saw us in action, but not, I imagine, he who heard us talking about courage just now.

La. That is most true.

Soc. And is this condition of ours satisfactory?

La. Quite the reverse.

Soc. Suppose, however, that we admit the principle of which we are speaking to a certain extent.

La. To what extent and what principle do you mean?

Soc. The principle of endurance. We too must endure and persevere in the enquiry, and then courage will not laugh at our faint-heartedness in searching for courage; which after all may, very likely, be endurance.

La. I am ready to go on, Socrates; and yet I am unused to investigations of this sort. But the spirit of controversy has been aroused in me by what has been said; and I am really grieved at being thus unable to express my meaning. For I fancy that I do know the nature of courage; but somehow or other, she has slipped away from me, and I cannot get hold of her and tell her nature.

Soc. But, my dear friend, should not the good sportsman follow the track, and not be lazy?

La. Certainly, he should.

Soc. And shall we invite Nicias to join us? he may be better at the sport than we are. What do you say?

La. I should like that.

Soc. Come then, Nicias, and do what you can to help your friends, who are tossing on the waves of argument, and at the last gasp; you see our extremity, and may save us and also settle your own opinion, if you will tell us what you think about courage.

Nic[ias]. I have been thinking, Socrates, that you and Laches are not defining courage in the right way; for you have forgotten an excellent saying which I have heard from your own lips.

Soc. What is it, Nicias?

Nic. I have often heard you say that 'Every man is good in that in which he is wise, and bad in that in which he is unwise.'

Soc. That is certainly true, Nicias.

Nic. And therefore if the brave man is good, he is also wise.

Soc. Do you hear him, Laches?

La. Yes, I hear him, but I do not very well understand him.

Soc. I think that I understand him; and he appears to me to mean that courage is a sort of wisdom.

La. What can he possibly mean, Socrates?

Soc. That is a question which you must ask of himself.

La. Yes.

Soc. Tell him then, Nicias, what you mean by this wisdom; for you surely do not mean the wisdom which plays the flute?

Nic. Certainly not.

Soc. Nor the wisdom which plays the lyre?

Nic. No.

Soc. But what is this knowledge then, and of what?

La. I think that you put the question to him very well, Socrates; and I would like him to say what is the nature of this knowledge or wisdom.

Nic. I mean to say, Laches, that courage is the knowledge of that which inspires fear or confidence in war, or in anything.

La. How strangely he is talking, Socrates.

Soc. Why do you say so, Laches?

La. Why, surely courage is one thing and wisdom another.

Soc. That is just what Nicias denies.

La. Yes, that is what he denies; but he is so silly.

Soc. Suppose that we instruct instead of abusing him?

Nic. Laches does not want to instruct me, Socrates; but having been proved to be talking nonsense himself, he wants to prove that I have been doing the same.

La. Very true, Nicias; and you are talking nonsense, as I shall endeavour to show. Let me ask you a question: Do not physicians know the dangers of disease? or do the courageous know them? or are the physicians the same as the courageous?

Nic. Not at all.

La. No more than the husbandmen who know the dangers of husbandry, or that other craftsmen, who have a knowledge of that which inspires them with fear or confidence in their own arts, and yet they are not courageous a whit the more for that.

Soc. What is Laches saying, Nicias? He appears to be saying something of importance.

Nic. Yes, he is saying something, but it is not true.

Soc. How so?

Nic. Why, because he does not see that the physician's knowledge only extends to the nature of health and disease: he can tell the sick man no more than this. Do you imagine, Laches, that the physician knows whether health or disease is the more terrible to a man? Had not many a man better never get up from a sick bed? I should like to know whether you think that life is always better than death. May not death often be the better of the two?

La. Yes certainly so in my opinion.

Nic. And do you think that the same things are terrible to those who had better die, and to those who had better live?

La. Certainly not.

Nic. And do you suppose that the physician or any other artist knows this, or any one indeed, except he who is skilled in the grounds of fear and hope? And him I call the courageous.

Soc. Do you understand his meaning, Laches?

La. Yes; I suppose that, in his way of speaking, the soothsayers are courageous. For who but one of them can know to whom to die or to live is better? And yet, Nicias, would you allow that you are yourself a soothsayer, or are you neither a soothsayer nor courageous?

Nic. What! do you mean to say that the soothsayer ought to know the grounds of hope or fear?

La. Indeed I do: who but he?

Nic. Much rather I should say he of whom I speak; for the soothsayer ought to know only the signs of things that are about to come to pass, whether death or disease, or loss of property, or victory, or defeat in war, or in any sort of contest; but to whom the suffering or not suffering of these things will be for the best, can no more be decided by the soothsayer than by one who is no soothsayer.

La. I cannot understand what Nicias would be at, Socrates; for he represents the courageous man as neither a soothsayer, nor a physician, nor in any other character, unless he means to say that he is a god. My opinion is that he does not like honestly to confess that he is talking nonsense, but that he shuffles up and down in order to conceal the difficulty into which he has got himself. You and I, Socrates, might have practised a similar shuffle just now, if we had only wanted to avoid the appearance of inconsistency. And if we had been arguing in a court of law there might have been reason in so doing; but why should a man deck himself out with vain words at a meeting of friends such as this?

Soc. I quite agree with you, Laches, that he should not. But perhaps Nicias is serious, and not merely talking for the sake of talking. Let us ask him just to explain what he means, and if he has reason on his side we will agree with him; if not we will instruct him.

La. Do you, Socrates, if you like, ask him: I think that I have asked enough.

Soc. I do not see why I should not; and my question will do for both of us.

La. Very good.

Soc. Then tell me, Nicias, or rather tell us, for Laches and I are partners in the argument: Do you mean to affirm that courage is the knowledge of the grounds of hope and fear?

Nic. I do.

Soc. And not every man has this knowledge; the physician and the soothsayer have it not; and they will not be courageous unless they acquire it—that is what you were saying?

Nic. I was.

Soc. Then this is certainly not a thing which every pig would know, as the proverb says, and therefore he could not be courageous.

Nic. I think not.

Soc. Clearly not, Nicias; not even such a big pig as the Crommyonian sow would be called by you courageous. And this I say not as a joke, but because I think that he who assents to your doctrine, that courage is the knowledge of the grounds of fear and hope, cannot allow that any wild beast is courageous, unless he admits that a lion, or a leopard, or perhaps a boar, or any other animal, has such a degree of wisdom that he knows things which but a few human beings ever know by reason of their difficulty. He who takes your view of courage must affirm that a lion, and a stag, and a bull, and a monkey, have equally little pretensions to courage.

La. Capital, Socrates; by the gods, that is truly good. And I hope, Nicias, that you will tell us whether these animals, which we all admit to be courageous, are really wiser than mankind; or whether you will have the boldness, in the face of universal opinion, to deny their courage.

Nic. Why, Laches, I do not call animals or any other things which have no fear of dangers, because they are ignorant of them, courageous, but only fearless and senseless. Do you imagine that I should call little children courageous, which fear no dangers because they know none? There is a difference, to my way of thinking, between fearlessness and courage. I am of opinion that thoughtful courage is a quality possessed by very few, but that rashness and boldness, and fearlessness, which has no forethought, are very common qualities possessed by many men, many women, many children, many animals. And you, and men in general, call by the term 'courageous' actions which I call rash; —my courageous actions are wise actions.

La. Behold, Socrates, how admirably, as he thinks, he dresses himself out in words, while seeking to deprive of the honour of courage those whom all the world acknowledges to be courageous.

Nic. Not so, Laches, but do not be alarmed; for I am quite willing to say of you and also of Lamachus, and of many other Athenians, that you are courageous and therefore wise.

La. I could answer that; but I would not have you cast in my teeth that I am a haughty Aexonian.

Soc. Do not answer him, Laches; I rather fancy that you are not aware of the source from which his wisdom is derived. He has got all this from my friend Damon, and Damon is always with Prodicus, who, of all the Sophists, is considered to be the best puller to pieces of words of this sort.

La. Yes, Socrates; and the examination of such niceties is a much more suitable employment for a Sophist than for a great statesman whom the city chooses to preside over her.

Soc. Yes, my sweet friend, but a great statesman is likely to have a great intelligence. And I think that the view which is implied in Nicias' definition of courage is worthy of examination.

La. Then examine for yourself, Socrates.

Soc. That is what I am going to do, my dear friend. Do not, however, suppose I shall let you out of the partnership; for I shall expect you to apply your mind, and join with me in the consideration of the question.

La. I will if you think that I ought.

Soc. Yes, I do; but I must beg of you, Nicias, to begin again. You remember that we originally considered courage to be a part of virtue.

Nic. Very true.

Soc. And you yourself said that it was a part; and there were many other parts, all of which taken together are called virtue.

Nic. Certainly.

Soc. Do you agree with me about the parts? For I say that justice, temperance, and the like, are all of them parts of virtue as well as courage. Would you not say the same?

Nic. Certainly.

Soc. Well then, so far we are agreed. And now let us proceed a step, and try to arrive at a similar agreement about the fearful and the hopeful: I do not want you to be thinking one thing and myself another. Let me then tell you my own opinion, and if I am wrong you shall set me right: in my opinion the terrible and the hopeful are the things which do or do not create fear, and fear is not of the present, nor of the past, but is of future and expected evil. Do you not agree to that, Laches?

La. Yes, Socrates, entirely.

Soc. That is my view, Nicias; the terrible things, as I should say, are the evils which are future; and the hopeful are the good or not evil things which are future. Do you or do you not agree with me?

Nic. I agree.

Soc. And the knowledge of these things you call courage?

Nic. Precisely.

Soc. And now let me see whether you agree with Laches and myself as to a third point.

Nic. What is that?

Soc. I will tell you. He and I have a notion that there is not one knowledge or science of the past, another of the present, a third of what is likely to be best and what will be best in the future; but that of all three there is one science only: for example, there is one science of medicine which is concerned with the inspection of health equally in all times, present, past, and future; and one science of husbandry in like manner, which is concerned with the productions of the earth in all times. As to the art of the general, you yourselves will be my witnesses that he has an excellent foreknowledge of the future, and that he claims to be the master and not the servant of the soothsayer, because he knows better what is happening or is likely to happen in war: and accordingly the law places the soothsayer under the general, and not the general under the soothsayer. Am I not correct in saying so, Laches?

La. Quite correct.

Soc. And do you, Nicias, also acknowledge that the same science has understanding of the same things, whether future, present, or past?

Nic. Yes, indeed, Socrates; that is my opinion.

Soc. And courage, my friend, is, as you say, a knowledge of the fearful and of the hopeful?

Nic. Yes.

Soc. And the fearful, and the hopeful, are admitted to be future good and future evils?

Nic. True.

Soc. And the same science has to do with the same things in the future or at any time?

Nic. That is true.

Soc. Then courage is not the science which is concerned with the fearful and hopeful, for they are future only; courage, like the other sciences, is concerned not only with good and evil of the future, but of the present and past, and of any time?

Nic. That, as I suppose, is true.

Soc. Then the answer which you have given, Nicias, includes only a third part of courage; but our question extended to the whole nature of courage: and according to your view, that is, according to your present view, courage is not only the knowledge of the hopeful and the fearful, but seems to include nearly every good and evil without reference to time. What do you say to that alteration in your statement?

Nic. I agree, Socrates.

Soc. But then, my dear friend, if a man knew all good and evil, and how they are, and have been, and will be produced, would he not be perfect, and wanting in no virtue, whether justice, or temperance, or holiness? He would possess them all, and he would know which were dangers and which were not, and guard against them whether they were supernatural or natural; and he would provide the good, as he would know how to deal both with gods or men.

Nic. I think, Socrates, that there is a great deal of truth in what you say.

Soc. But then, Nicias, courage, according to this new definition of
   yours, instead of being a part of virtue only, will be all virtue?
Nic. It would seem so.
Soc. But we were saying that courage is one of the parts of virtue?
Nic. Yes, that was what we were saying.
Soc. And that is in contradiction with our present view?
Nic. That appears to be the case.
Soc. Then, Nicias, we have not discovered what courage is.
Nic. We have not.

Like so many of the investigations guided by Socrates, the argument of this dialogue comes to no positive conclusion. But it is
clearly not a failure, for Socrates has succeeded in eliminating a
number of popular errors concerning the nature of courage. He has
also brought the argument to a resting place not far removed from
the final conclusions concerning courage that Plato reported years
later in *The Republic.* Consider the following passage, where the
argument is concerned primarily not with single individuals but
with the collective life of a Greek city-state.[4]

The city will be courageous in virtue of a portion of herself which
preserves under all circumstances that opinion about the nature of
things to be feared and not to be feared in which our legislator educated them; and this is what you term courage.
   I should like to hear what you are saying once more, for I do not
think that I perfectly understand you.
   I mean that courage is a kind of salvation.
   Salvation of what?
   Of the opinion respecting things to be feared, what they are and
of what nature, which the law implants through education; and I
mean by the words 'under all circumstances' to intimate that in
pleasure or in pain, or under the influence of desire or fear, a man
preserves, and does not lose this opinion. Shall I give you an illustration?
   If you please.
   You know, I said, that dyers, when they want to dye wool for
making the true sea-purple, begin by selecting their white colour
first; this they prepare and dress with much care and pains, in order that the white ground may take the purple hue in full perfec-

---

[4] Plato, *The Republic,* in *Dialogues,* trans. by Benjamin Jowett, Vol. III,
pp. 119-20.

tion. The dyeing then proceeds; and whatever is dyed in this manner becomes a fast colour, and no washing either with lyes or without them can take away the bloom. But, when the ground has not been duly prepared, you will have noticed how poor is the look either of purple or of any other colour.

Yes, he said; I know that they have a washed-out and ridiculous appearance.

Then now, I said, you will understand what our object was in selecting our soldiers, and educating them in music and gymnastic; we were contriving influences which would prepare them to take the dye of the laws in perfection, and the colour of their opinion about dangers and of every other opinion was to be indelibly fixed by their nurture and training, not to be washed away by such potent lyes as pleasure—mightier agent far in washing the soul than any soda or lye; or by sorrow, fear, and desire, the mightiest of all other solvents. And this sort of universal saving power of true opinion in conformity with law about real and false dangers I call and maintain to be courage, unless you disagree.

But I agree, he replied; for I suppose that you mean to exclude mere uninstructed courage, such as that of a wild beast or of a slave —this, in your opinion, is not the courage which the law ordains, and ought to have another name.

Most certainly.

Thus we learn that for Plato and Socrates courage is knowledge, but knowledge of a special sort that can preserve itself under pressure.

The problem of definition, as Socrates conceives it, stands out clearly in the quotation from Plato's *Laches*. He is not interested in special cases. The courageous behavior of heavy-armed soldiers is no more significant than that of light-armed skirmishers. Socrates tries to push through all these instances and find the general term that lies behind—to formulate the concept of courage which applies equally well to all cases that must be considered. Thus courage in resisting pleasure, in resisting, say, the thrill of running spectacular risks, must be considered as well as the courage that scorns unavoidable danger. Socrates is talking about courage in general.

There is an unhappy tendency in modern thought whereby we sometimes speak of courage "in general" as if it were something vague and undetermined. Indeed, the terms "abstract" and "general" are often used today, even by educated people, as synonyms of "vague" or "indefinite." This is certainly to be regretted. There is really very little vagueness about a term that has been put through the mill of Socratic analysis, at any rate there is much less vagueness than there would otherwise have been. Thought is vague when it overlooks distinctions and lumps many things together without seeing just what these things have in common and where they differ. Socrates, of course, advocates no such procedure. When we do class objects together, we should not rest until the method of inductive definition has made clear just what common element they possess. It is only after such analysis that we use words with any precision or know at all clearly what it is we are talking about.

The method of inductive definition follows a logical principle that may be expressed as follows: A definition should be neither too wide nor too narrow. It should not include more subject matter than our use of the term allows, nor should it exclude any subject matter conceded by widespread usage. Thus Laches' definition that courage is sticking at one's post is clearly too narrow. It excludes certain types of behavior that we should all term brave. On the other hand, Nicias' attempt to identify courage with knowledge of the truly dangerous includes too much, as Socrates points out. There is a certain type of cynical humor that is based upon use of pseudo-definitions, intentionally chosen too wide for the subject matter usually conceded to the terms defined. Thus to call violin music "the sound produced by drawing horsehair over catgut" is to offer a pseudo-definition that includes too much.

SOCRATES' METHOD OF SPECULATION

Socrates' discontent with Materialism was directed especially against the curious Atomism of Anaxagoras, with whose works he was at one time well acquainted. Anaxagoras had tempered the extreme Materialism of other Pre-Socratics by teaching that the arrangement of the particles is not wholly a matter of chance and necessity. He believed that an intelligence (*nous*) guided the courses of the atoms, at least in the beginning, and rescued them from chaos.

Again Anaxagoras differs from other Atomists in emphasizing the quality of each atom. For him, the atoms—"seeds," as he called them—are not mere physical units, such as those Democritus was soon to describe, each with its unique size and shape. On the contrary, each one carries with it, or is identical with, a perceptible quality. A concrete perceptible thing is a mixture of "seeds," all qualities being represented in each thing, but only a few dominant ones clearly recognizable. Here Anaxagoras seems to draw something from the teaching of Heraclitus, who insisted that since "it is the cold things that become warm, and the warm things that become cold," opposites must interpenetrate one with another. For Anaxagoras this becomes the somewhat presumptuous dogma that each concrete thing contains all qualities. Otherwise, he might say, how can vegetable foods be changed into flesh, or wood into ashes and smoke? Even intelligence cannot change like into unlike.

Socrates was disappointed to find that Anaxagoras really made very little use of the intelligence he postulated, reverting continually to Materialism. Apparently Anaxagoras invoked intelligence only to remove his original chaos, when the "seeds" lay in a purely random mixture and there were no concrete things.[5]

Socrates came to look upon his interest in Anaxagoras as an extravagance of his "salad days." But he felt that in outgrowing Anaxagoras and thinkers of similar stamp he had learned much, and had been forced to formulate his own principles clearly—that he had in fact come in sight of a new method of speculation. This method is described in the following passage from Plato's *Phaedo*.[6]

When I was young, Cebes, I had a prodigious desire to know that department of philosophy which is called the investigation of nature; to know the causes of things, and why a thing is and is

[5] Some modern scholars feel that Socrates misread Anaxagoras, who really intended to assign a more important role to intelligence. But that need not trouble us here. See Professor R. K. Hack's study *God in Greek Philosophy* (Princeton University Press, 1931).

[6] Plato, *Phaedo*, in *Dialogues*, trans. by Benjamin Jowett, Vol. II, pp. 241-45.

created or destroyed appeared to me to be a lofty profession; and I was always agitating myself with the consideration of questions such as these:—Is the growth of animals the result of some decay which the hot and cold principle contracts, as some have said? Is the blood the element with which we think, or the air, or the fire? or perhaps nothing of the kind—but the brain may be the originating power of the perceptions of hearing and sight and smell, and memory and opinion may come from them, and science may be based on memory and opinion when they have attained fixity. And then I went on to examine the corruption of them, and then to the things of heaven and earth, and at last I concluded myself to be utterly and absolutely incapable of these enquiries, as I will satisfactorily prove to you. For I was fascinated by them to such a degree that my eyes grew blind to things which I had seemed to myself, and also to others, to know quite well; I forgot what I had before thought self-evident truths; e.g. such a fact as that the growth of man is the result of eating and drinking; for when by the digestion of food flesh is added to flesh and bone to bone, and whenever there is an aggregation of congenial elements, the lesser bulk becomes larger and the small man great.... [I am no] longer satisfied that I understand the reason why one or anything else is either generated or destroyed or is at all, but I have in my mind some confused notion of a new method, and can never admit the other.

Then I heard some one reading, as he said, from a book of Anaxagoras, that mind was the disposer and cause of all, and I was delighted at this notion, which appeared quite admirable, and I said to myself: If mind is the disposer, mind will dispose all for the best, and put each particular in the best place; and I argued that if any one desired to find out the cause of the generation or destruction or existence of anything, he must find what state of being or doing or suffering was best for that thing, and therefore a man had only to consider the best for himself and others and then he would also know the worse, since the same science comprehended both. And I rejoiced to think that I had found in Anaxagoras a teacher of the causes of existence such as I desired, and I imagined that he would tell me first whether the earth is flat or round; and whichever was true, he would proceed to explain the cause and the necessity of this being so, and then he would teach me the nature of the best and show that this was best; and if he said that the earth was in the centre, he would further explain that this position was the best, and I should be satisfied with the explanation given, and not want any other sort of cause. And I thought that I would then go on and ask him about the sun and moon and stars, and that he would explain to me their comparative swiftness, and their returnings and various states, active and passive, and how all of them were for the best. For I could not imagine that when he spoke of mind as the disposer of them, he would give any other account of their being as they are, except that this was best; and I thought that when he had explained to me in detail the cause of each and the cause of all, he would go on to explain to me what was best for each and what was good for all. These hopes I would not have sold for a large sum of money, and I seized the books and read them as fast as I could in my eagerness to know the better and the worse.

What expectations I had formed, and how grievously was I disappointed! As I proceeded, I found my philosopher altogether forsaking mind or any other principle of order, but having recourse to air, and ether, and water, and other eccentricities. I might compare him to a person who began by maintaining generally that mind is the cause of the actions of Socrates, but who, when he endeavoured to explain the causes of my several actions in detail, went on to show that I sit here because my body is made up of bones and muscles; and the bones, as he would say, are hard and have joints which divide them, and the muscles are elastic, and they cover the bones, which have also a covering or environment of flesh and skin which contains them; and as the bones are lifted at their joints by the contraction or relaxation of the muscles, I am able to bend my limbs, and this is why I am sitting here in a curved posture—that is what he would say; and he would have a similar explanation of my talking to you, which he would attribute to sound, and air, and hearing, and he would assign ten thousand other causes of the same sort, forgetting to mention the true cause, which is, that the Athenians have thought fit to condemn me, and accordingly I have thought it better and more right to remain here and undergo my sentence; [7] for I am inclined to think that these muscles and bones of mine would have gone off long ago to Megara or Boeotia—by the dog they would, if they had been moved only by their own idea of what was best, and if I had not chosen the better and nobler part, instead of playing truant and running away, of enduring any punishment which the state inflicts. There is surely a strange confusion of causes and conditions in all this. It may be said, indeed, that without bones and muscles and the other parts of the body I cannot execute my purposes. But to say that I do as I do because of them, and that this is the way in which mind acts, and not from the choice of the best, is

___

[7] Socrates is in prison, awaiting execution.

a very careless and idle mode of speaking. I wonder that they cannot distinguish the cause from the condition, which the many, feeling about in the dark, are always mistaking and misnaming. And thus one man makes a vortex all round and steadies the earth by the heaven; another gives the air as a support to the earth, which is a sort of broad trough. Any power which in arranging them as they are arranges them for the best never enters into their minds; and instead of finding any superior strength in it, they rather expect to discover another Atlas of the world who is stronger and more everlasting and more containing than the good;—of the obligatory and containing power of the good they think nothing; and yet this is the principle which I would fain learn if any one would teach me. But as I have failed either to discover myself, or to learn of any one else, the nature of the best, I will exhibit to you, if you like, what I have found to be the second best mode of enquiring into the cause

I should very much like to hear, he replied.

Socrates proceeded:—I thought that as I had failed in the contemplation of the true existence, I ought to be careful that I did not lose the eye of my soul; as people may injure their bodily eye by observing and gazing on the sun during an eclipse, unless they take the precaution of only looking at the image reflected in the water or in some similar medium. So in my own case, I was afraid that my soul might be blinded altogether if I looked at things with my eyes or tried to apprehend them by the help of the senses. And I thought that I had better have recourse to the world of mind and seek there the truth of existence. I dare say that the simile is not perfect—for I am very far from admitting that he who contemplates existences through the medium of thought, sees them only "through a glass darkly," any more than he who considers them in action and operation. However, this was the method which I adopted: I first assumed some principle which I judged to be the strongest, and then I affirmed as true whatever seemed to agree with this, whether relating to the cause or to anything else; and that which disagreed I regarded as untrue.

In the last paragraph of this quotation Socrates outlines a method of investigation still employed in natural science, and indeed in all inquiry—the method of hypothesis. The human mind, he seems to say, is incapable of understanding the world directly, of reducing the manifold aspects of existence to a single pattern, all in one sweeping insight. He who tries this will only be dazzled and confused, and in despair he may join with the Sophists and renounce philosophy, thus losing the "eye of his soul." We can, however, make headway by setting up working hypotheses, or well-considered guesses, and then affirming as true those statements which the hypotheses require. We may, of course, find that we are thus forced to assert propositions that are clearly untenable, in which case the hypothesis must be discarded or in some measure reconstructed. In this way Socrates has been testing the hypothesis of the Materialists.

He is ready to discard it because it offers no intelligible account of something that we find prominent in his own life; namely, respect for purposes, ends, or ideals, and action undertaken or restrained for the sake of these. A purposive action is one prompted by a decision to the effect that this given alternative is, under the circumstances, the best. This implies that we act in such and such a way for the sake of certain standards or values. But atoms do not respect purpose. Their behavior is subject only to chance and necessity. Thus if nothing exists but atoms moving in the void, then purpose is something monstrous and inexplicable. Hence the repudiation of Materialism. In Socrates' day such a repudiation was certainly justified. Today we have to consider various attempts made by Materialists to explain how an organism or a person may act with an apparent interest in future possibilities.

So certain is Socrates of the reality of purposive acts of decision that he is willing to set up the great hypothesis that all things natural have a purpose behind them, even as human action. In Socrates' day this universal teleology, or theory of purpose, was hardly a very startling doctrine, it still being easier to urge, let us say, that horses have teeth in order to chew rather than that they chew because they have teeth, although the latter type of argument was not unknown to the Atomists. Certainly we may urge in Socrates' defense that this is easier to believe than the great rival hypothesis according to which human beings, themselves the products of chance and necessity, introduce value and purpose into a wholly mechanical world. When, however, Socrates carries the argument to explain the specific motions of the heavenly bodies, as he seems willing to do, the reader may have much greater difficulty in following him. It is perhaps hardly necessary to remind the reader that the method of hypothesis that Socrates advocates is today the method whereby many great principles, such as the doctrine of the evolution of organisms, are supported; but modern science and philosophy usually require a wider range of evidence than that which, in this case, seems to have contented Socrates.

Socratic analysis and its results are one thing; Socratic speculation and its hypotheses are another. One may accept, say, the conclusion of the *Laches* without sympathizing with the universal teleology of the passages just quoted. So Santayana attributes the following com· ment to the shade of Democritus in his delightful volume of dra matic essays entitled *Dialogues in Limbo:* [8]

An oracle admonished Socrates to know himself and not to dabble in natural philosophy; and in so far as he obeyed that admonition I honour him. For by self-knowledge he understood knowing his own mind or thoroughly discerning what he meant and what he loved; whereby he framed maxims excellent for the legislator, and fixed the grammar or logic of words. But when, forgetting the oracle, he averred that the sun and moon are products of reason, and are intended for human advantage,[9] he blasphemed against those gods, as if the blood and gall within him, proper to the health of his little body, had burst their bounds and filled the whole heaven. By this presumption he turned his inspiration into sophistry, and what should have been self-knowledge became madness and grotesque errors about the world.

[8] George Santayana, *Dialogues in Limbo,* p. 10. Constable & Co., London; Charles Scribner's Sons, New York; 1925. Reprinted by permission of the publishers.

[9] Does Socrates make this statement? If he is to answer this question, the reader must consider carefully Socrates' explicit commitments in the foregoing quotation. After all, does Socrates consider man to be in a specially privileged position?

CHAPTER III

Socrates and the Sophists

SOPHISTIC ETHICS

Although he outlined the great method of hypothesis, Socrates was himself little given to speculation upon the universe. The cosmic conjecture reported at the end of the previous chapter is probably the only one that he allowed himself during his intellectual maturity. Socrates' interests lay in human conduct and in describing what we mean by the various terms—"justice," "courage," "temperance," "piety," and so on—which describe the excellence of the good man. In this he was compelled to disagree with the leading Sophists, Protagoras,[1] Gorgias, Thrasymachus, Antiphon,[2] brilliant men who taught public speaking and the art of politics in a spectacular and popular fashion.

These men represent what Professor Cornford has so well termed the adolescence of Greek thought. Adolescence is the period in which the individual becomes, sometimes painfully, conscious of himself *as* an individual distinct from the family group. The adolescent often resents external authority, and is angered by efforts made to dominate him or to curb his own personal interests. The precocious adolescent, particularly if he is the product of a brilliant civilization, is cut to the quick if anyone presumes to do his thinking for him. If this attempt is made persistently and with any show of arbitrary authority, the brilliant adolescent becomes a bitter rebel, intent upon ridiculing the wisdom of his elders. The attitude of "modern youth" toward "Victorian" tradition is a case in point.

[1] Protagoras of Abdera (born about 480 B.C.) was the first thinker to call himself a Sophist.

[2] Antiphon the Sophist, was probably a follower of Protagoras. He is not to be confused with the more famous Antiphon the Orator.

Greek morality, the civilization against which the Sophists re-
acted, was a traditional one in which patriotism and piety were
united. The loyal act and the pious act were considered the handsome and the proper thing, the opposite was considered weak and
disgraceful. The codes of morals recognized in the several Greek
cities were advanced as becoming the dignity of a Hellene, a member of an exalted race, for whom action excusable in a "barbarian"
was unthinkable. (It was a Sophist who first suggested that the natural endowment of a Greek was perhaps no greater than that of a
barbarian.) Such racial conservatism might have withheld any people but the intellectually restless Greeks from all philosophical
freedom; as it was, the innovators were received by the more conservative aristocracy with the bitterest scorn and ridicule, of which
the comic poet Aristophanes is the most famous mouthpiece.

Plato has well portrayed the standards of the more conservative
gentlemen in the first book of his *Republic,* when the elderly Cepha-
lus insists that justice is "to speak the truth and to pay one's debts"
—that is, to fulfill one's obligations. The virtue of a gentleman lies
in administering his public and private duties in a sober manner,
supporting his friends and putting up a firm resistance to his enemies. The virtue of a woman is primarily obedience to her husband
and meticulous administration of his household. The virtues of the
lower classes are obedience and sobriety. This was the traditional
aristocratic code.

But Athens had become a democracy, although it occasionally
lapsed into oligarchic dictatorship, and many people had by the
time of the Sophists begun to think for themselves—people who
depended for their livelihood not directly upon the traditional land-
holding system, but who had, in the good or bad sense of the words,
to live by their wits and their initiative. Unfortunately much of this
thinking was motivated by self-interest rather than by the ideal of
individualism. But at any rate discussion of the matter stimulated
the growth of theories comparable to those of the Sophists.

The Sophist has the attitude of one who has "seen through"
morality, and is quite determined not to be imposed upon by laws
and ideals that, after all, can never be shown to possess any un-

46

questionable authority. He has read Herodotus and talked with travelers and merchants, and he is aware that standards and customs vary with geography. Morality seems to be a product of the time and the place, and the strong man is one who can surmount the restrictions of his immediate environment. The Sophist, ancient or modern—for the type is eternal—is the rebellious humanist, scorning the restrictions of tradition or supernatural authority.

Thus the ancient Sophist often taught a return to nature, or at least recommended this course to the stronger and more enlightened spirits. But their return to nature involved no sentimental faith in the natural goodness of man. There is a great difference between the Sophist and the modern romanticist. By "nature" the true Sophist, ancient or modern, means "human nature," or the collection of instincts, desires, and habits that would dominate the individual's life if he were free from the restraint of social custom. Since the Sophist is unable to find any absolute authority behind the imperatives enjoining justice, loyalty, or temperance, he considers most traditional moral codes as mere shackles hung upon the strong individual by a society that lives in constant fear of the strong man's "rugged individualism." Since the Sophist takes the point of view of his favorite pupil, the powerful leader who can exploit the multitude either through force or through persuasion, he tends to minimize the importance of social convention and restraint. After all, the young would-be statesmen who studied public speaking and political strategy from the Sophists were not adverse to a scheme of ethics that excluded all grounds for self-denial or self-sacrifice in the interest of society.

For the Sophist, there is really no point in speaking of a good man unless by that term we mean an able or a clever man. The successful man is he who wins some kind of power and is able to satisfy his desires by compelling others to bow to his demands. All men are at least secretly pleased by the possession of power, and prize it almost as an end in itself, however petty it may be. "Of gods we believe, and of men we know, that by necessary law of their own nature they rule whenever they can." [3]

[3] Thucydides, *The Peloponnesian War*, V, XVII, trans. by the authors.

The return to nature, then, is simply the strong man's refusal to accept the restraint of social convention or the self-denial founded upon a sentimental idealism. An idealist philosophy serves only to make the idealist subject to exploitation by clever realists who know how to mask their true will in noble concepts. This point of view is founded upon the argument of the following fragment from Antiphon the Sophist, which justifies what must seem to us a perverse indifference to any distinction between moral right and wrong.[4]

Justice [in the ordinary view] consists in not transgressing [or rather, in not being known to transgress] any of the legal rules of the State in which one lives as a citizen. A man, therefore, would practise justice in the way most advantageous to himself if, in the presence of witnesses, he held the laws in high esteem, but, in the absence of witnesses, and when he was by himself, he held in high esteem the rules of nature. The reason is that the rules of the laws are adventitious, while the rules of nature are inevitable [and innate]; and again that the rules of the laws are created by covenant and not produced by nature, while the rules of nature are exactly the reverse. A man, therefore, who transgresses legal rules, is free from shame and punishment whenever he is unobserved by those who made the covenant, and is subject to shame and punishment only when he is observed. It is otherwise with transgression of the rules which are innate in nature. If a man strains any of these rules beyond what it can bear, the evil consequences are none the less if he is entirely unobserved, and none the greater, if he is seen of all men; and this is because the injury which he incurs is not due to men's opinion but to the facts of the case.[5]

The work of the Sophists must not be considered as wholly destructive. A traditional morality requires some individualist reaction against itself; otherwise it degrades the very people who support it and sometimes tortures them in that most painful of human dead-

---

[4] Antiphon the Sophist, fragment, in Sir Ernest Barker, *Greek Political Theory: Plato and His Predecessors*, p. 83. Methuen & Co., London, 3d ed., 1947. Reprinted by permission of the publisher.

[5] Upon this passage Professor Barker offers the following note: "To transgress the rules of health, for instance (we may suppose the writer to mean), brings an inevitable reaction which proceeds inexorably from the facts of the case. To transgress a rule against perjury produces no inevitable reaction: only if one is observed is there any reaction, and then it is only a reaction of opinion."

locks, a conflict of two unquestioned and unexamined loyalties. Consider Sophocles' great tragedy *Antigone,* where the unhappy princess is torn between religious, family, and patriotic imperatives. The king has forbidden his people to give to a rebel, Antigone's brother, slain in battle, proper funeral rites. This was a very serious matter for the ancients, involving the soul of the deceased in great jeopardy. This Antigone recognizes, and she feels that she must save her brother from such disgrace and from a miserable immortality.

But from the traditional point of view the king's orders command as much respect as the dictates of such piety. Antigone is defiant, and refuses to respect the king's command. But the traditional attitude is made apparent in the choruses of the play. Here no standard of moral criticism is presented. The chorus insists that Antigone is doing wrong in violating a royal command, in which is embodied the civil law. This is true even though the command is harsh and although the slain prince deserves decent burial. The chorus, however, offers no standard whereby one command or custom can be valued above or below another. All are equally binding. This is the tragedy of a traditional morality, which the Greeks were probably the first people to understand and in part, at least, to overcome. The Sophists offer an important contribution to this reorientation. That they swing too far toward the other extreme is true, but thought often corrects itself by passing through such violent oppositions.

SOCRATES' CRITICISM OF THE SOPHISTS

Socrates' attitude toward the Sophists and something of the logical strategy he employed against them are evident in the following passage from Plato's *Gorgias.*[6]

Cal[*licles*].... how can a man be happy who is the servant of anything? On the contrary, I plainly assert, that he who would truly live ought to allow his desires to wax to the uttermost, and not to chastise them; but when they have grown to their greatest he should have courage and intelligence to minister to them and to satisfy all his longings. And this I affirm to be natural justice

[6] Plato, *Gorgias,* in *Dialogues,* trans. by Benjamin Jowett, Vol. II, pp. 379-82.

and nobility. To this however the many cannot attain; and they blame the strong man because they are ashamed of their own weakness, which they desire to conceal, and hence they say that intemperance is base. As I have remarked already, they enslave the nobler natures, and being unable to satisfy their pleasures, they praise temperance and justice out of their own cowardice. For if a man had been originally the son of a king, or had a nature capable of acquiring an empire or a tyranny or sovereignty, what could be more truly base or evil than temperance— to a man like him, I say, who might freely be enjoying every good, and has no one to stand in his way, and yet has admitted custom and reason and the opinion of other men to be lords over him?—must not he be in a miserable plight whom the reputation of justice and temperance hinders from giving more to his friends than to his enemies, even though he be a ruler in his city? Nay, Socrates, for you profess to be a votary of the truth, and the truth is this:—that luxury and intemperance and license, if they be provided with means, are virtue and happiness—all the rest is a mere bauble, agreements contrary to nature, foolish talk of men, nothing worth.

Soc[rates]. There is a noble freedom, Callicles, in your way of approaching the argument; for what you say is what the rest of the world think, but do not like to say. And I must beg of you to persevere, that the true rule of human life may become manifest. Tell me, then:—you say, do you not, that in the rightly-developed man the passions ought not to be controlled, but that we should let them grow to the utmost and somehow or other satisfy them, and that this is virtue?

Cal. Yes; I do.

Soc. Then those who want nothing are not truly said to be happy?

Cal. No indeed, for then stones and dead men would be the happiest of all.

Soc. But surely life according to your view is an awful thing; and indeed I think that Euripides may have been right in saying, 'Who knows if life be not death and death life;' and that we are very likely dead; I have heard a philosopher say that at this moment we are actually dead, and that the body is our tomb, and that the part of the soul which is the seat of the desires is liable to be tossed about by words and blown up and down; and some ingenious person, probably a Sicilian or an Italian...invented a tale in which he called the soul a vessel, and the ignorant he called the uninitiated or leaky, and the place in the souls of the uninitiated in which the desires are seated, being the intemperate and incontinent part, he compared to a vessel full of holes, because it can never be satisfied. He is not of your way of thinking, Callicles, for he declares, that of all the souls in Hades, meaning the invisible world, these uninitiated or leaky persons are the most miserable, and that they pour water into a vessel which is full of holes out of a colander which is similarly perforated. The colander, as my informer assures me, is the soul, and the soul which he compares to a colander is the soul of the ignorant, which is likewise full of holes, and therefore incontinent, owing to a bad memory and want of faith. These notions are strange enough, but they show the principle which, if I can, I would fain prove to you; that you should change your mind, and, instead of the intemperate and insatiate life, choose that which is orderly and sufficient and has a due provision for daily needs. Do I make any impression on you, and are you coming over to the opinion that the orderly are happier than the intemperate? Or do I fail to persuade you, and, however many tales I rehearse to you, do you continue of the same opinion still?

Cal. The latter, Socrates, is more like the truth.

Soc. Well, I will tell you another image, which comes out of the same school:—Let me request you to consider how far you would accept this as an account of the two lives of the temperate and intemperate in a figure:—There are two men, both of whom have a number of casks; the one man has his casks sound and full, one of wine, another of honey, and a third of milk, besides others filled with other liquids, and the streams which fill them are few and scanty, and he can only obtain them with a great deal of toil and difficulty; but when his casks are once filled he has no need to feed them any more, and has no further trouble with them or care about them. The other, in like manner, can procure streams, though not without difficulty; but his vessels are leaky and unsound, and night and day he is compelled to be filling them, and if he pauses for a moment, he is in agony of pain. Such are their respective lives:—And now would you say that the life of the intemperate is happier than that of the temperate? Do I not convince you that the opposite is the truth?

Cal. You do not convince me, Socrates, for the one who has filled himself has no longer any pleasure left; and this, as I was just now saying, is the life of a stone: he has neither joy nor sorrow after he is once filled; but the pleasure depends on the superabundance of the influx.

51

Soc. But the more you pour in, the greater the waste; and the holes must be large for the liquid to escape.

Cal. Certainly.

Soc. The life which you are now depicting is not that of a dead man, or of a stone, but of a cormorant; you mean that he is to be hungering and eating?

Cal. Yes.

Soc. And he is to be thirsting and drinking?

Cal. Yes, that is what I mean; he is to have all his desires about him, and to be able to live happily in the gratification of them.

Soc. Capital, excellent; go on as you have begun, and have no shame; I, too, must disencumber myself of shame: and first, will you tell me whether you include itching and scratching, provided you have enough of them and pass your life in scratching, in your notion of happiness?

Cal. What a strange being you are, Socrates! a regular mob-orator.

The Sophist takes for granted that men desire power and that the achievement of power is a thoroughly satisfying experience. This is because the powerful man is said to be in a position to take what he wants and thus to ensure a full satisfaction of his desires. Here Socrates disagrees, and by so doing introduces a wholly new concept into ethical discussion. Give a man unlimited power and you do not thereby ensure that he will get what he wants. He may not know what he wants. This statement sounds paradoxical even to-day, and that fact proves that we still stand in need of Socrates' teaching.

The Sophistic glorification of power is thus countered by Socrates' dictum: "Virtue is knowledge." By "knowledge" Socrates here means self-knowledge, as is evident by the fact that he often quotes the famous Delphic inscription "Know thyself." The ideal of culture and of education, in the broad sense of these terms, is simply self-knowledge, which means knowledge of one's desires and of the things that will fully and permanently satisfy them. This is by no means a simple matter. Many of us pass through life with only the vaguest idea of what things we consider truly worth while. Thus the way of life that we may occasionally praise is understood only in crudest outline, and we do not feel its appeal vividly enough to maintain any very concerted effort to live up to it. So we may strain every nerve to acquire power and wealth, which seemed to be sufficiently spectacular ideals to arouse our enthusiasm, only to be baffled and disappointed once we have acquired them, for the simple reason that since we do not know what we really want, we are unable to profit by our success.

This leads us to Socrates' interpretation of the phrase "a good man." Socrates here employs a favorite analogy of his. The good carpenter is one who knows the technique of his craft and is acquainted with the tools and materials with which he has to work. The good carpenter is the expert in carpentry. But a good carpenter is not necessarily a good man. Although competent in a specialty, he may be quite stupid in ordering his own life and achieving any genuine satisfaction. To accomplish this he must possess a self-knowledge comparable to his knowledge of his tools and his materials.

At first glance this ethical teaching seems extremely self-centered. Altruism seems to have been wholly ignored. But this is not strictly true. Socrates always thinks of man as an individual living in a society with other individuals without whose co-operation he would be helpless and without whose affection and esteem he would be miserable. No man who gives the matter thought really wants to treat his fellows merely as instrumental to his own success. If he is wise, he will know that he desires friendship and esteem, and that he will in the end enjoy gratitude more than suspicion and fear. It is this fact of human nature that the tyrant overlooks, and Socrates is never tired of showing us the true misery of the unrestrained tyrant. As Socrates puts it in Plato's *Gorgias,* the tyrant does what he thinks best at the moment, but it does not follow that as a human being he gets what he really wants.

Socrates may be said to have outdone the Sophists by pushing his theories toward their logical conclusions. The Sophist had suggested a return to nature, but he had failed to analyze human nature thoroughly, and Socrates was quick to see this weakness and to correct it. However, because of this interest in the Sophist's line of argument, Socrates was frequently classed as a Sophist by the less discerning of his contemporaries.

VIRTUE IS KNOWLEDGE

The Sophists' refusal to recognize any stable or unquestionable standard of value led them to take a laissez-faire attitude in ethics. "Every man to his humor," with the added memorandum that without power no man is in a position to indulge his humor. Socrates succeeded in pushing beyond this relativism to the doctrine of self-knowledge. Self-knowledge may be advocated without reservation as something of unquestionable worth, the very heart of virtue and the foundation of happiness. Such a high valuation of self-knowledge remains something of a surprise to the modern reader. But this need not be the case. What we must remember is that by self-knowledge Socrates does not mean merely a mass of information concerning oneself. Such information must be made part of one's character, so that it remains intimately apprehended in clear and vivid form, and so linked with one's ordinary trains of thought that it comes to mind almost habitually.

Knowledge of what we really want to do—of what we wish to gain for ourselves and for others, and knowledge of what we desire from other people—may exist rather vaguely in our consciousness and yet may remain unrelated to the immediate practical problems we have to face. Thus, as Ovid put it long after Socrates, "The better course I gaze on and approve: the worse I follow." For Socrates, such gazing and such approval do not constitute genuine ethical self-knowledge. To know in general that alcohol injures our health, and that we want to be healthy, is not always an active form of self-knowledge capable of restraining us from intemperance. This is because such self-knowledge is not sufficiently complete to meet the actual problem before us. We may say, "I shall make an exception of this one celebration." But what has the Socratic ethics to say to this? Only to ask again, "Do you really want to risk forming a dangerous habit that might by injuring your health thwart many of your deep-seated interests?" Most of us would probably answer No. And we must remember that a sincerely affirmative answer is almost inconceivable.

54

To be sure, very occasionally some man may discover that his interests have nearly all been thwarted anyway. Perhaps for a man who has been completely frustrated, whose normal way of life has been destroyed, whose ambitions are defeated and whose world has, so to speak, gone to pieces, the escape from reality that intoxication affords is, after all, a wise choice. Certainly, without having experienced such defeat we can hardly know what it is like, and are therefore not in a position to question the self-knowledge of one who makes such a decision. Tolerance would seem to be a corollary of the Socratic doctrine. But such a frustrated man must be able to believe that he no longer desires anything so much as passing exhilaration and hazy forgetfulness. Few human beings can sincerely say that they have no desires beyond these. Thus in the great majority of cases the drunkard is a man who fails to keep clearly before him what he really wants. He does not vividly and frequently recognize the price he pays for his pleasure.

The Socratic ethical ideal was expressed centuries later by none other than Rabelais in his famous *Fay ce que vouldras* (Do what you will). Such advice will be thought dangerous only by those who fail to attach the full Socratic force to the last word of the maxim.

THE VIRTUES ARE ONE

Virtue is knowledge, active knowledge, or as we might say, effective consciousness of ourselves and of our desires. Thus in a sense all the virtues are one, since each possesses the common core of knowledge. Thus courage, as we have seen, is enduring and effective consciousness of what we truly believe to be dangerous or fearful. Prudence accordingly would be the enduring and effective consciousness of what we truly believe to be useful. In the same way all the virtues may be defined. For once the habit of cogent self-knowledge has been developed, all the virtues follow as such knowledge is applied now to one practical problem, now to another. It is no plan of Socrates (or of any other great moralist) to prepare a rule of thumb for all possible emergencies of human conduct. On the

55

contrary, it is his purpose to show us the essential nature of virtue, by acquiring which we become capable of meeting moral emergencies on our own initiative.

If Socratic logic is the discovery of the concept, Socratic ethics is the discovery of consciousness as the arbiter of values, and the practice of Socratic wisdom is the effort the human being makes to preserve his individual consciousness in its rightful dominion over both inner and outward conduct. Thus conduct would not be guided by convention or tradition, but by the desires of the individual, provided only that these desires can stand the test of his own self-knowledge; that is, granted that the individual still finds these desires compelling after he fully understands them and the effects that they will have upon himself and upon others. Virtue is knowledge, but it is a self-knowledge that cannot be imparted in a classroom or even by many of the usual methods of family discipline. Socrates' attitude toward a sheer traditionalism which claims that sufficient ideas of good and evil may be imparted by one generation to another is made clear in the following passage from Plato's *Meno*.[7] (Notice the scandalized reaction of Anytus, who was later to accuse Socrates of corrupting the young through insidious and subversive teaching.)

Soc[*rates*]. You must be a diviner, Anytus, for I really cannot make out, judging from your own words, how, if you are not acquainted with them, you know about them. But I am not enquiring of you who are the teachers who will corrupt Meno (let them be, if you please, the Sophists); I only ask you to tell him who there is in this great city who will teach him how to become eminent in the virtues which I was just now describing. He is the friend of your family, and you will oblige him.

Any[*tus*]. Why do you not tell him yourself?

Soc. I have told him whom I supposed to be the teachers of these things; but I learn from you that I am utterly at fault, and I dare say that you are right. And now I wish that you, on your part, would tell me to whom among the Athenians he should go. Whom would you name?

Any. Why single out individuals? Any Athenian gentleman, taken

---

[7] Plato, *Meno*, in *Dialogues*, trans. by Benjamin Jowett, Vol. II, pp. 54-57.

at random, if he will mind him, will do far more good to him than the Sophists.

Soc. And did those gentlemen grow of themselves; and without having been taught by any one, were they nevertheless able to teach others that which they had never learned themselves?

Any. I imagine that they learned of the previous generation of gentlemen. Have there not been many good men in this city?

Soc. Yes, certainly, Anytus; and many good statesmen also there always have been and there are still, in the city of Athens. But the question is whether they were also good teachers of their own virtue;—not whether there are, or have been, good men in this part of the world, but whether virtue can be taught, is the question which we have been discussing. Now, do we mean to say that the good men of our own and of other times knew how to impart to others that virtue which they had themselves; or is virtue a thing incapable of being communicated or imparted by one man to another? That is the question which I and Meno have been arguing. Look at the matter in your own way: Would you not admit that Themistocles was a good man?

Any. Certainly; no man better.

Soc. And must not he then have been a good teacher, if any man was ever a good teacher of his own virtue?

Any. Yes, certainly; if he wanted to be so.

Soc. But would he not have wanted? He would, at any rate, have desired to make his own son a good man and a gentleman; he could not have been jealous of him, or have intentionally abstained from imparting to him his own virtue. Did you never hear that he made his son Cleophantus a famous horseman; and had him taught to stand upright on horseback and hurl a javelin, and to do many other marvellous things; and in anything which could be learned from a master he was well trained? Have you not heard from our elders of him?

Any. I have.

Soc. Then no one could say that his son showed any want of capacity?

Any. Very likely not.

Soc. But did any one, old or young, ever say in your hearing that Cleophantus, son of Themistocles, was a wise or good man, as his father was?

Any. I have certainly never heard any one say so.

Soc. And if virtue could have been taught, would his father Themistocles have sought to train him in these minor accomplishments, and allowed him who, as you must remember, was his own son, to be no better than his neighbours in those qualities in which he himself excelled?

Any. Indeed, indeed, I think not.

Soc. Here was a teacher of virtue whom you admit to be among the best men of the past. Let us take another,—Aristides, the son of Lysimachus: would you not acknowledge that he was a good man?

Any. To be sure I should.

Soc. And did not he train his son Lysimachus better than any other Athenian in all that could be done for him by the help of masters? But what has been the result? Is he a bit better than any other mortal? He is an acquaintance of yours, and you see what he is like. There is Pericles, again, magnificent in his wisdom; and he, as you are aware, had two sons, Paralus and Xanthippus.

Any. I know.

Soc. And you know, also, that he taught them to be unrivalled horsemen, and had them trained in music and gymnastics and all sorts of arts—in these respects they were on a level with the best—and had he no wish to make good men of them? Nay, he must have wished it. But virtue, as I suspect, could not be taught. And that you may not suppose the incompetent teachers to be only the meaner sort of Athenians and few in number, remember again that Thucydides had two sons, Melesias and Stephanus, whom, besides giving them a good education in other things, he trained in wrestling, and they were the best wrestlers in Athens: one of them he committed to the care of Xanthias, and the other of Eudorus, who had the reputation of being the most celebrated wrestlers of that day. Do you remember them?

Any. I have heard of them.

Soc. Now, can there be a doubt that Thucydides, whose children were taught things for which he had to spend money, would have taught them to be good men, which would have cost him nothing, if virtue could have been taught? Will you reply that he was a mean man, and had not many friends among the Athenians and allies? Nay, but he was of a great family, and a man of influence in Athens and in all Hellas, and, if virtue could have been taught, he would have found out some Athenian or foreigner who would have made good men of his sons, if he could not himself spare the time from cares of state. Once more, I suspect, friend Anytus, that virtue is not a thing which can be taught.

Any. Socrates, I think that you are too ready to speak evil of men: and, if you will take my advice, I would recommend you to be careful. Perhaps there is no city in which it is not easier to do men harm than to do them good, and this is certainly the case in Athens, as I believe that you know.

Soc. O Meno, I think that Anytus is in a rage. And he may well be in a rage, for he thinks, in the first place, that I am defaming these gentlemen; and in the second place, he is of opinion that he is one of them himself. But some day he will know what is the meaning of defamation, and if he ever does, he will forgive me.

Socratic criticism in any age is bound to be unpopular in many quarters. As John Dewey writes,[8] the traditional point of view:

...was deeply rooted in social habits and loyalties; it was surcharged with the moral aims for which men lived and the moral rules by which they lived. Hence it was as basic and as comprehensive as life itself, and palpitated with the warm glowing colors of the community life in which men realized their own being. In contrast, the positivistic (Socratic) knowledge was concerned [9] with merely physical utilities, and lacked the ardent associations of belief hallowed by sacrifices of ancestors and worship of contemporaries. Because of its limited and concrete character it was dry, hard, cold.

Socrates appeared to his contemporaries, at least to many of them, as a "subversive intellectual," a "negative critic."

But the Socratic attitude in ethics need not result in an extreme individualism that revolts against society. As we have seen, Socrates thinks of man as a social being, needing human companionship and support. Not only this, but Socrates insists also that the individual will, if sufficiently thoughtful, recognize his need of a law-abiding and orderly society in which he may pursue his happiness. He will not find it in his heart to contribute to the destruction of the laws by disobeying them. Thus Socrates devotes a loyalty directly to the laws themselves, and not to a ruler whose word carries authority. Authority is not to be conceived as something that can be vested in

---

[8] John Dewey, *Reconstruction in Philosophy,* p. 16, enlarged edition, The Beacon Press, Boston, 1948. Reprinted by permission of the publisher.

[9] I should prefer to say "seemed to the conservatives to be concerned with."

a person except as that person draws his authority from a legal system or a constitution. Neither absolute monarchy nor dictatorship
is consistent with the Socratic attitude. The state must be founded
upon the individual's respect for law and his loyalty to it. So deeply
did Socrates feel this devotion to the laws of his city that although,
as there can be little doubt, unjustly condemned to death by a hostile
majority who mistook him for an extreme Sophist, he refused to
attempt an escape that his influential friends could very easily have
effected, preferring to abide by the laws of his city and face death.
In the following passage from Plato's *Crito,* he states his reasons
for this decision.[10]

Soc[rates]. Then consider the matter in this way:—Imagine that
I am about to play truant (you may call the proceeding by any
name which you like), and the laws of the government come
and interrogate me: 'Tell us, Socrates,' they say; 'what are you
about? are you not going by an act of yours to overturn us—the
laws, and the whole state, as far as in you lies? Do you imagine
that a state can subsist and not be overthrown, in which the decisions of law have no power, but are set aside and trampled
upon by individuals?' What will be our answer, Crito, to these
and the like words? Any one, and especially a rhetorician, will
have a good deal to say on behalf of the law which requires a sen
tence to be carried out. He will argue that this law should not be
set aside; and shall we reply, 'Yes; but the state has injured us
and given an unjust sentence.' Suppose I say that?

Cr[ito]. Very good, Socrates.

Soc. 'And was that our agreement with you?' the law would answer;
'Or were you to abide by the sentence of the state?' And if I
were to express my astonishment at their words, the law would
probably add: 'Answer, Socrates, instead of opening your eyes—
you are in the habit of asking and answering questions. Tell us,
—What complaint have you to make against us which justifies
you in attempting to destroy us and the state? In the first place
did we not bring you into existence? Your father married your
mother by our aid and begat you. Say whether you have any objection to urge against those of us who regulate marriage?' None,
I should reply. 'Or against those of us who after birth regulate
the nurture and education of children, in which you also were

---

[10] Plato, *Crito,* in *Dialogues,* trans. by Benjamin Jowett, Vol. II, pp. 151-53.

trained? Were not the laws, which have the charge of education, right in commanding your father to train you in music and gymnastic?' Right, I should reply. 'Well then, since you were brought into the world and nurtured and educated by us, can you deny in the first place that you are our child and slave, as your fathers were before you? And if this is true you are not on equal terms with us; nor can you think that you have a right to do to us what we are doing to you. Would you have any right to strike or revile or do any other evil to your father or your master, if you had one, because you have been struck or reviled by him, or received some other evil at his hands?—you would not say this? And because we think right to destroy you, do you think that you have any right to destroy us in return, and your country as far as in you lies? Will you, O professor of true virtue, pretend that you are justified in this? Has a philosopher like you failed to discover that our country is more to be valued and higher and holier far than mother or father or any ancestor, and more to be regarded in the eyes of the gods and of men of understanding? also to be soothed, and gently and reverently entreated when angry, even more than a father, and either to be persuaded, or if not persuaded, to be obeyed? And when we are punished by her, whether with imprisonment or stripes, the punishment is to be endured in silence; and if she lead us to wounds or death in battle, thither we follow as is right; neither may any one yield or retreat or leave his rank, but whether in battle or in a court of law, or in any other place, he must do what his city and his country order him; or he must change their view of what is just: and if he may do no violence to his father or mother, much less may he do violence to his country.' What answer shall we make to this, Crito? Do the laws speak truly, or do they not?

Cr. I think that they do.

Soc. Then the laws will say: 'Consider, Socrates, if we are speaking truly that in your present attempt you are going to do us an injury. For, having brought you into the world, and nurtured and educated you, and given you and every other citizen a share in every good which we had to give, we further proclaim to any Athenian by the liberty which we allow him, that if he does not like us when he has become of age and has seen the ways of the city, and made our acquaintance, he may go where he pleases and take his goods with him. None of us [our] laws will forbid him or interfere with him. Any one who does not like us and the city, and who wants to emigrate to a colony or to any other city,

61

may go where he likes, retaining his property. But he who has experience of the manner in which we order justice and administer the state, and still remains, has entered into an implied contract that he will do as we command him. And he who disobeys us is, as we maintain, thrice wrong; first, because in disobeying us he is disobeying his parents; secondly, because we are the authors of his education; thirdly, because he has made an agreement with us that he will duly obey our commands; and he neither obeys them nor convinces us that our commands are unjust; and we do not rudely impose them, but give him the alternative of obeying or convincing us;—that is what we offer, and he does neither.

It is clear that Socrates does not think of human life as being wholly guided by law. Our decisions are rightfully our own, but the individual must recognize—if he is wise, he will desire to recognize —a minimum of legal restrictions and obligations without which social life would be impossible.

CONCLUSION

We shall presently examine later developments of ethical theory, all of which spring pretty largely from the Socratic starting point. Socrates' account of moral value as the desirable, as that which we really want, is the first approximation of the true nature of value made by moral philosophers. It is of course, a very general statement, useful, to be sure, in combating an extreme relativist such as Thrasymachus, but not very specific in details. Thus, even if we accept Socrates' position, we still have to ask: What is for us the truly desirable? How deeply do we desire pleasure and amusement? Are we really willing to forgo them altogether in the pursuit of some ambition? Is health, say, more desirable than friendship? And so on. The work of later thinkers, particularly that of Aristotle, although it does not usually add anything of great import to the Socratic notion of moral value, does aid us greatly in applying Socratic wisdom in actual moral practice. For instance, Aristotle's analysis of happiness, incomplete though it very probably is, will be of aid to anyone who is concerned to know what he really wants.

Socrates has come to be considered both in character and in achievement as the very incarnation of the philosophical ideal. He is the hero of philosophical history, and if he shares this high honor with anyone it is only with Spinoza, who in more modern times has re-embodied the Socratic virtues of absolute sincerity and independence of spirit. The persistence with which Socrates through his tireless questioning and challenging brought home to his fellow men the sad confusion of their unanalyzed opinions is a model for the philosophical reformer. No man who devotes himself wholly to exhibiting the errors, the prejudices, and the thoughtlessness of his contemporaries can avoid making bitter enemies. Many religious fanatics and political partisans are bound to unite against him. He may indeed offend all parties and find himself without any support. Socrates felt this opposition, and was unaffected by it. Always debonair and courteous, even when ironical, never for a moment fanatical, he allowed no consideration, even that of his personal safety —which in his later years was frequently threatened—to withhold him from accomplishing what he took to be his inspired destiny. It was, as he conceived it, his mission to force men to think and to examine their beliefs. No belief was too sacred to be questioned, but each man's sincere opinion deserved the same serious and thoughtful consideration.

His moral was as great as his intellectual integrity. Once when serving in public office, alone he defied the arbitrary authority of a dictatorial government—the oligarchic Council of Thirty—and refused to execute its illegal edicts. Again, he tried his best to foil an angry democratic assembly that had exceeded its authority in the trial of a group of inefficient officers. In war his endurance and cool courage were proverbial, and when finally he was on trial for his life, his defiance of his demagogic enemies was truly sublime.[11]

And therefore if you let me go now, and are not convinced by Anytus...if you say to me, Socrates, this time we will not mind Anytus, and you shall be let off, but upon one condition, that you are not to enquire and speculate in this way any more, and that if you are caught doing so again you shall die;—if this was the con-

[11] Plato, *Apology*, in *Dialogues*, trans. by Benjamin Jowett, Vol. II, pp. 122-23.

dition on which you let me go, I should reply: Men of Athens, I honour and love you; but I shall obey God rather than you, and while I have life and strength I shall never cease from the practice and teaching of philosophy, exhorting any one whom I meet and saying to him after my manner: You, my friend,—a citizen of the great and mighty and wise city of Athens,—are you not ashamed of heaping up the greatest amount of money and honour and reputation, and caring so little about wisdom and truth and the greatest improvement of the soul, which you never regard or heed at all? And if the person with whom I am arguing, says: Yes, but I do care; then I do not leave him or let him go at once; but I proceed to interrogate and examine and cross-examine him, and if I think that he has no virtue in him, but only says that he has, I reproach him with undervaluing the greater, and overvaluing the less. And I shall repeat the same words to every one whom I meet, young and old, citizen and alien, but especially to the citizens, inasmuch as they are my brethren. For know that this is the command of God; and I believe that no greater good has ever happened in the state than my service to the God. For I do nothing but go about persuading you all, old and young alike, not to take thought for your persons or your properties, but first and chiefly to care about the greatest improvement of the soul. I tell you that virtue is not given by money, but that from virtue comes money and every other good of man, public as well as private. This is my teaching, and if this is the doctrine which corrupts the youth, I am a mischievous person. But if any one says that this is not my teaching, he is speaking an untruth. Wherefore, O men of Athens, I say to you, do as Anytus bids or not as Anytus bids, and either acquit me or not; but whichever you do, understand that I shall never alter my ways, not even if I have to die many times.

Socrates expressed his ideal of human life very beautifully in the prayer with which Plato closes his great dialogue *Phaedrus*.[12]

Beloved Pan, and all ye other gods who haunt this place, give me beauty in the inward soul; and may the outward and inward man be at one. May I reckon the wise to be the wealthy, and may I have such a quantity of gold as a temperate man and he only can bear and carry.—Anything more? The prayer, I think, is enough for me.

[12] Plato, *Phaedrus*, in *Dialogues*, trans. by Benjamin Jowett, Vol. I, p. 489.

CHAPTER IV

Plato

PLATO AND SOCRATES

Socrates left no written statement of his philosophy. But the impact of his personality upon Greek thought was so great that within a few years of his death perhaps half a dozen interpretations of his work and even of his life were offered to the Greek world by men who were proud to be known as his pupils. Several of these men we shall have to mention in the sequel. The greatest was Plato,[1] who carried Socratic method and Socratic concepts to a magnificent conclusion in one of the sanest and most comprehensive philosophies that mankind has ever produced.

Plato's mode of presentation of his ideas is an unusual one. Wishing to preserve the spirit of a Socratic investigation, he cast his arguments in dialogue form. In these dialogues, or conversations, Socrates, the questioner, guides his companions, as indeed we have already seen, toward clearer and more consistent ideas. In the earlier dialogues, it is generally supposed that Plato incorporated in somewhat polished form actual discourses that had been carried on by Socrates and the members of his circle. There can be no doubt that in the later dialogues Plato advances ideas that the actual Socrates never entertained. As he grows older, Plato becomes more and more boldly speculative and less and less Socratic, although Socrates appears as a character in nearly all the dialogues.

Socrates' fate at the hands of his fellow citizens bitterly disillu-

---

[1] Plato (427-347 B.C.) came of an aristocratic Athenian family. He was a wide traveler, visiting not only Italy but Sicily and Egypt. In Sicily he made an unsuccessful attempt to establish much-needed political and social reforms. In 387 he founded the Academy at Athens. This school was the first institution of higher learning in Europe, a great center of research and of instruction.

sioned the young Plato, who at that time withdrew from any actual part in the political affairs of his own country. This was for him a truly drastic step to take, as he came of a family distinguished in political life. His own aristocratic relatives, among others, had attempted a dictatorship and failed because of their own selfishness. Later on, the people, returned to power and in the flush of triumph too ready to listen to demagogues, had put Socrates to death. Thus both parties, aristocratic and popular, were found wanting in his eyes, and in misery of spirit Plato left Athens for a period of over ten years. In an "open letter" justifying his part in the political affairs of Syracuse, Plato explains his decision not to enter public life as follows: [2]

In the days of my youth my experience was the same as that of many others. I thought that as soon as I should become my own master I would immediately enter into public life. But it so happened, I found, that the following changes occurred in the political situation.

In the government then existing, reviled as it was by many, a revolution took place; and the revolution was headed by fifty-one leaders, of whom eleven were in the City and ten in the Piraeus—each of these sections dealing with the market and with all municipal matters requiring management—and Thirty were established as irresponsible rulers of all. Now of these some were actually connexions and acquaintances of mine; and indeed they invited me at once to join their administration, thinking it would be congenial. The feelings I then experienced, owing to my youth, were in no way surprising: for I imagined that they would administer the State by leading it out of an unjust way of life into a just way, and consequently I gave my mind to them very diligently, to see what they would do. And indeed I saw how these men within a short time caused men to look back on the former government as a golden age; and above all how they treated my aged friend Socrates, whom I would hardly scruple to call the most just of men then living, when they tried to send him, along with others, after one of the citizens, to fetch him by force that he might be put to death—their object being that Socrates, whether he wished or no, might be made to

[2] Plato, *Epistle VII*, trans. by R. G. Bury in *Plato with an English translation*, vol. VII, 479, 481, 483. Loeb Classical Library. Harvard University Press, Cambridge, 1929. Reprinted by permission of the publisher.

share in their political actions; he, however, refused to obey and risked the uttermost penalties rather than be a partaker in their unholy deeds. So when I beheld all these actions and others of a similar grave kind, I was indignant, and I withdrew myself from the evil practices then going on. But in no time the power of the Thirty was overthrown, together with the whole of the government which then existed. Then once again I was really, though less urgently, impelled with a desire to take part in public and political affairs. Many deplorable events, however, were still happening in those times, troublous as they were, and it was not surprising that in some instances, during these revolutions, men were avenging themselves on their foes too fiercely; yet, notwithstanding, the exiles who then returned exercised no little moderation. But, as ill luck would have it, certain men of authority summoned our comrade Socrates before the law-courts, laying a charge against him which was most unholy, and which Socrates of all men least deserved; for it was on the charge of impiety that those men summoned him and the rest condemned and slew him—the very man who on the former occasion, when they themselves had the misfortune to be in exile, had refused to take part in the unholy arrest of the friends of the men then exiled.

When therefore, I considered all this, and the type of men who were administering the affairs of State, with their laws too and their customs, the more I considered them and the more I advanced in years myself, the more difficult appeared to me the task of managing affairs of State rightly. For it was impossible to take action without friends and trusty companions; and these it was not easy to find ready to hand, since our State was no longer managed according to the principles and institutions of our forefathers; while to acquire other new friends with any facility was a thing impossible. Moreover, both the written laws and the customs were being corrupted, and that with surprising rapidity. Consequently, although at first I was filled with an ardent desire to engage in public affairs, when I considered all this and saw how things were shifting about anyhow in all directions, I finally became dizzy; and although I continued to consider by what means some betterment could be brought about not only in these matters but also in the government as a whole, yet as regards political action I kept constantly waiting for an opportune moment; until, finally, looking at all the States which now exist, I perceived that one and all they are badly governed; for the state of their laws is such as to be almost incurable without some marvellous overhauling and good luck to boot. So in my

67

praise of the right philosophy I was compelled to declare that by it one is enabled to discern all forms of justice, both political and individual. Wherefore the classes of mankind (I said) will have no cessation from evils until either the class of those who are right and true philosophers attains political supremacy, or else the class of those who hold power in the States becomes, by some dispensation of Heaven, really philosophic.

Traveling in Italy during his self-imposed exile, Plato came in contact with a school of philosophy that had been established for nearly two centuries, the religious cult of Pythagoras. Plato learned then from the Pythagoreans that number is an important ingredient of nature. A numberless or unmeasurable nature would seem as strange to us as a colorless or a lifeless nature. This was a most important step for Plato to take, for to say that number is an ingredient of the world is to introduce an element which cannot be seen with the eye or touched with the hand. It is to recognize what we so often call abstractions as important constituents of reality. Remove tangible stuff or matter from nature and we are left with an unfamiliar world; remove number or measure and we are equally baffled. Thus the latter is at least as real as the former, as much a part of the world. This insight prepared Plato for his doctrine of forms, in which he combines the teaching of Socrates and Pythagoras.

THE THEORY OF FORMS

We have seen that Socrates discovered the concept and contributed the analytic method of inductive definition, which we might call a technique for determining and clarifying our concepts. To this Plato adds a very important consideration, which requires a good deal of patient study. Put very briefly it is this: The object that the concept contemplates is not quite the same object [3] that our less

---

[3] To avoid confusion, we offer the following definition of "object" or better, a statement of the way in which we shall be using the term. An object is anything to which we can pay attention in perception, memory, or thought. It may be, for instance, a sound, a body, or something often considered less tangible, such as the law of gravitation or the square root of 2. The object, be it noted, is not the act of awareness whereby said object is apprehended, but the *thing* that the awareness selects for

precise methods of thinking touch upon, although the two types of object, conceptual and subconceptual, are somehow related. In the dialogue *Laches,* quoted in part above, the first attempts at describing courage fail to achieve generality or true conceptual scope and accordingly they fail to grasp the true nature of courage. Laches does not penetrate at first to the true structure of his subject matter. He does not think about courage in general, but confines himself to certain special cases he has happened to observe. Socrates forces him toward recognition of the true structure of courage by insisting upon consideration of other instances. He presses Laches toward insight into the general pattern of courage that is embodied equally in all the instances which can be brought to mind. This general pattern Plato calls a *form.*

The Greek word for "form" is "idea," and often this is translated by the English word "idea." This is unfortunate, because we now tend to think of an idea as an event in our stream of consciousness or as an act of mind. What Plato means by "form" is the object that can be grasped only by conceptual thinking, what we might call the objective or goal toward the comprehension of which the Socratic method of analysis is directed. To employ Plato's terms, we have knowledge of the form but only opinions concerning the instances, considered without a grasp of the forms. This point is the very essence of Platonism and the reader must make every effort to understand it fully. Definitions of geometrical structures afford examples. Thus we have no knowledge of the straight line derived simply from inspection, but we may acquire this knowledge through a definition, such as "A straight line is one which, when rotated upon its own length as axis, remains unmoved."

Let us present a further example to illustrate the relation of opinion and knowledge.[4] Consider two arithmetical series. First, that of the whole numbers and their squares in order of magnitude. Second, the series of odd numbers:

---

consideration. In introspection, I can make one of my own feelings an object, but the feeling then remains distinct from my act of noticing it.

[4] Two of the following examples are not derived from Plato's writings. Insofar as they involve algebra and the Arabic system of notation, they lie beyond the frontiers of Plato's thought. But they do illustrate his method.

1	2	3	4	5	6	7	8	etc.
1	4	9	16	25	36	49	64	etc.

	3	5	7	9	11	13	15	etc.

We notice that the odd numbers fill the gaps between the square numbers. Thus $1 + 3 = 4$; $4 + 5 = 9$; $9 + 7 = 16$; and so on.[5] The

[5] This progression may be represented geometrically:

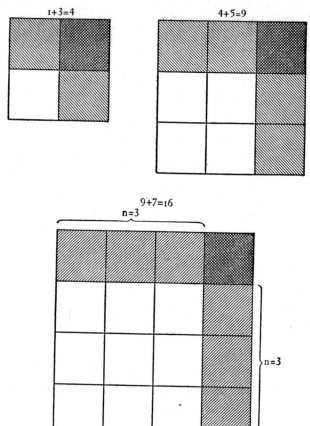

If n represents the side of the original square, then we must add $2n + 1$ to construct the next square, for we must build a border around two edges of the square in order to increase its side by one unit.

70

reader can prolong this operation ad libitum and come to the conclusion that the nth odd number fills the gap between the nth square
and the $(n + 1)$th square; in other words, that the relation discovered continues to hold no matter how far we prolong the series. But
do we know that this *must* be the case? How do we know in advance that after we pass, say, the number 10^{15} the relation may not
cease to apply? We can know nothing of the sort if we confine ourselves to examining single instances. To be sure, we may have great
confidence in such opinion, but we have no knowledge of the sort
that Plato is seeking.

Such knowledge can be obtained, but only after we have recognized another object that was at first beyond our grasp. This object
is the *general term* of the series:

1	4	9	16	25	36	49	64
	3	5	7	9	11	13	15

It is the general pattern whereby any triad of the type of

1	4, or 4	9, or 49	64, etc.
	3	5	15

is built up.

Notice the relations of the terms:

2	3	7	8
4	9	49	64
	5		15

The number 15 fills the gap between 7^2 and 8^2 and it is equal to
$7 + 8$.

This pattern may be represented symbolically as:

$$n \qquad\qquad n + 1$$
$$n^2 \qquad\qquad (n + 1)^2$$
$$2n + 1$$

A little algebra makes clear that this relation will hold for any
value of n. For $n^2 + (2n + 1) = (n + 1)^2$. Once we grasp this

general pattern or form we *know* that the odd numbers in order of magnitude must fill the gap of the square numbers in their order of magnitude.

A second example of this recognition of a form is given in the following quotation from the *Meno,* in which Socrates leads a slave boy who is untrained in mathematics to recognize that the square of the diagonal is double the square of the side of a given square (algebraically, $d^2 = 2s^2$).[6]

Soc[*rates*]. It will be no easy matter, but I will try to please you to the utmost of my power. Suppose that you call one of your numerous attendants, that I may demonstrate on him.

Men[*o*]. Certainly. Come hither, boy.

Soc. He is Greek, and speaks Greek, does he not?

Men. Yes, indeed; he was born in the house.

Soc. Attend now to the questions which I ask him, and observe whether he learns of me or only remembers.

Men. I will.

Soc. Tell me, boy, do you know that a figure like this is a square? [Fig. II] [7]

Boy. I do.

Soc. And you know that a square figure has these four lines equal? [AB, CD, AC, BD of Fig. II].

Boy. Certainly.

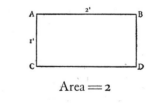

Area = 2

FIGURE I

Soc. And these lines [EF, GH, Fig. II] which I have drawn through the middle of the square are also equal?

Boy. Yes.

Soc. A square may be of any size?

---

[6] Plato, *Meno,* in *Dialogues,* trans. by Benjamin Jowett, Vol. II, pp. 41-46.

[7] Figures from W. C. Greene, *Scholia Platonica* (Monograph No. 8). American Philological Association, Lancaster, Penna., 1939. Reprinted by permission of the publisher.

Boy. Certainly.

Soc. And if one side of the figure be of two feet, and the other side be of two feet, how much will the whole be? Let me explain: if in one direction the space was of two feet, and in the other direction of one foot, the whole would be of two feet taken once? [Fig. I].

Boy. Yes.

Soc. But since this side is also of two feet, there are twice two feet? [Fig. II].

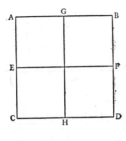

Area = 4

FIGURE II

Boy. There are.

Soc. Then the square is of twice two feet?

Boy. Yes.

Soc. And how many are twice two feet? count and tell me.

Boy. Four, Socrates.

Soc. And might there not be another square twice as large as this, and having like this the lines equal?

Boy. Yes.

Soc. And of how many feet will that be?

Boy. Of eight feet.

Soc. And now try and tell me the length of the line which forms the side of that double square: this is two feet—what will that be?

Boy. Clearly, Socrates, it will be double.

Soc. Do you observe, Meno, that I am not teaching the boy anything, but only asking him questions; and now he fancies that he knows how long a line is necessary in order to produce a figure of eight square feet; does he not?

Men. Yes.

Soc. And does he really know?

Men. Certainly not.

Soc. He only guesses that because the square is double, the line is double.

Men. True.

Soc. Observe him while he recalls the steps in regular order (*To the Boy.*) Tell me, boy, do you assert that a double space comes from a double line? Remember that I am not speaking of an oblong, but of a figure equal every way, and twice the size of this—that is to say of eight feet; and I want to know whether you still say that a double square comes from a double line?

Boy. Yes.

Soc. But does not this line become doubled if we add another such line here? [IH, Fig. III].

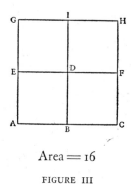

Area = 16

FIGURE III

Boy. Certainly.

Soc. And four such lines will make a space containing eight feet? [□ACGH, Fig. III].

Boy. Yes.

Soc. Let us describe such a figure: Would you not say that this is the figure of eight feet? [Figure. III].

Boy. Yes.

Soc. And are there not these four divisions in the figure [□ DEGI, □ DFHI, □ ABDE, □ BCDF, Fig. III], each of which is equal to the figure of four feet?

Boy. True.

Soc. And is not that four times four?

Boy. Certainly.

Soc. And four times is not double?

Boy. No indeed.

Soc. But how much?

74

Boy. Four times as much.

Soc. Therefore the double line, boy, has given a space, not twice, but four times as much.

Boy. True.

Soc. Four times four are sixteen—are they not?

Boy. Yes.

Soc. What line would give you a space of eight feet, as this gives one of sixteen feet;—do you see?

Boy. Yes.

Soc. And the space of four feet is made from this half line? [AB Fig. III].

Boy. Yes.

Soc. Good; and is not a space of eight feet twice the size of this, and half the size of the other?

Boy. Certainly.

Soc. Such a space, then, will be made out of a line greater than this one [AB], and less than that one [AC]? [Fig. III].

Boy. Yes; I think so.

Soc. Very good; I like to hear you say what you think. And now tell me, is not this a line of two feet and that of four?

Boy. Yes.

Soc. Then the line which forms the side of eight feet ought to be more than this line of two feet, and less than the other of four feet?

Boy. It ought.

Soc. Try and see if you can tell me how much it will be.

Boy. Three feet.

Soc. Then if we add a half to this line of two, that will be the line of three [AB Fig. IV]. Here are two [AE] and there is one [EB]; and on the other side, here are two also [EF] and there is one [FG]: and that makes the figure of which you speak?

Boy. Yes.

Soc. But if there are three feet this way and three feet that way, the whole space will be three times three feet?

Boy. That is evident.

Soc. And how much are three times three feet?

Boy. Nine.

Soc. And how much is the double of four?

Boy. Eight.

Soc. Then the figure of eight is not made out of a line of three?

Boy. No.

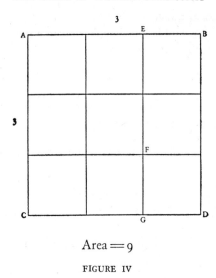

Area = 9

FIGURE IV

Soc. But from what line?—tell me exactly; and if you would rather not reckon, try and show me the line.

Boy. Indeed, Socrates, I do not know.

Soc. Do you see, Meno, what advances he has made in his power of recollection? He did not know at first, and he does not know now, what is the side of a figure of eight feet: but then he thought that he knew, and answered confidently as if he knew, and had no difficulty; now he has a difficulty, and neither knows nor fancies that he knows.

Men. True.

Soc. Is he not better off in knowing his ignorance?

Men. I think that he is.

Soc. If we have made him doubt, and given him the 'torpedo's shock,' have we done him any harm?

Men. I think not.

Soc. We have certainly, as would seem, assisted him in some degree to the discovery of the truth; and now he will wish to remedy his ignorance, but then he would have been ready to tell all the world again and again that the double space should have a double side.

Men. True.

Soc. But do you suppose that he would ever have enquired into or learned what he fancied that he knew, though he was really ignorant of it, until he had fallen into perplexity under the idea that he did not know, and had desired to know?

Men. I think not, Socrates.

Soc. Then he was the better for the torpedo's touch?

Men. I think so.

Soc. Mark now the further development. I shall only ask him, and not teach him, and he shall share the enquiry with me: and do you watch and see if you find me telling or explaining anything to him, instead of eliciting his opinion. Tell me, boy, is not this a square of four feet which I have drawn? [□ AEBI, Fig. V]

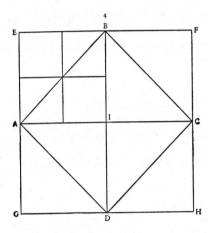

Area ABCD = ½EFHG = 8

FIGURE V

Boy. Yes.

Soc. And now I add another square equal to the former one? [□ BFCI, Fig. V.]

Boy. Yes.

Soc. And a third, which is equal to either of them? [□ AIDG, Fig. V.]

Boy. Yes.

Soc. Suppose that we fill up the vacant corner? [□ CHDI, Fig. V]

Boy. Very good.

Soc. Here, then, there are four equal spaces?

Boy. Yes.

Soc. And how many times larger is this space than this other?

Boy. Four times.

Soc. But it ought to have been twice only, as you will remember.

Boy. True.

Soc. And does not this line [AB, Fig. V], reaching from corner to corner, bisect each of these spaces?

Boy. Yes.

Soc. And are there not here four equal lines [□ ABCD] which contain this space?

Boy. There are.

Soc. Look and see how much this space is.

Boy. I do not understand.

Soc. Has not each interior line cut off half of the four spaces?

Boy. Yes.

Soc. And how many such spaces are there in this section?

Boy. Four.

Soc. And how many in this?

Boy. Two.

Soc. And four is how many times two?

Boy. Twice.

Soc. And this space is of how many feet?

Boy. Of eight feet.

Soc. And from what line do you get this figure?

Boy. From this.

Soc. That is, from the line which extends from corner to corner of the figure of four feet?

Boy. Yes.

Soc. And that is the line which the learned call the diagonal. And if this is the proper name, then you, Meno's slave, are prepared to affirm that the double space is the square of the diagonal?

Boy. Certainly, Socrates.

The reader may employ another example. The digits in the multiples of 9 add up to 9 or to a multiple of 9—9, 18, 27, 36, 45, 54, 63, 72, 81, 90, 99, 108, 117...[8] We have an opinion concerning this arithmetical fact. How achieve knowledge of this? Simply by grasping the general pattern involved in adding 9 to any number: $9 =$

---

[8] This example, while it may seem to be anachronistic in its dependence on Arabic notation, is really thoroughly Pythagorean. The Pythagorean designated the equivalent of the sum of digits for his alphabetic numbers by the term *pythmen*, and several theorems are preserved in which the Pythagoreans worked out such properties of digital sums. See Sir Thomas Heath, *History of Greek Mathematics*, Vol. I, pp. 115-17; "The *pythmen* and the rule of nine or seven."

$(10 - 1)$. To add $(10 - 1)$ to any whole number involves, in general, subtracting 1 from the digit column (borrowing when necessary) and adding 1 to the 10 column (carrying over to the next column when necessary). Thus the digit column will decrease by 1 except where, as in the passage from 90 to 99, it increased by 9. Also the 10 column will increase by 1 except where it decreases by 9, as in the passage from 99 to 108, or where it remains the same, as in the passage from 90 to 99 (and here the digits change is $+9$). It will readily be seen that the possible combinations are the following:

Change in 10 Column	Change in Digit Column
$+1$	-1
-9	-1
$+0$	$+9$

Cases one and three fit readily into our scheme; the total sum remains unchanged or grows by 9. In the second case the change in the total sum of all columns will not be -10 but -9 or minus a multiple of 9, because when the 10 column decreases by 9 the column on the left (the 100 column) will be increased by 1, giving $+1 -9 -1$ as the total alteration, as in passing from 891 to 900; or the 100 column will be decreased by 9 (in case the 100 column originally read 9). But in this latter case there will be a gain of 1 in a column still farther to the left, giving $+1 -9 -9 -1$ as the total alteration, as in the passage from 8991 to 9000.

Since we began our multiplication table with 9 itself, and either add nothing to the sum of the digits or else increase by 9 or decrease by 9 or a multiple of 9, it is clear that we will have either 9 or some multiple of 9 as the sum of the digits in any member of the table.

Is it not clear that in grasping this general pattern of the multiplication table for 9, we grasp an object that we were not aware of when we saw the table simply as 9, 18, 27, 36 etc.? This object is a Platonic form, schematized as $+(10-1)$, and its apprehension is a concept that grasps structure common to many instances. Of course the instances themselves can be witnessed without apprehension of the full structure of the form, but this is opinion and not knowledge.

The reader should now be able to understand Plato's proof of the reality of the form or the object of genuine—that is, conceptual—knowledge. Such an object is called *self-existent;* that is, it has a definite structure of its own that can be considered without reference to any given particular instance. This structure is permanent, since it does not change as one particular instance after another comes to our attention. So manhood or courage remains unaltered with the passing of any particular brave man. We quote from the *Timaeus:* [9]

... do all those things which we call self-existent exist? or are only those things which we see, or in some way perceive through the bodily organs, truly existent, and nothing whatever besides them? And is all that which we call an intelligible essence [form] nothing at all, and only a name? Here is a question which we must not leave unexamined or undetermined, nor must we affirm too confidently that there can be no decision; neither must we interpolate in our present long discourse a digression equally long, but if it is possible to set forth a great principle in a few words, that is just what we want:

Thus I state my view:—If mind and true opinion are two distinct classes, then I say that there certainly are these self-existent ideas [forms] unperceived by sense, and apprehended only by the mind; if, however, as some say, true opinion differs in no respect from mind, then everything that we perceive through the body is to be regarded as most real and certain. But we must affirm them to be distinct, for they have a distinct origin and are of a different nature; the one is implanted in us by instruction, the other by persuasion; the one is always accompanied by true reason, the other is without reason: the one cannot be overcome by persuasion, but the other can: and lastly, every man may be said to share in true opinion, but mind is the attribute of the gods and of very few men. Wherefore also we must acknowledge that there is one kind of being which is always the same, uncreated and indestructible, never receiving anything into itself from without, nor itself going out to any other, but invisible and imperceptible by any sense, and of which the contemplation is granted to intelligence only. And there is another nature of the same name with it, and like to it, perceived by sense, created, always in motion, becoming in place and again vanishing out of place, which is apprehended by opinion and sense.

[9] Plato, *Timaeus,* in *Dialogues,* trans. by Benjamin Jowett, Vol. III, pp. 471-72.

Thus instances of courage come to be and pass away. But the pattern of courage is permanent and remains the same regardless. So also, to return to our recent example, if we count by 9's to 999, or as far as we like, and find each number mentioned to be related to its neighbors according to the permanent principle of $+(10-1)$, we will pass in counting from even to odd. Further, 18 is divisible by 6, but 27 is not. So the numbers in the table vary in their characteristics, but their property of yielding a sum of digits divisible by 9 remains throughout. But just so long as we continue to treat numbers as objects of opinion, we fail to comprehend these permanent principles, although opinion may guess them without fully comprehending. Numbers seem then to be like partially understood events in nature. As we proceed to examine new instances, we do not know whether familiar characteristics will continue to appear.[10] We are, then, at the mercy of experience; we must wait to see whether our principle continues to hold. With knowledge we grasp a permanent structure that we know must hold true. This makes the study of number an excellent illustration of Plato's distinction between opinion and knowledge. As Plato himself insisted, the study of even elementary mathematics affords an excellent introduction to philosophical problems.

Courage and the general term of a series are as genuine objects of thinking as is the battle of Marathon or the number 981. For Plato they possess more reality, because in understanding either of them we must penetrate further into the permanent structure of human nature or of the number system than we do when we apprehend particular instances without the aid of general concepts, purified by analysis. Thus we have a greater insight into the permanent structure of the physical world when we comprehend Newton's law of the inverse square of the distance than when we notice apples falling to the earth.

Although they are genuine objects, the forms are not, like so

---

10 For purposes of elementary study we may think of the succession of numbers as an example of change. The numbers may be said to grow in size as we proceed. Today we might demur at this analogy and say that the numbers remain unchanged in a series along which we move. But in a famous passage in his *Phaedo* Plato has chosen to think of numbers as growing when one is added to another.

many concrete physical things, open to sensuous perception. Geometers do not observe the properties of the right triangle through their senses. They form intellectual judgments concerning these problems. It is only through such judgment that we escape from opinion. So, if we tried to establish the Pythagorean theorem by measuring a figure constructed on the blackboard, we would gain nothing but opinion. This is true for several reasons. First, the figure on the board is not a perfect triangle; for instance, the sides are not true straight lines. Furthermore, and much more important, the figure presents but one case of the right triangle and not *any* right triangle. It presents a right triangle of special dimensions, with sides of certain lengths, angles of certain magnitudes.

What is true of this figure need not, so far as mere observation can determine, be true of other right triangles. If we are to grasp the form, or *any* right triangle, we must discriminate between non-essential characteristics of the particular instance and the essential feature of the right triangle. This requires something more than merely seeing what is on the blackboard. The act of judgment whereby we refrain from considering any property of the figure that is not essential to the right triangle—as a general form—is something quite distinct from sheer sensuous perception, whereby we entertain in our minds what the sense organs offer us. This judgment or discrimination is indispensable to the apprehension of the forms. Of course we could not become aware of the forms or of anything else if we had no sense organs. But again, without judgment and discrimination we should not be able to grasp the forms. As Plato says in his *Theaetetus,* "We see *through* our eyes not *with* them."

Plato considers knowledge as something different in kind from opinion. In his earlier writings he advances a doctrine, which most scholars assert should not be interpreted literally, to the effect that in apprehending a form the mind is recalling something seen long ago in a premundane existence, when the unembodied soul was wholly free from opinion and saw the forms, so to speak, face to face. Thus we are said to be reminded of the forms by the particular instances we encounter in our earthly experience. We never, of course, find the form "triangle" on the blackboard, but what does appear on the blackboard may recall the form to our intellectual attention. Today, the great majority of philosophers would look with suspicion upon so bold a hypothesis as this, which requires us to postulate a previous life.

But there can be no doubt that this analogy of Plato is worth consideration, in that it forces us to contrast opinion and knowledge and to attempt to understand the connections between them. When, after considering many separate instances of a form, we finally grasp the pattern itself, it is true that the mind has transcended or gone beyond the material presented to it. It has caught something that none of the instances makes absolutely manifest. The doctrine of reminiscence expresses the fact that the mind reaches beyond the mass of particulars offered it to touch a general pattern, just as in memory proper, or ordinary recall, the mind is carried beyond the word or phrase to some scene that is associated with it. This is, of course, only an analogy. Plato never suggests that the reminiscence of form is actually a case of the association of ideas in the stream of our consciousness.

Plato develops his theory of knowledge and of the levels of think-ing in *The Republic,* especially in the following famous passage, that is usually spoken of as the "analogy of the divided line." [11] Here he refrains from any mention of reminiscence.

Suppose you take a line divided into two unequal parts,—one tc represent the visible class of objects, the other the intellectual,— and divide each part again into two segments on the same scale. Then, if you make the lengths of the segments represent degrees of distinctness or indistinctness, one of the two segments of the part which stands for the visible world will represent all images:—mean-ing, by images, first of all, shadows; and, in the next place, reflec-tions in water, and in close-grained, smooth, bright substances, and everything of the kind, if you understand me.

Yes, I do understand.

Let the other segment stand for the real objects corresponding to these images,—namely, the animals about us, and the whole world of nature and of art.

[11] Plato, *Republic,* trans. by J. L. Davies and D. J. Vaughan, pp. 231-34. Mac-millan & Co., London, 3d ed., 1866.

Very good.

Would you also consent to say that, with reference to this class, there is, in point of truth and untruthfulness, the same distinction between the copy and the original, that there is between what is matter of opinion and what is matter of knowledge?

Certainly I should.

Then let us proceed to consider how we must divide that part of the whole line which represents the intellectual world.

How must we do it?

Thus: one segment of it will represent what the soul is compelled to investigate by the aid of the segments of the other part, which it employs as images, starting from hypotheses, and travelling not to a first principle, but to a conclusion. The other segment will represent the objects of the soul, as it makes its way from an hypothesis to a first principle which is not hypothetical, unaided by those images which the former division employs, and shaping its journey by the sole help of real essential forms.

I have not understood your description so well as I could wish.

Then we will try again. You will understand me more easily when I have made some previous observations. I think you know that the students of subjects like geometry and calculation, assume by way of materials, in each investigation, all odd and even numbers, figures, three kinds of angles, and other similar data. These things they are supposed to know, and having adopted them as hypotheses, they decline to give any account of them, either to themselves or to others, on the assumption that they are self-evident; and, making these their starting point, they proceed to travel through the remainder of the subject, and arrive at last, with perfect unanimity, at that which they have proposed as the object of investigation.

I am perfectly aware of the fact, he replied.

Then you also know that they summon to their aid visible forms, and discourse about them, though their thoughts are busy not with these forms, but with their originals, and though they discourse not with a view to the particular square and diameter which they draw, but with a view to the absolute square and the absolute diameter, and so on. For while they employ by way of images those figures and diagrams aforesaid, which again have their shadows and images in water, they are really endeavouring to behold those abstractions which a person can only see with the eye of thought.

True.

This, then, was the class of things which I called intellectual; but

84

I said that the soul is constrained to employ hypotheses while engaged in the investigation of them,—not travelling to a first principle, (because it is unable to step out of, and mount above, its hypotheses,) but using, as images, just the copies that are presented by things below,—which copies, as compared with the originals, are vulgarly esteemed distinct and valued accordingly.

I understand you to be speaking of the subject-matter of the various branches of geometry and the kindred arts.

Again, by the second segment of the intellectual world understand me to mean all that the mere reasoning process apprehends by the force of dialectic, when it avails itself of hypotheses not as first principles, but as genuine hypotheses, that is to say, as stepping-stones and impulses, whereby it may force its way up to something that is not hypothetical, and arrive at the first principle of everything, and seize it in its grasp; which done, it turns round, and takes hold of that which takes hold of this first principle, till at last it comes down to a conclusion, calling in the aid of no sensible object whatever, but simply employing abstract, self-subsisting forms, and terminating in the same.

I do not understand you so well as I could wish, for I believe you to be describing an arduous task; but at any rate I understand that you wish to declare distinctly, that the field of real existence and pure intellect, as contemplated by the science of dialectic, is more certain than the field investigated by what are called the arts, in which hypotheses constitute first principles, which the students are compelled, it is true, to contemplate with the mind and not with the senses; but, at the same time, as they do not come back, in the course of inquiry, to a first principle, but push on from hypothetical premises, you think that they do not exercise pure reason on the questions that engage them, although taken in connection with a first principle these questions come within the domain of the pure reason. And I believe you apply the term understanding, not pure reason, to the mental habit of such people as geometricians,—regarding understanding as something intermediate between opinion and pure reason.

You have taken in my meaning most satisfactorily; and I beg you will accept these four mental states, as corresponding to the four segments,—namely pure reason corresponding to the highest, understanding to the second, belief to the third, and conjecture to the last; and pray arrange them in gradation, and believe them to partake of distinctness in a degree corresponding to the truth of their respective objects.

I understand you, said he. I quite agree with you, and will arrange them as you desire.

DIAGRAM

	4	
		pure forms
		pure reason (dialectic)
knowledge		————————eternal being
	3	
		hypothesis
		understanding
	2	
		things
		belief
opinion		————————temporal becoming
	1	
		images
		conjecture

1:2 = 3:4

We may interpret "images" in section 1 of our diagram pretty literally, and think of objects apprehended through only one of the senses. Thus when we hear a sound without seeing the cause of it, or see a distant object that we cannot compare in size with other familiar objects, we have to do with images. On the other hand, we might also interpret "image" more freely and refer to any object of judgment about which we must hazard a guess without any broad sweep of evidence to support it. By "things," in section 2, we may understand objects apprehended in groups concerning which we believe certain generalizations to hold true. Thus *All men are mortal* would be for Plato an example of belief. This way of thinking about objects carries much greater weight than mere conjecture. It may be based upon a vast array of evidence. Belief is frequently a case of *right opinion*. The weakness of belief lies not in the fact that it is false—it may indeed be true enough—but in that we do not see the reason for its being true. Since in belief we do not grasp the reason or general pattern, we may be said to be thinking about

86

a mere group of objects and not knowing a form. Thus when we first concluded that the odd numbers occupy the gap between the square numbers, we did not grasp the reason or the general term of the series. We were then thinking of the numbers as groups of entities that can be experienced by counting, and not as exemplifications of a general form. This contrast between opinion and the object of opinion on the one hand, and knowledge and the object of knowledge on the other hand is the very core of Platonic philosophy.

Plato argues that if there are no forms, then knowledge cannot differ from opinion, for knowledge is to be distinguished from opinion by the fact that it grasps a general pattern. And if there is no difference between knowledge and opinion, there is no distinction between, say, a mathematical demonstration and a happy guess made without complete understanding. Now we know that there is such a distinction and therefore we cannot deny that there are forms.

By "hypothesis," [12] in section 3 of our diagram, we may understand any form containing undefined terms. Thus even our analytical thinking concerning square and odd numbers apprehends only hypotheses, and is therefore called "understanding," for the simple reason that we have not as yet defined number. In attempting to do this we push toward the very frontier of science and philosophy and seek to apprehend their first principles. So in natural science we remain on the level of hypothesis and of understanding, in Plato's sense of these terms. When we say that 'a causes b,' to reach first principles a definition of causation is required. Such definitions are the goals of the Socratic method of analysis in its most lofty and difficult enterprise. It is this enterprise which Plato calls *dialectic* or *pure reason*.

FORMS AND THE PROBLEM OF CHANGE

There are for Plato various types of forms. We have remarked already such forms as courage, which is a permanent ideal of hu-

12 The reader should distinguish this use of the term "hypothesis" from that employed at the close of Chapter II.

man life, and such mathematical structures as a right triangle or the general term of a series. We must also recognize such forms as *man* or *plant* or *animal,* generic types that offer a problem in inductive definition. (Thus we may define man with the ancients as an animal having the power of rational speech or discourse.) We must also admit such patterns as those which are embodied, say, in the motion of the heavenly bodies, or in any phase of natural process. The laws of nature known to modern science may be interpreted as Platonic forms, although Plato, living in the infancy of such science, says little concerning these.[13]

It is important to remember that Plato considered his method applicable rather to mathematics, pure philosophy, and the Socratic study of ethics than to what we should nowadays term "natural science." In some quarters it is thought to be one of the profound weaknesses of Platonism that its master looked with considerable suspicion upon contemporary study of the actual events of nature, upon study of what we today call phenomena. Such study, Plato insists, deserves only passing consideration. Serious attention should be devoted to philosophy and mathematics, where a certainty of the type that distinguishes knowledge from opinion may be at least occasionally achieved. Natural science can never attain anything beyond a certain probability. Today many of us may look upon this notion as almost perverse, but we must remember that in Plato's day the conclusions of the students of natural phenomena hardly deserved the attention which Plato himself was willing to bestow upon them, whereas the geometrists were offering a firm foundation for further work and establishing a successful and a fruitful science.

For Plato, the natural sciences can never attain the exactness of pure mathematics and dialectic, reaching at best only a high probability; but this is no reason for neglecting them. They should be developed as accurately as possible. Plato's choice of a Pythagorean, Timaeus the Locrian, as the chief speaker in the *Timaeus,* the dia-

[13] The reader is advised, if he wishes to read Plato's work on natural science, to use some translation of the *Timaeus* other than that of Jowett. R. G. Bury's translation, in the Loeb Classical Library, is suggested.

logue most concerned with natural science, reflects his conviction of the most profitable method of scientific procedure. To describe and understand nature, we must look for its underlying mathematical structure. Granting that dialectic will enable one to discover the *nature,* use, and *right function* of things, mathematics is still the tool for finding and describing the mechanism by which such right functions or natures are embodied in the matrix of space and time. Thus one of the problems studied in Plato's Academy was to discover the simplest accurate mathematical explanation of the complex apparent motions of the stars and planets. This conception of "science" as a mathematical enterprise is so modern that some scholars have been led to credit Plato with the invention of our Western idea of "science." This credit must however be tempered by the reflection that for Plato, while mathematics can answer the question "How are things arranged?" only dialectic can arrive at an answer to the question "Why?"

We have said with Plato that there are forms or that the forms exist. How does this use of the verb "to be" and "exist" differ from that we employ when we say, "The Washington monument *exists*" or "There *is* a house on the island?" To answer this question requires use of dialectic. When I say that there *is* a house on the island, I recognize that the house has a history; it is subject to time. There once was no house on the island and in time there may be none. Again, the house changes more or less slowly as it stands. What is true of it today may not be true of it tomorrow.

But this does not apply to the forms. They do not alter. Thus they do not exist in a historical present belonging between a past and a future that are to be contrasted with it. But they belong in a changeless present, or what we might call the *present eternal,* a tense not recognized by the grammarian but one employed by the mathematician and well known to the philosopher. When we prove that the altitude of an isosceles triangle bisects the base, our tense is the present eternal, and we are talking about a permanent form. Thus eternity, in this sense—the Platonic sense—refers not to an everlasting flux that is never exhausted, to something that "goes on and on," but to a type of object that undergoes in itself absolutely no change. Thus the right triangle is eternal not because of its great age, but because, strictly speaking, it has no age.

We see from the diagram on page 86 that Plato employs the term "being" to refer to the eternal forms, and the term "becoming" to refer to images and things that are subject to time or change and so have history.

Plato expresses his certainty that the forms enjoy more reality than the object in time by saying that the forms really *are* while the transitory object *never really is,* but is always becoming. In general we may say that knowledge is awareness of being, opinion, awareness of becoming. In the case, however, of right opinion, it is true that we may be actually aware of permanent structure, but our thinking remains opinion because we cannot be sure that we are face to face with something permanently and necessarily true. We do not clearly recognize the forms as genuine beings.

Plato is at this point ready to offer his answer to the problem produced by the deadlock of Greek philosophy, of which Parmenides and Heraclitus represent the conflicting tendencies. The forms abide, the many instances of the forms change and pass in the flux. The passing show of things is not sheer change; it embodies or reflects the permanence of an oft-repeated structure. Being, that which can be understood exhaustively, does not change. Thus Parmenides has much reason on his side. But the world of becoming, the usual object of opinion—namely the realm of concrete particulars—is always changing. So Heraclitus' intuition is not wholly false.

However, the concrete thing in becoming cannot be exhaustively understood. We can fully understand forms and forms only. Thus it is not unreasonable to say that man can know everything about the form of the plane triangle, but it is folly to say that anyone can know everything about this particular piece of brass that is cut in triangular form. In the first place, the shape is not perfectly triangular, any more than the triangle on the blackboard is an absolute triangle, being bounded as it is by little mountain ranges of chalk-dust rather than by sheer straight lines. Again, our piece of brass has a history, and the ingredients of the brass have histories, and these histories cannot be exhausted. *The* triangle—the form—can be completely understood because it has no history, because its entire being is concentrated in the present eternal.

Plato is still enough a follower of Parmenides to look upon the actual world of change as opaque and imperfect, but he will not call it a sheer delusion, and thus he acknowledges that there is some justice in Heraclitus' position. Change is actual. Our experience to that effect cannot be doubted; but when we come to try to understand change and the particular objects in it, we find that we can proceed only by appealing to principles that do not change but enjoy the permanence of pure forms. Thus Plato in his *Timaeus* calls time the "moving image of eternity." By this he seems to say that change can be explained only when it is thought of as reflecting or embodying eternal or changeless structure. This teaching seems to be after all very reasonable when we consider that Plato describes the situation in which all thinking about the world, including modern science, finds itself. We understand events—insofar as we *do* understand them, and that is imperfectly—only by recognizing them as instances of this or that law, or we understand concrete objects as members of this or that group or class. The law and the class are permanent.

That sheer change would be unknowable is a central doctrine of Platonism, which is well expressed in the following passage from the *Phaedo*.[14]

And were we not saying long ago that the soul when using the body as an instrument of perception, that is to say, when using the sense of sight or hearing or some other sense (for the meaning of perceiving through the body is perceiving through the senses)— were we not saying that the soul too is then dragged by the body into the region of the changeable, and wanders and is confused; the world spins round her, and she is like a drunkard, when she touches change?

Very true.

But when returning into herself she reflects, then she passes into the other world, the region of purity, and eternity, and immortality,

14 Plato, *Phaedo*, in *Dialogues*, trans. by Benjamin Jowett, Vol. II, p. 222.

and unchangeableness, which are her kindred, and with them she
ever lives, when she is by herself and is not let or hindered; then
she ceases from her erring ways, and being in communion with the
unchanging is unchanging. And this state of the soul is called wisdom?

Thus Plato teaches us that only those things which possess or embody something permanent can be knowable. Without eternity or
the changeless, time would be sheer chaos.

FORMS AND THINGS

The theory of the forms arises from an analysis of knowing. It is
not itself a speculative theory. A careful inspection of the activity of
knowing reveals the forms as clearly as inspection of language reveals parts of speech and, say, the mood, tense, or voice of verbs.
The form is a type of object that we have only to describe clearly if
we would make its presence evident. But connected with any discussion of the forms there are speculative problems that cannot
be solved by inspection and analysis. We know that there are
two great classes of objects, objects of opinion and objects of knowledge or forms. Let us now put this question: How are these two
objects connected or related one to another? How comes the general
pattern to reside in or be reflected in the particular thing? We
know well enough that if the general objects were not in some way
intimately connected with the particular, knowledge would be out
of the question. The many particulars are recognizable only insofar
as they present similarity one to another, and they can be studied
only insofar as they embody a common structure or general pattern.
But this does not answer our question: How is the general present
with or in the particular? This question may also be put in the
form: How can the eternal be present in the temporal, the permanent in the changing?

It was to this problem that Plato devoted the best energies of his
later period. And in this search he was spurred on by the comments
of his hostile critics who rejoiced to find that the question is not an
easy one either to answer or to dismiss. Plato prefaces his answer

with an exposition of certain errors common to many discussions of the relation of general to particular. The great dialogue entitled *Parmenides* is devoted to this topic. In the first place, we must not think of this relation as one of spatial juxtaposition or inclusion. The general is not *in* the particular as the core is in the apple. Nor is the relation spatial in any sense. How could the form "man" be in two places at once? Yet this would be necessary if the form were a spatial entity included in many particulars. Furthermore, we must not say that the particular participates in the general if by "partici-pate" we mean to "have a share in." Plato has very cleverly disposed of this possibility.[15]

Suppose that you divide absolute greatness, and that of the many great things, each one is great in virtue of a portion of greatness less than absolute greatness—is that conceivable?

No.

Or will each equal thing, if possessing some small portion of equality less than absolute equality, be equal to some other thing by virtue of that portion only?

Impossible.

Or suppose one of us to have a portion of smallness; this is but a part of the small, and therefore the absolutely small is greater; if the absolutely small be greater, that to which the part of the small is added will be smaller and not greater than before.

How absurd!

Nor will Plato tolerate the notion that the forms are only thoughts or ideas in the modern sense of the word. Some might argue that only particulars exist independently of mind and that the form is only the concept our mind fastens on after having examined many particulars. This is quite counter to the spirit of Platonism. For Plato the form is the object attended to by the concept. To be sure, if the forms are thought, they clearly cannot be merely our thought, for they must belong or refer to the particular objects, whether or not we happen to be thinking of them. Therefore if the forms are thoughts, they must be thoughts in some way *possessed* by the par-ticulars. And Plato feels that this is equivalent to saying that all

[15] Plato, *Parmenides*, in *Dialogues*, trans. by Benjamin Jowett, Vol. IV, p. 51.

particulars think—that the concrete world is a wholly mental one. This last proposition is dismissed as absurd.[16]

But may not the ideas, asked Socrates, be thoughts only, and have no proper existence except in our minds, Parmenides? For in that case each idea may still be one, and not experience this infinite multiplication.

And can there be individual thoughts which are thoughts of nothing?

Impossible, he said.

The thought must be of something?

Yes.

Of something which is or which is not?

Of something which is.

Must it not be of a single something, which the thought recognizes as attaching to all, being a single form or nature?

Yes.

And will not the something which is apprehended as one and the same in all, be an idea?

From that, again, there is no escape.

Then, said Parmenides, if you say that everything else participates in the ideas, must you not say either that everything is made up of thoughts, and that all things think; or that they are thoughts but have no thought?

Thus the form is not an idea or a thought; it is not the product of mind. But this does not mean that Plato is to account for the relation of form to particular without reference to mind. Mind does not make the forms. We discover the forms, we do not construct them. Plato insists upon this, but when he tries to explain the relation of form to particular he turns to a speculative theory involving mind. Mind is the link between the eternal and the temporal. Through mental activity the forms are embodied in a world of concrete particulars. Plato does not succeed in proving—in fact he hardly attempts to prove—that mind must play such a role in the universe. His approach is boldly speculative, and he is usually conscious of this. He seems to be saying: Mind is of such a nature that we may quite consistently consider the presence of the eternal in the

16 *Ibid.*, p. 52.

temporal, of form in the flux, as the outcome of mental activity, and this seems to be the most likely hypothesis to account for that fundamental aspect of things. In framing this hypothesis, Plato has much reason on his side. Mind not only recognizes the presence of the general in the particular, but can and often does work toward the embodiment of some general pattern in a given particular situation.

An artist may embody a general pattern, theme, or idea—some religious subject, for instance—that has been exploited by earlier artists in other ways. The artist will use his own medium and technique. Thus through the agency of his creative activity the artist individualizes a general topic, gives it, as Shakespeare would say, a "local habitation" and a particular concrete life under the special conditions of his own work. In this way active mind enriches the concrete flux by infusing it with a form that it would otherwise not have embodied. A medium becomes significant—that is, bears form —only as it is controlled by mind.

Plato's insistence that the world is subject to the dominion of mind is very clear in the following selection from his *Philebus*.[17]

Soc[*rates*]. Yet the answer is easy, since all philosophers assert with one voice that mind is the king of heaven and earth—in reality they are magnifying themselves. And perhaps they are right. But still I should like to consider the class of mind, if you do not object, a little more fully.

Phi[*lebus*]. Take your own course, Socrates, and never mind length; we shall not tire of you.

Soc. Very good; let us begin then, Protarchus, by asking a question.

Pro[*tarchus*]. What question?

Soc. Whether all this which they call the universe is left to the guidance of unreason and chance medley, or, on the contrary, as our fathers have declared, ordered and governed by a marvellous intelligence and wisdom.

Pro. Wide asunder are the two assertions, illustrious Socrates, for that which you were just now saying to me appears to be blasphemy; but the other assertion, that mind orders all things, is worthy of the aspect of the world, and of the sun, and of the moon, and

17 Plato, *Philebus,* in *Dialogues,* trans. by Benjamin Jowett, Vol. IV, pp. 596-99.

of the stars and of the whole circle of the heavens; and never will I say or think otherwise.

Soc. Shall we then agree with them of old time in maintaining this doctrine,—not merely reasserting the notions of others, without risk to ourselves,—but shall we share in the danger, and take our part of the reproach which will await us, when an ingenious individual declares that all is disorder?

Pro. That would certainly be my wish.

Soc. Then now please to consider the next stage of the argument.

Pro. Let me hear.

Soc. We see that the elements which enter into the nature of the bodies of all animals, fire, water, air, and, as the storm-tossed sailor cries, 'land' (i.e. earth), reappear in the constitution of the world.

Pro. The proverb may be applied to us; for truly the storm gathers over us, and we are at our wit's end.

Soc. There is something to be remarked about each of these elements.

Pro. What is it?

Soc. Only a small fraction of any one of them exists in us, and that of a mean sort, and not in any way pure, or having any power worthy of its nature. One instance will prove this of all of them; there is fire within us, and in the universe.

Pro. True.

Soc. And is not our fire small and weak and mean? But the fire in the universe is wonderful in quantity and beauty, and in every power that fire has.

Pro. Most true.

Soc. And is the fire in the universe nourished and generated and ruled by the fire in us, or is the fire in you and me, and in other animals, dependent on the universal fire?

Pro. That is a question which does not deserve an answer.

Soc. Right; and you would say the same, if I am not mistaken, of the earth which is in animals and the earth which is in the universe, and you would give a similar reply about all the other elements?

Pro. Why, how could any man who gave any other be deemed in his senses?

Soc. I do not think that he could—but now go on to the next step. When we saw those elements of which we have been speaking gathered up in one, did we not call them a body?

Pro. We did.

Soc. And the same may be said of the cosmos, which for the same reason may be considered to be a body, because made up of the same elements.

Pro. Very true.

Soc. But is our body nourished wholly by this body, or is this body nourished by our body, thence deriving and having the qualities of which we were just now speaking?

Pro. That again, Socrates, is a question which does not deserve to be asked.

Soc. Well, tell me, is this question worth asking?

Pro. What question?

Soc. May our body be said to have a soul?

Pro. Clearly.

Soc. And whence comes that soul, my dear Protarchus, unless the body of the universe, which contains elements like those in our bodies but in every way fairer, had also a soul? Can there be another source?

Pro. Clearly, Socrates, that is the only source.

Soc. Why, yes, Protarchus; for surely we cannot imagine that of the four classes, the finite [or form], the infinite [or flux], the composition of the two, and the cause, the fourth, which enters into all things, giving to our bodies souls, and the art of self-management, and of healing disease, and operating in other ways to heal and organize, having too all the attributes of wisdom;—we cannot, I say, imagine that whereas the self-same elements exist, both in the entire heaven and in great provinces of the heaven, only fairer and purer, this last should not also in that higher sphere have designed the noblest and fairest things?

Pro. Such a supposition is quite unreasonable.

Soc. Then if this be denied, should we not be wise in adopting the other view and maintaining that there is in the universe a mighty infinite and an adequate limit, of which we have often spoken, as well as a presiding cause of no mean power, which orders and arranges years and seasons and months, and may be justly called wisdom and mind?

Pro. Most justly.

Soc. And wisdom and mind cannot exist without soul?

Pro. Certainly not.

Soc. And in the divine nature of Zeus would you not say that there is the soul and mind of a king, because there is in him the power of the cause? And other gods have other attributes, by which they are pleased to be called.

Pro. Very true.

Soc. Do not then suppose that these words are rashly spoken by us, O Protarchus, for they are in harmony with the testimony of those who said of old time that mind rules the universe.

The reader may well ponder such a bold theory, and should neither accept nor discard it in haste. Certainly it is not a notion familiar to our modern consciousness. But as we grow better acquainted with the history of philosophy we shall learn that it is almost as difficult to do without the notion of cosmic mind as it is to explain the way in which that mind is related to the world of our experience. A modern Materialist, a truly great thinker, Samuel Alexander, has tried to treat the world as a vast system of motion, in which mind is of limited scope and a late arrival upon the scene. He does not recognize Plato's world soul. Accordingly we find him asking: "Why there should be finites (or actual things) within the general matrix (of motion or space-time) we can understand; for time and space, being indissolubly interwoven, do not remain extended blanks, but break each other up into differences. We cannot, however, see, at least I cannot, why these finites should exhibit actual repetition in their kinds. Perhaps we know too little at present about the repetition of individauls among organic forms to be able to face the more general and simpler problem." Alexander offers no answer and concludes:

"I can give no answer, and until the answer can be given I must admit that the scheme of things which has been suggested as a hypothesis, and has so far been verified, presents a grave defect; equally so, whether the actual multiplicity of individuals in their kinds is accepted as a purely empirical feature not admitting of explanation, or as an unsolved empirical problem." [18]

(See below, pp. 414-20.)

For Plato, form is embodied in the world because God's mind stands to the world as the artists's mind stands to the work of art

[18] Samuel Alexander, *Space, Time, and Deity*, Vol. II, pp. 312-13. The Macmillan Company, New York; 2 Vols., 1922. Reprinted by permission of the executors of the Alexander estate and the Macmillan Company.

he fashions. The Platonic scheme of the universe contains, then, three primal elements: the forms, God, and matter, which last is the stuff or medium in which the forms are embodied. We have already described the forms. We must now turn to the two remaining factors, God and matter. God is conceived as a soul who initiates the several phases of natural process or change. For the Greek, soul is nearly always thought of as that which initiates motion and gives it direction. Thus God may be thought of as the supreme soul, who has power over natural change. But this power is not exercised capriciously. God's intelligence contemplates the forms, and the world of concrete motion is subjected to them. Because of God's influence, the forms are apparent everywhere throughout nature, and there is no chaos or unintelligible flux.

If the reader desires a slightly more concrete picture of the relation of God to the world, let him employ the following analogy. We all possess in our power of speech an ability to initiate vocal sound, but thanks to our intelligence, this power is employed to embody meaning, and so the presence of intelligence establishes an orderly structure in our flow of speech. Thus, in a sense, God brings form into the moving world as we bring meaning into our use of words. Several points may be made in connection with this analogy. Mind looks toward meaning or form as an end or a goal, the concept or idea that one is trying to express. In this process other forms are employed as means. We refer in our analogy to the grammatical structures or patterns that we must employ in writing and in talking. Mind orders the secondary forms as means for the sake of an end.

Here we find Plato following the lead of Socrates and contributing support to the great hypothesis that nature is composed of many phases or passages of purposive development.

Matter may be described as the raw material in which God embodies the forms. Subtract the forms and God from our conception of the world and what we have left is matter. Plato's description of this matter in his *Timaeus* is as obscure as it is famous. Matter is described as composed of two elements: space and necessity. Plato seems to be describing a very significant feature of all intelligent and productive activity. Forms exist in their own isolation, undistorted by the contacts of actual existence. Actual entities do not exist in isolation, but overlap one another and, so to speak, blunt one another's edges. (Consider our example of the triangle done in chalk on the blackboard.) It is impossible to plunge a form into the welter of actual objects—that is, into the here and now of actual space and time—and preserve the logical rigor of its structure. Mathematical theory does not quite fit physical actuality; ideals must be compromised in practice. Space, the matrix of actuality in which concrete objects are fused together, resists the forms, and this resistance Plato calls *necessity,* against which the creator must always struggle.[19]

For the present we have only to conceive of three natures: first, that which is in process of generation; secondly, that in which the generation takes place; and thirdly, that of which the thing generated is a resemblance. And we may liken the receiving principle to a mother, and the source or spring to a father, and the intermediate nature to a child; and may remark further, that if the model is to take every variety of form, then the matter in which the model is fashioned will not be duly prepared, unless it is formless, and free from the impress of any of those shapes which it is hereafter to receive from without. For if the matter were like any of the supervening forms, then whenever any opposite or entirely different nature was stamped upon its surface, it would take the impression badly, because it would intrude its own shape.[20] Wherefore, that which is to receive all forms should have no form; as in making perfumes they first contrive that the liquid substance which is to receive the scent shall be as inodorous as possible; or as those who wish to impress figures on soft substances do not allow any previous impression to remain, but begin by making the surface as even and smooth as possible. In the same way that which is to receive perpetually and through its whole extent the resemblances of all eternal

[19] Plato, *Timaeus,* in *Dialogues,* trans. by Benjamin Jowett, Vol. III, pp. 470-71.

[20] To appreciate this reference to the "minting" of space, the reader would do well to handle and examine some Greek coins of Plato's period. The relative massiveness, intrusiveness, and recalcitrance of the medium, as well as the idealization of the design, contrasted with the technical mastery of medium and the realistic portraiture designs of our own coinage, will make Plato's metaphor more vivid, and help the reader to understand why in the philosopher's time it must have seemed a singularly apt one.

beings ought to be devoid of any particular form. Wherefore, the mother and receptacle of all created and visible and in any way sensible things, is not to be termed earth, or air, or fire, or water, or any of their compounds, or any of the elements from which these are derived, but is an invisible and formless being which receives all things and in some mysterious way partakes of the intelligible, and is most incomprehensible.

Plato's theory of matter is vague, although nearly always richly suggestive. Matter is at times described as something positive, not merely as a colorless matrix for the embodiment of the forms. In his *Philebus* Plato interprets matter as open opportunity, the indefinite sweep of possible production that faces a creative mind. Matter is to God what a blank sheet of paper is to the author, or the strings of a violin to the virtuoso. Matter is a challenge to creation. God, being in the language of the *Timaeus,* "perfectly good," wishes to enrich all things with the dignity of the forms, and so he accepts the challenge and constructs a world of harmony and order. But he can never be wholly successful in this, for matter is always a recalcitrant medium and *necessity,* or the resistance which the medium offers the creator, cannot be entirely overcome. Therefore God does not directly produce the evil and imperfections in the world. He is continually, although never completely, thwarted by matter. In order to indicate that God or the supreme productive mind is not directly responsible for the actual world just as it is, Plato calls him the *demiurge,* or contributing cause, who must employ both matter and the forms. The forms are never perfectly embodied, just as no human artifact ever quite embodies the full ideal principle upon which it is constructed. So no bedmaker perhaps quite achieves the embodiment of the perfect bed, which must be conceived as affording the maximum of comfort and of healthful sleep.

THE PLATONIC THEORY OF VALUE

The Platonic theory of value is a description of one form, usually called *the form of the good*. This form must in some measure be embodied in any object that possesses a degree of value. Thus a description of this form, if fully developed, amounts to a survey of the Platonic theories of logic, of conduct, and of art, of the various ways in which man may achieve value or do something worth while. We are, all of us, constantly concerned with values. We make implicit statements concerning them whenever we choose between alternatives or make a decision. Such decisions may involve moral, logical, or aesthetic standards, as our decisions concern conduct, reasoning, or the production or selection of objects of beauty.

Plato's theory of value, his description of the good, the true, and the beautiful, fits easily into his theory of forms. In fact some writers insist that the theory is founded directly upon Plato's faith in what we today call the objectivity of value. We believe that our judgments concerning the value of this or that object, practice, or institution are objective if we believe that we *discover* the importance or value of the object rather than producing it through fostering an opinion in its favor—so to speak, by giving it publicity. Our judgments must then be said to refer to a virtue or excellence that these judgments themselves do not produce or constitute. If we recognize this value as a Platonic form, we attribute to it an objectivity quite sufficient to justify our considering value judgments as acts of discovery rather than as arbitrary fiats whereby value is produced.

The Athenians were not unacquainted with such an interpretation of moral standards. Witness Sophocles' mention of the "unwritten and unfailing statutes of heaven," where "life is not of today or yesterday." In the face of Sophistic relativism, Plato defended the objectivity of moral values—not by listing a catalogue of indisputable imperatives, by insisting, so to speak, upon a list of "do's" and "dont's," but by describing as clearly as he could the common core of value that all genuine excellence must possess. In this way Plato presents to our consideration his understanding of the form of the good.

At first glance, Plato's theory of value seems strangely intellectual. It is perhaps best expressed by the statement that the embodiment of unity and complexity, of the one in the many, is the embodiment of value. Thus a picture gains by its detail provided only that this detail is caught up into the unifying pattern of the work as a whole, so that its elements may be seen to belong to one another. In this simple instance lies the essence of Plato's doctrine of value. The good man is he whose life has a pattern of unity into which is woven a wealth of varied activity, so that the elements of his nature, including his physical, mental, and spiritual needs, find a place in the order of his existence. No phase of his life may be neglected any more than a good artist may leave a "hole" in his canvas. Again, the good argument or turn of reasoning is one in which the evidence advanced stands together to support a central thesis, to make a coherent defense of a given point. No fact may be left unexplained or at loose ends. Unity and coherence are vital to reasoning. Consider these two examples from Plato's writings, where he has made the nature of value clear by describing objects where value is conspicuous by its absence. We quote from the *Phaedrus*.[21]

Soc[*rates*]. At any rate, you will allow that every discourse ought to be a living creature, having a body of its own and a head and feet; there should be a middle, beginning, and end, adapted to one another and to the whole?
Phaedr[*us*]. Certainly.
Soc. Can this be said of the discourse of Lysias? See whether you can find any more connexion in his words than in the epitaph which is said by some to have been inscribed on the grave of Midas the Phrygian.
Phaed. What is there remarkable in the epitaph?
Soc. It is as follows:—

'I am a maiden of bronze and lie on the tomb of Midas;
So long as water flows and tall trees grow,
So long here on this spot by his sad tomb abiding,
I shall declare to passers-by that Midas sleeps below.'

Now in this rhyme whether a line comes first or comes last, as you will perceive, makes no difference.

The balanced structure of classical poetry always contains form, and through its form it achieves beauty. The lines on the tomb of Midas offer but a sorry minimum of structure and so are beneath the contempt of a Platonist.

---

[21] Plato, *Phaedrus*, in *Dialogues*, trans. by Benjamin Jowett, Vol. I, pp. 472-73.

Again consider the life of a man whom Plato describes as follows in *The Republic:* [22]

> ...he lives from day to day indulging the appetite of the hour; and sometimes he is lapped in drink and strains of the flute; then he becomes a water-drinker, and tries to get thin; then he takes a turn at gymnastics; sometimes idling and neglecting everything, then once more living the life of a philosopher; often he is busy with politics, and starts to his feet and says and does whatever comes into his head; and, if he is emulous of any one who is a warrior, off he is in that direction, or of men of business, once more in that. His life has neither law nor order; and this distracted existence he terms joy and bliss and freedom; and so he goes on.
>
> Yes, he replied, he is all liberty and equality.
>
> Yes, I said; his life is motley and manifold and an epitome of the lives of many;—he answers to the State which we described as fair and spangled. And many a man and many a woman will take him for their pattern, and many a constitution and many an example of manners is contained in him.

Lack of structure, or of organization, is fatal to both beauty and virtue. In the purely intellectual realm, that of reasoning, it breeds error. Thus the good, the beautiful, and the true seem to possess a common core, or one essential structure. To exhibit this structure is the prime purpose of Plato's writings that concern value.

The most famous description of the form of the good occurs in *The Republic,* in a passage just before the equally famous figure of the divided line already quoted. In this passage Plato seems to be overcome by an intellectual humility. He hesitates to describe the form of the good as order or unity and variety, but speaks of it as the source of these things. This source of value cannot be described adequately in analytical fashion. Its nature can be perceived only through the use of metaphor. The philosopher must strain toward its apprehension as the poet strains for a figure of speech that will do his subject justice.

This emphasis upon suprarational insight appears, at least at first, to constitute a virtual repudiation of the Socratic method of inductive definition. Plato seems to be overreaching thought and

[22] Plato, *The Republic,* in *Dialogues,* trans. by Benjamin Jowett, Vol. III, p. 269.

working toward sheer insight or mystical illumination. He is not satisfied simply to observe what common element is to be found in those things which we usually consider of value. Such procedure would be purely a matter of Socratic analysis. What he seems to want is a vision whereby the forms of value described by analysis will actually appear as valuable; that is, of vital importance for all the things that come to be in the flux, a glorious and desirable goal toward which we all would tend freely and without reluctance if only we could see clearly what its true nature is.[23]

Are you aware, that whenever a person makes an end of looking at objects, upon which the light of day is shedding colour, and looks instead at objects coloured by the light of the moon and stars, his eyes grow dim and appear almost blind, as if they were not the seat of distinct vision?

I am fully aware of it.

But whenever the same person looks at objects on which the sun is shining, these very eyes, I believe, see clearly, and are evidently the seat of distinct vision?

Unquestionably it is so.

Just in the same way understand the condition of the soul to be as follows: Whenever it has fastened upon an object, over which truth and real existence are shining, it seizes that object by an act of reason, and knows it, and thus proves itself to be possessed of reason: but whenever it has fixed upon objects that are blent with darkness,—the world of birth and death,—then it rests in *opinion*, and its sight grows dim, as its opinions shift backward and forward, and it has the appearance of being destitute of reason.

True, it has.

Now, this power, which supplies the objects of real knowledge with the truth that is in them, and which renders to him who knows them the faculty of knowing them, you must consider to be the essential Form of Good, and you must regard it as the origin of science, and of truth, so far as the latter comes within the range of knowledge—and though knowledge and truth are both very beautiful things, you will be right in looking upon good as something distinct from them, and even more beautiful. And just as, in the analogous case, it is right to regard light and vision as resembling the sun, but wrong to identify them with the sun; so, in the case of science and truth, it is right to regard both of them as resembling

23 Plato, *Republic*, trans. by Davies and Vaughan, pp. 230-31.

good, but wrong to identify either of them with good; because, on the contrary, the quality of the good ought to have a still higher value set upon it.

That implies an inexpressible beauty, if it not only is the source of science and truth, but also surpasses them in beauty; for, I presume, you do not mean by it pleasure.

Hush! I exclaimed, not a word of that. But you had better examine the illustration further, as follows.

Show me how.

I think you will admit that the sun ministers to visible objects, not only the faculty of being seen, but also their vitality, growth, and nutriment, though it is not itself equivalent to vitality.

Of course it is not.

Then admit that, in like manner, the objects of knowledge not only derive from the good the gift of being known, but are further endowed by it with a real and essential existence; though the good, far from being identical with real existence, actually transcends it in dignity and power.

The sun or the fountain of value is the source of both light and heat. It renders the world intelligible and makes life possible. This figure of speech contains in compressed form a whole metaphysics of value. Light and power are seen as intimately related. Thus in social theory we can hardly expect to find Plato glorifying force on the one hand or free unrestrained competition on the other hand. Unenlightened energy can achieve no value.

The virtue and the excellence of the individual depend upon the way in which intelligence and tradition bring his needs, interests, and capacity into a harmonious economy or a unity. Plato considers the ethical equipment of the individual as subdivided into three types: intelligence, desire, and the capacity for moral effort, the will power that depends upon self-respect. In the well-developed personality this effort supports intelligence in its dominion over conduct, while in the evil or disorganized moral life it supports now one interest and now another, spurring the individual, who at last prides himself on his very excesses, to more and more unreasonable and self-damaging conduct. In this theory, Plato leans heavily upon the Pythagorean doctrine of harmony.

The following passage from *The Republic* presents Plato's doctrine of the four cardinal virtues: wisdom, courage, temperance, and justice, which last includes the first three as its component elements.[24]

What at the commencement we laid down as a universal rule of action, when we were founding our state, this, if I mistake not, or some modification if it, is justice. I think we affirmed, if you recollect, and frequently repeated, that every individual ought to have some one occupation in the state, which should be that to which his natural capacity was best adapted.

We did say so.

And again, we have often heard people say, that to mind one's own business, and not to be meddlesome, is justice; and we have often said the same thing ourselves.

We have said so.

Then it would seem, my friend, that to do one's own business, in some shape or other, is justice. Do you know whence I infer this?

No; be so good as to tell me.

I think that the remainder left in the state, after eliminating the qualities which we have considered, I mean temperance, and courage, and wisdom, must be that which made their entrance into it possible, and which preserves them there so long as they exist in it. Now we affirmed that the remaining quality, when three out of the four were found, would be justice.

Here then...after a hard struggle, we have, though with difficulty, reached the land; and we are pretty well satisfied that there are corresponding divisions, equal in number, in a state, and in the soul of every individual.

True.

Then does it not necessarily follow that, as and whereby the state was wise, so and thereby the individual is wise?

Without doubt it does.

And that as and whereby the individual is brave, so and thereby is the state brave; and that everything conducing to virtue which is possessed by the one, finds its counterpart in the other?

It must be so.

Then we shall also assert, I imagine, Glaucon, that a man is just, in the same way in which we found the state to be just.

This too is a necessary corollary.

But surely we have not allowed ourselves to forget, that what

[24] *Ibid.,* pp. 134-35; 146-48.

makes the state just, is the fact of each of the three classes therein doing its own work.

No; I think we have not forgotten this.

We must bear in mind, then, that each of us also, if his inward faculties do severally their proper work, will, in virtue of that, be a just man, and a doer of his proper work.

Certainly, it must be borne in mind.

Is it not then essentially the province of the rational principle to command, inasmuch as it is wise, and has to exercise forethought in behalf of the entire soul, and the province of the spirited principle to be its subject and ally?

Yes, certainly.

And will not the combination of music and gymnastic bring them, as we said, into unison; elevating and fostering the one with lofty discourses and scientific teachings, and lowering the tone of the other by soothing address, till its wildness has been tamed by harmony and rhythm?

Yes, precisely so.

And so these two, having been thus trained, and having truly learned their parts and received a real education, will exercise control over the concupiscent principle, which in every man forms the largest portion of the soul, and is by nature most insatiably covetous. And they will watch it narrowly, that it may not so batten upon what are called the pleasures of the body as to grow large and strong, and forthwith refuse to do its proper work, and even aspire to absolute dominion over the classes which it has no right according to its kind to govern, thus overturning fundamentally the life of all.

Certainly they will.

And would not these two principles be the best qualified to guard the entire soul and body against enemies from without; the one taking counsel, and the other fighting its battles, in obedience to the governing power, to whose designs it gives effect by its bravery?

True.

In like manner, I think, we call an individual brave, in virtue of the spirited element of his nature, when this part of him holds fast, through pain and pleasure, the instructions of the reason as to what is to be feared, and what is not.

Yes, and rightly.

And we call him wise, in virtue of that small part which reigns within him, and issues these instructions, and which also in its turn contains within itself a true knowledge of what is advantageous for the whole community composed of these three principles, and for each member of it.

Exactly so.

Again, do we not call a man temperate, in virtue of the friendship and harmony of these same principles, that is to say, when the two that are governed agree with that which governs in regarding the rational principle as the rightful sovereign, and set up no opposition to its authority?

Certainly, he replied; temperance is nothing else than this, whether in state or individual.

Lastly, a man will be just, in the way and by the means which we have repeatedly described.

We have seen that Plato conceives of the ideal unity of the state in terms similar to those employed in describing individual virtue. Plato's ideal society may be described as a form of socialism in that moral individualism, competition, and private ownership are discouraged; but unlike many modern socialisms, it does not include a liquidation of the upper classes; it undertakes to remove these classes from the abuses connected with family pride and ambitions and with the pursuit of wealth.

To nineteenth- and twentieth-century readers, it has usually seemed that Plato's social theory is strangely unappreciative of the potentialities and the social importance of technology. Although at least one scholar has contended that his frequent references to the arts show that Plato was interested and proficient in the skills and crafts of his time,[25] the "sidewalk-supervisor" tone and character of these references strongly suggest that he was not. It was the Sophists whom Plato sarcastically described as "adept at making a bed or flavoring a sauce" who prided themselves on their aptitude in crafts, and who thought that virtuous action and political science were crafts to be taught and mastered by precept and example just like pottery and cobbling. In several dialogues, Plato attacks this "technological" conception of politics and virtue. In the dialogue *Critias*, we have Plato's final commentary on the value of technol-

[25] In an article, R. S. Brumbaugh, "Note on the Numbers in Plato's *Critias*," *Classical Philology*, January 1948, it has been shown that the public-works program of Atlantis was not the result of rational social planning, and that it does not reflect any social unity or integration, a point sometimes questioned by scholars.

ogy. Here he describes the state of Altantis, which engaged in colossal technological enterprises, until at last (through the intervention of cosmic justice) the state was sunk beneath the sea by the weight of its own public works. The Atlantean engineers were masters of tunneling, bridging, and canalization, but their technology was employed in the service of a society with no central unifying body of moral principles or rational political institutions. The effect of the contribution of these technicians (whose works Plato describes as "superhuman"), applied in the service of a society of ten loosely federated tyrannies, in which the force of good traditions had been nullified by the prevalent urge to make everything "bigger and better," was simply to heighten the fever and hasten the disastrous end of the society on whose behalf their talent was exercised. It is not hard to see the moral of this story, or its cogency as Plato would have applied it to our own society.

In Plato's ideal society intelligence is the prime virtue of the governing class, courage that of the military, temperance that of the popular body or artisans class.[26] The active co-operation of these three classes constitutes social justice, even as the harmony of the three "parts" of the soul constitutes individual justice. After Socrates' death Plato had no respect for democracy and its popular whims, and after having witnessed the excesses of the dictatorial Council of Thirty, he was convinced that the aristocracy must be regenerated if it was to be trusted with power.

---

[26] Ancient and modern readers have often schematized Plato's picture of the ideal state:

Class	Social Function	Proper Virtue
Rulers	Deliberative	Wisdom
Auxiliaries	Executive	Courage
Artisans	Productive	Temperance

This is adequate insofar as "temperance" is the only excellence in which the artisan must share if he is to perform his proper social function. Plato, however, adds that temperance is "a right opinion about who should be ruler, and who be ruled, which harmonizes all the classes in the state," so that the rulers and the auxiliaries must also be temperate, and the above diagram is inadequate insofar as its form suggests that temperance is the *exclusive* or *distinctive* excellence of the artisan. This same qualification must be understood to apply to the statement about the temperance of the artisan, in the text above.

The following quotation from the *Timaeus* [27] presents a fairly thorough summary of Plato's social theories, with the exception of the educational provisions and the role of dialectical knowledge, topics that would not have been appropriate in this summary's cosmological context.

Soc[rates]....the chief theme of my yesterday's discourse was the State—how constituted and of what citizens composed it would seem likely to be most perfect.

Tim[aeus]. Yes, Socrates; and what you said of it was very much to our mind.

Soc. Did we not begin by separating the husbandmen and the artisans from the class of defenders of the State?

Tim. Yes.

Soc. And when we had given to each one that single employment and particular art which was suited to his nature, we spoke of those who were intended to be our warriors, and said that they were to be guardians of the city against attacks from within as well as from without, and to have no other employment; they were to be merciful in judging their subjects, of whom they were by nature friends, but fierce to their enemies, when they came across them in battle.

Tim. Exactly.

Soc. We said, if I am not mistaken, that the guardians should be gifted with a temperament in a high degree both passionate and philosophical; and that then they would be as they ought to be, gentle to their friends and fierce with their enemies.

Tim. Certainly.

Soc. And what did we say of their education? Were they not to be trained in gymnastic, and music, and all other sorts of knowledge which were proper for them?

Tim. Very true.

Soc. And being thus trained they were not to consider gold or silver or anything else to be their own private property; they were to be like hired troops, receiving pay for keeping guard from those who were protected by them—the pay was to be no more than would suffice for men of simple life; and they were to spend in common, and to live together in the continual practice of virtue, which was to be their sole pursuit.

Tim. That was also said.

27 Plato, *Timaeus*, in *Dialogues*, trans. by Benjamin Jowett, Vol. III, pp. 437-39.

Soc. Neither did we forget the women; of whom we declared, that their natures should be assimilated and brought into harmony with those of the men, and that common pursuits should be assigned to them both in time of war and in their ordinary life.

Tim. That, again, was as you say.

Soc. And what about the procreation of children? Or rather was not the proposal too singular to be forgotten? for all wives and children were to be in common, to the intent that no one should ever know his own child, but they were to imagine that they were all one family; those who were within a suitable limit of age were to be brothers and sisters, those who were of an elder generation of parents and grandparents, and those of a younger, children and grandchildren.

Tim. Yes, and the proposal is easy to remember, as you say.

Soc. And do you also remember how, with a view of securing as far as we could the best breed, we said that the chief magistrates, male and female, should contrive secretly, by the use of certain lots, so to arrange the nuptial meeting, that the bad of either sex and the good of either sex might pair with their like; and there was to be no quarrelling on this account, for they would imagine that the union was a mere accident, and was to be attributed to the lot?

Tim. I remember.

Soc. And you remember how we said that the children of the good parents were to be educated, and the children of the bad secretly dispersed among the inferior citizens; and while they were all growing up the rulers were to be on the look-out, and to bring up from below in their turn those who were worthy, and those among themselves who were unworthy were to take the places of those who came up?

Tim. True.

Soc. Then have I now given you all the heads of our yesterday's discussion? Or is there anything more, my dear Timaeus, which has been omitted?

The next quotation, from *The Republic,* although it shows us little of the detail of Plato's Utopian society, reveals the spirit of his social philosophy.[28]

Here Adeimantus interposed a question: How would you answer, Socrates, said he, if a person were to say that you are making these

[28] Plato, *The Republic,* in *Dialogues,* trans. by Benjamin Jowett, Vol. III, pp. 107-10.

people [the guardians] miserable, and that they are the cause of their own unhappiness; the city in fact belongs to them, but they are none the better for it; whereas other men acquire lands, and build large and handsome houses, and have everything handsome about them, offering sacrifices to the gods on their own account, and practising hospitality; moreover, as you were saying just now, they have gold and silver, and all that is usual among the favourites of fortune; but our poor citizens are no better than mercenaries who are quartered in the city and always mounting guard?

Yes, I said; and you may add that they are only fed, and not paid in addition to their food, like other men; and therefore they cannot, if they would, take a journey of pleasure; they have no money to spend on a mistress or any other luxurious fancy, which, as the world goes, is thought to be happiness; and many other accusations of the same nature might be added.

But, said he, let us suppose all this to be included in the charge.

You mean to ask, I said, what will be our answer?

Yes.

If we proceed along the old path, my belief, I said, is that we shall find the answer. And our answer will be that, even as they are, our guardians may very likely be the happiest of men; but that our aim in founding the State was not the disproportionate happiness of any one class, but the greatest happiness of the whole; we thought that in a State which is ordered with a view to the good of the whole we should be most likely to find justice, and in the ill-ordered State injustice: and, having found them, we might then decide which of the two is the happier. At present, I take it, we are fashioning the happy State, not piecemeal, or with a view of making a few happy citizens, but as a whole; and by-and-by we will proceed to view the opposite kind of State. Suppose that we were painting a statue, and some one came up to us and said, Why do you not put the most beautiful colours on the most beautiful parts of the body— the eyes ought to be purple, but you have made them black—to him we might fairly answer, Sir, you would not surely have us beautify the eyes to such a degree that they are no longer eyes; consider rather whether, by giving this and the other features their due proportion, we make the whole beautiful. And so I say to you, do not compel us to assign to the guardians a sort of happiness which will make them anything but guardians; for we too can clothe our husbandmen in royal apparel, and set crowns of gold on their heads, and bid them till the ground as much as they like, and no more. Our potters also might be allowed to repose on couches, and feast by the fireside, passing round the winecup, while their wheel is conveniently at hand, and working at pottery only as much as they like; in this way we might make every class happy—and then, as you imagine, the whole State would be happy. But do not put this idea into our heads; for, if we listen to you, the husbandman will be no longer a husbandman, the potter will cease to be a potter, and no one will have the character of any distinct class in the State. Now this is not of much consequence where the corruption of society, and pretension to be what you are not, is confined to cobblers; but when the guardians of the laws and of the government are only seeming and not real guardians, then see how they turn the State upside down; and on the other hand they alone have the power of giving order and happiness to the State. We mean our guardians to be true saviours and not the destroyers of the State, whereas our opponent is thinking of peasants at a festival, who are enjoying a life of revelry, not of citizens who are doing their duty to the State. But, if so, we mean different things, and he is speaking of something which is not a State. And therefore we must consider whether in appointing our guardians we would look to their greatest happiness individually, or whether this principle of happiness does not rather reside in the State as a whole. But if the latter be the truth, then the guardians and auxiliaries, and all others equally with them, must be compelled or induced to do their own work in the best way. And thus the whole State will grow up in a noble order, and the several classes will receive the proportion of happiness which nature assigns to them.

I think that you are quite right.

I wonder whether you will agree with another remark which occurs to me.

What may that be?

There seem to be two causes of the deterioration of the arts.

What are they?

Wealth, I said, and poverty.

How do they act?

The process is as follows: When a potter becomes rich, will he, think you, any longer take the same pains with his art?

Certainly not.

He will grow more and more indolent and careless?

Very true.

And the result will be that he becomes a worse potter?

Yes; he greatly deteriorates.

But, on the other hand, if he has no money, and cannot provide himself with tools or instruments, he will not work equally well himself, nor will he teach his sons or apprentices to work equally well.

Certainly not.

Then, under the influence either of poverty or of wealth, workmen and their work are equally liable to degenerate?

That is evident.

Here, then, is a discovery of new evils, I said, against which the guardians will have to watch, or they will creep into the city unobserved.

What evils?

Wealth, I said, and poverty; the one is the parent of luxury and indolence, and the other of meanness and viciousness, and both of discontent.

PLATO'S AESTHETICS

The appearance of the form through the medium of its embodiment in the flux is beautiful; the more radiantly the form is manifest, the more beautiful the object in which it is expressed. But sheer beauty is unembodied, being visible only to the man who can grasp pure form. Thus, if he is to be strictly consistent, the Platonist must believe that a mathematical theorem seen clearly in its full logical implication is more beautiful than, say, the "Hermes" of Praxiteles. The poet and the artist do not give us pure form, but form more or less distorted in matter. Such embodiment, if excellent, may arouse our enthusiasm for formal beauty, but it does not permanently satisfy the soul's demand for pure form. So Plato tends to evaluate art as one of the lower cultural activities, at best an introduction to more robust spiritual life, which is capable of enjoying supersensuous beauty or pure form.

The following passage from the *Symposium* [29] indicates Plato's conception of the ascent the soul may effect, passing from what we might call "heavy" sensuous beauty to "pure" formal beauty.

...For he who would proceed aright in this matter should begin in youth to visit beautiful forms; and first, if he be guided by his instructor aright, to love one such form only—out of that he should create fair thoughts; and soon he will of himself perceive that the

[29] Plato, *Symposium*, in *Dialogues*, trans. by Benjamin Jowett, Vol. I, pp. 580-82.

beauty of one form is akin to the beauty of another; and then if beauty of form in general is his pursuit, how foolish would he be not to recognize that the beauty in every form is one and the same! And when he perceives this he will abate his violent love of the one, which he will despise and deem a small thing, and will become a lover of all beautiful forms; in the next stage he will consider that the beauty of the mind is more honourable than the beauty of the outward form. So that if a virtuous soul have but a little comeliness, he will be content to love and tend him, and will search out and bring to the birth thoughts which may improve the young, until he is compelled to contemplate and see the beauty of institutions and laws, and to understand that the beauty of them all is of one family, and that personal beauty is a trifle; and after laws and institutions he will go on to the sciences, that he may see their beauty, being not like a servant in love with the beauty of one youth or man or institution, himself a slave mean and narrow-minded, but drawing towards and contemplating the vast sea of beauty, he will create many fair and noble thoughts and notions in boundless love of wisdom; until on that shore he grows and waxes strong, and at last the vision is revealed to him of a single science, which is the science of beauty everywhere. To this I will proceed; please to give me your very best attention:

He who has been instructed thus far in the things of love, and who has learned to see the beautiful in due order and succession, when he comes toward the end will suddenly perceive a nature of wondrous beauty (and this, Socrates, is the final cause of all our former toils)—a nature which in the first place is everlasting, not growing and decaying, or waxing and waning; secondly, not fair in one point of view and foul in another, or at one time or in one relation or at one place fair, at another time or in another relation or at another place foul, as if fair to some and foul to others, or in the likeness of a face or hands or any other part of the bodily frame, or in any form of speech or knowledge, or existing in any other being, as for example, in an animal, or in heaven, or in earth, or in any other place; but beauty absolute, separate, simple, and ever-lasting, which without diminution and without increase, or any change, is imparted to the ever-growing and perishing beauties of all other things. He who from these ascending under the influence of true love, begins to perceive that beauty, is not far from the end. And the true order of going, or being led by another, to the things of love, is to begin from the beauties of earth and mount upwards for the sake of that other beauty, using these as steps only, and from one going on to two, and from two to all fair forms, and from fair forms to fair practices, and from fair practices to fair notions, until from fair notions he arrives at the notion of absolute beauty, and at last knows what the essence of beauty is.

Platonic love, so much discussed without reference to Plato's own words, is the enthusiasm the soul feels in the presence of the form. In personal relations this enthusiasm may grow out of a friendship or an attachment based originally upon physical attraction. It must, however, transcend this if it is to be genuine Platonic love, which is finally inspired by beauty of character; that is, by the presence of human goodness or justice in the loved one rather than by physical attraction.

The doctrine of Platonic love is the most poetic of philosophical concepts, a constant source of inspiration to European poets and artists of all schools, the romantic and the classical in particular. The classicist—for instance, the poet Dryden or the poet Pope or the painter David—emphasizes Plato's love of form and order, while the romanticist—say, Shelley—emphasizes the emotional intensity and the ecstatic freedom from paltry, mundane considerations enjoyed by the person who is inspired by Platonic love.

CONCLUSION

Plato's philosophy stands as the first great "synthetic" philosophy of European civilization, a philosophy that draws its subject matter and its doctrines from many and widespread fields of human interest; for science, art, conduct, and religion are all included in the broad sweep of Plato's speculative vision. Plato is not, like so many of the Pre-Socratic philosophers, limited to one problem and to one type of insight. But the many problems he faces are drawn together in the vision that produces the theory of the form, and the sharp distinction between the permanent form and the changing actuality, the proper objects, the one of knowledge, the other of opinion. Here we find the reconciliation of the conflicting thought of Parmenides and Heraclitus. But there is a final emphasis decidedly in favor of Parmenides.

In this, Platonic philosophy summarizes the speculative genius of the ancient Greeks, for whom the perfect, the ideal, the worshipful, must be thought of as unchanging, and for whom that which comes to be and passes away can never be wholly admirable. This feeling—this prejudice, if you will—is common to the three speculative thinkers—Democritus, Plato, and Aristotle—who constructed the great systems of Greek thought. Against them stands the obscure figure of Heraclitus with his insistence upon the finality of change and the reality of plastic mobility. But Plato prevails and dominates Greek, Roman, and even Christian thought for centuries. It is not until very recent times that, under the influence of the modern notions of evolution and progress, and a belief in the vast import-ance of history as a human study, we turn again toward Heraclitus and with him doubt that perfection and immutability are synony-mous. In recent times, the philosophy of Henri Bergson, which it is fair to say dominated French thought for the past generation, is an example of a philosophy of change.

CHAPTER V

Aristotle[1]

ARISTOTLE AND PLATO

Aristotle's philosophy, while marked by many similarities to Plato's, involves a new interpretation of the problems of change and form. In general, Aristotle revises Plato's doctrine, with greater emphasis on the concept of concrete individuality. In his approach to any given problem, Plato tends to include more and more territory within the limits of his discussion and to find more and more topics relevant, until at last it becomes apparent that a man can really know anything, in Plato's phrase, only "when he knows what is true and false about the whole of being." In other words, for Plato, events take on significance only when we can view them in the total context of the universe, and forms can be defined and understood only when we see them, determined by principles, in their proper context among other forms. Discussion, too, proceeds by introducing more and more relevant information, and focusing it on the background of the problem at hand. Thus *The Republic,* which is an analytic discussion of justice, includes material from the fields of poetry, psychology, mathematics, astronomy, and theology.

For Aristotle, the opposite is true. Aristotle's method is fairly adequately described as systematic impatience with irrelevant information. Thus, for example, by distinguishing literary criticism from psychology before he starts, and sticking to this distinction, the critic

---

[1] Aristotle (384-322 B.C.) was born in Stagira in Macedonia, where his father was physician to the king. He studied at Plato's Academy from 367 to 347, and later became the tutor of the Macedonian Prince Alexander, who was to conquer Persia and to unite the Greek world. In 335, Aristotle founded at Athens the Lyceum, a school similar to the Academy. He was forced to leave Athens later because of the unpopularity of the Macedonian conquerors.

will avoid many of the errors and confusions of a more inclusive but muddled discussion, in which the work of art is confounded, say, with the soul of the artist. If the Platonic dialogue is thought of as a gradual illumination of a background, against which forms and problems emerge, an Aristotelian lecture is like a sharply focused bank of spotlights, in which the central point of interest is illuminated as brightly as possible by temporarily excluding the rest of the stage. It is this interest in precise distinction which makes the taste for Aristotle's philosophy an acquired one. But it is a taste that many people, impressed by the clarity and the practicality of the system it produces, have acquired.

Aristotle felt that his predecessors had oversimplified the speculative problem by assuming that "being" had a single, simple meaning, and that all "explanations" could be derived from a single method, which paid attention to the "real" aspect of each subject matter. In fact, however, we find that a biologist and a minister, or even a cook and a dietitian, are studying the same subject matter but using different techniques and arriving at different results. If one assumes that the work of specialists has nothing in common, because each is studying a radically different and isolated set of real things, philosophy becomes impossible. If, on the other hand, one assumes that all specialists have the same method and the same subject matter, but differ because some use the method unskillfully or in too restricted a context (as Plato suggests that poets, orators, and politicians are simply inferior philosophers, and the cook an inferior dietitian), this does not do justice to our experience of the real difference in the method and the kind of relevance that in fact exists between different fields of knowledge.

To the question "What is being?" the Platonists had answered that what a thing is, is determined by its form, and that the dialectical study of forms was the proper business of both philosophy and science. The Atomists, on the other hand, had answered that what a thing is, is determined by the material parts of which it is composed, and the analytical identification of elementary material parts was the proper business of both science and philosophy. Aristotle suggested that further analysis discloses a third, and different, significance.

What a thing is, is determined by four relevant aspects, rather than by one. These four determinants of the being of things Aristotle called *causes*. (In modern usage, we think of a cause as something separate and different in kind from its effect. But as Aristotle uses the term, a cause is an aspect that is constitutive of the thing that it causes. The cause is a component that makes each thing be what it is.)

Every real thing has an intelligible form, which is combined with a continuous matter. Both Platonists and Atomists were right in their interpretation of being, but the answer of neither was complete. A further incompleteness in the Platonists' position was that they gave no specific explanation of how a form and matter, entities completely diverse in kind, ever come to be combined together. For the Platonist, process and motion are not an intrinsic part of reality. Aristotle suggests that in nature the form exerts a kind of attraction on that matter which is capable of combining with it. But the actual process of matter taking on form requires some impact or energy exerted on the matter from an outside source, which is the impetus that starts off its development.

THE THEORY OF CAUSES

All these factors must be taken into account in a scientific explanation, since all four determine the "being" of things. As an example of the relevance of these "causes" to explanation, Aristotle takes an artificial object, a house. Four factors explain the nature and the existence of the house. The lumber, nails, and so on constitute the material cause. These materials are arranged in a form, given by the architect's plan; this is the constitutive form or formal cause of the house. To arrange the materials in this form, however, required a cause of motion—the material will not build itself into a house, but must be moved into shape and fastened together by builders. This source of motion is called the *efficient cause*. A complete explanation of the house also requires a reference to the purpose it is designed to serve. The house that is built for a dance hall will be a different building from the house designed to be a bank.

This element of purpose, which is built right into the house, and is the reason for the particular architect's plan chosen, is called the *final cause*.

The house differs from a plant, an animal, or any other natural object, by the relation in it of formal and final causes. While the purpose of the house can be thought of as different from its form, purpose is found in natural objects as the cause that makes each thing grow toward the realization of its complete form, which at the beginning of its growth it contains only incompletely. A young animal, for example, grows by a system of interconnected sequential stages, which lead directly, as if according to a plan, to its eventually becoming a full-grown adult member of its species. Aristotle says: [2]

Now that we have established these distinctions, we must proceed to consider causes, their character and number. Knowledge is the object of our inquiry, and men do not think they know a thing until they have grasped the 'why' of it (which is to grasp its primary cause). So clearly we too must do this as regards both coming to be and passing away and every kind of physical change, in order that, knowing their principles, we may try to refer to these principles each of our problems.

In one sense, then (1) that out of which a thing comes to be and which persists, is called 'cause,' e.g. the bronze of the statue, the silver of the bowl, and the genera of which the bronze and the silver are species.

In another sense (2) the form or the archetype, i.e. the statement of the essence, and its genera, are called 'causes' (e.g. of the octave the relation 2:1, and generally number), and the parts in the definition.

Again (3) the primary source of the change or coming to rest; e.g. the man who gave advice is a cause, the father is cause of the child, and generally what makes of what is made and what causes change of what is changed.

Again (4) in the sense of end or 'that for the sake of which' a thing is done, e.g. health is the cause of walking about. ('Why is he walking about?' we say, 'To be healthy,' and, having said that, we

---

[2] Aristotle, *Physics,* trans. by R. P. Hardie and R. K. Gaye, in *Works,* ed. by W. D. Ross, Vol. II, 194b15-195a25. Clarendon Press, 11 vols., Oxford, 1908-31. This and later quotations from the *Works* are reprinted by permission of the publisher.

think we have assigned the cause.) The same is true also of all the intermediate steps which are brought about through the action of something else as means toward the end, e.g. reduction of flesh, purging, drugs, or surgical instruments are means toward health. All these things are 'for the sake of' the end, though they differ from one another in that some are activities, others instruments.

This then perhaps exhausts the number of ways in which the term 'cause' is used.

As the word has several senses, it follows that there are several causes of the same thing (not merely in virtue of a concomitant attribute), e.g. both the art of the sculptor and the bronze are causes of the statue. These are causes of the statue *qua* statue, not in virtue of anything else that it may be—only not in the same way, the one being the material cause, the other the cause whence the motion comes. Some things cause each other reciprocally, e.g. hard work causes fitness and *vice versa,* but again not in the same way, but the one as end, the other as the origin of change. Further the same thing is the cause of contrary results. For that which by its presence brings about one result is sometimes blamed for bringing about the contrary by its absence. Thus we ascribe the wreck of a ship to the absence of the pilot whose presence was the cause of its safety.

All the causes now mentioned fall into four familiar divisions. The letters are the causes of syllables, the material of artificial products, fire, etc., of bodies, the parts of the whole, and the premises of the conclusion, in the sense of 'that from which.' Of these pairs the one set are causes in the sense of substratum, e.g. the parts, the other set in the sense of essence—the whole and the combination and the form. But the seed and the doctor and the adviser, and generally the maker, are all sources whence the change or stationariness originates, while the others are causes in the sense of the end or the good of the rest, for 'that for the sake of which' means what is best and the end of the things which lead up to it.

One of the most distinctive features of Aristotle's philosophy is his emphasis on the final cause. The form toward which each thing is developing seems to exert an attraction that gives direction to the process. Thus the stages of development of an animal may be viewed as the gradual realization of those functions of which an adult of the species is capable. The regularity with which growth patterns repeat, in an ordered sequence such that each step leads straight toward this end, seems to Aristotle to rule out the possibility that nature works "by chance," or that these things happen "accidentally," since the distinctive mark of "chance" or "accidental" events is exactly the absence in their history of such predictable, connected ordered stages.

ARTS OF LANGUAGE

Aristotle's meticulous care in applying this notion of relevance to language and words led him to write the first systematic treatment of the different forms of language suited to the various uses to which it is put—logic, rhetoric, and poetry—and in his treatment to exclude, as rigorously as possible, each use from the others. If we consider what things language can do, we may classify them into three: it may delight, persuade, or instruct. The use of language to delight is the province of poetry; to persuade, that of rhetoric; to instruct, that of logic; and putting the theorem of Pythagoras in rhymed hexameter does nothing to increase its instructive value. While Plato exiles from the community artists who delight without instructing, Aristotle begins by recognizing that the devices and the languages of the poet and the scientists are so different that no good can come from their confusion. The beautiful clarity and specific practicality that result from Aristotle's application of his method can be illustrated by considering his treatment, in the *logic,* of the conditions or rules of straight thinking, devices basic to the demonstrative use of language that neither delights nor merely persuades, but "proves."

A. Logic

Aristotle has profited from the experience of his predecessors enough to recognize the uselessness of speculations that have no sound analytic foundation. In his *Organon,* or *Logic,* he presents for the first time a systematic investigation of the analytic tools and procedures available to the speculative thinker. The effect of this investigation is to clarify the limits of legitimate speculation by indicating the kind of analytic foundation that any worth-while speculation will require.

The thinker begins with a set of words, each clearly defined. The word has a definite meaning; it stands for the direct recognition of the nature of some class of things or experiences; and it has only a single meaning in any given discussion. Single words by themselves, such as "Joe," "hits," or "runs," are neither true nor false; they tell us nothing about Joe, hitting, or running.

For purposes of analysis, statements or assertions are formed by combining words in such a way that one asserts something about the other. (The predicate is attributed to a subject.) All such judgments, called *propositions,* have a single subject and a single predicate, and each is either true or false. This is what distinguishes a proposition from a prayer; the prayer may have poetic and persuasive value, but it makes no assertion from which we can learn or prove something. "The grass is green" is a proposition; if the grass is green, it is true; if not, it is false. There are four main kinds of propositions: I may make a judgment that the predicate does belong to the subject, or that it does not belong. "All cats are black at night" and "No students are incurious" are judgments of these types. I may take in less territory when I know that the predicate belongs (or does not belong) to *some,* but not to *all* members of my subject class. If I attribute the predicate only to some, the proposition is called *particular;* if to all, it is called *universal.* (When I affirm the predicate, my proposition is called *affirmative, negative* when I deny it.) Aristotle thus provides for four types of propositions, usually abbreviated by the designations A, E, I, and O.

> Universal affirmative (A): All men are mortal.
> Universal negative (E): No men are mortal.
> Particular affirmative (I): Some men are mortal.
> Particular negative (O): Some men are not mortal.

Evidently, there is some connection between these different relations of mortal and man; for example, if A is true, E and O must both be false. An understanding of these relations is essential for any systematic work in logic, and can be obtained from any conventional treatment of the proposition.

"Thinking" proper, or "proof," however, takes place by connecting propositions in chains, to reach new conclusions. For instance:

> All men are mortal;
> Spaniards are men;
> Therefore Spaniards are mortal—

is a combination of two propositions the truth of which I know, to prove a third, which I did not know until I saw the connection. This is called the *syllogism,* and to it Aristotle claims we can reduce all constructive thinking. A syllogism is a set of three propositions, called *major premise, minor premise,* and *conclusion,* so related that the truth of the premises proves the truth of the conclusion. Not every set of three propositions has this relation, and Aristotle is able to separate those which have from those which have not. In this way, he establishes a set of specific rules for testing the validity of certain types of reasoning.

These rules will now be given—at the expense of the reader who feels that they do little to accelerate his acquiring a taste for Aristotle.

Obviously, two judgments that have nothing in common will give no new information, no matter how they are connected. Thus, knowing that "Night must follow day" and "Truth is ever victorious," I cannot draw the conclusion "Therefore always vote Republican." The rule here is that the two premises must have at least one term in common, which is the basis of their connection. This linking term, appearing in both premises, is called the *middle term;* it drops out in the conclusion. For example, in "Cats are mammals; Angoras are cats; therefore Angoras are mammals," "cats" is the middle term, and it drops out and does not appear in the conclusion.

Putting two negative premises together gives no proof, just as two pieces of ignorance won't add up to one piece of knowledge. Two things may not be the same thing, yet differ from each other. For example, I can't put together "No Democrat is a Communist" and "No Republican is a Communist" to conclude, as I might be naïvely tempted to do (since our minds habitually try to draw conclusions), that "Therefore all Democrats are Republicans."

It is the naïve tendency of the mind to extract a conclusion whenever it is given two premises to work on that fills our conversation and literature with so many instances of outrageous nonsense and misreasoning.

The most flagrant of these is the *fallacy of the undistributed middle*: for example, "Communists are prolabor; Jones is prolabor; therefore Jones is a Communist." Another example, more convincing to some readers, would be: "All men are animals; all dogs are animals, therefore all men are dogs." These errors may be explained by an examination of what is traditionally known as the *distribution of terms*.

Some statements tell us something about the whole class of the subject or predicate; others do not. Each type of proposition gives a different sort of information on this point. For example, "Some men are vicious creatures" clearly tells nothing about the whole class of vicious creatures (for men may be only a part of it), nor about the whole class of men (of which vicious men are only a part). Similarly, the proposition "All men are mammals," while it explicitly tells us something about the entire class of men, strictly speaking tells us nothing about the class of mammals taken as a whole, of which men form only a part. A term that refers to a class taken as a whole is called *distributed;* it is *undistributed* if it does not. Thus, in the examples given on page 125, the predicate of the A proposition, and both subject and predicate of the I proposition, are undistributed; but the subject of the A proposition is distributed. What about "No men are angels"? This clearly refers to the whole class of men, since not any one of the class in included; but it also refers to the whole class of angels, since men are being excluded completely from the whole class. So the E proposition has both a distributed subject and a distributed predicate. "Some men are not goats" refers only to some men, but to the entire class of goats, since the men referred to are being excluded from that whole class, so the O proposition distributes its predicate, but not its subject.

The rule that is violated by such statements as the proof that all men are dogs, above, is that the middle term must be distributed at least once in any valid piece of reasoning.

It is often helpful to visualize classes and their relations by circles and their exclusion or intersection. Thus "All men are animals" can be schematized:

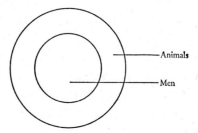

Since there are many animals that are not men, "animals" is an *undistributed* term.

If we let an *x* marked in the appropriate area represent an individual that is a member of a class, then "Some men are stupid creatures" is:

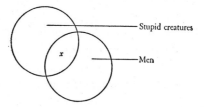

That is, at least one individual falls in the area of intersection of the two classes.

"No men are angels" becomes:

Here both terms are distributed, since every individual falling inside one circle must differ from every individual falling inside the other. Similarly, "Some men are not stupid beasts" might be thought to yield:

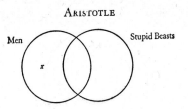

That is, at least one member of the one class falls *completely outside* the other. But on the basis of the information given, there is no way of telling whether the classes do or do not intersect. For example, "Some men are not stupid beasts" will be true with either of the following relations of the classes "stupid beasts" and "men":

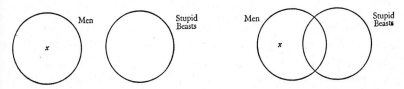

So this statement as it is interpreted in logic does not mean "Some men are not stupid beasts, *but others are*"; it leaves the question of whether any are an open one.

This O proposition clearly refers only to *some* men, hence "men" is an *undistributed* term; but it refers to *all* stupid beasts, since it tells us that, taking the class as a whole, no one of its members is included in the group of men who are not stupid beasts; "stupid beasts" is thus a *distributed* term.

We can now extend our diagrams, to show how the connecting middle term may establish legitimate connections. There are four possible types of valid linking by a middle term:

1. Two asserted inclusions (in which the middle is included by one term and includes the other):

> All men (B) are rational (C);
> all Frenchmen (A) are men (B);
> therefore all Frenchmen (A) are rational (C).

Identifying circles by abbreviations A, B, and C, instead of writing the terms out in full, this connection may be diagrammed as "B inside C and A inside B; hence A inside C":

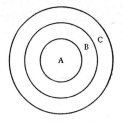

2. One exclusion and one inclusion:

> No men (M) are angels (P);
> all Chinese (S) are men (M);
> therefore no Chinese (S) are angels (P).

Abbreviating classes this time by S, M, and P, where M stands for the middle term, and S and P for the terms that are the subject and the predicate of the conclusion, we may diagram this: "Middle outside predicate; subject inside middle; hence subject outside predicate":

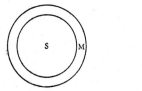

3. One inclusion and one intersection (the middle must be both included and intersected):

> All Republicans (M) are conservative (P);
> some of my best friends (S) are Republicans (M);
> therefore some of my best friends (S) are conservative (P).

This connection may be diagramed: "M inside P; some S inside M; hence, some S inside P," as shown:

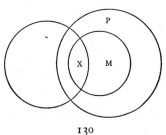

4. One exclusion and one intersection (the middle must be intersected):

> No philanthropists (M) are greedy (P);
> some wealthy men (S) are philanthropists (M);
> therefore some wealthy men (S) are not greedy (P).

This may be diagramed to show that the type of connection is: "M outside P; some S inside M; hence some S outside of P":

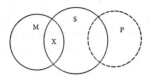

The reader can verify, by constructing diagrams or by analyzing the possible cases of inclusion, exclusion, and intersection algebraically, that these are the only ways in which known S-M and P-M connections can be linked to convey any certain information about the relation of S to P. In each case, the middle term is either once included or once excluded; but it can be included only by an A proposition, in which it is subject, hence distributed (for example, "all M is P"), and excluded only by an E proposition, in which it is distributed, too. This is the rationale of the rule: "In valid syllogisms, the middle term must be distributed at least once." On the other hand, as the next rule will show, the mere distribution of the middle class does not guarantee logical connection. An example would be:

> All American athletes (M) are strong (P);
> all American athletes (M) are Americans (S);
> therefore all Americans (S) are strong (P)—

which, when diagramed, shows the relation of classes to be: M inside P; M inside S; from which it certainly doesn't follow, as the example asserts, that all S must be inside P.

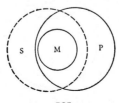

In this diagram, the dotted lines indicate that we have not enough evidence to tell whether the whole class of "Americans" as well as those members of it who are "American athletes" are included in the class of "strong men" or not. Hence we have no warrant for assuming that our evidence proves that they are all so included.

Two statements of intersection cannot make clear the relation of the total intersecting areas; take, for example:

> Some Americans (M) are cruel (P);
> some Indians (S) are Americans (M);
> therefore some Indians (S) are cruel (P).

From the statements given, we can't tell whether the relation of "cruel people" to "Indians" is (a) some Americans inside class of cruel persons, some Indians inside that part of the "Americans" which lies outside class of cruel persons; or (b) some Indians inside both classes simultaneously—that is, the x for some Indians falls in an area of intersection. But our asserted conclusion claims to have proved that the latter relation is the case; hence the reasoning is faulty.

Case A:

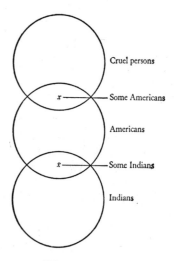

132

Case B:

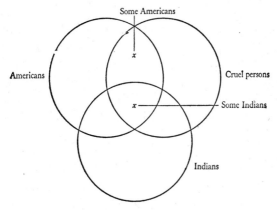

A fourth rule, invalidating such cases as "All men are animals; all men are rational; therefore all animals are rational," is the rule against jumping from part to whole—"No term may be distributed in the conclusion that was not distributed in the premises"—or, in case the concept of distribution still seems unfamiliar, we can say "No conclusion may be drawn about a whole class unless the information supporting the conclusion was also about that whole class, not just about a part of it." In the example given, while the conclusion claims to tell us something about all animals, only information about a part of that class (namely, those animals which are men) was provided in the major premise.

From these rules it is possible, once we have reduced an argument to its essential syllogistic form, to separate true reasoning from false.

The details of logic have been treated here, instead of generalizations about Aristotelianism, because the emphasis on specific cases and problems typical of the philosophy shows up to much greater advantage in its application than it does in generalization.

It must be clear, however, that the treatment of reasoning has omitted a good many features of language; for example, the words that we use are seldom as neutral as logical terms, and we do not typically converse with two premises for every asserted conclusion. The study of the use of language to persuade supplements logic by inquiring into cases where there is no possibility of proof, and where demands of a practical situation make the speaker interested in convincing his audience of something, not of proving it absolutely.

B. Rhetoric

Since the goal of the rhetorician is persuasion, his interest is centered in his audience (unlike that of the logician, who is interested in his proof primarily, not in what people think of it). Three things persuade audiences: the character of the speaker, the style of his speech, and their own opinions, with which the speech either will or will not agree. A speaker is most effective when his words convince the audience that he is well informed, intelligent, and well disposed toward his hearers. A speech is most effective when it shows this character in its speaker, and when it exhibits the conclusion as a proposed action that is a consequence of motives his audience has.

In rhetoric, usually reasoning is simplified from its full syllogistic form by not stating premises with which the opinions of the audience agree, and which, therefore, the hearer will automatically supply when such beliefs are needed as premises. For example, with an audience of prohibitionists, the argument "Johnson drinks; therefore he is a bad man" will be accepted, although only one premise has been stated; because the other premise needed to justify the conclusion "all men who drink are bad" is believed and automatically supplied by the group. Similar suppressed premises are often less evident; thus, arguments in favor of tariffs on the ground that "tariffs preserve the American standard of living" involve the assumed premise that everyone wants to do whatever will preserve our living standard. A syllogism in which one premise or the conclusion is not explicitly stated, but is automatically supplied by the audience, is called an *enthymeme*. Obviously, since the underlying form is the same, the same confusions that lead to fallacious proof may take place in enthymeme form, where they are much harder to track down, because there is no stated premise to examine.

Unlike scientific demonstration, speeches can produce certain effects very much like optical illusions. Primary among these is the *illusion of significance*. We are so used to thinking by connecting statements in sequential form that whenever we hear statements in sequence, we unconsciously assume that they represent real thought. For this reason, an orator who shouts loud "therefores" before his conclusions makes us feel that there must be some rational connection of these with the rest of his speech, whether there ever was or not. A second major source of optical illusion is what might be called *diffusion of emotional tone.* Our feeling about words is determined largely by the company they keep, and in the same way, when an unpalatable conclusion follows a speech in which many opinions that we find pleasant have been expressed, the speech loses some of its unacceptable character. Hence the standard formula for a political speech that our satirists have caricatured so often; a preamble of pleasant platitudes, with which the hearers all agree, a shouted "therefore," and a nonsequential political recommendation.

A proof is good if it proves; a speech, if it persuades. Therefore, as Aristotle treats it, a proof begins with known facts, and is indifferent to our wishes; a speech begins with our wishes, and tries to show that a given action furthers them.

C. Poetics

Having treated the speech and proof, Aristotle now turns to the poem. A peculiar property of poetry is that it has no purpose or final cause exterior to itself. Strictly speaking, a poet is not writing to prove anything or to persuade anyone, but because he finds certain combinations of words intrinsically appealing to his aesthetic sense. In poetry, it is the quality of ordered sequence, in which each part grows out of the one preceding it and leads to the one following it, that will best produce this aesthetic pleasure. As an adjunct to this sequence, we must not overlook the vividness of sensuous presentation, a fact that explains Aristotle's otherwise confusing treatment of the parts of speech.

Just as logical and rhetorical purposes of communication find their most effective forms of verbal expression in the syllogism and the enthymeme, so poetic communication has its own distinctive form in the *metaphor.* The metaphor embodies a recognition of resemblance that is valid. Unlike Plato and other earlier speculators, Aristotle is unwilling to accept metaphorical statements as the vehicle of his philosophical exposition. Since a metaphor basically involves "calling one thing by the name of another," it is not a tool adapted to produce results that are scientifically clear and significant. It does, however, embody and present insights of a type that have great aesthetic vividness and importance.[3]

Metaphor consists in giving the thing a name that belongs to something else; the transference being either from genus to species, or from species to genus, or from species to species, or on grounds of analogy. That from genus to species is exemplified in 'Here stands my ship'; for lying at anchor is the 'standing' of a particular kind of thing. That from species to genus in 'Truly ten thousand good deeds has Ulysses wrought,' where 'ten thousand,' which is a particular large number, is put in place of the generic 'a large number.' That from species to species in 'Drawing the life with the bronze,' and in 'Severing with the enduring bronze'; where the poet uses 'draw' in the sense of 'sever' and 'sever' in the sense of 'draw,' both words meaning 'to take away' something. That from analogy is possible whenever there are four terms so related that the second (B) is to the first (A) as the fourth (D) to the third (C); for one may then metaphorically put D in lieu of B, and B in lieu of D. Now and then, too, they qualify the metaphor by adding on to it that to which the word it supplants is relative. Thus a cup (B) is in relation to Dionysus (A) what a shield (D) is to Ares (C). The cup accordingly will be metaphorically described as the 'shield *of Dionysus*' (D plus A), and the shield as the 'cup of *Ares*' (B plus C). Or to take another instance: As old age (D) is to life (C), so is evening (B) to day (A). One will accordingly describe evening (B) as 'old age *of the day*' (D plus A)—or by the Empedoclean equivalent; and old age (D) as the 'evening' or 'sunset *of life*' (B plus C). It may be that some of the terms thus related have no special name of their own, but for all that they will be metaphorically described in just the same way....

And later:[4]

It is a great thing, indeed, to make a proper use of these poetical forms, as also of compounds and strange words. But the greatest

[3] Aristotle, *Poetics*, trans. by Ingram Bywater, in *Works*, Vol. XI, pp. 1457b 5-30.
[4] *Ibid.*, pp. 1459a5-6.

thing by far is to be a master of metaphor. It is the one thing that cannot be learnt from others; and it is also a sign of genius, since a good metaphor implies an intuitive perception of the similarity in dissimilars.

Aristotle's consistency in looking for the relevant aspect of each study leads him to classify the parts of speech differently in his treatments of rhetoric, logic, and poetry. The orator, concerned with agents and their actions, can get along very well with the simple distinction of nouns, verbs, and connectives. The logician needs a more elaborate separation of predicates into classes, corresponding to the kinds of things they signify,[5] while the individual letter, with its distinct aesthetic sound value, must be the poet's smallest element of speech.

The relation of poetry, argument, and oratory to their audiences as it has just been presented is in almost complete antithesis to Plato's philosophy. For Plato, politicians and poets are alike second-rate philosophers; only the true can be beautiful, and only when audiences forego judgment based on pleasure or passion can they reasonably determine what is true. For Aristotle, poetry and philosophy are wholly diverse enterprises, and it is unsound to expect both to have the same criteria or the same excellence.

It follows that for Aristotle, our evaluation of the same document will differ when we approach it in different frames of reference. A literary critic, for example, may highly praise a book that the judge orders suppressed because it is harmful to the public welfare; a volume of orations may be very poor as fine art, but excellent as an example of persuasive writing. The frame of reference we choose will depend upon our social function and professional interest; usually, a book gives more satisfactory results in one frame than another (thus the *Iliad,* which Aristotle finds superlative as poetry, he finds to be very poor as scientific exposition), but there is nowhere (as in Plato) a single privileged frame of reference within which every document must be read and evaluated.

---

[5] Most important of these is the distinctions of terms which signify "substance" ("substantives"), which are real independent individual things, from terms which signify attributes of these substances, such as their size, color, position, etc. ("predicates" and "adjectives").

This always leads to questions about the borderline case, which have been the standard attack on Aristotle's entire philosophy. "How shall one classify," it is asked, "a book equally amenable to analysis as aesthetics and as social commentary? Is it poetry or rhetoric?" The answer, which should be kept in mind when we come to discuss formal causes in nature, is: Both; a border-line case in this analysis falls simultaneously on both sides of the line.

D. Dialectic and Sophistry

Scientific knowledge is judgment about things that are universal and necessary, and the conclusions of demonstration, and all scientific knowledge, follow from first principles (for scientific knowledge involves apprehension of a rational ground). This being so, the first principle from which what is scientifically known follows cannot be an object of scientific knowledge, of art, or of practical wisdom; for that which can be scientifically known can be demonstrated, and art and practical wisdom deal with things that are variable. Nor are these first principles the objects of philosophic wisdom, for it is a mark of the philosopher to have *demonstration* about some things. If, then, the states of mind by which we have truth and are never deceived about things invariable or even variable are scientific knowledge, practical wisdom, philosophic wisdom, and intuitive reason, and it cannot be any of the three (i.e. practical wisdom, scientific knowledge, or philosophic wisdom), the remaining alternative is that it is *intuitive reason* that grasps the first principles.[6]

We have said that in rhetoric the starting points of arguments are given by the opinions of the audience. This suggests another question: "Where do the starting points in demonstration come from?" To this, there are three possible answers: from the nature of things, from opinions about the nature of things, or from verbal statements expressing opinions about the nature of things. Aristotle uses these three answers to divide logic into *demonstration, dialectic,* and *sophistic.* Science, which is knowledge that is necessarily so, has its basis in the nature of things. The terms of the logician represent a recognition, made directly by the mind, of the formal identities of

6 Aristotle, *Nicomachean Ethics,* trans. by W. D. Ross, in *Works,* Vol. IX, 1140b30-1141a5.

various classes of individual objects that the knower has encountered. Just as the Platonic recognition of a form involves a direct sudden vision or insight, so for Aristotle, the forms of the things we perceive are directly recognized.

The "form" here is of course the "formal cause," a distinctive nature or structure that makes the thing "what it is, rather than something else." This recognition is described as *intuition,* but unlike the meaning of "intuition" in other philosophies (such as Plato's, where the word is used to describe our vision of the form of the good, at the top of the divided line), Aristotle conceives of "intuition" not as giving a connected over-all picture of reality, but as providing individual direct insight into the natures of different kinds of things. A science begins with "principles" that express these insights, and the stages of a scientific demonstration must include causes throughout as middle terms. (When we remember that a cause is something that makes a thing be what it is, we can see that this causal connection will guarantee the necessity of scientific demonstration.)

Aristotle writes: [7]

Since in every class of things, as in nature as a whole, we find two factors involved, (1) a matter which is potentially all the particulars included in the class; (2) a cause which is productive in the sense that it makes them all (the latter standing to the former, as e.g. an art to its material) these distinct elements must likewise be found within the soul.

And, in fact mind as we have described it is what it is by virtue of becoming all things, while there is another which is what it is by virtue of making all things: this is a sort of positive state like light, for in a sense light makes potential colours into actual colours.

Mind in this sense of it is separable, impassible, unmixed, since it is in its essential nature activity (for always the active is superior to the passive factor, the originating force to the matter which it forms).

Actual knowledge is identical with its object: in the individual, potential knowledge is in time prior to actual knowledge, but in the universe as a whole it is not prior even in time. Mind is not at one

[7] Aristotle, *De anima* (*On the Soul*), trans. by J. A. Smith, in *Works,* Vol. III, 430a10-25.

time knowing and at another not. When mind is set free from its present conditions it appears as just what it is and nothing more: this alone is immortal and eternal (we do not, however, remember its former activity because, while mind in this sense is impassible, mind as passive is destructible), and without it nothing thinks.

While the mind possesses the capacity of apprehending the forms of things, this capacity is realized only through the experience, and with the materials, that the senses supply. As opposed to Plato's myths and metaphors of "recollection" and "innate ideas," Aristotle says flatly that "there is nothing in the intellect which was not first in (the experiences derived through) the senses." Unlike Anaxagoras, Aristotle does not mean that the colors, tastes, and so on of experienced objects constitute their essential reality; nor does he intend to say, as the Pythagoreans did, that perceived shapes and configurations constitute the essences of things. The essence or form of a substance is not perceived by the senses, but "grasped" by an intellectual insight that recognizes the intrinsic nature of the perceived object. The recognition of these forms, common to many individuals, comes about after repeated experience, which is constituted by the knower's contact with the external world through sensation. However, it may not always be clear from what starting point we should proceed, and other people may have formulated theories different from ours as to what the first principles of a science are.

Such differences must be matters not of fact, but of opinion. The fact can never be self-contradictory, since the intuitive insight of all men is the same; and this presents a difficult problem of method. Since the proofs of a science begin with principles, these principles themselves cannot be proved; otherwise, there would be an infinite regress of syllogisms and we would never have proved anything. Fortunately, at this point a second analytic instrument is available to the scientist, and *dialectic* is introduced as the art of demonstrations founded on asserted opinions.

Dialectic proceeds on the principle that a true opinion cannot be self-contradictory and cannot lead to false conclusions when it is taken as the major premise of valid logical demonstration. Consequently, in case of disagreement I may assume that my opponent's position is true, and see whether any false or self-contradictory consequences follow. If he is right, his position must be consistent; if his position is inconsistent, his premises cannot be right. Dialectic is thus of use to the scientist in checking his starting points, and to the moralist and the politician in establishing and defending positions in areas in which scientific demonstration is not possible. (It is interesting to recall that Plato saw in "dialectic" the sole and sufficient method of science and philosophy.)

It is also possible to reason, or to seem to reason, on the basis of purely verbal niceties. Aristotle felt that this legalistic approach to argument had been so refined and overworked by the Sophists that he called it sophistic. A "Sophist," as he appears here, becomes so interested in the wording of a statement that he completely loses sight of the opinion or the fact which that statement is trying to express. Characteristically, where Plato opposes the Sophists with metaphysical analysis, Aristotle opposes them by advocating clearcut verbal precision and distinction.

THE THEORY OF SUBSTANCES

Apparently, not all areas admit of equal scientific precision. "Science" depends, as we have said, on the mind's direct grasp of certain classes of natures; but not everything has a nature that can be grasped in this way. For example, colors and textures are always present as the colors and textures *of* something else, and we do not find them existing in their own right. Knowable forms belong only to those things which are capable of independent existence. These are called *substances*. This is very close to our own common-sense distinction (which is presumably of Aristotelian ancestry) between "things" and "qualities." A tree is a "real thing"—it doesn't need something else to support it or embody it; a color, on the other hand, is only a quality, and if there were no thing to support it, it could not exist. Plants, animals, the stars, the elements, almost exhaust the list of kinds of things that are "substantial," and which have a directly recognizable independent form.

These objects fall into classes, called *genera* and *species*. Man, for example, can be classed together with whales, cats, and dogs as mammalian; mammal is a genus, man one of its species. A species is a class of individuals having a common formal cause that the scientist defines. The causes are the basis of biology, though only two seem operative there. An animal has as its formal cause those distinctive abilities which an adult of its species possesses and exercises; various chemical elements constitute its material cause.

The final cause, the purpose at which animal life seems to aim, is a kind of drive toward maturity, toward realizing the potentialities of which it, as a member of its species, is capable; so the final cause and the formal cause are really identical in form. The efficient cause of the animal is to be found in its parents, members of the same species (for one criterion of defining a species for the Aristotelian biologist is that it breeds true to type),[8] but different individual members of it; hence, so far as their natures are concerned, the efficient and formal causes also become identical for the biologist. In his biology, Aristotle is very insistent that attention be paid to that drive toward mature development which all things share, and which we have identified with the purpose of each thing, as its final cause. Thus a baby is to be understood by seeing how his variously acquired co-ordinations aim at the development he will have attained as a mature man (and some of the most fruitful recent research in child behavior is developed from this same point of view).[9]

Aristotle writes:[10]

We must explain then (1) that Nature belongs to the class of causes that act for the sake of something; (2) about the necessary and its place in physical problems, for all writers ascribe things to this cause, arguing that since the hot and the cold, &c., are of such and such a kind, therefore certain things *necessarily* are and come to be—and if they mention any other cause (one his 'friendship and

---

[8] Consequently, the number of species must remain constant, since each animal is generated by a parent of the same species, and all animals are naturally fitted for procreation. It is against this view of the efficient cause in biology that the title of Darwin's *The Origin of Species* was directed.

[9] For example, the studies of Dr. Arnold Gesell in the field of child development; especially interesting is his *Infant and Child in the Culture of Today*, 1943.

[10] Aristotle, *Physics*, trans. by Hardie and Gaye, in *Works*, Vol. II, 198b10-199b5.

strife,' another his 'mind'), it is only to touch on it, and then good-bye to it.

A difficulty presents itself: why should not nature work, not for the sake of something, nor because it is better so, but just as the sky rains, not in order to make the corn grow, but of necessity? What is drawn up must cool, and what has been cooled must become water and descend, the result of this being that the corn grows. Similarly if a man's crop is spoiled on the threshing-floor, the rain did not fall for the sake of this—in order that the crop might be spoiled—but the result just followed. Why then should it not be the same with the parts in nature, e.g. that our teeth should come up *of necessity*—the front teeth sharp, fitted for tearing, the molars broad and useful for grinding down the food—since they did not arise for this end, but it was merely a coincident result; and so with all other parts in which we suppose that there is purpose? Wherever then all the parts came about just what they would have been if they had come to be for an end, such things survived, being organized spontaneously in a fitting way; whereas those which grew otherwise perished and continue to perish, as Empedocles says his 'man-faced ox-progeny' did.

Such are the arguments (and others of the kind) which may cause difficulty on this point. Yet it is impossible that this should be the true view. For teeth and all other natural things either invariably or normally come about in a given way; but of not one of the results of chance or spontaneity is this true. We do not ascribe to chance or mere coincidence the frequency of rain in winter, but frequent rain in summer we do; nor heat in the dog-days, but only if we have it in winter. If then, it is agreed that things are either the result of co-incidence or for an end, and these cannot be the result of coincidence or spontaneity, it follows that they must be for an end; and that such things are all due to nature even the champions of the theory which is before us would agree. Therefore action for an end is present in things which come to be and are by nature.

Further, where a series has a completion, all the preceding steps are for the sake of that. Now surely as in intelligent action, so in nature; and as in nature, so it is in each action, if nothing interferes. Now intelligent action is for the sake of an end; therefore the nature of things also is so. Thus if a house, e.g., had been a thing made by nature, it would have been made in the same way as it is now by art; and if things made by nature were made also by art, they would come to be in the same way as by nature. Each step then in the series is for the sake of the next; and generally art partly completes what nature cannot bring to a finish, and partly imitates her. If, therefore, artificial products are for the sake of an end, so clearly also are natural products. The relation of the later to the earlier terms of the series is the same in both.

This is most obvious in the animals other than man: they make things neither by art nor after inquiry or deliberation. Wherefore people discuss whether it is by intelligence or by some other faculty that these creatures work—spiders, ants, and the like. By gradual advance in this direction we come to see clearly that in plants too that is produced which is conducive to the end—leaves, e.g, grow to provide shade for the fruit. If then it is both by nature and for an end that the swallow makes its nest and the spider its web, and plants grow leaves for the sake of the fruit and send their roots down (not up) for the sake of nourishment, it is plain that this kind of cause is operative in things which come to be and are by nature. And since 'nature' means two things, the matter and the form, of which the latter is the end, and since all the rest is for the sake of the end, the form must be the cause in the sense of 'that for the sake of which.'

Now mistakes come to pass even in the operations of art: the grammarian makes a mistake in writing and the doctor pours out the wrong dose. Hence clearly mistakes are possible in the operations of nature also. If then in art there are cases in which what is rightly produced serves a purpose, and if where mistakes occur there was a purpose in what was attempted, only it was not attained, so must it be also in natural products, and monstrosities will be failures in the purposive effort. Thus in the original combinations the 'ox-progeny' if they failed to reach a determinate end must have arisen through the corruption of some principle corresponding to what is now the seed.

THE THEORETIC SCIENCES

A. Physics

Unfortunately from the point of view of the modern natural scientist Aristotle's penchant for distinctions led him to separate mathematics from natural science. Again, his treatment of physical phenomena seems to the modern scientist to include irrelevant concepts borrowed from biology. It is interesting to see how this fateful distinction looks from the inside of the philosophical system. Since science is about real things, and especially substances, there will be as many kinds of science as there are kinds of substance, and Aristotle finds three. We quote from the *Metaphysics:* [11]

And since natural science, like other sciences, is in fact about one class of being, i.e. to that sort of substance which has the principle of its movement and rest present in itself, evidently it is neither practical nor productive. For in the case of things made the prin-ciple is in the maker—it is either reason or art or some faculty, while in the case of things done it is in the doer—viz. will, for that which is done and that which is willed are the same. Therefore, if all thought is either practical or productive or theoretical, physics must be a theoretical science, but it will theorize about such being as admits of being moved, and about substance-as-defined for the most part only as not separable from matter. Now, we must not fail to notice the mode of being of the essence and of its definition, for, without this, inquiry is but idle. Of things defined, i.e. of 'what,' some are like 'snub,' and some like 'concave.' And these differ because 'snub' is bound up with matter (for what is snub is a concave *nose*), while concavity is independent of perceptible mat-ter. If then all natural things are analogous to the snub in their na-ture—e.g. nose, eye, face, flesh, bone, and, in general, animal; leaf, root, bark, and, in general, plant (for none of these can be defined without reference to movement—they always have matter), it is clear how we must seek and define the 'what' in the case of natural objects, and also that it belongs to the student of nature to study even soul in a certain sense, i.e. so much of it as is not independent of matter.

That physics, then, is a theoretical science, is plain from these considerations. Mathematics, also however, is theoretical; but whether its objects are immovable and separable from matter, is not at present clear; still, it is clear that *some* mathematical theorems *consider* them *qua* immovable and *qua* separable from matter. But if there is something which is eternal and immovable and separable, clearly the knowledge of it belongs to a theoretical science—not, however, to physics (for physics deals with certain movable things) not to mathematics, but to a science prior to both. For physics deals with things which exist separately but are not immovable, and some parts of mathematics deal with things which are immovable but presumably do not exist separately, but as embodied in matter; while the first science [metaphysics] deals with things which both

---

[11] Aristotle, *Metaphysics,* trans. by W. D. Ross, in *Works,* Vol. VIII, 1025b19–1026a20.

exist separately and are immovable. Now all causes must be eternal, but especially these; for they are the causes that operate on so much of the divine as appears to us [i.e. produce the movements of the heavenly bodies]. There must, then, be three theoretical philosophies, mathematics, physics, and what we may call theology [i.e. metaphysics].

Some things involve the presence of matter in their definitions; matter, which we have defined as the stuff out of which things are made, was viewed by Aristotle, with his dominant interest in form, as the possibility for future formal development, just as a rough block of marble would be seen by a sculptor as the raw possibility of statues. Things the natures of which involve change, or a changeable medium, are the subject matter of "natural philosophy," which embraces physics, chemistry, astronomy, and biology. There is, however, another class of objects, made familiar by the discussion of mathematical examples of forms in connection with Plato. These are the objects studied by the mathematician, which seem to be immune to the change that all other natural objects share.

Aristotle's most extensive work was done in natural philosophy, the study of "substances which contain an internal principle of change."

The type of motion in place that is natural to such substances suggested their classification into celestial and sublunary or terrestrial. A celestial substance moves in a circle; a terrestrial substance naturally moves in a straight line. The stars and planets are carried around by concentric celestial spheres, to which they are affixed, without interfering with each other, and with complete periodic regularity. (In developing this view, Aristotle redirected attention to celestial mechanics as opposed to the purer mathematical approach of the Academy.) When this celestial motion is transmitted to the region about the earth, it takes the form of linear movements that are irregular, and interfere with one another.

On the basis of the natural direction of their linear motion the four elements (earth, air, fire, and water) can be differentiated and classified; their constituent qualities provide a table of elements for an Aristotelian "chemistry."

Terrestrial substances, however, have many properties that cannot be described or explained simply by an analysis into their constitutive elements. Animals and plants, for example, show an over-all organization in which the parts have been so specialized that each has its own peculiar function in furthering the welfare of the organism as a whole.

Aristotle's classification of the species of animals, and his comparative analysis of their organs, laid the foundation of the science of biology, and still commands the admiration of biologists, both for the acuteness of observation shown, and for the clear-cut organization of data that a systematic use of the four causes made possible.

Various special treatises are devoted by Aristotle to particular biological functions, such as sleep and waking, respiration, and memory, which animals display.

To complete the system of biology and natural philosophy, it is necessary to have a scientific treatment of the peculiar nature and capacities of man, and Aristotle analyzes these in his work on psychology, the *De anima.* The mind in its operation seems to have the capacity of grasping the formal causes of objects that it contemplates. In a passage the meaning of which has been a storm center of scholarly controversy since Hellenistic times, Aristotle clearly brings out this identity of the mind and its object, and (evidently less clearly, since it is on this point the controversy centers) distinguishes the nature of mind as the biological capacity to know from the pure actuality of mind as knowing (See the passage quoted on page 139).

In the *Physics,* Aristotle explores some of the general principles of all natural philosophy. Here he shows the relevance of the causes to all natural change, and the ultimate dependence of natural process on the continuation of the celestial motion, a continuation caused by a *prime mover,* the nature and function of which will be indicated in the treatment of metaphysics, below.

B. Mathematics

Aristotle believed that the objects of mathematics are forms that have only a secondary or quasi-reality. We recognize figure and number, not by "intuition," but by "abstraction," and the objects of mathematics have no real independent existence. However, we are able to think of shapes and numbers *as though* they were capable of existing independently, not as shapes of this or that particular physical object; and it is with these abstractions that the geometer and the calculator have to do. However, since a form is the distinctive nature, not merely the spatial shape or appearance, of a species, any connection between abstracted quantities and immediately apprehended natures seemed to Aristotle arbitrary and accidental; hence he made no move toward applying mathematics to natural philosophy.

Aristotle's treatment of mathematics has been the least understood aspect of his philosophy. For no substance can exist without a shape, position, and motion, so that spatial and temporal existence does have a kind of nonaccidental connection with substantiality. However, shapes and numbers do not exist in nature except as the shapes and numbers of things; and the act by which we think the shape as though it were detached from its material container is called *abstraction;* it is very different from the *intuition* by which we recognize what the nature of a substance is. However, even in shapes and numbers, "we can recognize the final cause; for beauty is magnitude and order, and these are just what the mathematician studies." Only, the orders and magnitudes studied by the mathematician are accidentally connected (by the fact that certain laws of mathematics limit the growth of anything in space and time) with the natures of the self-sufficient entities containing them.

This view of mathematics leads Aristotle to say, very acutely, that Platonists "make mathematics the whole of philosophy." For Plato's forms are best illustrated by the abstractions of the mathematician; and mathematical beauty is constantly cited by Plato as an example of the kind of relation that constitutes the universal order.

C. Metaphysics

Substance, however, could conceivably be of a third kind—an independent reality, completely real, with no remaining raw possibilities, and consequently immune to change. His over-all view of nature and method led Aristotle to conclude that there were substances of this kind.

Looking at the universe as a whole—an operation, be it noted, that we as Aristotelians perform only when there is no particular part of it that we want to understand—we find a constant process of change, in which various species perpetuate themselves, and grow to maturity. We also find the stars, bodies which move with such uninterrupted cyclic regularity that their chemical composition must be supposed to be of a kind with which we are completely unfamiliar, since the bodies in our own field of immediate experience move in lines, not circles.

Throughout nature, we find possibility becoming realized, potentialities becoming actual. But, recognizing that there is this chain of efficient causes stretching back indefinitely into the past, the demands of logic require that there be some first cause. For the impetus that changes potentiality into actuality is always an *actual* cause (merely *possible* workmen can't arrange bricks to form a house, nor will the bricks build it by themselves). To start off and sustain the movements of nature, there must be some first actuality. Further, this first actuality must be unmixed with possibility, for whatever contains matter changes and decays and is irregular in its operation. This rules out the possibility that the first cause is an efficient cause, starting the movement of the world by impulsion, since "impulse" involves change, which in turn involves matter. It cannot be a material cause, since it must be actual, nor a formal cause, since it is a cause of change. The first cause must therefore be a final cause, which moves by its attraction.

This is Aristotle's doctrine of the *unmoved mover,* which he calls God. We come closest to imagining or experiencing such pure actuality when we consider our own acts of intuitive insight, for in the immediate recognition of a form, that form is present to our minds without any admixture of matter. In this direct, contemplative act of intellectual apprehension, then, we come as close as men can to the kind of pure actuality that constantly, by its attraction, starts and sustains cosmic motion. And if we try to imagine the life of God, the closest analogy we can find is a life of perfect, contemplative thought. Nevertheless, since "all things desire God," the presence of this unmoved mover explains why motions continue, and why actuality is constantly coming into being out of chaotic material possibility.

The differentiation of kinds of substances, and the relation of the causes to the cosmic scheme, is the work of *metaphysics,* forming, with mathematics and natural philosophy Aristotle's three kinds of theoretical knowledge, or pure sciences.

Before passing to the practical sciences of ethics, economics, and politics, it may be well to recapitulate what has been said about method, substances, and causes.

Aristotle summarizes these distinctions in a compressed passage, given here with a running commentary: [12]

1. Substances are distinguished from being of other kinds by their self-sufficiency (ability to exist apart):

Some things can exist apart and some cannot, and it is the former that are substances.

2. Therefore, all other things presuppose and depend on substantial existence, and the causes of substance are, directly or indirectly, the causes of all existent things:

And therefore all things have the same causes, because, without substances, modifications and movements do not exist.

3. (Animate substances are used here as an example. In animals, soul, and in man, reason, are the formal causes; the body is the material cause, and desire in man shows the influence of final causes.)

Further, these causes will probably be soul and body, or reason and desire and body.

4. In another sense, the basic natures of all things are the same, since all natural processes depend on the emergence of potentialities into actuality:

And in yet another way, analogically identical things are principles, i.e. actuality and potency;

[12] *Ibid.,* 1071a1-b1. Aristotle's text is italicized.

5. However, the extent of this sameness must be qualified by the fact that the specific potentiality and actuality are distinct in each individual case:

but these also are not only different for different things but also apply in different ways to them.

6. But the relation of actuality and potentiality even to the same thing is not constant; for example, when grape juice, which is wine potentially, has been fermented, it becomes wine actually:

For in some cases, the same thing exists at one time actually, at another potentially, e.g. wine or flesh or man does so.

7. The causes of substance include these two common principles of actuality and potentiality. The potentiality is in the material cause; the actuality is contributed by the form, whether thought of as combined with the matter, or separate from it, or as determining the actual nature of a substance by its absence (in which case the substance actually has, not the absent form, but its opposed contrary, the privation; as an actual "shapeless" stone is potentially a statue, but in actuality has the opposite of the clearly defined form of a statue). Forms and privations in themselves are regarded as actualizations of a matter in which they are present as potentiality, hence are here identified with actuality, though apart from a material embodiment, forms and privations do not exist except in a derivative sense:

(And these too fall under the above-named causes. For the form exists actually, if it can exist apart, and so does the complex of form and matter, and the privation, e.g. darkness or disease; but the matter exists potentially; for this is that which can become qualified either by the form or by the privation.)

8. The relation of actuality and potentiality to the efficient and final causes of substance is different from their relation to the material and formal causes. Other causes of substance exist besides actuality and potentiality. For example, a man is caused not only by the form and matter, but by his parents (the proximate efficient

cause) and less specifically by the life-giving heat of the sun (the remote efficient cause) :

But the distinction of actuality and potentiality applies in another way to cases where the matter of cause and of effect is not the same, in some of which cases the form is not the same but different, e.g. the cause of man is (1) the elements in man (viz. fire and earth as matter, and the peculiar form), and further (2) something else outside, i.e. the father, and (3) besides these the sun and its oblique course, which are neither matter nor form nor privation of man nor of the same species with him, but moving causes.

9. Not all the causes can be expressed in universal terms. While the formal cause, common to a species, can be expressed in this way (for example, humanity is the formal cause of man), the material and efficient causes cannot be, since they differ for the different individual members of the species. Thus the efficient causes of all men are not "paternity," but of each, his individual father:

Further, one must observe that some causes can be expressed in universal terms, and some cannot.

10. The universal causes operate only through concrete individuals, and apart from their embodiment in such concrete individuals, they have no separate efficacy or existence. Thus while we say, "Man is the cause of Mr. Jones," humanity can be operative as a cause of Jones only through its concrete embodiment of Jones's father.

The proximate principles of all things are the 'this' which is proximate in actuality, and another which is proximate in potentiality [for example, the proximate causes of a child are the individual father, who on Aristotle's view is the efficient and transmits the formal cause, and the germ contained in the individual mother, which is the material cause.] *The universal causes, then, of which we spoke do not* exist. *For it is the individual that is the originative principle of the individuals. For while man is the originative principle of man universally, there is no universal man, but Peleus is the originative principle of Achilles, and your father of you, and this particular* b *of this particular* ba, *though* b *in general is the originative principle of* ba *taken without qualification.*

11. Another qualification of the statement that "the causes of all things are the same" is that there are other kinds of "things" besides substances (for example, qualities, quantities, relations, and so on). Each of these kinds has causes of its own kind; the formal cause of a quantity is a quantity, that of a quality is itself a quality. (As an inelegant parallel, the statement "The final courses of all meals served in this restaurant are the same" is true in the sense that all the meals served end with a dessert course; but the statement must be qualified to show that these final courses are not absolutely and literally the same, since (1) there are many kinds of dessert on the menu, and (2) each diner choosing a given dessert receives his own individual serving, not the same dish as other customers, even though these others have also ordered dessert of the same kind.)

Further, if the causes of substances are the causes of all things, yet different things have different causes and elements, as was said; the causes of things that are not in the same class, e.g. of colours and sounds, of substances and quantities, are different except in an analogical sense;

12. And these differences extend to individual causes within the same class, for these differ for individuals:

and those things in the same species are different, not in species, but in the sense that the causes of different individuals are different, your matter and form and moving cause being different from mine, while in their universal definition they are the same.

13. The more specifically we interpret "sameness," the more clearly we see that the material and formal *causes* of things differ in kind when the *things* themselves differ in kind:

And if we inquire what are the principles and elements of substances and relations and qualities—whether they are the same or different—clearly when the names of the causes are used in several senses the causes of each are the same, but when the senses are distinguished the causes are not the same but different, except that in the following senses the causes of all are the same.

14. However, in certain senses the causes are the same. These similarities of the causes of all things are fundamental to Aristotle's view of the methods and the interrelation of the sciences. All things share in the formal, material, and efficient causes, of the kind appropriate to each:

They are (1) the same or analogous in this sense, that matter, form, privation, and the moving cause are common to all things;

15. Also, since substances are alone capable of independent existence, their causes are necessary conditions for the existence of the attributes that substances support:

and (2) the causes of substance may be treated as causes of all things in this sense, that when substances are removed all things are removed;

16. The prime mover, again, is a cause common to all things as a remote final cause:

further (3) that which is first in respect of complete reality is the cause of all things.

17. But although one can classify all the different forms and their privations together as causes of the same sort (that is, as formal causes), there are as many different forms and privations contrary to them as the contrary pairs of terms in language indicate:

But in another sense there are different first causes, viz. all the contraries which are neither generic nor ambiguous terms;

18. And, although we can say that the matter of each thing is a material cause like that of every other, each thing has its own individual matter, which is not common to anything else:

and, further, the matters of different things are different.

19. The conclusion is that the causes of all sensible things are four in number; that they are analogically the same for all, but specifically different for different kinds, and are individually distinct for different individuals. All natural sciences can therefore be oriented in analogous frames of causality, and their interrelations

shown by showing their relative emphasis on the four causes. This analogy is not, however, to be interpreted as denying distinctions in kind among the causes in each class, nor as denying that "to be" in its primary Aristotelian sense is to be a concrete individual substance:

We have stated, then, what are the principles of sensible things and how many they are, and in what sense they are the same and in what sense different.

For Aristotle, the only ultimate realities are individual substances. "Thus Peleus, and not man, is the father of Achilles, for, strictly speaking, nothing exists but individuals." These take on and lose various qualities without having their own identities affected thereby. Thus, I remain the same person when a sun tan changes my skin color. In nature, each substance owes its distinctive individuality to a combination of matter with a form; what this form is, the efficient cause will usually determine; and as it develops, the form exerts the kind of attraction and direction of the process that an ideal or goal exerts in the consciously directed life of a man. The causes of each account for the distinctive methods of the sciences.

In later treatments of this philosophy, usually the wrong conclusion is drawn from Aristotle's discussion of the nature of actuality, and its dependence on the unmoved mover. Christian theologians, for example, could take the statement "All things desire God" as a basic analogy or metaphor, and use the perfections of God to explain the natures of individual things. As we saw in the discussion of language, however, metaphor is the distinctive linguistic instrument of poetry, not of philosophy. God's attraction is exerted on the motions of the heavens, which are transmitted to the mundane region as efficient causes, and is effective on each thing through that individual thing's proximate efficient and final causes, not in any other less literal way.

The analysis of the world as a whole serves to disclose no separate forms or numbers which would contradict the conclusion that only individual substances exist in the truest sense. These individuals, however, have specific similarities through the chains of efficient causality that produce them, and science is possible precisely because the mind can recognize such similarity and invent words that stand for any individual member of a class indifferently. Individuals are made what they are, and are understandable, only through the individual causes of each. The task of science, therefore, is to discover the distinctive individualities and proximate causes of each class; and in this task, the over-all structure of nature and the prime mover are relevant only insofar as they determine *what the four kinds of causes of each explanation must be.*

The arts of language were cited as examples of this method at work. In each of these, the material causes are the parts of language; the efficient causes, users of language. The final causes are, in logic, making the mind grasp the nature of things adequately; in rhetoric, making the audience concur in certain practically oriented thoughts; and in poetry, displaying a coherent contexture of words. The formal causes represent the best disposal of the medium to perform these differentiated functions; the syllogism formally reproduces causal connection; the enthymeme, a practical decision; and the metaphor, an aesthetic and satisfying insight.

It has been said that mathematics will not serve as an instrument of the natural sciences, because substances are not made what they are simply by their size, shape, and motion, but by a potentiality present in each of them, which is coming into actuality.

Certain of Aristotle's ideas about substances have made a new appearance in contemporary philosophy. Among these is the notion that each substance stands by itself, is its own reason for being, and contains its causes in itself as determining its independent value and actuality. It is instructive to contrast the concrete, autonomous, individual substances of Aristotle with the abstract, interconnected, general forms of Plato.

The one thing that seems lacking in Plato's philosophy, some place of importance for the concrete, tangible individual, which appears only as the shadow of an eternal abstract form, has become in the Aristotelian treatment of the problem the one thing that stands out with most importance. The problem of change is resolved by the presentation of a world of individuals, each of which is developing autonomously toward the realization of the new possibilities that it contains, because the impact of its efficient cause on its matter starts it toward a specific kind of realized possibility. The qualities that vanish return into the realm or reservoir of possibility, whence they can emerge only on the occasion of a new interaction of their specifically appropriate material and efficient causes. Since only individuals, differentiated into distinctive kinds, exist, the role of the scientist is to describe the form of each kind, and to grasp those distinctions which make it be what it is, rather than a substance of another kind.

THE PRACTICAL SCIENCES

There are other kinds of knowledge besides the theoretical, however. Pure sciences differ among themselves because of the different natures of the things they study; but they agree in their ultimate purpose, which is pure disinterested knowledge of the way things are.

Just as differences of purpose separated the arts of language into three, so knowledge may be separated by its purposes into three kinds. Logic and proof are the proper tools of theoretical science; rhetoric suggests that there may be other fields of knowledge, directed toward practical action. The practical sciences, however, can never become completely "scientific" because of their problems and their subject matter. In the first place, since they are practical, these sciences regard everything from a peculiarly human point of view. "Men and fish," says Aristotle, "would agree as to what white and straight are; but as to the good, they would differ," since human values give no clue as to what would be to the natural practical benefit of fish.

In the second place, practical sciences have as their subject matter human customs and institutions, which, while arising from natural powers and needs, are artificial, and may and do vary indefinitely in form. Thus while each dogfish I may dissect is essentially like every other dogfish, the same cannot be said about customs or political institutions. Confronted with this problem, the social sciences must be developed dialectically, since there are no natural forms that we might intuitively grasp and use as starting points of our demonstration. The development is guided throughout, however, by relevant principles borrowed from other sciences, such as psychology and biology, and introduced to serve as starting points of dialectical investigation.

A third kind of knowledge is represented by technology, which aims not at happiness, nor at knowledge, but at making something. Technology may further be divided into two branches: one in which the thing made is designed as an instrument for some further purpose, such as a pruning knife; the other in which the thing made is valued as an end in itself. The former branch of technology is manufacturing or production; the latter is fine art, which includes poetry.

ETHICS

Aristotle's view of human life—of human virtue and human happiness—is profoundly consistent with his general philosophy of teleological development. Human conduct is, after all, only man's more or less conscious effort to secure those things which he finds he can value, and for Aristotle, the problem of the moralist is to discover what in human life is truly valuable, and to determine the conditions indispensable to its realization. The answer to the question: What is truly valuable? is implicitly indicated in the general scheme of Aristotle's thought. Man, like any developmental substance, tends toward a full maturity, the realization of his potentialities. This does not, of course, mean that all men or even a comparatively large group of men reach this full maturity of life. Development may be thwarted by any number of accidents. Aristotle calls the full maturity of human life *happiness* or *well-being,* and he applies the term *virtue* to those active habits of thought and conduct which make this full development possible.

Happiness is the end of human life, and from this bare definition we may learn a good deal concerning its nature. As a final end pursued for its own sake, happiness must not be thought of as instrumental, as a means to any further end. Happiness is good in itself, and accordingly good *for* nothing. Hence the possession of wealth cannot be identified with happiness. Wealth is, ethically speaking, an instrument to be employed as we spend our money, and hence it cannot be an end in itself. Further, happiness must be self-sufficient or as nearly so as possible. An end that depends for its realization upon a multitude of conditions external to the agent can hardly be an ideal goal of human life. "Development" that depends wholly upon external conditions is not true development, but merely a series of accidents that reveal no substantial growth of the individual. The individual's pursuit and achievement of happiness must be largely a matter of his own self-guided activity. If he depends upon external conditions for its realization, he is only giving hostages to fortune and inviting the most bitter disillusion. Hence, genuine happiness cannot be a matter of prestige or of honor. The end of a man's life cannot reside simply in the opinion that others have of him, and woe to him who thinks that it does!

The following passage from Aristotle's *Nicomachean Ethics* afford a summary of his theory of the highest good or happiness.[13]

Every art and every kind of inquiry, and likewise every act and purpose, seems to aim at some good; and so it has been well said that the good is that at which everything aims. . . .

If then in what we do there be some end which we wish for on its own account, choosing all the others as means to this, but not every end without exception as a means to something else (for so we should go on *ad infinitum,* and desire would be left void and objectless), this evidently will be the good or the best of all things.

And surely from a practical point of view it much concerns us to know this good; for then, like archers shooting at a definite mark, we shall be more likely to attain what we want. . . .

We see that there are many ends. But some of these are chosen only as means, as wealth, flutes, and the whole class of instruments. And so it is plain that not all ends are final.

But the best of all things must, we conceive, be something final.

If then there be only one final end, this will be what we are seeking—or if there be more than one, then the most final of them.

[13] Aristotle, *Nicomachean Ethics,* Bk. I, 1-7, Peters's translation, abridged, in Charles M. Bakewell, *Source Book of Ancient Philosophy,* pp. 251-53. Charles Scribner's Sons, New York, rev. ed., 1939. Reprinted by permission of the publisher and The Clarendon Press.

Now that which is pursued as an end in itself is more final than that which is pursued as means to something else, and that which is never chosen as means than that which is chosen both as an end in itself and as means, and that is strictly final which is always chosen as an end in itself and never as means.

Happiness seems more than anything else to answer to this description: for we always choose it for itself, and never for the sake of something else, while honor and pleasure and reason, and all virtue or excellence, we choose partly indeed for themselves (for, apart from any result, we should choose each of them), but partly also for the sake of happiness, supposing that they will help to make us happy. But no one chooses happiness for the sake of these things, or as a means to anything else at all.

We seem to be led to the same conclusion when we start from the notion of self-sufficiency.

The final good is thought to be self-sufficing (or all-sufficing). In applying this term we do not regard a man as an individual leading a solitary life, but we also take account of parents, children, wife, and, in short, friends and fellow-citizens generally, since man is naturally a social being. Some limit must indeed be set to this; for if you go on to parents and descendants and friends of friends, you will never come to a stop. But this we will consider further on; for the present we will take self-sufficing to mean what by itself makes life desirable and in want of nothing. And happiness is believed to answer to this description.

And further, happiness is believed to be the most desirable thing in the world, and that not merely as one among other good things; if it were merely one among other good things [so that other things could be added to it], it is plain that the addition of the least of other goods must make it more desirable: for the addition becomes a surplus of good, and of two goods the greater is always more desirable.

Thus it seems that happiness is something final and self-sufficing, and is the end of all that man does.

Accordingly, the happiness of man must be a truly human happiness. Otherwise it cannot be said to be a realization of human capacity. We may therefore expect it to contain something besides those satisfactions which are common to both man and the animals. To be well fed is not to be happy, nor can happiness be identified with sexual pleasure or even with the enjoyment of health and robust physical exercise. Man cannot realize himself and achieve happiness without the exercise of peculiarly human capacities.

Now man participates in three fundamental types of activity, or what in Aristotelian terminology we may call three souls or levels of soul. (For Aristotle, the soul of a living thing is its actual life, the co-ordinating function of its parts or members. "If the body were all eye, sight would be its soul.") There is a nutritive soul, which man possesses in common with both plants and animals. This soul is the co-ordination of activities whereby the body grows and maintains itself through the assimilation of food. There is also the sensitive soul or the co-ordination of functions (of the sense organs, and so on) whereby the body may respond to objects about it with which it is in immediate contact. This soul man shares with the lower animals, and to a much lesser degree with some plants. Finally, we have the rational soul whereby man is capable of shaping his conduct upon principles and laws quite beyond the reach of the lesser-endowed living beings. The life of the rational soul is indispensable to human happiness or well-being. Intelligence is the specific end of human life.[14]

But can we suppose that, while a carpenter, or a cobbler, has a function and a business of his own, man has no business and no function assigned him by nature? Nay, surely as his several members, eye and hand and foot, plainly have each its own function, so we must suppose that man also has some function over and above all these.

What then is it?

Life evidently he has in common even with the plants, but we want that which is peculiar to him. We must exclude, therefore, the life of mere nutrition and growth.

Next to this comes the life of sense; but this too he plainly shares with horses and cattle and all kinds of animals.

There remains then the life whereby he acts—the life of his rational nature, with its two sides or divisions, one rational as obeying reason, the other rational as having and exercising reason.

But as this expression is ambiguous, we must be understood to mean thereby the life that consists in the exercise of the faculties; for this seems to be more properly entitled to the name.

[14] *Ibid.*. Bk. I, 10, pp. 253-54.

The function of man, then, is exercise of his vital faculties [or soul] on one side in obedience to reason, and on the other side with reason.

When acting in obedience to reason, man follows his intelligence as a guide of conduct. When exercising reason without reference to conduct, man becomes the student of nature, the contemplative observer, whose joy is simply to understand. Aristotle seems tempted to *identify* happiness with the free exercise of intelligence, with scientific and philosophical contemplation. But the logic of his position really forbids this. Man must bring to full realization all his fundamental potentialities if he is to achieve human well-being completely. Intelligence is paramount as the function peculiar to human nature. But it cannot stand quite alone as an ideal. Thus Aristotle devotes whole chapters to other goods besides those of intelligence. For instance, friendship is a good without which life is hardly worth living, for man is by nature a social and sociable animal, and he must lead a sadly thwarted life if he is confined to solitude. Then too, both honor, or good repute, and health, although not by any means sufficient by themselves to constitute happiness, are not to be dismissed as of negligible value. But none of these can compare with the exercise of intelligence as the foundation of human well-being.

The reader may be at first puzzled by this doctrine, but actually there is much to be said in its favor. If we are to understand Aristotle, we must not think of intelligence as limited to the mental exercise employed in pure science and philosophy. This is perhaps its highest and purest expression—certainly Aristotle so considered it; but intelligence itself is involved whenever we seek "to put two and two together," or to solve the simplest practical problem. Let us remember that the worst thing that can befall a human being is complete loss of interest in his surroundings. No disappointment or reverse of fortune can wholly defeat a man unless it robs him of all desire to think about certain things and to understand them.

Such desire need not be motivated by scientific interest; in fact, it rarely is. Most of us are interested in the things that do attract us not directly for the sake of truth, but for one of a hundred other reasons. But the fact remains that when we cease to pay interested and sustained attention to some aspect of our environment, we fall into a miserable listlessness that is far worse than loss of health or reputation. To be free from intense physical desire or, say, from personal ambition, might seem to many a reasonable ideal. But let us try to conceive of life wholly devoid of any sort of curiosity about any thing or any event. This importance of mental activity as the embodiment of a human value will then be evident. Such indifference would be the very denial of the proper human excellence, which is the exercise of intelligence.

Having concluded that intelligence is man's proper excellence, Aristotle insists that the highest happiness will be based upon a life of serene and disinterested study, the pursuit of pure science; for this life embodies the purest form of intellectual activity. But Aristotle's account is not as clear as might be, and we are left wondering just how much happiness Aristotle would expect to find in a person not equipped by background or opportunity for the lifelong pursuit of pure science.[15]

But if happiness be the exercise of virtue, it is reasonable to suppose that it will be the exercise of the highest virtue; and that will be the virtue or excellence of the best part of us.

Now, that part or faculty—call it reason or what you will—which seems naturally to rule and take the lead, and to apprehend things noble and divine—whether it be itself divine, or only the divinest part of us—is the faculty the exercise of which, in its proper excellence, will be perfect happiness.

That this consists in speculation or contemplation we have already said.

This conclusion would seem to agree both with what we have said above, and with known truths.

This exercise of faculty must be the highest possible; for the reason is the highest of our faculties, and of all knowable things those that reason deals with are the highest.

Again, it is the most continuous; for speculation can be carried on more continuously than any kind of action whatsoever.

We think, too, that pleasure ought to be one of the ingredients of happiness; but of all virtuous exercises, it is allowed that pleasantest

[15] *Ibid.,* Bk. X, 7, pp. 264-66.

is the exercise of wisdom. At least philosophy is thought to have pleasures that are admirable in purity and steadfastness; and it is reasonable to suppose that the time passes more pleasantly with those who possess, than with those who are seeking knowledge.

Again, what is called self-sufficiency will be most of all found in the speculative life. The necessaries of life, indeed, are needed by the wise man as well as by the just man and the rest; but, when these have been provided in due quantity, the just man further needs persons towards whom, and along with whom, he may act justly; and so does the temperate and courageous man and the rest; while the wise man is able to speculate even by himself, and the wiser he is the more is he able to do this. He could speculate better, we may confess, if he had others to help him, but nevertheless he is more self-sufficient than anybody else.

Again, it would seem that this life alone is desired solely for its own sake; for it yields no result beyond the contemplation itself, while from all actions we get something more or less besides the action itself.

Again, happiness is thought to imply leisure; for we toil in order that we may have leisure, as we make war in order that we may enjoy peace....

This, then, will be the complete happiness of man, i.e. when a complete term of days is added; for nothing incomplete can be admitted into our idea of happiness.

But a life which realized this idea would be something more than human; for it would not be the expression of man's nature, but of some divine element in that nature—the exercise of which is as far superior to the exercise of the other kind of virtue [i.e. practical or moral virtue], as this divine element is superior to our compound human nature.

If then reason be divine as compared with man, the life which consists in the exercise of reason will also be divine in comparison with human life. Nevertheless, instead of listening to those who advise us as men and mortals not to lift our thoughts above what is human and mortal, we ought rather, as far as possible, to put off our mortality and make every effort to live in the exercise of the highest of our faculties; for though it be but a small part of us, yet in power and value it far surpasses all the rest.

And indeed this part would even seem to constitute our true self, since it is the sovereign and the better part. It would be strange, then, if a man were to prefer the life of something else to the life of his true self.

It is only the exceptional human being, capable, as Aristotle says, of transcending ordinary human nature and approaching the absolute freedom of the unmoved mover himself, who can realize the full happiness and freedom of the contemplative life. Contemplation then seems a sort of suprahuman happiness reserved for the very few. Here, the reader may notice what seems at least an inconsistency in Aristotle's system of ethics. Happiness has been described as the fulfillment of human capacity, the perfection of human function. But when happiness is at last fully described, it is spoken of as a suprahuman achievement, the fulfillment of a divine element in human nature. Still, a little reflection will show that this is perhaps after all consistent with the scheme of Aristotle's thought, according to which all things are moved toward the divine perfection of the unmoved mover, the ultimate final cause of all things.

Aristotle's theory of happiness will be more readily understood when we have made clear his distinction between happiness and pleasure. Pleasure is the mental and bodily state that accompanies any unimpeded activity of the organism. Thus we all tend to enjoy doing things we do well and without clumsiness, and we are apt to tire of activities that do not go smoothly. Any function if freely performed in a healthy state is pleasant. Digestion of a moderate meal affords an example. Pain is the result of conflict and inhibition, as when our listening to music is broken in upon by an external clatter. The enjoyment of pleasure is by no means to be identified with the achievement of happiness, since man may find pleasure in many activities not particularly human. Nonetheless, pleasure will be present in happiness, since the latter involves full and unimpeded exercise of certain capacities. But intensity of pleasure and the quantity of pleasure experienced are no criteria of happiness. A life full of pleasure need not, on Aristotelian principles, be a happy one. It is only because we tend to deny that the pleasures enjoyed by an unhappy man are truly pleasant that we have difficulty in grasping Aristotle's theory. Once we recognize the truth that many genuine pleasures can leave the personality as a whole unsatisfied, we have no further trouble in following Aristotle.

It is clear that blind pursuit of certain pleasures may actually jeopardize our happiness. If we could always keep before us the ideal of happiness, rightly understood, we would gladly forego any pleasure that stood in its way. But life is complex, and the relations of things are not always easily understood. So, although we all want to be happy, intense desire and confused thinking—the two are likely to go together, for man is easily led to believe what he desires intensely to believe—may often defeat our real purpose. On this point, Aristotle is not far removed from Socrates.

Thus far, we have completed a brief survey of what we might call the first principles of Aristotle's ethics, his theory of happiness, of what is worth while in human life. We have now to consider the remainder of his ethical thought, his theory of moral virtue or the human activity whereby happiness is made possible and is preserved. Aristotle's ethical thought is distinguished from that of many philosophers by the fact that he treats moral virtue as a means to an end and not as something of final and intrinsic value. He is thus to be contrasted with certain later thinkers—namely, the Stoics —who taught that virtue and not happiness is the final end of human life. This distinction is a fundamental one, which we shall encounter frequently in surveying the history of ethical theory.

For Aristotle, moral virtue may be described as intelligent self-guidance. This, of course, requires a mature and alert intelligence, but what Aristotle calls "intellectual virtue" may amount only to cleverness and brilliance of mind; sheer power of intellect is not by itself sufficient to control conduct. Man is a creature of habit as well as a rational animal, and intelligence must be supplemented by a foundation of disciplined habit. Moral virtue is a state of character whereby the good man is "apt to act" according to reason. Reason can see happiness as a goal, but by itself it is incapable of achieving it. Thus, Aristotle emphasizes a point that Socrates tended to treat with less insistence; namely, that knowledge, when divorced from a sound discipline of practical moral training, does not constitute moral virtue. Man grows strong by performing acts of strength, and he grows virtuous by performing virtuous actions; that is, through practice.

The early stages of such practice must be guided not by the individual himself but by his moral teacher. But no man may be said to have acquired moral virtue until he chooses the right course of his own uncoerced volition and until he tends to take pleasure in such a course. The importance of this last condition will be clear to anyone who carefully considers Aristotle's conception of pleasure as the enjoyment of unimpeded activity. So long as a virtue "comes hard," is impeded by unruly desire and imperfect habit, such moral virtue is not complete and the agent is in need of further moral training.

Virtue is a tendency to make effective decisions in accordance with right reason, and thus to further the happiness of the individual making the decision and of those in whose lives he plays a part. Since no reasonable man will desire to be without friends or to be looked upon as antisocial or dishonorable, he will consider the needs of his fellow citizens and respect their rights. These decisions will tend to find a middle path between the possible extremes of human conduct, and upon this path Aristotle builds his famous doctrine of the "golden mean."

Most of the significant alternatives that human choice faces may be so classified that the proper decision appears as a mean between undesirable extremes. Thus courage lies between timidity and foolhardiness, courtesy between an offensive forwardness and an awkward reserve, liberality between vulgar display and a selfish stinginess. Between such extremes it is impossible to find the proper means by the application of any quasi-mathematical formula. But experience and training will in time make possible the proper choice. When he is faced with alternatives, the good man's choice of the proper mean becomes at last a matter of taste or tact, the principles of which cannot be made wholly explicit. Here we discover the value of the classification of virtue and vice in terms of means and extremes. In a difficult situation, we may always ask ourselves whether we are falling too near an extreme, since it is easier to recognize an extreme form of conduct than it is to choose the mean itself directly. Thus we find ourselves saying, "I was a bit too hasty with so and so," or "I might have been less reserved in manner." It is by observing the extremes toward which we are tending that we at last hit the mean.

The doctrine of the mean is consistent with a momentous insight of the Greek moralists, who always emphasized the importance of moderation. This emphasis was a part of Greek religion as well as of Greek ethical common sense. Restraint and avoidance of all extremes of emotion and of conduct seem intrinsically admirable and pleasing to the gods. "Nothing too much," "The half is better than the whole," are proverbs expressing this attitude. In this matter, Aristotle is summing up the ancient wisdom of poets and religious teachers.

Throughout the Christian Middle Ages, this teaching of Aristotle's was highly esteemed, and it became known as the doctrine of the "golden mean." It is frequently treated as if it were the most important of Aristotle's contribution to ethics, although when we consider his masterly treatment of happiness as the end of life, we may well hesitate to accept this evaluation.

The following quotation includes Aristotle's summary of his doctrine of moral virtue: [16]

Virtue, then, is a habit or trained faculty of choice, the characteristic of which lies in observing the mean relatively to the persons concerned, and which is guided by reason, i.e., by the judgment of the prudent man.

And it is a moderation, firstly, inasmuch as it comes in the middle or mean between two vices, one on the side of excess, the other on the side of defect; and, secondly, inasmuch as, while these vices fall short of or exceed the due measure in feeling and in action, it finds and chooses the mean, middling, or moderate amount.

Regarded in its essence, therefore, or according to the definition of its nature, virtue is a moderation or middle state, but viewed in its relation to what is best and right it is the extreme of perfection.

The reader will notice that Aristotle's ethics differs from that of Plato only in matters of detail and emphasis. Both thinkers urge the supremacy of intelligence, whose function it is to guide man's needs and desires toward their fullest and most harmonious satisfactions. They both tend to consider social co-operation as an indispensable condition of the individual's complete development, al-

16 *Ibid.*, Bk. II, 6, p. 258.

though there is much less exhortation to self-sacrifice than in Christian ethics. Again, they both discount the importance of pleasure as in itself a reasonable end of human activity, but they both admit that the good life will contain pleasure. Each in his own way completes the picture of good character that Socrates sketched so brilliantly when he taught that "Virtue is knowledge," and "All the virtues are one." Plato does this with emphasis upon a social ideal, perhaps never to be realized; Aristotle, with his eye upon the empirical details of the actual moral experience of his day.

We do not find in Aristotle any Utopian scheme comparable to that of Plato's *Republic*. To be sure, Aristotle admires the ideal of the small, self-contained Greek city-state at a time when the Macedonian rule of Philip and Alexander was making such an ideal virtually impossible of realization. But insofar as social institutions, such as the family and private property, are concerned, Aristotle holds pretty closely to the already established customs and ideals, even to the extent of justifying the existence of a propertied leisure class, whose civilized life actually constitutes the raison d'être of the city itself.

Aristotle's choice of monarchy as the ideal form of government contrasts sharply with the Platonic scheme. This was perhaps in-fluenced by Aristotle's respect for the Macedonian constitution, which in the days of Philip and Alexander was showing itself to be at least more efficient than those of the existing democracies. But the two political theories have one fundamental feature in common. They both advocate the division of society into well-marked groups or classes, thus offering a profound contrast to the ideals of most modern democracies and socialisms. For Aristotle, slavery is justified on the ground that some men are born to obey, possessing what would seem to be almost an instinct for servitude.

Perhaps the most memorable contribution Aristotle makes to political theory lies in his comment upon the origin and purpose of social organization and the human need served by the state.[17]

Now, that man is more of a political animal than bees or any other gregarious animal is evident. Nature, as we often say, makes

[17] Aristotle, *Politics,* trans. by Benjamin Jowett, in *Works,* Vol. X, 1253a5-35.

nothing in vain, and man is the only animal whom she has endowed with the gift of speech. And whereas mere voice is but an indication of pleasure or pain, and is therefore found in other animals (for their nature attains to the perception of pleasure and pain and the intimation of them to one another, and no further), the power of speech is intended to set forth the expedient and inexpedient, and therefore likewise the just and the unjust. And it is characteristic of man that he alone has any sense of good and evil, of just and unjust, and the like, and the association of living beings who have this sense makes a family and a state.

Further, the state is by nature clearly prior to the family and to the individual, since the whole is of necessity prior to the part; for example, if the whole body be destroyed, there will be no foot or hand, except in an equivocal sense, as we might speak of a stone hand; for when destroyed the hand will be no better than that. But things are defined by their working and power; and we ought not to say that they are the same when they no longer have their proper quality, but only that they have the same name. The proof that the state is a creation of nature and prior to the individual is that the individual, when isolated, is not self-sufficing; and therefore he is like a part in relation to the whole. But he who is unable to live in society, or who has no need because he is sufficient for himself, must be either a beast or a god: he is no part of a state. A social instinct is implanted in all men by nature, and yet he who first founded the state was the greatest of benefactors. For man, when perfected, is the best of animals, but, when separated from law and justice, he is the worst of all; since armed injustice is the more dangerous, and he is equipped at birth with arms, meant to be used by intelligence and virtue, which he may use for the worst ends. Wherefore, if he have no virtue, he is the most unholy and the most savage of animals, and the most full of lust and gluttony. But justice is the bond of men in states, for the administration of justice, which is the determination of what is just, is the principle of order in political society.

AESTHETICS

Aristotle has not left us as complete an account of aesthetic value as that which is to be found in Plato's writings. There exists, however, an incomplete statement of his theory of literary criticism in his fragment known as the *Poetics*. The influence of this work has been enormous. For instance, criticism—or at least the theory of criticism—in the seventeenth and eighteenth centuries is frequently little more than an interpretation of this book. In this field, there are many renderings of Aristotle's thought, and we cannot hope to consider here its manifold interpretation. The reader who is interested should consult a work like *History of Esthetics* by Katherine E. Gilbert and Helmut Kuhn (Macmillan, 1939) or *Commentary on the* Poetics by Samuel H. Butcher (Macmillan, 1932). We can offer only the most cursory summary.

Art is an imitation of nature. At first glance, we may be tempted to interpret this statement as the first principle of an aesthetics according to which the artist is bound to describe things just as he finds them or else fail in his calling. But in all probability Aristotle has in mind no such nineteenth-century notion of art. For him, nature is, as we have seen, a theater of development wherein substances, especially living things, pass from potentiality to mature realization. If we take a cross section of nature at any given moment and ignore this natural tendency toward development, we distort nature. And this the artist should not do. Truly to imitate nature is to indicate its ideal direction as well as its actual status. Realism, in the modern sense of the word, can hardly belong to any philosophy so steeped in teleology as is Aristotle's.

Plato had recognized that art involves imitation. But he felt that this was a fault. For him, the artist imitates not nature in its development, but the objects and events present to a more or less uncritical experience. Such imitation contains no depth of interpretation. For Aristotle, imitation involves not only observation, but a sympathy with the essential tendency of the thing described. Aristotle makes this point when he tells us that poetry is more "philosophical" than history. Poetry is not primarily concerned with what has happened or is happening, but with the capacities or potentialities of the things described. Thus the idealism of Greek sculpture, and of the heroic poems that portray human beings as they might be if only nature were less subject to accident or material handicap, is a philosophical as opposed to a historical treatment. At least this is true for those who accept Aristotle's implied definition of history. Perhaps the greatest history, say, Thucydides' account of the decline of Athenian power, or the work of Polybius, is as much an imitation of nature, in Aristotle's sense, as a great tragedy. But Aristotle has not thought of this.[18]

It is the function of art to suggest man's possible greatness as well as to portray the actual stresses and tensions under which he must seek his fulfillment. The failure of potentially noble character to maintain itself because of a tragic flaw in its constitution is a favorite theme of Greek drama. Aristotle believes that in witnessing the failure of a splendid character—a failure brought about as the inevitable outcome of some one weakness, such as presumption or hasty passion—our human sympathies are enlarged and our understanding of human life is rendered more profound. In witnessing and comprehending such drama, we concentrate our attention upon the tragedy of existence—not, to be sure, upon the "seamy side of things," not, for example, upon unnatural vice or brutish cruelty, but upon the fact that nobility is rare and often subject to defeat because of the slight imperfection that it may contain.

Such defeat is a fearful and a pitiable thing. It is well to face this fact in its grim and fateful reality. Having done so, we are strangely freed, for a time at least, from the pessimistic foreboding that our awareness of the human predicament may inspire. Aristotle has called this sense of freedom which great tragedy produces a *katharsis* or purge, for we are purged of the very emotions that the tragedy arouses. Here Aristotle touches upon a fact that has often puzzled even the more enlightened members of the literary public. He suggests, by the way, an answer to the old question: "Why is tragedy so widely accepted as the greatest form of narrative or dramatic art?" Great tragedy can bring us a sense of acquiescence in and acceptance of life that lighter art, to say nothing of the literature of escape, wholly misses.

---

[18] Of course, as we have seen above, Aristotle does not in any sense *identify* poetry with philosophy. Poetry does not offer argument, it does not "prove" anything. Neither does a poem persuade us to undertake any specific action. Thus poetry is neither philosophy, science nor rhetoric. It does, however, at least when most successful, awaken a sense of values latent in our human life; and we may take delight in the intimation of these values.

SUMMARY: THE PROBLEM OF CHANGE

There is no particular reason to believe that the history of philosophy is logically ordered, as though its stages had been planned in advance. Nonetheless, selection of certain central problems characteristic of the several stages of speculation is indispensable as a pedagogical device to indicate a unity and sequence of intellectual events, which otherwise appear to the beginning student as a mass of episodic fact. We have found the problems of ancient philosophy centering about the interpretation of change, of the apparent fact of process or becoming.

In the philosophies of Democritus, Plato, and Aristotle, the problem of change seems to have reached three distinct, systematic resolutions. In each case, a refined analysis, along lines suggested by earlier speculation, has led to the recognition that something permanent and unchanging must be an ingredient of things that change. The atoms of Democritus, the forms of Plato, and the formal causes of Aristotle are such permanent ingredients, each lending pattern and intelligibility to an unstable matrix. This matrix is described as empty space; that is, the sheer possibility of motion, as an undulating material receptacle, or as a "raw" material composed of pure potentiality. In each of the three cases, the matrix supplies the fluctuating, unstable ingredient of process.

After Aristotle, the problem of change ceased to be the central theme of speculative philosophy. The three great systems seem to have exhausted the possibilities of its resolution. Later philosophers gradually turned to the problem of knowledge. A new skepticism and distrust of man's ability to attain adequate knowledge of nature initiated new ways of philosophy, limited by this very uncertainty. But in post-Aristotelian philosophy, even the problem of knowledge is subordinated, as we shall see, to practical and moral considerations.

CHAPTER VI

After Aristotle

HELLENISTIC ETHICS: PHILOSOPHIES OF DETACHMENT

By the time of Aristotle's death, the Greek world may be said to have been well launched upon a course of development whose tendencies are sharply to be contrasted with those of earlier centuries. The changes to be noticed are manifold, but they may be largely summarized in the statement that the city-state, in its social, political, religious, and cultural aspects, was ceasing to be the center of Greek life. The city-states had been seriously weakened by the disastrous and almost suicidal rivalry that culminated in the drawn-out Peloponnesian War between Athens, Sparta, and their allies. This conflict made impossible the survival of Hellenic civilization in its highest and most productive form.

The resulting historical contrast is a sharp one. The years that follow the decline are often described as comprising the Hellenistic rather than the Hellenic period of ancient history. At this time military and political supremacy passed to the Macedonians, the least cultivated of all the Greek peoples. Under the brilliant leadership of Philip and his son Alexander, often called the Great, there took place a most spectacular military expansion, during which the Macedonians briefly united the world of the eastern Mediterranean, ruling from the Adriatic to the frontiers of India. After Alexander's death, this widespread empire fell apart, and there arose a number of military despotisms, each under the control of one of Alexander's generals and thus superficially Greek in culture and way of life.

At this time Greece itself, Egypt, Asia Minor, and the whole of the Levant were subject to such dominion, except that the older Greek cities were classed as "allies" of the Macedonians. Under these conditions, local traditions and loyalties declined. These more centralized, more bureaucratic governments were often oppressive; and concentration of wealth and power often tended to impoverish and disenfranchise citizens whose ancestors in simpler and happier times had enjoyed a goodly measure of economic and political freedom. These people, deprived of their autonomy and their independence, came in time to consider themselves rather the victims than the agents of history. In the new metropolitan centers outside of old Greece, such as Antioch, Pergamum, or Alexandria, which rivaled the smaller cities like Athens or Corinth as centers of culture, the citizen enjoyed only an anonymous and impersonal status. Such passivity often reflected itself in a growing taste for "spectator" amusements of a very modern sort and, even among the poor, in a concern for luxuries and comforts, also comparable to our own.

The uncertainty and lack of security that characterized the Hellenistic world, especially from the time of the Second Punic War between Rome and Carthage (200 B.C.) until the establishment of the *Pax Romana* in the days of Augustus, undermined the intellectual life of happier centuries. Superstition and credulity, which at Athens had been in some measure held in check by the philosophical and sophistic spirit at the time of Anaxagoras, Protagoras, and Plato, spread widely throughout all classes. Even among those who resisted such intellectual decay the old interest in pure theory, the desire to understand and to contemplate, was replaced by more practical concerns.

So profound a change of orientation had somehow to be reflected in cultural and philosophical expression. Indeed, within a few years of the death of Aristotle a marked change in the spirit of Greek philosophy begins to make itself apparent. The very nature and function of philosophy, its place in the life of a thoughtful public, and the very purpose which it seeks to fulfill undergo transformation. The word itself gradually changes its significance for many writers. "Philosophy" and "philosophical" take on something of the popular meaning that they have ever since carried in general literature. A "philosophy" is recognized as a set of maxims to steady and support the human spirit against the pressures of a threatening, a frustrating, or an uncongenial world. Philosophy, so conceived, is often a source of consolation for the inevitable and perennial ills of life. It can also be recognized as an effort to enliven one's sense of the importance of human life itself and to dispel a feeling of futility that so often accompanies the more tedious routine of a metropolitan existence. Philosophy is thus primarily devoted to building and maintaining morale, to combating what has been described as a certain "loss of nerve" and of self-confidence, characteristic of overcentralized and metropolitan civilizations, where the citizen is often reduced to being a frustrated spectator.

So conceived, a sound philosophy must help us to see the harsh or drab realities, the misfortunes and brutal contingencies, even the tiresome details of our existence, in what we may come to believe is their proper perspective. Above all, philosophy must teach its devotees to make their terms with despair. We must always remember that the course of events lies mostly beyond our control. Certainly no man should think of reforming the world before he has mastered himself, for this latter undertaking requires a lifetime of thoughtful self-discipline, and until self-mastery has been achieved, control of the outward environment is profitless. Furthermore, philosophy is man's inner bulwark of defense against circumstance, which, it is obvious enough, no philosopher or group of intellectuals can hope to control. Having despaired of establishing a Utopia, having despaired even of preserving the solid and political achievements of his ancestors, the Hellenistic philosopher undertakes to save himself by learning to face the necessities of life with cheerful dignity. As a rule he is not eager to make converts, but he is gratified if his life and writings offer a helpful example to others. The wise man will be content to limit his demands upon life to those few and unspectacular but lasting goods that it lies within his power to achieve and to retain.

These negative aspects of Hellenistic philosophy are somewhat relieved by the cosmopolitanism—what we should today call the "internationalism" and the "equalitarianism"—of the ethical thinkers who followed Aristotle. The distinction between Greek and barbarian, and also that between free man and slave, which had survived the analysis of Plato and Aristotle, break down completely. From the moral point of view, all human beings stand together, facing a common destiny. A sense of human fellowship, transcending racial, political, social, and economic distinctions, begins to characterize philosophical discussion. The solidarity of the small city-state having passed, the human individual, recognized as such and respected, begins to command greater attention. In this respect, Hellenistic ethics often suggests the liberalism of nineteenth- and twentieth-century thought. The warrior and the hero, so dear to Homeric legend, even the philosopher king or the magnificent public benefactor, so respected by Aristotle, no longer appear as ideally admirable types. The less spectacular virtues of prudence, patience, and tolerance, the attributes of the reasonable man who accepts his lot with an even-tempered and quiet dignity, receive the commendation of the philosopher.

The Hellenistic philosopher is usually quite ready to admit that the world, as we know it, is a sorry place and that its major ills are incorrigible. Accordingly, the wise man will seek detachment: he will seek to avoid emotional entanglement in such a world, at least insofar as his own human nature can be persuaded to do so. Thus the Platonic and Aristotelian ideals of human happiness as the full realization of human capacities are too naïvely optimistic in conception. Their widespread achievement in the complex world of Hellenistic despotism is unlikely, and if they should ever be attained, they would, in large measure, be owing to some freakish vagary of history.

The philosophies of detachment take two forms, which are frequently rather too sharply contrasted with one another in popular estimate and even in some scholarly appraisals. These two forms of thought may be described as the philosophies of *contentment* and of *self-respect,* the Epicurean and the Stoic schools of morality. The follower of Epicurus [1] frankly admits that as a human being he

---

[1] Epicurus (341-270 B.C.) was born on the island of Samos. He taught at Athens from 306 B.C.

pursues pleasure and that without pleasure of some sort his life would be empty. But he recognizes two dangers attendant upon this pursuit, which any philosophy of pleasure must consider. In the first place, many pleasures defeat themselves when enjoyment gives way to indulgence, and the aftermath of such pleasure is often painful. Furthermore, to be checked or thwarted in a pleasant or satisfying pursuit or to be deprived of an object in which we take pleasure can often make us regret bitterly our having known the enjoyments that are taken from us. To cultivate preferential tastes and interests is only to concern ourselves too deeply with contingencies over which we have little or no control. Never, in any case, should we allow ourselves to become so involved that we cannot face with acquiescence the loss of whatever has enthralled us. This seems to be the meaning of Aristippus' famous remark *"Habeo, non habeor"* —"I possess, but I am not possessed"—with which he is said to have characterized his relation to his mistress.[2]

The Epicurean ideal of detachment is not completely realized until the philosopher recognizes clearly that for the man who has wisely interpreted the place of human life in its world, the very absence of pain, of fear, and of anxiety becomes a positive pleasure. It is the purpose of philosophy to develop man's prudence and teach him to realize his practical evaluations, so that he may achieve this contentment. The quiet and noncompetitive pleasures of genuine friendship based upon common intellectual interests are recommended. Ambition of all sorts, especially political ambition, must be forsworn. Above all, if we are to reach the philosopher's goal, we must banish fear. Thus it is all-important that we be able to consider our future with equanimity. To assist us in attaining such self-possession, the Epicurean philosophers prepared and defended a number of maxims about which was centered a whole philosophy of life, including a cosmology borrowed from Democritus and a

---

[2] Aristippus of Cyrene (435?-?356 B.C.) was a member of the Socratic circle, famed throughout antiquity for his wit and for his extreme formulation of the pleasure philosophy. He is said to have frankly preferred physical to mental pleasure. He warned, however, that no pleasure should be allowed to dominate the desires of the individual. The philosophy of Epicurus is a much modified version of the Cyrenaic's code.

modified form of polytheism prepared for the purpose. This philosophy, which was presented as a virtual way of salvation, was finally summarized in the following quatrain: [3]

> There is nothing to fear from the gods;
> There is nothing to feel in death;
> The good lies within our grasp;
> And evil can always be borne.

The gods of Olympus are doubtless real enough, but their lives are too rich and their enjoyment of existence too comprehensive to make likely any serious concern on their part with the virtues or the shortcomings of relatively insignificant human beings. Certainly the gods will not stoop to reward or punish human beings. They will not even notice human existence. Thus we have nothing to fear from the gods, and our dread of divine punishment is nothing but a troublesome and superstitious fantasy.

There is no afterlife of any sort. Death involves the complete annihilation of consciousness. It is less even than a dreamless sleep. This is made inevitable as the Democritean atoms, composing the human frame, fall from one another at our body's death. Since life *is* the concourse of these atoms, at their dispersal all vital activity, including consciousness, vanishes. Thus, although "we" shall die, we shall never *experience* death. "Where *we* are death is not; where death is, we are not." If we can school ourselves to accept the analogy of dreamless sleep, death ceases to be a concern of ours. There is nothing to fear and nothing to anticipate.

The good that reasonable human beings pursue lies in this life or it lies nowhere—and there is in this life a real possibility of our achieving contentment, if only we are schooled in prudence and wisdom. To be sure, the world was never made for our happiness, and we may at any moment be stricken with disease or subjected to the caprices of fortune or of despotism. Suffering and disappointment must be accepted. But, in general, we may say that intense anguish is by its very nature short-lived and that long-enduring

---

[3] Diogenes of Oenoanda, a comparatively late Epicurean of the third century A.D., who carved these verses on a stone wall to symbolize their availability to all mankind.

pain is less intense and may, with fortitude, be borne. Life can be rendered tolerable if it is accepted in a reasonable spirit.

It is obvious that such a philosophy has nothing to do with the licentious pursuit of physical pleasure, so often identified with the Epicurean ideal. The Epicureans have often been thus slandered by critics who, despising human nature, feared the reaction they believed would follow upon man's release from superstitious inhibition. In this one respect—and it is an important one—the Epicurean remains an optimist. Like Socrates, whom he profoundly respects, the Epicurean has enough confidence in his fellow men and enough sympathy for them earnestly to desire their enlightenment.[4]

> 'Tis sweet, when, down the mighty main, the winds
> Roll up its waste of waters, from the land
> To watch another's labouring anguish far,
> Not that we joyously delight that man
> Should thus be smitten, but because 'tis sweet
> To mark what evils we ourselves be spared;
> 'Tis sweet, again, to view the mighty strife
> Of armies embattled yonder o'er the plains,
> Ourselves no sharers in the peril; but naught
> There is more goodly than to hold the high
> Serene plateaus, well fortressed by the wise,
> Whence thou may'st look below on other men
> And see them ev'rywhere wand'ring, all dispersed
> In their lone seeking for the road of life;
> Rivals in genius, or emulous in rank,
> Pressing through days and nights with hugest toil
> For summits of power and mastery of the world.
> O wretched minds of men! O blinded hearts!
> In how great perils, in what darks of life
> Are spent the human years, however brief!—
> O not to see that nature for herself
> Barks after nothing, save that pain keep off,
> Disjoined from the body, and that mind enjoy
> Delightsome feeling, far from care and fear!

[4] Lucretius. *On the Nature of Things,* trans. by William Ellery Leonard, pp. 45, 47. (Bk. II, lines 1-28, 54-62). (Everyman's Library) J. M. Dent & Sons, London; E. P. Dutton & Co., New York; 1921. Reprinted by permission of the publishers.

Titus Lucretius Carus (98-54 B.C.) presented the philosophy of Epicurus in Latin verse. His poem *De rerum natura* is one of the masterpieces of Latin literature.

Therefore we see that our corporeal life
Needs little, altogether, and only such
As takes the pain away, and can besides
Strew underneath some number of delights....
For just as children tremble and fear all
In the viewless dark, so even we at times
Dread in the light so many things that be
No whit more fearsome than what children feign,
Shuddering, will be upon them in the dark.
This terror then, this darkness of the mind,
Not sunrise with its flaring spokes of light,
Nor glittering arrows of morning can disperse,
But only nature's aspect and her law.

The Stoics demand no more of the world than the Epicureans, but their notion of contentment is a deeper one, requiring an active commitment or engagement in life and affairs. They do, it is true, cultivate a detachment, an emotional acquiescence or resignation, even, as they call it, an "apathy." But for the Stoic, the good man is not permitted to withdraw from the world. He is even committed to take part in public affairs if his abilities and opportunities make it seem reasonable to do so. In fact, Stoicism, despite its nonpolitical origin, has often appealed to the most thoughtful and conscientious administrators. The greatest of these include the Roman statesmen Cato, Cicero, and the Emperor Marcus Aurelius. These men, after all, were more clearly aware than any others of the insecurity of the Hellenistic world and of the inequities it contained.

The satisfaction that the Stoic seeks is the sense that, insofar as it has lain in his power, he has played out the role and has fulfilled the personal destiny that his reason has made manifest to him. It is not for him to complain that his efforts have been thwarted, that his achievements have been pulverized by circumstance or squandered by human folly. And if he is in some measure successful, he should not hope for recognition of his work. He must devote his best efforts in a spirit of disinterested sincerity to the tasks that seem most appropriate to his abilities and situation. The intelligence that apprehends the role "assigned" to each individual is, after all, but a spark from the central world wisdom, which, like the fiery *logos* of Heraclitus, guides from within the course of life and history. We cannot hope fully to understand the purposes of this cosmic intelligence. We see but a fragment of the whole sweeping strategy, and we often feel that it is without a central purpose or direction. For the Stoic, however, this doubt is interpreted as an act of presumption based on our failure to recognize the limits of our own knowledge and the finitude of our powers of thought. If we maintain an impartial detachment, we shall find that our own mental powers are sufficient to indicate where our duty lies. Our conduct is meritorious only insofar as it is motivated by a recognition of duty. The Stoic is a stern moralist and an astute critic of human motives, including his own. He is studious to avoid

> The last temptation...the greatest treason
> To do the right deed for the wrong reason.

The following passages are quoted from the *Meditations* of Marcus Aurelius.[5]

5. Every moment think steadily as a Roman and a man, to do what thou hast in hand with perfect and simple dignity, and feeling of affection, and freedom, and justice; and to give thyself relief from all other thoughts. And thou wilt give thyself relief, if thou doest every act of thy life as if it were the last, laying aside all carelessness and passionate aversion from the commands of reason, and hypocrisy, and self-love, and discontent with the portion which has been given to thee. Thou seest how few the things are, the which if a man lays hold of, he is able to live a life which flows in quiet, and is like the existence of the gods; for the gods on their part will require nothing more from him who observes these things.

*　　*　　*　　*

[5] Marcus Aurelius Antoninus, *Meditations*, Bk. II, 5, and Bk. X, 2-6, translated by George Long. George Bell & Sons, London, 1862. Marcus Aurelius Antoninus (121-180 A.D.), Roman emperor and Stoic philosopher. Marcus was an excellent administrator distinguished by a strong sense of what we would today call social responsibility. He was deeply beloved by his people, appearing in history as one of the most attractive examples of the "philosopher king." Like most Roman administrators of his age, he saw in Christianity nothing but a threat to the solidarity of the Empire and accordingly treated his few Christian subjects with an unfortunate severity that seems inconsistent with the humane wisdom of his life and writings.

2. Observe what thy nature requires, so far as thou art governed by nature only: then do it and accept it, if thy nature, so far as thou art a living being shall not be made worse by it. And next thou must observe what thy nature requires so far as thou art a living being. And all this thou mayst allow thyself, if thy nature, so far as thou art a rational animal, shall not be made worse by it. But the rational animal is consequently also a political [social] animal. Use these rules then and trouble thyself about nothing else.

3. Everything which happens either happens in such wise as thou art formed by nature to bear it, or as thou art not formed by nature to bear it. If then it happens to thee in such a way as thou art formed by nature to bear it, do not complain, but bear it as thou art formed by nature to bear it. But if it happens in such wise as thou art not formed by nature to bear it, do not complain, for it will perish after it has consumed thee. Remember however that thou art formed by nature to bear everything, with respect to which it depends on thy own opinion to make it endurable and tolerable, by thinking that it is either thy interest or thy duty to do this.

4. If a man is mistaken, instruct him kindly and show him his error. But if thou art not able, blame thyself, or blame not even thyself.

5. Whatever may happen to thee, it was prepared for thee from all eternity; and the implication of causes was from eternity spinning the thread of thy being, and of that which is incident to it.

6. Whether the universe is [a concourse of] atoms, or nature [is a system], let this first be established, that I am a part of the whole which is governed by nature; next, I am in a manner intimately related to the parts which are of the same kind with myself. For remembering this, inasmuch as I am a part, I shall be discontented with none of the things which are assigned to me out of the whole; for nothing is injurious to the part, if it is for the advantage of the whole. For the whole contains nothing which is not for its advantage; and all natures indeed have this common principle, but the nature of the universe has this principle besides, that it cannot be compelled even by any external cause to generate anything harmful to itself. By remembering, then, that I am a part of such a whole, I shall be content with everything that happens. And inasmuch as I am in a manner intimately related to the parts which are of the same kind with myself, I shall do nothing unsocial, but I shall rather direct myself to the things which are of the same kind

with myself, and I shall turn all my efforts to the common interest, and divert them from the contrary. Now if these things are done so, life must flow on happily, just as thou mayst observe that the life of a citizen is happy, who continues a course of action which is advantageous to his fellow-citizens, and is content with whatever the state may assign to him.

These two schools of morality found widespread acceptance among educated people and for some centuries characterized the more thoughtful spiritual life of the ancient world. Although their doctrines were sometimes twisted by professional apologists of the status quo, who deliberately compromised their ideals and confused their application to practical problems, the spirit of the two great philosophies remains clear enough in retrospect. The gentle, if somewhat aloof, cheerfulness of the Epicureans and the unconditional self-dedication of the Stoics, who faced failure and catastrophe with indifference or contempt, has fascinated the imagination of many centuries. Both schools have been frequently celebrated in literature, sometimes even by the same author, as in the works of the Roman poet Horace and the English A. E. Housman.

HELLENISTIC LOGIC

The hesitancy toward commitment or self-surrender of any sort typical of Hellenistic philosophy is reflected in the new developments of logic. In the Hellenistic age experience did not engender confidence in man's ability to understand or control the world around him. Hellenistic logic parallels Hellenistic ethics by emphasizing extreme caution and admonishing the student of nature to avoid overreaching himself. Scientific and philosophical ambition is seen to be as dangerous as its counterpart in the moral life. In all enterprises, the Hellenistic philosopher advocates restraint and detachment and warns the enthusiast to shorten sail. Thus in the development of Stoic logic one can see the intellectual confidence of Aristotle give way to a new, more skeptical timidity. It is reason that constitutes the real internal identity of man, and lends him its dignity; the external world, on the other hand, interferes with this internal harmony by constant shocks which produce the disturbing passions that mislead the mind, and which the sage has schooled himself to disregard.

But if our passions, which are internal interpretations of contact with outer objects, are contrary to reason, and must be disregarded, how far are the reports of the senses trustworthy? Sensation, too, is the registration of an impact; and just as we do not think the pain in a bumped shin is a property of the chair on which it was bumped, we may reasonably wonder whether the color of the rose exists in the rose itself, or only in the mental picture of it that sensation presents to our consciousness. Once the question has been raised, it cannot be answered, for obviously there is no way to observe what the rose would be like in the absence of any observer. A more accurate description of sensation therefore seemed to the Stoics to be one that avoided any commitment concerning the existence of objects corresponding to our perception of them, and simply treated perceptions as sequences of "presentations" in the mind. However, while we can doubt the truth of any given presentation, certain sequences force us to assent to their truth through the form of their connection. We may be entirely unsure as to whether our belief that it is raining is true; the senses are unreliable; perhaps we only think we feel the rain. But we cannot resist believing that "if it is raining, then it is raining"; the connection of these concepts creates a statement that is irresistible and indubitable for any rational being.

With this reorientation, the hypothetical argument becomes the central concern of Stoic logic. For an "if ... then" proposition avoids commitment about an external set of facts as to the real existence or natures of which we are unsure, but states relations of concepts in a form that is completely consistent and reasonable. Thus insofar as intelligible syntactical structures are common to reason and nature, we can know true propositions about the world as a whole; I am sure that if there are two apples in a basket, and I add two more, there will then be four apples in the basket. Experience however, never presents situations that permit the kind of absolute intellectual assurance which goes with the proposition that $2 + 2 = 4$.

Perhaps I overlooked an apple in the bottom of the basket when I started; perhaps someone has crept up and stolen one while I was putting them in. I can give no conclusive reason proving that no such interference has taken place. If, then, the rule of life is to be "follow reason," and reason accepts only those statements which from their form it is impossible to doubt, not much room is left for sense experience.

The Aristotelian demonstrative syllogism, which was thought to express the mind's grasp of certain invariant essences recognized through perception of changing concrete things, gives way to the more timid hypothetical syllogism in which no commitment is made as to the mind's ability to extract *reasonable* propositions from the inconsistent and inexact reports of sensation. The urge to withdraw from a hostile external world has led to a retreat into the recesses of pure reason, where it is even possible to doubt such a world's objective existence, and no room is left for experiment or experience in philosophy.

Epicurean Logic

The Epicurean development of logic reflects a temperament and an outlook that share the mistrustfulness of the Stoic. The Epicurean also beats a retreat but this retreat leads him toward commitment in the opposite intellectual direction. To the Epicurean, it seems that men often destroy their chance for happiness by an overactivity of speculative imagination; they think of hostile forces as lurking behind the scenes of nature, and imagine an unhappy immortality as being their destiny. Not only do they think these things as possible intellectual constructions, but they mistake them for actual fact, an illusion which causes them so much fear of death and of the gods that their lives become terror-ridden, perturbed, and painful. These extreme cases show very clearly that the constructions of human intelligence need not correspond to experienced fact, and that they often lead to practical results directly counter to man's own best interests. The mind has a tendency to create artificial fictions from the materials experience supplies, which go far beyond the evidence, and then to mistake these constructions for the real nature of fact.

What a logician needs, then, is a discipline in separating his belief in fact from his innate propensity to believe in fabrication. To this end, the Epicurean "canonic," which held the place of logic in their system, was developed as a corrective to human credulity. The objections raised by such intellectuals as the Stoics against the reliability of perception seemed to the Epicurean really to apply to the mind. It is not my senses which deceive me, but the judgments which I construct from the materials they provide, and the erroneous expectations to which those judgments lead. My expectation that the oar which looks bent under water will continue to look bent when I take it out is not based directly on perception, but represents an erroneous expectation created by my intellectual interpretation of the report of the senses.

To correct normal overcredulity, one must attribute existence in fact only to those things which can be perceived; that is, experimentally demonstrated. All theories about the nature of the world must be held meaningless unless one can confirm them by perceived experimental evidence; the fact that a certain concept carries "irresistible conviction" to the mind is no adequate test of its correspondence with reality. This position is diametrically opposed to that of the Stoic, who believes that since the logical structure of reasoning and the logical structure of fact correspond, there must be some divine mind responsible for nature. This inference, which the Stoic finds completely convincing, the Epicurean regards with profound mistrust and can easily resist.

All philosophical hypotheses must explain observed fact by processes and inferences of the sort we can verify experimentally in perception. Experimental evidence is not available to demonstrate the conclusions of the Stoic. Only direct perception can serve as a warrant for assertions about reality; only extensions of the processes we perceive about us can be entertained as plausible hypotheses about entities or regions that cannot be inspected directly.

Thus, in the logical theories of the Hellenistic period, the uncertainty and loss of confidence of the age as a whole and its representative philosophers have been projected into logic, by the Stoics as a doubt of anything of which we do not see the intellectual necessity, by the Epicureans as a doubt of everything of which we do not see the perceivable experimental evidence. For the Stoic, this changes the emphasis in logical form to an investigation of the rational structure of hypotheses; for the Epicurean, into a calculation of probabilities based on analogy with past experience.

The defense of each of these positions against the other, if one combines them, obviously constitutes the basis for a thoroughgoing skepticism, a type of philosophy that also flourished during this period. The Stoics, in the interest of their conviction that only the rational can be real, develop extensive arguments to establish the unreliability of unreasoning perception; the Epicureans, in their attempt to destroy morally undesirable beliefs in gods and immortality, develop equally extensive arguments to discredit the reliability of overcredulous reason. By adducing the absence of any experimental evidence for such Stoic beliefs as those in human dignity and divine providence, then by showing that there is a difference between appearance and reality that the Epicureans have left out of account, the skeptic can derive a picture of human fallibility in which complete suspension of judgment with absence of definite commitment seems the only reasonable attitude.

MYSTICISM

The Stoics and the Epicureans, despite their fundamental disagreement on certain points, are at one in that they cling to a philosophy that does not overstep what we might call the limits of common sense. Accordingly, their metaphysics seems at times overcautious and pedestrian, and they rarely tax severely the credulity of their supporters. At least the supernatural and the miraculous are pretty consistently avoided. We have seen that critics and scholars are often willing to describe the Stoics and the Epicureans as timidly seeking a consistent philosophy of escape. But we must not forget that they respect reason, and curb the flights of uncontrolled speculation, which a philosophy of escape so often affects.

At last the ancient world grew weary of its cautious and logical mentors. Uncontrolled imagination and speculative ingenuity came more and more to the fore. Roman skepticism and Greek clarity of thought gave way again and again to dreamlike speculation. Platonism joined hands with mythology and with prophecy. The Platonic myth, which in Plato's hands had been an excellent means of foreshadowing possible solutions of the darker problems that always lie along the frontier of philosophy, appeared in a less responsible and more fantastic form. Magic and miracle were once more considered philosophically respectable, and ancient mythologies were plundered, so that philosophy was burdened with the most doubtful products of Oriental "wisdom" and popular superstition. This tendency, which by the end of the second century A.D. was well under way, was a complex one, and by no means without a brighter side.

It is during this period that Christianity, already established, despite official disapproval, as a powerful religious movement, was seeking to work out a philosophical world view to supplement its faith. And there appeared—not only in Christian quarters—a thirst for spiritual life free of the rigid formalism and ritual of the moribund polytheism of Greece and Rome. In its early days, ancient philosophy had been an enemy of the established religion. In this earlier period ancient mythology had failed to satisfy the analytical curiosity of the philosophers, and conflict had resulted. Now, in a later time, philosophy sought a substitute for the religion that it had aided in displacing. The result was that in these later centuries philosophy grew more and more otherworldly and religious in character.

Belief in a mysterious and wonderful unseen world that is the home of the human soul, and which contains man's higher destiny, grew among all classes of people. Indeed, after the fall of the Greek city-state the natural world had less and less to offer the high-minded and reflective thinker. By the time the Roman Empire had degenerated into what we might nowadays call a military dictatorship, in which the dynasties grew more and more unstable, the "world" appeared not only to lack any spark of idealism but to be really little more than a den of avaricious and bloodthirsty ruffians. To be free from the savage ambitions, bitter disappointments, and unstable victories that participation in worldly life afforded became more and more the ideal of all "men of good will." At first, it was mostly the poor and the downtrodden who had sought the kingdom of heaven, but before long men and women of every degree, some of them fleeing from the heavy and stupefying luxury of an empty age, were seeking "salvation" and "rebirth." These concepts indeed are not entirely limited to Christianity, but also appear in some rival religions, for instance in Mithraism.

People sought spiritual peace and certainty. Many of them found it, and many failed because they made their new religion a ground of bitter contention and too subtle controversy, being unhappily as eager to dominate in the world of the spirit as their ancestors had been in the world of affairs. Spiritual life tended all too frequently to caricature itself in the most bitter theological and philosophical controversies, which seem at one time to have held the place that is today occupied by economic and political theorizing.

The ideal of the ancient sage had been understanding of nature. As the poet Lucretius wrote: *"Felix qui potuit rerum cognoscere causas"*—"Happy is he who knows the causes of things," and patterns his life in harmony with nature and its law. But that ideal had perished, and was not to be reborn in the heart of European man for many centuries; for the time being thoughtful people were convinced that the "kingdom is not of this world." The aim of eager inquiry was to penetrate the supernatural. Many of those who possessed a complete singleness of purpose forgot the world and sought the unseen. Mysticism flourished, and many people, both Christian and pagan, cultivated as never before the inner life of spiritual intuition.

The glory of the world of the spirit, where God is enthroned, was often termed ineffable or inexpressible, and the concepts of philosophy, even those of the Platonist, were held by many to be inadequate to describe the celestial mysteries. So we hear much of the "deep yet dazzling darkness" of the Godhead toward which the human spirit is drawn and where the restless questioning of the human intellect is finally silenced. On the other hand, those who could not even for a time completely forget the world tended nonetheless to believe that all life is subject to supernatural authority, the source of eternal reward and punishment. These people pursued a less-exalted ideal of salvation. They sought peace through virtue and an assurance of an afterlife free from the turmoil of earthly needs and desires, and they were willing to sacrifice much to achieve this end.

The new religious consciousness, whether Christian or pagan, turned away from Stoic pantheism and Epicurean materialism This, as we have mentioned, was not without its drawbacks. The Stoic and Epicurean philosophies, especially the latter, had offered a bulwark against superstition, a bulwark that neither Christianity nor later pagan philosophy was always able to maintain, so that in later times even the learned frequently sought the miraculous, the more obvious and spectacular manifestations of the supernatural.

The spiritual leaders of the age, men who it would be stupid to say were dominated by superstition, sought nothing less than a re-interpretation of the universe and of man's place in it. These thinkers were often guided or inspired by mystical insight as much as by logic, so that to understand their thought we must know something of the meaning and the content of mysticism. The mystic professes to have learned important truths concerning the nature of the universe and the destiny of the human soul not by inductive generalization or logical deduction, but by an immediate acquaintance or intuition.

Perhaps for most of us today the nearest approach to mysticism occurs in the enjoyment of beauty, when we assert confidently that a certain work of art is beautiful even though we are without a critical theory and a vocabulary with which to defend our lively certainty. But the mystic is not concerned with matters of taste: he seeks a vision of what philosophers call "ultimate truth." In the mystic consciousness or trance, as it is sometimes called, this truth is said to be revealed. Unhappily, translation of such insight into words is a difficult if not an impossible task, and the mystics themselves often warn us against their own most strenuous efforts to communicate a wisdom that surpasses understanding.

The object of mystical insight is reality itself. The mystic usually

recognizes this object as God, however inadequately he may be able
to describe what he has seen. To know God directly in an intuition
is for the mystic the highest goal and the highest happiness of
human life. The vision of God is an immediate revelation of beauty
and goodness as well as of truth, a standard of value as well as of
reality. It is also a revelation of power, the creative power upon
which the world depends for its existence. God, although the source
of all power, is himself steadfast and unmoved. The mystical experience may involve recognition of either one of these attributes.
Thus the English mystical poet William Wordsworth has described
both experiences most vividly: [6]

> [I] felt
> Incumbencies more awful, visitings
> Of the Upholder of the tranquil Soul,
> *Which underneath all passion lives secure*
> *A steadfast life.* But peace! it is enough
> To notice that I was ascending now
> To such community with highest truth....
>
> Our destiny, our nature, and our home
> Is with infinitude, and only there;
> With hope it is, hope that can never die,
> *Effort, and expectation, and desire,*
> *And something evermore about to be.*

To achieve the mystic consciousness, the human mind must free
itself from its usual absorbing interest and desires. As the German
mystic Jakob Boehme has put it, "He who can make his will stand
still shall see God." Such an attitude of the spirit may be brought
about in various ways. The bemused state of mind following an
intense aesthetic experience, and the relaxation after sustained intellectual concentration, are two of them. In either case the mind has
freed itself from all distraction by concentrated attention upon one
object or upon one problem. When this concentration is relin-
quished, there may be a moment when the "will stands still," before the world and its business once more claims the soul. If this

---

[6] Wordsworth, *The Prelude*, (1805 text) Bk. III, ll. 114 ff; Bk. VI, ll. 538 ff. Italics
added.

moment is prolonged, the mystical consciousness may assert itself. This consciousness may be induced voluntarily, and it is frequently the goal of monastic devotions. The concentration and detachment of prayer and religious meditation are often preludes to mysticism. Today mystical consciousness is very occasionally produced by the incomplete administration of an anesthetic. Here, if consciousness survives the deadening of all physical feeling and the temporary obliteration of all personal interests, a mystical state may supervene.

Mystics frequently, although by no means always, despise or fear the body and all worldly pursuits. One can well understand why. These things are likely to appear to the mystic primarily as sources of a distraction that renders the mystical consciousness impossible. Hence the suspicion of nature, and of the body, that is so deeply rooted in certain religious traditions. This attitude, strangely enough, may survive the mysticism that originally produced it.

Mysticism penetrated nearly all philosophical thought in the final centuries of Graeco-Roman life. Both pagan and Christian thinkers cultivated mystical insight, the pagan followers of Plato and the Christian Fathers of the Church. In the third century A.D. there arose a new school of mystical pagan thought, known to history as Neo-Platonism.

THE NEO-PLATONISTS

The Neo-Platonists relied upon mystical intuition for the solution of certain of the central problems of philosophy. Their thinking was a strange combination of rigorous rationalism and suprarational mysticism. In its later stages Neo-Platonism degenerated into a potpourri of occultism and superstition, but in its earlier and healthier state it had a contribution to make to the interpretation of Platonic idealism.

The Platonic universe is a system of levels. The form of the good, the true, and the beautiful occupies the highest level and is the apex of the system. Below this we find the lesser forms in their dialectical order. These lower forms are less general and "nearer" the concrete world than are the higher. Beneath the form stands the world of concrete particulars, and in turn beneath these lie matter and space. These lower entities are subject to change, while the forms are eternal or immutable. Mind, we recall, stands at the center of the system and is responsible for the exemplification of form and order in the flux of material or spatial existence.

Through the centuries Platonists have sought to describe just how the eternal order is related to the temporal order, how form and flux are present together. This is the problem to which Plato devotes his attention in the dialogue *Parmenides*. As the student will recall, he there tells us how *not* to consider this relation. We are left with the feeling that the relation is sui generis; that is, not to be compared with other relations of which we have experience. Most emphatic is Plato's insistence that the relation of form to particular is not a spatial one, and furthermore that the forms are not to be identified with thoughts in any mind, divine or human. However, we are told that mind is able to bring about a union of form and flux. But the precise manner of this union has never been explained to the full satisfaction of all Platonists.

Here the Neo-Platonist turns his back on logic and appeals to intuition, although he warns us not to desert intelligence until it has yielded us all that it can give. Plotinus [7] describes the relation of form to the world in figurative and imaginative language, this being the only way by which such intuition can be communicated. The great principle so apprehended is this: The simple produces the complex, not by an assemblage or piecing together of parts, but by an incomprehensible expansion or overflow of the simple being into a complexity of a lower order. Strangely, this overflow in no way exhausts its simple source, which is always capable of further production and remains quite unaltered. So a teacher in "giving"

[7] Plotinus (204-269 A.D.) first studied philosophy at Alexandria under Ammonius Saccas, who was also the teacher of the Christian theologian Origen. He was deeply interested in Oriental philosophy and religion, and in the hope of learning something of them he joined the ill-starred campaign of the Emperor Gordian against the Persians. Upon Gordian's death and the failure of the campaign, Plotinus journeyed to Rome, where he enjoyed great success as a teacher, counting the new Emperor Gallienus and the Empress Salonnica among his disciples. Plotinus was a brilliant lecturer, but a careless and reluctant author. Hence his writings, even as edited by his faithful disciple Porphyry, are often obscure.

an idea to his students does not himself lose it or lessen its clarity in his own mind. So the god of mysticism is a source of power and of change, but himself quite steadfast and unmoved.

The forms are produced by the simple One, or the good (Plotinus sometimes calls the One, "God"), and the forms produce nature, or the soul of the world, which in turn produces the finite creatures with whom we are acquainted. So the simplicity of the eternal descends to become the complexity of the temporal. The world was not created once and for all. It flows forever from the ultimate and incomprehensible simplicity of the One. This simplicity is by nature creative. So all goodness is creative or constructive, and evil, the privation or absence of goodness, is sterile or even actively destructive.

We cannot hope to explain or analyze this act of *emanation* whereby the complex flows from the simple. Nor can we describe it by framing a speculative hypothesis. Plotinus insists that the thinker who has purified his vision beholds this ultimate mystery directly and without passing through the steps of an argument. As Emerson [7a] would put it "the highest truth on this subject remains unsaid ... for all that we say is the far-off remembering of the intuition." One cannot criticize Plotinus on this point, although those who possess the power of mystical contemplation may test his wisdom in terms of their own vision. But even those who, like the present author, lack the gift of illumination cannot fail to be impressed, at times even overwhelmed, by the splendor and sincerity of Plotinus' thought.

If we cannot wholly explain, we can at any rate vaguely picture or imagine, Plotinus' principle. And this will be of value if only in that it aids us to remember what Plotinus has to say. A great modern philosopher has described the Neo-Platonist's world picture as follows. Henri Bergson writes: [8]

[7a] "Self-reliance," par. 21.

[8] Henri Bergson, *Creative Evolution,* trans. by Arthur Mitchell, pp. 320-21. Henry Holt & Co., New York, 1911. This and a later quotation are reprinted by permission of the publisher.

If immutability is more than becoming, form is more than change, and it is by a veritable fall that the logical system of Ideas [Platonic forms], rationally subordinated and coördinated among themselves, is scattered into a physical series of objects and events accidentally placed one after another. The generative idea of a poem is developed in thousands of imaginations which are materialized in phrases that spread themselves out in words. [This represents *emanation*.] And the more we descend from the motionless idea, wound on itself, to the words that unwind it, the more room is left for contingency and choice. Other metaphors, expressed by other words, might have arisen; an image is called up by an image, a word by a word. All these words run now one after another, seeking in vain, by themselves, to give back the simplicity of the generative idea. Our ear only hears the words: it therefore perceives only accidents. [Thus the farther we descend in the scale of being, the less orderly, the less "logical," the world appears. Pure form gives way to chance. Since for Plotinus, as for Plato, order is an embodiment of value, the farther we descend in the scale of being, the less perfect the world appears]. But our mind, by successive bounds, leaps from the words to the images, from the images to the original idea, and so gets back, from the perception of words—accidents called up by accidents—to the conception of the Idea [Platonic form] that posits its own being. So the philosopher proceeds, confronted with the universe. Experience makes to pass before his eyes phenomena which run, they also, one behind another in an accidental order determined by circumstances of time and place. This physical order— a degeneration of the logical order—is nothing else but the fall of the logical into space and time. But the philosopher, ascending again from the percept to the concept, sees condensed into the logical all the positive reality that the physical possesses. His intellect, doing away with the materiality that lessens being, grasps being itself in the immutable system of Ideas [forms]. [This represents the opposite of emanation, what Plotinus called *ecstasy,* the return of the soul toward the simple eternity whence it sprang. The goal of ecstasy is the intuition of the One itself.] Thus Science [the vision of the forms] is obtained, which appears to us, complete and ready-made, as soon as we put back our intellect into its true place, correcting the deviation that separated it from the intelligible. Science is not, then, a human construction. It is prior to our intellect, independent of it, veritably the generator of Things.

This "ready-made" science—that is, truth which is, so to speak, "waiting for us"—being in no wise created by us, appears in Plotinus' writings as the intelligence that apprehends all the forms in one great system, somewhat as an ideally gifted mathematician might survey all the theorems of a system of geometry complete with their corollaries and their interwoven implications. Since Plotinus declines to consider the forms as distinct from the intelligence that apprehends them,[9] we may speak of the forms as together constituting an ideal science. This science is an eternal intellect, superior to our intelligence, which is intermittent and mixed with much consciousness that is not purely intellectual in nature. Science, or Truth—that is, intellect including the forms—comprises the first stage of emanation from the One. Without the One, or at least without the energy received from the One, nothing could exist. So Emerson interprets Plotinus in his essay "Self-Reliance."[10]

This is the ultimate fact which we so quickly reach on this, as on every topic, the resolution of all into the ever-blessed One. Self-existence is the attribute of the Supreme Cause, and it constitutes the measure of good by the degree in which it enters into all lower forms. All things real are so by so much virtue as they contain. Commerce, husbandry, hunting, whaling, war, eloquence, personal weight, are somewhat, and engage my respect as examples of its presence and impure action. I see the same law working in nature for conservation and growth. Power is in nature the essential measure of right. Nature suffers nothing to remain in her kingdoms which cannot help itself. The genesis and maturation of a planet, its poise and orbit, the bended tree recovering itself from the strong wind, the vital resources of every animal and vegetable, are demonstrations of the self-sufficing, and therefore self-relying soul.

The following passages, which present Plotinus' doctrine concerning the One, are selected from his *Enneads*.[11]

[9] If Plotinus put intelligence and thought below the forms as emanating from them, he would have to admit that no intelligence can apprehend the forms as they really are, since that which emanates from form must be less perfect than form, and this would be to desert Platonism entirely.

[10] Paragraph 23.

[11] Plotinus, *Enneads*, Bk. VI, 9, trans. by Thomas Taylor. London, 1817.

On the Good, or the One

All beings are beings through the One, both such as are primarily beings, and such as in any respect whatever are said to be classed in the order of beings. For what would they be, if they were not one? For if deprived of unity, they are no longer that which they were said to be. For neither would an army, or a choir, exist (as such), unless each of them was one. Nor would a herd exist, if it were not one. But neither would a house or a ship have an existence, unless they possess the One; since a house is one thing, and also a ship, which one if they lose, the house will no longer be a house, nor the ship a ship. Continued magnitudes, therefore, unless the One is present with them, will not have an existence. Hence, when they are divided, so far as they lose the One, they change their existence. The bodies, also, of plants and animals, each of which is one, if they fly from the One, in consequence of being broken into multitude, lose the essence which they before possessed, no longer being that which they were, but becoming instead of it other things, and continuing to be these so long as they are one. Health, likewise, then has a subsistence, when the body is congregated into one (i.e., when it possesses symmetry), and beauty then flourishes when the nature of the One confines the parts of the body.... For of the things which are denominated one, each is in such a manner one as is the being which it possesses. So that things which are in a less degree beings, possess in a less degree the One; but those that have more of entity have also more of the One. Moreover, soul being different from the One, possesses more of it in proportion as it is more truly soul, yet is not the One itself. For soul is one, and in a certain respect the One which it possesses is an accident. And these are two things, soul and one, in the same manner as body and one. That indeed which is discrete multitude, as a choir, is more remote from the One, but that which is continuous is nearer to it. But soul which has more alliance with, participates more abundantly of the One. If, however, because soul cannot exist unless it is one, it should be said that soul and the One are the same, we reply in the first place, that other things also are what they are in conjunction with being one, but at the same time the One is different from them. For body and one are not the same; but body participates of the One. In the next place, each soul is a multitude, though it does not consist of parts. For there are many powers in it, viz., those of reasoning, appetition, and apprehension, which are connected by unity as by a bond. Soul, therefore, being itself one imparts the

One, to other things. But she also suffers (i.e. participates) this one from something else.

Shall we say, therefore, that in each of the things which subsist according to a part, the essence of it and the One are not the same? In true being indeed, and true essence, essence, being, and the One, are the same. So that he who discovers being in these, will also discover the One, and will find that essence itself is the One itself. Thus, for instance, if essence is intellect, the One also is here intellect, viz., an intellect which is primarily being, and primarily one. And when it imparts existence to other things, thus, and so far as it imparts this, it also imparts the One. For what else besides intellect and being, can the One of these be said to be? For either the One is the same with being, as a man is the same thing as one man; or it is as a certain number of each thing, as when you speak of a certain two. And thus the One is asserted of a certain thing alone. If, therefore, number pertains to beings, it is evident that the One also pertains to them: and what it is must be investigated. But if the One is nothing more than the energy of the soul attempting to number, the One will have no existence in things themselves. Reason however has said, that whatever loses the One, loses entirely at the same time its existence....

In order to perceive the One, it is necessary to receive from intellect a declaration of what intellect is able to accomplish. Intellect, however, is able to see either things prior to itself, or things pertaining to itself, or things effected by itself. And the things indeed contained in itself, are pure; but those prior to itself are still purer and more simple; or rather this must be asserted of that which is prior to it. Hence, that which is prior to it, is not intellect, but something more excellent. For intellect is a certain one among the number of beings; but the One is not a certain one, but is prior to every thing. Nor is it being; for being has, as it were, the form of the One. But the One is formless, and is even without intelligible form. For the nature of the One being generative of all things, is not any one of them. Neither, therefore, is it a certain thing, nor a quality, nor a quantity, nor intellect, nor soul, nor that which is moved, nor again that which stands still. Nor is it in place, or in time; but is by itself uniform, or rather without form, being prior to all form, to motion and to permanency. For these subsist about being which also cause it to be multitudinous. Why, however, if it is not moved, does it not stand still? Because it is necessary that one or both of these should subsist about being. And that which stands still, stands still through permanency, and is not the same with it. Hence permanency is accidental to it, and it no longer remains simple. For when we say that the One is the cause of all things, we do not predicate anything as an accident to it, but rather as something which happens to us, because we possess something from it, the One in the meantime subsisting in itself. It is necessary, however, when speaking accurately of the One, neither to call it that nor this. But we running as it were externally round it, are desirous of explaining the manner in which we are affected by it. And at one time, indeed, we draw near to it, but at another time fall from it, by our doubts about it.

Plotinus considered himself primarily as a student and an expositor of the works of Plato. But in his own writings he tends, more or less consciously, to alter Platonic doctrine on a number of points. The inseparable union of form and intellect mentioned above is one of these. His theory of matter is another. For Plotinus, matter is not a raw material in which the forms are exemplified or embodied. There is nothing, so to speak, waiting for the emanation of the forms. Matter is rather closer to Aristotle's pure potentiality than to the material world of Plato's *Timaeus*. It is the product of emanation, not a medium which emanation employs. It is the fact of diversity, of otherness, opposed to productive simplicity. Each stage of emanation involves the appearance of matter. Thus there is a material aspect even of the forms themselves. The One is alone free of anything material, being in itself pure simplicity. Perhaps matter is but a way of looking at the emanation of the One. If we consider not the simplicity of the One, but the fact that it tends always to overflow into complexity, we are compelled to fashion some notion of matter.

There is one further point of significant difference between Plato and Plotinus. Plotinus, true to a tendency of his age, is far more impressed with the personality of the individual than was Plato. Thus each individual human being possesses a Platonic form of his own. He is not a mere reflection of manhood, but possesses a unique pattern of his own in which manhood is an ingredient. Thus there is a form of Socrates as well as of man or of philosopher. Concrete individuality has become an object of interest. This interest Neo-Platonism and Christianity share in common.

The later Neo-Platonists delighted in finding symbols or reflections of the One and of emanation throughout all nature, in literature, and even in the study of mathematics. It was thought to be the function of the philosopher to reveal these many images or reflections of the great truth. The works of Homer were treated as philosophical allegory, and the figures of geometry were seen to yield spiritual analogies. Accordingly the circle was held to be [12]

the one perfect figure, the very symbol of the totality of the spritual world; which, like it, is invisible, except at its circumference, where it is limited by the dead, gross phenomena of sensuous matter. And even as the circle takes its origin from one centre, itself unseen—a point, as Euclid defines it, whereof neither parts nor magnitude can be predicated,—does not the world of spirits revolve round one abysmal being unseen and undefinable,—in itself ... nothing, for it is conceivable only by the negation of all properties, even those of reason, virtue, force; and yet, like the centre of the circle, the cause of all other existences?

[12] Charles Kingsley, *Hypatia,* Chap. XV, p. 217. The Macmillan Company, New York, 13th ed., 1885.

⇥⇥ CHAPTER VII ⇤⇤

Christianity and Its Influence
upon Philosophical Thought
in the Middle Ages

After the time of Plotinus and his brilliant pupil Porphyry many
of the greater intellects were Christians; and after the conversion of
the Emperor Constantine in 324, Christian philosophy and theology
became the great intellectual concern of the period. There were a
few who felt that Christianity could stand without any intellectual
support. Christian truth is revealed truth, and if we believe what
God has made evident in the inspired writing of the Old and New
Testaments, we shall have no need of philosophy. But this attitude
could not entirely satisfy a civilization whose intellectual leaders had
for centuries pored over the wisdom of Plato and Aristotle. Certainly revealed truth, although revealed directly and not requiring
the accord of reason, cannot be in itself unreasonable. Reason is a
gift of God, not so precious, to be sure, as the way of life revealed
in the person of Jesus, but still far from being despicable. It is true
that toward the end of the second century Tertullian,[1] intellectually
a convinced materialist, but spiritually an ardent Christian, had explained *"Credo, quia impossibile"!*—"I believe because it is impossible (or absurd)." The point being that if Christianity were not
logically absurd I should not need faith, but should possess some
rational knowledge of its truth. Tertullian seems to have thought of
faith as a kind of direct intuition. In this he must have been some-

---

[1] Tertullian (160-220 A.D.) a Carthaginian lawyer, was converted to Christianity
during his early manhood. He devoted his brilliant intellect, trained in the subtleties
of Roman law, to the defense of his new faith.

thing of a mystic. But his attitude came finally to seem perverse, and in the long run faith tended to seek the support of reason.

REASON AND FAITH

For centuries, however, the precise relation between faith and reason has remained a matter of considerable dispute. We shall mention three typical answers to this delicate problem.

The first is that of St. Augustine, who, as we shall see, dominated Christian philosophy throughout the early Middle Ages.[2] For Augustine, Christian philosophy is produced when "faith seeks understanding." He attempts to evaluate fairly both faith and reason when he writes, "I believe that I may understand, and I understand that I may believe." This statement is easily misinterpreted. Augustine does not mean that understanding takes the tenets of faith for granted and then deduces doctrine from them, although this is often supposed to be his meaning. Professor Gilson interprets as follows:[3]

What he asks himself is simply this: whether, among those propositions which by faith he believes to be true, there are not a certain number which reason may know to be true. In so far as the believer bases his affirmations on the intimate conviction gained from faith he remains purely and simply a believer, he has not yet entered the gates of philosophy; but when amongst his beliefs he finds some that are capable of becoming objects of science then he becomes a philosopher, and if it is to the Christian faith that he owes this new philosophical insight, he becomes a Christian philosopher.

Thus faith may be said to guide reason toward important fields of investigation, and reason in turn may be said to strengthen and

[2] St. Augustine (354-430 A.D.), after his conversion to the Catholic faith, was made Bishop of Hippo in northern Africa. In his earlier beliefs, Augustine had inclined toward the Manichaeism of Faustus, according to which, as in the religion of the ancient Persians, the world is subject to two principles, one good, the other evil.

[3] Etienne Gilson, *The Spirit of Medieval Philosophy*, p. 36. Sheed & Ward, London; Charles Scribner's Sons, New York; 1936. Reprinted by permission of the publishers.

enrich faith by showing the rational ground of some, if not of all, the revealed truths. Augustine attempts to prove the existence of God without recourse to scriptural authority. But it is most important to notice that Augustine and his followers derive their philosophical problems from the content of Christian faith. Augustine himself insisted, "I am interested in God and in the human soul, *and in nothing else.*" The true Augustinian has little or no interest in nature or the "world," considered apart from deity.

The second or rationalist answer is to be found in the writings of Scotus Erigena [4] and in those of Peter Abelard.[5] These men tend to consider revelation as inadequate until it has been accepted by reason and thoroughly established on philosophical grounds. Only the ignorant will accept doctrine on faith and not seek to establish it rationally. Thus Erigena holds that in the end there can be no distinction between philosophy and religion. "True philosophy is the true religion, and true religion is the true philosophy." This doctrine had been known centuries earlier to the Christians of Alexandria. But it terrified Erigena's contemporaries, who considered his ideas either "insane or blasphemous."

Abelard held the same position, but was perhaps more ready to advance to extremes than Erigena. He was willing to say explicitly that we cannot believe what we do not find intelligible. We accept revelation only because we find it reasonable. Since revelation purports to disclose truth, it must be intelligible. We might interpret Abelard by saying that for him an uncomprehended revelation is

[4] Johannes Scotus Erigena (c. 810-c. 880) was an Irish scholar and philosopher, who was brought to Paris to teach in the famous School of the Palace founded by Charlemagne. He was well acquainted with Greek thought at a time when very few western Europeans could read Greek. Accordingly he has by some historians been described as the last of the ancient philosophers. Although a devout Christian, he was impatient of ecclesiastical restrictions upon philosophy, and his writings were often much too bold for their day. They were condemned by the Church.

[5] Peter Abelard (1079-1142) was a most brilliant and popular lecturer on philosophy and theology in Paris. His life constituted a tragic effort to break through the rigid dogmatism of the established religion of his day. His works were condemned and publicly burned. Abelard's name is also famous in connection with his ill-starred love affair, which is preserved in the correspondence that passed between him and his wife Héloïse.

as futile as an uncomprehended demonstration in geometry. He writes as follows concerning his treatise on the Trinity: [6]

They (my students) were calling for human and philosophical arguments and insisting upon something intelligible, rather than mere words, saying that there has been more than enough of talk which the mind could not follow; that it was impossible to believe what was not understood in the first place; and that it was ridiculous for anyone to set forth to others what neither he nor they could rationally conceive.

For Abelard, then, reason seems ready to criticize faith. He paid dearly for his opinions. He was haled before two Church Councils, and his works were condemned and burned.

The student must not forget that these medieval rationalists, independent as they seem in attitude, never doubted that the basic essentials of Christianity could stand the test of rational examination. They sometimes seemed, indeed, more convinced of the truth of their religion than more cautious thinkers who found it necessary or expedient to keep faith and reason asunder.

The third answer was developed during the great period of medieval philosophy, when European thought was as robust and as acute as it has ever been. It is the answer of St. Thomas Aquinas,[7] the great systematizer of medieval Christian doctrine. His position is as follows: We may rest assured that revelation and rational truth will never conflict. There cannot, in the very nature of things, be two conflicting truths, one of faith and the other of reason. (This suggestion had actually been made by certain desperate medieval thinkers who accepted the works of Aristotle as embodying rational truth and the Bible as setting forth the truths of faith.) Some of the tenets that we accept on faith can be established also by reason. The exist-

[6] Abelard, *Historia Calamitatum,* quoted in H. O. Taylor, *The Medieval Mind,* V. I, p. 328. Harvard University Press, Cambridge, 1949. Reprinted by permission of the publisher.

[7] St. Thomas Aquinas (1225?-1274), greatest of Catholic philosophers and theologians, was born of an aristocratic Italian family. His relatives attempted unsuccessfully to keep him from entering the monastic order of the Dominicans. Aquinas studied and taught philosophy in Cologne, in Paris, and in Italy. By the time of the Council of Trent, in the sixteenth century, his writings had become recognized as the dominant philosophy of Catholicism.

ence of God is one of these. The immortality of the soul is another. Such truths are of so tremendous an importance to the welfare of the human soul that God has seen fit to reveal them, even though man is capable in his profoundest researches of discovering them for himself. There are, however, other truths of faith that man could never have discovered unaided. Thus man could never have shown by pure reason that God created the world out of nothing, nor could he have discovered the way of salvation that Jesus teaches. He need not assert that these latter truths are unintelligible or unreasonable in themselves, but rather that man possesses neither the evidence nor the mental power to arrive at them unaided.

The position of Aquinas may be considered a healthy one in that it assures the rational investigator, the philosopher or the scientist, that he need not fear to pursue his independent studies. Nothing he can firmly establish can possibly be counter to true religion. Some historians have thought that this attitude of Aquinas has helped to free European thought from the fear of undermining religion and so has helped to make possible the independent pursuit of natural science. Certainly Aquinas says nothing to discourage purely secular and rational inquiry. In this respect he is perhaps more liberal than Augustine.

In the later Middle Ages, after the time of Aquinas, there arose a tendency on the part of philosophers and theologians to separate faith from reason more sharply than before, and philosophy hesitated to accept rational proofs of many religious teachings that had been advanced by such men as Augustine and Aquinas. But at this time, medieval thought, at least insofar as it is to be considered as an interpretation of Christianity, was declining. And many clerical writers feared to trust the philosophical argument, which they suspected might at any time get out of hand and turn against the religion it had once seemed to serve.

THE THEORY OF GOD AS SUPREME BEING

Before the fall of Rome and the collapse of ancient civilization in western Europe, Christian philosophy had developed along Platonic lines. The great thinkers of the Greek and Latin churches, whose work may be said to culminate in the writings of Augustine, had reworked the concepts of Plato and Plotinus and produced a Christian Platonism. There is much subtle and closely reasoned thinking, valuable for its rigor and profundity, that we must omit here. We shall notice only the broadest outline of this philosophy, treating only those doctrines which are quite indispensable for an understanding of modern thought.

The personal God of Christianity is described as the Supreme Being. He occupies the highest position in a metaphysical scheme like that of Plotinus, and he is also the object of the mystic's contemplation. God alone possesses full and perfect reality. Of God alone can we say without reservation "He *is*," for the soul of man and the very world he inhabits are not wholly real. According to one interpretation of the Biblical text, which however some modern scholars hesitate to accept, the words I AM THAT I AM, with which God revealed himself to Moses (*Exodus* 3:14) indicate that God possesses being in a way that his creatures do not. No creature has the right to say "I am that I am." This is because creaturely beings are not self-contained; they depend for their existence upon other things. Thus a man depends upon his ancestry for his existence, and also upon an environment from which he must draw his sustenance. Isolate a human being from his world and he would be nothing at all. Without an environment he could never exist. God is not so limited. He is what he is without dependence upon other things. God does not depend upon the world, nor would he be essentially other than he is had he created no world.

According to the teaching of the *Shepherd of Hermas,* one of the earliest of Christian writings, God must be conceived as wholly independent or unconditioned.[8]

First of all believe that God is one, 'who made all things and perfected them, and made all things to be out of that which was not,'

---

[8] *Shepherd of Hermas,* Mandate I, from *The Apostolic Fathers,* trans. by Kirsopp Lake, Vol. II, p. 71. (Loeb Classical Library), 1919. Reprinted by permission of the Harvard University Press. We have substituted "conditions" for "contains" and "unconditioned" for "uncontained" (*achoretos*).

and conditions all things, and is himself alone unconditioned. Believe then in him, and fear him, and in your fear be continent.

Furthermore, we are assured in Scripture that God does not change. He is subject to no Heraclitean flux. On the other hand, *we* are always changing in some respect, and our world changes continually. What being we possess now we have not always possessed, nor will it always be ours. We are limited and conditioned by an unalterable past and an unknown future. But God dwells in an eternal present. This is what is meant by the fullness or perfection of his Being. He is limited neither by past nor by future: he *is* what he is. To put it more technically, after the manner of such thinkers as Thomas Aquinas, God's *essence* is identical with his *existence*. God exists *a se,* since he depends on nothing beyond himself. In contrast, human beings and all created substances or individuals exist *per se;* that is, they possess genuine concrete existence but they *receive* it from without. Qualities and attributes of these created substances exist *through* the substances and so do not exist even *per se.* To summarize: God possesses, or is, necessary being; created things enjoy only a dependent or contingent being.

This is Platonism transformed. The reader will recall that for Plato pure being, or the form, the object of understanding and reason, is eternal: it neither comes to be nor does it pass away. But all exemplification or embodiments of this form that exist in an actual concrete world are steeped in the flux of constant change. Now according to Christian Platonism, God is truly eternal, like the Platonic form, but unlike the form, he possesses actual concrete existence as well as intelligible subsistence, and unlike the form, he can speak out in the first person. He is the one ultimate condition of both intelligibility or order and of existence.

The God of Aristotle determines the *order* of nature. He is the final cause of all development. But he has not created or given existence to the world that he influences. Much the same thing may be said of the demiurge in Plato's *Timaeus.* The Christian God, on the other hand, is not only the source of order, he is the *creator* of the world. Thus we say that God has created the world *out of nothing,* in order to indicate that in this act of creation he is in no way limited. He is an artist who creates his own medium of expression. This conception of God is magnificently expressed in the following passages from the *Confessions* of St. Augustine: [9]

Behold heaven and earth have a being, and they cry out that they were made; for they do change and vary. Whereas whatsoever hath not been made, and yet is, hath nothing in it now that was not before; and this is to be changed and to vary. They also cry out that they did not make themselves; but they say, "For this reason we are, because we are made; we were not therefore, before we were made, that so we might give a being to ourselves." Now this voice of them that speak, is the evidence of the thing itself. Thou therefore, O Lord, who art beautiful, didst make them, for they are beautiful; who art good, for they are good; who Art, for they also are; yet are they neither so beautiful, so good, nor are they in such wise as thou, their Creator, art; in comparison with whom they are neither beautiful, nor good, *nor are they at all.* These things we know, thanks be to thee; yet this knowledge of ours, in comparison with thine, is but mere ignorance....

For out of the fulness of thy goodness doth thy creature subsist, that the good, which could in nothing profit thee, nor was of thee in such wise as to be equal to thee, might yet not be wanting, since it could be made of thee. For what could that heaven and earth, which thou madest in the beginning, merit at thy hands? Let those spiritual and corporeal natures, which thou didst make in thy Wisdom, say how they deserved of thee, that so everything that was but begun and formless might in its several kind depend upon thy Wisdom; whether it were spiritual or corporeal, ready to fall away into an immoderate kind of flux and an extreme dissimilitude of thee—the spiritual, though without form, superior to the corporeal, though formed; and the corporeal, though not formed, yet better than if it were a mere nothing—and might so depend upon thy Word, they being formless; unless by the same Word they were brought back to thy Unity, and so were formed, and made to be very good, by thee the only sovereign Good? Nay, how could they deserve at thy hands to be so much as without form, seeing they could not be even this, except of thee?

[9] St. Augustine, *Confessions,* Mathews trans., rev. by Dom Roger Hudleston, pp. 297, 364. Burns, Oates & Washbourne, London, 1923. Reprinted by permission of the publisher.

This idea of creation, difficult as it is to conceive, is of capital importance, since it establishes the primary relation between God and the world, and between God and man. Many philosophies founded upon the concept of a supreme or unconditioned being describe this being as "containing" as parts of itself all lesser entities as an organism contains and conditions its organs. For them, the Supreme Being is the universe, the total environment upon which any finite or limited entity depends for its existence. This results in pantheism. According to this doctrine, God contains all finite beings. The human soul is then an idea, or a grouping of ideas, in God's mind. According to more orthodox doctrine, the soul is a creature, distinct from its creator although dependent upon him. Thus Christian philosophy commits itself to what is often called *spiritual pluralism*. Each creaturely soul possesses a proper individuality, if not an independence, of its own. Thus, as we shall see, the decisions and deeds of a human being are said to be his own and not God's, although the human being is dependent upon God for his very existence.

GOD AND THE PLATONIC FORMS

The Supreme Being of Christian philosophy is thought of as an infinite mind possessing will and intellect, although we are warned that the human soul stands so far below the divine in the scale of being that it is most dangerous to argue from the one to the other when we seek to describe God. The eternal word or wisdom or intellect of God appears often in Augustinian philosophy. It constitutes a reinterpretation of Plato's theory of the forms, not unlike that offered by Plotinus. Augustine thinks of the form as constituting truth. Like the Neo-Platonists, he cannot separate truth from mind. For him, form is inseparable from idea or concept. Thus God's wisdom, which constitutes the form, is the final standard of intellectual truth. In our most rigorous thinking we are attempting to make our idea correspond with this perfect wisdom.

Once we identify Plato's form with idea or concept, it is indeed very difficult for us to doubt the existence of an all-knowing God corresponding to Augustine's conception. Plato has shown that without the forms there can be no genuine knowledge, but only opinion. Thus if we believe in genuine knowledge, as the Augustinian most emphatically does, we must believe in the forms. But we cannot think of the forms except as truths; that is, as true ideas in the wisdom or intelligence of God. Thus to believe that genuine knowledge is possible is to believe in the existence of God. Augustine repeats this argument again and again in various forms. But the ultimate propriety of his identifying the Platonic form with mental act or state is at least open to question. If Augustine is right, mathematics has to do only with the concept of the circle, with the idea of triangle—with God's idea, of course, but with idea nonetheless.[10]

By such argument Augustine has attempted to put God above the Platonic forms that his wisdom contains. Plato himself recognized a cosmic mind that treats the forms as objects, but not as its own ideas. Thus the cosmic mind or demiurge described by Plato is not the Supreme Being upon whose existence all else depends. We shall see that this step of Augustine's, whereby Platonism is recast, is to have an enormous effect upon the history of philosophy.[11]

THE PROBLEM OF FREE WILL

This exaltation of deity to the highest point in the scheme of things has difficult consequences. If God as Supreme Being upon whose creative will all else depends is the all-knowing author of the

[10] Let us briefly examine this notion of Augustine's. If "idea" or "concept" means anything, it means a mental act or state referring to an object. Thus the mathematicians' idea of circle refers to an object, the Platonic form of circle. Now Augustine has equated the Platonic form with God's idea. But if God's idea is a genuine one, it too must refer to some object, an object distinct from God's idea. Unhappily Augustine makes no allowance for this, and he cannot do so, for God's wisdom is, according to him, final truth, beyond which there is no appeal. But if the Platonic form cannot refer beyond itself, why call it an idea at all? Why not recognize that it is an extramental object?

[11] The reader should note that Augustine, although he puts God above the forms in the scale of being, does not consider the forms as creatures. The forms are coeternal with deity itself, constituting the logos or wisdom of God. The relation of this wisdom to God himself is one of the problems faced by the theolgian in formulating the doctrine of the Holy Trinity.

world, what freedom or responsibility is left for his creatures? The ultimate decision upon which all events, both physical and mental, must depend would seem to lie exclusively with God. Nonetheless theologians and philosophers alike have been reluctant to accept such a conclusion. Although *dependent* upon the Creator, from whom he receives his existence, the creature is conceived as *distinct* from God. Thus creaturely decisions and conduct are not God's decisions, and God cannot be held in any way responsible for them.

We are told that God is not responsible for the sins of man, or indeed for earthly evil in any form. Evil is always a limitation, a dilution of being or full perfection. It is essentially negative in character and hence not the direct product of a supreme or perfect will. This conception is difficult enough to grasp, but it is rendered even more puzzling by the theory of divine providence, according to which the divine understanding is fully aware not only of the hierarchy of Platonic forms but also of the created world and all that it contains. God is fully aware of the embodiment or exemplification of the forms in our lives. He sees or foresees these lives as a whole and in detail. He does not have to "wait for" future consequences. They are all envisaged, along with their conditions. For God nothing is unknown, not even the future. Perfect knowledge need not wait upon circumstance; it foresees all circumstance and its outcome. Thus God sees the sins that his creatures will commit, and these are present to his vision when he creates. Still, all moral fault is said to lie with the creature. And this is true even though the creature receives his whole existence from the Creator who foresees the sin. Thus we face the paradox that perfection produces moral imperfection, being fully aware of what it does. Or if we view the situation from the human standpoint, we must say that our actions are morally our own, for which we merit reward or punishment, even though he who made us what we are foresaw clearly what our actions would be from the very first.

Virtually without exception, medieval philosophers held that the Supreme Being must possess unlimited knowledge, and this is thought to require providence, which includes all the events of universal history, even the detailed lives and thoughts of each individual creature. But on the other hand, God must possess infinite goodness and justice. This of course requires that he be free of any moral responsibility for the sins of his creatures. Orthodox theology has attempted to escape this cruel dilemma by insisting that God's foresight or time-transcending vision does not render him the author of his creatures' sins. Just so those students of history who were able to foresee the World War of 1914-18 were in no way responsible for it.

But the skeptic might reply, "These students of whom you speak had not created the forces they studied." Nonetheless theology, both medieval and modern, has been either unbelievably subtle or unusually stubborn on this point, and theologians have rarely retreated from this very difficult position.[12]

In all fairness to the theologians, we must recognize that for most of them, including especially Augustine and Erigena, our understanding of God is recognized as very incomplete. No creature can fully comprehend the Supreme Being, whose essence surpasses both the experience and the concepts of the finite mind. Thus there must always be something dark and incomplete in theological speculation, a residue of mystery that can never be expelled.

---

[12] The Jesuit theologians of early modern times attempted to exempt God from all responsibility for man's sins by formulating the subtle and ingenious doctrine of *scientia media,* or God's knowledge of possible or contingent events, many of which as mere possibilities never actually take place. God sees clearly what *would* be the outcome of any complex of circumstance that he might choose to decree. Thus he knows, quite aside from his decree establishing any set of actual conditions, how any given creature would choose to act in face of any given set of circumstances. In this knowledge the creature is considered as free, in the sense that he is thought of as following his own nature, not compelled by external force. Now when God decrees a chain of circumstances and the creature chooses, he acts as God foresaw that he would act if, so to speak, he were left to himself in the face of the circumstances. Thus God's infallible prevision is maintained, but God is not responsible for the creature's choice. It is not God's choice but one that God foresaw that under certain conditions the creature would make of his own nature. This argument is an admirable logical edifice, but the fact still remains that according to our theologians the creature owes his existence and his nature wholly to the God who both creates and foresees. God, fully aware of what he does, creates a human nature liable to sin and knows in detail how this weakness may manifest itself. He then supplies the conditions of this manifestation. But the creature must bear the punishment.

THE DISPUTE CONCERNING UNIVERSALS

It should be clear that despite Augustine's transformation of the theory of forms, this type of Christian philosophy is wholly committed to the Platonic thesis that genuine knowledge penetrates beyond concrete particulars and is aware of sheer form, however the nature of this form may be interpreted. Repudiate this central doctrine of Platonism and you tear the very heart from Augustinian philosophy. Thus for many centuries Christian thinkers stood guard over Platonism, defending it zealously against all comers. To defend Platonism was to defend the faith. And when the opponents of Platonism began, as they did in the twelfth century, to make headway, it seemed to many that Antichrist himself was at hand. It is small wonder then that later Augustinians were inclined to exaggerate the claims of Platonism. In this way they brought about the famous dispute concerning universals.

The Platonic form is frequently described as a *universal*. Broadly speaking, a universal is something that can be exemplified in many concrete situations which are discontinuous and remote one from another. The universal is not itself limited to any one situation: "manhood" is not limited to Tom, Dick, or Harry, nor are the possibilities of human nature exhausted in any one of them. Impressed as they were by a study of grammar, the medieval Schoolmen often spoke of the universals in Aristotelian terms as *predicables;* that is, something that may be predicated of things. As Abelard put it, the universal is that which by its very nature is predicable of a number of things. A concrete thing can never be a predicate, but can only appear properly as a subject. (Thus even when we say "Great is the temple," "temple" remains the subject or concrete substantival term, whereas "great" is the predicate or universal. On the other hand, in "That building is a temple," "temple" is a predicate and hence a universal.)

A thorough knowledge of Platonism introduces the form or universal as the indispensable object of genuine knowledge that is opposed to opinion, and in this way presents an excellent background for the discussion of the question "What is the universal?" But unhappily many students of Plato have failed to find Platonic teaching wholly unequivocal on this point. Even Porphyry, the disciple of Plotinus, himself steeped in Platonic and Neo-Platonic studies, considers the question too abstruse to be included in his work on logic. Porphyry writes in the last sentences of his introduction to *Aristotle's Categories:* [13]

Now, concerning genera and species [that is, more general and less general universals, such as *animal,* more general, and *dog,* less general].

(1) Whether they are independent of the knowing mind or mere products of that mind; and if independent of the mind,

(2) Whether they are corporeal or incorporeal, and if incorporeal,

(3) Whether they exist apart from sensible things or whether they are in and of sensible things—

All this I will decline to say, for this problem is a lofty business, unsuited to an elementary work.

Medieval thinkers tended to work from this formulation of the problem presented to them in a Latin translation of Porphyry's work. The genuine Platonist is ready to answer Porphyry's first two questions without hesitation. Universals are independent of the knowing mind, since we recognize or come upon forms that we do not arbitrarily create. The Pythagorean theorem is not created at the fiat of a mathematician. And again the forms are incorporeal, for, unlike bodies, they are not subject to change and dissolution. Finally, the true Platonist is ready to say that the universal is exemplified or reflected in the world of becoming; but if he remembers his *Parmenides,* he will not want to say that the universal is to be found in sensible things, for that is to suggest that the relation is a spatial one, and he well knows that the universal is not "inside" the particular or, like the sailcloth of Parmenides, "above" it. The relation of form to becoming is sui generis: it cannot be described in terms derived from other fields of inquiry, say from geometry or the study of the properties of spatial relations.

Had the earlier medieval thinkers kept all this in mind, they would have saved themselves a great deal of confusion. But under

---

[13] Paraphrased by the author.

the circumstances they can hardly be held at fault. After the prolonged disorders that had attended the disintegration of the Roman Empire, they possessed only three dialogues of Plato, the *Timaeus,* the *Phaedo,* and the *Meno,* and these in Latin translation. Had they possessed the *Parmenides* and the *Philebus,* they would have been more clearly aware of the difficulties that threatened them. But as it was, speculation once more outran analysis, and the result was an intellectual bedlam, which has never been wholly quieted. Medieval Platonism tended at times almost to parody or caricature the theory of forms, and some of the followers of Augustine outdid Plato in their eagerness to make the universal or the form the most prominent object in the universe. Their view is known as *extreme realism.*[14] According to this theory, universals are the only true realities. Particulars are literally reduced to universals. William of Champeaux (died 1121) tended to see in the particular *nothing* but an accident or a property of the universal. And for Erigena, the particular is simply the intersection of several universals. Thinghood or individuality, the concept that had so preoccupied Aristotle, was virtually lost from view. So the universal usurped the status and the dignity of the concrete thing. This amounts to a confusion of first principles that Plato would never have tolerated—a confusion, furthermore, the consequences of which are apt to involve the theologian in most embarrassing difficulties.

As we have already noted, Christian doctrine is committed to a defense of the reality of the individual soul. This individual soul must also be considered to be of infinite or absolute importance and value. Thus any theory that reduces the individual human being to an intersection of universal patterns or types will in the long run prove distasteful to Christian thinkers. Furthermore, since the universals are often conceived as ideas in God's intellect, the human soul, along with all other concrete entities, seems on the point of being reduced to a fragment of God's being—and that of course amounts to pantheism.

---

[14] This use of the word "realism" must not be confused with the modern use, common in both literature and philosophy. This latter use has nothing to do with the problem of universals.

In the discussion of the status of universals, the nature of the knowing process assumed a new importance. It seemed clear to the Augustinian realists that sense experience produces mental images, which serve in Platonic fashion to "remind" the soul of the real world of forms when these images are illuminated by the light of grace coming from God. The concepts in our minds represent various possible combinations of forms; some of these possible combinations God has chosen to make actual in the Creation; and it is through our understanding of God's choice that we are able to identify some of our mental images as representing actual, concrete (as opposed to abstract, possible) things. God thus provides the mediation between our subjective concepts and the events in the natural order that those concepts represent.

"Knowledge" results from our being reminded by experience of the eternal forms that happen, by their intersection, to define an individual object or fact. On this view, while the subjective moment of illumination can never be expressed in language, the parts and devices of language, standing for forms and their various relations, are an adequate mirror of the concepts in the mind. Thus such a realist is led to insist that the parts of language correspond to distinctions in the nature of things, since they reflect the sets of forms that are combined in the creation. Both the word and the concept are conventional signs, which take on meaning only through illumination. Hence to doubt that universal words refer to real entities seems almost the same as doubting whether the concepts which those words express refer to a real world or are only an illusion. And this, in turn, is to doubt the perfection of God.

The Arab commentators on Aristotle, many of whose commentaries were translated and studied along with Aristotle's text, managed to press this analysis of knowledge to the theologically unwelcome conclusion that it is *only* the mind of God that thinks, men from time to time sharing in and catching glimpses of the divine thought. This conclusion is theologically unwelcome because (1) it breaks the distinction between Creator and creature to allow men to participate in God's thought, and (2) it destroys the notion of personal free will and moral responsibility that underlies the theological doctrines of salvation, the last judgment, and personal immortality.

There are several alternatives to *extreme realism*. One is known as *moderate realism*. This is virtually the position of Aristotle, according to which the forms or universals do not enjoy any reality distinct from concrete particulars or from human or divine thinking. This position does not involve the serious theological difficulties we have just noted, and it is really closer to Plato than is the extreme realism of Erigena and William of Champeaux. In the end, this view was combined with an Augustinian Platonism according to the great compromise drafted by Aquinas and his teacher Albert the Great.[15] This compromise runs as follows: We recognize that Platonism is true insofar as we must admit that God's intelligence contains exemplars or patterns that his will brings to creation. These exemplars have their being quite independent of the creaturely world. They may be described as *universalia ante rem,* or universals as they exist without reference to the created world.

But at this point Aquinas breaks with the Augustinian tradition. The universals that we, as creatures, are capable of apprehending are not the divine exemplars themselves but something much more humble in the scale of being, although nevertheless dependent upon them. The universals we apprehend are *universalia post rem,* forms that are to be apprehended only by the aid of the sensuous experience of concrete objects. We may also think of the forms as constituting the structure or embodied pattern of the created world. These may be called *universalia in re.*

Since he is pure intelligence, God apprehends the exemplars directly. But we as creaturely beings, dependent for our knowledge upon sensibility as well as upon intelligence, apprehend only *universalia post rem.* We may come to know them only by abstracting the common qualities or similarities from the particular, sensible things with which we become acquainted. *Universalia post rem* must never be confused with the divine exemplars, which are in no

---

[15] Albert the Great (Albertus Magnus; 1193-1280), a Dominican monk, and for a time Bishop of Ratisbon. His greatest work was the editing of the writings of Aristotle. Albert and Aquinas were together at Paris and Cologne from 1245 to 1252.

way subject to the conditions of a created world or of creaturely understanding. *Universalia post rem* are, we might say, the nearest that the human mind can come to the pure form that God envisages directly. We live and pursue understanding in the twilight of a created world. By insisting that the universals open to our minds and resident in natural objects are not identical with the exemplars in God's intelligence, Aquinas protects religion from the menace of the pantheism that had threatened the extreme realists. By insisting that the forms are, insofar as they are exemplified in creation, fundamentally or primarily in the world and formally or secondarily in the human mind, Aquinas teaches that the mind can acquire true knowledge only by recognizing observation of nature as an indispensable starting point.

Aquinas was careful in preparing his theory of moderate realism to describe individuals, particularly individual human beings, as containing in their make-up elements other than embodied universals. In this way he distinguished a concrete individual from a mere intersection of universals, even of exemplified or embodied universals. These other elements are material. They are constituted by Aristotelian matter, which is subject to quantity or measurement. The idiosyncrasies of the individual, the marks of its unique and exclusive particularity, are owing neither to the forms nor to any combination of the forms, but to the presence in the constitution of the individual of Aristotelian matter and quantitative order (size, weight, and so on). The presence of matter distinguishes the individual very sharply from any mere combination of divine exemplars, and so helps to avoid pantheism.

This compromise is an excellent example of what Henry Osborn Taylor has called Aquinas's "all-balancing and all-considering" method. Theories are drawn from Plato, Aristotle, and Augustine, and these are woven together into a system consistent with the requirements of Christian teaching. This procedure has made Aquinas the official philosopher of Catholicism. His theories constitute today the rational system through which Catholic faith is rendered consistent with a comprehensive interpretation of the universe.

The remaining alternatives to extreme realism are as heavily laden with unorthodox possibilities as are the works of Scotus Erigena himself. These alternatives involve the denial of Realism. They are known as *Nominalism* and *Conceptualism;* on these theories universals are considered either as mere names or words, or again as concepts proper only to the mind. According to these theories the real is the individual and the concrete. Universals are instruments of the mind whereby we may speak intelligently of many individuals, considered, so to speak, en masse, as when we assert the proposition: All men are mortal. Statements that employ these instruments are true, as far as they go, even of individuals taken singly, but they indicate only what we might call the distant *outline* of the individual. Only direct observation and sensuous experience can bring the individual before us in its full reality. Accordingly, knowledge of universals does not carry the mind upward in the scale of being. Observation captures more reality than does dialectic.

In the fourteenth century, despite the great formulation of Christian doctrine already accomplished by Aquinas, these antirealistic theories were widespread. They corresponded with a reawakening interest in nature at this time and with some of the first attempts since ancient times to formulate anew the principles of mechanics, the theory of weight, and the general principle governing the motion of bodies.

The medieval Aristotelian philosophers who were least influenced by the Arab interpreters of Aristotle mentioned above accepted the view that the concept may be a direct, habitual recognition by the mind of the nature of some actual thing, present in experience. Consequently language, which is only a set of conventional symbols standing for these immediate and indivisible acts of mind, is neither an adequate means for representing the real nature of thought, nor yet that of things. The greater confidence in the mind's direct grasp of actual objects, characteristic of this tradition, is reflected in a greater sense of the weakness of language, and indeed of symbolism in general as a key to nature. "Universal" terms refer to habitual indivisible acts of recognition by the human mind, not to forms or exemplars in the mind of God.

Because of the divergent theories of knowledge in the background, one must use some care in evaluating discussions of medieval "Nominalism" and "Realism." The Aristotelian "Nominalist" is not at all the skeptic some historians would make him out; in fact, his distrust of language may come from a more dogmatic confidence in the adequacy of unaided human reason than that which his realistic Augustinian opponent shares.

Perhaps the most famous of the fourteenth-century antirealists is William of Occam.[16] He is not so extreme in his theories as his twelfth-century predecessor Roscellinus, but his formulation of the great principle of antirealist method, known as *Occam's razor,* has become a byword among cautious and skeptical students of science and philosophy. The principle reads as follows: *Entities must not be multiplied beyond necessity.* It may be interpreted to mean that in scientific or philosophical investigation we must never admit the existence of any entities lying beyond actual observation, unless these are absolutely indispensable in explaining the situation that we encounter in the world of concrete particulars. Always accept, in other words, the simplest explanation that introduces the smallest number of unknown or unperceived causes. It is clear that reference to demons, angels, even to rational belief in God, can easily be rendered questionable upon such a principle. For what particular concrete situations are to be explained *only* by reference to such entities? Occam was a devout Christian and a good churchman, but he accepted such doctrines as the existence of God and the immortality of the soul purely on faith. Occam's razor is sometimes called the principle of parsimony, by which the theorist is admonished to be very stingy with his concepts, and to take nothing for granted. This principle is probably more popular today than ever before.

A little reflection will show that a principle like Occam's razor is likely to be formulated only in an atmosphere of extremely antirealistic thought. Here philosophy is invited, so to speak, to begin

---

[16] William of Occam (1300-1349), an English thinker educated at Oxford, was a follower of Duns Scotus (1270?-1308), and accordingly inclined to suspect many of the principles of Thomism. Occam's theory of knowledge in many ways approximates the theories of John Locke, the seventeenth-century leader of English Empiricism.

at the bottom rather than at the top of our world. If we take this hint, we shall not begin our philosophizing with a concept like that of the Supreme Being, which after all cannot be termed absolutely indispensable from a logical point of view. But we shall begin with the observable features of our own natural environment. In observing this environment, we must be satisfied at first with what we can sense directly. Hence universals will appear only as schemes of thought whereby we characterize the more common features of the things we observe. Thus we observe that horses have four legs, and then formulate the universal "quadruped" as a class that includes the horse and many other species of animal. We seem to be working up from particulars. Individual horses are real things. "Quadruped" is only a word, a term, or a concept. The case against realism can be made very impressive in this way. But before coming even to a tentative conclusion, the reader should consider once more the Platonic argument that leads to a recognition of the forms as genuine objects of thought, without which we are unable to distinguish clearly between knowledge and opinion. Antirealistic teaching is likely to slur over this important distinction.

ARGUMENTS FOR THE EXISTENCE OF GOD

Antirealistic philosophy is not characteristic of the intellectual enterprise of the Middle Ages, which was after all founded on an attempt to unite Christian faith with the philosophy of Greek idealism. There are, then, two types of thought that belong properly to the philosophical enterprise of the Middle Ages. The first is the Augustinian, which dominated from the day of Augustine himself to about the time of the Norman Conquest of England, when the tradition was weakened by the excessive zeal of the extreme realists. The second is the Aristotelian, a tradition firmly established after the crusades, when Aristotle's writings were brought to western Europe in Latin translation. (The first of these translations were made, strangely enough, not from the Greek but from the Arabic, the Saracens having preserved the works of Aristotle, translated them, and commented upon them at a time when Christendom was too disorganized to maintain the scholarship necessary for such an undertaking, even had the manuscripts been available.) The tone of Arabian philosophy caused much concern to the philosophers of western Europe, who feared its tendency toward open and avowed pantheism. At one time the works of Aristotle were condemned because they were thought to contain the origins of this pantheism.

The characteristics of the two types of medieval thought, the Augustinian and the Aristotelian, are clearly reflected in the arguments they offer for the existence of God. The Augustinian begins by describing the human soul and searching in human consciousness for evidences of God. Thus, as we have already seen, an argument is developed that leads from our respect for knowledge and truth to the existence of God. For the Augustinian, the consciousness of the individual is the great treasure house whence we may draw knowledge of God and his universe, to supplement our faith in revelation. Augustine was himself a very skillful introspectionist. Only writers like Pascal, Amiel, or Wordsworth are comparable to him in this respect. It is significant that his most famous work, the *Confessions,* which contains in its later portions a summary of his philosophy, is written in autobiographical form. In all this the Augustinian is closer to the Protestant and to the modern Romanticist than is the Thomist, the follower of Thomas Aquinas. The Thomist favors an Aristotelian approach. Accordingly he does not emphasize the inner life of the individual to such a degree, but follows Aristotle in trying to establish the existence of God as a necessary condition of the presence of motion, growth, and development in the world about us.

There are two outstanding arguments that belong properly to the Augustinian tradition. The first is Augustine's own proof derived from the nature of truth itself. This we have already examined (see above, page 211). The second was formulated by St. Anselm, who is sometimes called the "second Augustine." [17] It is called the

[17] St. Anselm (1033-1109) ended his career as Archbishop of Canterbury. He is distinguished not only for his work in pure philosophy, but also for his interpretation of the Christian world drama, which he describes in his interesting and picturesque work on the Incarnation, *Cur Deus homo.* Anselm was a zealous defender of the prerogatives of the Church against the expansion of secular power.

ontological argument, which signifies that its reasoning has to do with the theory of being—in this case with the Supreme Being, for God is described throughout in terms of the latter concept. Anselm undertakes to show that no one can intelligently deny the existence of God without falling into contradiction. When we deny the existence of God, we do not clearly know what we are talking about. We are using words, not framing concepts. "The fool hath said in his heart, There is no God" (Psalm 14), and Anselm undertakes to show the fool that he is closer to a proof of God's existence than he thinks. This is in accordance with the Augustinian procedure, which probes even the consciousness of doubt for evidence of God's existence.

The Ontological Argument

God is identified with the Supreme Being, which Anselm terms "a being than which nothing greater can be conceived." Now even he who denies the existence of God understands the meaning of this expression. There may be some room for doubt here, but certainly a medieval Augustinian would understand what is meant— namely, the concept of the Supreme Being that has been derived through a fusion of Platonism with the Scriptures. This being than which nothing greater can be conceived is the Supreme Being, who depends upon nothing beyond himself in order to exist. If this being than which nothing greater can be conceived can be thought of as dependent upon anything beyond itself, then we are in a position to form another concept of a being not so dependent, and this would be a concept of a "greater" being. Therefore we must think of our greatest being as the Supreme Being. The question then presents itself, "Does this being exist as independent of, or at least not produced by, our understanding?"

Anselm answers in the affirmative. Let us suppose that this being exists *only* in our understanding. Then surely anyone may think of a greater being; namely, one that exists *both* in our understanding *and* in reality. But here we face a contradiction. According to our supposition, the being than which nothing greater can be conceived exists only in the understanding, and recognition of this fact leads us to recognize an even *greater* being. But to recognize—that is, of course, to conceive of—a being greater than the being than which nothing greater can be conceived is quite absurd. Hence we must abandon our presupposition that the Supreme Being exists only in the understanding. Therefore the Supreme Being exists in reality.

Anselm concludes with pious enthusiasm, "and this Being thou art, O Lord, our God." And perhaps in this last phrase he reveals the incomplete nature of his proof. Insofar as the ontological argument is concerned, Anselm certainly has not established that this greatest being is by nature comparable to the God of the Scriptures, the merciful and just God of the Christian revelation. Of course, we may argue that God reveals himself in the Scriptures as Supreme Being. Certainly Anselm accepted this interpretation of the I AM THAT I AM. But for Anselm, as for any Augustinian, philosophy is "faith seeking understanding." A proof that does not involve reference to any scriptural authority, even on what may seem to be a very minor point, is to be preferred. Anselm undertakes to provide such proof in the sequel, but with only a somewhat questionable success. He insists that the Supreme Being must be lacking in nothing and must possess all those attributes which it is better to possess than not to possess.

This amounts to the assertion that the Supreme Being is the standard of all value as well as of reality, but Anselm never explores this notion as thoroughly as it deserves. He does say enough, however, to indicate an important train of thought. One who does not admit, he writes, that a horse is more perfect than a stick of wood, or a man than a horse, hardly himself deserves the name of man, of *Homo sapiens*. This is not the sort of argument that we usually look for in philosophy, but Anselm's drift can be detected even so. Man stands higher in the scale of being than a horse or a stick of wood, because he is more independent. By this we do not mean that man has fewer needs than a horse, for the contrary is probably true. What we do mean is that man is more autonomous, he can determine his life more completely than the horse can. He can control his own future more fully. So a good man is a better creature than a good horse. God, the one fully independent being, is accordingly the best of all beings. He possesses not only the fullest reality but the highest value or goodness. From this Anselm passes confidently to the assertion that God is just, compassionate, and merciful in the highest degree. This can be maintained, however, only if we establish that justice, sympathy, and mercy are virtues high in the scale of independence. And this last, at least in the mind of a conscientious skeptic, may remain a matter of argument.

But there is another and more serious criticism of Anselm's reasoning. This was pointed out in his own lifetime by the monk Gaunilon of Marmoutier near Tours, with whom Anselm carried on a courteous controversy. Gaunilon supposed that the fool who presumes to deny the existence of God and who professes an inability to understand the Augustinian tradition, replies to Anselm's argument somewhat as follows: "I grant that there exists in my understanding some idea of a Supreme or Perfect Being than whom nothing greater can be conceived, but this idea is very incomplete and can afford no factual details. I can honestly give you no information concerning this being, for I have no *acquaintance* with it. I possess at most its mere name or definition. And I am unable to identify any real things as corresponding to this conception of mine. Under these circumstances, I cannot say that the Supreme Being clearly exists or resides even in my mind. Certainly, it exists therein no more truly than the idea of a perfect island than which no more delightful dwelling place can be conceived. And still on this argument on one would believe in the existence of such an island. From such an idea, which is wholly divorced from experience, no reality can be inferred."

Anselm replied that mention of the island is wholly irrelevant. An island is not an independent or a supreme being, it is not something that even in thought may be made to appear as greater or more perfect than all other entities. On the other hand, our idea of the Supreme Being is our idea of supreme worth or goodness itself, and resides clearly in the faith and conscience of Gaunilon as well as of Anselm. The fact that we have never experienced the presence of this Supreme Being as indubitably as we experience the presence of a concrete object in our environment Anselm passes over. He has much more confidence in the power and the validity of the sheer concept than has Gaunilon. And here, after all, lies the crux of the argument, which neither thinker has thoroughly exhibited. The point at issue is fundamentally this: Can we trust in sheer reason that transcends or goes beyond the possibility of all verification by what we call experience? Anselm says Yes, Gaunilon says No. We shall come upon this problem later when we study the philosophy of Immanuel Kant, who makes this topic the very center of his thinking.

The Cosmological Argument

The Aristotelian tradition, headed by Albert the Great and Thomas Aquinas, repudiates the ontological argument. Only angelic intelligence or mind freed from dependence upon sense organs and the material conditions of an earthly environment could know that God exists simply by examining the *idea* of God that it possesses. The human soul is not a pure intelligence, but a rational being requiring sensation and experience as well as pure logic to guide its researches. Accordingly, Albert and Aquinas tend to argue from observable phenomena. They single out as their starting point the presence of motion, change, or development in the world, and try to show that the indisputable facts connected with these imply the existence of God. They pass, however, almost at once beyond the realm of sensible phenomena into the Aristotelian theory of potentiality and actuality, and their proof is not very different from that whereby Aristotle claimed to have established the existence of the unmoved mover. The argument turns upon Aristotle's conception of all process as a passage from potentiality to actuality.

All motion or change involves a potentiality that is realized and rendered actual. Such motion can be initiated only by something actual. Thus only an *actually* hot stove will boil water—that is, initiate the process whereby water, as potential steam is rendered into actual steam. Nor could the water boil of itself. Nothing can be at once mover and moved. This point is crucial. Entities in motion are hereby recognized as being dependent upon causes for the very reason that they are in motion. In other words, we are asked to repudiate the hypothesis that motion is a fundamental state or condition of the universe requiring no explanation. Even today there are many who would accept this hypothesis and assume that everything in motion is moved by something else.

Our argument begins now to indicate its conclusion. If everything in motion is moved by something else, this something else must either be unmoved or in turn be moved by yet another, and this in turn must be unmoved or be moved by another being, and so on. But we must not allow ourselves to play with the idea of an infinite regress of moving agents, for that would involve a contradiction. There would be no first mover and therefore no movers at all, because the second mover imparts movement only because the first mover sets it in motion, and so on.[18] Therefore we must expect a first or unmoved mover, and this we identify with God. An unmoved mover is a Supreme Being, since the fact that it exists unmoved indicates that it exists wholly independent of any environment.

This argument is today called cosmological, as distinct from Anselm's ontological argument. This is to indicate that it does not deal directly with the nature of being but with the way in which beings influence one another. Aquinas goes beyond Aristotle, since he thinks of God not only as final cause of the world, which he is, but also as efficient cause or Creator. The reader will remember that for Aristotle, God is the final cause of the continuity of natural process. For Aquinas, God is also the ultimate agent who initiates all motion by his creation of the world. That this creation of the world takes place in time, or better, that the world has had a temporal beginning, is a truth that we can know only by revelation. Philosophy cannot show that the world is not coeternal with God,

---

[18] The reader should examine this step in the argument very carefully. That the second mover depends upon the first mover is true only if it is granted that *there is* a first mover; that is, if there is no infinite regress. If there is an infinite regress, there is no point in numbering the movers at all, and hence there is no second mover. How can we use a proposition dependent, as it is, upon the denial of an infinite regress to show that this very denial is sound? Do we not thereby assume what we are trying to prove?

who would then *continually* create or support the world's existence, instead of giving it existence at the beginning of time.[19]

The Teleological Argument

There is still another argument, the most popular of all, which has flourished in medieval as well as in modern times. This is the *teleological argument*, sometimes called the *argument from design* and sometimes the *argument from the government of the world*. Consider, for instance, living organisms whose members must be nicely adapted one to another so that they can function together and in harmony. This co-ordination is teleological, means being ordered for the sake of ends; that is, man's hands, feet, eyes, ears, and so on being designed to fulfill specific functions. To say that this order and arrangement of parts have come to pass by accident is to admit the existence of an effect without a cause.[20] Aquinas insists that in such a case things which of their own nature are opposed and disparate are brought into co-ordination by an influence external to themselves. Life itself is an influence descending upon the nonliving and bringing with it an order and a discipline of which the nonliving shows no sign if left to itself. This influence may be called divine, since it seems to come from above the world and is imposed upon elements from without.

We shall see that this argument, in one form or another, is to stand for many centuries as the most popular and impressive attempt to establish God's existence. It is not seriously challenged until the eighteenth century, and is in no quarter wholly discredited until the middle of the nineteenth. This train of thought is committed to a stubborn defense of teleology, the doctrine that nature is subject to purposive control, or that a tendency toward ends or

[19] The above sketch of Aquinas's reasoning oversimplifies his complex and closely wrought argument to a very considerable degree. The reader who is willing to cope with very compact and therefore difficult reasoning may consult Gilson: *The Philosophy of St. Thomas Aquinas*, 2d ed. rev. and enl., Chaps. III-V (W. Heffer & Sons, London, 1929), where all Aquinas's arguments for the existence of God are stated in full.

[20] This statement should be examined carefully. How do we know that this order *is an effect?* Besides, some people are willing to say that man sees because he has eyes rather than that he has eyes in order to see.

goals has been instilled into the goings-on of nature. Now it is easy to catch a glimpse of teleology let us say, in the great teeth and claws of a beast of prey, in the powerful hind legs of a rabbit, or the protective coloration of a frog. But the thought of the Middle Ages goes much further. The natural elements, earth, water, air, and fire, have each its proper place, one above the other, and they tend to seek these places, somewhat as a plant seeks light, fire rises, earth falls. This is Aristotle's doctrine, and the medieval Schoolmen find it much to their liking, as it satisfies their feeling that nature is through and through the embodiment of purpose rather than of chance.

Aristotle of course had thought of this tendency toward ends as an eternal or uncreated aspect of nature. To the medieval mind, it was the product of a creative wisdom, one of the many lines of evidence that manifest the glory of God. Hence the Democritean philosophy of chance and necessity appeared as only a shallow and stupid interpretation of the world, seeming indeed almost blasphemous. A source of conflict lay in the fact that even in the later Middle Ages thinkers were already beginning to study the motion of bodies from a mechanical point of view. This actually occurred in the great center of Christian theology, the University of Paris. This work was, however, often ignored, and had to be repeated two centuries later.

CHAPTER VIII

The Beginnings of Modern Philosophy

TRANSITION

Between William of Occam and Descartes—that is, between distinctly medieval and distinctly modern philosophy—lies a period of nearly three hundred years. It would be stupid to call this a gap in the history of philosophy. There has been only one real gap in the history of European thought, and that lies between the time of the fall of Rome and Charlemagne's School of the Palace, from Boëthius to Scotus Erigena. This was not so much a break in philosophical thought as a virtual suppression of civilization. After Occam's time no such breakdown occurred. But the age was not suitable for the production of important systems of thought, although many attempts in that direction were made. The age was one of marked transition. And in such an age, one cannot produce a broad interpretation of things that will possess lasting value. One cannot synthesize new ideas until the ideas themselves have become purified and afford the philosopher fairly definite material with which to work. And in the meantime philosophy must mark time.

The problem of the Middle Ages had been to adjust the great principles of Greek idealism to Christian doctrine. The problem of modern philosophy was to be the adjustment of Greek thought, including, however, its materialist and mechanist side, along with medieval Christian thought, to the world view offered the European mind by the development of modern science. This latter development was very slow in getting under way. A new interest in nature and a new way of observing nature were necessary. These advanced slowly, and both were subject to the pressure of traditional opposition. In combating this opposition, philosophy did yeoman service.

It helped to turn interest upon nature and natural phenomena. It did so by interpreting the whole intricate order of nature as a manifestation of the wisdom of God and insisting that the supreme perfection of deity can be fully understood only through a concomitant understanding of its reflection in the world.

Ideas of this sort may be derived from Plato, if only we are willing to identify Plato's form of the good with deity. Therefore, as the complete works of Plato became once more available in western Europe (especially after the fall of Constantinople, which drove eastern European scholars to seek employment in the West) philosophy drew from them the notion that the order and the beauty of the natural world deserve the attention of the religious enthusiast. These thinkers tended toward pantheism, and they were certainly unorthodox in the eyes of the Church, but they aided in making modern science possible.

Consider Robert Browning's free but penetrating interpretation of these ideas in his early poem *Paracelsus*. Here Browning has caught the spirit of enthusiasm, at once pantheist and humanist, that inspired the freethinking philosophers who stood at the dawn of modern natural science. The creative power of nature and the intelligence of man are recognized as divine incarnations.[1]

> I knew, I felt, (perception unexpressed,
> Uncomprehended by our narrow thought,
> But somehow felt and known in every shift
> And change in the spirit,—nay, in every pore
> Of the body, even,)—what God is, what we are,
> What life is—how God tastes an infinite joy
> In infinite ways—one everlasting bliss,
> From whom all being emanates, all power
> Proceeds; in whom is life forevermore,
> Yet whom existence in its lowest form
> Includes; where dwells enjoyment there is he,
> With still a flying point of bliss remote,

[1] Browning, *Paracelsus*, V. Philippus Aureolus Paracelsus (Theophrastus Bombast von Höhenheim; 1493-1541), physician, alchemist, philosopher, and mystic, was hounded by the authorities throughout his life because of what they considered to be his suspicious and subversive theories of God, nature, and man. He lived for a time in Basel.

A happiness in store afar, a sphere
Of distant glory in full view; thus climbs
Pleasure its heights forever and forever.
The centre-fire heaves underneath the earth,
And the earth changes like a human face;
The molten ore bursts up among the rocks,
Winds into the stone's heart, outbranches bright
In hidden mines, spots barren river-beds,
Crumbles into fine sand where sunbeams bask—
God joys therein. The wroth sea's waves are edged
With foam, white as the bitten lip of hate,
When, in the solitary waste, strange groups
Of young volcanos come up, cyclops-like,
Staring together with their eyes on flame—
God tastes a pleasure in their uncouth pride.
Then all is still; earth is a wintry clod:
But spring-wind, like a dancing psaltress, passes
Over its breast to waken it, rare verdure
Buds tenderly upon rough banks, between
The withered tree-roots and the cracks of frost,
Like a smile striving with a wrinkled face;
The grass grows bright, the boughs are swoln with blooms
Like chrysalids impatient for the air,
The shining dorrs are busy, beetles run
Along the furrows, ants make their ado;
Above, birds fly in merry flocks, the lark
Soars up and up, shivering for very joy;
Afar the ocean sleeps; white fishing-gulls
Flit where the strand is purple with its tribe
Of nested limpets; savage creatures seek
Their loves in wood and plain—and God renews
His ancient rapture. Thus he dwells in all,
From life's minute beginnings, up at last
To man—the consummation of this scheme
Of being, the completion of this sphere
Of life; whose attributes had here and there
Been scattered o'er the visible world before,
Asking to be combined, dim fragments meant
To be united in some wondrous whole,
Imperfect qualities through creation,
Suggesting some one creature yet to make,
Some point where all those scattered rays should meet
Convergent in the faculties of man.

It is interesting to note the fact that despite his great interest in nature, Paracelsus considers man or human nature as the flower or culmination of the created universe. Most striking is his conception of the presence *in nature* and in life of the thought and the will of God. As the Italian Campanella [2] put it, "The world is the book in which the eternal Sense has written his own thoughts."

At about this time a revival of Pythagorean ideas may be said to have inspired modern astronomy. A true Pythagorean will insist that the universe is to be understood primarily in terms of precise mathematical relations, and that in general the more systematic and harmonious explanations are, the more are they correct. In other words, mathematical elegance is a criterion of truth. Such speculative notions led men like Copernicus [3] and Kepler [4] to search for the great geometrical proportions immanent in the motions of the heavenly bodies. Copernicus discovered the solar system and denied the ancient principle that the earth is the center of a finite physical universe. Kepler confirmed Copernicus' work and demonstrated further that the orbits of the planets about the sun are elliptical. By so doing, he laid the foundation both of modern astronomy and of Newtonian physics.

From the time of his earliest researches Kepler was inspired by the belief that God created the world in accordance with some pre-existent [mathematical] harmony, certain manifestations of which might be traced in the number and sizes of the planetary orbits and in the motion of the planets therein.[5]

[2] Tommaso Campanella (1568-1639), although a Dominican monk and a very devout Catholic, caught the rising spirit of the scientific age. He was a friend of the scientist Galileo.

[3] Nicolaus Copernicus (1473-1543) was a Polish (or Prussian) astronomer, also a physician and a canon of Frauenburg cathedral. His great work was *Concerning the Revolutions of the Celestial Spheres.*

[4] Johann Kepler (1571-1630) somewhat reluctantly combined the professions of astronomer and astrologer at the court of Rudolf II of Bohemia. At Prague he worked with the Danish astronomer Tycho Brahe, upon whose observations Kepler's hypotheses were constructed.

[5] Adrian Wolf, *History of Science, Technology, and Philosophy in the Sixteenth & Seventeenth Centuries,* p. 133. Macmillan & Co., London; The Macmillan Company, New York; 1935. Reprinted by permission of the publishers.

It was therefore with a genuine religious enthusiasm that Kepler published his conclusions, which seemed to be the dream of Pythagoras come true. In fact, his laws of planetary motion do reveal the mathematical interconnection of things that the Pythagoreans had dimly foreseen.[6]

The intensity of Kepler's religious Pythagoreanism is revealed in the words with which he announced his discovery.[7]

It is not eighteen months since the first glimpse of light reached me, three months since the dawn, very few days since the unveiled sun, most admirable to gaze upon, burst out upon me. Nothing holds me; I will indulge in my sacred fury; I will triumph over mankind by the honest confession that I have stolen the golden vases of the Egyptians to build up a tabernacle for my God, far away from the confines of Egypt. If you forgive me, I rejoice; if you are angry, I can bear it; the die is cast; the book is written; to be read either now or by posterity, I care not which; it may well wait a century for a reader, as God has waited 6,000 years for an observer.

Kepler saw in the mathematical order of the heavens a manifestation of divine wisdom. But there were many who could find in the new astronomy only a denial of man's dignity and cosmic significance. Mankind had been once thought to dwell at the very center of a finite physical universe, which might easily be imagined to have been planned for him. With the inception of the new astronomy man appears, physically at any rate, to be lost in a limitless universe "whose center is everywhere and whose circumference is nowhere." He does not even inhabit the center of the little solar system in which he dwells. His earth is but one of several planets traveling around the sun and the sun but one of an infinitude of

[6] Kepler's three laws of planetary motion may be stated as follows:

1. All the planets move around the sun with elliptical orbits, the sun being at one focus of the ellipse.

2. The line joining the planet to the sun sweeps out equal areas in equal intervals of time.

3. For all planets, the square of the time of one complete revolution or "year" is proportional to the cube of the mean distance of the planet from the sun.

[7] Ivan B. Hart, *Makers of Science*, p. 91. Clarendon Press, Oxford, 1924. Reprinted by permission of the publisher. Our treatment of Kepler and Galileo follows that of Hart.

stars. To be sure, this emotional reaction now seems to many students little more than sentimental nonsense. It seemed, however, to be anything but that to many a thinker of the sixteenth and seventeenth centuries, and so the Church set itself squarely in opposition to the new astronomy. On the other hand, this astronomy was enthusiastically accepted by the mystical pantheist Giordano Bruno, who delighted in a physical universe whose limitless immensities seemed to declare its divinity.[8] Bruno was burned at the stake.

Walter Pater summarized Bruno's pantheism as follows:[9]

Returning to this ancient "pantheism," after the long reign of a seemingly opposite faith, Bruno unfalteringly asserts "the vision of all things in God" to be the aim of all metaphysical speculation, as of all enquiry into nature. The Spirit of God, in countless variety of forms, neither above, nor in any way without, but intimately within, all things, is really present, with equal integrity and fulness, in the sunbeam ninety millions of miles long, and the wandering drop of water as it evaporates therein. The divine consciousness has the same relation to the production of things as the human intelligence to the production of true thoughts concerning them. Nay! those thoughts are themselves actually God in man: a loan to man also of His assisting Spirit, who, in truth, is the Creator of things, in and by His contemplation of them. For Him, as for man in proportion as man thinks truly, thought and being are identical, and things existent only in so far as they are known. Delighting in itself, in the sense of its own energy, this sleepless, capacious, fiery intelligence evokes all the orders of nature, all the revolutions of history, cycle upon cycle, in ever new types. And God the Spirit, the soul of the world, being therefore really identical with the soul of Bruno also, as the universe shapes itself to Bruno's reason, to his imagination, ever more and more articulately, he too becomes a sharer of the divine joy in that process of the formation of true ideas, which is really parallel to the process of creation, to the evolution of things. In a certain mystic sense, which some in every age of the world have understood, he, too, is the creator; himself ac-

[8] Giordano Bruno (1548-1600) in his early career entered the Dominican order. The severity of the Inquisition referred to above may have been influenced by what the orthodox with reason considered as apostasy. Bruno was unwilling to attend Mass and lost an appointment at the University of Paris because of this.

[9] Pater, *Gaston de Latour,* pp. 181-84. Macmillan & Co., London; The Macmillan Company, New York; 1896. This and a later quotation are reprinted by permission of the publishers.

tually a participator in the creative function. And by such a philosophy, Bruno assures us, it was his experience that the soul is greatly expanded: *con questa filosofia l'anima mi s'aggrandisce: mi se magnifica l'intelletto!*

For, with characteristic largeness of mind, Bruno accepted this theory in the whole range of its consequences. Its more immediate corollary was the famous axiom of "indifference," of "the coincidence of contraries." To the eye of God, to the philosophic vision through which God sees in man, nothing is really alien from Him. The differences of things, those distinctions, above all, which schoolmen and priests, old or new, Roman or Reformed, had invented for themselves, would be lost in the length and breadth of the philosophic survey: nothing, in itself, being really either great or small; and matter certainly, in all its various forms, not evil but divine. Dare one choose or reject this or that? If God the Spirit had made, nay! was, all things indifferently, then, matter and spirit, the spirit and the flesh, heaven and earth, freedom and necessity, the first and the last, good and evil, would be superficial rather than substantial differences.

Enthusiastic pantheism aided the rise of modern science. But the first supreme scientist of modern times held himself wholly aloof from such ebullient speculation. Galileo is in a sense the prototype of the modern scientific investigator.[10] He declined to attempt a comprehensive philosophy of nature, although his friend Campanella urged him to undertake this. He preferred to contribute a few principles that he had thoroughly demonstrated and tested by observation and experiment. He himself commented upon his choice: "For the sake of a hundred or more propositions of natural things, I have no desire to discredit and to lose the merits of the ten or twelve that I have discovered and know by demonstration to be true."

Galileo bequeathed to Europe the firm beginnings of physical science: the principle of the pendulum, that of the acceleration of falling bodies, a finished and coherent proof of the earth's mobility,

---

[10] Galileo Galilei (1564-1642), the Florentine mathematician, physicist, and astronomer, is the father of modern exact science. Galileo espoused the Copernican theory of the heavens, already defended by Kepler. By asserting that the earth moved he aroused the anger of the Holy Office (the Inquisition). He was forced to recant. His fate broke the spirit of Italian science in the Renaissance, which languished for many years under arbitrary ecclesiastical restriction.

and the pregnant hypothesis that bodies on earth and in the heavens are subject to the same laws. All this is to say nothing of his observations of the mountains of the moon and of sun spots, which latter phenomenon reveals the fact that the sun is itself in rotation. From the point of view of the history of philosophy, Galileo's most important contribution lies in his introducing a type of investigation that makes no use of Aristotle's conception of a teleological physics. In other words, final cause plays no part in his scheme of explanation. He found it possible to measure certain things, acceleration of falling bodies, for instance, that had never been accurately measured before. But why these things are as they are, what end or purpose they served, lies quite beyond the scope of such studies. A more speculative intellect—and one less subject to persecution— might easily have gone further and denied the reality of final cause altogether. This, indeed, was soon to happen in the philosophy of Spinoza.

In his famous inquiry concerning the acceleration of falling bodies, Galileo established a method of experiment. His purpose was to test a hypothesis that observation had suggested to him, namely, that velocity is proportional to the time of falling, or that a falling body gathers equal increments of velocity in equal increments of time. Galileo tested this hypothesis experimentally in an ingenious way. He made use of an inclined plane twelve yards long, down the center of which ran a trough one inch wide. This trough was lined with smooth parchment to minimize friction. A polished brass ball was released at the head of the plane, and the time it took to cover given distances was recorded, for a wide range of varying inclinations, by an ingeniously contrived water clock. As a result of these experiments, Galileo concluded that the distance covered is proportional to the square of the time. This experiment applies not only to bodies moving on an inclined plane, but is also relevant to falling bodies. This is because we many consider "falling" a special case where the steepness of the slope has been increased to ninety degrees.

In this way Galileo conducted experimental observations under artificially simplified physical conditions. And in this way he founded exact physical science; such science recognizes physical nature as rigidly mathematical in its habits. All events are seen as subject to formula. Nothing takes place for the sake of any end or ideal. Nothing takes place that is not subject to law. Nature forever repeats in varying context its precise routine, like a great machine that continues to perform set operations without reference to their outcome. In fact, the analogy of the machine soon fascinates the consciousness of the scientist and of the philosopher, although if the latter has Platonic or Aristotelian allegiances, he is often depressed by this notion.

Such a concept is closer to the theory of Democritus than to that of other ancient philosophers. To be sure, after the work of Kepler and Galileo science employs so many mathematical instruments that it assumes a markedly Pythagorean aspect. Even so, the growing tendency to suspect all teleological methods of thought that characterizes the rise of modern science is clearly Democritean. The history of modern philosophy, at least in its first period, is largely the history of the impact of this concept of mechanical science upon the European consciousness.

THE PHILOSOPHY OF DESCARTES

The first outstanding statement of the method and the philosophical implications of the new science is contained in the first great "system" of modern philosophy. This system was the work of René Descartes, a man who combined the powers of a brilliant and successful mathematician, a somewhat too-speculative theorist in physics, and a student of philosophy, if not widely read, at least with his wits sharpened by the best Jesuit teachers in Europe.[11] His

---

[11] René Descartes (1596-1650) came of a noble French family. He was educated by the Jesuits at the famous school of La Flèche. For a time he devoted himself to the fashionable life of the French capital, and then, hoping to see the world, "went to the wars" in Germany. He soon, however, devoted himself wholly to study, pursuing his researches in mathematics, physics, astronomy, anatomy, and philosophy. He is the inventor of the Cartesian co-ordinates, and the founder of analytic geometry. Descartes preferred to spend much of his life in Holland, where freedom of thought was more secure than elsewhere. He died in Sweden, where Queen Christina had called him to lend distinction to her court.

system was formulated in an effort to outline the broadest aspects of the world as a student of the new sciences saw it. Its author hoped that this outline might turn out to be acceptable to the religious authorities, and so he hoped to close the breach that was ever widening between science and religion. But, despite this hope, Descartes never admitted any ecclesiastical or religious authority superior to reason.

What we may without question call *modern* philosophy begins with Descartes, and it is from him that we inherit the background against which the problems of philosophy are discussed today. Thus it is highly important to understand Descartes's contribution and to see clearly his presuppositions as well as his conclusions. These presuppositions are in great measure those of the new scientific attitude. Both the method and much of the subject matter of Descartes's thinking is derived from or lies parallel with the work of such men as Kepler and Galileo. Both the physical world and the attitude of mind maintained by the student of physics and astronomy attracted Descartes's attention and guided his thought.

Descartes himself was not inclined to admit the existence of any external influence upon his thinking. He even had the temerity to assert that he was beginning to philosophize afresh without any presuppositions. But he advanced this rather preposterous boast in his eagerness to make clear that he accepted no scriptural or ecclesiastical authority. For Descartes, philosophy is not faith seeking understanding, nor is it reason putting faith to the test. On this point Descartes broke completely with medieval thought, and in so doing he declared philosophy's complete independence of orthodox revelation, a course, incidentally, that the astronomers and physicists from Copernicus on had actually been following. Descartes did, however, make this independence explicit.

For Descartes, then, philosophy should depend upon no revelation, upon no authority, and upon no tradition, but is to be guided only by the good sense and the logical acumen of its author. As a matter of fact, Descartes was himself well endowed with both these qualities, but, genius as he was, he could hardly be expected to create a new intellectual world by his own fiat, although this is what he seems to be undertaking in his famous *Discourse on Method* and in his *Meditations*.

Descartes has been rightly called the father of modern philosophy. But recognition of this truth should not blind us to the fact that modern philosophy has more remote ancestors; namely, the thinkers by whom Descartes was influenced despite himself, to mention only a few: Pythagoras; Euclid and the mathematicians; Plato, Augustine, and Anselm; Democritus and the founders of modern science, such as Copernicus, Kepler, and Galileo. It may be convenient to consider Descartes's thought as composed of several ingredients, no one of which can be said to be wholly original with him. Descartes is a very original thinker, but his philosophical originality lies in his attempt to synthesize these elements, nearly all of which were centuries old in his day. The "ingredients" we have, perhaps rather arbitrarily, selected for discussion are as follows:

1. The method of mathematical deduction

2. Augustinian Platonism, including the theory of the Supreme Being

3. Galileo's theory of physical mechanism

4. Dualism of mind and body

5. A new analysis of knowledge, resulting in the theory of *representative perception,* whereby we know or are directly aware of only our own ideas, which in their turn "represent" the "external world."

These ingredients need not all be considered as of equal priority. The second and third, Platonism and mechanism, together determine the fourth and fifth. If Plato is right concerning the mind, and Democritus and Galileo are right concerning the body, body and mind must be two very different things. This constitutes point 4 in our scheme. Again, if all body is wholly mechanical in nature but often appears quite otherwise, we must frequently be aware of body in a very indirect way. This constitutes point 5 of our scheme.

Furthermore, these ingredients are not all consistent with one another. Platonism and mathematical method can live together in harmony. But Platonism and universal mechanism are "mighty opposites"; their conflicting tendencies are all but irreconcilable. In attempting to serve both Plato and Democritus, modern thought has committed itself to centuries of internal conflict, which has not been wholly overcome even today. Only a fool or a genius would have undertaken such a task. Yet the task had to be undertaken if modern philosophy was to survive. Modern science, that of Galileo, for example, was in its earliest developments mechanistic. Modern ethical and religious consciousness was frequently Platonic and Augustinian in its early orientation. Thus modern culture started life with a mechanistic body and an Augustinian soul. Somehow the two had to be reconciled. Science on the one hand, ethics and religion on the other, were at war; and at times each side seemed ready or at least willing to destroy the other.

This desperate need of reconciliation has called forth all the imagination, genius, and learning that a brilliant age has had at its command. But the conflict has become so deeply rooted in our thinking that in many quarters the very possibility of reconciliation is treated with scorn. Even today competent philosophers of science delight in telling us that the propositions of ethics and of ethical theory are neither true nor false but meaningless; and in the other camp there have always been idealists only too willing to divorce philosophy wholly from natural science. And, worst of all, many who do believe in the general possibility of a reconciliation are quite baffled, and unable to offer any explicit scheme whereby it may be effected.

All the elements of this age-long conflict are to be found in Descartes's thinking. Needless to say, he does not even approach a consistent resolution of the conflict, but bequeaths the problem to his successors. Descartes raised more problems than he solved, but he succeeded in making recognition of these problems inescapable.

Let us now consider in order the ingredients of Descartes's thought.

1. *Mathematical method*. Descartes's logical method is derived from his work in mathematics. One must, he insists, keep one's intellectual house in order, and make only the most judicious addi-

tions. Indubitable starting points, subject only to the authority of "good sense," comparable to the axioms of arithmetic and geometry, must be uncovered, and from these step by step a system of true propositions deduced. One must never accept anything as true that one does not grasp in a "clear and distinct idea." The theory of the clear and distinct idea is the center of Cartesian methodology. It is also the guiding principle in the work of Spinoza and Leibniz, Descartes's great successors.

Descartes divided ideas into those which are obscure, those which are clear, and those which are distinct as well as clear. "I call that clear," he says, "which is present and manifest to the attentive mind, as we say we see an object clearly when it is present to the eye looking on, and when it makes on the sense of sight an impression sufficiently strong and definite; but I call that distinct which is *clear and at the same time so definitely distinguished from everything else* that its essence is evident to him who properly considers it." [12]

The clear and distinct idea must be so simple that it is free of all confusion or indefinite outlines. Thus all complex problems, such as those which most interest the philosopher, must be broken up into their simpler parts, which can be comprehended in clear and distinct ideas. There is no point in trying to prove, say, the Pythagorean theorem at first glance. One must start on a lower plane of axioms and definitions and proceed slowly by clear and distinct ideas toward comprehension of so complex a truth. This method affords a gradual advance, each step of which we take only as we recognize its absolute certainty. It is quite different from the

---

[12] *Principles of Philosophy,* i. 45. This is taken from the translation by Robert Latta of Leibniz, *The Monadology.* Oxford, Clarendon Press, 1898, p. 48. Galileo had already employed a method strikingly similar to this in the thinking which preceded some of his most brilliant experiments. Thus when he formed the hypothesis that heavy bodies would fall no more rapidly than lighter bodies, he formed a clear conception of the heavy body as composed of a number of elements comparable to lighter bodies. He saw no reason why the combination of a number of lighter bodies should increase the speed with which these bodies fall. It is interesting to notice that Galileo thought it necessary to verify his clear and distinct idea by experiment. In practice as well as in theory, Descartes often tended, unfortunately, to overlook this very necessary safeguard.

method of speculation suggested by Socrates (see above, page 38 ff.), whereby we provisionally accept a broad hypothesis as true and then search for means of verifying it. Descartes's method may be of value in much philosophical analysis, but it is very doubtful that any broad speculative conclusions can be obtained in this way. Certainly Descartes at times overlooked the strict requirements of his method when constructing his system.

Furthermore, when this method is successfully followed, it results in a singularly rigid philosophy, according to which we must claim that we possess sun-clear and final conclusions concerning the nature of things. These conclusions are unfortunately not pliable hypotheses that can be readjusted to fit new discoveries. They must stand or fall as the inevitable conclusions of certain so-called self-evident starting points. So rigid and dogmatic a system has grown more and more to seem out of place in modern times, when philosophy has had to meet unexpected scientific developments.

Descartes's conception of this method is stated in the first pages of his famous *Discourse on Method,* the publication of which in 1637 is often described as the first event in modern philosophy.[13]

Good sense is, of all things among men, the most equally distributed; for every one thinks himself so abundantly provided with it, that those even who are the most difficult to satisfy in everything else, do not usually desire a larger measure of this quality than they already possess. And in this it is not likely that all are mistaken: the conviction is rather to be held as testifying that the power of judging aright and of distinguishing Truth from Error, which is properly what is called Good Sense or Reason, is by nature equal in all men; and that the diversity of our opinions, consequently, does not arise from some being endowed with a larger share of Reason than others, but solely from this, that we conduct our thoughts along different ways, and do not fix our attention on the same objects. For to be possessed of a vigorous mind is not enough; the prime requisite is rightly to apply it. The greatest minds, as they are capable of the highest excellencies, are open likewise to the greatest aberrations; and those who travel very slowly may yet

[13] *The Method, Meditations, and Selections from the Principles of Descartes,* ed. and trans. by John Veitch, pp. 3-4. William Blackwood and Sons, Edinburgh and London, 10th ed., 1890.

make far greater progress, provided they keep always to the straight road, than those who, while they run, forsake it.

Some pages below, Descartes formulates his method more precisely: [14]

And as a multitude of laws often only hampers justice, so that a state is best governed when, with few laws, these are rigidly administered; in like manner, instead of the great number of precepts of which Logic is composed, I believed that the four following would prove perfectly sufficient for me, provided I took the firm and unwavering resolution never in a single instance to fail in observing them.

The *first* was never to accept anything for true which I did not clearly know to be such; that is to say, carefully to avoid precipitancy and prejudice, and to comprise nothing more in my judgment than what was presented to my mind so clearly and distinctly as to exclude all ground of doubt.

The *second,* to divide each of the difficulties under examination into as many parts as possible, and as might be necessary for its adequate solution.

The *third,* to conduct my thoughts in such order that, by commencing with objects the simplest and easiest to know, I might ascend by little and little, and, as it were, step by step, to the knowledge of the more complex; assigning in thought a certain order even to those objects which in their own nature do not stand in a relation of antecedence and sequence.

And the *last,* in every case to make enumerations so complete, and reviews so general, that I might be assured that nothing was omitted.

The long chains of simple and easy reasonings by means of which geometers are accustomed to reach the conclusions of their most difficult demonstrations, had led me to imagine that all things, to the knowledge of which man is competent, are mutually connected in the same way, and that there is nothing so far removed from us as to be beyond our reach, or so hidden that we cannot discover it, provided only we abstain from accepting the false for the true, and always preserve in our thoughts the order necessary for the deduction of one truth from another. And I had little difficulty in determining the objects with which it was necessary to commence, for I was already persuaded that it must be with the simplest and

[14] *Ibid.,* pp. 19-20.

easiest to know, and, considering that of all those who have hitherto sought truth in the Sciences, the mathematicians alone have
been able to find any demonstrations, that is, any certain and evident reasons, I did not doubt but that such must have been the rule
of their investigations. I resolved to commence, therefore, with the
examination of the simplest objects, not anticipating, however, from
this any other advantage than that to be found in accustoming my
mind to the love and nourishment of truth, and to a distaste for all
such reasonings as were unsound.

2. *Augustinian Platonism.* Despite all this, Descartes was by no
means so free from tradition as statements like the above would
lead us to believe. From Augustine, or at least from the Augustinian
tradition, with which he seems to have become acquainted despite
the fact that his teachers, as Jesuits, viewed Augustine with suspicion, Descartes inherited a willingness to consider seriously, although of course not to accept on authority, the doctrine of God
as the Supreme Being, or absolutely independent reality. But he was
even more Augustinian than this by itself indicates. He found the
Augustinian emphasis upon the inner life thoroughly to his liking,
and he looked within the human consciousness for a starting point
upon which to build his philosophy. Descartes even follows Augustine's method as presented in his *Confessions* and develops his
ideas in autobiographical form as meditations. Then again, he put
much store in the ontological argument for the existence of God,
which was first developed by Anselm, who is known as the "second
Augustine." The individual's awareness of his own reality as a
center of consciousness and of God as perfect or Supreme Being
are made the foundation of such an investigation.

The Platonic forms, in a new incarnation, are included in Descartes's system, but they have become conscious ideas, as in Plotinus
and Augustine, and Descartes finds them in *our own* consciousness
as *innate ideas* the truth of which it is virtually impossible for a
human being to question. He does, however, occasionally drive
himself, out of sheer conscientious rigor, to doubt their validity,
so to speak, as an intellectual experiment. These ideas or eternal
truths are not, as with Plato, identified with types or universals.

They are propositions holding true of things throughout all space and time; and, even more un-Platonic, they are ideas resident in the mind of a finite individual thinker. Descartes never supplies an exhaustive list of these innate ideas, but we shall come upon several of them; for instance, every event and every finite being owes its existence to some cause other than itself.

3. *Mechanism*. Descartes's interest in the infant sciences of physics and astronomy led him to repudiate the notion of teleology in nature. No doubt God has created the world with purposes and an end in view, but we are not capable of grasping these, and must study efficient rather than final causes, for it would be presumptuous to consider ourselves as sharing the councils of the Deity. Accordingly Descartes emphatically repudiated Aristotle's teleological theory of development, his theory of substance and of the four causes, and of celestial and terrestial or sublunary motion.

All of these doctrines had occupied a position of great prominence in the writings of the medieval Schoolmen, in particular those of Thomas Aquinas. Descartes accepted a mechanism much closer to that of Democritus than to any theory of nature tolerated by Plato or Aristotle, although he was always eager to indicate the points upon which he disagreed with Democritus. There are several of these which are important as matters of detail, but both schemes of thought accept an out-and-out mechanist interpretation of the physical world. Descartes's mechanism, like that of Democritus, applies not only to the world of physical objects but also to the realm of living things. Unlike Democritus, Descartes does not hold a mechanist theory of the human mind.

Descartes belonged, as we have just seen, to the period that culminated in the discovery of the first principles of mechanics, a period when the radical thinkers were interested in seeing natural process analyzed into elements—mass, force, velocity, acceleration, and so on—that might be interrelated as functions of one another, varying relatively to each other according to various laws or formulas, and thus revealing the ground pattern of a natural determinism. Hence Descartes was interested in a world whose operations are regular and law-abiding. He never determined satisfactorily what these laws are, but he was convinced of their existence and their universal application. Now if nature is to be conceived as thus regular and orderly in its physical process, it seemed obvious to the mathematical Descartes that we must consider this process as measurable. The entities in which this order is to be discovered must be measurable entities, such things as mass, force, velocity, acceleration, must be subject to measurement if we are to recognize any thoroughly orderly relation or ratio between them. Further, it is obvious that there are many things in the world that are not measurable, at least not accurately so, as for instance desire, will, love, and hate, and the emotions and sentiments in general.

But unfortunately for Descartes and his fellow thinkers, the older medieval conception of nature had been, so to speak, saturated with ideas very similar to those just mentioned. Vitalist or biological ideas of an old school had overrun the realm of physics. For instance, it was taught that heavy bodies fall because they have within them a downward tendency, just as a child has within him a manward tendency and, so to speak, "loves to become" a man even as an Aristotelian acorn "loves to become" an oak. In this scheme motion was not considered simply as change of place. It was rather change of condition or change of state or of quality. Thus when a body falls, it is not so much a change of place as a change of condition. This change is a passage of the "downward tendency" from potentiality to actuality, from possibility to active function. Just so, in a child the characters of manhood reside as potential; that is, as a possible outcome that will be realized if natural function goes unthwarted. In such growth, it was thought that change of place,— that is, of position of one body as relative to other bodies—plays a minor role, even though it is involved in all development.

But Descartes was inspired by the thought that all matter, all physical bodies whether animate or inanimate, might successfully be studied as composed of moving particles, and their relative positions plotted according to definite laws of motion. From this point of view, clear and distinct conclusions might be obtained concerning the structure of animate and inanimate bodies, and useful knowledge, for instance in the fields of medicine and mechanics, might be developed. Such inquiry requires analysis of compound bodies into their simple units and a study of the behavior of such units. All this has little to do with the tendencies or potentialities that the Schoolmen of the Middle Ages had believed to be concealed somehow in animate and inanimate bodies. So Descartes wished to ignore everything but the spatial and the measurable in the study of the physical world; hence he wished to rule out of consideration all factors save those involved in change of place. He did not wish to be embarrassed by occult or concealed tendencies or forces that he could not handle in terms of such motion.

Following this lead, Descartes denied the ultimate independence of qualitative change. He taught that change of color or of temperature is really change of movement among the particles which compose the body in question. In this, modern science has borne him out, and has strengthened his thesis that knowledge gained through the senses cannot stand by itself as final, but must be explained by rational and often mathematical inquiry. This assumption of Descartes's made his world a much simpler and a more orderly one, but the assumption was, in his day, by no means a necessary nor an obvious one to make.

Furthermore, Descartes fled from the notion of final cause. For if *man* is the final cause or "end" of a boy's growth, how can this be included in a spatial analysis of the boy's physiology? Descartes thought that study of this physiological pattern could be carried on fruitfully only with reference to the motion of the particles involved. Knowledge of these bodies and their behavior might be developed without reference to "where they were going." This, Descartes thought, was a much more adequate method. And in a sense he was right, because laws of motion are more easily treated than laws of growth, since motion is more readily measurable than growth.

In order to frame a reasonably clear conception of Descartes's mechanist interpretation of biology, let us examine the following passages from J. S. Haldane's Gifford Lectures, *The Sciences and*

Philosophy. Here the great physiologist summarizes Descartes's views and presents concisely the chief difficulty involved.[15]

The leadership of Descartes has been recognized on all hands by those who have subsequently maintained that the proper line to take in the study of biology is to aim at a complete physico-chemical account of the phenomena of life, thus placing biology in the position of a branch of physics and chemistry.

The attempt of Descartes is contained in his two short books *De homine* and *De formatione foetus.* The aim of these books was to show that life may, in so far as it is not deliberately directed by the soul, be regarded as consisting of mechanical or physico-chemical processes, the living body itself being also produced from its material elements by mechanical processes. As regards the details of these processes, he says that they may be different from what he suggests, and that his only concern was to demonstrate that they may be regarded as mechanical processes of some sort. Thus his general argument was in no way compromised by the subsequent demonstration that many of the particular mechanical processes which he hypothetically suggested are non-existent. He had put forward a general hypothesis as to the nature of life, and this hypothesis has gained very widespread support. To many scientific men of the present time, and to a multitude of popular writers, its truth seems, indeed, to be self-evident.

Even in the time of Descartes it was already clear that much of what occurs within the living body is susceptible of clear mechanical explanation. Thus the movements, whether voluntary or involuntary, of the limbs, etc., had been rendered intelligible by showing how, when muscles contract, the tendons attached to them act on the bones to which they are also attached, thus bringing about mechanically the various voluntary and involuntary movements of the bodily parts attached to these bones. Kepler had shown how the crystalline lens of the eye, acting just like a glass lens, produces an image on the retina. Harvey had shown how the blood, driven mechanically by pressure from the heart, and guided by valves, is circulated round the body, carrying nutriment to and removing waste products from all parts. No one questioned successfully the mechanical explanations applied in connexion with these and various other processes occurring within the living body. It therefore

15 J. S. Haldane, *The Sciences and Philosophy*, pp. 19-21. Doubleday, Doran and Company. 1929; Hodder & Stoughton, London, 1930. This and the following quotation are reprinted by permission of the publishers.

seemed natural enough to adopt the belief that all physiological processes are ultimately susceptible of similar mechanical or physico-chemical explanation.

Against this point of view Haldane submits the following evidence.[16]

The further stage of development to which I have referred as characterizing more recent physiology concerns the attention now directed on the co-ordination, or, as it is often termed, regulation of life-processes. The development of physical chemistry and accurate methods of physical measurement, and of analysis of blood and other liquids, have made it possible to see far more clearly certain outstanding facts with regard to the exact co-ordination of familiar physiological processes, and the essential importance of this co-ordination. To some of these facts attention was first clearly directed by the experiments and writings of Claude Bernard [1813-1878, a French physiologist]; and since then their importance has come to stand out more and more prominently in every department of physiology.

In experiments on the oxidation of sugar in the living body Bernard started with the expectation that when sugar and other carbohydrates which are converted into sugar by the digestive ferments are withheld from an animal, the sugar which he had found to be present in the blood would disappear. He found, however, that this was not the case: the sugar was still present in the blood after prolonged starvation. Moreover, if very large amounts of sugar were given, there was only a slight increase in the percentage present in the blood, since rise in this percentage was prevented owing to the disappearance of the sugar, or its copious excretion by the kidneys. He was thus led, on the one hand to the search for and discovery of glycogen as an immediate source of and repository for sugar in the body, and on the other hand to the conception that the blood, and particularly its plasma, is a general internal medium which is kept remarkably constant in composition and amount, owing to the co-ordinated regulating influence upon it of various organs, such as the kidneys, liver, lungs, etc. On a wide survey of what was then known of animal physiology he even went so far as to conclude that "all the vital mechanisms, varied as they are, have only one object, that of preserving constant the conditions of life in the internal environment."

[16] *Ibid.*, pp. 38-39.

The conception embodied in these words has proved an extraor dinarily useful one in guiding physiological work into fruitful channels, and in uniting what would otherwise be no better than a chaotic collection of isolated observations. Furthermore, side by side with increased knowledge of the co-ordination of physiological activities in maintaining the "conditions of life," there has grown up a correspondingly increased knowledge of the biological im portance of the maintenance of these very conditions.

Perhaps, after all, the Aristotelian concepts of developmental substance, of formal and final cause, are closer to the self-adjusting and self-maintaining organism than is Descartes's concept of the living machine. The organism may be expected at least always to *attempt* to maintain the normal conditions of its life, and this requires a continuous flow of self-adjustment not to be expected from a machine.

4. *Dualism of mind and body.* Believing as he did that the body's behavior can be in no way guided by purpose, Descartes was naturally eager to show that there exists a sharp distinction between body and mind. He had gone so far as to say that animals are only machines, their bodies displaying what we should now call reflex action, being quite without consciousness or will. But he was not willing to describe man in this way. Man possesses a conscious will and a power of free choice, although his body, like all animal bodies, is a part of the mechanical process of nature.

In this exception made in man's favor Descartes was dominated by a notion that seemed to him of the greatest importance. He was inspired by the thought that the human will is absolute and master of its situation once it is given the opportunity to operate deliber ately. A moment's reflection will show that such a notion has as sure a grip upon a philosophy like Descartes's as has the notion of a regular and measurable order of nature. Suppose we deny this freedom of the will and admit that the mind "obeys" the "motions" of the "fluids" in the brain—that our mind is like that of the animals without the power of will. What, then, of our opinions concerning the problems of philosophy and of science? Are they genuine opinions? Or are they part of a course of events that itself is but the regular unfolding of a natural process? If the latter alternative be the true one, how can we believe that our assertions have any logical value? If judgment is an event in the spatial world that proceeds without reference to values, how may we expect to find the value of sound reasoning respected or embodied in our thinking?

Sound thinking is not a result of submental or mechanical order. Sound thinking has a goal it endeavors to reach. It is always trying to express itself according to principles of logic with which it does not easily conform. Descartes felt sure that it presupposed a free will that could accept and reject ideas as they were weighed and judged. On this side, Descartes was wholly teleological. Reasoning is an *adaptive* activity. Man must adjust his thoughts to what he realizes are the norms of good thinking and valid investigation. This Descartes believed, and he emphasized the importance of an independent will as the activity that makes for such "adaptation," although of course he never used so modern a term.

Hence Descartes, true to his faith in human reasoning and to his interest in physical science, split the world into two types of being, volitional thought and spatial matter or extension. To the first he attributed the power of free decision and purposive development; to the second he denied these attributes without any qualification. This constitutes *Cartesian dualism*.

Descartes's sharp and uncompromising insistence that body and mind are absolutely distinct, the one being wholly mechanical and extended in space, the other spontaneous, teleological, and unextended, came as a most unwelcome teaching to the followers of Aristotle. These students had come to take for granted the theory that the human being is a developmental substance which manifests an intrinsic unity or harmonious co-operation of mental and bodily functions. These functions had been described as the "soul" of Aristotle's system: the vegetative or nutritive, the sensitive, and the rational souls that in man are, so to speak, woven together in what the Schoolmen came to call the "substantial form" of each individual. For Aristotle and for Aquinas, the soul of the individual is manifest in the integrated function of his mind and body, of the parts of his organism as a whole. Only God and the angels possess sheer intelligence, free from matter and beyond the need of bodily support. In separating mind and body, Descartes was again turning toward the Augustinian position and deserting the Aristotelian principles of the later Scholastics.

Today the interplay of mind and body as aspects of the activity of a single organism, or as Aristotle would say, a single substance, seems much closer to the trend of scientific investigation than does the sharp dualism of Descartes. On the other hand, the Aristotelian insistence that the organism is teleological is received with somewhat less enthusiasm, and there are many biologists who are quite happy to dispense with the concept of final cause. Aristotle stands against the dualism of body and mind and against mechanism. Descartes stands for dualism and for physical mechanism. Modern science tends to disapprove of dualism and, despite the attitude of such theorists as J. S. Haldane, just quoted, hesitates when facing the question of mechanism versus teleology with reference to both the mental and the physical aspects of the organism. But we may surmise that the more recent tendency is away from Descartes toward Aristotle. After all, Aristotle himself allowed room for efficient and material causes as well as for final causes. And biology and physiology both recognize something very close to final cause when they speak of the organism as a self-adjusting and self-maintaining unit.

At any rate, we may be sure that Descartes was altogether too hasty in repudiating the Aristotelian theory of development and in banishing final causes from biology. He was probably very wise, certainly in his day, to dismiss final cause from physics and from astronomy, although Leibniz was soon to challenge even this move. There can be no doubt, however, that in framing his system Descartes went too far in this direction and was too enthusiastic a mechanist.

5. *Analysis of knowledge resulting in the doctrine of representative perception.* For Descartes, awareness or the act of knowing is the entertaining of an idea by the mind. All that is immediately and directly present to the mind is the idea. When we analyze consciousness, we need not consider the question whether there is a

world of things corresponding to our ideas. All that we have before us is the idea that the mind entertains. Strictly speaking, we are aware of our ideas and then we infer that there is an extramental object corresponding to them and in some measure producing them. Grounds for this inference are presented at length in Descartes's writings. Perhaps the greatest weakness of this theory lies in that those of us who have not studied a philosophy similar to Descartes's are quite unaware of any such act of inference. This theory of knowledge is known as *representative perception* because the ideas are said to represent to us the things in the world. An alternative theory is that in which the idea is identified with the mental activity whereby we are aware of things in the world. According to this view, the idea does not stand like a screen between the mind and the "external" world, but is the mind's focusing of attention upon things. According to Descartes, we can attend only to our own ideas, a very different doctrine.

Descartes's thinking was confirmed in this theory by his above-mentioned belief that the sensuous or *secondary* qualities of color, sound, and so on exist only in the perceiving mind. The world external to the mind possesses only *primary* or mathematical and physical properties. In this Descartes is very close to Democritus. The color green as perceived stands for or represents a certain physical situation in which light and the surface texture of a physical object are involved. Aside from the perceiving mind, there is no quality of greenness attached to the situation.

So at the beginning of modern philosophy we come upon a type of thought that does not hesitate to depart from the common sense of every man. It has come to be a platitude in the writings of many modern philosophers that things are not at all what they seem to be. What appears to be teleological often proves to be mechanical, qualities that seem to belong to objects prove to be purely mental, and as modern philosophy develops, even graver departures from common sense are contemplated. Descartes himself was capable of entertaining doubts concerning the existence of a world of objects independent of our consciousness and, what is probably even more radical, the dictum that every event must have a cause came to be challenged within the space of a century after Descartes's work.

Scholastic philosophy tends on the whole to pride itself on its interpreting and completing common sense rather than repudiating it as a gross misinterpretation of the world. To be sure, the medieval Scholastics never granted common sense any authority over philosophy, for common sense can offer no reasoned arguments for its beliefs. But it is thought to contain many sound principles, perceived not clearly and completely, but even so by no means wholly distorted. According to this view, a philosopher should feel uncomfortable when he is forced to deny many propositions that common sense seems to support. This Scholastic principle has only very rarely been appreciated in modern thought.

CARTESIAN DOUBT

Descartes's mathematical method aims always at complete certainty. No suspicion of doubt can be tolerated either in first principles or in conclusions. It is therefore absolutely essential that the Cartesian uncover an indubitable starting point, one that can resist our most persistent efforts to doubt its validity.

To find such a principle is not easy, and in Descartes's day it seemed more than usually difficult. There had arisen a tradition of skepticism into which many enlightened thinkers retreated, disgusted and bewildered as they were by the heated religious controversies between Catholic and Protestant, between the several Protestant sects, and between the parties within the Catholic Church. These controversies all too often led to bloody persecutions. Endless disputes, frequently wholly verbal and without substance, produced a tedious racket in the ears of one in whom the *odium theologicum* was lacking. But such disputes, like the endless economic and political debates of today, were often contagious, and many peaceful-minded people were in time drawn into them, almost against their will and certainly against their better judgment.

Accordingly, Montaigne [17] had recommended that the wise man

[17] Michel Eyquem de Montaigne (1533-1592), a courtier at the court of Charles IX of France, retired to his estate, and there wrote his *Essays*, which had important influence on English and French literature and philosophy.

protect himself against all form of dogmatic and rhetorical zeal by schooling himself to recognize his own ignorance and by rehearsing frequently the shortcomings of human judgment and noting how the mind is constitutionally prone to error and is never in a position to assert indubitable conclusions. Thus for Montaigne, doubt had almost taken the place of faith. It was from doubt or the suspension of judgment that he derived his peace of mind, and his sense of spiritual security was founded upon a despair of reasoning. At least, he was sure that he would wander no further in search of answers to human problems. He was through with all such problems, and so finally at peace. Faith itself had become in his eyes so disputatious and quarrelsome that no man could tolerate it without forfeiting his serenity.

Still, the panorama of human belief attracted Montaigne's attention and held his interest. Walter Pater has interpreted Montaigne as follows: [18]

The diversity, the undulancy, of human nature!—so deep a sense of it went with Montaigne always that himself too seemed to be ever changing colour sympathetically therewith. Those innumerable differences, mental and physical, of which men had always been aware, on which they had so largely fed their vanity, were ultimate. That the surface of humanity presented an infinite variety was the tritest of facts. Pursue that variety below the surface!—the lines did but part further and further asunder, with an ever increasing divergency, which made any common measure of truth impossible. Diversity of custom!—What was it but diversity in the moral and mental view, diversity of opinion? and diversity of opinion, what but radical diversity of mental constitution? How various in kind and degree had he found men's thoughts concerning death, for instance, "some (ah me!) even running headlong upon it, with a real affection"? Death, life; wealth, poverty; the whole sum of contrasts; nay! duty itself, "the relish of right and wrong"; all depend upon the opinion each one has of them, and "receive no colour of good or evil but according to the application of the individual soul." Did Hamlet learn of him that "there is nothing either good or bad but thinking makes it so"?—"What we call evil is not so of itself: it depends only upon us, to give it another taste and complexion.— Things, in respect of themselves, have peradventure their weight,

18 Pater. *op. cit.,* pp. 117-20.

measure, and conditions; but when once we have taken them into us, the soul forms them as she pleases.—Death is terrible to Cicero, courted by Cato, indifferent to Socrates.—Fortune, circumstance, offers but the matter: 'tis the soul adds the form.—Every opinion, how fantastic soever to some, is to another of force enough to be espoused at the risk of life."

For opinion was the projection of individual *will,* of a native original predilection. Opinions!—they are like the clothes we wear, which warm us, not with their heat, but with ours. Track your way (as he had learned to do) to the remote origin of what looks like folly; at home, on its native soil, it was found to be justifiable, as a proper growth of wisdom. In the vast conflict of taste, preference, conviction, there was no real inconsistency. It was but that the soul looked "upon things with another eye, and represented them to itself with another kind of face; reason being a tincture almost equally infused into all our manners and opinions; though there never were in the world two opinions exactly alike." And the practical comment was, not as one might have expected, towards the determination of some common standard of truth amid that infinite variety, but to this effect rather, that we are not bound to receive every opinion we are not able to refute, nor to accept another's refutation of our own; these diversities being themselves ultimate, and the priceless pearl of truth lying, if anywhere, not in large theoretic apprehension of the general, but in minute vision of the particular; in the perception of the concrete phenomenon, at this particular moment, and from this unique point of view—that for you, this for me—now, but perhaps not then.

Now; and not then! For if men are so diverse, not less disparate are the many men who keep discordant company within each one of us, "every man carrying in him the entire form of human condition." "That we taste nothing pure": the variancy of the individual in regard to himself: the complexity of soul which there, too, makes "all judgments in the gross" impossible or useless, certainly inequitable, he delighted to note. Men's minds were like the grotesques which some artists of that day loved to joint together, or like one of his own inconstant essays, never true for a page to its proposed subject. "Nothing is so supple as our understanding: it is double and diverse; and the matters are double and diverse, too."

Descartes set himself to find some principle which even such a past master of skepticism could not impugn. He admitted from the start that one may cast doubt upon nearly all the articles of belief which constitute our common sense and our experience of the world. One may doubt, at least if he holds the Cartesian theory of knowledge, that he has a body. He may indeed be no more than a disembodied mind somehow dreaming of a body. It may well be that the people whom he sees in the streets have no souls, no consciousness. They may be automata or puppets. After all, he never directly experiences the consciousness of another human being. There is no conclusion of scientific thought, even of mathematics itself, about which an error owing to inattention, or to some hidden confusion, is not at least conceivable. And after all, when one calls to mind the scientific conclusions that he has come to accept, he does not at the same time call to mind all the evidence that supports them. This he perhaps remembers having examined; but he does not see it in detail, and memory is notoriously untrustworthy.

Descartes asks: What is there, then, that I cannot doubt? His answer is just this: The fact that I doubt. My doubting is something real. Just so a dream is real as a state of consciousness, if not as a representation of further reality. Certainly my doubting consciousness exists. At least the doubter cannot doubt his own existence as a thinking, doubting being. Thought, of which doubt is a variety, exists without any question. And since I think, I exist. My thinking ego is an actual thing, and I cannot doubt its existence. Nearly everything *about* which I think may be illusory. Every external object may be something other than what I take it to be. But the fact that I think about something is unquestionable. Whereupon Descartes summarizes: I have a clear and distinct idea of myself as a thinking being, *res cogitans*. Here follows Descartes's argument, as stated in his *Discourse on Method*.[19]

I had long before remarked that, in relation to practice, it is sometimes necessary to adopt, as if above doubt, opinions which we discern to be highly uncertain, as has been already said; but as I then desired to give my attention solely to the search after truth, I thought that a procedure exactly the opposite was called for, and that I ought to reject as absolutely false all opinions in regard to which I could suppose the least ground, for doubt, in order to ascertain whether

[19] Descartes, *op. cit.*, pp. 32-33.

after that there remained aught in my belief that was wholly indubitable. Accordingly, seeing that our senses sometimes deceive
us, I was willing to suppose that there existed nothing really such as
they presented to us, and because some men err in reasoning, and
fall into paralogisms, even on the simplest matters of Geometry, I,
convinced that I was as open to error as any other, rejected as false
all the reasonings I had hitherto taken for demonstrations; and
finally, when I considered that the very same thoughts (presentations) which we experience when awake may also be experienced
when we are asleep, while there is at that time not one of them true,
I supposed that all the objects (presentations) that had ever entered
into my mind when awake, had in them no more truth than the
illusions of my dreams. But immediately upon this I observed that,
whilst I thus wished to think that all was false, it was absolutely
necessary that I, who thus thought, should be somewhat; and as I
observed that this truth, *I think, hence I am,* was so certain and of
such evidence, that no ground of doubt, however extravagant, could
be alleged by the Sceptics capable of shaking it, I concluded that I
might, without scruple, accept it as the first principle of the Philosophy of which I was in search.

At this point Descartes's powers of analysis have failed him, and
he proceeds to take a step of which he can hardly have formed a
clear and distinct idea. He concludes that he is a thing or substance
that thinks. Have we after all a clear and distinct idea of the self as
a thing or substance that is, so to speak, an agent that thinks? We
cannot doubt that there is thinking. But a thing that *does* the thinking is perhaps another matter. How do I know that thinking belongs to an ego? And what does "belong" mean in this context?
Descartes makes no effort to discover a clear and distinct idea of
this relation, and so he passes over a problem that is to cause,
within a century, no end of difficulty and embarrassment (see below,
page 311).

The thinking thing is for Descartes a purely spiritual substance.
It is not a body or a living organism that thinks. Thought—and
accordingly the thinker—is absolutely unextended. It has no spatial
dimensions or relations. Thus my idea of "peace" is neither right
nor left, above or below, my idea of "truth." Nor is my *idea* of the

Pennsylvania Station in New York City larger or smaller than my *idea* of the physical atom. Spatial properties do not belong to ideas, not even to ideas *about* spatial objects. My idea of the triangle does not possess three sides. In the same way, my idea of fire is not hot. Thought is bound together by the logical relations of implication, the relations of "if" and "therefore," not by spatial or even temporal relations. Nor is my thinking located in any part of my body, or even vaguely within my body as a whole. The isosceles triangle does not exist within any spatial limits proper to my organism. Certainly it is not "in my head."

Descartes, then, refuses to doubt the existence of himself as a purely spiritual thinking being. So far he has escaped the universal skepticism of Montaigne. But this step is only a beginning. If Descartes is to banish doubt completely and to establish a philosophical foundation for the new sciences of physics and astronomy, he must believe in more than his own existence. He must offer sound reasons for dismissing any doubt, however refined, in the existence of a physical world external to or distinct from the mind. It is true that we all may say, "I possess a clear and distinct idea of the geometrical properties of space." But Descartes admits that, however carefully we examine this idea, we have no reason to suppose that it refers to something lying beyond or independent of the thinking self. He then undertakes to prove the existence of this external world by means of a rather lengthy argument. He first proves the existence of God, and from this truth he deduces the existence of his external world.

The proof of the existence of God, which is in all probability taken from Augustine, runs somewhat as follows: Since I doubt—that is, admit that I do not possess truth—I at least know what truth is. I am then aware of an ideal of a perfect knowledge that I do not myself possess. How comes it then that I possess this ideal? Can I, a very imperfect being, subject to illusion and to doubt, construct any ideal of perfection—of perfect knowledge, of perfect character, or of perfect power? The answer is simply that I cannot. Yet unquestionably I must possess such an ideal or I should not know that I doubt. The ideal must therefore come to me from another source, from a being capable of entertaining perfectly true knowledge. This being we may call God.

Descartes conceives of his deity as the Supreme Being of the Augustinian tradition, who is in no way limited or confined by any entity beyond himself. In order to strengthen this position, Descartes offers further arguments for the existence of God. One of these arguments is the ontological (see above, page 224) and another what we may call the argument from the nature of time. This is an auxiliary argument that supports Descartes's primary contention. This argument may be outlined as follows: I at least exist. Now supposing, for the sake of argument, that in some way my being (including the great ideal of perfection which I entertain) exists at the present moment independent of any created agency or supporting cause, the question still remains: Could my being then continue to exist without external assistance? Descartes feels that it could not. He argues as follows in the *Meditations:* [20]

For the whole time of my life may be divided into an infinity of parts, each of which is in no way dependent on any other; and, accordingly, because I was in existence a short time ago, it does not follow that I must now exist, unless in this moment some cause create me anew as it were,—that is, conserve me. In truth, it is perfectly clear and evident to all who will attentively consider the nature of duration, that the conservation of a substance, in each moment of its duration, requires the same power and act that would be necessary to create it, supposing it were not yet in existence; so that it is manifestly a dictate of the natural light that conservation and creation differ merely in respect of our mode of thinking [and not in reality]. All that is here required, therefore, is that I interrogate myself to discover whether I possess any power by means of which I can bring it about that I, who now am, shall exist a moment afterwards: for, since I am merely a thinking thing (or since, at least, the precise question, in the meantime, is only of that part of myself), if such a power resided in me, I should, without doubt, be conscious of it; but I am conscious of no such power, and thereby I manifestly know that I am dependent upon some being different from myself.

[20] *Ibid.,* p. 129.

But Descartes returns a moment later to his favorite argument, that drawn from the idea of perfection.[21]

There remains only the inquiry as to the way in which I received this idea from God; for I have not drawn it from the senses, nor is it even presented to me unexpectedly, as is usual with the ideas of sensible objects, when these are presented or appear to be presented to the external organs of the senses; it is not even a pure production or fiction of my mind, for it is not in my power to take from or add to it; and consequently there but remains the alternative that it is innate, in the same way as is the idea of myself. And, in truth, it is not to be wondered at that God, at my creation, implanted this idea in me, that it might serve, as it were, for the mark of the workman impressed on his work; and it is not also necessary that the mark should be something different from the work itself; but considering only that God is my creator, it is highly probable that he in some way fashioned me after his own image and likeness, and that I perceive this likeness, in which is contained the idea of God, by the same faculty by which I apprehend myself,—in other words, when I make myself the object of reflection, I not only find that I am an incomplete, [imperfect] and dependent being, and one who unceasingly aspires after something better and greater than he is, but, at the same time, I am assured likewise that he upon whom I am dependent possesses in himself all the goods after which I aspire, [and the ideas of which I find in my mind], and that not merely indefinitely and potentially, but infinitely and actually, and that he is thus God. And the whole force of the argument of which I have here availed myself to establish the existence of God, consists in this, that I perceive I could not possibly be of such a nature as I am, and yet have in my mind the idea of a God, if God did not in reality exist,—this same God, I say, whose idea is in my mind—that is, a being who possesses all those lofty perfections, of which the mind may have some slight conception, without, however, being able fully to comprehend them,—and who is wholly superior to all defect, [and has nothing that marks imperfection]: whence it is sufficiently manifest that he cannot be a deceiver, since it is a dictate of the natural light that all fraud and deception spring from some defect.

From this last proposition Descartes proceeds carefully to show that our belief in an external world is justified. Let us follow his

21 *Ibid.*, pp. 131-32.

lengthy argument in detail. We may do this most easily if we turn
to the text of his *Principles of Philosophy,* where he presents his
ideas in a form rather more precise than that of his *Meditations,*
from which we have just quoted. Here in the First Part of the *Principles,* having already exhibited his proofs of the existence of God,
Descartes sets out to draw conclusions from this great truth which
he has established to his own satisfaction.[22]

XXIX. That God is not the cause of our errors.
The first attribute of God which here falls to be considered, is
that he is absolutely veracious and the source of all light, so that it
is plainly repugnant for him to deceive us, or to be properly and
positively the cause of the errors to which we are consciously subject; for although the address to deceive seems to be some mark of
subtlety of mind among men, yet without doubt the will to deceive
only proceeds from malice or from fear and weakness, and consequently cannot be attributed to God.
XXX. That consequently all which we clearly perceive is true,
and that we are thus delivered from the doubts above proposed.
Whence it follows, that the light of nature, or faculty of knowledge given us by God, can never compass any object which is not
true, in as far as it attains to a knowledge of it, that is, in as far as
the object is clearly and distinctly apprehended. For God would
have merited the appellation of a deceiver if he had given us this
faculty perverted, and such as might lead us to take falsity for
truth [when we used it aright]. Thus the highest doubt is removed,
which arose from our ignorance on the point as to whether perhaps
our nature was such that we might be deceived even in those things
that appear to us the most evident. The same principle ought also
to be of avail against all the other grounds of doubting that have
been already enumerated. For mathematical truths ought now to be
above suspicion, since these are of the clearest. And if we perceive
anything by our senses, whether while awake or asleep, we will
easily discover the truth, provided we separate what there is of
clear and distinct in the knowledge from what is obscure and
confused....
XXXII. That there are only two modes of thinking in us, viz.,
the perception of the understanding and the action of the will.
For all the modes of thinking of which we are conscious may be
referred to two general classes, the one of which is the perception or

[22] *Ibid.,* pp. 206-10.

operation of the understanding, and the other the volition or operation of the will. Thus, to perceive by the senses (*sentire*), to imagine,
and to conceive things purely intelligible, are only different modes
of perceiving (*percipiendi*); but to desire, to be averse from, to
affirm, to deny, to doubt, are different modes of willing.

XXXIII. That we never err unless when we judge of something
which we do not sufficiently apprehend.

When we apprehend anything we are in no danger of error, if we
refrain from judging of it in any way; and even when we have
formed a judgment regarding it, we would never fall into error,
provided we gave our assent only to what we clearly and distinctly
perceived; but the reason why we are usually deceived, is that we
judge without possessing an exact knowledge of that of which we
judge.

XXXIV. That the will as well as the understanding is required
for judging.

I admit that the understanding is necessary for judging, there
being no room to suppose that we can judge of that which we in
no way apprehend; but the will also is required in order to our
assenting to what we have in any degree perceived. It is not necessary, however, at least to form any judgment whatever, that we
have an entire and perfect apprehension of a thing; for we may
assent to many things of which we have only a very obscure and
confused knowledge.

XXXV. That the will is of greater extension than the understanding, and is thus the source of our errors.

Further, the perception of the intellect extends only to the few
things that are presented to it, and is always very limited: the will,
on the other hand, may, in a certain sense, be said to be infinite,
because we observe nothing than can be the object of the will of any
other, even of the unlimited will of God, to which ours cannot also
extend, so that we easily carry it beyond the objects we clearly perceive; and when we do this, it is not wonderful that we happen to
be deceived....

XXXIX. That the liberty of our will is self-evident.

Finally, it is so manifest that we possess a free will, capable of
giving or withholding its assent, that this truth must be reckoned
among the first and most common notions which are born with us.
This, indeed, has already very clearly appeared, for when essaying
to doubt of all things, we went so far as to suppose even that he
who created us employed his limitless power in deceiving us in
every way, we were conscious nevertheless of being free to abstain

from believing what was not in every respect certain and undoubted. But that of which we are unable to doubt at such a time is as self-evident and clear as any thing we can ever know.

Descartes is now ready finally to prove the existence of a physical world that exists distinct from our knowledge of it. The closing argument is based on the principle that God would be deceiving us if he allowed sensation that apparently comes upon us from without to arouse in us ideas of a world that does not really exist beyond our minds. The following selections from the Second Part of the *Principles* contain this argument and also describe Descartes's conception of the physical world.[23] (Descartes was in his day considered to be as outstanding in the field of physics as in that of philosophy. Today, however, his physical conceptions are primarily of historical importance, Descartes's works having been superseded in his own century by the great theories of Isaac Newton.)

I. The grounds on which the existence of material things may be known with certainty.

Although we are all sufficiently persuaded of the existence of material things, yet, since this was before called in question by us, and since we reckoned the persuasion of their existence as among the prejudices of our childhood, it is now necessary for us to investigate the grounds on which this truth may be known with certainty. In the first place, then, it cannot be doubted that every perception we have comes to us from some object different from our mind; for it is not in our power to cause ourselves to experience one perception rather than another, the perception being entirely dependent on the object which affects our senses. It may, indeed, be matter of inquiry whether that object be God, or something different from God; but because we perceive, or rather, stimulated by sense, clearly and distinctly apprehend, certain matter extended in length, breadth, and thickness, the various parts of which have different figures and motions, and give rise to the sensations we have of colours, smells, pain, etc., God would, without question, deserve to be regarded as a deceiver, if he directly and of himself presented to our mind the idea of this extended matter, or merely caused it to be presented to us by some object which possessed neither extension, figure, nor motion. For we clearly conceive this

[23] *Ibid.*, pp. 232-45.

matter as entirely distinct from God, and from ourselves, or our mind; and appear even clearly to discern that the idea of it is formed in us on occasion of objects existing out of our minds, to which it is in every respect similar. But since God cannot deceive us, for this is repugnant to his nature, as has been already remarked, we must unhesitatingly conclude that there exists a certain object extended in length, breadth, and thickness, and possessing all those properties which we clearly apprehend to belong to what is extended. And this extended substance is what we call body or matter.

II. How we likewise know that the human body is closely connected with the mind.

We ought also to conclude that a certain body is more closely united to our mind than any other, because we clearly observe that pain and other sensations affect us without our foreseeing them; and these, the mind is conscious, do not arise from itself alone, nor pertain to it, in so far as it is a thing which thinks, but only in so far as it is united to another thing extended and moveable, which is called the human body. But this is not the place to treat in detail of this matter.

III. That the perceptions of the senses do not teach us what is in reality in things, but what is beneficial or hurtful to the composite whole of mind and body.

It will be sufficient to remark that the perceptions of the senses are merely to be referred to this intimate union of the human body and mind, and that they usually make us aware of what, in external objects, may be useful or adverse to this union, but do not present to us these objects as they are in themselves, unless occasionally and by accident. For, after this observation, we will without difficulty lay aside the prejudices of the senses, and will have recourse to our understanding alone on this question, by reflecting carefully on the ideas implanted in it by nature.

IV. That the nature of body consists not in weight, hardness, colour, and the like, but in extension alone.

In this way we will discern that the nature of matter or body, considered in general, does not consist in its being hard, or ponderous, or coloured, or that which affects our senses in any other way, but simply in its being a substance extended in length, breadth, and depth. For, with respect to hardness, we know nothing of it by sense farther than that the parts of hard bodies resist the motion of our hands on coming into contact with them; but if every time our hands moved towards any part, all the bodies in that place receded as quickly as our hands approached, we should never feel hardness;

and yet we have no reason to believe that bodies which might thus recede would on this account lose that which makes them bodies. The nature of body does not, therefore, consist in hardness. In the same way, it may be shown that weight, colour, and all the other qualities of this sort, which are perceived in corporeal matter, may be taken from it, itself meanwhile remaining entire: it thus follows that the nature of body depends on none of these....

VIII. That quantity and number differ only in thought (*ratione*) from that which has quantity and is numbered.

For quantity differs from extended substance, and number from what is numbered, not in reality but merely in our thought; so that, for example, we may consider the whole nature of a corporeal substance which is comprised in a space of ten feet, although we do not attend to this measure of ten feet, for the obvious reason that the thing conceived is of the same nature in any part of that space as in the whole; and, on the other hand, we can conceive the number ten, as also a continuous quantity of ten feet, without thinking of this determinate substance, because the concept of the number ten is manifestly the same whether we consider a number of ten feet or ten of anything else; and we can conceive a continuous quantity of ten feet without thinking of this or that determinate substance, although we cannot conceive it without some extended substance of which it is the quantity. It is in reality, however, impossible that any, even the least part, of such quantity or extension, can be taken away, without the retrenchment at the same time of as much of the substance, nor, on the other hand, can we lessen the substance, without at the same time taking as much from the quantity or extension.

IX. That corporeal substance, when distinguished from its quantity, is confusedly conceived as something incorporeal.

Although perhaps some express themselves otherwise on this matter, I am nevertheless convinced that they do not think differently from what I have now said: for when they distinguish (corporeal) substance from extension or quantity, they either mean nothing by the word (corporeal) substance, or they form in their minds merely a confused idea of incorporeal substance, which they falsely attribute to corporeal, and leave to extension the true idea of this corporeal substance; which extension they call an accident, but with such impropriety as to make it easy to discover that their words are not in harmony with their thoughts....

XVI. That a vacuum or space in which there is absolutely no body is repugnant to reason.

With regard to a vacuum, in the philosophical sense of the term, that is, a space in which there is no substance, it is evident that such does not exist, seeing the extension of space or internal place is not different from that of body. For since from this alone, that a body has extension in length, breadth, and depth, we have reason to conclude that it is a substance, it being absolutely contradictory that nothing [nonbeing] should possess extension, we ought to form a similar inference regarding the space which is supposed void, viz., that since there is extension in it there is necessarily also substance....

XXIII. That all the variety of matter, or the diversity of its forms, depends on motion.

There is therefore but one kind of matter in the whole universe, and this we know only by its being extended. All the properties we distinctly perceive to belong to it are reducible to its capacity of being divided and moved according to its parts; and accordingly it is capable of all those affections which we perceive can arise from the motion of its parts. For the partition of matter in thought makes no change in it; but all variation of it, or diversity of form, depends on motion. The philosophers even seem universally to have observed this, for they said that nature was the principle of motion and rest, and by nature they understood that by which all corporeal things become such as they are found in experience.

XXIV. What motion is, taking the term in its common use.

But motion (viz., local, for I can conceive no other kind of motion, and therefore I do not think we ought to suppose there is any other in nature), in the ordinary sense of the term, is nothing more than the *action by which a body passes from one place to another*. And just as we have remarked above that the same thing may be said to change and not to change place at the same time, so also we may say that the same thing is at the same time moved and not moved. Thus, for example, a person seated in a vessel which is setting sail, thinks he is in motion if he look to the shore that he has left, and consider it as fixed; but not if he regard the ship itself, among the parts of which he preserves always the same situation. Moreover, because we are accustomed to suppose that there is no motion without action, and that in rest there is the cessation of action, the person thus seated is more properly said to be at rest than in motion, seeing he is not conscious of being in action.

The reader should contrast this theory of the external world with the conceptual framework within which Isaac Newton successfully erected his laws of motion and his principle of gravitation. Descartes considers space and matter to be identical, so that matter possesses only geometrical properties. He denies the existence of a vacuum or empty space, into which bodies seem to move. He prefers a theory of relative motion, bodies being in motion only *with relation to other bodies,* each unit gliding or swimming through a plenum of displaceable bodies so that no vacuum is ever produced, each body being thought to be always in contact with the surfaces of surrounding bodies. To this Descartes adds that one body can impart motion to another only by coming in actual contact with it. There is no "action at a distance" whereby one body may attract another.[24]

On the other hand, Newton accepts space as an entity independent of matter in which bodies move and exercise a mutual attraction upon one another, proportional to their masses and to the inverse square of the distance between them. In fact, space is the medium through which this attraction at a distance is propagated. Such absolute space existing as independent of the bodies it contains is not an object of experience. We perceive only the spatial relation of one body to another. Absolute space can be known only to mathematical intelligence.

However, only the aspects of Newton's work that can be checked by calculation and observation remain essential to the science of physics. Thus his theory of an absolute, empty space, an entity that cannot be observed and whose presence cannot influence our calculations need not be accepted as equally necessary to physical theory, as is the Newtonian mathematics of gravitation. On this one point more recent physical theory has turned toward Descartes, who stands in some ways closer to Einstein than to Newton.

[24] Being without a theory of action at a distance, Descartes was compelled to interpret the solar system as a sort of whirlpool, or vortex, in which the planets are carried around the sun, bathed in a moving ether or "light matter." The vortex has been formed by the collision of moving particles, because of which the smaller units are driven toward a center, where they are compressed together to form a central sun, while the larger ones revolve about this center. These particles or units are the product of friction that movement introduces into extension.

∗» CHAPTER IX «∗

The Cartesian Problem of Interaction

BODY AND MIND

St. Augustine had gladly limited his philosophical interests to an understanding of God and the human soul. To these Descartes added, as we have just seen, an interest in the physical world. Accordingly he directed his curiosity toward these three objectives: God, the human mind, and the physical world. He conceived of the universe as containing three kinds of things or, as he preferred to say, substances: God, thought, and extension or matter. We have already followed his attempts to establish the existence of each type of substance. It is now our purpose to learn how he related the three substances one to another in a systematic scheme.

Let us quote again from the *Principles*, Part One.[1]

LI. What substance is, and that the term is not applicable to God and the creatures in the same sense.

But with regard to what we consider as things or the modes of things, it is worth while to examine each of them by itself. By substance we can conceive nothing else than a thing which exists in such a way as to stand in need of nothing beyond itself in order to its existence. And, in truth, there can be conceived but one substance which is absolutely independent, and that is God. We perceive that all other things can exist only by help of the concourse of God. And, accordingly, the term substance does not apply to God and the creatures *univocally*, to adopt a term familiar in the schools; that is, no signification of this word can be distinctly understood which is common to God and them.

LII. That the term is applicable univocally to the mind and the body, and how substance itself is known.

[1] *The Method, Meditations, and Selections from the Principles of Descartes*, pp. 215-17.

Created substances, however, whether corporeal or thinking, may be conceived under this common concept; for these are things which, in order to their existence, stand in need of nothing but the concourse of God. But yet substance cannot be first discovered merely from its being a thing which exists independently, for existence by itself is not observed by us. We easily, however, discover substance itself from any attribute of it, by this common notion, that of nothing there are no attributes, properties, or qualities: for, from perceiving that some attribute is present, we infer that some existing thing or substance to which it may be attributed is also of necessity present.

LIII. That of every substance there is one principal attribute, as thinking of the mind, extension of the body.

But, although any attribute is sufficient to lead us to the knowledge of substance, there is, however, one principal property of every substance, which constitutes its nature or essence, and upon which all the others depend. Thus, extension in length, breadth, and depth, constitutes the nature of corporeal substance; and thought the nature of thinking substance. For every other thing that can be attributed to body, presupposes extension, and is only some mode of an extended thing; as all the properties we discover in the mind are only diverse modes of thinking. Thus, for example, we cannot conceive figure unless in something extended, nor motion unless in extended space, nor imagination, sensation, or will, unless in a thinking thing. But, on the other hand, we can conceive extension without figure or motion, and thought without imagination or sensation, and so of the others; as is clear to any one who attends to these matters.

LIV. How we may have clear and distinct notions of the substance which thinks, of that which is corporeal, and of God.

And thus we may easily have two clear and distinct notions or ideas, the one of created substance, which thinks, the other of corporeal substance, provided we carefully distinguish all the attributes of thought from those of extension. We may also have a clear and distinct idea of an uncreated and independent thinking substance, that is, of God, provided we do not suppose that this idea adequately represents to us all that is in God, and do not mix up with it anything fictitious, but attend simply to the characters that are comprised in the notion we have of him, and which we clearly know to belong to the nature of an absolutely perfect Being. For no one can deny that there is in us such an idea of God, without groundlessly supposing that there is no knowledge of God at all in the human mind.

According to such reasoning, man is a union of two substances, of *res cogitans* and *res extensa*. Between these two substances there must take place what is known as interaction. When I will to lift my hand and succeed in doing so, my mind has influenced my body. And when I recognize that I feel pain, my body has influenced my mind. In other words, thinking substance and extended substance seem to be linked by cause and effect. Descartes had formed what he considered clear and distinct ideas of thought and of body. The further task lay before him of forming such an idea of the union or interaction of thought and body. He did not clarify the situation when he located interaction in the pineal gland, a small organ to be found just above the cerebral lobes of the brain.

Consider any spatially extended body being moved not by impact of another body, but by the action of a nonspatial idea. When we consider bodily motion, we expect to find the cause of this motion located somewhere in space along with the moving body; moreover, we expect to find the effects which this moving body produces also localized. But according to Cartesian principles this is most difficult to conceive. Space is of the essence of body, and an idea is nonspatial. Interaction between the two seems inconceivable. We may as well talk of shooting the square root of 2 with a popgun.

It is important to notice that before Descartes's time the problem of interaction had not received the attention that the seventeenth-century thinkers bestowed upon it. This was not because earlier thinkers were any less astute in their reflections, but because Descartes had virtually produced the problem by his way of describing body and mind. Between these two substances Descartes tried to establish efficient causation. Had he followed Aristotle and thought of the mind as a formal cause of the organism's behavior, he might have avoided much difficulty. The formal cause, pattern of behavior, or "manner of go" of an organism may be thought of as unextended without difficulty. But Descartes was far from Aristotle. He wished to make consciousness something quite independent of the organism and its body. Otherwise he could not describe it as indubitably real, since the very existence of bodily organism was still subject to question at the beginning of Descartes's meditations.

Descartes's contemporaries were quick to notice that there was a flaw in his thinking on this subject. The atomist Gassendi challenged him in the following words: [2]

How may the union of the corporeal with the incorporeal be conceived? ... How will that which is corporeal seize upon that which is incorporeal, so to hold it conjoined with itself, or how will the incorporeal grasp the corporeal, so as reciprocally to keep it bound to itself.... ? I ask you how you think that you, if you are incorporeal and unextended, are capable of experiencing the sensation of pain? ... The general difficulty always remains, how the corporeal can have anything in common with the incorporeal, or what relationship may be established between the one and the other.

Two decades later Spinoza objected in even more telling fashion. Having briefly sketched the Cartesian theory of interaction between mind and body, Spinoza proceeds: [3]

So far as I can gather from his own words, this is the opinion of that distinguished man, and I could scarcely have believed it possible for one so great to have put it forward if it had been less subtle. I can hardly wonder enough that a philosopher who firmly resolved to make no deduction except from self-evident principles, and to affirm nothing but what he clearly and distinctly perceived, and who blamed all the schoolmen because they desired to explain obscure matters by occult qualities, should accept a hypothesis more occult than any occult quality. What does he understand, I ask, by the union of the mind and body? What clear and distinct conception has he of thought intimately connected with a certain small portion of matter? I wish that he had explained this union by its proximate cause. But he conceived the mind to be so distinct from the body that he was able to assign no single cause of this union, nor of the mind itself, but was obliged to have recourse to the cause of the whole universe, that is to say, to God.

In the last sentence Spinoza refers to a suggestion made casually by Descartes, and not strictly characteristic of his thought, to the

[2] Letter from Pierre Gassendi to Descartes, 1641, quoted by Descartes in *Objections and Replies*. See *The Philosophical Works of Descartes*, trans. E. S. Haldane and G. R. T. Ross, Cambridge University Press, 1912, v. 2, pp. 201-202.

[3] Spinoza, *Ethics*, trans. by William Hale White, p. 251. Macmillan & Co., London; The Macmillan Company, New York; 1883. This and later quotations are reprinted by permission of the publishers.

effect that God has so constructed the world that upon the occasion of a certain change taking place in our bodies a corresponding change takes place in our minds. Thus interaction is to us a mystery. Only God can bring about an intercourse between body and mind, and only God can understand it.

Thus we see that Descartes's system cannot stand up under the scrutiny of a very Cartesian criticism. The two types of created substance cannot be of such diverse nature as Descartes had considered to be possible. The outcome, in its general outline at least, is not hard to foresee. The successors of Descartes must join together what he had put asunder. Now if we leave out of consideration the possibility of a return to an Aristotelian theory that relates body to mind as form to matter, there remain four alternatives open. These are materialism, parallelism, idealism, and occasionalism.

1. *Materialism* avoids the Cartesian problem of interaction by reducing mind to body. This is undertaken by the English thinker Thomas Hobbes.

2. *Parallelism* interprets body and mind as two closely corresponding aspects of one and the same fundamental reality and so avoids the necessity of interaction. Parallelism is characteristic of the philosophy of Spinoza.

3. *Idealism* avoids the problem of interaction by reducing body to mind. This is the alternative chosen by Leibniz.

4. *Occasionalism* denies interaction but maintains that body and mind "keep step" with one another, behaving just as if they did actually interact. This harmony is maintained by God's omnipotent interference. On the occasion that I will to arise, God alters the motions of my muscles to make this possible. And on the occasion that I cut my finger, God alters my consciousness so that it includes pain. We have already seen that Descartes himself at one time considered this theory. It was also advanced by Geulincx and Malebranche.

The first three of these alternatives overrule the Cartesian notion that there can be two wholly distinct types of created or finite substance. The fourth alternative finds us still within the Cartesian philosophy invoking the omnipotence of deity in order to overcome its difficulties. This alternative is no longer considered seriously, since it explains one mystery merely by appeal to another. Let us consider the remaining three.

We have in another context already examined the materialist's position. It involves all the difficulties into which Democritus fell when he attempted to identify thinking with the motion of atoms (see above, p. 22). Modern materialism brings no new solution of these difficulties.

THE PARALLELISM OF SPINOZA [4]

Let us now consider parallelism in some detail. According to this theory, consciousness and extension are always inseparable and intimately reflect one another's structure. There is in the universe no body without a corresponding mind and no mind without a corresponding body. This amounts to panpsychism, or the theory that all things are animated, possessing some degree of psychic activity. There is no moment of human consciousness that has not a correlate in the bodily state of the agent, and no physiological condition that is not somehow reflected in consciousness. The term "parallelism,' although widely used, is hardly strong enough to characterize Spinoza's view. Spinozism really depends upon the assumption that

[4] Baruch (Benedictus de) Spinoza (1632-1677), a Portuguese Jew whose family had fled to Amsterdam to escape persecution, quarreled with his own people on religious grounds and was excommunicated from the synagogue at Amsterdam. After this he lived quietly and obscurely in Amsterdam, in Rijnsburg, and in The Hague, supporting himself by grinding lenses. Most of his work remained unpublished during his lifetime and was circulated among his friends in manuscript form. His pantheism was generally taken for atheism, and he lived in constant danger of persecution, even in Holland. The gentleness and sincerity of his character made him beloved not only by his fellow students with whom he talked and corresponded but also by the simple people among whom he lived. He was quite without avarice, twice relinquishing his hold upon considerable fortunes, one coming from his father, which he yielded to his sisters, and another that he returned to the family of an enthusiastic admirer who had impulsively made him his heir. Although living in poverty, Spinoza refused a comfortable appointment at the University of Heidelberg because there was some question concerning the freedom of instruction to be accorded him.

Spinoza was influenced by certain Hebrew thinkers of the Middle Ages, but more profoundly by Descartes himself. He was so fascinated by Descartes's mathematical method that he undertook to present or "demonstrate" his own thought in "geometrical form," with axioms, definitions, theorem, corollaries, such as we find in Euclid.

body and mind are related to one another as the convex and concave "sides" of a curve, as two genuine aspects of one and the same thing; that is, in the case of the curve, of one set of points. This image is more helpful than that of two parallel lines. There is no need to talk of interaction. The two sides of a curve do not interact, one does not cause the other, but both are determined by one formula or by one sweep of the pencil. But of course, although the two do not interact, we cannot have one without the other. Nor is one purposive while the other is mechanical. In fact, Spinoza denies final causes in the orders of both mind and matter.

With this bold assumption as a background, Spinoza brings Descartes's theory of the three substances into a closely knit system, much simpler than Descartes's own, although Descartes had been very close to the Spinozist solution when he asserted that God is the only true substance.

To return to the analogy of the curve just mentioned, we may say that God is the curve itself, the one true substance, or independent reality, requiring nothing beyond itself in order to exist. Accordingly, mind and extension are attributes, properties, or aspects of the one substance; that is, following our analogy, the inside and the outside of the curve. Substance as a whole is present in each of its attributes. Just so, the whole curve may be considered in its concave or its convex aspects. There are other attributes, thus other ways at looking at substance, but we are not aware of these. Thought and extension exhaust our perspectives of the universe, but for the infinite intellect of God other perspectives—an infinite number of them according to Spinoza—are apparent.

The universe is as much a system of thought as one of extended body. The logical relations of implication, the structures of ground and consequent, characterize the world quite as truly as do the laws of motion. The infinite intellect of God corresponds to the total system of motion and rest. The former is the systematic organization of truth, the latter that of motion. This correspondence can be found on lower levels.

Our own finite thought may be described as the "idea" of our body. Thus the mind of each organism is said to apprehend the universe as the setting or background which includes the body of that organism. This body through its many forms of sensitivity participates in the structure of the world, and the mind that is the idea of this body apprehends the nature of things accordingly.

Human behavior may be studied fruitfully either from the point of view of the subject's consciousness or from that of his overt actions and physiological processes.

The things of our ordinary experience, indeed all finite entities— sticks, stones, stars, plants, animals, and people, things that in another context we might call "substances"—are for Spinoza "modes" or modifications of the one substance. They are incomplete details of substance, inseparable from it. Each mode is present in each attribute, being repeated from a new point of view in each one of the perspectives of reality. The mode stands to substance as a whole as waves and currents belong to the ocean. Apart from substance, the one self-existing reality, there can be no modes, and conversely there can be no substance without modes of some sort. No mode can exist by itself. It requires the environment of substance as a whole to support its existence. Substance or God alone constitutes or includes all of the conditions required by any single mode. Thus God merits the name of "perfect" or "complete" being. Spinoza argues that God is a substance of this sort, whose existence is established by the ontological argument. For Spinoza, the perfect being does not create the world. It includes the detail of the world as its own modification. In Spinoza's theory the pantheistic implications of the Augustinian tradition are at last made explicitly manifest.

The framework of Spinoza's thought is contained in the definitions with which he opens his greatest work, the *Ethics*. The full title of this work is especially illuminating: *Ethics, Demonstrated after the Fashion of Geometry*. The argument of the *Ethics* opens with a set of definitions and axioms, from which are deduced a body of propositions, arranged as in a textbook of geometry. The definitions follow.[5]

I. By the self-caused (*causa sui*) I understand that, whose essence involves existence; or that, whose nature cannot be conceived un-

[5] *Ibid.*, p. 1. We have made slight changes in I and IV.

less existing. (By the ontological argument Spinoza shows that God or substance is *causa sui*.)

II. That thing is called finite in its own kind which can be limited by another thing of the same nature. For example, a body is called finite, because we always conceive another which is greater. So a thought is limited by another thought; but a body is not limited by a thought, nor a thought by a body. (Spinoza is here referring to the modes, which he defines below, definition V.)

III. By substance, I understand that which is in itself and is conceived through itself; in other words, that, the conception of which does not need the conception of another thing from which it must be formed.

IV. By attribute, I understand that which the intellect perceives of substance, as constituting its essence.

V. By mode, I understand the affections of substance, or that which is in another thing through which also it is conceived.

VI. By God, I understand Being absolutely infinite, that is to say, substance consisting of infinite attributes, each one of which expresses eternal and infinite essence.

Explanation.—I say absolutely infinite but not infinite in its own kind; for of whatever is infinite only in its own kind, we can deny infinite attributes; but to the essence of that which is absolutely infinite pertains whatever expresses essence and involves no negation.

Spinoza proves by a number of arguments that God or the infinite being must exist. The simplest of these arguments appears below. Its close similarity to the reasoning of Anselm will be obvious.[6]

Inability to exist is impotence, and, on the other hand, ability to exist is power, as is self-evident. If, therefore, there is nothing which necessarily exists excepting things finite, it follows that things finite are more powerful than the absolutely infinite Being, and this (as is self-evident) is absurd; therefore either nothing exists or Being absolutely infinite also necessarily exists. But we ourselves exist, either in ourselves or in something else which necessarily exists. Therefore the Being absolutely infinite, that is to say, God, necessarily exists. Q.E.D.

6 *Ibid.*, p. 10.

There is a serious difficulty in the interpretation of definition IV that has caused trouble to many students of Spinoza. Attribute is defined as "that which the intellect perceives of substance." But intellect, as a mode of thought, is itself a modification of one of the attributes. Therefore attribute must be prior to intellect. Certainly intellect cannot then be the cause of attribute. Hence intellect does not produce the attribute, which must then exist as an extramental constituent of substance. In that case, substance must be in some way divided into an infinite number of corresponding members. We may well ask what causes this division. Can we say, as Spinoza does occasionally, that these attributes are "aspects" or "expressions" of substance? But what is an aspect without a knowing mind? And for Spinoza, mind is itself an attribute. This is a very serious obscurity, perhaps fatal to Spinoza's system.

The determinism of Spinoza's system allows no exceptions. Both God and man are involved in it. God does not choose the detail of his world, nor does he create anything by "fiat." The lives of human beings are determined in detail. There is for Spinoza no such thing as the Cartesian free will, spontaneous in its decisions. Every human act or decision is in every detail wholly conditioned, and follows from the nature of substance just as the truth that the sum of the angles of a triangle is equal to two right angles follows from the nature or definition of a triangle.

It is interesting and important to notice this attitude. Spinoza thought of concrete things and actual events as "following" upon the nature of substance just as certain propositions in mathematics follow upon other propositions. Thus any item of finite existence is as completely determined by and dependent upon God or nature as a segment of a circumference is dependent upon the rotation of the radius that generates it.

Both Spinoza and Descartes seem to have been willing to consider the world as if it were virtually a system of mathematics, a web of geometrical relations. Thus they seem to have confused the implications whereby theorems are bound together with the principles or powers that activate the concrete world. They tended to ignore Plato's warning that the concrete world may contain but an imperfect exemplification of mathematical law and order, and that this world may be subject to powers other than purely logical principles. Accordingly they found themselves facing a determinism or necessitarianism of the most rigorous sort.

Spinoza, unlike Descartes, made no effort to escape from this. While Descartes insisted upon an indeterminist theory of the human will, the spontaneous nature of which he believed was evident to our intuition, Spinoza built his philosophy of conduct squarely upon the presupposition of determinism. Thus Spinoza treats the moral agent, considered as mind and as physical organism, in terms of his theory of finite modes. Spinoza's moral philosophy may be interpreted as a persistent effort to reconcile the notion of autonomy and moral freedom with the determinism to which his metaphysics had committed him. We shall consider this important phase of his thought in another chapter.

We have already noticed that the speculative systems of early modern philosophy tend to be strikingly anti-Aristotelian in spirit. Of these, Spinoza's system may be considered the most extreme. For Aristotle, nothing exists but individual substances, co-ordinated within the limits of a world system. For Spinoza, the world system is itself the one and only true individual. It is the one substance. All finite things depend upon it for their essential character as well as for the fact of their existence. These finite entities, or modes, are literally quite unthinkable without reference to the one background of reality that they all share. Spinoza summarizes this situation in his famous formula "All determination is negation." This statement is not merely a logical principle. It is the reflection of an attitude toward the world, a recognition of the common presence of all things in a single togetherness.

Spinoza's view of nature reminds one of the curious statement once made by the American mystic Paul Benjamin Blood: "Indeed we may fancy an intelligence which, instead of regarding things as simply owning entity, should regard chiefly their background as affected by the holes which they are making in it." [7]

---

[7] Quoted by William James in "A Pluralistic Mystic," *Memories and Studies,* Longmans, Green & Co., New York, 1911, p. 380.

Spinoza has been called a "God-intoxicated" man. This description is true enough, but we must remember that for him, God is identified with nature, or the world as a whole. Nature, so intuited and so conceived, entails not only all thought and all extension but also the full duration or history proper to them. What to us appears as *past, present,* or *future* must be realized in one closed system of interrelation that itself has no history. The sublimity of this concept of eternity gradually dawns upon us as we study Spinoza. His contemporary Pascal once spoke with awe of the astronomical universe as a sphere "whose center is everywhere and whose circumference nowhere." Spinoza contemplates such a universe "under the aspect of eternity," recognizing temporal duration as well as spatial immensity as its partial manifestation.

Eternity is recognized as constituting "existence itself." Thus no finite entity or mode can be considered fully real as it stands in a moment of time, against a background of history with an indeterminate future extending vaguely before it. The true reality of this finite mode is inseparable from the world as a whole that encompasses it. There is no open or unfinished future or field of alternative possibility. There is nothing in the world undetermined or contingent—no lacunae and no loose ends.

Spinoza finds in his concept of substance as eternal perfection or fullness of being, which depends upon nothing beyond itself, a satisfying object of religious contemplation. But his religion stands far removed from most popular creeds. As the following passage makes evident, Spinoza finds it necessary to repudiate any sort of final cause or purpose as characterizing the world. Spinoza's universe—by name, substance, God, or Nature—*contains* its details. It does not plan or create them. We quote from the appendix to the first book of the *Ethics*.[8]

In the foregoing I have explained the nature and properties of God. I have shown that he necessarily exists, that he is one: that he is, and acts solely by the necessity of his own nature; that he is the free cause of all things, and how he is so; that all things are in God,

[8] Spinoza, *Ethics,* trans. by R. H. M. Elwes, pp. 70-75. Bohn Library. George Bell & Sons, London, 1884. Reprinted by permission of the publisher.

and so depend on him, that without him they could neither exist nor be conceived; lastly, that all things are predetermined by God, not through his free will or absolute fiat, but from the very nature of God or infinite power. I have further, where occasion offered, taken care to remove the prejudices, which might impede the comprehension of my demonstrations. Yet there still remain misconceptions not a few, which might and may prove very grave hindrances to the understanding of the concatenation of things, as I have explained it above. I have therefore thought it worth while to bring these misconceptions before the bar of reason.

All such opinions spring from the notion commonly entertained, that all things in nature act as men themselves act, namely, with an end in view. It is accepted as certain, that God himself directs all things to a definite goal (for it is said that God made all things for man, and man that he might worship him). I will, therefore, consider this opinion, asking first, why it obtains general credence, and why all men are naturally so prone to adopt it? secondly, I will point out its falsity; and, lastly, I will show how it has given rise to prejudices about good and bad, right and wrong, praise and blame, order and confusion, beauty and ugliness, and the like.

I. This is not the place to deduce these misconceptions from the nature of the human mind: it will be sufficient here, if I assume as a starting point, what ought to be universally admitted, namely, that all men are born ignorant of the causes of things, that all have the desire to seek for what is useful to them, and that they are conscious of such desire. Herefrom it follows first, that men think themselves free, inasmuch as they are conscious of their volitions and desires, and never even dream, in their ignorance, of the causes which have disposed them to wish and desire. Secondly, that men do all things for an end, namely, for that which is useful to them, and which they seek. Thus it comes to pass that they only look for a knowledge of the final causes of events, and when these are learned, they are content, as having no cause for further doubt. If they cannot learn such causes from external sources, they are compelled to turn to considering themselves, and reflecting what end would have induced them personally to bring about the given event, and thus they necessarily judge other natures by their own. Further, as they find in themselves and outside themselves many means which assist them not a little in their search for what is useful, for instance, eyes for seeing, teeth for chewing, herbs and animals for yielding food, the sun for giving light, the sea for breeding fish, etc., they come to look on the whole of nature as a means for obtaining such conveniences. Now as they are aware, that they found these conveniences and did not make them they think they have cause for believing, that some other being has made them for their use. As they look upon things as means, they cannot believe them to be self-created; but, judging from the means which they are accustomed to prepare for themselves, they are bound to believe in some ruler or rulers of the universe endowed with human freedom, who have arranged and adapted everything for human use. They are bound to estimate the nature of such rulers (having no information on the subject) in accordance with their own nature, and therefore, they assert that the gods ordained everything for the use of man, in order to bind man to themselves and obtain from him the highest honors. Hence also it follows, that everyone thought out for himself, according to his abilities, a different way of worshipping God, so that God might love him more than his fellows, and direct the whole course of nature for the satisfaction of his blind cupidity and insatiable avarice. Thus the prejudice developed into superstition, and took deep root in the human mind; and for this reason everyone strove most zealously to understand and explain the final causes of things; but in their endeavor to show that nature does nothing in vain, i.e., nothing which is useless to man, they only seem to have demonstrated that nature, the gods, and men are all mad together. Consider, I pray you, the result: among the many helps of nature they were bound to find some hindrances, such as storms, earthquakes, diseases, etc.: so they declared that such things happen, because the gods are angry at some wrong done them by men, or at some fault committed in their worship. Experience day by day protested and showed by infinite examples, that good and evil fortunes fall to the lot of pious and impious alike; still they would not abandon their inveterate prejudice, for it was more easy for them to class such contradictions among other unknown things of whose use they were ignorant, and thus to retain their actual and innate condition of ignorance, than to destroy the whole fabric of their reasoning and start afresh. They therefore laid down as an axiom, that God's judgments far transcend human understanding. Such a doctrine might well have sufficed to conceal the truth from the human race for all eternity, if mathematics had not furnished another standard of verity in considering solely the essence and properties of figures without regard to their final causes...

II. Further, this doctrine does away with the perfection of God: for, if God acts for an object, he necessarily desires something which he lacks. Certainly, theologians and metaphysicians draw a distinction between the object of want and the object of assimilation; still they confess that God made all things for the sake of himself, not for the sake of creation. They are unable to point to anything prior to creation, except God himself, as an object for which God should act, and are therefore driven to admit (as they clearly must), that God lacked those things for whose attainment he created means, and further that he desired them ...

III. After men persuaded themselves, that everything which is created is created for their sake, they were bound to consider as the chief quality in everything that which is most useful to themselves, and to account those things the best of all which have the most beneficial effect on mankind. Further, they were bound to form abstract notions for the explanation of the nature of things, such as *goodness, badness, order, confusion, warmth, cold, beauty, deformity,* and so on; and from the belief that they are free agents arose the further notions *praise* and *blame, sin* and *merit.*

I will speak of these latter hereafter, when I treat of human nature; the former I will briefly explain here.

Everything which conduces to health and the worship of God they have called *good,* everything which hinders these objects they have styled *bad;* and inasmuch as those who do not understand the nature of things do not verify phenomena in any way, but merely imagine them after a fashion, and mistake their imagination for understanding, such persons firmly believe that there is an *order* in things, being really ignorant both of things and their own nature. When phenomena are of such a kind, that the impression they make on our senses requires little effort of imagination, and can consequently be easily remembered, we say that they are *well-ordered;* if the contrary, that they are *ill-ordered* or *confused.* Further, as things which are easily imagined are more pleasing to us, men prefer order to confusion—as though there were any order in nature, except in relation to our imagination—and say that God has created all things in order; thus, without knowing it, attributing imagination to God, unless, indeed, they would have it that God foresaw human imagination, and arranged everything, so that it should be most easily imagined. If this be their theory they would not, perhaps, be daunted by the fact that we find an infinite number of phenomena, far surpassing our imagination, and very many others which confound its weakness. But enough has been said on this subject. The other abstract notions are nothing but modes of imagining, in which the imagination is differently affected, though they are considered by the ignorant as the chief attributes of things, inasmuch as they believe that everything was created for the sake of themselves; and, according as they are affected by it, style it good or bad, healthy or rotten and corrupt. For instance, if the motion whose objects we see communicate to our nerves be conducive to health, the objects causing it are styled *beautiful;* if a contrary motion be excited, they are styled *ugly.*

Things which are perceived through our sense of smell are styled fragrant or fetid; if through our taste, sweet or bitter, full-flavored or insipid, if through our touch, hard or soft, rough or smooth, etc. Whatsoever affects our our ears is said to give rise to noise, sound, or harmony. In this last case, there are men lunatic enough to believe that even God himself takes pleasure in harmony; and philosophers are not lacking who have persuaded themselves, that the motion of the heavenly bodies gives rise to harmony—all of which instances sufficiently show that everyone judges of things according to the state of his brain, or rather mistakes for things the forms of his imagination. We need no longer wonder that there have arisen all the controversies we have witnessed and finally skepticism: for, although human bodies in many respects agree, yet in very many others they differ; so that what seems good to one seems bad to another; what seems well ordered to one seems confused to another; what is pleasing to one displeases another, and so on. I need not further enumerate, because this is not the place to treat the subject at length, and also because the fact is sufficiently well known. It is commonly said: "So many men, so many minds; everyone is wise in his own way; brains differ as completely as palates." All of which proverbs show, that men judge of things according to their mental disposition, and rather imagine than understand: for, if they understood phenomena, they would, as mathematics attest, be convinced, if not attracted, by what I have urged.

We have now perceived, that all the explanations commonly given of nature are mere modes of imagining, and do not indicate the true nature of anything, but only the constitution of the imagination; and, although they have names, as though they were entities imaginary rather than real; and, therefore, all arguments against us drawn from such abstractions are easily rebutted.

Many argue in this way. If all things follow from a necessity of the absolutely perfect nature of God, why are there so many imperfections in nature? such, for instance, as things corrupt to the point of putridity, loathsome deformity, confusion, evil, sin, etc. But these reasoners are, as I have said, easily confuted, for the perfection of things is to be reckoned only from their own nature and power:

things are not more or less perfect, according as they delight or offend human senses, or according as they are serviceable or repugnant to mankind. To those who ask why God did not so create all men, that they should be governed only by reason, I give no answer but this: because matter was not lacking to him for the creation of every degree of perfection from highest to lowest; or, more strictly, because the laws of his nature are so vast, as to suffice for the production of everything conceivable by an infinite intelligence.

THE IDEALISM OF LEIBNIZ

Spinoza built his philosophy upon the first of Descartes's three substances, the independent or perfect being. Hobbes, the materialist, built his upon the second Cartesian substance, body or extension. Leibniz undertook to construct a philosophy wholly upon the third, the thinking substance or *res cogitans,* of Descartes.[9] For Leibniz, matter is not sheer extension or in any way the opposite of thought. It is a very dull or undeveloped form of mentality. Hence Leibniz is an idealist. Spinoza had brought Cartesian thought into the rigid mold of a strict monism. Leibniz, on the other hand, emphasized heavily the pluralism latent in the Cartesian system. For him, the world was a vast society of thinking substances of all grades of perfection. God, the creator, is the highest thinking substance. His perception is completely illuminated, nothing being left obscure or confused. God's complete vision includes not only all that exists but also all possibility, or all that might have existed had God so willed. Possibilities are orderly and conceivable. Thus one can describe them without falling into contradiction. But many of them are incompatible with the actual course of things that God has chosen and allowed to enjoy the status of existence. These, although conceivable, are unrealized.

[9] Gottfried Wilhelm von Leibniz (1646-1716), of Bohemian descent, born in Leipzig, son of a university professor, was distinguished as mathematician, physicist, philosopher, historian, jurist, and diplomat. He shares with Newton the distinction of having discovered the infinitesimal calculus. He was attached to the court of the Duke of Hanover later to become George I of England, as librarian, and he was for a time employed on diplomatic missions by the Prince Bishop of Mainz. Although at the height of his career loaded with honors—he was created a Baron of the Holy Roman Empire—Leibniz died in obscurity, for the time being forgotten by the world.

Below God there are many less perfect thinking substances. These perceive the world—that is, God and the universe that he has chosen to create—less and less clearly. For the lower beings, details of the world seem more and more confused into an indiscriminate mass. (Thus the roar of the sea may be heard as one surge of sound, al- though it is actually composed of innumerable yet distinct elements.) The lowest substances are hardly aware of the contrast between themselves and the world. They possess but a vague sense of their own identity. They have perception but neither memory nor reason. Their perceptions are then uninterpreted, being divorced from mem- ory of the past and from the possibilities with reference to which reason can tentatively predict the future. These lowest substances must live wholly in the present, unable to look before and after. But even so, they differ from fully conscious substance only in degree. There is no sharp difference of kind. Thus even what we call inert matter thinks after its own dull fashion. Descartes speaks of matter as sheer extension. Leibniz insists that sheer extension is sheer nothing, and finds reality in the exercise of perception and thought.

All these substances or *monads,* as Leibniz calls them, share one and the same object of thought and perception, but each grasps and interprets this object according to its own powers. The object is the world as God has chosen it from the many possibilities that he con- templates. The life of each monad is a vision or a representation of this order of things more or less completely entertained in detail. Each monad has a point of view or station at which its perception of the world is centered. And each monad "makes its living" by per- ceiving the world.

It may surprise us to learn that Leibniz considers perception as the essential activity of all things, whether they are inorganic, living, or rational. We may be surprised to find the great thinker describ- ing, say, a pebble as a center of perception. We may be even more puzzled to find him describing our own conscious life as primarily a cognitive rather than a voluntary matter. After all, action and decision seem every bit as important as perception.

As regards the first point, what Leibniz has done is to convert Descartes's dictum "I perceive, therefore I exist" to read "It exists, therefore it perceives." Whether or not this is permissible can be judged only with reference to the adequacy and the consistency of Leibniz's system as a whole. As regards the second point, we must remember that all perception insofar as it involves a focusing of attention on a given object is a voluntary matter, and further, that all acts of will or expenditure of mental effort must involve the holding of our attention or perception upon one problem or upon one practical issue, volition thereby depending upon cognition. The power of attention is the power behind both thinking and action.

There is no interaction between monads and no direct perception of one monad as such by another. Thus I do not directly perceive my friend's ego as a stream of consciousness. I do not directly share his thoughts. Even less am I aware of the monads composing the furniture of my room, or of those constituting the material out of which the heavenly bodies are composed. But despite this isolation of the monads, their perceptual activity is harmonized and the universe of monadic activity is held together. This is because all the monads live by perceiving or representing the same objects; namely, God's chosen possibilties of creation. These representations of the world, which constitute the life histories of the monads, fit together consistently as, for instance, the members of a series of photographs of the same object taken from different angles could be consistently related one to another, although in the making of them no photographer has paid any attention to his fellow workers. There is, then, a *pre-established harmony* of monadic activity, owing to the common motivation of all monadic perception.

Unlike most of the innovators of seventeenth-century thought, Leibniz refused to repudiate final cause, but he found both final and mechanical causes of importance in investigation. In his *Discourse on Metaphysics* Leibniz writes: [10]

As I do not wish to judge people in ill part I bring no accusation against our new philosophers who pretend to banish final causes from physics, but I am nevertheless obliged to avow that the con-

[10] Leibniz, *Discourse on Metaphysics*, trans. by George R. Montgomery, pp. 33-35. Open Court Publishing Co., La Salle, Ill., 1902. This and a later quotation are reprinted by permission of the publisher.

sequences of such a banishment appear to me dangerous, especially when joined to that position which I refuted at the beginning of this treatise. That position seemed to go the length of discarding final causes entirely as though God proposed no end and no good in his activity, or as if good were not to be the object of his will. I hold on the contrary that it is just in this that the principle of all existences and of the laws of nature must be sought, hence God always proposes the best and most perfect. I am quite willing to grant that we are liable to err when we wish to determine the purposes or councils of God, but this is the case only when we try to limit them to some particular design, thinking that he has had in view only a single thing, while in fact he regards everything at once....

All those who see the admirable structure of animals find themselves led to recognize the wisdom of the author of things and I advise those who have any sentiment of piety and indeed of true philosophy to hold aloof from the expressions of certain pretentious minds who instead of saying that eyes were made for seeing, say that we see because we find ourselves having eyes. When one seriously holds such opinions which hand everything over to material necessity or to a kind of chance (although either alternative ought to appear ridiculous to those who understand what we have explained above) it is difficult to recognize an intelligent author of nature. The effect should correspond to its cause and indeed it is best known through the recognition of its cause, so that it is not reasonable to introduce a sovereign intelligence ordering things, and in place of making use of the wisdom of this sovereign being, to employ only the properties of matter to explain phenomena. As if in order to account for the capture of an important place by a prince, the historian should say it was because the particles of powder in the cannon having been touched by a spark of fire expanded with a rapidity capable of pushing a hard solid body against the walls of the place, while the little particles which composed the brass of the cannon were so well interlaced that they did not separate under this impact,—as if he should account for it in this way instead of making us see how the foresight of the conqueror brought him to choose the time and the proper means and how his ability surmounted all obstacles.

Leibniz points out that consideration of final causes is sometimes of value even in the study of physics. We quote again from the *Discourse on Metaphysics*.[11]

[11] *Ibid.,* pp. 38-39.

God is ... a workman able enough to produce a machine still a thousand times more ingenious than is our body, by employing only certain quite simple liquids purposely composed in such a way that ordinary laws of nature alone are required to develop them so as to produce such a marvellous effect. But it is also true that this development would not take place if God were not the author of nature. Yet I find that the method of efficient causes, which goes much deeper and is in a measure more immediate and *a priori,* is also more difficult when we come to details, and I think that our philosophers are still very frequently far removed from making the most of this method. The method of final causes, however, is easier and can be frequently employed to find out important and useful truths which we should have to seek a long time, if we were confined to that other more physical method of which anatomy is able to furnish many examples. It seems to me that Snellius, who was the first discoverer of the laws of refraction, would have waited a long time before finding them if he had wished to seek out first how light was formed. But he apparently followed that method which the ancients employed for Catoptrics, that is, the method of final causes. Because, while seeking for the easiest way in which to conduct a ray of light from one given point to another given point by reflection from a given plane (supposing that that was the design of nature) they discovered the equality of the angles of incidence and reflection, as can be seen from a little treatise by Heliodorus of Larissa and also elsewhere. This principle Mons. Snellius, I believe, and afterwards independently of him, M. Fermat, applied most ingeniously to refraction. For since the rays while in the same media always maintain the same proportion of sines, which in turn corresponds to the resistance of the media, it appears that they follow the easiest way, or at least that way which is the most determinate for passing from a given point in one medium to a given point in another medium. That demonstration of this same theorem which M. Descartes has given, using efficient causes, is much less satisfactory. At least we have grounds to think that he would never have found the principle by that means if he had not learned in Holland of the discovery of Snellius.[12]

---

12 Willebrord Snellius (1591-1626), Dutch mathematician. Snell's law of refraction is a formulation of the fact, observed by Heliodorus, that a ray of light follows the path that will lead it from its origin to a given point through refracting media in the least time. This statement treats the path as a whole rather than the forces acting at any given moment, and looks in that path for a kind of aesthetic simplicity that a mechanistic Cartesian would not admit as a legitimate scientific concept. In

In this, as in so much, Leibniz makes his way back toward Aristotle, who recognized that both efficient and final causes are present throughout nature. Again, in undertaking the great task of reconciling teleology with mechanism, Leibniz points the way toward much of the speculation of the eighteenth and nineteenth centuries. He indicates two considerations drawn from his study of the mechanical order that are not incompatible with a purposive or teleological world system. In the first place, Leibniz submits, as we have just seen, that mechanical entities are primarily instruments subject to the employment of mind. The very analogy of the machine suggests this. According to this view, the mechanical complexity we find in nature is always accompanied by purposive direction, even though this is often not obvious to us. Again, what is apparently mechanical may be interpreted as being in itself a low order of mind. Mechanism need not be thought of as the absolute opposite of mind, but as a stupefied or dull expression of mind, in which memory and reason are so weak that pursuit of ends and the employment of means are virtually imperceptible. Entities on this level "represent" less clearly the end and the values of God's world than some measure of its order. Just so, a man too exhausted to make plans may still perform certain routine operations based upon habit and so "blindly" pursue his ends. For these actions a low order of perception is necessary, but not memory and reason.

There is nothing in nature that is strictly and purely mechanical, nothing that quite corresponds to the external world of Cartesian thought. There is finality or purpose embodied in every phenomenon. If one likes, one may use, despite Descartes and the mechanists, the very analogy of the machine to present this proof. The

---

the history of science, however, the results of Kepler and Copernicus in astronomy, Dalton in chemistry, and Maupertuis in physics have been based on the method of "final causes." Leibniz chooses his illustrations of this point from physics, but his meaning becomes clearer as we transfer the problem to biology (after all, for Leibniz, physics is a kind of biology of the monads). It is much easier to analyze the physical and chemical structure of a given organ when we have a sound preliminary idea of what the function of that organ is in the whole organism. Here the determination of proper functions as wholes must precede, and serves to guide, the analysis of the mechanical behavior of parts through which the organ is efficiently caused to perform this function.

following quotation is taken from Leibniz' outstanding philosophical work, *The Monadology:* [13]

Thus the organic body of each living being is a kind of divine machine or natural automaton, which infinitely surpasses all artificial automata. For a machine made by the skill of man is not a machine in each of its parts. For instance, the tooth of a brass wheel has parts or fragments which for us are not artificial products, and which do not have the special characteristics of the machine, for they give no indication of the use for which the wheel was intended. But the machines of nature, namely, living bodies, are still machines in their smallest parts *ad infinitum.* It is this that constitutes the difference between nature and art, that is to say, between the divine art and ours.

And the Author of nature has been able to employ this divine and infinitely wonderful power of art, because each portion of matter is not only infinitely divisible, as the ancients observed, but is also actually subdivided without end, each part into further parts, of which each has some motion of its own; otherwise it would be impossible for each portion of matter to express the whole universe.

Whence it appears that in the smallest particle of matter there is a world of creatures, living beings, animals, entelechies, souls.

Each portion of matter may be conceived as like a garden full of plants and like a pond full of fishes. But each branch of every plant, each member of every animal, each drop of its liquid parts is also some such garden or pond.

And though the earth and the air which are between the plants of the garden, or the water which is between the fish of the pond, be neither plant nor fish; yet they also contain plants and fishes, but mostly so minute as to be imperceptible to us.

Thus there is nothing fallow, nothing sterile, nothing dead in the universe, no chaos, no confusion save in appearance, somewhat as it might appear to be in a pond at a distance, in which one would see a confused movement and, as it were, a swarming of fish in the pond, without separately distinguishing the fish themselves.

To make such a reconciliation of mechanism and teleology more explicit and more persuasive is the chosen task of many of Leibniz's successors. We shall have occasion to examine some of these attempts later.

[13] Leibniz, *The Monadology,* trans. by Robert Latta, pp. 254-57. Clarendon Press, Oxford, 1925. Reprinted by permission of the publisher.

Empiricism: Locke, Berkeley, and Hume

THE PHILOSOPHY OF EXPERIENCE

Descartes, and his great followers, Spinoza and Leibniz, are usually spoken of as *Rationalists,* not to indicate that their powers of reasoning were necessarily any greater than those of other thinkers, but in order to emphasize the fact that they believed human reason to be capable of framing a comprehensive theory of the world, and of man's place in it, simply by following out the implications of certain indubitable starting points, which are always open to a reflective intelligence disposed to careful analysis. These thinkers begin their philosophy, or at least profess to do so, not with some observed aspect of nature but with certain unquestioned, and for them unquestionable, insights, such as Descartes's certainty that he possessed a clear and distinct idea of perfection. But many philosophers refuse to honor such starting points, and it is to such thinkers that we shall now turn.

The conflict between these two types of philosophy is known historically as the dispute between *Rationalism* and *Empiricism,* between the philosophies of reason and the philosophies of experience. (By "experience" is meant nonrational or noninferential awareness, such as hearing a noise or seeing a color, feeling pain or being aware of one's own emotional state, say, of anger, in its several mental and physical manifestations.) This dispute occupies in the late seventeenth century and in the eighteenth the place that the conflict between Realism, Conceptualism, and Nominalism had held during the medieval period. The medieval thinkers had centered their dispute upon the status of universals, which were usually thought of as classes or types. The presence of modern scientific theory somewhat altered the setting if not the nature of the problem. Mere classification no longer seemed the most important feature of science. The interest of scientists had turned toward the study of cause and effect in the physical world.

The nature and status of the causation of physical matter had become an important object of discussion. The Rationalist insisted that we can be directly aware of mental and physical substance and of causation, just as the medieval Realist had insisted that we can be directly aware of universals. Recall Descartes's confidence in his clear and distinct idea of the physical or extended world and his assumption that there must be a cause of any actual entity, for instance of his own idea of perfection. On the other hand, the Empiricists or philosophers of experience come gradually to insist that we cannot be acquainted with or directly experience such things as substance and causal law, but that in the case of the latter, we can know only sequences of events, and in the case of the former, clusters of sensuous qualities, such as color and hardness, which we are wont to call physical things. Thus for example we really should not say that A causes or necessitates B, but that B, insofar as we have observed, has always followed after A and has never appeared without it and that we are led to expect that B will continue to do so. At most causation is a concept that we employ to interpret the sequence of events. Just so the medieval anti-Realist had often considered universals as instruments of our thinking but not as objective realities in the order of things.

The Empiricists have always built their arguments upon the principle that there must be nothing in our intellect or reason that has not first appeared to the senses: *Nihil est in intellectu quod non prius fuerit in sensu.* This sentence might be called the battle cry of the Empiricist. The Empiricists tend, perhaps inconsistently, to consider their battle cry as a self-evident truth. To put it in other words, the intellect or reason has no right to *add* anything to experience or to alter the dictates of experience beyond certain minimal corrections, as for instance when we discover that our senses actually disagree, as in the case of the stick appearing bent in water, or the parallel lines that seem to converge in a colonnade or along a railroad right of way.

The full consequences of this theory of reason are slow to make themselves manifest. In fact the early Empiricists never wholly perceived them. Reason can only arrange or sort the results of observation, recognizing cases of regular sequence or frequent coexistence of observable phenomena, or noting when one phenomenon varies in the presence of another. Scientific law finally comes to be thought of as a body of convenient formulas whereby we indicate that granted A, B may be expected to appear, or if A varies in such a way, B may be expected to vary in another way. But these laws, says the Empiricist, are not by themselves proper objects of knowledge any more than were universals in the eyes of the medieval opponents of Realism. If with the Empiricist we do not consider law itself as a genuine object of thought, we do not recognize such a thing as causal necessity—that B *must* follow upon A,—but only that it very often has and that we expect it will continue to do so, since no one seems to have experienced the contrary. Here Plato's contrast between opinion and knowledge should come once again to the attention of philosophers (see above, page 71).

This empirical interpretation of knowledge begins in the seventeenth century when it is proposed, although by no means fully developed, in the writings of Francis Bacon and John Locke. It is further developed by Bishop Berkeley and by David Hume in the eighteenth century, and it is carried on in the nineteenth by John Stuart Mill and his allies. It is at present being most carefully restated by a school of thinkers known as the "Logical Positivists." These recent writers recognize, however, much more clearly than their predecessors the indispensable role that mathematics plays in scientific investigation. By and large, Empiricism has always been more at home in Britain and the United States than on the continent of Europe, and even the present Austrian school of Logical Positivists are willing to recognize in the eighteenth-century figure of the Scot, David Hume, their great forerunner and teacher.

The Empiricist repudiates the theory that the clear and distinct idea guarantees its own validity. Ideas are true only insofar as they can be traced back to experience through the most rigorous analysis and verified in experiential terms. Knowledge is trustworthy and genuine only when it is supported throughout by experience. Thus Empiricism is characterized by a suspicion of the intellect when it operates undisciplined by frequent experiments and observation. On the other hand, the great Rationalists were men who stood close to the growth of modern mathematics, which is the most impressive instance of nonexperimental thought. Descartes invented analytic geometry and Leibniz shared the honors of the infinitesimal calculus with Isaac Newton. Accordingly these men were well acquainted with the deductive powers of the human mind when it procedes from postulates to theorems, and they put confidence in thought as distinct from observation. This mathematical confidence the Empiricists did not possess, and they loved to indicate what seemed to them the inadequacy of pure thought. Thus Francis Bacon, the forerunner of all the English Empiricists, writes in his *Novum Organum:* [1]

The human understanding is of its own nature prone to suppose the existence of more order and regularity in the world than it finds. And though there be many things in nature which are singular and unmatched, yet it devises for them parallels and conjugates and relatives which do not exist....

The human understanding when it has once adopted an opinion (either as being the received opinion or as being agreeable to itself) draws all things else to support and agree with it. And though there be a greater number and weight of instances to be found on the other side, yet these it either neglects and despises, or else by some

---

[1] Francis Bacon, *Novum Organum,* in *Works,* ed. by James Spedding, Robert Leslie Ellis, and Douglas D. Heath, Vol. VIII, p. 79. Houghton Mifflin Co., 15 vols., Boston, 1870-82.

Francis Bacon (1561-1626), English philosopher, was an important figure in the courts of Elizabeth and James I. Under the latter he became Lord Chancellor and was made Baron Verulam and Viscount St. Albans. In 1621 he confessed that he was guilty of bribery and corrupt dealing, and was fined, and banished from Parliament and the court. Later James remitted the fine, and pardoned him. His *Essays* are his chief literary work, and the *Novum Organum* and *The Advancement of Learning* are his chief contributions to philosophy.

distinction sets aside and rejects; in order that by this great and pernicious pre-determination the authority of its former conclusions may remain inviolate. And therefore it was a good answer that was made by one who when they showed him hanging in a temple a picture of those who had paid their vows as having escaped shipwreck, and would have him say whether he did not now acknowledge the power of the gods,—'Aye,' asked he again, 'but where are they painted that were drowned after their vows?' And such is the way of all superstition, whether in astrology, dreams, omens, divine judgments, or the like; wherein men having a delight in such vanities, mark the events where they are fulfilled, but where they fail, though this happen much oftener, neglect and pass them by. But with far more subtlety does this mischief insinuate itself into philosophy and the sciences; in which the first conclusion colours and brings into conformity with itself all that come after, though far sounder and better. Besides, independently of that delight and vanity which I have described, it is the peculiar and perpetual error of the human intellect to be more moved and excited by affirmatives than by negatives; whereas it ought properly to hold itself indifferently disposed towards both alike. Indeed in the establishment of any true axiom, the negative instance is the more forcible of the two.

The human understanding is moved by those things most which strike and enter the mind simultaneously and suddenly, and so fill the imagination; and then it feigns and supposes all other things to be somehow, though it cannot see how, similar to those few things by which it is surrounded. But for that going to and fro to remote and heterogeneous instances, by which axioms are tried as in the fire, the intellect is altogether slow and unfit, unless it be forced thereto by severe laws and overruling authority....

The human understanding is no dry light, but receives an infusion from the will and affections; whence proceed sciences which may be called 'sciences as one would.' For what a man had rather were true he more readily believes. Therefore he rejects difficult things from impatience of research; sober things, because they narrow hope; the deeper things of nature, from superstition; the light of experience, from arrogance and pride, lest his mind should seem to be occupied with things mean and transitory; things not commonly believed, out of deference to the opinion of the vulgar. Numberless in short are the ways, and sometimes imperceptible, in which the affections colour and infect the understanding.

These comments constitute Bacon's discussion of what he calls the "Idols," or false notions, "of the tribe"; that is, of mankind as a whole. For Bacon, the human understanding is by its very nature an imperfect mirror of the world, and only the most cautious pro-cedure with constant checking by observation can preserve it from error. Besides the sources of error already mentioned, there are the "Idols of the cave," or errors peculiar to individuals because of their prejudices, ambitions, and so on; the "Idols of the market place," or errors resulting from the unobserved ambiguity of words and phrases; and the "Idols of the theater," or errors resulting from the prestige acquired by outworn modes of thought.

Spinoza read Bacon, and his comment is enlightening. He was shocked to find that the English thinker supposed the human in-tellect to be by its very nature fallible, picturing the world after the analogy of its own nature, and not after the analogy of the universe. We need not follow Spinoza's argument on this point, but we may notice that such suspicion of intelligence seems to him monstrous.[2] And we can well understand why. If intelligence errs because of its very nature, how can we hope to free ourselves from error? After all, even an Empiricist philosophy is the product of intelligence, as are also the rules of procedure or of method the scientist follows. Thus, if intelligence is essentially untrustworthy, Empirical philos-ophy, as well as natural science and Rationalist metaphysics, would seem to stand in peril. The wise Empiricist will not, therefore, allow his enthusiasm for observation and experiment to undermine his respect for pure thought. But in its beginnings Empiricism often knew little restraint, and the Empiricist's eagerness sometimes left him open to this criticism. Of course, on the other hand, there is no doubt that the Rationalists continually overplayed their hands

[2] Spinoza seems perhaps to have overlooked Bacon's comment with which he introduces his treatment of the idols: "The doctrine of those who have denied that certainty could be attained at all, has some agreement with my way of proceeding at the first setting out; but they end in being infinitely separated and opposed. For the holders of that doctrine assert simply that nothing can be known; I also assert that not much can be known in nature by the way which is now in use. But then they go on to destroy the authority of the senses and understanding; whereas I proceed to devise and supply helps for the same."—Nonetheless we can understand the diffi-culty that Spinoza, as a true rationalist, was quick to sense.

and advertised as clear and distinct ideas many unanalyzed notions, to which they clung on purely controversial grounds.

The proper conduct of thought involves both reason and experience, and the mind of the investigator is constantly shifting from one to the other. To slight observation in order to honor reason or vice versa is to ignore their true interdependence. Observation must always be guided by intelligence. The observer, whether physicist, biologist, or economist, must always decide what to look for; he must at least decide upon some area in which he may expect to find significant material. Observation, alone and unaided, would be wholly lost before the infinite multiplicity of phenomena. On the other hand, without observation intelligence is left, at least in natural science, without a means of choosing between two or three equally plausible hypotheses.

Science has been described as "putting questions to nature." Without intelligence there would be no questions or tentative hypotheses to put to the test, and without observation there would be no answer to the questions. According to this point of view, neither the Empiricist nor the Rationalist has the last word. The Empiricist is wrong in arguing that there can be nothing in intelligence that was not first in the senses. It is the function of intelligence to frame hypotheses before they can be verified—that is, to ask questions— and the questions *when asked* always exceed observational evidence Again the Rationalist is somewhat too hasty in supposing that there are self-evident starting points in philosophy and in science that require no verification and are immune from any form of criticism. Even my awareness of myself as a thinking being lacks this authority, for, as we have seen, there is some question as to the nature of the ego or thinking being. It was in fact largely owing to the Rationalist's too eager insistence that the human mind is equipped with many absolutely indubitable principles that the Empiricist's countermovement found such ready welcome in many quarters.

The earlier Empiricist tends to appear as a crusader who combats many unfounded and illegitimate notions beneath which he finds philosophy and common sense held in an inglorious servitude. His avowed purpose is to free the intelligence of the race from such subjection. Actually, however, in accomplishing this liberation he often leaves common sense confused and indignant and strips philosophy of every one of its traditionally cherished ideas. During the eighteenth century the Empiricists attempted to rid philosophy of many principles long thought to be indispensable. The attempt was, on the whole, a failure, but it served an important purpose in that the destructive criticism of the Empiricists awakened a renewed and more painstaking investigation on the part of other philosophers.

As we have seen, the Empiricists turned their analysis chiefly on two problems, that of substance and that of causation. Examination of the nature of substance through analysis of our awareness of substance led them to formulate radical theories concerning the nature of the mind or the self, that is, concerning thinking substance, and again concerning the nature and status of the so-called external world and the objects existing therein; that is, concerning physical or corporeal substance. By the time Empiricism had run its course, Empiricists had "reduced" both the mind and the world to mere bundles and sequences of atomic impressions or sensations. The universe seemed to have "come apart" under the analysis of the Empiricist.

But this process of destruction was a gradual one, and there were times when Empiricism for a brief time deserted its rigorous analysis and indulged in metaphysical hypothesis of a most spectacular sort. There are three clearly marked stages of British Empiricism, which we may call:

1. The Representative Dualism of John Locke
2. The Subjective Idealism of Bishop Berkeley
3. The Atomic Empiricism of David Hume

Each of these philosophies involves some destructive criticism of Descartes's world scheme. Locke discards the innate ideas of Descartes, but otherwise follows Descartes in many things. Berkeley eliminates corporeal substance, and presents a spectacular theory of the world as entirely mental; finally Hume goes on to repudiate the concept of thinking substance, the *res cogitans* of Descartes, and also reduces our concepts of cause and effect and of causal necessity, which had been for Descartes clear and distinct ideas, to a notion of mere sequence accentuated by our habitual and customary faith in the recurrence of such sequence.

LOCKE'S THEORY OF REPRESENTATIVE DUALISM

In his own day Locke was looked upon as a destroyer.[3] Just as many supposed that Descartes had destroyed medieval Scholasticism, so there were many who supposed that Locke had destroyed the Cartesian philosophy. This belief was founded upon Locke's famous refutation of the Cartesian theory of innate ideas. Mind, Locke insists, possesses no knowledge that it has not, so to speak, earned by working its way from the raw material of experience. No knowledge is given ready-made, unless it be perhaps our immediate intuitive awareness that we exist; certainly there is no innate knowledge of God, nor is there any such knowledge of the properties of extension, as Descartes had thought.

Ideas, according to Locke, can exist only in consciousness, and it is absurd to suppose that a child is born conscious of Cartesian ideas; and since an idea can exist in the mind only when we are aware of it, there is no way by which innate ideas can be, so to speak, stored away in the mind. We do know certain propositions to be valid upon inspection, as in the case of the axioms of mathematics, but this is because we have here to do with material so simple that the mind is able to grasp its truths at one stroke. But even so children do not recognize these truths until they have had some opportunity to test the propositions in question by inspection.

---

[3] John Locke (1632-1704), physician and diplomatist as well as philosopher, studied at Oxford before embarking upon a public career, much of which was pursued under the protection of the Earl of Shaftesbury, the outstanding political leader of the reign of Charles II. Locke shared the fortunes of his patron, and spent some time as an exile in Holland, where he worked upon his great book, *An Essay concerning Human Understanding,* finally published in 1690. Locke is also famous for his contribution to political theory and for his defense of political and religious tolerance.

It is certainly not necessary to suppose that these propositions are in any way established in the mind by biological inheritance.[4]

Locke refuses to consider the existence of a perfect being or Cartesian God as established by our confidence in any innate idea. Some Anglican churchmen who had come to found their theology upon Cartesian principles took alarm at this statement of Locke's. The Bishop of Worcester inquired: "If there is no innate idea of God, how are we to refute the atheist?" Locke's answer is typical of his lively spirit in controversy: If there really were an innate idea of God, no man would be an atheist. And, as Professor Gilson has put it, that was enough to settle the whole question—at least in the mind of the average reader.

The following quotations from Locke's *Essay concerning Human Understanding* exemplify his theories of knowledge and of the relation of knowledge to experience.[5]

[Book I, Chapter I] 8. . . . I must here in the entrance beg pardon of my reader for the frequent use of the word idea, which he will find in the following treatise. It being that term, which, I think, serves best to stand for whatsoever is the object of the understanding when a man thinks; I have used it to express whatever is meant

---

[4] Locke is quite right on this point, but he does leave open the question: Upon just what authority do we accept as true many propositions concerning the actual world that are not referred to sensuous experience? Consider for example Locke's argument for the existence of God: "There was a time then, when there was no knowing being, and when knowledge began to be; or else there has been also a knowing being from eternity. If it be said, there was a time when no being had any knowledge, when that eternal being was void of all understanding; I reply, that then it was impossible there should ever have been any knowledge: it being as impossible that things wholly void of knowledge, and operating blindly, and without any perception, should produce a knowing being, as it is impossible that a triangle should make itself three angles bigger than two right ones. For it is as repugnant to the idea of senseless matter, that it should put into itself, sense, perception, and knowledge, as it is repugnant to the idea of a triangle, that it should put into itself greater angles than two right ones."—*Op. cit.,* Bk. 4, Chap. 10, par. 5. After all, how can such teaching be derived from experience? Do we ever experience the origin of mind or the relation of mind to corporeal things? Locke occasionally exceeds the limits of his empiricism. We must remember that he stands at the beginning of the movement. Hume, for instance, would never resort to an argument such as the above. The fact that no one of our ideas seems "repugnant" to another affords a true empiricist no foundation for argument.

[5] John Locke, *An Essay concerning Human Understanding,* 1690. Selections from Books I and II.

by phantasm, notion, species, or whatever it is which the mind can be employed about in thinking; and I could not avoid frequently using it.

I presume it will be easily granted me, that there are such ideas in men's minds; every one is conscious of them in himself, and men's words and actions will satisfy him that they are in others.

Our first enquiry then shall be, how they come into the mind....

[Book II, Chapter I] 1. Every man being conscious to himself that he thinks, and that which his mind is applied about, whilst thinking, being the ideas that are there, it is past doubt, that men have in their minds several ideas, such as are those expressed by the words, Whiteness, Hardness, Sweetness, Thinking, Motion, Man, Elephant, Army, Drunkenness, and others. It is in the first place then to be inquired, how he comes by them. I know it is a received doctrine, that men have native ideas, and original characters, stamped upon their minds, in their very first being. This opinion I have, at large, examined already; and, I suppose, what I have said, in the foregoing book, will be much more easily admitted, when I have shewn, whence the understanding may get all the ideas it has, and by what ways and degrees they may come into the mind; for which I shall appeal to every one's own observation and experience.

2. Let us then suppose the mind to be, as we say, white paper, void of all characters, without any ideas; how comes it to be furnished? Whence comes it by that vast store which the busy and boundless fancy of man has painted on it, with an almost endless variety? Whence has it all the materials of reason and knowledge? To this I answer, in one word, from experience; in all that our knowledge is founded, and from that it ultimately derives itself. Our observation employed either about external sensible objects, or about the internal operations of our minds, perceived and reflected on by ourselves, is that which supplies our understandings with all the materials of thinking. These two are the fountains of knowledge, from whence all the ideas we have, or can naturally have, do spring.

3. First, Our senses, conversant about particular sensible objects, do convey into the mind several distinct perceptions of things, according to those various ways wherein those objects do affect them: and thus we come by those ideas we have, of Yellow, White, Heat, Cold, Soft, Hard, Bitter, Sweet, and all those which we call sensible qualities; which when I say the senses convey into the mind, I mean, they from external objects convey into the mind what produces there those perceptions. This great source of most of the ideas

we have, depending wholly upon our senses, and derived by them to the understanding, I call SENSATION.

4. Secondly, The other fountain, from which experience furnisheth the understanding with ideas, is the perception of the operations of our own mind within us, as it is employed about the ideas it has got; which operations when the soul comes to reflect on and consider, do furnish the understanding with another set of ideas, which could not be had from things without; and such are Perception, Thinking, Doubting, Believing, Reasoning, Knowing, Willing, and all the different actings of our own minds; which we being conscious of and observing in ourselves, do from these receive into our understandings as distinct ideas, as we do from bodies affecting our senses. This source of ideas every man has wholly in himself: and though it be not sense, as having nothing to do with external objects, yet it is very like it, and might properly enough be called internal sense. But as I call the other sensation, so I call this REFLECTION, the ideas it affords being such only as the mind gets by reflecting on its own operations within itself. By reflection then, in the following part of this discourse, I would be understood to mean that notice which the mind takes of its own operations, and the manner of them; by reason whereof there come to be ideas of these operations in the understanding. These two, I say, viz. external material things, as the objects of sensation; and the operations of our own minds within, as the objects of reflection; are to me the only originals from whence all our ideas take their beginnings. The term operations here I use in a large sense, as comprehending not barely the actions of the mind about its ideas, but some sort of passions arising sometimes from them, such as is the satisfaction or uneasiness arising from any thought.

5. The understanding seems to me not to have the least glimmering of any ideas, which it doth not receive from one of these two. External objects furnish the mind with the ideas of sensible qualities, which are all those different perceptions they produce in us: and the mind furnishes the understanding with ideas of its own operations.

These, when we have taken a full survey of them and their several modes, combinations, and relations, we shall find to contain all our whole stock of ideas; and that we have nothing in our minds which did not come in one of these two ways. Let anyone examine his own thoughts, and thoroughly search into his understanding; and then let him tell me, whether all the original ideas he has there, are any other than of the objects of his senses, or of the operations of his mind, considered as objects of his reflection; and how great a mass of knowledge soever he imagines to be lodged there, he will, upon taking a strict view, see that he has not any idea in his mind, but what one of these two have imprinted; though perhaps, with infinite variety compounded and enlarged by the understanding, as we shall see hereafter....

9. To ask at what time a man has first any ideas, is to ask when he begins to perceive; having ideas, and perception, being the same thing. I know it is an opinion, that the soul always thinks, and that it has the actual perception of ideas in itself constantly as long as it exists; and that actual thinking is as inseparable from the soul, as actual extension is from the body: which if true, to inquire after the beginning of a man's ideas is the same as to inquire after the beginning of his soul. For by this account soul and its ideas, as body and its extension, will begin to exist both at the same time....

20. I see no reason therefore to believe, that the soul thinks before the senses have furnished it with ideas to think on; and as those are increased and retained, so it comes, by exercise, to improve its faculty of thinking, in the several parts of it, as well as afterwards, by compounding those ideas, and reflecting on its own operations; it increases its stock, as well as facility, in remembering, imagining, reasoning, and other modes of thinking....

22. Follow a child from its birth, and observe the alterations that time makes, and you shall find, as the mind by the senses comes more and more to be furnished with ideas, it comes to be more and more awake; thinks more, the more it has matter to think on. After some time it begins to know the objects, which, being most familiar with it, have made lasting impressions. Thus it comes by degrees to know the persons it daily converses with, and distinguish them from strangers; which are instances and effects of its coming to retain and distinguish the ideas the senses convey to it. And so we may observe how the mind, by degrees, improves in these, and advances to the exercise of those other faculties of enlarging, compounding, and abstracting its ideas, and of reasoning about them, and reflecting upon all these; of which I shall have occasion to speak more hereafter....

24. ... Thus the first capacity of human intellect is, that the mind is fitted to receive the impressions made on it; either through the senses by outward objects; or by its own operations when it reflects on them. This is the first step a man makes towards the discovery of any thing, and the ground-work whereon to build all those notions which ever he shall have naturally in this world. All those sublime

thoughts which tower above the clouds, and reach as high as heaven itself, take their rise and footing here: in all that good extent wherein the mind wanders, in those remote speculations, it may seem to be elevated with, it stirs not one jot beyond those ideas which sense or reflection have offered for its contemplation.

25. In this part the understanding is merely passive; and whether or no it will have these beginnings, and as it were materials of knowledge, is not in its own power. For the objects of our senses do, many of them, obtrude their particular ideas upon our minds whether we will or no: and the operations of our minds will not let us be without, at least, some obscure notions of them. No man can be wholly ignorant of what he does when he thinks. These simple ideas, when offered to the mind, the understanding can no more refuse to have, nor alter, when they are imprinted, nor blot them out, and make new ones itself, than a mirror can refuse, alter, or obliterate the images or ideas which the objects set before it do therein produce. As the bodies that surround us do diversely affect our organs, the mind is forced to receive the impressions, and cannot avoid the perception of those ideas that are annexed to them....

[Chapter II] 1. The better to understand the nature, manner, and extent of our knowledge, one thing is carefully to be observed concerning the ideas we have; and that is, that some of them are simple, and some complex.

Though the qualities that affect our senses are, in the things themselves, so united and blended, that there is no separation, no distance between them; yet it is plain, the ideas they produce in the mind enter by the senses simple and unmixed. For though the sight and touch often take in from the same object, at the same time, different ideas; as a man sees at once motion and colour; the hand feels softness and warmth in the same piece of wax: yet the simple ideas, thus united in the same subject, are as perfectly distinct as those that come in by different senses: the coldness and hardness which a man feels in a piece of ice-being as distinct ideas in the mind, as the smell and whiteness of a lily; or as the taste of sugar, and smell of a rose. And there is nothing can be plainer to a man, than the clear and distinct perception he has of those simple ideas; which, being each in itself uncompounded, contains in it nothing but one uniform appearance, or conception in the mind, and is not distinguishable into different ideas.

2. These simple ideas, the materials of all our knowledge, are suggested and furnished to the mind only by those two ways abovementioned, viz. sensation and reflection. When the understanding

is once stored with these simple ideas, it has the power to repeat, compare, and unite them, even to an almost infinite variety; and so can make at pleasure new complex ideas. But it is not in the power of the most exalted wit, or enlarged understanding, by any quickness or variety of thought, to invent or frame one new simple idea in the mind, not taken in, by the ways aforementioned: nor can any force of the understanding destroy those that are there. The dominion of man, in this little world of his own understanding, being much-what the same as it is in the great world of visible things; wherein his power, however managed by art and skill, reaches no farther than to compound and divide the materials that are made to his hand; but can do nothing towards the making the least particle of new matter, or destroying one atom of what is already in being. The same inability will every one find in himself, who shall go about to fashion in his understanding any simple idea, not received in by his senses from external objects, or by reflection from the operations of his own mind about them. I would have any one try to fancy any taste, which had never affected his palate; or frame the idea of a scent he had never smelt: and when he can do this, I will also conclude that a blind man hath ideas of colours, and a deaf man true distinct notions of sounds.

3. This is the reason why, though we cannot believe it impossible to God to make a creature with other organs, and more ways to convey into the understanding the notice of corporeal things than those five, as they are usually counted, which he has given to man: yet I think, it is not possible for any one to imagine any other qualities in bodies, howsoever constituted, whereby they can be taken notice of, besides sounds, tastes, smells, visible and tangible qualities. And had mankind been made but with four senses, the qualities then, which are the object of the fifth sense, had been as far from our notice, imagination, and conception, as now any belonging to a sixth, seventh, or eighth sense, can possibly be: which, whether yet some other creatures, in some other parts of this vast and stupendous universe, may not have, will be a great presumption to deny. He that will not set himself proudly at the top of all things, but will consider the immensity of this fabrick, and the great variety that is to be found in this little and inconsiderable part of it which he has to do with, may be apt to think, that in other mansions of it there may be other and different intelligent beings, of whose faculties he has as little knowledge or apprehension, as a worm shut up in one drawer of a cabinet hath of the senses or understanding of a man: such variety and excellency being suitable to the wisdom and power of the maker.

Although bitterly opposed to the Cartesian theory of innate ideas, Locke owes more to Cartesian thought than is at first apparent. Indeed, Locke's philosophy may be best described as a restatement of Descartes's position made from the point of view of an Empiricist. This restatement contains certain inconsistencies, owing to the fact that Descartes's scheme of God, man, and the physical world was worked out upon a supposition that our knowledge of these things depends upon our innate ideas and intuitive insight, and acquired quite independently of sensuous experience. Locke is forced to supply empirical foundations for propositions that were originally offered as clear and distinct ideas, and the result is not very happy. This his keener followers soon recognized, and they tended to simplify his philosophy in order to render it empirically sound. There soon appeared to be very few limits that could be put to this process of simplification. Concept after concept of the Lockian scheme fell before Empiricist analysis. In the end, Locke's system was literally torn to pieces by those who clung not to his conclusions but to the spirit of his method.

Perhaps Locke's most vulnerable point lies in his notion of *idea* and its relation to the mind on one hand and to the world on the other. From the texture of experience we abstract, or more literally withdraw, certain ideas, primarily by ignoring irrelevant details. Knowledge arises as the comparison or contrast of these ideas is carried out by the mind as it frames propositions and makes assertions. Locke insists that, properly speaking, ideas and not things are the *objects* of our knowledge. In other words, and this seems to many modern thinkers almost monstrous, we think *about* our own ideas.[6]

1. Since the mind, in all its thoughts and reasonings, hath no other immediate object but its own ideas, which it alone does or can contemplate; it is evident, that our knowledge is only conversant about them.

2. Knowledge then seems to me to be nothing but the perception of the connexion and agreement, or disagreement and repugnancy, of any of our ideas. In this alone it consists. Where this perception

[6] *Ibid.,* Bk. 4, Chap. I.

is, there is knowledge; and where it is not, there, though we may fancy, guess, or believe, yet we always come short of knowledge. For when we know that white is not black, what do we else but perceive that these two ideas do not agree? When we possess ourselves with the utmost security of the demonstration, that the three angles of a triangle are equal to two right ones, what do we more but perceive, that equality to two right ones does necessarily agree to and is inseparable from the three angles of a triangle?

According to Locke, then, ideas and ideas alone are the objects of the knowing mind. Accordingly ideas stand *between* the mind and the reality known. Both in perception and in thought ideas appear as representatives of something beyond them, but since we do not know anything beyond the ideas, we cannot say how accurately these latter represent the world; and a hardened skeptic may even question their credentials as representatives and suggest that there is really nothing beyond them to be represented. Descartes avoided this difficulty by appealing to our innate idea of a truthful deity; this avenue of escape is closed for Locke.

It is one thing to say that sensuous images, patches of color, and so on merely represent but do not accurately reflect the world lying beyond them, but quite another thing to say that all ideas, including concepts as well as perceptual images, actually come between us and reality. After all, images may not be wholly accurate, but if we know this to be the case, we make some allowance in the judgment we pass upon their representative value. However, if *all* ideas are to be questioned in this way, we are left in an unhappy skepticism, not knowing what to trust and what to doubt. Even knowledge of ourselves, and that of our mental powers, involves ideas. Thus instead of knowing directly that we know, we entertain ideas representing knowledge. Ideas, then, seem to veil our own mentality as well as cutting us off from a direct vision of the world beyond.

Acceptance of such a theory clearly involves skepticism, or the admission that we can never know the world of mind or matter as it really is. Locke goes halfway to meet this skepticism by confessing that we do not know what substance, mental or physical, really is. We know, thinks Locke, that there are physical substances or concrete realities to which the primary qualities belong and to which secondary qualities refer. But what such things are, aside from these qualities, we do not know. We can only say that substance in some way "underlies" the qualities. Locke's critics are soon to point out that the word "underlies" is in this context a very vague one, and Locke himself admits that our idea of substance is "confused." Berkeley is to point out with gusto that such a confused idea is not derived from experience, for we do not experience corporeal substance in the same way that we are aware of the simple idea of *yellow* or of *bitter*.

Even Locke must admit that his substance is a "something I know what" and Berkeley quite correctly insists that an Empiricist has no right to talk of such an unexperienced and unexperienceable entity. Berkeley himself, however, rather inconsistently clings to the concept of spiritual substance or the thinking self, the ego of our self-awareness and the agent of our conduct. But Hume finds no evidence to support our belief in either corporeal or mental substance. In this he is an absolutely consistent Empiricist, who will allow nothing to appear in science or philosophy that has not entered our knowledge as a bona-fide object of sensuous experience or of direct introspection.

In 1637, Descartes published his *Discourse on Method,* and thereby established the "new" philosophy. This philosophy was indeed new in many ways, but it centered about a concept as old as Aristotle, one that had been cherished by medieval thinkers. This was the idea of substance. Within the century following Descartes, this concept was subjected to the most rigorous analysis, and was in time interpreted as anything but the indispensable concept that Aristotle had considered it to be. By 1740, David Hume was attempting to construct some sort of philosophy without recognizing the validity of the concept of substance.

It is important to notice that in this first century of modern philosophy the concept of substance was never, except by Leibniz, given its Aristotelean teleological character as a vehicle of potentiality. It was not conceived according to organic analogies, but according to quasi-mathematical and spatial figures of speech. Particularly in Locke, substance appears as something inert, even without definite character. It is not difficult to eliminate such a concept from our thinking, although we may still stand in need of a concept comparable to Aristotle's.

THE SUBJECTIVE IDEALISM OF BISHOP BERKELEY

The following selections are taken from George Berkeley's *A Treatise concerning the Principles of Human Knowledge* (1710). (One will also find Berkeley's argument attractively presented in his *Three Dialogues between Hylas and Philonous* (1713), which is recommended for further reading.) The student who has followed the development of modern thought through Descartes and Locke should have little difficulty in understanding Berkeley's argument, despite its bold departure from the tenets of common sense or popular belief.[7]

1. It is evident to any one who takes a survey of the *objects of human knowledge* that they are either *ideas* actually imprinted on the senses; or else such as are perceived by attending to the passions and operations of the mind; or lastly, *ideas* formed by help of memory and imagination—either compounding, dividing, or barely representing those originally perceived in the aforesaid ways. By sight I have the ideas of light and colours, with their several degrees and variations. By touch I perceive hard and soft, heat and cold, motion and resistance; and of all these more and less either as to quantity or degree. Smelling furnishes me with odours; the palate with tastes; and hearing conveys sounds to the mind in all their variety of tone and composition.

[7] George Berkeley, *A Treatise concerning the Principles of Human Knowledge,* 2nd ed. 1734.

George Berkeley (1685-1753) was born in Ireland and educated at Trinity College, Dublin. He enjoyed a successful career in the Church of England, ending his days as the Anglican Bishop of Cloyne in Ireland. He was a friend of Dean Swift and belonged to the circle of Addison and Steele, the chief literary group in the London of Queen Anne. Berkeley made an unsuccessful effort to induce Parliament to found a Church of England university in the American colonies, and he even journeyed to America in the hope of furthering his scheme. Berkeley's most important philosophical writing was completed well before he was thirty.

And as several of these are observed to accompany each other, they come to be marked by one name, and so to be reputed as one thing. Thus, for example, a certain colour, taste, smell, figure and consistence having been observed to go together, are accounted one distinct thing, signified by the name apple; other collections of ideas constitute a stone, a tree, a book, and the like sensible things; which as they are pleasing or disagreeable excite the passions of love, hatred, joy, grief, and so forth.

2. But, besides all that endless variety of ideas or objects of knowledge, there is likewise Something which knows or perceives them; and exercises divers operations, as willing, imagining, remembering, about them. This perceiving, active being is what I call *mind, spirit, soul,* or *myself.* By which words I do not denote any one of my ideas; but a thing entirely distinct from them, wherein they exist, or, which is the same thing, whereby they are perceived—for the existence of an idea consists in being perceived.

3. That neither our thoughts, nor passions, nor ideas formed by the imagination, exist without the mind is what everybody will allow. And to me it is no less evident that the various sensations or ideas imprinted on the Sense, however blended or combined together (that is, whatever objects they compose), cannot exist otherwise than in a mind perceiving them. I think an intuitive knowledge may be obtained of this by any one that shall attend to what is meant by the term *exist* when applied to sensible things. The table I write on I say exists, that is, I see and feel it; and if I were out of my study I should say it existed; meaning thereby that if I was in my study I might perceive it, or that some other spirit actually does perceive it. There was an odour, that is, it was smelt; there was a sound, that is, it was heard; a colour or figure, and it was perceived by sight or touch. This is all that I can understand by these and the like expressions. For as to what is said of the *absolute* existence of unthinking things, without any relation to their being perceived, that is to me perfectly unintelligible. Their *esse* is *percipi*; nor is it possible they should have any existence out of the minds or thinking things which perceive them.

4. It is indeed an opinion strangely prevailing amongst men, that houses, mountains, rivers, and in a word all sensible objects, have an existence, natural or real, distinct from their being perceived by the understanding. But, with how great an assurance and acquiescence soever this Principle may be entertained in the world, yet whoever shall find in his heart to call it in question may, if I mistake not, perceive it to involve a manifest contradiction. For, what

are the forementioned objects but the things we perceive by sense? and what do we perceive besides our own ideas or sensations? and is it not plainly repugnant that any one of these, or any combination of them, should exist unperceived?

5. If we thoroughly examine this tenet it will, perhaps, be found at bottom to depend on the doctrine of *abstract ideas*. For can there be a nicer strain of abstraction than to distinguish the existence of sensible objects from their being perceived, so as to conceive them existing unperceived? Light and colours, heat and cold, extension and figures—in a word the things we see and feel—what are they but so many sensations, notions, ideas, or impressions on the sense? and is it possible to separate, even in thought, any of these from perception? For my part, I might as easily divide a thing from itself. I may, indeed, divide in my thoughts, or conceive apart from each other, those things which perhaps I never perceived by sense so divided. Thus, I imagine the trunk of a human body without the limbs, or conceive the smell of a rose without thinking on the rose itself. So far, I will not deny, I can abstract; if that may properly be called *abstraction* which extends only to the conceiving separately such objects as it is possible may really exist or be actually perceived asunder. But my conceiving or imagining power does not extend beyond the possibility of real existence or perception. Hence, as it is impossible for me to see or feel anything without an actual sensation of that thing, so is it impossible for me to conceive in my thoughts any sensible thing or object distinct from the sensation or perception of it.

6. Some truths there are so near and obvious to the mind that a man need only open his eyes to see them. Such I take this important one to be, viz. that all the choir of heaven and furniture of the earth, in a word all those bodies which compose the mighty frame of the world, have not any subsistence without a mind; that their *being* is to be perceived or known; that consequently so long as they are not actually perceived by me, or do not exist in my mind or that of any other created spirit, they must either have no existence at all, or else subsist in the mind of some Eternal Spirit: it being perfectly unintelligible, and involving all the absurdity of abstraction, to attribute to any single part of them an existence independent of a spirit. To be convinced of which, the reader need only reflect, and try to separate in his own thoughts the *being* of a sensible thing from its *being perceived*.

7. From what has been said it is evident there is not any other Substance than *Spirit,* or that which perceives. But, for the fuller

proof of this point, let it be considered the sensible qualities are colour, figure, motion, smell, taste, and such like, that is, the ideas perceived by sense. Now, for an idea to exist in an unperceiving thing is a manifest contradiction; for to have an idea is all one as to perceive; that therefore wherein colour, figure, and the like qualities exist must perceive them; hence it is clear there can be no unthinking substance or *substratum* of those ideas.

8. But, say you, though the ideas themselves do not exist without the mind, yet there may be things like them, whereof they are copies or resemblances; which things exist without the mind in an unthinking substance. I answer, an idea can be like nothing but an idea; a colour or figure can be like nothing but another colour or figure. If we look but never so little into our own thoughts, we shall find it impossible for us to conceive a likeness except only between our ideas. Again, I ask whether those supposed *originals* or external things, of which our ideas are the pictures or representations, be themselves perceivable or no? If they are, then *they* are ideas, and we have gained our point: but if you say they are not, I appeal to any one whether it be sense to assert a colour is like something which is invisible; hard or soft, like something which is intangible; and so of the rest.

9. Some there are who make a distinction betwixt *primary* and *secondary* qualities. By the former they mean extension, figure, motion, rest, solidity or impenetrability, and number; by the latter they denote all other sensible qualities, as colours, sounds, tastes, and so forth. The ideas we have of these they acknowledge not to be the resemblances of anything existing without the mind, or unperceived; but they will have our ideas of the *primary qualities* to be patterns or images of things which exist without the mind, in an unthinking substance which they call *Matter*. By Matter, therefore, we are to understand an inert, senseless substance, in which extension, figure, and motion do actually subsist. But it is evident, from what we have already shewn, that extension, figure, and motion are only ideas existing in the mind, and that an idea can be like nothing but another idea; and that consequently neither they nor their archetypes can exist in an unperceiving substance. Hence, it is plain that the very notion of what is called *Matter* or *corporeal substance,* involves a contradiction in it.

10. They who assert that figure, motion, and the rest of the primary or original qualities do exist without the mind, in unthinking substances, do at the same time acknowledge that colours, sounds, heat, cold and suchlike secondary qualities, do not; which they tell

us are sensations, existing in the mind alone, that depend on and are occasioned by the different size, texture, and motion of the minute particles of matter. This they take for an undoubted truth, which they can demonstrate beyond all exception. Now, if it be certain that those *original* qualities are inseparably united with the other sensible qualities, and not, even in thought, capable of being abstracted from them, it plainly follows that *they* exist only in the mind. But I desire any one to reflect, and try whether he can, by any abstraction of thought, conceive the extension and motion of a body without all other sensible qualities. For my own part, I see evidently that it is not in my power to frame an idea of a body extended and moving, but I must withal give it some colour or other sensible quality, which is acknowledged to exist only in the mind. In short, extension, figure, and motion, abstracted from all other qualities, are inconceivable. Where therefore the other sensible qualities are, there must these be also, to wit, in the mind and nowhere else. . . .

16. But let us examine a little the received opinion. It is said extension is a *mode* or *accident* of Matter, and that Matter is the *substratum* that supports it. Now I desire that you would explain to me what is meant by Matter's *supporting* extension. Say you, I have no idea of Matter; and therefore cannot explain it. I answer, though you have no positive, yet, if you have any meaning at all, you must at least have a relative idea of Matter; though you know not what it is, yet you must be supposed to know what relation it bears to accidents, and what is meant by its supporting them. It is evident *support* cannot here be taken in its usual or literal sense, as when we say that pillars support a building. In what sense therefore must it be taken?

17. If we inquire into what the most accurate philosophers declare themselves to mean by *material substance,* we shall find them acknowledge they have no other meaning annexed to those sounds but the idea of Being in general, together with the relative notion of its supporting accidents. The general idea of Being appeareth to me the most abstract and incomprehensible of all other; and as for its supporting accidents, this, as we have just now observed, cannot be understood in the common sense of those words; it must therefore be taken in some other sense, but what that is they do not explain. So that when I consider the two parts or branches which make the signification of the words *material substance,* I am convinced there is no distinct meaning annexed to them. But why should we trouble ourselves any farther, in discussing this material

substratum or support of figure and motion and other sensible qualities? Does it not suppose they have an existence without the mind? And is not this a direct repugnancy, and altogether inconceivable? ...

25. All our ideas, sensations, notions, or the things which we perceive, by whatsoever names they may be distinguished, are visibly inactive: there is nothing of power or agency included in them. So that one idea or object of thought cannot produce or make any alteration in another. To be satisfied of the truth of this, there is nothing else requisite but a bare observation of our ideas. For, since they and every part of them exist only in the mind, it follows that there is nothing in them but what is perceived: but whoever shall attend to his ideas, whether of sense or reflexion, will not perceive in them any power or activity; there is, therefore, no such thing contained in them. A little attention will discover to us that the very being of an idea implies passiveness and inertness in it; insomuch that it is impossible for an idea to do anything, or, strictly speaking, to be the cause of anything: neither can it be the resemblance or pattern of any active being, as is evident from sect. 8. Whence it plainly follows that extension, figure, and motion cannot be the cause of our sensations. To say, therefore, that these are the effects of powers resulting from the configuration, number, motion, and size of corpuscles, must certainly be false.

26. We perceive a continual succession of ideas; some are anew excited, others are changed or totally disappear. There is therefore *some* cause of these ideas, whereon they depend, and which produces and changes them. That this cause cannot be any quality or idea or combination of *ideas,* is clear from the preceding section. It must therefore be a *substance*; but it has been shewn that there is no corporeal or material substance: it remains therefore that the cause of ideas is an incorporeal active substance or Spirit.

27. A Spirit is one simple, undivided, active being—as it perceives ideas it is called the *understanding,* and as it produces or otherwise operates about them it is called the *will.* Hence there can be no *idea* formed of a soul or spirit; for all ideas whatever, being passive and inert (*vid.* sect. 25), they cannot represent unto us, by way of image or likeness, that which acts. A little attention will make it plain to any one, that to have an idea which shall be *like* that active Principle of motion and change of ideas is absolutely impossible. Such is the nature of Spirit, or that which acts, that it cannot be of itself perceived, but only by the effects which it produceth. If any man shall doubt of the truth of what is here delivered, let him but reflect

and try if he can frame the idea of any power or active being; and whether he has ideas of two principal powers, marked by the names *will* and *understanding,* distinct from each other, as well as from a third idea of Substance or Being in general, with a relative notion of its supporting or being the subject of the aforesaid powers—which is signified by the name *soul* or *spirit.* This is what some hold; but, so far as I can see, the words *will, soul, spirit,* do not stand for different ideas, or, in truth, for any idea at all, but for something which is very different from ideas, and which, being an agent, cannot be like unto, or represented by, any idea whatsoever. Though it must be owned at the same time that we have some *notion* of soul, spirit, and the operations of the mind, such as willing, loving, hating—inasmuch as we know or understand the meaning of these words.

28. I find I can excite ideas in my mind at pleasure, and vary and shift the scene as oft as I think fit. It is no more than willing, and straightway this or that idea arises in my fancy; and by the same power it is obliterated and makes way for another. This making and unmaking of ideas doth very properly denominate the mind active. Thus much is certain and grounded on experience: but when we talk of unthinking agents, or of exciting ideas exclusive of volition, we only amuse ourselves with words.

29. But, whatever power I may have over my own thoughts, I find the ideas actually perceived by Sense have not a like dependence on *my* will. When in broad daylight I open my eyes, it is not in my power to choose whether I shall see or no, or to determine what particular objects shall present themselves to my view; and so likewise as to the hearing and other senses; the ideas imprinted on them are not creatures of *my* will. There is therefore some other Will or Spirit that produces them.

30. The ideas of Sense are more strong, lively, and distinct than those of the Imagination; they have likewise a steadiness, order, and coherence, and are not excited at random, as those which are the effects of human wills often are, but in a regular train or series —the admirable connexion whereof sufficiently testifies the wisdom and benevolence of its Author. Now the set rules, or established methods, wherein the Mind we depend on excites in us the ideas of Sense, are called the *laws of nature;* and these we learn by experience, which teaches us that such and such ideas are attended with such and such other ideas, in the ordinary course of things.

31. This gives us a sort of foresight, which enables us to regulate our actions for the benefit of life. And without this we should be

eternally at a loss: we could not know how to act anything that might procure us the least pleasure, or remove the least pain of sense. That food nourishes, sleep refreshes, and fire warms us; that to sow in the seedtime is the way to reap in the harvest; and in general that to obtain such or such ends, such or such means are conducive—all this we know, not by discovering any *necessary connexion* between our ideas, but only by the observation of the *settled laws* of nature, without which we should be all in uncertainty and confusion, and a grown man no more know how to manage himself in the affairs of life than an infant just born.

32. And yet this consistent uniform working, which so evidently displays the Goodness and Wisdom of that Governing Spirit whose Will constitutes the laws of nature, is so far from leading our thoughts to Him, that it rather sends them wandering after second causes. For, when we perceive certain ideas of Sense constantly followed by other ideas, and we know this is not of our own doing, we forthwith attribute power and agency to the ideas themselves, and make one the cause of another, than which nothing can be more absurd and unintelligible. Thus, for example, having observed that when we perceive by sight a certain round luminous figure, we at the same time perceive by touch the idea or sensation called heat, we do from thence conclude the sun to be the *cause* of heat. And in like manner perceiving the motion and collision of bodies to be attended with sound, we are inclined to think the latter the *effect* of the former.

33. The ideas imprinted on the Senses by the Author of nature are called *real things:* and those excited in the imagination, being less regular, vivid, and constant, are more properly termed *ideas,* or *images of things,* which they copy and represent. But then our *sensations,* be they never so vivid and distinct, are nevertheless ideas: that is, they exist in the mind, or are perceived by it, as truly as the ideas of its own framing. The ideas of Sense are allowed to have more reality in them, that is, to be more strong, orderly, and coherent than the creatures of the mind; but this is no argument that they exist without the mind. They are also less dependent on the spirit or thinking substance which perceives them, in that they are excited by the will of another and more powerful Spirit: yet still they are *ideas:* and certainly no idea, whether faint or strong, can exist otherwise than in a mind perceiving it....

135. Having despatched what we intended to say concerning the knowledge of *ideas,* the method we proposed leads us in the next place to treat of *spirits:* with regard to which, perhaps, human

knowledge is not so deficient as is vulgarly imagined. The great reason that is assigned for our being thought ignorant of the nature of Spirits is our not having an *idea* of it. But, surely it ought not to be looked on as a defect in a human understanding that it does not perceive the idea of Spirit, if it is manifestly impossible there should be any such idea. And this if I mistake not has been demonstrated in section 27. To which I shall here add that a Spirit has been shewn to be the only substance or support wherein unthinking beings or ideas can exist: but that this *substance* which supports or perceives ideas should itself be an idea or like an idea, is evidently absurd.

136. It will perhaps be said that we want a *sense* (as some have imagined) proper to know substances withal; which, if we had, we might know our own soul as we do a triangle. To this I answer, that in case we had a new sense bestowed upon us, we could only receive thereby some new *sensations* or *ideas of sense*. But I believe nobody will say that what he means by the terms *soul* and *substance* is only some particular sort of idea or sensation. We may therefore infer that, all things duly considered, it is not more reasonable to think our faculties defective, in that they do not furnish us with an idea of Spirit, or active thinking substance, than it would be if we should blame them for not being able to comprehend a *round square*.

137. From the opinion that Spirits are to be known after the manner of an idea or sensation have risen many absurd and heterodox tenets, and much scepticism about the nature of the soul. It is even probable that this opinion may have produced a doubt in some whether they had any soul at all distinct from their body; since upon inquiry they could not find they had an idea of it. That an *idea* which is inactive, and the existence whereof consists in being perceived, should be the image or likeness of an agent subsisting by itself, seems to need no other refutation than barely attending to what is meant by those words. But, perhaps you will say that though an idea cannot resemble a Spirit in its thinking, acting, or subsisting by itself, yet it may in some other respects; and it is not necessary that an idea or image be in all respects like the original.

138. I answer, If it does not in those mentioned, it is impossible it should represent it in any other thing. Do but leave out the power of willing, thinking, and perceiving ideas, and there remains nothing else wherein the idea can be like a spirit. For, by the word *spirit* we mean only that which thinks, wills, and perceives; this, and this alone, constitutes the signification of that term. If therefore

it is impossible that any degree of those powers should be represented in an idea, it is evident there can be no idea of a Spirit.

139. But it will be objected that, if there is no *idea* signified by the terms *soul, spirit,* and *substance,* they are wholly insignificant, or have no meaning in them. I answer, those words do mean or signify a real thing; which is neither an idea nor like an idea, but that which perceives ideas, and wills, and reasons about them. What I am *myself,* that which I denote by the term *I,* is the same with what is meant by *soul* or *spiritual substance.* If it be said that this is only quarrelling at a word, and that, since the immediate significations of other names are by common consent called *ideas,* no reason can be assigned why that which is signified by the name *spirit* or *soul* may not partake in the same appellation, I answer, all the unthinking objects of the mind agree in that they are entirely passive, and their existence consists only in being perceived; whereas a *soul* or *spirit* is an active being, whose existence consists, not in being perceived, but in perceiving ideas and thinking. It is therefore necessary, in order to prevent equivocation and confounding natures perfectly disagreeing and unlike, that we distinguish between *spirit* and *idea.* See sect. 27.

140. In a large sense indeed, we may be said to have an idea, or rather a notion of *spirit.* That is, we understand the meaning of the word, otherwise we could not affirm or deny anything of it. Moreover, as we conceive the ideas that are in the minds of other spirits by means of our own, which we suppose to be resemblances of them, so we know other spirits by means of our own soul—which in that sense is the image or idea of them; it having a like respect to other spirits that blueness or heat by me perceived has to those ideas perceived by another.

141. [The natural immortality of the soul is a necessary consequence of the foregoing doctrine. But before we attempt to prove this, it is fit that we explain the meaning of that tenet.] * It must not be supposed that they who assert the natural immortality of the soul are of opinion that it is absolutely incapable of annihilation even by the infinite power of the Creator who first gave it being, but only that it is not liable to be broken or dissolved by the ordinary laws of nature or motion. They indeed who hold the soul of man to be only a thin vital flame, or system of animal spirits, make it perishing and corruptible as the body; since there is nothing more easily dissipated than such a being, which it is naturally impossible should survive the ruin of the tabernacle wherein it is inclosed. And

* Omitted from the second edition.

this notion hath been greedily embraced and cherished by the worst part of mankind, as the most effectual antidote against all impressions of virtue and religion. But it hath been made evident that bodies, of what frame or texture soever, are barely passive ideas in the mind, which is more distant and heterogeneous from them than light is from darkness. We have shewn that the soul is indivisible, incorporeal, unextended; and it is consequently incorruptible. Nothing can be plainer than that the motions, changes, decays, and dissolutions which we hourly see befal natural bodies (and which is what we mean by the *course of nature*) cannot possibly affect an active, simple, uncompounded substance: such a being therefore is indissoluble by the force of nature; that is to say, *the soul of man is naturally immortal.*

142. After what has been said, it is, I suppose, plain that our souls are not to be known in the same manner as senseless, inactive objects, or by way of *idea.* *Spirits* and *ideas* are things so wholly different, that when we say 'they exist,' 'they are known,' or the like, these words must not be thought to signify anything common to both natures. There is nothing alike or common in them; and to expect that by any multiplication or enlargement of our faculties we may be enabled to know a spirit as we do a triangle, seems as absurd as if we should hope to *see* a *sound.* This is inculcated because I imagine it may be of moment towards clearing several important questions, and preventing some very dangerous errors concerning the nature of the soul.

We may not, I think, strictly be said to have an *idea* of an active being, or of an action; although we may be said to have a *notion* of them. I have some knowledge or notion of *my mind,* and its acts about ideas; inasmuch as I know or understand what. is meant by these words. What I know, that I have some notion of. I will not say that the terms *idea* and *notion* may not be used convertibly, if the world will have it so. But yet it conduceth to clearness and propriety, that we distinguish things very different by different names. It is also to be remarked that, all *relations* including an act of the mind, we cannot so properly be said to have an idea, but rather a notion of the relations and habitudes between things. But if, in the modern way, the word *idea* is extended to *spirits,* and *relations,* and *acts,* this is, after all, an affair of verbal concern.

143. It will not be amiss to add, that the doctrine of *abstract ideas* has had no small share in rendering those sciences intricate and obscure which are particularly conversant about spiritual things. Men have imagined they could frame abstract notions of the *powers*

and *acts* of the mind, and consider them prescinded as well from the mind or spirit itself, as from their respective objects and effects. Hence a great number of dark and ambiguous terms, presumed to stand for abstract notions, have been introduced into metaphysics and morality; and from these have grown infinite distractions and disputes among the learned.

144. But, nothing seems more to have contributed towards engaging men in controversies and mistakes with regard to the nature and operations of the mind, than the being used to speak of those things in terms borrowed from sensible ideas. For example, the will is termed the *motion* of the soul: this infuses a belief that the mind of man is as a ball in motion, impelled and determined by the objects of sense, as necessarily as that is by the stroke of a racket. Hence arise endless scruples and errors of dangerous consequence in morality. All which, I doubt not, may be cleared, and truth appear plain, uniform, and consistent, could but philosophers be prevailed on to retire into themselves, and attentively consider their own meaning.

145. From what hath been said, it is plain that we cannot know the existence of *other spirits* otherwise than by their operations, or the ideas by them, excited in us. I perceive several motions, changes, and combinations of ideas, that inform me there are certain particular agents, like myself, which accompany them and concur in their production. Hence, the knowledge I have of other spirits is not immediate, as is the knowledge of my ideas; but depending on the intervention of ideas, by me referred to agents or spirits distinct from myself, as effects or concomitant signs.

146. But, though there be some things which convince us human agents are concerned in producing them, yet it is evident to every one that those things which are called the Works of Nature, that is, the far greater part of the ideas or sensations perceived by us, are *not* produced by, or dependent on, the wills of *men*. There is therefore some other Spirit that causes them; since it is repugnant that they should subsist by themselves. See sect. 29. But, if we attentively consider the constant regularity, order and concatenation of natural things, the surprising magnificence, beauty, and perfection of the larger, and the exquisite contrivance of the smaller parts of creation, together with the exact harmony and correspondence of the whole; but above all the never-enough-admired laws of pain and pleasure, and the instincts or natural inclinations, appetites, and passions of animals;—I say if we consider all these things, and at the same time attend to the meaning and import of the attributes

One, Eternal, Infinitely Wise, Good, and Perfect, we shall clearly perceive that they belong to the aforesaid Spirit, 'who works all in all,' and 'by whom all things consist.'

147. Hence, it is evident that God is known as certainly and immediately as any other mind or spirit whatsoever, distinct from ourselves. We may even assert that the existence of God is far more evidently perceived than the existence of men; because the effects of Nature are infinitely more numerous and considerable than those ascribed to human agents. There is not any one mark that denotes a man, or effect produced by him, which does not more strongly evince the being of that Spirit who is the Author of Nature. For, it is evident that, in affecting other persons, the will of man hath no other object than barely the motion of the limbs of his body; but that such a motion should be attended by, or excite any idea in the mind of another, depends wholly on the will of the Creator. He alone it is who, 'upholding all things by the word of His power,' maintains that intercourse between spirits whereby they are able to perceive the existence of each other. And yet this pure and clear light which enlightens every one is itself invisible.

148. It seems to be a general pretence of the unthinking herd that they cannot *see* God. Could we but see Him, say they, as we see a man, we should believe that He is, and believing obey His commands. But alas, we need only open our eyes to see the Sovereign Lord of all things, with a more full and clear view than we do any of our fellow-creatures. Not that I imagine we see God (as some will have it) by a direct and immediate view; or see corporeal things, not by themselves, but by seeing that which represents them in the essence of God; which doctrine is, I must confess, to me incomprehensible. But I shall explain my meaning. A human spirit or person is not perceived by sense, as not being an idea. When therefore we see the colour, size, figure, and motions of a man, we perceive only certain sensations or ideas excited in our own minds; and these being exhibited to our view in sundry distinct collections, serve to mark out unto us the existence of finite and created spirits like ourselves. Hence it is plain we do not see a man, if by *man* is meant, that which lives, moves, perceives, and thinks as we do: but only such a certain collection of ideas as directs us to think there is a distinct principle of thought and motion, like to ourselves, accompanying and represented by it. And after the same manner we see God: all the difference is that, whereas some one finite and narrow assemblage of ideas denotes a particular human mind, whithersoever we direct our view we do at all times and in all

places perceive manifest tokens of the Divinity: everything we see, hear, feel, or anywise perceive by sense, being a sign or effect of the power of God; as is our perception of those very motions which are produced by men.

149. It is therefore plain that nothing can be more evident to any one that is capable of the least reflexion than the existence of God, or a Spirit who is intimately present to our minds, producing in them all that variety of ideas or sensations which continually affect us, on whom we have an absolute and entire dependence, in short 'in whom we live, and move, and have our being.' That the discovery of this great truth, which lies so near and obvious to the mind, should be attained to by the reason of so very few, is a sad instance of the stupidity and inattention of men, who, though they are surrounded with such clear manifestations of the Deity, are yet so little affected by them that they seem, as it were, blinded with excess of light.

It requires no very lengthy reflection to recognize that Berkeley's thought is not entirely devoted to a destructive analysis of previous philosophy. It is true that he dispenses with the concepts of corporeal substance and reduces nature to a mere surface of appearance. where the sequence and coexistence of primary and secondary qualities are observable. But Berkeley's speculative sense of reality is much richer than this, as his theory of deity and his "notion" of the active self makes manifest. The physical world may be no more than a cluster of "inert" ideas, passive data of our observation; but the reality which encompasses them involves an interplay of spiritual activities. Thus Berkeley's speculative philosophy is a spiritual realism, introduced by a skeptical Empiricism. Despite his own statement, the proposition "To be is to be perceived" does not adequately summarize his position. "To be is to perceive" would almost seem a more adequate statement. To quote from Henri Bergson's summary of Berkeley's philosophy: [8]

If a body is made of "ideas" or, in other words, if it is entirely passive and determinate, having neither power nor virtuality, it

---

[8] Henri Bergson, "Philosophical Intuition," in *The Creative Mind*, trans. by Mabelle L. Andison, pp. 138-39. Philosophical Library, New York, 1946. Reprinted by permission of the publisher. Italics added.

cannot act on other bodies; and consequently the movements of bodies must be the effect of an active power, which has produced these bodies themselves and which, because of the order which the universe reveals, can only be an intelligent cause. If we are mistaken when under the name of general ideas we set up as realities the names that we have given to groups of objects or perceptions more or less artificially constituted by us on the plane of matter, such is not the case when we think we discover, behind this plane, the divine intentions: the general idea which exists only on the surface and which links body to body is no doubt only a word, but the general idea which exists in depth, relating bodies to God or rather descending from God to bodies, is a reality.... Finally, if God imprints in each one of us perceptions, or as Berkeley says, "ideas," the being which gathers up these perceptions, or rather which goes to meet them, is quite the reverse of an idea: it is a will, though one which is constantly limited by divine will. *The meeting-place of these two wills is precisely what we call matter.* If the *percipi* is pure passivity the *percipere* is pure activity. Human mind, matter, divine mind therefore become terms which we can express only in terms of one another.

THE ATOMIC EMPIRICISM OF DAVID HUME

The following passages are taken from David Hume's own abstract of his major work *A Treatise of Human Nature.*[9] The abstract was published anonymously in 1740, the year following the publication of the *Treatise* itself, which had attracted little attention. It contains a remarkably precise and compact summary of the more original features of Hume's contribution. This *Abstract* has been recently brought to light and its authorship identified by the late J. M. Keynes, the logician and economist, in collaboration

[9] David Hume, *Abstract of a Treatise of Human Nature,* 1740, pp. 5-11.

David Hume (1711-1776) was born of a distinguished Scottish family and educated at the University of Edinburgh, which he entered at the age of twelve. Like Locke, Hume became an active diplomatist, being for a time chargé d'affaires at the British Embassy in Paris, where he was greatly admired and much flattered and entertained. In his own Scotland, however, Hume's skeptical views were held suspect, and he sought in vain for university appointments. He devoted the leisure of his later years to writing history. At this time he was well acquainted with Edmund Burke, whose advocacy of a reconciliation between England and the American colonies he shared and endeavored to further.

with P. Sraffa. It was reprinted in 1938 by the Cambridge University Press.

This book seems to be wrote upon the same plan with several other works that have had a great vogue of late years in England. The philosophical spirit, which has been so much improved all over Europe within these last fourscore years, has been carried to as great a length in this kingdom as in any other. Our writers seem even to have started a new kind of philosophy, which promises more both to the entertainment and advantage of mankind, than any other with which the world has been yet acquainted. Most of the philosophers of antiquity, who treated of human nature, have shewn more of a delicacy of sentiment, a just sense of morals, or a greatness of soul, than a depth of reasoning and reflection. They content themselves with representing the common sense of mankind in the strongest lights, and with the best turn of thought and expression, without following out steadily a chain of propositions, or forming the several truths into a regular science. But 'tis at least worth while to try if the science of *man* will not admit of the same accuracy which several parts of natural philosophy are found susceptible of. There seems to be all the reason in the world to imagine that it may be carried to the greatest degree of exactness. If, in examining several phaenomena, we find that they resolve themselves into one common principle, and can trace this principle into another, we shall at last arrive at those few simple principles, on which all the rest depend. And tho' we can never arrive at the ultimate principles, 'tis a satisfaction to go as far as our faculties will allow us.

This seems to have been the aim of our late philosophers, and, among the rest, of this author. He proposes to anatomize human nature in a regular manner, and promises to draw no conclusions but where he is authorized by experience. He talks with contempt of hypotheses; and insinuates, that such of our countrymen as have banished them from moral philosophy, have done a more signal service to the world, than *my Lord Bacon,* whom he considers as the father of experimental physicks. He mentions, on this occasion, *Mr. Locke, my Lord Shaftsbury, Dr. Mandeville, Mr. Hutchison, Dr. Butler,* who, tho' they differ in many points among themselves, seem all to agree in founding their accurate disquisitions of human nature intirely upon experience.

Beside the satisfaction of being acquainted with what most nearly concerns us, it may be safely affirmed, that almost all the sciences are comprehended in the science of human nature, and are dependent on it. *The sole end of logic is to explain the principles and Operations of our reasoning faculty, and the nature of our ideas,* morals and criticism *regard our tastes and sentiments; and* politics *consider men as united in society, and dependent on each other.* This treatise therefore of human nature seems intended for a system of the sciences. The author has finished what regards logic, and has laid the foundation of the other parts in his account of the passions.

The celebrated *Monsieur Leibnitz* has observed it to be a defect in the common systems of logic, that they are very copious when they explain the operations of the understanding in the forming of demonstrations, but are too concise when they treat of probabilities, and those other measures of evidence on which life and action intirely depend, and which are our guides even in most of our philosophical speculations. In this censure, he comprehends *the essay on human understanding, le recherche de la verité,* and *l'art de penser.* The author of the *treatise of human nature* seems to have been sensible of this defect in these philosophers, and has endeavoured, as much as he can, to supply it. As his book contains a great number of speculations very new and remarkable, it will be impossible to give the reader a just notion of the whole. We shall therefore chiefly confine ourselves to his explication of our reasonings from cause and effect. If we can make this intelligible to the reader, it may serve as a specimen of the whole.

Impressions and Ideas

Our author begins with some definitions. He calls a *perception* whatever can be present to the mind, whether we employ our senses, or are actuated with passion, or exercise our thought and reflection. He divides our perceptions into two kinds, *viz. impressions* and *ideas.* When we feel a passion or emotion of any kind, or have the images of external objects conveyed by our senses; the perception of the mind is what he calls an *impression,* which is a word that he employs in a new sense. When we reflect on a passion or an object which is not present, this perception is an *idea. Impressions,* therefore, are our lively and strong perceptions; *ideas* are the fainter and weaker. This distinction is evident; as evident as that between feeling and thinking.

The first proposition he advances, is, that all our ideas, or weak perceptions, are derived from our impressions, or strong perceptions, and that we can never think of anything which we have not seen without us, or felt in our own minds. This proposition seems to be equivalent to that which Mr. *Locke* has taken such pains to establish, *viz. that no ideas are innate.* Only it may be observed, as an inaccuracy of that famous philosopher, that he comprehends all our perceptions under the term of idea, in which sense it is false, that we have no innate ideas. For it is evident our stronger perceptions or impressions are innate, and that natural affection, love of virtue, resentment, and all the other passions, arise immediately from nature. I am perswaded, whoever would take the question in this light, would be easily able to reconcile all parties. *Father Malebranche* would find himself at a loss to point out any thought of the mind, which did not represent something antecedently felt by it, either internally, or by means of the external senses, and must allow, that however we may compound, and mix, and augment, and diminish our ideas, they are all derived from these sources. *Mr. Locke,* on the other hand, would readily acknowledge, that all our passions are a kind of natural instincts, derived from nothing but the original constitution of the human mind.

Our author thinks, "that no discovery could have been made more happily for deciding all controversies concerning ideas than this, that impressions always take the precedency of them, and that every idea with which the imagination is furnished, first makes its appearance in a correspondent impression. These latter perceptions are all so clear and evident, that they admit of no controversy; tho' many of our ideas are so obscure, that 'tis almost impossible even for the mind, which forms them, to tell exactly their nature and composition." Accordingly, wherever any idea is ambiguous, he has always recourse to the impression, which must render it clear and precise. And when he suspects that any philosophical term has no idea annexed to it (as is too common) he always asks *from what impression that idea is derived?* And if no impression can be produced, he concludes that the term is altogether insignificant. 'Tis after this manner he examines our idea of *substance* and *essence;* and it were to be wished, that this rigorous method were more practised in all philosophical debates.

LOGICAL POSITIVISM
NOTE ON THE THEORY OF MEANING:

Hume's language here is very important in the light of more recent forms of Empiricism. Hume tells us that a term that cannot be traced back to an impression is insignificant; that is, without meaning. It is, in other words, a piece of mere nonsense. Thus a sentence containing such a term is not a genuine assertion. Strictly speaking, it is neither true nor false, being in this respect like a line from nonsense poetry. The implications of this theory are startling indeed. A philosophy like that of Spinoza centers about a concept of substance that is described as *self-caused*. But the latter concept cannot be reduced to sensuous impressions. Therefore it has no meaning, and accordingly some of the chief propositions in Spinoza's philosophy are nonsense—that is, neither true nor false but meaningless.

In very recent years this line of attack has come to the fore and is employed by a new school of Empiricists known as *Logical Positivists*. In its modern form Hume's theory of meaning is expressed somewhat as follows: No statement that cannot be tested or verified by means of sensuous observation can be said to have meaning or *sense*. We quote from Professor Carnap's *Philosophy and Logical Syntax:* [10]

Every assertion P in the wide field of science has this character, that it either asserts something about present perceptions or other experiences, and therefore is verifiable by them, or that propositions about future perceptions are deducible from P together with some other already verified propositions. If a scientist should venture to make an assertion from which no perceptive propositions could be deduced, what should we say to that? Suppose, *e.g.,* he asserts that there is not only a gravitational field having an effect on bodies according to the known laws of gravitation, but also a *levitational field,* and on being asked what sort of effect this levitational field has, according to his theory, he answers that there is no observable effect; in other words, he confesses his inability to give rules according to which we could deduce perceptive propositions from his assertion. In that case our reply is: your assertion is no assertion at all; it does not speak about anything; it is nothing but a series of empty words; it is simply without sense.

It is true that he may have images and even feelings connected with his words. This fact may be of psychological importance; logically, it is irrevelant. What gives theoretical meaning to a proposi-

[10] Rudolf Carnap, *Philosophy and Logical Syntax,* pp. 13-15. Kegan Paul, Trench, Trübner & Co., London, 1935. Reprinted by permission of the Orthological Institute, London.

tion is not the attendant images and thoughts, but the possibility of deducing from it perceptive propositions, in other words, the possibility of verification. To give sense to a proposition the presence of images is not sufficient; it is not even necessary. We have no actual image of the electro-magnetic field, nor even, I should say, of the gravitational field. Nevertheless the propositions which physicists assert about these fields have a perfect sense, because perceptive propositions are deducible from them. I by no means object to the proposition just mentioned about a levitational field that we do not know how to imagine or conceive such a field. My only objection to that proposition is that we are not told how to verify it.

According to this view, all metaphysical and theological speculation is condemned as meaningless. All statements that assert ideals of conduct are similarly to be discarded as meaningless. Since we cannot verify through sensuous perception such statements as "It is wrong to tell a falsehood," the logical positivists insist that such value judgments are equivalent to imperatives. Thus "It is wrong to tell a falsehood" is equivalent to an imperative: "Do not lie!" And this sentence obviously cannot be verified. Hence the extreme Logical Positivist considers all discussion of ethical principles meaningless.

In the case of mathematics, however, the Logical Positivist reports favorably. Mathematics is not an empirical science based upon sensuous perception. But this is because it attempts, unlike philosophical speculation, only to frame a language system that may be employed when we undertake to make statements in other sciences. Mathematics is an elaborate grammar or system of syntax employed in framing all sorts of verifiable propositions. Thus

$$(5 \text{ plus } 2) \text{ equals } (3 \text{ plus } 4)$$

means that wherever we come upon one expression we may substitute the other, as we may substitute "healthier" for "in better health" without altering the truth or the falsity of our statement. Thus we may in any piece of empirical, scientific reasoning substitute for the expression "The plane figure ABC is triangular" the expression "The sum of the angles of the plane figure ABC is equal to two right angles" without altering the truth or the falsity of our statement.

According to this interpretation, mathematical propositions do not widen the scope of our real knowledge, but clarify certain expressions by indicating that they mean the same thing as other expressions already familiar. Hence the equation, which is based on the notion of identity, is the fundamental form of mathematical discourse. The symbol of identity, the "equality sign," is interpreted as indicating that the expressions so joined are synonymous. Accordingly equations contain information concerning one language system. They do not refer directly to things.

Let us return to Hume's Abstract: [11]

Matters of Fact and Causation

'Tis evident, that all reasonings concerning *matter of fact* are founded on the relation of cause and effect, and that we can never infer the existence of one object from another, unless they be connected together, either mediately or immediately. In order therefore to understand these reasonings, we must be perfectly acquainted with the idea of a cause; and in order to that, must look about us to find something that is the cause of another.

Here is a billiard-ball lying on the table, and another ball moving towards it with rapidity. They strike; and the ball, which was formerly at rest, now acquires a motion. This is as perfect an instance of the relation of cause and effect as any which we know, either by sensation or reflection. Let us therefore examine it. 'Tis evident, that the two balls touched one another before the motion was communicated, and that there was no interval between the shock and the motion. *Contiguity* in time and place is therefore a requisite circumstance to the operation of all causes. 'Tis evident likewise, that the motion, which was the cause, is prior to the motion, which was the effect. *Priority* in time, is therefore another requisite circumstance in every cause. But this is not all. Let us try any other balls of the same kind in a like situation, and we shall always find, that the impulse of the one produces motion in the other. Here therefore is a *third* circumstance, *viz.* that of a *constant conjunction* between the cause and effect. Every object like the cause, produces always some object like the effect. Beyond these three circumstances of contiguity, priority, and constant conjunction, I can discover nothing in this cause. The first ball is in motion; touches the second; immediately the second is in motion: and when I try the experi-

---

[11] Hume, *op. cit.*, pp. 11-25.

ment with the same or like balls, in the same or like circumstances, I find, that upon the motion and touch of the one ball, motion always follows in the other. In whatever shape I turn this matter, and however I examine it, I can find nothing farther.

This is the case when both the cause and effect are present to the senses. Let us now see upon what our inference is founded, when we conclude from the one that the other has existed or will exist. Suppose I see a ball moving in a streight [sic] line towards another, I immediately conclude, that they will shock, and that the second will be in motion. This is the inference from cause to effect; and of this nature are all our reasonings in the conduct of life: on this is founded all our belief in history: and from hence is derived all philosophy, excepting only geometry and arithmetic. If we can explain the inference from the shock of two balls, we shall be able to account for this operation of the mind in all instances.

Were a man, such as *Adam,* created in the full vigour of understanding, without experience, he would never be able to infer motion in the second ball from the motion and impulse of the first. It is not anything that reason sees in the cause, which make us *infer* the effect. Such an inference, were it possible, would amount to a demonstration, as being founded merely on the comparison of ideas. But no inference from cause to effect amounts to a demonstration. Of which there is this evident proof. The mind can always *conceive* any effect to follow from any cause, and indeed any event to follow upon another; whatever we *conceive* is possible, at least in a metaphysical sense: but wherever a demonstration takes place, the contrary is impossible, and implies a contradiction. There is no demonstration, therefore, for any conjunction of cause and effect. And this is a principle, which is generally allowed by philosophers.

It would have been necessary, therefore, for *Adam* (if he was not inspired) to have had *experience* of the effect, which followed upon the impulse of these two balls. He must have seen, in several instances, that when the one ball struck upon the other, the second always acquired motion. If he had seen a sufficient number of instances of this kind, whenever he saw the one ball moving towards the other, he would always conclude without hesitation, that the second would acquire motion. His understanding would anticipate his sight, and form a conclusion suitable to his past experience.

It follows, then, that all reasonings concerning cause and effect, are founded on experience, and that all reasonings from experience are founded on the supposition, that the course of nature will continue uniformly the same. We conclude, that like causes, in like

circumstances, will always produce like effects. It may now be worth
while to consider, what determines us to form a conclusion of such
infinite consequence.

Custom as the Guide of Life

'Tis evident, that *Adam* with all his science, would never have
been able to *demonstrate,* that the course of nature must continue
uniformly the same, and that the future must be conformable to the
past. What is possible can never be demonstrated to be false; and
'tis possible the course of nature may change, since we can conceive
such a change. Nay, I will go farther, and assert, that he could not
so much as prove by any *probable* arguments, that the future must
be conformable to the past. All probable arguments are built on the
supposition, that there is this conformity between the future and
the past, and therefore can never prove it. This conformity is a
matter of fact, and if it must be proved, will admit of no proof but
from experience. But our experience in the past can be a proof of
nothing for the future, but upon a supposition, that there is a resemblance betwixt them. This therefore is a point, which can admit
of no proof at all, and which we take for granted without any proof.

We are determined by CUSTOM alone to suppose the future conformable to the past. When I see a billiard-ball moving towards
another, my mind is immediately carry'd by habit to the usual effect,
and anticipates my sight by conceiving the second ball in motion.
There is nothing in these objects, abstractly considered, and independent of experience, which leads me to form any such conclusion:
and even after I have had experience of many repeated effects of
this kind, there is no argument, which determines me to suppose,
that the effect will be conformable to past experience. The powers,
by which bodies operate, are entirely unknown. We perceive only
their sensible qualities: and what *reason* have we to think, that the
same powers will always be conjoined with the same sensible
qualities?

'Tis not, therefore, reason, which is the guide of life, but custom.
That alone determines the mind, in all instances, to suppose the
future conformable to the past. However easy this step may seem,
reason would never, to all eternity, be able to make it.

This is a very curious discovery, but leads us to others, that are
still more curious. *When I see a billiard ball moving towards another, my mind is immediately carried by habit to the usual effect,
and anticipate[s] my sight by conceiving the second ball in motion.*
But is this all? Do I nothing but CONCEIVE the motion of the second

334

ball? No surely. I also BELIEVE that it will move. What then is this *belief?* And how does it differ from the simple conception of any thing? Here is a new question unthought of by philosophers.

Ideas and Matters of Fact

When a demonstration convinces me of any proposition, it not only makes me conceive the proposition, but also makes me sensible, that 'tis impossible to conceive anything contrary. What is demonstratively false implies a contradiction; and what implies a contradiction cannot be conceived. But with regard to any matter of fact, however strong the proof may be from experience, I can always conceive the contrary, tho' I cannot always believe it. The belief, therefore, makes some difference between the conception to which we assent, and that to which we do not assent.

To account for this, there are only two hypotheses. It may be said, that belief joins some new idea to those which we may conceive without assenting to them. But this hypothesis is false. For *first,* no such idea can be produced. When we simply conceive an object, we conceive it in all its parts. We conceive it as it might exist, tho' we do not believe it to exist. Our belief of it would discover no new qualities. We may paint out the entire object in imagination without believing it. We may set it, in a manner, before our eyes, with every circumstance of time and place. 'Tis the very object conceived as it might exist; and when we believe it, we can do no more.

Secondly, the mind has a faculty of joining all ideas together, which involve not a contradiction; and therefore if belief consisted in some idea, which we add to the simple conception, it would be in a man's power, by adding this idea to it, to believe anything, which he can conceive.

Since therefore belief implies a conception, and yet is something more; and since it adds no new idea to the conception; it follows, that it is a different MANNER of conceiving an object; *something* that is distinguishable to the feeling, and depends not upon our will, as all our ideas do. My mind runs by habit from the visible object of one ball moving towards another, to the usual effect of motion in the second ball. It not only conceives that motion, but *feels* something different in the conception of it from a mere reverie of the imagination. The presence of this visible object, and the constant conjunction of that particular effect, render the idea different to the *feeling* from those loose ideas, which come into the mind without any introduction. This conclusion seems a little surprizing; but we

335

are led into it by a chain of propositions, which admit of no doubt. To ease the reader's memory I shall briefly resume them. No matter of fact can be proved but from its cause or its effect. Nothing can be known to be the cause of another but by experience. We can give no reason for extending to the future our experience in the past; but are entirely determined by custom, when we conceive an effect to follow from its usual cause. But we also believe an effect to follow, as well as conceive it. This belief joins no new idea to the conception. It only varies the manner of conceiving, and makes a difference to the feeling or sentiment. Belief, therefore, in all matters of fact arises only from custom, and is an idea conceived in a peculiar *manner*.

Our author proceeds to explain the manner or feeling, which renders belief different from a loose conception. He seems sensible, that 'tis impossible by words to describe this feeling, which every one must be conscious of in his own breast. He calls it sometimes a *stronger* conception, sometimes a more *lively*, a more *vivid*, a *firmer*, or a more *intense* conception. And indeed, whatever name we may give to this feeling, which constitutes belief, our author thinks it evident, that it has a more forcible effect on the mind than fiction and mere conception. This he proves by its influence on the passions and on the imagination; which are only moved by truth or what is taken for such. Poetry, with all its art, can never cause a passion, like one in real life. It fails in the original conception of its objects, which never *feel* in the same manner as those which command our belief and opinion.

Our author presuming, that he had sufficiently proved, that the ideas we assent to are different to the feeling from the other ideas, and that this feeling is more firm and lively than our common conception, endeavours in the next place to explain the cause of this lively feeling by an analogy with other acts of the mind. His reasoning seems to be curious; but could scarce be rendered intelligible, or at least probable to the reader, without a long detail, which would exceed the compass I have prescribed to myself.

I have likewise omitted many arguments, which he adduces to prove that belief consists merely in a peculiar feeling or sentiment. I shall only mention one; our past experience is not always uniform. Sometimes one effect follows from a cause, sometimes another: in which case we always believe, that that will exist which is most common. I see a billiard-ball moving towards another. I cannot distinguish whether it moves upon its axis, or was struck so as to skim along the table. In the first case, I know it will not stop after the shock. In the second it may stop. The first is most common, and therefore I lay my account with that effect. But I also conceive the other effect, and conceive it as possible, and as connected with the cause. Were not the one conception different in the feeling or sentiment from the other, there would be no difference betwixt them.

The Notion of Power

We have confin'd ourselves in this whole reasoning to the relation of cause and effect, as discovered in the motions and operations of matter. But the same reasoning extends to the operations of the mind. Whether we consider the influence of the will in moving our body, or in governing our thought, it may safely be affirmed, that we could never foretel the effect, merely from the consideration of the cause, without experience. And even after we have experience of these effects, 'tis custom alone, not reason, which determines us to make it the standard of our future judgments. When the cause is presented, the mind, from habit, immediately passes to the conception and belief of the usual effect. This belief is something different from the conception. It does not, however, join any new idea to it. It only makes it be felt differently, and renders it stronger and more lively.

Having dispatcht this material point concerning the nature of the inference from cause and effect, our author returns upon his footsteps, and examines anew the idea of that relation. In the considering of motion communicated from one ball to another, we could find nothing but contiguity, priority in the cause, and constant conjunction. But, beside these circumstances, 'tis commonly suppos'd, that there is a necessary connexion between the cause and effect, and that the cause possesses something, which we call a *power,* or *force,* or *energy.* The question is, what idea is annex'd to these terms? If all our ideas or thoughts be derived from our impressions, this power must either discover itself to our senses, or to our internal feeling. But so little does any *power* discover itself to the senses in the operations of matter, that the *Cartesians* have made no scruple to assert, that matter is utterly deprived of energy, and that all its operations are perform'd merely by the energy of the supreme Being. But the question still recurs, *What idea have we of energy or power even in the supreme Being?* All our idea of a Deity (according to those who deny innate ideas) is nothing but a composition of those ideas, which we acquire from reflecting on the operations of our own minds. Now our own minds afford us no more notion of energy than matter does. When we consider our will or volition a *priori,* abstracting from experience, we should never be able to infer any effect from it. And when we take the assistance of experience, it only shows us objects contiguous, successive, and constantly conjoined. Upon the whole, then, either we have no idea at all of force and energy, and these words are altogether insignificant, or they can mean nothing but that determination of the thought, acquir'd by habit, to pass from the cause to its usual effect. But who-ever would thoroughly understand this must consult the author himself. 'Tis sufficient, if I can make the learned world apprehend, that there is some difficulty in the case, and that who-ever solves the difficulty must say something very new and extraordinary; as new as the difficulty itself.

By all that has been said the reader will easily perceive, that the philosophy contain'd in this book is very sceptical, and tends to give us a notion of the imperfections and narrow limits of human under-standing. Almost all reasoning is there reduced to experience; and the belief, which attends experience, is explained to be nothing but a peculiar sentiment, or lively conception produced by habit. Nor is this all, when we believe any thing of *external* existence, or suppose an object to exist a moment after it is no longer perceived, this belief is nothing but a sentiment of the same kind. Our author insists upon several other sceptical topics; and upon the whole concludes, that we assent to our faculties, and employ our reason only because we cannot help it. Philosophy would render us entirely *Pyrrhonian,* [i.e., skeptical] were not nature too strong for it.

The Soul a Train of Perceptions

I shall conclude the logics of this author with an account of two opinions, which seem to be peculiar to himself, as indeed are most of his opinions. He asserts, that the soul, as far as we can conceive it, is nothing but a system or train of different perceptions, those of heat and cold, love and anger, thoughts and sensations; all united together, but without any perfect simplicity or identity. *Des Cartes* maintained that thought was the essence of the mind; not this thought or that thought, but thought in general. This seems to be absolutely unintelligible, since everything, that exists, is particular: And therefore it must be our several particular perceptions, that compose the mind. I say, *compose* the mind, not *belong* to it. The mind is not a substance, in which the perceptions inhere. That notion is as unintelligible as the *Cartesian,* that thought or perception in general is the essence of the mind. We have no idea of substance of any kind, since we have no idea but what is derived from some impression, and we have no impression of any substance either material or spiritual. We know nothing but particular qualities and perceptions. As our idea of any body, a peach, for instance, is only that of a particular taste, color, figure, size, consistence, &c. So our idea of any mind is only that of particular perceptions, without the notion of anything we call substance, either simple or compound....

Freedom of the Will [12]

It may perhaps be more acceptable to the reader to be informed of what our author says concerning *free-will*. He has laid the foundation of his doctrine in what he said concerning cause and effect, as above explained. " 'Tis universally acknowledged, that the operations of external bodies are necessary, and that in the communication of their motion, in their attraction and mutual cohesion, there are not the least traces of indifference or liberty."—"Whatever therefore is in this respect on the same footing with matter, must be acknowledged to be necessary. That we may know whether this be the case with the actions of the mind, we may examine matter, and consider on what the idea of a necessity in its operations are founded, and why we conclude one body or action to be the infallible cause of another.

"It has been observed already, that in no single instance the ultimate connexion of any object is discoverable either by our senses or reason, and that we can never penetrate so far into the essence and construction of bodies, as to perceive the principle on which their mutual influence is founded. 'Tis their constant union alone, with which we are acquainted; and 'tis from the constant union the necessity arises, when the mind is determined to pass from one object to its usual attendant, and infer the existence of one from that of the other. Here then are two particulars, which we are to regard as essential to *necessity, viz.* the constant *union* and the *inference* of the mind, and wherever we discover these we must acknowledge a necessity." Now nothing is more evident than the constant union of particular actions with particular motives. If all actions be not constantly united with their proper motives, this uncertainty is no more than what may be observed every day in the actions of matter, where by reason of the mixture and uncertainty of causes, the effect is often variable and uncertain. Thirty grains of opium will kill any man that is not accustomed to it; tho' thirty grains of rhubarb will not always purge him. In like manner the

[12] *Ibid.,* pp. 28-32.

fear of death will always make a man go twenty paces out of his road; tho' it will not always make him do a bad action.

And as there is often a constant conjunction of the actions of the will with their motives, so the inference from the one to the other is often as certain as any reasoning concerning bodies: and there is always an inference proportioned to the constancy of the conjunction. On this is founded our belief in witnesses, our credit in history, and indeed all kinds of moral evidence, and almost the whole conduct of life.

Our author pretends, that this reasoning puts the whole controversy in a new light, by giving a new definition of necessity. And, indeed, the most zealous advocates for free-will must allow this union and inference with regard to human actions. They will only deny, that this makes the whole of necessity. But then they must shew, that we have an idea of something else in the actions of matter; which, according to the foregoing reasoning, is impossible.

The Association of Ideas

Thro' this whole book, there are great pretensions to new discoveries in philosophy; but if anything can intitle the author to so glorious a name as that of an *inventor,* 'tis the use he makes of the principle of the association of ideas, which enters into most of his philosophy. Our imagination has a great authority over our ideas; and there are no ideas that are different from each other, which it cannot separate, and join, and compose into all the varieties of fiction. But notwithstanding the empire of the imagination, there is a secret tie or union among particular ideas, which causes the mind to conjoin them more frequently together, and makes the one, upon its appearance, introduce the other. Hence arises what we call the *apropos* of discourse: hence the connection of writing: and hence that thread, or chain of thought, which a man naturally supports even in the loosest *reverie.* These principles of association are reduced to three, *viz. Resemblance;* a picture naturally makes us think of the man it was drawn for. *Contiguity;* when *St. Dennis* is mentioned, the idea of *Paris* naturally occurs. *Causation;* when we think of the son, we are apt to carry our attention to the father. 'Twill be easy to conceive of what vast consequence these principles must be in the science of human nature, if we consider, that so far as regards the mind, these are the only links that bind the parts of the universe together, or connect us with any person or object exterior to ourselves. For as it is by means of thought only that anything operates upon our passions, and as these are the only ties of our thoughts, they are really *to us* the cement of the universe, and all the operations of the mind must, in a great measure, depend on them.

SUMMARY AND CONCLUSION

Hume brought Empiricism to a logical resting place, but he was so far ahead of his contemporaries that he encountered no very cordial reception, at least in Britain. Indeed, as he himself admitted, his Atomic Empiricism is not a philosophy that anyone is likely to believe except when he is plunged deeply in meditation and is momentarily unconscious of practical concerns. All that Hume leaves of the world scheme of Descartes and Locke is a flux of distinct impressions and ideas that combine and recombine in pattern after pattern. The self is a stream of such entities, where the units are attracted one to another according to the principles of association. The "external world" is a system of clustered impressions following upon one another so as to produce the feeling of causal necessity. Substances or enduring and unified objects, whether mental or physical, have no reality, *insofar as we can tell,* beyond that granted by the grouping together of impressions and ideas. Things are groups of impressions, minds are groups of impressions and ideas; that is all we can say. No layman is likely to accept such a philosophy with enthusiasm, but the question remains: What is wrong with it?

From the point of view of recent Logical Positivism, there is *nothing* wrong with Hume's philosophy. For this school of thought, it is impossible to formulate an important criticism of Hume without employing unverifiable or meaningless statements. This is because all statements having to do with the "real" self or the "real" external world go beyond the possibility of verification in terms of perception or sensuous data.

-»» CHAPTER XI «««-

The Critical Philosophy of Immanuel Kant

KANT'S "COPERNICAN REVOLUTION"

In the development of eighteenth-century ideas, Rationalism and Empiricism are succeeded by a new mode of thought, known to history as *Philosophical Criticism*. This philosophy is initiated and inspired by the great German thinker Immanuel Kant.[1] Kantian criticism undertakes to sketch the limits of trustworthy human knowledge; and in this sense it may be said to continue in a rigorous and very systematic way an enterprise upon which John Locke had already rather cautiously embarked. But the Kantian criticism goes far beyond that of Locke in that it requires not only reason but experience itself to present credentials and to justify its claims as a reliable instrument in our apprehension of the human environment. Kant's masterpiece, the *Critique of Pure Reason,* which is,

---

[1] Immanuel Kant (1724-1804) is said to have been of Scottish ancestry. He lived his entire life in East Prussia, where he was born in very humble circumstances at Königsberg. He taught at the University of Königsberg from 1775 to 1797. His was a life outwardly most uneventful, the life of a bachelor, a tutor and professor, who never traveled and never entered public affairs. He is, however, said to have implanted liberal ideas in the minds of his students, several of whom were in later life active in the abolition of serfdom. Kant was a very wide reader, a good conversationalist, and a splendid lecturer on a variety of subjects, including such unphilosophical topics as the architecture of fortifications. Indeed the great difficulty of Kant's major philosophical writings arises from the novelty and the profundity of his subject matter. When he writes on less abstruse topics, his style can be very clear and compact. He was well acquainted with the natural science of his day, and he was a serious student of astronomy, in which field he actually anticipated Laplace's nebular hypothesis. Despite the profoundly religious training received from his Pietist parents, he withdrew from all formal religious affiliations in later life. Although he was a subject of Frederick the Great, Kant was a pacifist, and discussed at length the cause and cure of international warfare in his essay on *Eternal Peace.*

indeed, the central monument of modern philosophy, constitutes just as much a critical evaluation of experience as of reason and philosophical speculation. Thus Kant cuts beneath the investigations of both Rationalism and Empiricism.

The *Critique of Pure Reason* may be characterized as constituting an astute and remarkably thoroughgoing analysis of the human situation, considered from the cognitive or "theoretical" point of view. It is thus primarily a criticism of science and of metaphysics. In his later works, Kant re-examines this human situation from other points of view, from that of ethics and of value theory in general, including reference to aesthetic value in nature and the arts and to the idea of teleology.

Kant reminds us that our knowledge of the world arises within the human situation and is subject to human limitations; accordingly we must recognize that human knowledge is very different from the synoptic vision that we may suppose would belong to a god or an archangel. Man does not apprehend the world with its detail extending before his attention in the systematic complexity of a map. On the contrary, he begins with the most fragmentary and the most fleeting glimpses of the world, which his limited sensibility helps him to grasp. From these shreds of incomplete vision, he may very gradually construct a tentative picture of the world as a whole, but the world in its fullness of detail is never present to human attention. We never *experience* the *universe* as such. In our apprehension of things, diversity far outruns unity, and the ultimate fact of unity, if it be a fact, appears to us as no more than an assumption, albeit one to which we are committed in a most uncompromising way, by the very shape of our thinking.

We are presented, through the several avenues of our sensibility, with a confused manifold of data. It is from this almost chaotic multiplicity that our awareness must rise toward comprehension of a world order. These data, at first jumbled together and mutually irrelevant, may, if apprehended together in relevant groups and series, reveal aspects or perspectives of nature. Nature is, after all, the system of phenomenal objects open to our apprehension—as Kant says, it is an order of "possible experience."

In order to apprehend nature and to penetrate beyond the surface of the fluent multiplicity that is given us, we must somehow recognize that the many data belong together as representative elements characterizing the structure of a world. The presence of a world, the ultimate and inclusive unity of phenomena, is not directly open to the sensibility. We enjoy no sensuous datum that indicates the presence of a cosmic unity or systematic world order. The very possibility of such an order is brought home to us not through the flux of data, but through the interpretative activity of the understanding. Such interpretation proceeds from the very cast of our thinking. It is brought by our understanding to the manifold of sensibility. Through its own acts of interpretative judgment, the understanding grasps ways of relating sensuous data to one another. In so doing, it reaches beyond them to the comprehension of objective situations. These objective situations, or more simply objects, cannot be entertained exclusively by the sensibility. It is with reference to these objects, whose apprehension is made possible through the interpretative concepts of the understanding, that we order or unite the manifold of sensibility and become aware of nature.

The most prominent concepts of modern philosophy, such as substance and causality, are justified precisely insofar as they can be shown to be indispensable to the activity whereby we apprehend enduring objective situations, as distinct from the fleeting data of our sensibility. They justify themselves insofar as they are indispensable to our mental life; and Kant is eager to show that our mental life would be quite impossible without them. Only as these concepts make possible our apprehension of objective situations do we possess a unity of consciousness. Our very existence as conscious beings is involved with them. We cannot be conscious of a mere flux of data the multiplicity of which overwhelms us. We are conscious only of objective situations the framework of which offers us an enduring unity of some sort. For Kant, consciousness is no mere state of feeling, but an interpreted awareness of things and events.

The guiding concepts of interpretation whereby we unite the manifold of sensibility, apprehend objects, and maintain our consciousness may be said to characterize our mentality rather more than they characterize ultimate reality itself. To be sure, a supra-human intelligence, like that of a god, which does not have to fight its way toward unity from an initial diversity, might well find the ultimate reality of things characterized by a pervasive structure that we are unable to apprehend. But we are incapable of such vision. Thus the Kantian philosophy contains a strong element of skepticism. The critical philosophy remains skeptical even of those principles which can be shown to be indispensable in our experience and interpretation of the world—and this for the excellent reason that our interpretation of the world is an incomplete one and based upon an incomplete contact with reality. Our very concept of the "world" or "nature" is itself a principle of interpretation peculiar to our finite mental activity.

Kant introduces this new and difficult thought to his readers by comparing his theory of knowledge and experience to the work of Copernicus in astronomy. Copernicus, we may recall, reoriented students of astronomy by rejecting the ancient assumption that the stars revolve around the terrestrial spectator and by accepting the contrary position that the spectator is in motion and the stars at rest. Accordingly, Kant undertakes to change the orientation of the theory of knowledge. He makes the intelligibility of the world that is open to our awareness depend not wholly upon the nature of the world but, in large measure, upon the activity of our own understanding.

In carrying out his program, Kant completely reconsidered the nature of human knowledge and its relation to the world. One of his primary concerns while so doing lay in his desire to re-establish the prestige of philosophy, which by the mid-eighteenth century had reached a low ebb. This decline was largely owing to the fact that the deadlock between Rationalism and Empiricism seemed a final one, and the cultivated public had grown at last inclined to view the conflict with indifference. This historical situation was similar, in broad outline, to that which had preceded the Socratic philosophy centuries before. At both periods, philosophical thought had exhausted the more obvious possibilities, and advance was impossible without a new orientation and a new method.

KANT'S RELATION TO RATIONALISM AND EMPIRICISM

The philosophy of Kant is accordingly a meeting of extremes, a historical crossroads of European thought. Here Rationalism and Empiricism meet and are transformed; and here lie the beginnings of many modern schools of thought, of Idealism and Pragmatism among others. The Kantian philosophy is neither Empiricist nor Rationalist, but it derives important truths from both of these traditions. Empiricism, for Kant, is valuable only as a counterargument to offset the excesses of Rationalism, and Rationalism is significant as a check upon Empiricism. Kant digs beneath them both to find principles more fundamental than any perceived by these earlier schools.

It is not true, as Empiricism teaches, that every genuine element in knowledge is derived from the senses. But again it is not true, as Rationalism insists, that certain fundamental aspects of the universe as a whole are given to us directly by suprasensuous insight. Concerning the world as a whole, thinks Kant, its structure, its origin, its destiny, and its relation to God, we know nothing with logical certainty. Thus the goal of speculative philosophy is unattainable.

Our suprasensuous insights are important only insofar as they serve to interpret and enlighten the welter of sensuous data that we are always receiving. Accordingly, Descartes's innate ideas are not genuine revelations of ultimate reality, but some of them are nonetheless valuable forms for interpreting the raw material of experience. As such, they help us to organize and systematize our sensuous perception and to render it intelligible. They may not, indeed, help us to gain a vision of the ultimately real. But these guiding concepts do help us to arrange and relate our impressions and to bring a measure of order out of what would otherwise be chaos. This order may not—Kant is very sure that it does not—correspond very closely to ultimate reality. But it is a coherent order and one that holds firm throughout the whole extent and duration of our experience. In this respect, it is dependable.

Impressions must always be supplemented by suprasensuous acts of interpretation if we are to enjoy an intelligible experience of things and events. Thus such pervasive relationships as spatial distance and contiguity and causal connection are not given us directly through sensuous impressions. The statement, familiar to our common sense, and by Descartes considered an innate idea, "Every event must have a cause," is, among others, the result of a suprasensuous act of interpretation, which, Kant tries to prove, is based neither upon empirical observation nor upon direct vision of ultimate reality. But Kant insists that it remains an indispensable guide of our experience and comprehension of the world about us. Remove it, and what would be left of our common sense and of our awareness of the environment in which we live? As we shall see presently in detail, Kant undertakes to show that there would be virtually nothing left of our awareness of things or enduring objects spread out in space and changing in time, nor would our knowledge of ourselves as centers of consciousness aware of sequences of Humean impressians be possible.

For Kant, an idea like that of causation applies *within* our experience of things and is absolutely indispensable to such experience. It is therefore clearly *not* the product or outcome of our experience, for experience cannot exist without it. We may even argue that in a sound theory of knowledge, experience itself may be "derived" from our apprehension of causality and not vice versa. Hence Empiricism is false. But on the other hand, the fact that we can show causation to be indispensable to our awareness of things in space and time, so that without it our whole way of looking at things would be quite impossible, does not establish as an unquestionable truth the Rationalistic doctrine that causation as we know it is an ultimate character of reality. It is valid only *within* our experience, which depends upon it. This theory of knowledge depends upon recognition of the delicate relationship between sensibility and understanding.[2]

2 Kant, "Transcendental Logic," in *Critique of Pure Reason,* in G. T. Whitney and P. H. Fogel, *An Introduction to Kant's Critical Philosophy.* Macmillan & Co., London; The Macmillan Company, New York; 1914. Reprinted by permission of the publishers. Italics added.

Our knowledge arises from two fundamental sources of the mind, the first of which is the reception of representations (the receptivity of impressions), the second the power of knowing an object through these representations (spontaneity of concepts); through the first an object is given to us, through the second, this object is thought in relation to that representation (as mere determination of mind). Intuition and concepts, therefore, constitute the elements of all our knowledge, so that neither concepts which are without any corresponding intuition, nor intuition without concepts can result in knowledge ...

We would call the receptivity of our mind, that is, its power of receiving representations, whenever it is in any wise affected, sensibility, while the understanding, on the contrary, is the power of producing representations, or the spontaneity of knowledge. Our nature is so constituted, that intuition can never be other than sensuous, that is, it contains only the way in which we are affected by objects. On the contrary, the understanding is the power of thinking the object of sensuous intuition. *Neither of these powers is to be preferred over the other.* Without sensibility no object would be given to us, and without understanding no object could be thought by us. *Thoughts without content are empty, and intuitions without concepts are blind.* Consequently it is just as necessary to make one's concepts sensuous (that is, to add to them the object in intuition) as to make one's intuitions intelligible (that is, to bring them under concepts). Neither of these powers or capacities can exchange its proper functions. The understanding cannot intuit anything, and the senses cannot think anything. Only through their union can knowledge arise.

Kant called his philosophical method *critical* in that he offers a criticism or an examination of all experience and of all thinking, with special emphasis upon all the latent and tacit assumptions that our way of looking at things involves. We must be allowed to take nothing for granted, without noticing that we do so. We must be completely aware of every act of judgment and of every assumption upon which our way of looking at things depends. Nothing can be taken as self-evident or as beyond question. This distinguishes Kant from his Rationalist predecessors.

Kant's method may also be called *transcendental;* and this distinguishes him from the Empiricist. A transcendental investigation is one in which we attempt to justify our employment of notions, like that of substance and causation, that cannot, as Hume has shown, be founded wholly upon sensuous experience. In general, Kant attempts to show that these notions are indispensable to the very existence of *our* experience, as actual centers of consciousness aware of a world of objects established in space and in time.

KANT'S THOUGHT AS AN ANSWER TO HUME

Kant's philosophy is a complex one, and may profitably be approached from many angles. For the beginner, perhaps the most illuminating approach is that which interprets Kant's thought as an answer to Hume's Atomic Empiricism. Kant attempts to supply what this Empiricism has overlooked, and by so doing he corrects Hume's conclusions, which are unsatisfactory in that they leave quite unjustified many common-sense beliefs and reduce to the status of an unsupported and illogical assertion a primary assumption of natural science. For Hume, all our knowledge of the world about us is empirical or derived from generalizations upon the sequence and coexistence of impressions. For Hume, there is no knowledge of the world about us given a priori; that is, independent of our experiences based upon impressions. This Kant denies; he finds that much of our knowledge of this world is a priori. For instance, he argues that our belief in causation—that is, our acceptance of the proposition that every event has both causes and effects—is a priori. The relation of knowledge to experience is well outlined in the following passage from the *Critique of Pure Reason*.[3]

Of the Difference between Pure and Empirical Knowledge

That all our knowledge begins with experience there can be no doubt. For how should the faculty of knowledge be called into activity, if not by objects which affect our senses, and which either produce representations by themselves, or rouse the activity of our understanding to compare, to connect, or to separate them; and

---

[3] Kant, *Critique of Pure Reason,* trans. by Max Müller, pp. 715-16. Macmillan & Co., London; The Macmillan Company, New York; 2nd ed., 1896. This and the following quotation are reprinted by permission of the publishers.

thus to convert [i.e., work up] the raw material of our sensuous impressions into a knowledge of objects, which we call experience? In respect of time, therefore, no knowledge within us is antecedent to experience, but all knowledge begins with it.

But although all our knowledge begins with experience, it does not follow that it arises from experience. For it is quite possible that even our empirical experience [experience or empirical awareness of things] is a compound of that which we receive through impressions, and of that which our own faculty of knowledge (incited only by sensuous impressions), supplies from itself, a supplement which we do not distinguish from that raw material, until long practice has roused our attention and rendered us capable of separating one from the other.

It is therefore a question which deserves at least closer investigation, and cannot be disposed of at first sight, whether there exists a knowledge independent of experience, and even of all impressions of the senses? Such *knowledge* is called *a priori*, and distinguished from *empirical* knowledge, which has its sources *a posteriori*, that is, in experience.

This term *a priori*, however, is not yet definite enough to indicate the full meaning of our question. For people are wont to say, even with regard to knowledge derived from experience, that we have it, or might have it, *a priori*, because we derive it from experience, not *immediately*, but from a general rule, which, however, has itself been derived from experience. Thus one would say of a person who undermines the foundations of his house, that he might have known *a priori* that it would tumble down, that is, that he need not wait for the experience of its really tumbling down. But still he could not know this entirely *a priori*, because he had first to learn from experience that bodies are heavy, and will fall when their supports are taken away.

Kant proceeds to select criteria whereby we may clearly distinguish between a priori and a posteriori knowledge. Since experience can never show that a statement is *necessarily* true or that something *had* to happen, but only that the statement is true or that the event has happened, Kant considers all necessary knowledge to be a priori. Again he recognizes that all universal statements which refer without exception to members of a class of which all the members have not been observed, contain an a priori element that overreaches experience. This means, of course, that all scientific conclusions, all our knowledge of natural law, are a priori and exceed actual observation.[4]

We Are in Possession of Certain Cognitions a priori, and Even the Ordinary Understanding Is Never without Them.

All depends here on a criterion, by which we may safely distinguish between pure and emipirical knowledge. Now experience teaches us, no doubt, that something is so or so, but not that it cannot be different. *First,* then, if we have a proposition, which is thought, together with its necessity, we have a judgment *a priori;* and if, besides, it is not derived from any proposition, except such as is itself again considered as necessary, we have an absolutely *a priori* judgment. *Secondly,* experience never imparts to its judgments true or strict, but only assumed or relative universality (by means of induction), so that we ought always to say, so far as we have observed hitherto, there is no exception to this or that rule. If, therefore, a judgment is thought with strict universality, so that no exception is admitted as possible, it is not derived from experience, but valid absolutely *a priori.* Empirical universality, therefore, is only an arbitrary extension of a validity which applies to most cases, to one that applies to all: as, for instance, in the proposition, all bodies are heavy. If, on the contrary, strict universality is essential to a judgment, this always points to a special source of knowledge, namely a faculty of knowledge *a priori.* Necessity, therefore, and strict universality are safe criteria of knowledge *a priori,* and are inseparable one from the other. As, however, in the use of these criteria, it is sometimes easier to show the contingency than the empirical limitation of judgments, and as it is sometimes more convincing to prove the unlimited universality which we attribute to a judgment than its necessity, it is advisable to use both criteria separately, each being by itself infallible.

That there really exist in our knowledge such necessary, and in the strictest sense universal, and therefore...*a priori* [judgments] is easy to show. If we want a scientific example, we have only to look to any of the propositions of mathematics; if we want one from the sphere of the ordinary understanding, such a proposition as that each change must have a cause, will answer the purpose; nay, in the latter case, even the concept of cause contains so clearly the concept of the necessity of its connection with an effect, and of the strict universality of the rule, that it would be destroyed altogether if we

---

[4] *Ibid.,* pp. 716-18.

attempted to derive it, as Hume does, from the frequent concomi-
tancy of that which happens with that which precedes, and from a
habit arising thence (therefore from a purely subjective necessity),
of connecting representations. It is possible even, without having
recourse to such examples in proof of the reality of pure propositions
a priori within our knowledge, to prove their indispensability for
the possibility of experience itself, thus proving it *a priori*. For
whence should experience take its certainty, if all the rules which it
follows were always again and again empirical, and therefore contingent and hardly fit to serve as first principles? For the present,
however, we may be satisfied for having shown the pure employment of the faculty of our knowledge as a matter of fact, with the
criteria of it.

Not only in judgments, however, but even in certain concepts, can
we show their origin *a priori*. Take away, for example, from the
concept of a body, as supplied by experience, everything that is empirical, one by one; such as colour, hardness, or softness, weight, and
even impenetrability, and there still remains the space which the
body (now entirely vanished) occupied: that you cannot take away.
And in the same manner, if you remove from your empirical concept of any object, corporeal or incorporeal, all properties which experience has taught you, you cannot take away from it that property
by which you conceive it as a substance, or inherent in a substance
(although such a concept contains more determinations than that of
an object in general). Convinced, therefore, by the necessity with
which that concept forces itself upon you, you will have to admit
that it has its seat in your faculty of knowledge *a priori*.

Kant introduces another distinction equally as central to his
thought as that between a priori and a posteriori knowledge. This is
the distinction between analytic and synthetic judgment or assertion.
An analytic judgment is one based strictly upon a definition, so that
the predicate adds nothing to the subject not already included in it
by accepted definition. Thus "All bodies are extended" is an analytic
judgment for those who accept Descartes's definition of the corporeal world. But "All bodies gravitate according to Newton's law
of the inverse square of the distance" is a synthetic judgment, since
the predicate is not included in the subject by definition or tacit
understanding. "Every event has causes" is a synthetic judgment,
since "cause" is not included by definition in "event." It is also a

priori; it cannot be satisfactorily derived from experience, as, in fact, Hume himself has shown.[5]

Thus the chief propositions that Hume has insisted cannot be derived from our experience of impressions (propositions such as "Every event has causes") turn out to be in Kantian terminology synthetic judgments a priori. Hume would deny the validity of such judgments. Thus he reduces our acceptance of causality to a mere feeling of expectation. But Kant undertakes to establish their validity, and indeed considers this problem the very center of his philosophy. How are synthetic judgments a priori possible? is the great question with which Kant introduces his theory of knowledge.[6]

In *a priori* synthetic judgments, I can get no aid whatever from experience. But, if it is here vain to look to experience for aid, on what other support am I to rely, when I seek to go beyond a certain conception A, and to connect B synthetically with it? Take the proposition, that every event must have its cause. No doubt I cannot have the conception of an event i.e., of something that happens without thinking of something as having a moment of time before it, and from this certain analytic judgments may be derived. But the conception of a cause lies entirely outside the conception of an event, and introduces an idea not contained in it. By what right, then, do I pass from the conception of an event to the totally different conception of a cause? How do I know that there is a necessary connection between the two conceptions, when I can perfectly well think the one without the other? What is here the unknown *x,* which gives support to the understanding, when it seems to have discovered an entirely new predicate B to belong necessarily to the subject A? Experience it cannot be, because the principle has a degree of universality that experience can never supply, as it is supposed to connect the new conception with the old in the way of necessity, and must do so entirely *a priori,* and on the basis of mere conceptions. And yet our speculative *a priori* knowledge must rest upon such synthetic or ampliative propositions.

[5] "Yesterday at ten o'clock my car was in the garage" is synthetic, since by definition my car does not have to be so located, and it is a posteriori, since my statement is based directly upon my observation. "*All* men must die" is a priori, since I have not observed *all* human beings and found them to be mortal, and it is synthetic, since the notion of death does not follow from our concept of "man" by rigorous deduction.

[6] Kant, *Critique of Pure Reason,* in *The Philosophy of Kant, as Contained in Extracts from His Own Writings,* selected and trans. by John Watson, pp. 14-15. James Maclehose & Sons, Glasgow, new ed., 1894.

Hume denies the validity of synthetic judgments a priori because he has ignored an element of first importance. He recognizes "experience" interpreted as sequences of empirical data, or impressions, as a trustworthy foundation of knowledge. This is because impressions are unquestionably actual. But he recognizes nothing else as possessing equal authority. Thus space and time, substance, causation, the external world, and the self, as we ordinarily understand them, cannot be accorded an empirical status comparable to that enjoyed by impressions. In fact, the underlying reality of these entities turns out to be no more than a grouping together of impressions under the guidance of custom and habit. Accordingly, impressions are indispensable to our concept of substance, causality, and so forth, but the latter are not considered indispensable to our apprehension of empirical data. Thus the reality of empirical data cannot be challenged without our further challenging the reality of substance, causality, and so on. But we may, according to Hume, challenge substance, causality, and so on without challenging the reality of the atomic impressions. The latter are, after all, on Hume's view, absolutely beyond reproach, constituting the *one* set of elements that the human mind can recognize without question as offering a reliable starting point for inquiry.

This position Kant undertakes to modify. Our apprehension of a flux, or sequence, of events, is, as we shall see in detail later, impossible without our reliance upon guiding principles of perception or thought, such as space and time, substance and causality, and the unity of the self. Therefore Kant is in a position to maintain that the above-mentioned suprasensuous aspects of our world are just as indispensable as are the empirical data. Impressions are accordingly not the only building blocks out of which our knowledge of things is constructed. Substance, causality, and so on are genuine and pervasive patterns in what Kant calls the "phenomenal world" or the system of possible human experience. This phenomenal world is *objective,* although not ultimately real. Thus it is not an illusion. It is not a product of irresponsible or faulty thinking. It is a genuine human perspective of reality. That it is the only perspective, Kant never maintained. Furthermore, he insists that ultimate reality, the "thing-in-itself" considered as stretching far beyond human experience, cannot be described, even in outline, by terms and methods applicable to the phenomenal world.

THE STRUCTURE OF THE PHENOMENAL WORLD:
SPACE, TIME, AND THE CATEGORIES

It is now our purpose to present the detail of Kant's theory of the phenomenal world and to show how he establishes his views concerning its nature. Hitherto we have mentioned his theories concerning this realm without offering his arguments in support of them. This phenomenal world, or the order of possible human experience, is composed of objects that stand to one another in spatial relation and that undergo change. Distance and direction are important and omnipresent relations in this scheme of things. Furthermore, events or moments of change are related to one another temporally. Any event may be said to be before or after or simultaneous with some other event. Kant argues that we must recognize space and time as the outstanding and pervasive characters of the phenomenal world; these characters are presented to us as a priori intuitions. Kant believes that these intuitions are valid only of this phenomenal world, and that reality, considered as apart from our experience, is neither spatial nor temporal. He is convinced that space and time are merely forms of our intuition or sensibility; that is, they do not belong to a world existing independently of the human mind. They are accordingly limited to the phenomenal world of possible human experience. Kant's reasons for this belief, which seems to be at odds with common sense, are as follows:

Space and time are not concepts derived from experience. Thus we do not form our idea of space by generalizing upon our experience of *right-left, above-below, east-west, north-south, nearer than, farther than,* and so on; nor do we form our idea of time by generalizing upon our experience of *before and after, earlier than, later than,* and so on. These propositions can be proved in several ways. In the first place, we do not recognize one object as being at the left of another, or one event as being before another, until we have been aware of them as spatially or temporally related. Therefore we cannot derive space and time from these relations, for we need our awareness of space and time in order to grasp the relations themselves. Again, we are aware of *one* great space in which all objects bound to one another by such relations as *above, below, right left,* are situated. This space contains all *places* or spatial situations of which we can be aware. Also we are aware of one great time that contains all periods of world history. This distinguishes our knowledge of space and time from ordinary concepts derived from experience, for ordinary concepts, say, "house" or "mountain," do not *contain* all their particular examples or instances as parts of themselves.

Furthermore, we are aware of space and time as infinite or boundless; that is, we feel that no distance is so great that a greater does not extend beyond it, that no chronological period is so long that a longer one does not include it. But we certainly do not learn this by generalizing upon our experience of distances actually traveled or periods of time actually measured. Besides, we think of space and time as indefinitely divisible. Thus no distance and no lapse of time can be considered as the shortest one possible; and this of course is not the result of observation. Therefore the ideas of space and time cannot be considered as the outcome of empirical thinking. They are prior to such thinking.

Again, space and time appear to us as prior to experience and to the generalizations based upon experience. We know this because we find that we cannot think about things at all without being aware of space and time. We cannot think of space and time as nonexistent; we cannot imagine our world without them. But we can "think away" any typical object of sensuous experience without difficulty. In doing so, we consider the wholes of space and time as free from the entities in question. But of course we cannot do this with reference to space and time themselves. It is, however, questionable whether, as Kant insists, we can entertain the ideas of *empty* space and *empty* time—that is, time and space containing no things or events. Nonetheless, the structure of space and time is present to us in such a way that we can formulate synthetic, a priori judgments concerning mathematical and chronological relations. These judgments are supported by our direct contemplation of space and time themselves. Empirical verification, based upon inspection of many and diverse instances, is not required. If space and time were not given to us as wholes in intuition, prior to experience, this would, Kant believes, be impossible.

Kant summarizes this position by declaring that space and time are "empirically real" as inseparable and indispensable aspects of the phenomenal world; but that they are "transcendentally ideal," since their presence in the phenomenal world is owing to their intimate connection with human sensibility. Aside from such sensibility, space and time, as we know them, would be nothing at all.

The structure of the phenomenal world contains much more than space and time. These latter, after all, constitute only its skeleton or, let us say, its warp and woof or most general outline. Such an outline is grasped by what Kant calls pure intuition. Such intuition is not limited to any one of the special senses. Thus we do not see, hear, or feel space and time, although we say with conviction that we see, hear, and feel objects in space and time. Space and time supply the broadest possible background for such experience. The more detailed structure of the phenomenal world is apprehended through the assistance of the understanding. The understanding is less closely related to sensibility than are the pure intuitions.

Nonetheless, it is indispensable to coherent perception of things and of events. Substance and causation constitute the outstanding features of the content so apprehended, and they are accordingly described as *categories* of the understanding. By means of these we grasp, not the general outline of the phenomenal world, but the presence of things and events and the way in which these are related to one another within that outline. Without the categories, the elements of the phenomenal world would not "belong together" and we should not be aware of series of events, or of enduring things, although we might perhaps be aware of space and time themselves as the pure forms of intuition.

In other words, by means of the categories we apprehend the *objective* content of space and time. An object may be defined as "that under the concept of which we unite the manifold of sensibility." The categories are the most general concepts in terms of which we recognize the meaning of objectivity. They are clearly a priori, for without them no recognition of objects, and hence no experience, would be possible.

In working out this theory of the categories, Kant throws light upon several topics at once. Not only does he further our knowledge of the constitution of our self-consciousness, which after Hume's analysis of the self had remained a subject of considerable dispute; but he also advances a theory of the causal connection of events, which topic Hume had also brought into prominence. The linking together of these two topics is one of the most characteristic features of Kant's philosophy, and constitutes its most original contribution. The organization of the human mind and the organization of the phenomenal objects open to that mind cannot be discussed separately. The unity of the self and the order of the phenomenal world are, at least for the inquiring philosopher, closely interrelated. This discovery is one of the manifestations of what Kant describes as his "Copernican revolution," or new orientation, in philosophy.

Kant believes that unless we are aware of a phenomenal world in which substances and events are interrelated in orderly sequence, we cannot be aware of the knowing self as in any sense a unity. Again, unless we can be aware of the self as such a unity of experience, we cannot be aware of an objective order of phenomena. In other words, unless we are in a position to recognize clearly the continuity of our present experience with our past experience, we can speak neither of the personal identity of our minds nor of the historical identity of things in the world. These two identities are, insofar as our knowledge is concerned, inseparably united. I cannot be aware of my personal identity unless I recognize that I have been witnessing events or continued "stories" as opposed to a jumble of data.

The ego is always the center of an awareness of *something,* and a jumble of unrelated data does not constitute a *something.* I must, at the very least, be aware of my own body as the same body that I "possessed" some moments ago. Nor, on the other hand, can I be aware of a continuity of events unless I am able to recognize an event as something closely related to and, so to speak, continuing another event which I know that I have previously apprehended. In order to know this, I must be in a position to recognize that *I* have had previous experience; that is, that my awareness is an egocentric continuity. Accordingly, while conscious, I must always be capable of making the statements "I am the I that I was" and "These present events are continuations of those things, now passed, which I once experienced or might presumably have experienced." The conditions of such recognition are the indispensable conditions of our apprehension of phenomena as distinguished from mere data.

Kant describes at some length the way in which data are interpreted, and their relations apprehended, so that we see through them to the structure of the phenomenal world that they manifest. Thus, in order to perceive a sequence of events or an object that endures against a background of change, I must recognize many data, which come to me in a more or less confused manner beset with much irrelevant material, as belonging to one another or as comprising, despite their apparent separation, the manifestation of one concrete object or story. Accordingly data must be apprehended and then retained in consciousness, so that they may be seen as relevant to other data following after them. *Apprehension* and *retention* of data and *recognition* of their mutual relevance are indispensable to significant perception.

The categories are, to put it simply, the modes of relevance whereby one datum can be apprehended as pertinent to another, which it may in no way resemble and which may have preceded it by some time. This data may be seen as united by the category of *substance* and *attribute,* as when we interpret a mass of data presented to us through several avenues of sensation, as manifesting the presence of a familiar object, the data appearing as qualities or attributes of the object. Data may also be seen as united by the category of cause and effect, as when, for instance, we relate a sound heard unexpectedly with the discovery of a fallen body that we had not previously noted. *The all-important point to grasp is that data themselves do not constitute the relations between other data.* We cannot relate one impression to another by adding several other impressions. We cannot perceive relations merely by employing our sensibilities. We must have recourse to understanding, and the categories are the types of interrelation of phenomena open to the human understanding. These concepts are involved in our recognition of objects. Accordingly, such notions as whole and part, substance and attribute, cause and effect, are indispensable to our understanding of the phenomenal world in its organization and with the interconnections of its parts. Also they are indispensable to our awareness of ourselves as unified and continuous egos, possessing personal identity.

There are four groups of categories whereby data may be seen as related in such a way as to indicate the presence of phenomenal objects. These are the categories of *quantity, quality, relation,* and *modality.* Notions expressed in the words "one," "some," and "all" indicate the concept of *quantity* that the understanding constantly employs in interpreting its environment. Certainly "all," the notion of totality, is not the direct product of sensuous data. It is not comparable, let us say, to a shade of blue or to a certain flavor. It is not a sensuous datum, but it is used constantly to interpret data—and so are the other categories.

Notions expressed in the words like "real," "unreal," and "to a certain degree" are classed under the head of *quality.* Here we find the understanding employing the notion of degree, so important in all qualitative distinctions. Thus when we compare broad daylight with utter darkness and then recognize many degrees of intervening twilight, we employ categories of reality (in this case daylight), unreality (in this case darkness as the absence of daylight), and, referring to intervening stages, the category of limitation or degree. Perhaps the terms *presence, absence,* and *degree of intervening quality* are more easily understood. At any rate, what Kant insists upon is this: When we compare sense data and arrange them in a scale between two limiting extremes, we are adding something to the brute data themselves—mainly, the very fact that they can be so arranged. The data we succeed in interpreting do not in their isolation carry this information with them, although they are consistent with it. Thus the notion of intense pain contains more than the sheer stab of pain; it contains the idea that pain is subject to a comparative scale.

The so-called categories of *relation* (strictly speaking, all the categories involve relation of some sort) are *substance and attribute, cause and effect,* and *reciprocity.* We are reasonably familiar with the meaning of the first two of these. The last leads us to recognize that in an objective situation open to our experience, things will be so arranged that they are at the same time cause and effect of one another, as for instance in the case of the celestial bodies that compose the solar system, and which mutually influence one another's paths of motion. Hume has shown most adequately that the relations of substance and attribute and cause and effect are not directly given us by sensuous data.

The last group of categories appear under the title of *modality,* and these may offer the student more difficulty than the others, since they represent concepts less likely to be recognized in casual reflection. These categories are listed as *possibility, existence, necessity,* with their opposites *impossibility, nonexistence,* and *contingency.* Just as causal connection is an idea that does not arise directly from sensuous experience, so also the notion of necessity cannot be thus derived. Nor can that of mere possibility, as distinct from necessity. Nor is the idea of existence, let us say of the center of the earth or the farther side of the moon, purely a product of sensuous observation. Like all categorial ideas, these notions are absolutely indispensable to our apprehension of the phenomenal world, for without such ideas to guide us we can make neither head nor tail of the welter of data with which our sensibilities are, so to speak, flooded.

The categories may be predicated of the phenomenal world be-cause the phenomenal world is the realm of our possible experience, and without the categories our egocentric temporal experience would be impossible. Since the categories are not impressions or even generalizations from our experience, Kant calls them nonempirical or a-priori elements. They are not apprehended by a passive mentality open to impressions, but by an *act* of interpretation or synthesis whereby data are made to reveal objects belonging together in comprehensible patterns. Without this act there would be no experience of phenomena, mental or physical. Thus the phenomenal world, including the stream of human consciousness, depends for its structure upon the synthesis (sometimes called the synthetic unity) that unites space and time, the categories, and Humean impressions.

This synthesis is not a personal mental act, in the sense that my decision to purchase a certain book is such an act. It is an act in which all human minds must participate as long as they are conscious, and it is an act upon which all experience depends. Nothing that fails to conform to the requirements of this synthesis can enter the realm of possible experience; that is, can be part of our phenomenal world, mental or physical. No datum that escapes interpretation according to a scheme of space, time, and the categories can contribute to the phenomenal order. Thus Kant would say to Hume: No event will ever appear in our phenomenal world without causal connections that will also be present at least as *possible* experiences, for causality is a category of the understanding, a sine qua non of possible experience. What escapes causal connection escapes all possible human experience and must lie outside of the phenomenal world, if, indeed, it exists at all. The same is true of the other categories.

The fact that the phenomenal world is thus subject to the categories makes possible our pursuit of the natural sciences. The categories supply the minimum of order in nature without which any attempt to discover the pattern of natural process would be futile. Imagine, for instance, the effect upon scientific inquiry of the belief that there are many typical and recognizable events in nature that have no causes, events which, so to speak, "just happen." Whenever faced by a difficult problem of explanation, the scientist would have to consider the possibility that the phenomena in question had no causal background and therefore lay beyond the pale of scientific investigation altogether. This embarrassing possibility no true scientist is ever willing to consider seriously. In refusing to do so, he is supported by the very conditions of human experience, as interpreted by Kant.

Kant has summarized his theory of the categories as follows: [7]

What has been shown in the deduction of the categories is that the pure conceptions of understanding, on which all *a priori* knowledge of nature is based, are principles that make experience possible. In other words, they are principles for the general *determination* of phenomena in space and time, a determination that ultimately flows from the principle of the *original* synthetic unity ...as the form of understanding in relation to space and time, the original forms of sensibility.

Concerning the category of causality itself Kant advances the following special considerations by which he shows that causality is one of the indispensable elements involved in our apprehension of any objective sequence of phenomena. It is quite obvious that any experience that takes time to complete itself must possess a continuity of conformation, some order in terms of which one temporal element is related to another. This continuity provides a more or less abiding pattern through which we can recognize one element as "belonging" to another or following upon it as a continuation of the order inherent in the situation. Such continuity can be supplied in one of two ways. Its temporal form may be subjective, or private, insofar as it is a result of our method of observation; that is, in this case, conditioned by the fact that we are studying an unchanging situation, as for instance, surveying in a succession the details of a mansion. Here the *sequence* of items observed may be varied in many ways at our will. Or the element of continuity may be objective, as when we follow with our eyes the movements of a ship that is in motion against a background. Here the *sequence* of details is irreversible and beyond our control.

Now it is clear that in these two situations we must emphasize different categories or primary forms of organization of data. We recognize that the gables, windows, and so on of the mansion are parts of its relatively permanent structure. Thus we find an objective order in the situation studied. In doing so, we emphasize the category of substance and that of quantity. But when we follow the motion of the ship, we must realize that the various positions noted are related to one another *objectively* as moments of the ship's motion. This, unlike the house, cannot be conceived as remaining stable throughout a time span. For in the case of the ship's motion, the order of succession in our apprehension does not depend upon our way of approach to the object, as it did in the case of the mansion. Rather, the successive character is objective and belongs to the motion itself. Our object *contains* change.

It is reasonable to express this fact of objective sequence by stating that every element in an objectively successive situation must follow upon another according to a rule. Here the rule, or group of rules, underlying the motion supplies the system of organization that in our former illustration was supplied by the presence of the house. In the case of the ship's motion, the system is guaranteed by the fact that the positions of the ship occur as they do owing to a causal principle. Causality, we are told, is the principle of such temporal organization, in terms of which we can distinguish between subjectively and objectively ordered succession.

Kant does not believe that mind creates or wholly constitutes the objects in the phenomenal world. But he recognizes that the phenomenal world and the human mind are mutually adapted to one another, the one being incomprehensible without the other. It is a case of mutual interdependence. Thus Hegel misrepresents Kant when in his *Lectures on the History of Philosophy* he writes as follows, while discussing the Kantian a priori: [8]

The fact that we crave for universality and necessity as that which first constitutes the objective, Kant thus undoubtedly allows. But if universality and necessity do not exist in external things, the question arises "Where are they to be found?" To this Kant, as against Hume, maintains that they must be *a priori,* i.e. that they must rest on reason itself, and on thought as self-conscious reason; their source is the subject, "I" in my self-consciousness. This, simply expressed, is the main point in the Kantian philosophy.

Kant is quite ready to assert, at least in his later and more mature position, that the phenomenal world is not mental. This makes

[8] Hegel, *Lectures on the History of Philosophy,* Vol. III, pp. 427-28. K. Paul, Trench, Trübner & Co., 3 vols., 1894-96.

quite impossible any rapprochement between the followers of Kant and those of Berkeley. Kant makes quite clear that a phenomenon is not a figment of the mind, not simply an idea, but an *object* of possible experience. Accordingly, one cannot identify *esse* and *percipi*. To do this is to consider the whole phenomenal world to be as evanescent as our sense impressions themselves. Impressions are fleeting, but they manifest something more permanent, which we recognize as the structure of the phenomenal world.

Even so, we must remember that phenomena are not ultimate realities. The fullness of being contains more than is manifest in the world of our possible experience. We enjoy a limited surface of reality, and if we attempt to account for reality *as a whole* by means of information gathered from our experience and study of the phenomenal world, we are bound to fail. The phenomenal world no more constitutes the full reality of the universe than the façade of a building constitutes or reveals the total architecture of the edifice.

The phenomenal world is the order of objectivity or possible experience. Experience comprises an interplay of sensibility and understanding. Sensibility supplies the manifold data of empirical or sensuous intuition, subject to the minimal patterns of interrelation supplied by the pure or nonsensuous intuitions of space and time. Understanding recognizes these spatial and temporal data as manifesting the presence of phenomena, or what constitute for us objective situations, interpreted by the categories. So constituted, the phenomenal world is the field of objectivity explored in detail by natural science. It is indeed what we ordinarily mean by "nature." It is the world of causal reciprocity, the structure of which may be explained by quantitative methods. It comes very close to being identical with Descartes's extended world, although Kant prefers the Newtonian mechanics to the Cartesian. It is a world of strict causal determinism, and Kant finds no place in it for teleology or freedom.

It is possible, however, to conceive another order of reality, open to intelligence but beyond the reach of our very limited mode of experience, bounded as it is by space, time, and the categories. Such a world may be thought to contain the ultimate realities of which we clearly experience, so to speak, only the surface. In such a universe freedom and teleology may be central principles. God, freedom, the immortal soul, may be thought of as the ideas about which such a world is organized. Much of our daily living assumes the validity of notions such as these. Moral life, the practice of religion, our sense of the purposiveness of the structure and the functions of living beings, all point in this direction.

But we cannot determine with certainty whether these notions are more than convenient assumptions or merely helpful fictions. Our experience is not broad enough or rich enough to supply exhaustive verification of them. Viewed in this light, the Kantian philosophy, despite minor imperfections, clearly reflects the predicament of our modern age, in which quantitative science has so far outrun the development of moral and spiritual insight. Natural science and technology have invaded the phenomenal world with brilliant success, while the great problems of religion and philosophy remain obscure. Here, as Tennyson once put it, "all [our] mind is clouded with a doubt," and we wait in forlorn hope for further insight.

BEYOND PHENOMENA

One of the first questions that a critic of Kant's philosophy is likely to phrase runs as follows: "How do we know that this so-called phenomenal world is not, after all, the ultimately real world? Are we not going too far and raising unnecessary difficulties when we insist that the familiar world in which we live and move is not wholly real?" To this question Kant has a definite answer. We know that the phenomenal world is not composed of ultimate realities because we have found that its structure depends upon the synthesis or act of interpretation that we all, as conscious beings, are constantly sharing during our waking hours. Of an ultimate reality, considered as distinct from and uninterpreted by this synthesis, we can form no certain idea.

If, however, we persist in believing that the phenomenal world is ultimately real, Kant insists that we examine what he calls the *antinomies,* or conflicts of reasoning, which arise when we undertake to complete our description of this phenomenal world. These conflicts have appeared frequently in the history of philosophy and they have remained unsolved. So long as we suppose that the phenomenal world is ultimately real, we can entertain no hope of removing them.

FIRST CONFLICT

Thesis	*Antithesis*
The world has a beginning in time, and is enclosed within limits of space.	The world has no beginning in time, and no limits in space, but is infinite as regards both time and space.

SECOND CONFLICT

Thesis	*Antithesis*
Every composite substance in the world is made up of simple parts, and nothing whatever exists but the simple, or that which is composed out of the simple.	No composite thing in the world is made up of simple parts, nor does anything simple exist anywhere in the world.

THIRD CONFLICT

Thesis	*Antithesis*
Causality in conformity with laws of nature is not the only causality, from which all the phenomena of the world can be derived. To explain those phenomena it is necessary to suppose that there is also a free causality.	There is no freedom, but all that comes to be in the world takes place entirely in accordance with laws of nature.

FOURTH CONFLICT

Thesis	*Antithesis*
There exists an absolutely necessary being, which belongs to the world either as a part or as the cause of it.	There nowhere exists an absolute necessary being, either in the world or outside of the world, as its cause.

The antinomies indicate that the phenomenal order does not constitute a consistent and harmonious system. When we attempt to consider the phenomenal world as a whole and to complete, even in broadest outline, the conditions to which the description of every phenomenal object commits us, we find ourselves in serious difficulties. These difficulties develop as follows:

If we believe that a conditioned phenomenon can arise only when all of its conditions have been established, then we cannot believe that these conditions are infinite in number. On the other hand, we encounter real difficulty in setting limits to the number of conditions, at any rate if we remain within the scope of the phenomenal order. The resulting conflicts have often been felt by philosophers and can be discovered by any thoughtful person. Kant formulates a report upon them; we need not say that he discovers them.

In each conflict, Kant seeks to establish both thesis and antithesis by considering each in turn to be false and in each case reducing this denial to an absurdity. Kant's arguments are involved, and are not always accepted today, at least in the form which he gave them. Nonetheless these arguments do indicate difficulties that still disturb scientists and philosophers. We cannot undertake here to discuss all the Kantian arguments connected with the antinomies. A brief comment on the first antinomy must suffice. We shall also consider the argument of the third antinomy in due time.

Let us consider the proposition "The world has no beginning in time." This constitutes the first part of the antithesis of the first conflict. It may be clarified by an examination of the notion of "beginning in time." This notion applies to any finite entity conditioned by other entities, but it does not apply to the world as a whole. How could the world as a whole arise from *empty* time? Yet if the world as a whole has had a beginning in time, this must have happened. But this is impossible, therefore the world has had no beginning in time.

On the other hand, let us now consider the thesis of this conflict; namely, the proposition "The world *has* a beginning in time." We may then ask, following Kant in spirit if not in letter: Can we conceive of a world process that has *never* had a beginning? Certainly not as we conceive of processes that we claim to understand. We never consider these as unlimited in time. We assume a point of departure. Can we, indeed, admit as the temporal background of a given event an unlimited time? Can we say that before a given event is possible an infinite number of previous events must have taken place? The difficulty remains a real one. Solution of such difficulties is conceivably possible only insofar as we admit that a fully complete understanding must involve considerations not open to us.

Kant insists that if we limit ourselves by the notion that the phenomenal world of space, time, and the categories is ultimately real, so that there can be no appeal to an order of reality lying beyond it, we must admit that since there is as much evidence for each thesis as for each antithesis, reason is utterly baffled. If, however, we admit that the phenomenal world is not a real world, but only our limited perspective of the real world, the presence of these contradictions need cause us no such concern, for we may suppose that with reference to the real or noumenal world these conflicts may somehow be resolved. In such a world, space, time, and causality may well enjoy a less prominent position, or may indeed have yielded to other patterns of relation.

There are, according to Kant, a number of questions that our intelligent curiosity urges us to ask, but which we can never hope fully to answer. Kant formulates these questions systematically. They are questions concerning the origin of the world system, the ultimate nature of its structure, and its relation to a Supreme Being or God. Also there are unanswerable questions concerning man himself, particularly concerning the human soul, its chances for immortality and the freedom of its acts and decisions. Insofar as these questions require discussion of realities lying beyond the phenomenal realm, they are strictly unanswerable. This does not, however, prevent us from sketching consistent and entirely possible answers concerning the final truth of which we must suspend judgment. Thus religious faith can never command the absolute support of philosophical reason; but it may nonetheless find that its assertions, although they cannot be proved, cannot be refuted or dismissed, and that in fact at least some of them can be shown to be internally consistent and thus to constitute a reasonable surmise concerning the persistent problems of God, the freedom of the will, and the immortality of the soul.

Thus as regards the problem of human freedom, we may suppose that the noumenal conditions of human decision allow an element of individual autonomy and initiative, but that no sign of this autonomy is manifest in the phenomenal order, in which *every* event is subject to the determinist categories of causation and causal reciprocity. One of Kant's chief concerns in speculation concerning the noumenal world is to make plausible the notions of human autonomy and of volitional initiative.

Kant insists that no *exhaustive* explanation of a natural event can ever be offered in terms of causation alone. In his discussion of the third antinomy, he argues that such explanation forces us back indefinitely, and our search for causes and causes of causes is then quite unlimited. On the other hand, reference to a free, autonomous decision based on a sense of intrinsic value, rationally tested, does not require us to search indefinitely for determining conditions. The decision may be considered as itself *initiating* a course of action. Unfortunately, the categories of causation and causal reciprocity, as we recognize them, will not tolerate our recognition of such an autonomous act of will, which originates a course of events within the phenomenal world. But the phenomenal world is not reality. Ultimate reality, or the noumenal world, may be such that freedom is possible within it. But in that case, Kant should admit that our moral decisions take place in the noumenal order, with the principles of which we, as agents of decision, should then be in intimate contact. We must postpone discussion of this difficulty until we examine in detail Kant's system of ethics.

Kant's teaching concerning ultimate reality should be divided under two heads: negative teaching whereby he warns us against the common pitfalls of thinking concerning this realm; and positive teaching whereby he undertakes, as we have mentioned above, to suggest tentatively a possible theory of reality. One of the most important elements characterizing Kant's negative teaching concerning the noumenal order is his denial of the possibility of what was commonly known as rational theology; that is, the philosophy which proves the existence of God. This denial amounts to a criticism of the theory of the Supreme Being that, as we have seen, Christian thinkers had developed by uniting Platonism and Scripture.

Kant is not eager to show that such a theology is an impossible account of things, but only that it lacks any necessary and compelling validity. He admits that our reason, if left to itself, uncriticized by a rigorous philosophy, tends to find, even upon purely intellectual grounds, the concept of the Supreme Being an attractive one. This was the case, for instance, with Descartes, Spinoza, and Leibniz. By means of such a notion we reduce our view of the world to an orderly system, in which the self-sufficient and unconditioned Supreme Being is the ultimate background of all finite or contingent beings. This is true whether we reach the concept of the Supreme Being by following the argument from design or by following the argument from the first cause (see above, page 227-9). Kant finds imperfections in both these arguments.

But the more pressing question arises: How do we know that this idea of ours of the Supreme Being represents any reality beyond our own thinking, to which it brings so considerable a measure of order and system? How do we know that it is anything more than an interesting hypothesis convenient as an aid in systematizing our ideas? We cannot support the idea of the Supreme Being, as we can the categories of the understanding, by showing that it is *indispensable* to our everyday experience of events. But there is one argument known to philosophy which passes directly from idea to reality, and that is the ontological argument of Anselm, Descartes, Spinoza, and Leibniz. According to this argument, we are assured that the Supreme Being must be more than an idea. This argument Kant proceeds to examine and to reject.

The ontological argument runs, as we may recall, somewhat as follows: We cannot deny the existence of God, for God as the Supreme Being must possess the property of existence, without which he would be lacking in the very perfection or fullness of being that we recognize as characterizing his nature. If we define God, with the

371

theologians and philosophers, as the Supreme Being, the most real being, or the perfect being, we must recognize existence as one of his attributes.

Kant's criticism may be briefly outlined as follows: We may invoke the hypothesis that a Supreme Being exists. The idea of this being, considered as the ultimate condition or first cause of natural events and as the source of the teleology apparent among living things, is a helpful concept that aids us in ordering our thinking. But we must still ask the question: Does this idea refer to an object? Now the Supreme Being as object cannot be present before our attention, as for instance a triangle can be. Thus the reality or the existence of God can be entertained by us only as a concept. It must be advanced as the predicate of a judgment—and only as the predicate of a synthetic judgment. As such, we cannot assert it simply by invoking the principle of contradiction.

But, upon further examination, we discover that *being, reality,* or *existence* is not a genuine predicate at all. It neither displays the structure of the conceived entity nor presents something that can be added to the original concept. Thus my idea of God as existing and my idea of God as nonexisting are exactly the same. The only way in which we, as finite minds, can judge cogently concerning the existence of any conceived entity requires our apprehension of that entity in the context of experience. But we cannot, at least according to Kant, experience God.

It is interesting to notice in passing that perhaps the only theologians who can withstand the Kantian criticism are those who believe that in some way we do experience or intuit the presence of God. In the last years of his life, Kant himself seems to have felt that we do perhaps in free moral decisions feel the presence of a divine power. But this notion is not characteristic of his earlier work, and it is never elaborated systematically by Kant himself.

The following quotations from the *Critique of Pure Reason* contain Kant's attack upon the ontological proof for the existence of God.[9]

9 *Ibid.,* pp. 204-10.

From what has been said it is obvious that the conception of an absolutely necessary being is a pure conception of reason. It is a mere idea, the objective reality of which is by no means proved by the fact that reason requires it. All that we can say is that the idea of an absolutely necessary being points to a certain ideal completeness, but as this completeness is unattainable, the idea really limits the sphere of understanding instead of extending its knowledge to new objects.

People have at all times [i.e., in all ages] spoken of an absolutely necessary being, but they have begun by seeking to prove its existence without first asking whether and how a thing of that sort could even be conceived. It is certainly easy enough to give a verbal definition of it, as something the non-existence of which is impossible. But this throws no light upon the conditions which force us to regard the non-existence of a thing as absolutely unthinkable. Now it is just these conditions that we really wish to know. We wish to know whether under the conception of a necessary being we are thinking anything at all or not. To speak of the "unconditioned," and thus to take away all the conditions by means of which understanding is able to regard anything as necessary, does not help us to understand, whether in the conception of an unconditionally necessary being we are thinking of a real being, or, as may perhaps be the case, of nothing at all.

It has commonly been supposed that this conception, now so familiar to us, but originally hit upon by accident, might be justified by bringing forward a number of examples, and that thus all further inquiry into its intelligibility was rendered superfluous. Every geometrical proposition, it was said, as, for instance, that a triangle has three angles, is absolutely necessary; and people talked as if such examples entitled them to say that they had a perfectly clear conception of what they meant by an object that lay entirely beyond the sphere of human understanding.

The examples brought forward were, however, all without exception taken from *judgments,* not from *things* and their existence. But the unconditioned necessity of a judgment is not the same thing as an absolute necessity of a thing. The absolute necessity of a judgment is only a conditioned necessity of the thing predicated, that is, of the predicate in the judgment. The proposition just cited does not say that three angles are absolutely necessary, but only that, if a triangle exists, that is, is presented in perception, it must contain three angles. But this mere logical necessity has proved a fruitful source of illusion. People have framed *a priori* the conception of a thing that seems to include existence within its content, and have then assumed that, because existence belongs necessarily to the object as conceived, it must also belong necessarily to the thing itself. Thus it is inferred that there is an absolutely necessary being, because the existence of that being is thought in a conception that has been arbitrarily assumed, and assumed under the supposition that there is an actual object corresponding to it.

If in an identical judgment [i.e., a judgment asserting identity] I retain the subject after rejecting the predicate, a contradiction arises, and hence I say that the predicate belongs to the subject necessarily. But if I reject the subject as well as the predicate, there is no contradiction, for nothing is left to which a contradiction could apply. To assume that there is a triangle, and yet to deny that it has three angles, is contradictory, but there is no contradiction in denying both the triangle and its three angles. It is exactly the same with the conception of an absolutely necessary being. If the existence of that being is denied, the thing itself with all its predicates is at the same time denied. How can this be shown to involve a contradiction? The contradiction cannot come from without [i.e., arise from considerations external to the thing in question], for the thing is not said to be necessary because of its relation to anything external; nor can it come from within, for, in denying the reality of the thing itself, the reality of all that it contains is at the same time denied. "God is almighty" is a necessary judgment. The predicate "almighty" cannot be denied, so long as the subject "God" is affirmed, for the conception of God, that is, of an infinite being, is identical with the conception of a Being that is "almighty." But if you say, "There is no God," neither the predicate "almighty" nor any other predicate remains: in the denial of the subject every possible predicate is denied, and there is therefore not the least contradiction in saying that God does not exist.

At this point, however, I am told that there is one conception, although only one, the object of which cannot without contradiction be denied to exist. The conception is that of an absolutely necessary Being. This Being, it is said, possesses all reality, and such a Being, as I am willing to admit, we are justified in assuming to be possible. Now that which comprehends all reality, the objector goes on, must also comprehend existence. Hence existence is in this case involved in the conception of a thing as possible. If, therefore, the thing is denied to exist, even its internal possibility is denied, and this is self-contradictory.

Now I simply ask, whether the proposition, that *this or that thing*

374

exists, is an analytic or a synthetic proposition. If it is analytic, nothing is added to the thought of a thing by predicating existence of it. Either the thought in you must itself be the thing, or you have simply assumed existence to be implied in mere possibility, and then derived existence from internal possibility, which is nothing but a wretched tautology. It does not mend matters to use the word "reality" in speaking of the conception of a thing, and the word "existence" in speaking of the conception of the predicate. Call all that is assumed "reality," and in the conception of the subject the thing with all its predicates is already assumed to be actual, and this assumption is simply repeated in the predicate. Admit, on the other hand, as every rational being must admit, that every proposition which affirms existence is synthetic, and how can it be any longer maintained that the predicate of existence cannot be denied without contradiction? That is the privilege of analytic propositions only, and is bound up with their very nature.

The illusion which arises from confusing a logical predicate with a real predicate, that is, with one that determines an actual thing, stubbornly resists almost all attempts to correct it. As logic abstracts from all content, anything at all may serve as a *logical* predicate; nay, the subject may even be predicated of itself. But a *determination* is a real predicate, which adds something to the conception of the subject and enlarges it. Hence it must not be assumed in the conception of the subject.

Being is evidently not a real predicate, that is, a conception of something that is capable of being added to the conception of a thing. It is merely the ungrounded assertion of a thing or of certain determinations as an object of thought. In logic *being* is simply the copula of a judgment. The proposition, *God is omnipotent,* contains two conceptions, the objects of which are respectively *God* and *omnipotence;* and the word *is* adds no new predicate, but is merely a sign that the predicate omnipotent is asserted in relation to the subject *God.* If, then, I take the term *God,* which is the subject, to comprehend the whole of the predicates, including the predicate *omnipotent,* and say, *God is,* or *There is a God,* I do not enlarge the conception of God by a new predicate, but I merely bring the subject in itself with all its predicates, in other words, the *object,* into relation with my conception. The content of the object and of my conception must be exactly the same, and hence I add nothing to my conception, which expresses merely the possibility of the object, by simply placing its object before me in thought, and saying that it *is.* The real contains no more than the possible. A

375

hundred real dollars do not contain a cent more than a hundred possible dollars. The one signifies the conception, the other the object as it is set over against the conception; but if the object contained more than the conception, the conception would not express the whole object, and would therefore be an inadequate conception. No doubt there is in my purse a hundred dollars more if I actually possess them, than if I have merely the conception, that is, have merely the possibility of them. As real, the object is not simply contained in my conception analytically, but it is added to it synthetically, the conception as such being merely a determination of my own state. But the hundred dollars do not become more than a hundred whether they exist outside of my conception or not....

And here we come upon the true source of the difficulty. Were it an object of sense that was in question, we should never think of identifying the existence of the thing with the mere conception of it. In that case we at once see that the conception of a thing signifies merely the agreement of the object with the universal conditions of all possible empirical knowledge; whereas, by the existence of a thing we mean that the object is thought as contained in the context of experience as a whole [as an object of possible observation]....

The labour and energy spent upon the famous ontological or Cartesian proof from mere conceptions of the existence of a Supreme Being are therefore thrown away, and a man has no more chance of extending his knowledge by means of mere ideas than a merchant can better his position by adding a few noughts to his cash account.

The above passage brilliantly exemplifies Kant's attitude toward the Rationalists, just as his discussion of the categories of the understanding presents his case against the Empiricists. Kant's repudiation of the ontological argument illustrates his skepticism concerning our knowledge of ultimate reality, which lies beyond the limits of our experience. In our inquiry concerning the noumenal world we have no dependable guiding thread comparable to space, time, and the categories that make possible genuine synthetic judgment concerning phenomena. Thus concerning the noumenal world or reality as a whole we can, according to Kant, make no statements with certainty.

This is true not only of our knowledge of the universe as a whole and of its relation to God, but also of our self-knowledge. The true nature of the human soul, as it exists in the noumenal world, quite escapes us. What the soul is, aside from the fact that it must somehow be connected with the maintenance of the synthetic unity of our experience, we do not know. Thus, for instance, we cannot say whether the soul is, as Plato and the Scholastics taught, simple and indivisible and accordingly indestructible. We know nothing about the soul except what we may call the empirical or phenomenal self; that is, the continuity of our awareness in the synthetic unity. We can be aware of the soul only as we observe its "surface," which is our own consciousness of the phenomenal world. But the ontology of the soul escapes our understanding.

There are two difficulties that arise when a Kantian considers critically the question of our knowledge of ourselves as thinking beings. In the first place, is the self given to us through any intuited data? Certainly not through sensuous data, and it seems questionable whether we are directly aware, as Kant would say, through "intellectual intuition" of an active self. Besides, even if some dark sense of selfhood, reaching beyond the synthetic unity of consciousness, were available, systematic knowledge of such a self would be extremely difficult. We could hardly interpret it by means of the categories, which apply not to consciousness and the conditions of its origin, but only to the objects of consciousness as manifest through sensuous data. Thus the self or soul, considered as a real entity or power distinct from phenomena, is beyond the reach of our understanding. We cannot describe it as a substance, nor can we think of it as exercising or receiving causal influence.

A CRITICISM OF KANTIAN SKEPTICISM

According to Kant, the scientists explore the details of the phenomenal world. Mathematics explores the nature of space and time, and the natural sciences examine the types of recurring objects to be found in the phenomenal world and the laws by which their processes are related to one another. But speculative philosophy can offer only dark guesses concerning the nature of things that lie "beyond" this phenomenal world which the sciences study. The phenomenal world is open to mind, because it is subject to space, time, and the categories. We know that it is subject to these conditions because these are essential to the synthetic unity without which egocentric experience of a sequence of events would be quite impossible. Since this synthesis is uniformly indispensable to our every perception of phenomena, we may speak of it as "suprapersonal mind," or a phase of human awareness that does not depend upon the personal interests, ideals, or general background of the individual. "The whole phenomenal world of science is simply the contents of one ideal human experience; for it is the real world, not as it is in itself, but as it must appear to all minds which share the same form of sensibility and of thought." (Paton) [9a] Kant's profoundest difficulties center in his theory of the nature and function of mind, of the process without which there would be no distinction between phenomena and noumena, between the world as we must perceive it and the world as it really is, the thing-in-itself. Let us quote from the late Professor Hoernlé's criticism of Kant's theory of knowledge: [10]

I start from what is common ground, *viz.*, that Kant's *Critique [of Pure Reason]* is "a philosophical analysis of human experience on its cognitive side." ...

I prefer to argue from the nature and function assigned to mind in the context of the theory. What is that context? Fundamentally, it seems to me, it is that of a dualism of knower and known as two distinct existents. The knower is characterised as "mind" or "self"; the known as "reality." If the question is asked: But is not the mind itself part of reality in the most inclusive sense? the point is met by adding that mind knows itself, so that mind is also part of the known, *i.e.*, of reality. Reality, then, as known, consists of mind (or minds) and the non-mental part of reality, a scheme which fits the traditional distinction between mind and matter, and allows the realm of bodies in space to be assigned to the physical sciences, whilst psychology deals with the realm of minds. Attention next

[9a] H. J. Paton, *Kant's Metaphysic of Experience,* New York, Macmillan, 1936, vol. I, p. 542.

[10] R. F. A. Hoernlé, review of H. J. Paton, *Kant's Metaphysic of Experience,* in *Mind,* n.s., Vol. XLVI (1937), pp. 500-02. Reprinted by permission of the editor of *Mind.*

turns to what is meant by reality *as known, i.e.,* reality as object of a knower, as object of perception and thought to a mind or self. Here is introduced the theory that whatever is object of perception and thought is determined by the constitution of the perceiving and thinking mind, and therefore "appearances." This applies to all reality as known: both physical bodies and minds, as objects of knowledge, are "appearances." What they are in themselves remains unknown and unknowable. The world which is object of knowledge is thus, as appearance, suspended, as it were, between two unknown "things-in-themselves," both of which are, however, its "conditions" (in the sense that, without them, there could be no appearances at all). In all appearances, we can distinguish "matter" and "form": the "matter" is contributed by things-in-themselves, and is "given to inner and/or outer sense" [sensibility]; the form is contributed, as *a priori* synthetic principles, by mind as knower.

Now, my difficulty with a theory of this type is the double and ambiguous rôle which mind has to play as, at once, knower and known. Mind, as object to itself, is "appearance": mind, as "thing-in-itself," is unknown. Why is mind, as known, appearance? Because every object of knowledge, and therefore mind as object, is determined by the "constitution" of mind as knower. Does mind know its own constitution as knower? Can mind bring before itself —by reflection on itself, by self-conscious self-objectifying thought— its own constitution as knower? Yes, it must be able to do so. For, is it not precisely the achievement of Kant's *Critique* to exhibit the constitution of the knowing mind as *a priori* forms, giving rise to *a priori* synthetic propositions, which are known independently of all sense-experience? But, if this be so, we have to face the crucial question: If mind thus knows itself in its constitution as knower, is mind thus known "appearance" or "phenomenon"? Clearly not. Is it, then, thing-in-itself? This, too, is impossible, for the thing-in-itself is unknown and unknowable. What then is this mind as knower and where does it fit in? It is the central hero of Kant's story; for the world of appearances, as distinct from the world of things-in-themselves, depends on it. But, being itself neither appearance nor thing-in-itself, it has no intelligible place in the scheme of the universe for which it is none the less the chief argument.

As Professor Hoernlé makes quite clear, Kant must admit that we know a good deal about minds, and also that, despite this, mind cannot be classed as phenomenal. He rules out the possibility that we do not or cannot understand the nature of mind. Suppose, however, for the sake of the argument, that a defender of Kant's theory should accept this alternative and assert that we know no more about mind than we do about noumena, or things-in-themselves. In that case Kant's philosophy is in no sense an answer to Hume's. If all that we know about mind is limited to a mere classification of mental *phenomena,* how do we know that space, time and the categories are indispensable to our mode of thinking? Under such circumstances we should know this with no more certainty than, according to Hume, we know that gravitation is a constant character of the physical world, or that the sun must rise tomorrow. Once we call mind unknowable, along with the thing-in-itself, we must admit that space, time, and the categories need no longer be recognized as *necessary* characters of our mode of awareness, for we cannot determine what is necessary to something unknowable. And with that admission Kant's system crumbles.

There seems, then, to be but one alternative left to the Kantian. He must admit that mind is somehow supraphenomenal, and yet at the same time that it is knowable. Along these lines, and along these lines only, can he proceed with safety. This, of course, does not compel the Kantian to admit that mind is the only reality, or even the only knowable reality. It does not force him into pure idealism, but it does compel him to realign his fundamental concepts.

CHAPTER XII

Kant and German Idealism

KANT'S DEFENSE OF TELEOLOGY

In his later writings, Kant further explores the possibility of our framing conjectual hypotheses concerning the supraphenomenal order. This is undertaken in his last great work, the *Critique of Judgment*. In this book he discusses two closely related types of thought, that whereby we recognize the embodiment of purpose, and that whereby we recognize the presence of beauty in the world about us. These types of awareness suggest the possibility of an outlook upon the world from which we may apprehend something of the supraphenomenal order of things. In these pages we can do no more than briefly sketch the broad conclusions of this work.

This suprasensible world is a world of organization, a world of teleology, not one of mechanical causation. The relation between whole and part that is established in it is rather purposive than mechanical. Just so a phrase exists in a composition not because of any vis a tergo production, but for the sake of the whole meaning, which would be imperfect without it. So the organs of a living body, although perhaps in a lesser degree, are related to the organism, which in turn makes their existence possible.

Why is it that we do not become directly aware of our membership in such a realm? Kant argues that this is because of the way in which our minds cut into reality. Our experience is temporal, essentially inseparable from change. The content of our "sensuous intake" is limited, and we have to piece our knowledge together out of a series of glimpses, one following another. Such a limited way of knowing must miss certain aspects of things, and Kant undertakes to show just how the importance of final cause is over-looked.

Let us employ the following analogy to illustrate Kant's use of ideas drawn from his philosophy of art and beauty. Suppose that we have through some paralysis of our mental functions to consider the words of a poem as isolated and disparate. Suppose that instead of "reading" in the full sense we move from word to word in a series of leaps, recognizing the audible qualities of each syllable, and noticing whether it is stressed or unstressed. Suppose also that the meaning of the words is confined to their dictionary definitions, which we fail to weave together into a continued significance, somewhat as we fail to handle a language whose syntactical forms are beyond us. Now in even a simple stanza there would be a considerable amount of linear order to be discovered by this method. The sequence of stressed and unstressed syllables composing each line might be schematically expressed and a special type of order revealed. If we move, antlike, from one word to another, we may be tempted to suspect that the whole stanza in all its aspects is to be explained in terms of formulas such as those which we have used to describe rhythm and rhyme.

We might believe this if we had not enjoyed the poem; that is, if we had not been aware of its meaning and felt the force of its expression. For such an aesthetic experience, "running through" the lines word for word is not enough; whole phrases must be taken together, and the meaning of the several words dovetailed—or better, fused together—to yield continued and coherent significance. To be sure, the incomplete vision might reveal something of the artist's technique. But technique aside from aesthetic effect is a sadly incomplete vision of poetry, something like the American schoolboy's appreciation of Virgil. To apprehend the verse, we must see all the parts as caught into a whole, within which the parts are significant. Such apprehension is totally different from the schoolboy's piecing together. Whereas in the latter we have sequences of words, in the former we have meaning that is diffused throughout a number of words and which is a factor in the interpretation and appreciative comprehension of these words, just as it has been a factor in their selection by the poet. Only then does the apt choice of words manifest itself and the rhythm seem to melt into the meaning and the atmosphere of the whole.

For Kant, the enjoyment of beauty involves a harmony of the understanding and the sensibility. Here sense and meaning support one another in so complete and subtle an interplay that no analysis, paraphrase, or discursive description can do adequate and exhaustive justice to the beautiful object. In the beautiful object, form and matter are united in a unique and individual or exemplary realization. Beauty is a realization of purpose, although of a purpose that could not have been fully stated in advance.

Somewhat in this way, we may contrast the realm of phenomenal order and the realm of teleological organization. Man's understanding is thoroughly at home only in the realm of order. We can be much surer of observed sequences that can be schematized than of any meaning we may discover in "life" or in history. This is because we can never have a view of the "verses" of life or of history except by running through series of events the juxtaposition of which seems almost arbitrary when we begin to creep from point to point. Hence we grasp no significance or purpose, nor can we be absolutely sure that there is any. Order of a sort we do finally discover, but it is the order of regular patterns of sequence that can be schematized rather than appreciated.

Kant develops this distinction with wonderful subtlety. We cannot see the world as the embodiment of purpose or meaning. Strictly speaking, this is because we must begin in experience with partial glimpses and derive wholes, or patterns of combined elements, from these; whereas it is possible to conceive of a mind for which the whole is the first datum, or at the very least a datum given along with the parts. If we do not begin with the whole, it will not seem an essential ingredient in the life of its parts—it will seem to be a resultant of the parts. Hence causation will take the place of organization in our interpretation. Now, owing to the form of our experience, we never do begin with a whole, we begin with glimpses. Hence causation, rather than embodiment of meaning, seems the universal form of world order, although this is interrupted here and there by the appearance of adaptation in biology, by our sense of our freedom in moral decisions, and by the idea of value in aesthetics.

Kant suggests, however, that another form of knowledge is at least thinkable, in which *whole* is as primary a datum as *part.* For this experience the meaning, purpose, and value of events is suffused throughout their apprehension. In such a way does God know the world, the true world that our manner of experience obscures from us. In a world organized according to such a principle, ends and purposes are the moving forces.

We quote from Kant's *Critique of Judgment:* [1]

It is the nature of our intelligence to proceed in knowledge from an *analytical universal,* or a conception, to the particular as given in empirical perception. The multiplicity of the latter thus remains undetermined, until judgment has determined it by bringing the perception under the conception. We may, however, conceive of an intelligence different in kind from ours, an intelligence which is perceptive and not discursive, and which therefore proceeds from a *synthetic universal* to the particular, that is, *from a perceived whole to the parts.* For such an intelligence, the connection of the parts which form a determinate whole would not be, or appear, contingent as it is for us.... But, from the peculiar character of *our* intelligence, a real whole in nature is regarded only as the effect of the combined motive forces of the parts. We may, however, instead of viewing the whole as dependent on the parts, after the manner of our discursive intelligence, *take a perceptive or archetypal intelligence as our standard, and seek to comprehend the dependence of the parts on the whole,* both in their specific nature and in their interconnection.

Of especial significance is Kant's treatment of genius and his comparison of genial apprehension or invention to "archetypal" knowledge. Genius produces its creations according to no preconceived abstract pattern, the pattern of the work being complete only with the work itself, whose finality or purpose is fully manifest only with the realization and embodiment of the work and not in preliminary conception. Thus the work of the genius is exemplary, not

[1] Kant, *Critique of Judgment,* in *The Philosophy of Kant, as Contained in Extracts from His own Writings,* selected and trans. by John Watson, p. 340. Italics added.

subject to rule, but giving the law to itself as it develops. Hence, we may add, it can be appreciated only by an act of genius that grasps the unique and proper life of the whole along with the parts. Thus *we* can hardly appreciate nature's genius.

Kant's contribution is then essentially this: It may well be that scientific order is not really irreconcilable with value and the realization of finality or purpose. The two may stand together, as do technique and meaning in a successful work of art. It is owing to man's ontological predicament that in nature he can see only the "technique" with satisfying clarity.

A similar view is expressed with profound insight into the psychology of creation by Kant's follower Schelling. But this attitude is peculiar to an important movement in literature and philosophy and cannot be confined strictly to the writings of individual thinkers. This movement is known as Romanticism. Insofar as it has real philosophical value, Romanticism may be summed up as follows: To understand, in the usual sense of the term, is not the culmination of knowledge. There is something more revealing and more significant than understanding. Understanding is limited to the apprehension of comparatively superficial principles. To know fully and intimately, we must surpass all principles and abstractions and apprehend the concrete thing itself.

Some Romanticists call the faculty of true knowledge reason, some imagination, others intuition, and there is a wealth of interpretation advanced concerning all these. Wordsworth and William Blake call this faculty imagination, and Wordsworth indicts understanding with the statement that "we murder to dissect." Blake tells us that reason (for him, the term refers to understanding) can move only on the "same dull round." Imagination alone makes real discoveries. And the nucleus of the new thought seems to be in Goethe's belief that life is a process which makes its way in some measure independent of rational principles. Thus in art, the customary, the regular, the universal, is only the skeleton that is carried along in a plastic development.

In such a philosophy there is always the danger that the concrete reality will be hailed as something entirely opposed to logical principles. At times we hear philosophers crying out against all logical thought, since it does little more than distort its object. The relation of purely discursive to intuitive or creative thinking is one of the nicest problems the philosophy of Romanticism has to face.

But the Romantic contribution in its lasting form is essentially this: The beautiful things we create and the beauty we perceive in nature (and at last we learn that everything real is beautiful if seen directly) are, so to speak, suprarational, because they are unique. We cannot exhaust their meaning by classifying them, nor can we treat them as functions of something other than themselves. If we do this, they will cease to be beautiful. They will seem to lose the intimate selfhood that we once recognized as beautiful. Here in the unique life of each object is something that quite surpasses determination, something that does not *belong* to an order, although of course it may contain much order. Thus when Blake tells us that reason sees but the circumference of things, he means to say that reason, or understanding, touches only the boundaries, the definitions, the relations of things rather than their reality. This reality is present only to the mind that creates these things or appreciates the act of creation which first produced them.

ROMANTIC IDEALISM: SCHELLING [2]

This creative act receives the most careful study from Kant's brilliant follower Schelling, whom we have just mentioned. Schelling, like most Romanticists, lacks Kant's circumspection and cau-

[2] Friedrich Wilhelm Joseph von Schelling (1775-1854) was educated at the University of Tübingen, where his father was a professor of theology. Here the young Schelling was in company with Hegel. At this time he was deeply moved by the radical political movement in France, and he was involved in some minor revolutionary agitation. He became deeply interested in the history of mythology, and he was also a constant, if unorthodox, student of the Bible. He also followed the developments in natural science, although in this field his judgment was often uncritical. Himself something of a poet, Schelling was an eager champion of Romanticism in art and literature, and his private life reflects the somewhat undisciplined freedom of early Romanticism. Besides, his spectacular and brilliant personality was marred by his conceit. But Schelling was probably the most brilliant, although not the soundest, of the German Romantic thinkers. His circle has been described as living in a "whirligig of wit and philosophy, conversation on art and on everything under the

tion. He advances, even when he speculates concerning ultimate reality, propositions that he considers to be unquestionably true rather than reasonable surmises. Although he is not an orthodox Rationalist, Schelling approaches the self-assurance of Descartes and Spinoza. He substitutes the artist's intuition for the Cartesian clear and distinct idea, and in this way he claims absolute certainty for his conclusions. In his philosophy, the sharp Cartesian distinction between the voluntary activity of mind and unconscious natural order is retained; but it is made the starting point of philosophy rather than the last word. For Schelling, this sharp distinction cannot be ultimate. It is apparent that acts of will culminate in objective situations that are suffused with unconscious or objective order.

Further, in successful aesthetic activity, will is at last identical with its object. Value and structure are found together. Subjective will is at peace with objective form, and the artist loses himself in his work, which though embodying itself in a physical medium remains part of himself. But although will and order often cannot be separated in actual life, they are upon inspection very different things. Teleology and structural causation are "absolutely" different, one from another, as different as syntax from an emotion that calls for expression in words. This difference Schelling presents without overmuch exposition or argument. He relies implicitly upon a common sense charged with the Cartesian feeling of the distinction between objective mechanism and subjective purpose.

Schelling's philosophy is presented as a transcending of this absolute dualism. This form of statement, which suggests that creative activity performs the "impossible" by harmonizing the two aspects of things, somewhat obscures Schelling's meaning for the modern student and conceals the actual derivation of his ideas from the common human experience of beauty. Now this experience does

---

sun." Schelling taught for a time at Jena, where he was close to both Fichte and Hegel, and he lectured later at Berlin. The development of his philosophical ideas was rapid, almost headlong, and he tended to shift his position frequently. His influence has been great, surpassed only by that of Kant and Hegel themselves. Such men as the English poet and philosopher Samuel Taylor Coleridge, and the great naturalist Louis Agassiz may be counted among his followers.

clearly suggest the way in which the reconciliation may be made apparent. The only union of will and order of which we possess obvious concrete evidence lies in the aesthetic activity. This activity is the synthesis of two tendencies, manifest respectively in the artist's feeling for technique and form and in his desire to say or express something. Thus creation is an act of realization that unites these two tendencies, whereby certain ends or objects of the will are at times successfully embodied in a concrete structure. This act of embodiment Schelling considers as resolution of conflict, the conflict the artist feels to exist between his medium and his ideal. The stubborn resistance of the medium and its final surrender to a desired pattern is the life of creation. To recognize that in a certain object such conflict has been overcome is to enjoy beauty. To do this, we must see structure enlivened by the presence of meaning. Without such insight, our view of things can be only superficial.

In such a way, we may suppose, God surveys his creation; and, even to us, if we are properly enlightened by a true philosophy, and free of pedantry, the world may appear as the realization of creative power. Thus for man, as for Goethe's angels, the unfathomed and triumphant works of creation are magnificent as on the first day—

Die unbegreiflich hohen Werke
Sind herrlich wie am ersten Tag.

This romantic idealism, derived via Schelling from the Kantian *Critique of Judgment,* enjoyed a wide and a fruitful influence. Samuel Taylor Coleridge, the English poet, Ralph Waldo Emerson in the United States, and Félix Ravaisson, the lesser known student of art and philosophy in France, were prominent as defenders of this way of thought. In the United States, this type of Idealism has often been described as Transcendentalism. These thinkers felt with Schelling that they could surmount the barriers of Kant's more cautious skepticism, which had withheld him from presenting the philosophy of the *Critique of Judgment* as anything more than a tentative surmise. They share this speculative confidence with other schools of post-Kantian Idealism.

REALITY AS EGOCENTRIC: FICHTE [3]

The philosophy immediately following upon Kant tends, as we have seen, to affirm the Idealism of the *Critique of Judgment,* but to affirm it in an unqualified fashion, quite ignoring the caution and the suspicion of all dogmatic assertion so characteristic of the Kantian attitude. Kant has shown that what we call the external world of phenomena is by no means independent of our thinking process. Mind, by its very nature, helps to determine what features of reality are to constitute our phenomenal world. Phenomena owe their most general patterns to the mode of interpretation maintained by the synthetic unity that inspires all human thinking. Thus substance and causality, for example, are pervasive features of this phenomenal world and the prominence of these features depends upon our mode of apprehension. From this point, it is not a great step to the suggestion that the world of external phenomena is in some way produced or created by mind, not perhaps my mind or your mind, but a cosmic mind, perhaps a sort of pantheistic deity. Thus the very existence and the full structure of phenomena may be thought to depend upon the activity of consciousness, in this case not merely selective and interpretative in function but actually creative.

Against this view, we may argue that while we can, through careful reflection and analysis, become to some degree aware of the powers of selection and interpretation that our minds exercise, we are not in the least aware of any tendency on our part to create phenomena out of nothing. Even so, there have been thinkers willing to resort to the hypothesis that mind produces the full content

---

[3] Johann Gottlieb Fichte (1762-1814) was considered at one time Kant's most brilliant successor. Born of peasant stock, Fichte spent much of his boyhood as a gooseherd. He acquired an education at Jena and Leipzig, despite great poverty. From 1794 to 1799 he taught at the University of Jena under the patronage of the Duke of Saxe-Weimar, at whose court the poet Goethe resided. He left Jena because of opposition to his unorthodox religious views. His later life was spent in Berlin, where he was very active in arousing the Germans to resist the domination of the French, who, under Napoleon, had quite overrun the disorganized German principalities. Fichte's social philosophy was highly colored by patriotism and by his intense faith in the exalted destiny of the German people.

and texture of its object. For these philosophers, there is nothing prior to mental activity and nothing "given" to it from without. From this point of view, mind may be said to produce the very background against which it works and the material that it employs. The ego is said to produce the nonego; mind is said to produce nature.

The evidence that can be offered in defense of such a conclusion is largely indirect, and may be surveyed under two heads.

1. If we remain within the presuppositions of the Kantian system, we shall experience the greatest difficulty in describing any datum or element "given" to mind from without. We seem to be aware of phenomena only as they are subjected to space, time, and the categories—that is, as they are interpreted by consciousness. The raw material upon which this interpretation is said to work never appears in its sheer givenness. By this we mean that we are never aware of sheer sensation or of absolutely uninterpreted data. Why then should we suppose that there is any absolutely raw material given to mind from without? Many thinkers prefer to dismiss the possibility of such a datum, somewhat as Berkeley dismissed Locke's notion of the unperceived corporeal substance.

2. In all reasoning we suppose that reality is subject to the general principles which the logic of investigation is constrained to respect. Reality must be such that we may describe it without contradicting ourselves. Accordingly it must manifest patterns each of which possesses an enduring and recognizable identity. Thus the principles of mental integrity or consistency, the laws of thought themselves, must be reflected in nature, or logical inquiry into nature would be impossible. Nature must, for instance, be such that two contradictory assertions cannot at the same time be true of one and the same set of objects. Nature itself must respect the mind's standard of truth or there can be no successful thinking concerning nature. Hence nature must be subject to mind.

This line of argument was first worked out in brilliant detail by Fichte, who argues that the first principles of intelligibility are the first products of self-consciousness, which must produce them in order to assert itself. The principle of identity, for instance, is involved in the synthetic unity itself; that is, in the conditions whereby I can assert "I am the I that I was." The archetype of all identity is the identity of self-consciousness, and identity exists in nature because nature is the product of conscious mind. Thus things endure throughout change without melting into a chaos because they are ultimately subject to mind. This is true of all logical order, which is, so to speak, the signature with which mind marks its products.

According to this argument, mind must produce the full detail of the world, which must be in every respect subject to the laws of thought. Fichte's opponents scornfully retorted that he had quite confused man or the human mind with God, who creates a world out of nothing; and it is true that he was always willing to dismiss the fact that mind is not productive of objects in general but must always work, like the human artist, within a given medium that it does not create. After all, if I create my world and you create your world, how is our mental agreement and communication with one another possible? If our minds are not disciplined by the presence of a common reality, how are they, so to speak, kept in step with one another? Fichte is inclined to answer this by saying that finite selves—that is, you and I—are manifestations of one and the same productive principle, the creative ego or God that is the same in all selves, the core or essence of each individual mentality. Finite personality, including personal interests and modes of thought, is produced by this ego just as the so-called external world is produced.

In recent years, a philosophy very similar to that of Fichte has been taught by the Italian idealist Giovanni Gentile.

THE DIALECTICAL OR ABSOLUTE IDEALISM OF HEGEL

Fichte interprets the logically disciplined order of nature as the product of mind. There is another approach, differing at least in orientation, according to which this very order may be recognized as mind itself, actually present in the world. According to this view, that of Hegel, nature is not so much the product of mind as its outward appearance. Reason is immanent in all things, and logic is virtually identified with cosmology.[4]

If thought tries to form a notion of things, this notion ... cannot be composed of articles and relations which are alien and irrelevant to the things. Reflection, it was said above, conducts to the universal of things: which universal is itself one of the constituent factors of a notion. To say that Reason or Understanding is in the world, is equivalent in its import to the phrase 'Objective Thought'. The latter phrase however has the inconvenience that *thought* is usually confined to express what belongs to the mind or consciousness only, while *objective* is a term applied, at least primarily, only to the non-mental.

To speak of thought or objective thought as the heart and soul of the world, may seem to be ascribing consciousness to the things of nature. We feel a certain repugnance against making thought the inward function of things, especially as we speak of thought as marking the divergence of man from nature. It would be necessary, therefore, if we use the term *thought* at all, to speak of nature as the system of unconscious thought, or, to use Schelling's expression, a petrified intelligence. And in order to prevent misconception, thought-form or thought-type should be substituted for the ambiguous term *thought*.

From what has been said the principles of logic are to be sought in a system of thought-types or fundamental categories, in which the

[4] Hegel, *The Encyclopaedia of the Philosophical Sciences*, trans. by William Wallace, pp. 46-47. Clarendon Press, Oxford, 2nd ed., 1892. Reprinted by permission of the publisher.

George Wilhelm Friedrich Hegel (1770-1831) son of a minor government official, was educated at Stuttgart and Tübingen, where he was in the company of Schelling, who by far outshone him as a student. The two men were also at Jena in the company of Fichte. Together, Schelling and Hegel edited a philosophical periodical, the *Critical Journal*, which Hegel afterward conducted alone. Hegel's stay at Jena was terminated by the Napoleonic invasion in 1807. He taught later at Nuremberg as a schoolmaster and, after 1816, as a professor of philosophy at Heidelberg, and finally from 1818 to 1831 at Berlin. Lacking in Kant's originality and in Schelling's brilliance, Hegel is distinguished for the thoroughness of his work, which includes pertinent and systematic comment upon almost every aspect of European culture. He had an especially broad knowledge of history, including the development of the arts and of religion. He wrote one of the first comprehensive histories of European philosophy. His writing is characterized by a fondness for philosophical terms derived solely from the German without reference to Latin and Greek. This adds something to the difficulty of his style, which some critics have described as "barbarous." Despite this, his thought may be said to have conquered the philosophical world and to have ruled it, despite many insurrections, for nearly a century.

opposition between subjective and objective, in its usual sense, vanishes. The signification thus attached to thought and its characteristic forms may be illustrated by the ancient saying that 'nous governs the world,' or by our own phrase that 'Reason is in the world': which means that Reason is the soul of the world it inhabits, its immanent principle, its most proper and inward nature, its universal. Another illustration is offered by the circumstance that in speaking of some definite animal we say it is (an) animal. Now, the animal, *qua* animal, cannot be shown; nothing can be pointed out excepting some special animal. Animal, *qua* animal, does not exist: it is merely the universal nature of the individual animals, whilst each existing animal is a more concretely defined and particularised thing. But to be an animal,—the law of kind which is the universal in this case,—is the property of the particular animal, and constitutes its definite essence. Take away from the dog its animality, and it becomes impossible to say what it is. All things have a permanent inward nature, as well as an outward existence. They live and die, arise and pass away; but their essential and universal part is the kind; and this means much more than something *common* to them all.

The reader will notice that Hegel interprets universals very much as Augustine and Plotinus did centuries before; that is, he thinks of them as acts of a mental power rather than as eternal objects, after the fashion of Plato.

According to the philosophy of Hegel, the world is active thought, manifesting itself in many ways, of which nature, history, religion, and philosophy itself are significant examples. These manifestations are not perfect mirrors of world thought; one may be said to be higher or more adequate than another. Thus nature—that is, the world that is studied by the natural scientist—is not as adequate a manifestation of reality as, say, history and religion are. But for all that, nature is one expression of ultimate truth. There are, indeed, degrees of truth or degrees of adequacy in the manifestation of reality. Each degree of adequacy actually tends to contradict lower degrees, but these contradictions can always be resolved if we turn to higher and more inclusive levels of interpretation.

These levels or degrees of truth need not, in fact must not, be thought of simply as stages in *our* thinking. They are "moments" in the self-revelation of the absolute reality. Nature, or the system of cause and effect, is real in a sense that it is objective, being in no way the product of irresponsible thinking. But it is less real than mind and autonomous freedom in that it manifests less adequately the core of absolute reality.

This core of absolute reality may be characterized as self-sufficient and internally consistent, since it depends on nothing that lies beyond it. In this it resembles the *ens a se* or the fullness of being that Christian theologians attribute to God, and also the *causa sui* of Spinoza. It differs from the first of these in that it does not create the world out of nothing, and from the second in that it is more adequately manifest through mind than through matter. It may best be described as independent and autonomous; that is, it exists *in* itself and *through* itself.

If we undertake to offer a complete description of any entity short of absolute reality itself, we are bound to fall sooner or later into antinomies of the sort that Kant has described. These antinomies are insoluble so long as we continue to discuss the conflict as an isolated problem. The contradiction can be resolved only if we "transcend" the situation and view it in a more ample perspective. In this way, we draw more closely toward knowledge of the self-sufficient or absolute reality that is in itself a resolution of the contradictions which we have observed on lower levels. *Dialectic,* or the reconciliation of opposites, which at a given level are really and truly contradictory of one another, is the essence of thought; and this thought is present both in our lives and in the world. Thought understands itself as the unity of a variety that contains conflict; and it recognizes things as the variety of the unity.

Pure or dialectical reason will, as it develops, criticize itself by positing antinomies or conflicts, and it will climb toward a richer philosophy upon a ladder of opposition and reconciled contradictions. The advance of philosophical thought will then proceed by way of many three-cornered zigzags, in which thought passes from one proposition to its contrary and then to a third proposition that reconciles the two and opens a new array of problems. This movement is described as a passage from *thesis* through *antithesis* to *synthesis*.

The true Hegelian believes that this method of thought depends upon or corresponds to the very nature of reality itself, which involves the truth that every finite entity or situation produces its own opposite. This is certainly true of the psychology of human opinion, where under the guidance of one concept or ideal, the thinking public for a time ignores all opinions conflicting with its favorite notions. But these ignored points of view accumulate, until there comes a time when we pay for our one-sidedness by being driven to accept an opposite doctrine. Then only careful reconsideration of all evidence can bring us to a new solution that transcends both the earlier thesis and the antithesis.

Hegel was convinced that there are many important antinomies besides the few Kant had presented. For the Hegelian, every great period in the history of thought has to face antinomies and work out solutions by transcending the concept they represent. In this way every great period of thought is conceived as attaining a new perspective and a new orientation of problems. We may think of the opposition of Rationalism and Empiricism, which represent respectively a thesis and an antithesis, and the way in which the whole problem was recast in Kant's critical philosophy, which in this case constitutes a synthesis. Or, going back to ancient times, we may recall the philosophy of permanence presented by Parmenides, the philosophy of flux advanced by Heraclitus, and the revision of the problem by Plato, the latter being a synthesis wherein the earlier philosophies are transcended and the deadlock is overcome.

According to Hegel, a philosophy need not achieve absolute truth in order to be counted a successful one. It accomplishes its purpose if it pushes beyond the conflicts of thought that characterize its epoch. Almost inevitably it will bequeath further conflicts to its successors, but these will not be immediately apparent. This limitation applies not only to traditional philosophies, but also to the development of religion and the attitudes of human culture in general.

According to Hegel, the religious point of view is by no means false, yet it does not include absolute truth. The philosophy of the higher religions of the Western world, with its theory of a personal God who created the world out of nothing, is not wholly false. In fact, it reveals much that is true, insofar as its emphasizes the importance of creative mind in the scheme of things. But insofar as such philosophy distinguishes God from the world it fails to perceive the fundamental principle of the philosophy of organic monism that Hegel advances. Religious philosophy is likely to think of God as capable of existing independent of the world: as we shall see, according to Hegel, no such independence is possible. The philosophy that results from the development of ideas in Western religion must in the end be transcended. But this does not mean that religious thinking is therefore invalid. It is rather an incomplete view of the world indispensable for those who do not see beyond it.[5]

In Hegel's view, reality in its full organization of detail must be free of unresolved conflicts. The last word cannot lie with the antinomies, but with a harmonizing unity. The real is the rational, and the rational is the real. It is true that we cannot see such reason as immanent everywhere, because we isolate fragments and tend to treat them as independent realities when in truth there are no independent realities but only one system of reality, the parts of which condition and influence one another. Thus to discuss causality apart from a study of the human understanding, such as we find in Kant, is to distort our subject matter.

Again, to discuss an organism without recognizing its relation to the environment in which it lives, or a moral code without reference to the conditions it has had to meet, is to discuss an isolated, what

[5] A sincere believer may well prefer to reject this "concordat" which Hegel offers to religion. If we know that the religious point of view must in the end be transcended, we can hardly believe that our feelings of awe and our impulse to worship are very important things. Furthermore, it raises an interesting question whether we can feel religious awe when contemplating an absolute reality that includes ourselves, as the Hegelian organic world unity is said to do. The object of worship is usually thought of as a "something not ourselves." Accordingly any pantheism as complete as the Hegelian is often distasteful to a person of profoundly religious feeling.

Hegel called an "abstract," fragment of a concrete and delicately interwoven reality. In so doing, we cannot even see clearly the fragment upon which we concentrate our attention. Just so, we miss much of the significant structure of an organ about the function of which we know little or nothing. We do not know what to consider essential and what accidental, for we consider our object without reference to its place in the economy of the organism as a whole.

This is true not only of our thinking, but of reality in general: entities cannot exist in isolation any more than they can be understood *in abstracto*. What, for example, would become of the kidneys apart from the other organs of the body? What would be left of the organism once it was removed from heat and food? Without the solar system, the earth would not be the moving sphere that it is. Nor would physical entities in general be what they are were it not for such principles as gravitation and the laws of motion, which after all only describe the ways in which bodies are related one to another. Any finite entity depends for its nature and its existence upon the system of things that condition it. Any finite entity is constituted by its relations to its environment, and in turn the environment itself is, in a lesser measure, constituted by these very relations. Reality is thus a close-knit system of reciprocity. The relations that finite entities bear to one another are organic or *internal,* since they cannot change without essentially altering the very nature of the finite beings involved.

According to Hegel and his many followers, it is the presence of this system of internal relations which makes reasoning possible. If relations were external,[6] rather than internal, the intellectual enterprise would be thwarted. It is only because the character of a fragmentary object implies the presence of a wider system of internal relations, and vice versa, that inference is possible. If there were no such systematic connections, reality would not be rational; that is, it would be without systematic unity and accordingly unknowable. For Hegel, then, the presupposition of reasoning is not the Platonic form, an isolated and independent unit, a universal apart from par-

---

[6] An *external* relation is one that does not alter or constitute the essential nature of the terms which it relates.

ticulars, but a systematic union of particular finite entities—what the Hegelian calls the *concrete universal*. This ultimate organization of all finitude into one self-consistent and logically independent reality deserves the name of the *infinite* or *unconditioned,* what Hegelians usually describe as the *Absolute.*

Of this Absolute, there are many finite manifestations. Of these, human social life is an outstanding example. Accordingly, Hegelian moral theory repudiates the concept of the abstract individual. Personality is realized only as the individual is drawn out of his loneliness, his abstract or false freedom, and participates in the life of the family, of the community, and of the state. Only through such membership and such participation does the individual realize for himself a life of significant content. Divorced from such a background, there is no human nature, no personality, no truly human individual. On the other hand, society or the state itself is no more than the "actually existing, realized moral life" of its members.

This doctrine, asserting as it does the almost organic interrelation of individual and society, can lead to many things in moral philosophy and in political theory. Emphasize society and an authoritarian theory is forthcoming; emphasize the individual and a centralized program of universal education and social welfare emerges. Thus Hegelian ethics can contribute to both the Right and the Left in political thought. But according to an orthodox Hegelian, both Right and Left falsify the doctrine by committing themselves to abstractions.

Nonetheless liberals have always felt uneasy when considering the Hegelian doctrine that the state, although affording the realization of the moral lives of its citizens, is not itself subject to moral obligation or to the moral judgment of an individual. This seems to the liberal to open the door to the least attractive form of absolutism, at once authoritarian and irresponsible. We must remember, however, that the Hegelian philosophy was viewed with suspicion and hostility by the reactionary European governments of the 1840's. This was partially because its emphasis upon the organic nature of society made difficult a defense of special interests pertaining to a landed aristocracy or to private institutions.

SUMMARY

Modern philosophy begins in Descartes with many distinct substances and with two opposed types of being, mind and extension,
the second subject to the strictest determinism, the first the seat of a
spontaneous and undetermined freedom. Furthermore, in its beginnings modern philosophy recognizes plurality and division everywhere, and is consistently baffled by the problem of explaining the
interaction of these many distinct substances which possess such
differing constitutions. Hegel denounces this pluralism as counter
to the spirit of reason, and accordingly impossible in a thoroughly
intelligible world. All entities are interdependent, and no one of
them exists or is truly knowable outside the systematic interconnection of them all, which interconnection *is* the Absolute itself. All
diversity or wealth of detail must be complemented by a unity that
overrules it, and it is the nature of this unity which the dialectical
method slowly reveals to us.

Mind and nature, subject and object, cannot be departmentalized
in Cartesian fashion. They must stand together. Mind or subject
appears as the organizing unity of nature, life, and history; thing or
object, as the variety of detail so organized. Mind is autonomous
when it realizes its inner nature to the full. Thus the Absolute
possesses complete autonomy or freedom, yet this does not conflict
with the law-abiding nature of its content, for such law is one of
the ways in which autonomous mind organizes its content. Final
cause is another.

For Hegel, it is clear, the Absolute Idea, the world spirit itself, is
an idea of development and progress. But it is important to recognize that, on the other hand, there is no progress of the Idea.
Consider as an instance of this the following mention of progress,
which indicates its prominence in the Hegelian scheme of things.[7]

The religious mind ... views the world as ruled by Divine Providence, and therefore correspondent with what it ought to be. But
this harmony between the 'is' and the 'ought to be' is not torpid
and rigidly stationary. Good, the final end of the world, has being,

[7] Hegel, *The Encyclopaedia of the Philosophical Sciences*, p. 373.

only while it constantly produces itself. And the world of spirit and the world of nature continue to have this distinction, that the latter moves only in a recurring cycle, while the former certainly also makes progress.

(The last sentence indicates that, for all his interest in develop-ment, Hegel did not anticipate the notion of organic evolution.)

Nullity and transitoriness constitute only the superficial features and not the real essence of the world. That essence is the notion *in posse* and *in esse:* And thus the world is itself the Idea, and all unsatisfied endeavor ceases when we recognize that the final pur-pose of the world is accomplished no less than ever accomplishing itself. Generally speaking, this is the man's way of looking; while the young imagine that the world is utterly sunk in wickedness, and that the first thing needful is a thorough transformation.

We may, accordingly, summarize Hegel's attitude toward process and development in the words of the English Hegelian, Bernard Bosanquet, who maintained that [8]

the foundational nature of all that is, while containing the infinite changes which are the revelation of its inexhaustible life, not con-finable within a single direction or temporal career, is not itself and as such engaged in a progress and mutation. . . .

As I have argued elsewhere, a being that has a purpose, a career, an alteration in time, is a different sort of being from the universe. It is one among others, a finite, a partial nature which, in the con-ditions which meet it in the world of all there is, finds stimuli, ends to attain, defects to make good, positive but partial conditions call-ing for completion. The universe is the *raison d'être* of all this. It is the ultimate real in which lies the fact that anything at all is and can be, and the ultimate characters which are, in virtue of that fact. Starting from the common ground that the universe is full of change and movement, we have staring us in the face the problem whether it can be described as, taken altogether, a movement or engaged in a movement. That would mean, as I understand, on any reasonable rendering, whether it was, to put it quite roughly at first, more like the ocean, or more like a river; whether it is, in its entire and funda-

[8] Bosanquet, *The Meeting of Extremes in Contemporary Philosophy*, p. 210, pp. 180-81. Macmillan & Co., London; The Macmillan Company, New York; 1921. Reprinted by permission of Ellen Bosanquet and The Macmillan Company.

mental being, engaged in a passage and departure from one type or determination of being to another which succeeds the former and excludes it.

Here we face St. Augustine's difficult statement, *"Non* in *tempore sed* cum *tempore finxit deus mundum."* God creates the world not *in* time but *along with* time. This is austere doctrine, extraordinarily difficult to conceive and impossible to picture in imagination. As we shall see, the philosophy of the last hundred years is profoundly concerned with these difficulties.

A little reflection will make clear that we are faced here with all the old problems of determinism and predestination in a new form.

A HEGELIAN POSTSCRIPT:
THE DIALECTICAL MATERIALISM OF KARL MARX

The Hegelian philosophy has enjoyed a wide influence and has contributed both form and matter to many schools of thought that are not usually classified as Hegelian. In some cases, this influence extends to ways of thought that deny the essentially Hegelian contribution. Outstanding among these is the theory of *dialectical materialism,* which has supplied a philosophical background for the social theory of modern Communism.

Hegelians have always been eager to apply the pattern of the dialectic to the historical development of social institutions and to the concepts of social value that accompany them. In short, it is in human history that the dialectic is found to be most clearly manifest. In later years, the Communists, who are in some respects followers of Hegel, have interpreted the opposition between social classes and the resolution of such conflict in social theory and practice as a dialectical development. The dominant class tends in time to undermine its own supremacy, and by the inadequacy of its vision and the narrowness of its practice to invite a movement that eventually supersedes it. The final synthesis in which all such class conflict would be overcome is conceived of as a society without class distinctions and without the institution of private property, upon which these distinctions are usually based. The Communists, however, under the leadership of Karl Marx, tend to interpret dialectical development along materialist lines.[9] They have no sympathy with Hegel's concept of the world mind, which they find much too close to the teaching of established religion to suit their anticlerical taste.

Whatever its value may be in the fields of economics and sociology, this truncated version of Hegel's dialectic lacks any great philosophical importance. It makes no significant or characteristic contribution to metaphysical or epistemological theory, and its champions, in this resembling their reactionary opponents, frequently substitute abuse for argument. Aside from reminding us emphatically that our religious and philosophical beliefs are often colored by our social and economic status, the Dialectical Materialist has little of philosophical significance to offer. But his ideas have taken on great historical importance, since they are now included in the ideology of Russian socialism. They therefore require some attention from the student of modern philosophy.

Dialectical Materialism was founded by Karl Marx, who began his philosophical career with a prolonged study of Hegel's work. Always suspicious of Hegel's concept of absolute spirit, Marx soon came to the conclusion that mind is a product of natural process. His friend Engels once summarized this position as follows: [10]

.. the material, sensuously perceptible world to which we ourselves belong is the only reality ... Our consciousness and thinking, however supra-sensuous they may seem, are the product of a material, bodily organ, the brain. Matter is not a product of mind, but mind itself is merely the highest product of matter.

[9] Karl Marx (1818-1883) studied law, then philosophy. His association with the various beginnings of labor movements forced him to change profession and residence often. He moved from Germany to Paris, to Belgium, to England. His analysis of economic history and his philosophical theories of the eventual downfall of capitalism inspired the Russian Revolution of 1919, and the vitality and contemporary importance of his philosophy are a spectacular proof that ideas may have far-reaching social consequences, that philosophy is not entirely divorced from practical affairs.

[10] Engels, *Ludwig Feuerbach and the Outcome of Classical German Philosophy*, ed. by C. P. Dutt, p. 25. International Publishers, New York, 1941. Reprinted by permission of the publisher. These lines are quoted from Engels by Joseph Stalin in his *Dialectical and Historical Materialism*, Eng. trans., International Publishers, New York, 1940.

Matter is described as the "objective reality given to us in sensation," also as "that which produces sensation." The Dialectical Materialists are not sufficiently interested in the theory of knowledge to concern themselves very seriously with the problem of reconciling these two descriptions of matter. After all, for them, philosophy is rather more an ideology supporting social action than a theory of being. Marx insisted upon this in his famous remark:

The philosophers have *interpreted* the world in various ways; the point however is to *change* it.[10a]

Engels describes Marx's reconstruction of the Hegelian philosophy as follows:[11]

The separation from the Hegelian school was here also the result of a return to the materialist standpoint. That means it was resolved to comprehend the real world—nature and history—just as it presents itself to everyone who approaches it free from preconceived idealist fancies. It was decided relentlessly to sacrifice every idealist fancy which could not be brought into harmony with the facts conceived in their own and not in a fantastic connection. And materialism means nothing more than this. But here the materialistic world outlook was taken really seriously for the first time and was carried through consistently—at least in its basic features—in all domains of knowledge concerned.

Hegel was not simply put aside. On the contrary, one started out from his revolutionary side, from the dialectical method. But in its Hegelian form this method was unusable. According to Hegel, dialectics is the self-development of the concept. The absolute concept does not only exist—where unknown—from eternity, it is also the actual living soul of the whole existing world.... According to Hegel, therefore, the dialectical development apparent in nature and history, i.e., the causal interconnection of the progressive movement from the lower to the higher, which asserts itself through all zigzag movements and temporary setbacks, is only a miserable copy of the self-movement of the concept going on from eternity, no one knows where, but at all events independently of any thinking human brain. This ideological reversal had to be done away with. We comprehended the concepts in our heads once more material-

[10a] *Ibid*. p. 84.
[11] *Ibid.*, pp. 43-44.

403

istically—as images of real things instead of regarding the real things as images of this or that stage of development of the absolute concept. Thus dialectics reduced itself to the science of the general laws of motion—both of the external world and of human thought—two sets of laws which are identical in substance, but differ in their expression in so far as the human mind can apply them consciously, while in nature and also up to now for the most part in human history, these laws assert themselves unconsciously in the form of external necessity in the midst of an endless series of seeming accidents. Thereby the dialectic of the concept itself became merely the conscious reflex of the dialectical motion of the real world and the dialectic of Hegel was placed upon its head; or rather, turned off its head, on which it was standing before, and placed upon its feet again.

For Marx, the laws governing the behavior of matter in motion produce a development comparable to Hegel's dialectic of history. This is not the result of the plan of any world spirit, nor of the attraction of some cosmic final cause, but simply the way in which matter changes from one relatively stable configuration to another. Marx thus constructed his philosophy of history in terms of efficient and material causes, without recourse to the final causality of Hegel's system. For Marx, matter is characterized by mass, extension, and inertia. It is the *subject* of all change, the principle of continuity in the world process. The states and configurations of matter in motion constitute the detail of the world system. This motion manifests a dialectical pattern. The dynamic configurations of matter tend to generate forces that undermine their stability and initiate new configurations markedly in contrast to their predecessors. We may recall the Ionian theory of natural process as swinging from one "opposite" to another. Indeed, Dialectical Materialists frequently quote Heraclitus with approval, despite his doctrine of *logos*. But the denial of final causation stands without qualification.

Even when surveying human history, Dialectical Materialists allow no exception to the metaphysical principle of the primacy of material and efficient causes. Ultimately, changes in thought and society are caused by changes in the material conditions and structures of social life. Thought and evaluation are simply more complex aspects of material process, conditioned and conditionable by adjustment within the environment that is their causal origin. Since thought is part of a historical, material process, it is not surprising that the stages of this process reappear as the laws of thought.

Social (and physical) history is a record of the constant dissolution of the relatively stable configurations of matter by the forces of their environments, and the following recombination, in the face of these environmental forces, of new configurations of greater stability. Past stabilities have constantly set up new environmental stresses that require a greater complexity and integration of every future stable configuration. The passage of time thus involves a constant progress toward complexity and integration, simply from the character of the material constituents of nature. This is reflected in the relation of the conditions and methods of agricultural and industrial production to the development of social life.[12]

In the social production which men carry on they enter into definite relations which are indispensable and independent of their will; these relations of production correspond to a definite stage of development of their material powers of production. The sum total of these relations of production constitutes the economic structure of society—the real foundation, on which rise legal and political forms of social consciousness.

The mode of production in material life determines the general character of the social, political, and spiritual processes of life. *It is not the consciousness of men that determines their existence, but on the contrary their social existence determines their consciousness.*

At a certain stage in their development, the material forces of production in society come into conflict with the existing relations of production—or—what is but a legal expression for the same thing—with the property relations within which they had been at work before. From forms of development of the forces of production, these turn into their fetters. Then comes the period of social revolution. With the change of the economic foundation, the entire immense superstructure is more or less rapidly transformed.

In considering such transformations the distinction should always be made between the material transformation of the economic con-

[12] Marx, *A Contribution to the Critique of Political Economy,* in *Selected Works of Karl Marx and Friedrich Engels,* ed. by C. P. Dutt, Vol. I, 356-57. International Publishers, 2 vols., 1939. Reprinted by permission of the publisher.

ditions of production, which can be determined with the precision of natural science, and the legal, political, religious, aesthetic or philosophical—in short, the ideological forms in which men become conscious of this conflict and fight it out. Just as our opinion of an individual is not based on what he thinks of himself, so can we not judge of such a period of transformation by its own consciousness; on the contrary, this consciousness must rather be explained from the contradictions of material life, from the existing conflict between the social forces of production and the relations of production.

This recognition of an inevitable dialectical pattern in history, combined with the conviction that changes in social thinking and law follow upon changes of the material conditions of their generating environment, provides a strong position from which to advocate material reform, in the interest of aiding the development of a more stable and tolerable future situation—which the passage of time will inevitably bring about. For any given present, however, the nature of this future social structure can be known only insofar as it can be seen in the present as the antithesis of the status quo. This antithesis will provide the impetus for altering the present system.

Marx's philosophy has retained practical importance largely because of the expression it gives to dissatisfaction with the inequities of any given present, backed by the conviction that their destruction will inevitably lead to a brighter future. The disequilibrium through which Marx thought that modern industrial society would bring about its own downfall was the class conflict resulting from the economic institution of capital. It seemed to him that the practice of granting an economic reward to persons who were nonproductive, but who claimed a lion's share of goods because they "owned" the means of production, would, as their profit was used to acquire further ownership, create an intolerable situation. As the concentration of wealth in the hands of a very few capitalistic monopolists was increased, a sense of common interests would be more keenly felt by the noncapitalist groups, under increasing economic pressure. This class consciousness on the part of the wage laborers (the proletariat) would lead to concerted demands for a share in ownership and in control of the means of production, which would be met with sharp repressive measures by the capitalist class. The upshot would be a revolution in which the proletariat (led by those technicians and intelligentsia whom economic hardships had cured of their habit of thinking of themselves as capitalists) would forcibly take over ownership of the means of production, and destroy the repressive political institutions that the capitalists had set up in their last-ditch defense of their class interests.[13]

Along with the constantly diminishing number of the magnates of capital, who usurp and monopolise all the advantages of this process of transformation, grows the mass of misery, oppression, slavery, degradation, exploitation; but with this too grows the revolt of the working-class, a class always increasing in numbers, and disciplined, united, organized by the very process of capitalist production itself. The monopoly of capital becomes a fetter upon the mode of production which has sprung up and flourished along with, and under it. Centralization of the means of production and socialisation of labour at last reach a point where they become incompatible with their capitalist integument. This integument is burst asunder. The knell of capitalist private property sounds. The expropriators are expropriated.

The capitalist mode of appropriation, the result of the capitalist mode of production, produces capitalist private property. This is the first negation of individual private property, as founded on the labour of the proprietor. But capitalist production begets, with the inexorability of a law of Nature, its own negation. It is the negation of negation. This does not re-establish private property for the producer, but gives him individual property based on the acquisitions of the capitalist era—*i.e.,* on co-operation and the possession in common of the land and of the means of production.

The transformation of scattered private property, arising from individual labour, into capitalist private property is, naturally, a process, incomparably more protracted, violent, and difficult, than the transformation of capitalistic private property, already practically resting on socialised production, into socialised property. In the former case, we had the expropriation of the mass of the people by a

[13] Marx, *Capital*, ed. by Friedrich Engels, trans. by Samuel Morse and Edward Aveling, pp. 836-37. Modern Library, 1936. Reprinted by permission of Random House.

few usurpers; in the latter, we have the expropriation of a few usurpers by the mass of the people.

As indicated above, Marx sees the dialectical flaw of capitalism, the source of its fundamental instability, as lying in its tendency toward monopoly of ownership and power. But, for Marx, this one-sided movement will necessarily be overcome by counter tendencies. The whole process is thought of as an inexorable, dialectical determinism, manifesting itself in irreconcilable social conflict. Many thinkers, whether liberal or conservative, who are interested primarily in the intelligent and cooperative solution of complex and delicate social and economic problems will view such a theory of determinism with suspicion and distaste. They will question both its historical authenticity and its social usefulness. After all, it may be argued, we surrender to a deterministic necessity only when we renounce any effort at solving our problems and "let nature take her course."

It is very likely true that capitalism, at least capitalism as we have known it in the last two centuries or so, is an unstable form of social organization. Its internal weakness is, in general, what the Marxist finds it to be. Capitalism is thus bound to be transformed dialectically *unless,* with a foresight and an intelligence that the Marxist refuses to recognize, it reforms itself and escapes a violent end, thus suspending the blind necessity of Dialectical Materialism. We may hope that the future of our civilization will not be left to the workings of uncontrolled forces, however "historical" or dialectical in nature. Such a development would involve unlimited and warlike conflict. After all, the violent destruction of the capitalist system through war and civil war seems unlikely to yield a new order more adequate and more stable than the old. Despite the doctrinaire predictions of the Dialectical Materialist, such drastic treatment might well be expected to kill the patient before effecting a cure. This seems especially true when we consider the extraordinarily destructive form that the warfare of the future appears likely to take. So considered, the outcome of modern European history seems hardly so certain a consummation as that which Marx envisaged a hundred years ago.

CHAPTER XIII

The Last Hundred Years

CRITICISM OF HEGELIAN MONISM

Throughout the nineteenth century, and in England and the United States until about the time of World War I, the Hegelian philosophy, in its several interpretations and reformulations, enjoyed a great prestige. Its comparatively recent decline has seemed to many people still active in philosophical circles something of a tragedy. A revival of Idealism based in principle upon Hegelian theory is still possible, although the present trend is away from this type of thought. This decline is owing largely to a fundamental difficulty that the Hegelians never succeeded in removing from their systems. This difficulty may be stated somewhat as follows:

According to the theory of internal relations, the Absolute or concrete universal cannot be adequately known *in abstracto;* that is, in schematic outline that omits detail. It follows, although Hegelians often dislike to admit it, that we cannot know what the Absolute is, because, lacking omniscience, we are not acquainted with the encyclopedic detail of information necessary for such a comprehensive vision. Can we then be quite certain that there *is* an Absolute? This is a grave problem for the Hegelian.

If the world is a system of reciprocity wholly internal in its interrelations, we can know it adequately only as a complete or concrete whole. To abstract any aspect from this whole is to falsify both that aspect and the world. But since we cannot avoid some measure of such abstraction, we can know nothing truly. Hegelian dialectic seems to leave us in skepticism. We do not know how far our present conclusions must be altered by further knowledge. So we hardly know where we stand. The Hegelian method undermines

Hegelian doctrine. We have been told by the Hegelians that there are degrees of truth. How true, then, is the theory of the degrees of truth? [1]

Hegelian Monism tended from the very start to invite a Pluralistic opposition. Many times throughout the nineteenth century the Pluralists attacked Hegelian idealism. In the early twentieth century, English and American Pluralists met with considerable success. They usually gathered under the banner of Realism. In modern times this term carries a new meaning. It does not necessarily indicate some form of Platonism, as it did in the Middle Ages. Rather it refers to any theory which holds that mind and its objects are distinct, in the sense that the knowing mind does not necessarily condition its object or in any way constitute its nature. The object known is not organically connected with the knowing mind, but is externally related to it.

We may argue that objects must be externally related to the activity of knowing mind; for, if the object depends in some way upon the act of knowing, then we may argue that the knower, by his very act of knowing, alters the object. But this seems to be counter to the very nature of reasoning, which must attempt not to alter the object studied, but to report upon the nature of things that it leaves unchanged. If the knowing mind changes its object by the very act of knowing, there will be no completely true knowledge, for the production of this knowledge will have altered the object known. Accordingly there must be some type of thinking that does not alter its object but simply apprehends it, just as it is in itself, even as it is when it stands wholly unknown.

If it is true that the mind is externally related to the object, the close-knit unity of the Hegelian Absolute is irreparably shattered. Furthermore, on this view nature has not depended upon mind, but can exist as quite independent of mind. This, we may suppose,

[1] To apply the theory of the degrees of truth to the very proposition that states the theory itself may seem to many a captious sort of criticism. But it is a type of criticism that the Hegelian philosophy seems especially to invite, for according to Hegel, the philosophy of absolute Idealism is itself a stage in the dialectical development of human thought. Hence it must be transcended; but we do not know in what direction the new advance will be made.

it must have done during the vast reaches of time before mind appeared in the evolution of life.

REALISM

Modern Realism teaches that objects may exist quite isolated from any mind that knows them. But when asked to define objects, when asked the question, "Just where shall we draw the line between extramental object and mental representation or interpretation of this object?" the Realists begin to disagree. Some follow Descartes and Locke in their distinctions between primary or extramental and secondary or representative qualities. A very few insist that even the secondary qualities of color and so on belong to the concrete, extramental objects; while others follow Kant in believing that strictly extramental properties of the object are to us unknown. Some recognize time or change as extramental as well as mental in its scope while they deny this in the case of space, which is said to be a matter of representative appearance. In fact, during this dispute, at one time or another virtually every possibility has been explored and every conceivable thesis has been maintained and again repudiated. Thus we cannot hope to report on all the shades of opinion concerning this problem. We may suggest, however, a few propositions that seem too reasonable to be dismissed.

1. There is something in the world besides the finite mind, and this something is not produced by that mind. Thus we *recognize* some aspects of the world instead of *creating* them.

2. There is no aspect of the world recognized by the finite mind which that mind does not interpret as well as recognize. But this interpretation is not sheer creation, since the mind may go astray if it is careless and fails to respect the objective elements before it.

3. This objective element is not the product of our minds; but whether it is itself ultimately mental or nonmental is a problem that we cannot solve solely by examining the nature of the cognitive situation or the relation of mind to object. If the objective element is mental, it is presumably teleological, and vice versa; but we can determine this, if at all, only by reading the evidence offered

by many branches of research. And many of these researches have little to do with the question of mind and object, of primary and secondary qualities, of appearance and reality and related problems.

Modern Realism in its minimal form—that is, as stated in proposition 1 above—is almost unquestionably true; yet we cannot from this proposition deduce the further proposition that reality is ultimately nonmental in nature. Nor, of course, can we establish the contrary—that reality as a whole is mental.

Modern Realism has hardly succeeded in constructing so complete and all-inclusive a philosophy as that of the Idealist followers of Hegel. Realism commanded attention at a time when the chief interest of the philosophical public was centered upon criticism of Idealism. In this negative or destructive phase of their work, the Realists were distinguished as keen critics. Once, however, the Idealist philosophy lost its dominant position, it became evident that Realism had fewer positive contributions to offer than many had supposed. There is, however, at least one contribution of importance for philosophical speculation that the modern Realists have originated.

This contribution is concerned with interpreting the biological theory of the evolution of living forms, which in the mid-nineteenth century so profoundly transformed European thinking. All modern philosophy has been in contact with the development of the special sciences, and the thinking of the last hundred years has been no exception. The first period of modern philosophy stood in reciprocal influence with the astronomical theories of Copernicus and Kepler. The work of these men resulted in a new understanding of the spatial structure of the physical world. The attention and the interest of philosophers were accordingly directed toward the concept of an infinite space or of an infinitely extended matter; and in such writers as Descartes and Spinoza the relation of this entity to other realities or aspects of reality was considered at length.

The seventeenth century had been deeply concerned with the geometry of the universe, and this preoccupation had a significant influence upon the beginnings of modern philosophy. In the nineteenth century, the attention of the learned world was gradually redirected. Time succeeded space in the center of philosophical attention. The vast age of the earth and of the solar system suggested by Laplace—and, even more disturbing at first, the vast age of life on the earth suggested by Lamarck and Cuvier, and rendered undeniable at last by Darwin and his successors—emphasized in a very spectacular way the importance of change, of development, and of growth.

This new world picture has gradually been included in our philosophy during the past century. Time or process has superseded space or extension, and occupies the more central position in our thought. We are now less inclined to identify a thing with the measurable extension or physical matter that "underlies" it. We are gradually recognizing that a thing is a process, a past proceeding into a future. We think in terms of temporal and historical backgrounds, of origins, and of destinations. In some systems of thought, the concept of events has taken the place formerly held by substance. If the term "substance" continues to be employed, its meaning is altered to indicate that it refers rather more to a continuity of change than to an underlying permanence.

Such a view of things reminds one at first glance of the flux philosophy of Heraclitus. This we have mentioned above. But there is a significant difference. For Heraclitus, change appears as a periodic fluctuation between opposites. But in recent years, cosmic change has been interpreted as opening upon an unknown, even an undetermined, future. Profound transformation of a nonrepetitive type is its very essence, as the panorama of organic evolution so spectacularly illustrates. Repetitive cycles may be included, but they characterize only the surface texture of cosmic process.

In the following pages we shall have occasion to mention four thinkers whose work illustrates the new attitude just described. These are Samuel Alexander, William James, Henri Bergson, and Alfred North Whitehead. Let us first examine Alexander's theory of emergent evolution and consider it in the light of the foregoing comments.

The theory of *emergent evolution* is but one of several attempts that have been made since the middle of the nineteenth century to include the great biological theory of the evolution of organisms and the origin of living species within the limits of a comprehensive philosophy of nature. In the form given it by Charles Darwin in 1859, this theory recognized the appearance of new species, descended from older ones, as the result of the many slight and fortuitous variations whereby offspring tend to differ from their forebears from generation to generation. Of these variants the less sturdy examples are eliminated in the competitive struggle for existence. The elimination of the unfit or the survival of the fittest (better of the more fit) became the watchwords of all philosophy drawing its inspiration from biological theory.

Since in general only the stronger or better-equipped members of a species survive, and since, at least according to Darwinian theory, variations that render these members stronger tend to be inherited, there is a progress toward the appearance of organisms better equipped or better adapted to their environment. This progress constitutes evolution. On the Darwinian theory this evolution is the result of no conscious plan or purpose but of the virtually automatic elimination of weaker organisms. Thus for many years the theory of evolution seemed to support a philosophy opposed to theism, and to any theory that recognizes plan or purpose in the development of living species.

Emergent evolutionists do not deny the fundamentals of this theory of natural selection, just mentioned. Many stages of evolution are to be explained in this way. But the emergent evolutionists point to certain crises in the development of life, say, the origin of life itself, or the appearance of consciousness, or such lesser phenomena as the origin of pure science, or the origin of the sense of beauty. All these developments may be called emergents in that they present something quite distinct from what has gone before them and do not seem to be the result of a very gradual accumulation of minor and fortuitous variations. On the contrary, they involve the emergence of a new principle of organization. Hence an interpretation of evolution is advanced that recognizes a principle of development quite distinct from the Darwinian theory, which it supplements.

Let us consider Alexander's work in greater detail.[2] He begins not with a theory of evolution, nor even with a theory of life, but with certain propositions concerning the nature of being in general. As a philosopher interested in evolution, Alexander is naturally impressed by the fact of change. He finds change at the very heart of all reality. This change or motion he describes as *space-time*.

ALEXANDER'S THEORY OF EMERGENT EVOLUTION

For Alexander, the universe is composed of events. Events happen or occur. The togetherness of events is space-time. Neither space nor time exists without the other, nor is either conceivable apart from the other. The two are united as motion. Without space, time would have to be, as in Descartes's universe, constantly and completely recreated, for the past would perish completely. The past is with the present, owing to the fact that its pattern endures from one time to another; and Alexander sees such pattern as fundamentally spatial. Without time, nothing would happen in space; and for Alexander, this means that there would be in space no principle of differentiation, no structure. Together space and time appear as motion, which is the stuff of all things. Separated, space and time are lifeless abstractions of no significance. If we care to employ the "human metaphor," Alexander thinks that we may call time the "mind" of space and space the "body" of time. Time is the active and productive, space the passive and conservative, element. Remove space and the moments of time, disembodied, are without orientation and background. Remove time and space, unnerved, is without initiative, change, or structure.

According to Alexander, any existing thing is a *substance*. By this Alexander means that it is a piece of space which is the scene of succession. Thus "a straight line is an extreme instance of the life of a substance." But, generally speaking, substances have more body to them than straight lines can boast of. Such complex sub-

[2] Samuel Alexander (1859-1938) an English philosopher, studied under the Idealists at Oxford before becoming a leader of Realist thought. He taught philosophy at the University of Manchester.

stances are things or contours of space within which take place the motions correlated to the qualities of the things.

A substance, then, is an enduring contour of space time. Alexander at times calls substances singular universals, for their very presence in space-time or motion bears witness to the fact that they bear a plan or pattern within them that is not exhausted at any point or at any instant. Now throughout space time we find that substances bear distinct resemblances to one another; this fact drives us to the contemplation of the generic universals. The nature of these may be also expressed in terms of space time. Hence a generic universal is a constitutive plan of motion or action, as Alexander phrases it, a "habit of space-time." Thus universals are spatiotemperal in character, although not limited to any given portion of space-time. Substance is a context of motion that develops within itself—what Alexander calls empirical qualities, such as color, sound, life. Each quality is in correlation with certain motions. (Alexander consciously speaks in Spinozistic terms.) As the path of evolution is traversed, configurations of motion attain such a complexity that new qualities arise. Thus life emerges from the inorganic and thought from living things. These qualities we must accept as purely empirical, unpredictable features, accept with "natural piety," as Alexander puts it.[3]

The higher emergent has been described as based on a complexity of the lower existents; thus life is a complex of material bodies and mind of living ones. Ascent takes place, it would seem, through complexity. But at each change of quality the complexity as it were gathers itself together and is expressed in a new simplicity. The emergent quality is the summing together into a new totality of the component materials. Just in this way, as our thoughts become more and more complex, some new conception arises in the mind of a discoverer which brings order into the immense tangle of facts and simplifies them and becomes the starting-point for fresh advances in knowledge; or in social affairs some vivifying idea like democracy arises to create as it were a new moral order, in

[3] Samuel Alexander, *Space, Time, and Deity*, Vol. II, pp. 70-71. Macmillan & Co., London; The Macmillan Company, New York; 2 vols., 1922. Reprinted by permission of the executors of the Alexander Estate and The Macmillan Company.

which distinctions and divergences arise which demand in their turn a new practical key. Somewhat in this fashion complexes of one stage of existence gather themselves for a new creation, and additional complexities mean new simplifications.

It follows as part of this relation of the higher level to the lower, as an empirical emergent from "material" already endowed with its own quality, that the empirical qualities of the "material" are carried up into the body of the higher level but not into its new quality. Life is based on material existents which have colour or smell or weight. But life is not itself coloured, nor, except in a metaphor, sweet.

Thus Alexander tries to undermine the materialist reduction of life and mind to inorganic matter while avoiding the necessity of postulating a vital or mental energy.[4]

The thing called mind has not in respect of its mentality the lower empirical qualities. Energy is an empirical quality of matter and does not belong to mind or life. Yet it is easy to interpret the phrases "vital" or "mental energy" as the energy of the material equivalents; and in this way, be it observed, the difficulties of the application of the principle of conservation of energy to life and mind disappear.

The novel nature of each emergent cannot be predicted. In this matter Alexander holds true to his analogy of the growth of knowledge and artistic creation. However, the spatiotemporal configuration of the world seems to him predetermined and, granted a calculator with sufficient breadth of insight, predictable. But unless he lived to observe them, this calculator could not predict what qualities would be evoked by the complexes he predicts in space-time.

Mind plays a comparatively limited role in Alexander's universe. He maintains that even the secondary qualities are not dependent upon mind but actually resident in their objects. Thus although the objects are presented to the mind, they are not subject to it. To say that they are, he thinks, involves a failure to recognize the distinction between the act of mind, which is stimulated by a medium, such as light or sound, and the nonmental external object.

4 *Ibid.*, p. 71.

Although denying that mind is more than an empirical quality of space-time, Alexander finds in reality as a whole a nisus toward better things. The world, he thinks, is always working to give birth to new qualities better than those it has already produced. He finds in the qualities a rising scale of perfection. Perfection is a matter of wealth of organization and close interrelation of parts. In the life of man, perfection is most manifest in moral autonomy or self-legislation. Toward a fuller perfection, which is to be expressed in new qualities, the world is being drawn into the nisus. The new quality with which the universe is big Alexander calls deity. God is the universe possessing deity; and religion is based upon "a brute sentiment for deity," by which we feel that we are being drawn toward the next emergent and that we contribute toward it. In the religious sentiment we realize through our whole constitution of body and mind, rather than through any specific faculty, that in the forward movement [5]

due to the onward sweep of Time our minds with their substructure of body are caught, and our religious response is at once the mark that we are involved in that nisus, and that our minds contribute in their part towards it. . . . The whole world with its real tendency to deity stirs in us from the depths of our nature a vague endeavour or desire which shadows forth its object. Then intellect comes into play, and discovers in detail the characters of this object, and finds at last what it truly is, the tendency of the world forwards towards a new quality.

Each quality is related to one below it as mind to body, the lower quality having been drawn to an intricate spatiotemporal complexity out of which sprang the new emergent. Mind, thinks Alexander, will be related to the next emergent as body is in its turn related to mind. Religion is, then, an elemental feeling that the world is making something out of us that will surpass us in perfection. It is, of course, impossible to predict the new emergent. There is, as we have noticed, in Alexander's universe an element of the unpredictable, but this is confined to the nature of the empirical qualities. Within the limits of emergence, even the qualities behave with an

[5] *Ibid.*, Vol. II, p. 377.

orderly necessity. Accordingly Alexander does not shoot his universe full of the unpredictable, but limits its scope to the emergence of certain qualities.

The nisus of space-time is not reflective nor even mental in character. Nonetheless space-time "elaborates without forethought a 'hierarchy of ministration' which if it were produced by mind would imply a vast or all-wise forethought or providence." In the course of evolution some types of life are crushed by others. "Competition is the means to the supremacy of the adapted over the unadapted types and brings value into being by the rejection of unvalue. Deity, the new emergent, arises as the outcome of the onward sweep of all that is persistent and counts in the economy of the world." Thus by a sort of blind natural selection space-time perfects the type of its offspring.

We have seen that the restless productivity of primordial motion, inspired though it is by the nisus toward deity, is unreflective and unconscious. On the question: Is there mind at the root of things? Alexander comments: [6]

For we who ask the question are products of the process of creation, and we dare not speak of the universe in terms of its parts.... But if we think of the world as primordially a spirit, and not less of a spirit than ourselves but more of one, as we necessarily do if we indulge in such description as I have named, we are not securing simplicity, but only interpreting the simple by the complex.... The simple world [the ultimate] may still contain its analogue to mind, but that mind will be more and not less elementary than ours.

Bertrand Russell has advanced a shrewd objection to the theory of emergence with particular emphasis upon its religious aspect.[7]

[6] Samuel Alexander, "Artistic Creation and Cosmic Creation," in *Proceedings of the British Academy,* Vol. XIII (1927), p. 262. Reprinted by permision of the British Academy and the Oxford University Press. For critical comment on Alexander's treatment of the place of mind in reality, see above, page 98.

[7] Bertrand Russell, Earl Russell (1872-   ), logician, mathematician, and prolific writer on social problems, his views on which are almost uniformly radical. Along with A. N. Whitehead, Russell published the now famous *Principia Mathematica,* in which an effort was made to treat mathematical axioms as identical with the first principles of logic. Russell stood for a time in defense of a reconstruction of Platonic realism. He now stands closer to the Logical Positivists.

His argument runs something as follows: The defenders of this theory tell us that each new emergent quality is unpredictable; in other words, that nature is advancing into the unknown. Still, they seem quite certain that each new emergence as it hovers over the horizon of futurity deserves to be styled deity. As Russell tersely expresses it, "in order to escape from determinism, prediction is made impossible, and yet the adherents of this theory predict the future existence of god." Perhaps it is wiser to admit that the emergent evolutionists' belief in deity is as much a matter of mystical faith as of reasoning.

ABSOLUTISM AND THE "BLOCK UNIVERSE"

One of the more popular and more widely discussed issues involved in the conflict of Absolutism, Realism, and Pluralism is that of time and eternity, or becoming and being. This problem is aggravated by our modern concern for the reality of motion, change, and time. We are inclined to suspect that Hegel and the absolutists have been too willing to ignore this reality, or to transmute it into something else. If, after all, sensuous perception and practical experience are to be our chief guides, we must recognize temporal change as the most spectacular feature of our world, whose existence seems to be the constant production of an unalterable past. If, on the other hand, we acknowledge reason or understanding as an autonomous power of the mind that reflects the most prominent outlines and the essential structure of the world, we are likely to think of change as the object of our incomplete, sensuous apprehension. As we advance from sensuous experience to a rational comprehension, the world is revealed as an unchanging reality of which process is but an appearance. Mathematical forms and natural laws are then looked upon as unalterable, and our ability to predict the future leads us to treat it as an existent object, out of reach of our senses but actually open to reason and to understanding and even as present to them.

Thus the great medieval thinkers such as Augustine and Aquinas thought of world history as present to God's eternal vision. According to Boëthius, such eternity may be described as the "interminable and perfect possession of life as a simultaneous whole." Spinoza and Leibniz are in essential agreement. But by the Empiricist and the Pluralist, who consider experience to be sounder than rational speculation, the fact of change tends to be acknowledged as final, in no sense as the appearance of a simultaneous or nontemporal reality. Hegel sides with the Rationalists in this matter. He advances even further when he tells us that every bit of reality, past, present, or future, is inseparably bound up with every other bit in a network of internal, organic relation.

The Absolutist's conception of eternity in its contrast with our experience of time may be crudely illustrated in the following way: Suppose that we are in a canoe paddling around the bend in a river. As we paddle along, we see, say, first a stand of trees, then a house, and then, as we come fully around the bend, a little hill on the horizon. These objects appear to us one after the other; that is, in temporal series. Suppose, however, that we survey the same landscape from above, as from an airplane. River, trees, house, and hill will appear all at once. Now let us stretch our imaginations and suppose that from our airplane, now of course a "metaphysical" airplane, we can survey all at once not only the features of the land-scape but also the *trip* of a canoe on the river, the incidents of the trip being present to us all at once just as the features of the land-scape were seen from the airplane. In the Absolute mind, however, the incidents of the trip are related internally one to another, so that the mutual interpenetration and dependence is greater than that which we might observe among the objects of the landscape. According to such theory, which follows directly upon Hegelian doctrine, all history, both what we call past and what we call future, may be considered as a single dramatic whole, not unfinished and in the making, but completely present or "given" to the cosmic mind.

By many Pluralists this view is held to be equally as distasteful as it is erroneous. It seems to involve the thesis that for God or the cosmic mind "nothing happens." The world appears then to be what William James chose to call a "block universe" without an "open" future; past, present, and future existing all of a piece. According to this view, all events enjoy but one status, which seems to us identical with that which we attribute to the events of past history, where the outcome of every event is as definitely fixed as are its previous conditions. It is hard to think of human beings as choosing between alternatives in such a world, where every outcome is as fixed as every past event. But it is hard to believe that we do not in our decisions actually contribute to the growth of a future world. We all believe that as conscious agents we influence our world instead of being carried along in a predetermined stream. Thus arises a new form of anti-Rationalism and anti-Absolutism: the philosophy of novelty, which insists that there is something new about every event so that it transcends its past. This means that although the new event is in contact with its past, and to some degree conforms to limitations already established, it is not wholly determined by anything, past or future. It enjoys an individuality of its own that is not predictable from any vantage point in the past. Here the central idea of emergence has been applied not only to the origin of new species and of new living forms but to the nature of every concrete event.

Thus, for example, a line of poetry may carry on the meanings that earlier lines have introduced; also its metrical scheme and its rhymed ending may fit into a pattern already set up; but if it is a successful one, the line has a character that adds something to the poem. In this sense it has independence, and it has individuality. It is a creation and nowise a mere restatement of something established in the past. In the production of such a central novelty, time and change appear as ultimately real. If such novelty did not arise, the "block universe" would be an unquestionable fact. Let us consider Henri Bergson's discussion of this point.[8]

[8] Henri Bergson, *Creative Evolution*, pp. 340-41, trans. by Arthur Mitchell, pp. 340-41. Henry Holt & Co., New York, 1911. This and a later quotation are reprinted by permission of the publisher. The first italics in paragraph two are added.

Henri Bergson (1859-1941), French philosopher and psychologist, from 1901 to 1921 taught at the Collège de France. He carried on the Romantic tradition of philosophy, not only in doctrine but also in the highly imaginative style of his prose, which abounds in metaphor and analogy and in happily chosen examples. The student will find his *Introduction to Metaphysics* (1912) a helpful work with which to begin a study of Bergson.

When a child plays at reconstructing a picture by putting together the separate pieces in a puzzle game, the more he practices, the more and more quickly he succeeds. The reconstruction was, moreover, instantaneous, the child found it ready-made, when he opened the box on leaving the shop. The operation, therefore, does not require a definite time, and indeed, theoretically, it does not require any time. That is because the result is given. It is because the picture is already created, and because to obtain it requires only a work of recomposing and rearranging—a work that can be supposed going faster and faster, and even infinitely fast, up to the point of being instantaneous. But, to the artist who creates a picture by drawing it from the depths of his soul, time is no longer an accessory; it is not an interval that may be lengthened or shortened without the content being altered. The duration of his work is part and parcel of his work. To contract or to dilate it would be to modify both the psychical evolution that fills it and the invention which is its goal. The time taken up by the invention, is one with the invention itself. It is the progress of a thought which is changing in the degree and measure that it is taking form. It is a vital process, something like the ripening of an idea.

The painter is before his canvas, the colors are on the palette, the model is sitting—all this we see, and also we know the painter's style: do we foresee what will appear on the canvas? We possess the elements of the problem; we know in an abstract way, how it will be solved, for the portrait will surely resemble the model and will surely resemble also the artist; but the *concrete solution brings with it that unforeseeable nothing which is everything in a work of art.* And it is this nothing that takes time. Nought as matter, it creates itself as form. The sprouting and flowering of this form are stretched out on an unshrinkable duration, which is one with their essence. So of the works of nature. Their novelty arises from an internal impetus which is progress or succession, which confers on succession a peculiar virtue or which owes to succession the whole of its virtue—which, at any rate, makes succession, or *continuity of interpenetration* in time, irreducible to a mere instantaneous juxtaposition in space. This is why the idea of reading in a present state of the material universe the future of living forms, and of unfolding now their history yet to come, involves a veritable absurdity. But this absurdity is difficult to bring out, because our memory is accustomed to place alongside of each other, in an ideal space, the terms it perceives in turn, because it always represents *past* succession in the form of juxtaposition. It is able to do so, indeed, just because the past belongs to that which is already invented, to the dead, and no longer to creation and to life. Then, as the succession to come will end by being a succession past, we persuade ourselves that the duration to come admits of the same treatment as past duration. that it is, even now, unrollable, that the future is there, rolled up, already painted on the canvas. An illusion, no doubt, but an illusion that is natural, ineradicable, and that will last as long as the human mind!

Bergson concludes: *"Time is invention or it is nothing at all."*

What is true of the work of art is in lesser degree true of every event, and especially true of the decisions or voluntary actions of every human being. As Professor Whitehead, in this respect almost a disciple of Bergson, put it: [9]

My unity—which is Descartes's 'I am'—is my process of shaping this welter of material into a consistent pattern of feelings. The individual enjoyment is what I am in my role of a natural activity, as I shape the activities of the environment into a new creation, which is myself at this moment; and yet, as being myself, it is a continuation of the antecedent world. If we stress the role of the environment, this process is causation. If we stress the role of my immediate pattern of active enjoyment, this process is self-creation. If we stress the role of the conceptual anticipation of the future whose existence is a necessity in the nature of the present, this process is the teleological aim at some ideal in the future. This aim, however, is not really beyond the present process. For the aim at the future is an enjoyment in the present. It thus effectively conditions the immediate self-creation of the new creature.

This creative or productive activity of the self is thought to be incompatible with Absolutism, which can hardly grant such independence to the concrete individual. The passage from Whitehead just quoted is important in that it presents his belief that causation,

[9] Alfred North Whitehead, *Modes of Thought,* p. 228. The Macmillan Company, New York, 1938. Reprinted by permission of the publisher.

Alfred North Whitehead (1861-1947) has been a lecturer at Trinity College, Cambridge, and in later years a professor at Harvard University. Besides offering an acute criticism of scientific methods and formulating the presuppositions of modern science, Whitehead constructed a brilliant system of speculative philosophy, of which the above quotation is an example. One beginning an examination of Whitehead's thought will do best to turn to his *Science and the Modern World,* where both the analytical and the speculative sides of his work are present in their simpler form.

creation, purpose, and selfhood are not distinct from one another as regards the locus of their embodiment in the world. One and the same pattern of events can be seen as embodying causality, selfhood, and purpose. No one of these is more fundamental or "more real" than the others. Every event is partially the continuation of some pattern already present in the actual world. It is also itself, it has qualities of its own, and it "makes toward" the future, in which its fundamental patterns may be preserved. Thus for Whitehead the concourse of events in nature is at once equally deterministic, pluralistic, and teleological. We need not talk of nature as if it were wholly *subject* to causal law. Nature is just as much subject to selfhood and to purpose as it is to causation. The attempts to reduce purpose to causation, and causation to purpose, are the vices of Materialists and Idealists respectively. We have no reason to emphasize one at the expense of the other. Both are primary.

Again, nature is essentially a matter of process. We must not think of nature as something that *undergoes* change, but as something actually made up of events. There is no concrete reality that is not essentially both changeable and changing in all its concrete aspects. Such a philosophy need not, as its enemies argue, deny that reality offers any aspect of permanence. The point is simply that every concrete event, as well as every concrete thing, has an individuality of its own that is distinct from and not wholly dependent upon eternal laws and principles. But this does not reduce the latter to the status of an illusion. As a matter of historical fact, a philosophy of change is not incompatible with Platonism, or at least with acceptance of the reality of the Platonic forms, those "eternal objects" which, themselves not subject to change, are forever reflected in the concrete flux.

A NEW CONCEPT OF SPACE

Whitehead sometimes describes his philosophy as a theory of nature conceived as a "creative advance." The importance of time as the emergence of novelty is emphasized. A new concept of space is also involved. He recognized that the concept of "location" or "place" is basic to any application of philosophical theory to concrete experience. One of the most striking and basic speculative suggestions in his philosophy is that our traditional notion of location requires revision. Since Aristotle included the "place where" among his categories, no basic revision of the notion of place has been widely accepted until Whitehead's time. Much of our thinking operates through spatial diagrams and metaphors. Thus a new notion of location may be expected to mark a break with tradition, and to open new ways of relating concepts in our thought.

Our common sense in the twentieth century includes the notion that space is "separative," that is, disconnecting or holding apart things which exist in different places. (This is very likely a belated acceptance by common sense of Descartes's conviction that the realm of extended substance was made up of separate locations, like the points of a co-ordinate grid, so that the relations of spatial events were exactly like the relations of points in his analytic geometry.) Whitehead's basic objections to this view were twofold. First, our immediate experience with nature seems to indicate that events are more closely connected than the traditional notion that a radically different place contains a radically different event can explain. Second, if time is thought of as similar to space, the future, having a different "location" from the present, will be essentially disconnected from it, and scientific prediction will be inexplicable.

The error involved, according to Whitehead, is the result of our paying attention to only one of the aspects of space as it enters into our concrete experience—"abstracting" its separative character, and then mistakenly believing that the abstraction contains everything that is to be found in the concrete picture. A spatial point is not one of the elements we encounter in concrete experience; it is a high-order abstraction, which we derive from experience by leaving a great deal out; and by adding togther many such abstractions, we cannot recapture the important aspects of reality that were deliberately omitted in their formation. It is a conviction of certain romantic poets, and one which our own experience will confirm, that space not only holds concrete things apart, but also in some sense fuses them together.

An event and its context are not really completely independent. Thus a poet sees the barren mountain as giving an air of somberness to the entire surrounding landscape; a historian sees society as giving a certain color to the imagination of the individual in each historical era. Recent research in biology suggest that an individual organism cannot be simply separated from its environment; the two interpenetrate in such a way that the environment helps to make the organism what it is, and the organism in turn helps to make the environment what *it* is. Experience acquaints us with a "prehensive" as well as a "separative" character of space—things are held and fused together by proximity, as well as held sharply apart by distance.

If we were to abstract the prehensive instead of the separative character of space, we should have to say that all events in space and time interpenetrate so tightly that one cannot describe an entity without describing its entire environment, since the environment entity separation is not a sharp one, although our common-sense notion of simple location leads us to overlook their real interpenetration. We would then have to think about each thing as present throughout space, as diffusely located, since we can say what it is only by describing its diffused effect on other things, and their converse effects on it. The "thing" then ceases to be thought of as exactly here and now. On the contrary, it is thought of as existing throughout a diffused network of relationships in space and time.

Such a view of location would, of course, also be an abstraction that would overlook part of our concrete experience. It would not do justice to the separative character that space certainly possesses. A purely prehensive space would be too chaotic to make any unified account of thought or nature possible. If we again compare this abstract view with concrete fact, we find that while aspects of a thing are spread through space as a whole, and are there effective in making other things what they are, there is nonetheless a center of disturbance, a source of diffusion, which, while we cannot give it an exact simple location, unifies and holds together the diffused pattern of aspects.

For example, the chair at which I am looking is, as a part of my experience, really influencing my present physical state and making it what it is. The prehensive character of space is effective here, involving my nature with a part or aspect of the near-by chair. But although the chair is a constitutive part of my total existence at the moment, I am not tempted nor likely to *confuse* myself with the chair, and think of it as an indispensable part of me. On the contrary, while I experience the chair as present to my mind, it appears to have come in from the outside, so to speak; the separative character of space allows me to feel my relation to the chair as one of difference; I somehow perceive that I am not at the center of the radiating influences which constitute the chair, whereas I am at the center of the pattern of effects on my environment which constitutes *me*.

This joint perception of presence and difference Whitehead calls the *modal* character of space; patterns of influence are held together about a unifying center, and differ in intensity as we approach their periphery. This concept of modal location seems to take account of both of the characteristics of space that are important in our concrete experience. The things in my environment are present in the pattern unified and held together about the center of my experience; but some of these ingredients of my experience carry with them a feeling of external reference, a felt pull toward another center of unity to which they belong.

If we inspect some of our common ways of thinking about things, we can see that it makes a good deal of difference whether our location of them is simple or modal. Traditional logic, for example, is geared to operate in a world of separate, simply located substances (Aristotle names isolation in place and in thought as two characteristics of substance), which retain their complete identities regardless of variation in the relations into which they enter. If George sits next to Jane, he still will be "substantially" the same old George.

On the contrary, if there are no simple, separately boxed things in concrete fact, and if the identity of each thing involves the relations into which that thing enters with objects around it, then logical description must give up the sharp break between substances (conveniently made by nature to serve as the subjects of propositions) and attributes, including relations (conveniently made to serve as predicates). Not nature, but the abstracting activity of the mind, paying attention to space as separative at the expense of space as modal, is responsible for this sort of logical classification. A satisfactory logic for Whitehead's philosophy must therefore be relational; that is, the concept of relation must be central in logic, as it is basic in nature.

When we think about the relation of the students to an elementary-school class, we think of each student as "simply located" at his desk, and may preserve the neatness of this abstract way of representing the student's relation to the class as a whole by nailing the desk to the floor. One of the discoveries of contemporary educators is that if classroom equipment is left movable, the spatial arrangements can be adapted to influences in the teaching situation, and pupils will participate more effectively in a group where they are not so mechanically isolated as members.

When we think about the relation of the individual as part to society as a whole, we again employ a metaphor of space. If we conceive the members of a community, though close together, as separated within their community's spatial organization, our social concepts presuppose a real independence of the individual and society, which does not adequately take account of concrete fact. Thus we overlook the very features of life that make the difference between a society and an anarchy. Sometimes, on the other hand, this relation has been conceived in terms of community as a spatial relation of pure prehension, an abstract way of thinking that leaves no room for independence or individuality; and in practice this is totalitarian.

If we think of an individual as modally located in the community, our metaphor escapes both these distorted oversimplifications of the concrete situation. He is not simply an isolated creature who lives at 16 West 20th Street, third floor rear, with a completely self-contained personality and physique that are only accidentally related to environment. His actions and their effect on other citizens cannot be simply localized in his apartment; by the things he does, he effects the whole community. Neither is the individual, however, to be thought of as an amorphous entity, molded by and entirely reflecting the external fields of force generated by the structure of the community as a whole, with its inherited customs and modes of thought. He is the center of a diffuse set of influences that lend their color to and help to form the entire community. He is made what he is partly by the fact that the materials from which he builds a unified personality are the constitutive effects on him of his society. But the unification of those constitutive effects which constitutes his individuality, and colors his environment, is distinctively the individual's own.

PRAGMATISM

The revolt against Absolutism that characterized the philosophy of the early twentieth century included, along with the several schools of Realism and evolutionary philosophy, a type of philosophy known as Pragmatism, which flourished especially in the United States. This way of thought constitutes as complete a reversal of the doctrine of Absolutism as it is possible to conceive. The philosophy of Hegel, as also that of Plato, is repudiated virtually in toto by the more extreme Pragmatists. Pragmatism resembles the philosophy of the ancient Sophists rather more closely than any other form of thought. Like the Sophist, the Pragmatist does not believe that mind is equipped to reflect or to reproduce the structure of the universe. But the Pragmatist goes beyond the ancient Sophist, since he is able to employ certain concepts borrowed from modern biology. Thus sensitivity, thought, and voluntary decision are described as instruments by means of which the organism guides itself in the struggle for survival. Mind is an organ of great power, since it aids the organism not only in adapting himself to his environment, but, by controlling nature, in shaping the environment itself to his own needs. But mind is a weapon, it is not a mirror, of nature.

The Pragmatist differs from the Sophist not only because he is able to draw upon modern biology, but also because he has, like so many modern thinkers, developed a deep sense of social obligation and of social solidarity. The Sophist combines his theory of knowledge, which is very like that of the Pragmatist, with an extreme individualism in ethics. The ancient Sophist boasted of his clever and self-seeking individualism, but the Pragmatist is likely to be a socialist in politics, and to be proud of the "social significance" of his work.

In its early stages, particularly in the writings of William James,[10] Pragmatism was committed to the thesis that any belief the acceptance of which seems to further the efficiency and abundance of human life is, for that reason, justified. Such beliefs were considered pragmatically sound, or even pragmatically "true." James included belief in God and in the freedom of the will among such pragmatically valuable doctrines. But more recent Pragmatism has veered away from such unorthodox apologies for traditional beliefs. The philosophy of William James may be called a humanistic Pragmatism, since it attempted to preserve those aspects of our culture which are essential to our ethical and religious beliefs; while the more recent type may be styled a skeptical or utilitarian Pragmatism, since it is primarily interested in furthering social efficiency and, in general, is suspicious of moral and religious tradition.

According to this latter type of Pragmatism, the hypotheses of science are important not because of their truth value (after all, their truth is never final), but because of the power over nature with which they equip us. Like the extreme Empiricist, the Pragmatist interprets a law of nature as a shorthand formula for the prediction of phenomena. All scientific thought, indeed all thought that has not been perverted by an outworn philosophy, looks toward the future as its natural field of interest. Purely disinterested contemplation of the past or of the "nature of reality" is biologically useless, and accordingly a perversion of thought. Mind is not built to picture past or present, but to control the future. Thus Pragmatism constitutes a philosophy of the practical, since it does not

10 William James (1842-1910) doctor of medicine, psychologist and philosopher, brother of the novelist Henry James, taught at Harvard from 1880 to 1907. In philosophy he furthered the development of Pragmatism, and in psychology raised many problems, particularly those concerning the nature of consciousness. James is famous for the informal clarity and the literary charm of his writings.

recognize the importance of "pure" or intellectual contemplation pursued for its own sake.

For the Pragmatist, there is no theory of the universe. Strictly speaking, there is no point in asking what the term "universe" means, and there are no grounds for inquiry concerning such a thing as "nature" or the "world as a whole." Science and culture can supply us only with instruments and attitudes for facing the future. So-called pure or theoretical philosophy, as opposed to practical technique, is neither true nor false. For truth belongs only to propositions as they are practically verified, when they lead to successful activity, when, so to speak, they "work."

A philosophy like that of Plato's theory of ideas, which describes an unseen world, cannot be practically tested. Such a philosophy can therefore be neither true nor false. Strictly speaking, it is not for the Pragmatist a product of genuine intellect. The pragmatic concept of intelligence is reflected in the following passage from John Dewey.[11]

Common sense regards intelligence as having a purpose, and knowledge as amounting to something. I once heard a physicist, quite innocent of the pragmatic controversy, remark that the knowledge of a mechanic or farmer was what the Yankee called gumption —acknowledgment of things in their belongings and uses, and that to his mind natural science was gumption on a larger scale: the convenient cataloguing and arranging of a whole lot of things with reference to their most efficacious services. Popularly, good judgment is judgment as to the relative values of things: good sense is horse sense, ability to take hold of things right end up, to fit an instrument to an obstacle, to select resources apt for a task. To be reasonable is to recognize things in their office as obstacles and as resources. Intelligence, in its ordinary use, is a practical term; ability to size up matters with respect to the needs and possibilities of the various situations in which one is called to do something; capacity

[11] John Dewey, *Philosophy and Civilization*, p. 41. G. P. Putnam's Sons, 1931, copyright by John Dewey. Reprinted by permission of the publisher.

John Dewey (1859-   ) has taught at the University of Chicago and at Columbia University. He may be considered the outstanding and, in a sense, the most typical, American philosopher. Dewey is a leader not only in philosophy, but also in educational theory and practice. It is interesting to notice that he began his philosophical writing under the influence of Hegel.

to envisage things in terms of the adjustments and adaptations they make possible or hinder. One objective test of the presence or absence of intelligence is influence upon behavior. No capacity to make adjustments means no intelligence; conduct evincing management of complex and novel conditions means a high degree of reason. Such conditions at least suggest that a reality-to-be-known, a reality which is the appropriate subject-matter of knowledge is reality-of-use-and-in-use, direct or indirect, and that a reality which is not in any sort of use, or bearing upon use, may go hang, *so far as knowledge is concerned.*

At best traditional philosophy affords an emotional satisfaction and is, in this respect, comparable to religious faith. To accept a congenial philosophy may give one a sense of poise, a feeling that one is "at home" in his world, but this is an emotional rather than a cognitive adjustment, and only too often such adjustment leads to a complacent conservatism that hinders rather than furthers progress toward more efficient control of the social and physical conditions of life. The human mind should look only toward control of the future. It is equipped only for action and for such thinking as is quite indispensable in practical activity. It is futile to consider the fundamental nature even of action itself; for this is only another form of pure contemplation that removes the mind from its true function. It is futile to examine the antecedents and the conditions of the human situation—in short, to discuss the nature of reality instead of formulating plans for human conduct and practical activity. The Pragmatist is not at all interested in understanding our cosmic background except as this offers a field for practical activity. To be sure, some Pragmatists admit that in the enjoyment of art and of beauty in general we consider our experience without any reference to its result and that we find some of it to be of intrinsic importance. But this is a matter of aesthetic enjoyment, and has little to do with knowledge. We quote again from John Dewey:[12]

A first-rate test of the value of any philosophy which is offered us is this: Does it end in conclusions which, when they are referred back to ordinary life-experiences and their predicaments, render

[12] John Dewey, *Experience and Nature*, Chapter I. Open Court Publishing Co., LaSalle, Ill., 2nd ed., 1929. Reprinted by permission of the publisher.

them more significant, more luminous to us, and make our dealings with them more fruitful? Or does it terminate in rendering the things of ordinary experience more opaque than they were before, and in depriving them of having in "reality" even the significance they had previously seemed to have? Does it yield the enrichment and increase of power of ordinary things which the results of physical science afford when applied in every-day affairs? Or does it become a mystery that these ordinary things should be what they are, or indeed that they should be at all, while philosophic concepts are left to dwell in separation in some technical realm of their own? It is the fact that so many philosophies terminate in conclusions that make it necessary to disparage and condemn primary experience, leading those who hold them to measure the sublimity of their "realities" as philosophically defined by remoteness from the concerns of daily life, which leads cultivated common sense to look askance at philosophy.

PRAGMATISM AND PRACTICAL VALUES

The Pragmatist insists that a philosophical doctrine such as Plato's theory of forms is worthless because it cannot meet the test described above. However, much of Plato's practical philosophy, his theory of society and of conduct, can be at one time or another pragmatically tested. Thus we may try to live according to Platonic maxims and test the quality and efficiency of the life that results In general, those maxims which further wholesome life are sound, those that result in unresolved conflict or friction are faulty. But it is true that maxims sound for one group may not be sound for another. Equalitarianism and a universal franchise seem by and large sound for Anglo-Saxon people, but not always feasible for people of other backgrounds and character. For the Pragmatist there is no point in asking whether equalitarianism is universally true; that is, whether it involves a true interpretation of human life. The question is rather: Under what human circumstances can equalitarianism be practically verified or rendered feasible, expedient, and fruitful?

Here a criticism seems to be in order. When he is trying to answer the question just formulated, the Pragmatist avoids commenting upon "human nature" in general, which he is apt to consider as vague and outworn a term as "universe" or "nature." He does not praise or blame, and he explains only by indicating that under certain conditions certain groups of people tend to react in this or that way. Nonetheless, if his reasoning is to be of any avail, he must be able to evaluate human situations, or he will be unable to tell whether, to return to our previous example, equalitarianism has been successful in this or that historical context. Now if the Pragmatist's evaluation is to be more than an expression of his own subjective and private prejudices and enthusiasms, his thinking must come upon some standard of value, and this value must be recognized as an end worthy of pursuit, not as a means to the achievement of something else. The Pragmatist must recognize something that is not merely instrumental, something the importance of which cannot be explained simply as furthering growth or development or rendering life more efficient. After all, the more efficient a man is, the more clearly should he see what he really wants to do, what it is that makes his activity worth while. Hence Pragmatism, if consistently pursued, seems about to merge, perhaps despite the intentions of some Pragmatists, with more conventional philosophy.

BERGSON'S PHILOSOPHY OF INTUITION

There is a compromise position, halfway between Pragmatism and Absolutism, one aspect of which we have already examined. This is the philosophy of *intuition* made famous in the early twentieth century through the writings of Henri Bergson, who has combined a pragmatic interpretation of reason with a philosophy of romanticism comparable to Schelling's. For Bergson, intellect is pretty much what the Pragmatists say it is. It is aimed at action rather than at contemplation. It apprehends nothing fully, rather it manipulates and controls. In fact, from a purely theoretical standpoint, intellect distorts certain aspects of its subject matter. For instance, intellect is interested only in those aspects of nature which repeat themselves. It is interested only in causal sequences and in correlations. These are important because they make prediction and control possible, but they do not exhaust the nature of the concrete. Intellect ignores the individual and the unique, and it prepares an account of nature which omits these omnipresent aspects. Thus pragmatic intelligence ignores the full wealth of nature. But it is supplemented by an aesthetic sense that cultivates an intuition of the unique aspects of the particular individual thing. It is in these concrete things that all causation and all functional relations find a medium in which to exist. Hence the latter, important as they are, cannot be adequately understood apart from the tissue of the concrete world.

Intuition, then, cherishes the concrete and the unique; intellect ignores these and notices only those formal elements that can repeat themselves. At this point, the Bergsonian argument takes a characteristic turn. In apprehending the unique as such—that is, in emphasizing the approach of the artist rather than that of the scientist—we are said to experience an aspect of things that is for the most part lost from the view of quantitative science. Here we find quality as opposed to quantity, the individual's effort and intention as opposed to his measurable, overt behavior, and above all we strengthen our sense of our own continuity as living, conscious beings *possessing* a past and facing an unsettled future through the activities of our purposeful choice.

Now it is Bergson's belief, which he has most eloquently set forth with many brilliant analogies and examples, that intuitive inspection of the concrete world, especially where that world contains life and consciousness, can transform philosophy. And for many modern students, Bergson has succeeded in doing just this. He has persuaded many of his readers to accept his intuitive insight that the concrete world in its enduring concreteness has a character of its own, which no system of concepts can quite discern. This character, once it has been intuitively experienced—and it must be intuitively experienced to be known—undermines our willingness to accept any system of determinism, whether mechanist or teleological.

Bergson prefers to describe the concrete world, much as Whitehead has done, as creative or productive process. The past, which is real, presses toward the future and, overreaching itself, constitutes a new present. This element of unique and unpredictable novelty is always present and open to our intuition. If we recognize this element, we will come to admit that process or duration is always in some measure changing its course, and we may come to believe that the real is essentially a "continuous change of direction," a "ceaseless upspringing of something new." This intuitive recognition of omnipresent and unpredictable novelty led Bergson toward his famous theory of *creative evolution*. Evolution, like all concrete process, is undetermined and unpredictable. The wealth of individual forms, the free play of variation along any line of development, suggests some sort of creative experiment. A power persistent in the direction of its activity, ingeniously prolific of relevant detail, enlivens the world, organizing matter into life even as the imagination of an artist enlivens his medium. To be sure, the work of art may possess a vast network of technical, even of routine, order. This order is the proper object of intelligence. But the artist is concerned with the creation and organization of such order.

Bergson warns us we must not suppose evolution to have culminated in the production of man, nor must we suppose that the evolutionary trend moving toward *Homo sapiens* is the only one which embodies great value. Life expands in all directions, of which expansion such developments as plant life, insect life, and human life are characteristic achievements.

The following quotations from Bergson's writings indicate his view of intuition and its relations to intellect.[13]

Thinking usually consists in passing from concepts to things, and not from things to concepts. To know a reality, in the usual sense of the word "know," is to take ready-made concepts, to portion them out and to mix them together until a practical equivalent of the reality is obtained. But it must be remembered that the normal work of the intellect is far from being disinterested. We do not aim generally at knowledge for the sake of knowledge, but in order to take sides, to draw profit—in short, to satisfy an interest. We inquire up to what point the object we seek to know is *this* or *that*, to what

---

13 Henri Bergson, *An Introduction to Metaphysics*, trans. by T. E. Hulme, pp. 40-42. G. P. Putnam's Sons, New York, 1912. Reprinted by permission of the publisher.

known class it belongs, and what kind of action, bearing, or attitude it should suggest to us. These different possible actions and attitudes are so many *conceptual directions* of our thought, determined once for all; it remains only to follow them: in that precisely consists the application of concepts to things. To try to fit a concept on an object is simply to ask what we can do with the object, and what it can do for us. To label an object with a certain concept is to mark in precise terms the kind of action or attitude the object should suggest to us. All knowledge, properly so called, is then oriented in a certain direction, or taken from a certain point of view. It is true that our interest is often complex. This is why it happens that our knowledge of the same object may face several successive directions and may be taken from various points of view. It is this which constitutes, in the usual meaning of the terms, a "broad" and "comprehensive" knowledge of the object; the object is then brought not under one single concept, but under several in which it is supposed to "participate." How does it participate in all these concepts at the same time? This is a question which does not concern our practical action and about which we need not trouble. It is, therefore, natural and legitimate in daily life to proceed by the juxtaposition and portioning out of concepts; no philosophical difficulty will arise from this procedure, since by a tacit agreement we shall abstain from philosophizing. But to carry this *modus operandi* into philosophy, to pass here also from concepts to the thing, to use in order to obtain a disinterested knowledge of an object (that this time we desire to grasp as it is in itself) a manner of knowing inspired by a determinate interest, consisting by definition in an externally-taken view of the object, is to go against the end that we have chosen, to condemn philosophy to an eternal skirmishing between the schools and to install contradiction in the very heart of the object and of the method. Either there is no philosophy possible, and all knowledge of things is a practical knowledge aimed at the profit to be drawn from them, or else philosophy consists in placing oneself within the object itself by an effort of intuition.

That [14] an effort of this kind is not impossible, is proved by the existence in man of an aesthetic faculty along with normal perception. Our eye perceives the features of the living being, merely as assembled, not as mutually organized. The intention of life, the simple movement that runs through the lines, that binds them together and gives them significance, escapes it. This intention is

---

[14] Bergson, *Creative Evolution*, pp. 176-78.

just what the artist tries to regain, in placing himself back within the object by a kind of sympathy, in breaking down, by an effort of intuition, the barrier that space puts up between him and his model. It is true that this aesthetic intuition, like external perception, only attains the individual. But we can conceive an inquiry turned in the same direction as art, which would take life *in general* for its object, just as physical science, in following to the end the direction pointed out by external perception, prolongs the individual facts into general laws. No doubt this philosophy will never obtain a knowledge of its object comparable to that which science has of its own. Intelligence remains the luminous nucleus around which instinct, even enlarged and purified into intuition, forms only a vague nebulosity. But, in default of knowledge properly so called, reserved to pure intelligence, intuition may enable us to grasp what it is that intelligence fails to give us, and indicate the means of supplementing it. On the one hand, it will utilize the mechanism of intelligence itself to show how intellectual molds cease to be strictly applicable; and on the other hand, by its own work, it will suggest to us the vague feeling, if nothing more, of what must take the place of intellectual molds. Thus, intuition may bring the intellect to recognize that life does not quite go into the category of the many nor yet into that of the one; that neither mechanical causality nor finality [teleology] can give a sufficient interpretation of the vital process. Then, by the sympathetic communication which it establishes between us and the rest of the living, by the expansion of our consciousness which it brings about, it introduces us unto life's own domain, which is reciprocal interpenetration, endlessly continued creation. But, though it thereby transcends intelligence, it is from intelligence that has come the push that has made it rise to the point it has reached. Without intelligence, it would have remained in the form of instinct, riveted to the special object of its practical interest, and turned outward by it into movements of locomotion.

For Bergson, all intellectualist philosophies tend to take either one of two general forms, mechanical materialism or what Bergson calls *Finalism*. Finalism is Absolutism of a Hegelian type in which the notion of teleology is preserved, but in which all change and process are ultimately absorbed in an eternity comparable to the "block universe" of William James. In other words, all intellectualist philosophies fail to include the ultimate reality of process and growth, the reality of what Bergson calls "duration." Both theories "do away with time," while intuition perceives duration directly.[15]

If everything is in time, everything changes inwardly, and the same concrete reality never recurs. Repetition is therefore possible only in the abstract: what is repeated is some aspect that our senses, and especially our intellect, have singled out from reality, just because our action, upon which all the effort of our intellect is directed, can move only among repetitions. Thus, concentrated on that which repeats, solely preoccupied in welding the same to the same, intellect turns away from the vision of time. It dislikes what is fluid, and solidifies everything it touches. We do not *think* real time. But we *live* it, because life transcends intellect. The feeling we have of our evolution and of the evolution of all things in pure duration is there, forming around the intellectual concept properly so-called an indistinct fringe that fades off into darkness. Mechanism and finalism agree in taking account only of the bright nucleus shining in the centre. They forget that this nucleus has been formed out of the rest by condensation, and that the whole must be used, the fluid as well as and more than the condensed, in order to grasp the inner movement of life.

Indeed, if the fringe exists, however delicate and indistinct, it should have more importance for philosophy than the bright nucleus it surrounds. For it is its presence that enables us to affirm that the nucleus is a nucleus, that pure intellect is a contraction, by condensation, of a more extensive power. And, just because this vague intuition is of no help in directing our action on things, which action takes place exclusively on the surface of reality, we may presume that it is to be exercised not merely on the surface, but below.

As soon as we go out of the encasings in which radical mechanism and radical finalism confine our thought, reality appears as a ceaseless upspringing of something new, which has no sooner arisen to make the present than it has already fallen back into the past; at this exact moment it falls under the glance of the intellect, whose eyes are ever turned to the rear. This is already the case with our inner life. For each of our acts we shall easily find antecedents of which it may in some sort be said to be the mechanical resultant. And it may equally well be said that each action is the realization of an intention. In this sense mechanism is everywhere, and finality everywhere, in the evolution of our conduct. But if our action be one that involves the whole of our person and is truly ours, it could

[15] *Ibid.*, pp. 46-48.

not have been foreseen, even though its antecedents explain it when once it has been accomplished. And though it be the realizing of an intention, it differs, as a present and *new* reality, from the intention, which can never aim at anything but recommencing or rearranging the past. Mechanism and finalism are therefore, here, only external views of our conduct. They extract its intellectuality. But our conduct slips between them and extends much further. Once again, this does not mean that free action is capricious, unreasonable action. To behave according to caprice is to oscillate mechanically between two or more ready-made alternatives and at length to settle on one of them; it is no real maturing of an internal state, no real evolution; it is merely—however paradoxical the assertion may seem—bending the will to imitate the mechanism of the intellect. A conduct that is truly our own, on the contrary, is that of a will which does not try to counterfeit intellect, and which, remaining itself—that is to say, evolving—ripens gradually into acts which the intellect will be able to resolve indefinitely into intelligible elements without ever reaching its goal. The free act is incommensurable with the idea, and its "rationality" must be defined by this very incommensurability, which admits the discovery of as much intelligibility within it as we will. Such is the character of our own evolution; and such also, without doubt, that of the evolution of life.

CONCLUSION

Such in briefest outline are the schools of contemporary philosophy. Whether the future is to be dominated by a speculative philosophy like that of Whitehead, by a philosophy of sheer intuition like that of Bergson, or by an ultimately skeptical philosophy based upon the pragmatic interpretation of scientific method and of social practice, it is impossible to say. At the present moment perhaps the last type of thought is the most fashionable, although it often appears without describing itself as pragmatic. But the future may well belong to some mode of thought that has not yet clearly asserted itself. At any rate it is clear that the next few years will witness many philosophical enterprises. But that any of these will be as outwardly successful as the Hegelian Idealism proved itself to be in the nineteenth century is very doubtful. Perhaps we shall witness the unhappy emergence of a provincial nationalism in philosophical thought, owing to mistaken ideas of patriotism and racial pride. If this is to be the case, there will be little "meeting of the minds" among philosophical students in official positions, and international civilization will suffer accordingly.

CHAPTER XIV

Moral Philosophy in the Modern Period

The great themes of ancient ethical theory repeat themselves in modern times. The ideals of the Stoic, the Epicurean, and of Plato and Aristotle reappear continually. These ideals often require fresh statement to fit the interests, theories, and conditions of a new world, but in essence the ancient notions endure: autonomy, or self-control, indifference to fortune, the dominion of intelligence, the ideal of inner justice or the harmony and balance of the "parts" of the soul, the ideal of moderation or the "middle path"—all these recur in modern thought.

But they find themselves in a new setting so saturated with Christian doctrine that even the deliberate efforts of philosophical students cannot wholly isolate classical and Christian. The basic concepts are many of them classical in origin, and the style of discussion, being as it is free from any external authority, is Greek in spirit; but many of the topics discussed, for instance the relation of benevolence to self-love, the importance of sympathy and the central position of obligation and the sense of duty, are largely Christian and Hebraic in background. The conclusions reached are often orthodox neither in letter nor in spirit, but the subject matter discussed often owes its prominence to the religious tradition. This is sometimes true even when the theories advanced actually conflict with the teaching of contemporary ecclesiastical institutions.

But on the whole modern ethics is closer to the ancient Greeks than to early Christianity, or even to the Christianity of the Middle Ages, for the notions of salvation and rebirth have ceased to dominate modern ethical theories. To put it briefly, modern thought seeks the perfecting of the natural man, not his transfiguration. In other words, the ethics of the modern philosopher is primarily secular, even though the modern thinker may find some place for religion in his scheme of values and even though many of our ethical judgments owe their existence to a religious background.

Modern ethical thought is often utopian in spirit; it seeks to describe an ideal of the good life, which, as is often, although not universally, admitted, can rarely be completely realized or even very closely approximated. In order to discuss the possible perfection of human nature, we need a broad conception of what such human nature is. Ethics is accordingly in large measure an attempt to define the meaning of the word "human," to determine whether man is primarily a creature of intelligence, of creative imagination, of voluntary effort, of sense of duty, of social sympathy, or of self-assertion. Of coure every man possesses each one of these characteristics to some extent. The problem is, which of these attributes deserves the center of the stage, which one of them, or which group of them, is indispensable to the full development of the moral life? Nearly all modern students of ethics are inclined to emphasize the sense of duty and of social sympathy far more heavily than did the ancient Greeks.

Again, although reason continues to play an important role in modern ethics, it gradually changes its aspect, becoming more and more a purely practical function, a power that controls nature and determines the future rather than one that contemplates truth, so that by "reason" or "intelligence" contemporary writers mean something not wholly identical with the *nous* of Plato and his followers. This emphasis upon practical outcome, which is characteristic of much nineteenth- and twentieth-century ethics, leads us sometimes to consider for evaluation actions and their consequences rather than ethical attitudes, motives, and intentions. This is, however, not true of the earlier masters of modern ethical thought. In fact the greatest of these, Spinoza and Kant, describe freedom, which is for them, as for so many of the moderns, the ultimate ideal, as entirely a matter of inner attitude and clarity of mind. In this they both owe much to the influences of Stoicism and Christianity.

444

THE ETHICS OF SPINOZA

For Spinoza, freedom has its modern political as well as its pro-
founder metaphysical meaning. As a radical leader of seventeenth-
century thought, Spinoza defends the freedom of the individual
from external restraint. He argues with energy in defense of freedom
of speech and of scientific thought. But for Spinoza, a man might
well remain essentially free even if his political and economic freedom were wholly taken from him. And on the other hand, no
formal grant of political franchise or even the fact of economic independence can make men truly free. For freedom, insofar as it is
the quality of man, is an inner power, whereby intelligence enlightens the emotions. This freedom has nothing whatsoever to do with
indeterminism. On this point Spinoza repudiates Descartes. For
Spinoza, cause and effect appear in human behavior as clearly and
as rigidly as in the inanimate world. A free action is not an un-
caused action, but one belonging to a personality that is in great
measure self-caused or self-contained. This concept requires elucida-
tion.

Insofar as our interests and desires are what they are owing to the
guiding activity of our intelligence, they may be said to be caused
by us, being then truly our own. Insofar as they are not so determined, insofar as they are matters of impulse or passion, they are in
a sense forced upon us: [1]

The desires which follow from our nature in such a manner that
they can be understood through it alone, are those which are related
to the mind, in so far as it is conceived to consist of adequate ideas.
The remaining desires are not related to the mind, unless in so far
as it conceives things inadequately, whose power and increase cannot be determined by human power, but by the power of objects
which are without us. The first kind of desires, therefore, are properly called actions, but the latter passions; for the first always indicate our power, and the latter, on the contrary, indicate our
impotence and imperfect knowledge.

Actions are free, passions are in bondage. Actions are caused by
our true selves, passions are forced upon us by the influence that the

[1] Spinoza, *Ethics*, trans. by White, p. 241.

445

world exercises upon our desires. Both of course are subject to causation, but to causations of different types. No man is ever completely free throughout a whole lifetime. No man leads, in Spinoza's sense of the word, a wholly active life. This is the privilege of God only, who alone can satisfy the conditions of Spinoza's definition of freedom: [2]

That thing is called free which exists from the necessity of its own nature alone, and is determined to action by itself alone. That thing, on the other hand, is called necessary, or rather compelled, which by another is determined to existence and action in a fixed and prescribed manner.

Spinoza's ideal of human freedom is that of a life of action, in his sense of the term. Much of his ethical writing is devoted to describing the way in which such active freedom can be maintained by the individual. Spinoza's freedom depends directly upon intelligent self-control and reflective self-possession. These enable the human being to lead a life that is as genuinely human as it is individually his own. In other words, reason may assist each person to "seek his own profit and to persevere in his own being"; that is, to be active and free. We shall see presently that this does not involve a defense of selfishness, despite the individualistic terminology in which the idea is expressed.

For Spinoza, human desires are not to be controlled through sheer discipline based upon denial and constant curbing. True freedom involves a reshaping of the desires, and this takes place primarily through enlightenment. The free man does what he wants to do, but this is because his very desires as well as his overt practical decisions are enlightened by reason and insight. This ethical ideal is clearly Socratic in essence. Spinoza's moral philosophy is in many ways a modern restatement of the Socratic "Virtue is knowledge." And Spinoza gives a richer and more concrete meaning to the Socratic "Know thyself" than have many writers more directly influenced by Socrates.

For Spinoza, the growth of an individual's freedom is the growth

[2] *Ibid.*, p. 2.

of his ability to employ his reason profitably in guiding his conduct. When subject to passion, we are guided by inadequate ideas and are driven into action without the benefit of ample thought, and hence we have no opportunity of determining whether the action in question is truly desirable, or even whether we are likely to regret it after its performance. To be subject to emotional pressure that thwarts our rational freedom is to live in what Spinoza calls "human bondage." To be sure, the free man feels emotions, but for him the presence of emotion does not stifle intelligence. Spinoza's free man is most eager to avoid any emotional disturbance that tends to distort his thinking. He is also most suspicious of any emotion that tends to shake his confidence in his powers as a rational human being. Thus Spinoza is as suspicious of all types of worry as he is of the more usually recognized forms of unruly emotion. His moral disapproval of worry leads him to a somewhat startling conclusion. Repentance, even when considered as conscientious disapproval of our own actions, is found to be harmful in its effects and evil in nature. Repentance is described as pain, or sorrow that is accompanied by the idea of one's own behaviour as cause. Now pain always involves our passage from a greater to lesser "perfection," or state of power and efficiency. In this case, it produces a depression of spirit which makes a truly confident and rational fortitude impossible.[3]

As Spinoza writes:[4]

Repentance is not a virtue, that is to say, it does not spring from reason; on the contrary, the man who repents of what he has done is doubly wretched or impotent.... For, in the first place, we allow ourselves to be overcome by a depraved desire, and, in the second place, by sorrow.

But he somewhat tempers his doctrine in the sequel:[5]

Inasmuch as men seldom live as reason dictates, therefore these two emotions, humility and repentance, together with hope and fear, are productive of more profit than disadvantage, and therefore,

[3] See *Ethics,* III, Definition of the emotions, 27, and IV, prop. 44.
[4] *Ibid.,* p. 223.
[5] *Ibid.,* p. 223

since men must sin, it is better that they should sin in this way. For if men impotent in mind were all equally proud, were ashamed of nothing, and feared nothing, by what bonds could they be united or constrained? The multitude becomes a thing to be feared if it has nothing to fear. It is not to be wondered at, therefore, that the prophets, thinking rather of the good of the community than of a few, should have commended so greatly humility, repentance and reverence. Indeed, those who are subject to these emotions can be led much more easily than others, so that, at last, they come to live according to the guidance of reason, that is to say, become free men, and enjoy the life of the blessed.

The power of intelligence as a guide of life depends not only upon logical accuracy but upon the way in which the truths of intelligence are presented. We may know objects (and the relations pertaining between them), Spinoza teaches, in one of three ways. We may apprehend them through mere experience without grasping the rationale of their activity or of their relations to other objects. Thus, to use Spinoza's example, if we solve a problem in proportion by applying the rule that the product of the means is equal to the product of the extremes—a rule that we have seen in successful operation without discovering the reason of its validity—we depend upon mere experience. Such knowledge is prone to error and confusion, for it is based upon no insight into the nature of the objects known, and is perforce superficial.

But despite this, mere experience possesses a virtue that the second method of knowledge lacks; namely, the warmth and vividness of that which we sense immediately. For the second mode of knowledge, which is called reason, although infallible, deals only with the common properties of objects, of which the theorems of geometry and the laws of physics are examples. Thus if we solve the proportion by making use of the nineteenth proposition of the seventh book of Euclid, granted that we understand the demonstration, we employ reason to make use of the common properties of extended objects.

Such knowledge is abstract and gives us the rationale without the object, just as mere experience give us the object without the rationale. Intuition, the third mode of knowledge, combines the good qualities of both mere experience and reason, giving us the object and the rationale inseparably united. Thus, in solving at a glance the proportion 2: 4:: 3: x, we combine the certainty of the rational demonstration with the familiar vividness of experience.

Spinoza's intuition is concentrated thought that grasps the structure of particular subject matter clearly limited within very definite outlines. Thought need not pass beyond these outlines in order to comprehend its object. Thus, as we have seen, it need have recourse to no rule of thumb or scientific principle already established. In intuition everything is, so to speak, made to order, nothing is accepted as ready-made. Objects are seen as concrete rather than as instances of a law or a type. Hence the thinker experiences a lively sense of the immediate presence of his object. In intuition we are not aware of things by way of broad abstractions that distract our attention from the concrete objects themselves. Hence the great power intuition possesses of appealing directly to volition. Thus Spinoza thought intuition to be of greater power than reason in controlling the passions.

Intuition is also praised because of its close relation to a profoundly religious experience, which Spinoza describes as the "intellectual love of God." This may be summarized as a pantheistic sense of the unity of the world and of our unity with the world. But these aspects of the solidarity of things are more fully apparent to our intuitive knowledge than to our discursive reason or to our sensuous experience. The outcome of such insight seems to be a sense of value that discounts the importance of the temporary, the spectacular, and the narrowly personal in human affairs. This intellectual love of God frees the mind from the bondage of petty interests and supports a disinterested enjoyment and understanding of the human situation.

The action of intelligence and the inspiration of the intellectual love of God do not, according to Spinoza, destroy the emotions. But they do destroy passion, and they do this by transforming emotions from passions into active emotions or virtues. All virtue contains emotion; it would have no motive or driving power otherwise. But the active emotions of the virtues are not inclined to

449

hamper thinking, but to further it. In general, we may say that the passions are overcome when we understand them. It is a principle of Spinoza's psychology of morals that to know the cause of, let us say, a fit of anger or despair is actually to begin its conquest. For one thing, understanding prevents the emotion from completely filling and hence dominating our consciousness.

Understanding also helps us, once passion no longer stifles all reasoning, to comprehend the outcome of our succumbing to any given desire. Once our thinking has clarified itself, we may recognize that we do not really desire any such outcome. This is virtually a reaffirmation of the Socratic principle of morality. Thus the core of all virtue is for Spinoza pretty much what it is for Socrates, a steady presence of mind or amplitude of practical vision, which encompasses our immediate situation and its implications, thus enlightening our desires by confronting them with the true nature of the object that has attracted them.

The following quotations make clear Spinoza's conception of the relation of the individual to society and indicate his proposals for strengthening the foundation of genuine social co-operation.[6]

Anything that exists in Nature which we judge to be evil or able to hinder us from existing and enjoying a rational life, we are allowed to remove from us in that way which seems the safest; and whatever, on the other hand, we judge to be good or to be profitable for the preservation of our being or the enjoyment of a rational life, we are permitted to take for our use and use in any way we may think proper; and absolutely, every one is allowed by the highest right of Nature to do that which he believes contributes to his own profit.

Nothing therefore can agree better with the nature of any object than other individuals of the same kind, and so there is nothing more profitable to man for the preservation of his being and the enjoyment of a rational life than a man who is guided by reason. Again, since there is no single thing we know which is more excellent than a man who is guided by reason, it follows that there is nothing by which a person can better show how much skill and talent he possesses than by so educating men that at last they will live under the direct authority of reason.

[6] *Ibid.*, pp. 242-45.

In so far as men are carried away by envy or any emotion of hatred towards one another, so far are they contrary to one another, and consequently so much the more are they to be feared, as they have more power than other individuals of nature.

Minds, nevertheless, are not conquered by arms, but by love and generosity.

Above all things it is profitable to men to form communities and to unite themselves to one another by bonds which may make all of them as one man; and absolutely, it is profitable for them to do whatever may tend to strengthen their friendships.

But to accomplish this skill and watchfulness are required; for men are changeable (those being very few who live according to the laws of reason), and nevertheless generally envious and more inclined to vengeance than pity. To bear with each, therefore, according to his disposition and to refrain from imitating his emotions requires a singular power of mind. But those, on the contrary, who know how to revile men, to denounce vices rather than teach virtues, and not to strengthen men's minds but to weaken them, are injurious both to themselves and others, so that many of them through an excess of impatience and a false zeal for religion prefer living with brutes rather than amongst men; just as boys or youths, unable to endure with equanimity the rebukes of their parents, fly to the army, choosing the discomforts of war and the rule of a tyrant rather than the comforts of home and the admonitions of a father, suffering all kinds of burdens to be imposed upon them in order that they may revenge themselves upon their parents.

Although, therefore, men generally determine everything by their pleasure, many more advantages than disadvantages arise from their common union. It is better, therefore, to endure with equanimity the injuries inflicted by them, and to apply our minds to those things which subserve concord and the establishment of friendship.

The things which beget concord are those which are related to justice, integrity, and honor; for besides that which is unjust and injurious, men take ill also anything which is esteemed base, or that any one should despise the received customs of the State. But in order to win love, those things are chiefly necessary which have reference to religion and piety.

Concord, moreover, is often produced by fear, but it is without good faith. It is to be observed, too, that fear arises from impotence of mind, and therefore is of no service to reason; nor is pity, although it seems to present an appearance of piety.

Men also are conquered by liberality, especially those who have not the means wherewith to procure what is necessary for the support of life. But to assist every one who is needy far surpasses the strength or profit of a private person, for the wealth of a private person is altogether insufficient to supply such wants. Besides, the power of any man is too limited for him to be able to unite every one with himself in friendship. The care, therefore, of the poor is incumbent on the whole of society and concerns only the general profit.

CRITICISM OF SPINOZA'S POSITION

Spinoza's ethics comprise the clearest and the most comprehensive statement of what we may call the morality of intelligence. The secret of the moral life lies for Spinoza almost wholly in the awakening and the strengthening of man's intellectual power, by means of which he is enabled to protect his human nature. For Spinoza, ethics has absolutely no quarrel with natural science, not even with the assumption of causal determinism that the mechanistic science of Spinoza's day was inclined to accept. It is characteristic of Spinoza that he refuses to consider human nature in any way an exception to the order of nature as a whole. He feels that if this were the case, it would be impossible to apply understanding to human nature, and that as a result an ethics of intelligence would be quite impossible. Thus he writes of determinism: [7]

This doctrine contributes not a little to the advantage of common society, in so far as it teaches us by what means citizens are to be governed and led; not in order that they may be slaves, but that they may freely do those things which are best.

Determinism also inclines us to an intellectual acquiescence in the order of nature, and it teaches us to cultivate a stoical detachment when we are confronted by evil or troublesome people.

[The doctrine of determinism] is of service to us in so far as it teaches us how we ought to behave with regard to the things of fortune, or those which are not in our power, that is to say, which do not follow from our own nature; for it teaches us with equal mind to wait for and bear each form of fortune, because we know

[7] *Ibid.*, pp. 102-3.

that all things follow from the eternal decree of God, according to that same necessity by which it follows from the essence of a triangle that its three angles are equal to two right angles.

This doctrine contributes to the welfare of our social existence, since it teaches us to hate no one, to despise no one, to mock no one, to be angry with no one, and to envy no one. It teaches every one, moreover, to be content with his own, and to be helpful to his neighbor, not from any womanish pity, from partiality, or superstition, but by the guidance of reason alone, according to the demand of time and circumstance, as I shall show...

On this last point it is possible to disagree with Spinoza. Perhaps it is here that we come upon the most serious weakness of his highly intellectualized system of morality. It is very likely true that a belief in determinism has produced many admirable characters, even as Spinoza insists. In fact, there can be little doubt that Spinoza himself was one of these. But there is clearly another side to this. If the Spinozist is to be consistent, he must renounce value judgments altogether. However, when Spinoza writes of love, he tells us that only love which recognizes "freedom of the mind" as its cause is worth while and enduring. "Freedom" here means self-control, clarity of mind, and grace of conduct. Such virtues are essentially admirable. But if determinism undermines anger and scorn, what does it do to genuine admiration? To be sure, such a character as that which Spinoza describes would be of the greatest use to us, dependable and trustworthy. But only a depraved man would care to describe his friends as *merely* "useful." Disinterested enjoyment is essential to genuine friendship, and if disinterested anger or disappointment is impossible for a determinist, we may fail to see why disinterested admiration should be otherwise.

After all, it is difficult to comprehend the nature of individuality on Spinoza's terms. The human individual must be interpreted as a "finite mode," which is in every respect dependent upon and determined by its cosmic background. In Spinoza's metaphysics, the moral individual appears as little more than a wave in a stream; in his ethical theory, the individual appears as a center of autonomous and self-determined decision. It is questionable whether these two views of the moral agent are compatible.

THE ETHICS OF KANT

For Spinoza, reason is a source of enlightenment, and active intelligence guides our conduct by showing each desire what it is, how it arises, and what consequences it may expect. But for Spinoza, reason does not issue commands; it supplies pertinent information in a form that may appeal to the affections. But there is another point of view, according to which reason issues imperatives and requires obedience of the will. This tradition is Hebraic in background and looks toward the Old Testament for much of its inspiration, whereas the point of view that Spinoza presents is in spirit Greek. Immanuel Kant embodies this tradition, which in his day appears as a philosophical and rationalistic interpretation of Protestantism.

Protestantism contains within itself the sometimes incompatible elements of moral individualism and respect for higher authority. According to the Protestant scheme, the individual recognizes obligations that should by right determine his most important actions, but he reserves to himself the right to interpret such obligation in its application to his conduct. This attitude Kant maintains, and his philosophy is at once a statement of it and a defense. True to this background, Kant insists that no action is of moral value unless it is performed purely out of respect for some obligation that we recog-nize. An action performed on an impulse of kindness or generosity, while by no means an evil act, lacks strictly moral value, for morality is wholly a matter of obligation. Incidentally, Kant is certain that all human beings entertain some sense of obligation. They all recognize some things that should and some things that should not be done. But the content of obligation cannot be considered without an appeal to reason. It is from reason that the great imperatives of the moral life proceed.

In the first pages of Kant's *Metaphysic of Ethics* occurs a brief argument in defense of this point of view. Nature obviously did not intend man for happiness; for had she wished man to be happy and no more, she surely would have entrusted his happiness to instinct rather than to reason, which in man holds but a fluctuating supremacy. But since Nature has given man his reason to pilot him, we may assume that she intends him to live rationally rather than happily. Rational life, then, is the goal that we must endeavor to pursue.

In the *Metaphysic* Kant tries to present a formula, the famous *categorical imperative*,[8] by which we may test the rationality of our actions. The distinctive character of reason being, he thinks, its universal application, he decides that if we can universalize a contemplated action—if we can conceive of all men acting thus under similar conditions, without having to admit that the universality of the act undermines the possibility of its performance—we may consider it a good act.

This means that reason forbids any action the maxim or principle of which is not universal. In other words, reason forbids moral inconsistency. Thus in order to test the morality of a contemplated action, we must conceive of the principle involved as applying in general to all human situations of the type considered. If this conception involves no contradiction, our action is morally permissible. Perhaps Kant's most famous example is that of a man who considers making a promise that he knows he will not be able to fulfill:[9]

A man...finds himself forced by necessity to borrow money. He knows that he will not be able to repay it, but sees also that nothing will be lent to him, unless he promises stoutly to repay it in a definite time. He desires to make this promise, but he has still so much conscience as to ask himself: Is it not unlawful and inconsistent with duty to get out of a difficulty in this way? Suppose however that he resolves to do so, then the maxim of his action would be expressed thus: When I think myself in want of money, I will

[8] The commands of reason are called "categorical" in the sense that they are unconditionally binding for all human or rational beings. They admit of no hypothetical conditions. Thus the categorical imperatives of reason differ from hypothetical imperatives; for example, from such an imperative as the following: "If you wish to study engineering, you must learn to solve differential equations." Here the requirement applies only to those who are interested in pursuing a career in engineering. But a categorical imperative applies without conditions to all human beings.

[9] Kant, *Fundamental Principles of the Metaphysic of Ethics*, trans. by T. K. Abbott, pp. 47-49. Longmans, Green & Co., London, and New York, 1895. This and the following quotations are reprinted by permission of the publisher.

borrow money and promise to repay it, although I know that I never can do so. Now this principle of self-love or of one's own advantage may perhaps be consistent with my whole future welfare; but the question now is, is it right? I change then the suggestion of self-love into a universal law, and state the question thus: How would it be if my maxim were a universal law? Then I see at once that it could never hold as a universal law of nature but would necessarily contradict itself. For supposing it to be a universal law that everyone when he thinks himself in a difficulty should be able to promise whatever he pleases, with the purpose of not keeping his promise, the promise itself would become impossible, as well as the end that one might have in view in it, since no one would consider that anything was promised to him, but would ridicule all such statements as vain pretences . . .

[Another], who is in prosperity, while he sees that others have to contend with great wretchedness and that he could help them, thinks: What concern is it of mine? Let everyone be as happy as heaven pleases, or as he can make himself; I will take nothing from him nor even envy him, only I do not wish to contribute anything to his welfare or to his assistance in distress! Now no doubt if such a mode of thinking were a universal law, the human race might very well subsist, and doubtless even better than in a state in which every one talks of sympathy and good-will, or even takes care occasionally to put it into practice, but on the other side, also cheats when he can, betrays the rights of men, or otherwise violates them. But although it is possible that a universal law of nature might exist in accordance with that maxim, it is impossible to *will* that such a principle should have the universal validity of a law of nature. For a will which resolved this would contradict itself, inasmuch as many cases might occur in which one would have need of the love and sympathy of others, and in which, by such a law of nature, sprung from his own will, he would deprive himself of all hope of the aid he desires.

It is most important to mention that Kant does not always consider his categorical imperatives from a strictly social point of view. He does not always ask, "What if all men acted in this way?" Thus his discussion of suicide turns upon the fact that the usual motive of suicide, the desire to avoid pain and unhappiness, seems to have been intended to promote life, and that it is irrational to allow such a motive to defeat its own purpose by destroying life.

Kant is never weary of insisting that genuine morality can have only one origin in the human soul; namely, an unconditional respect for obligation as our reason makes this evident to us. Actions based upon sympathy or upon love are not, properly speaking, moral at all, although they may of course be beneficial to humanity. On this point, which has seemed to so many quite paradoxical, Kant is adamant. The principle of morality depends upon reason, which for Kant, as for the Stoics, is the universally human attribute that all men as human beings possess. Morality does not depend upon the sentiments or affections, which may vary from one individual to another. In this respect it is obvious that Kant stands very close to Stoicism. For the Stoics, the categorical imperative reads "Follow nature," which means "your essentially human nature or your reason": [10]

...it is of extreme importance to remember that we must not allow ourselves to think of deducing the reality of this principle from the *particular attributes of human nature.* For duty is to be a practical, unconditional necessity of action; it must therefore hold for all rational beings (to whom an imperative can apply at all) and *for this reason only* be also a law for all human wills. On the contrary, whatever is deduced from the particular natural characteristics of humanity, from certain feelings and propensions, nay even, if possible, from any particular tendency proper to human reason, and which need not necessarily hold for the will of every rational being; this may indeed supply us with a maxim, but not with a law; with a subjective principle on which we may have a propension and inclination to act, but not with an objective principle on which we should be *enjoined* to act, even though all our propensions, inclinations, and natural dispositions were opposed to it. In fact the sublimity and intrinsic dignity of the command in duty are so much the more evident, the less the subjective impulses favour it and the more they oppose it, without being able in the slightest degree to weaken the obligation of the law or to diminish its validity.

Here then we see philosophy brought to a critical position, since it has to be firmly fixed, notwithstanding that it has nothing to support it either in heaven or earth. Here it must show its purity as absolute dictator of its own laws, not the herald of those which are whispered to it by an implanted sense or who knows what tute-

[10] *Ibid.,* pp. 51-53.

lary nature. Although these may be better than nothing, yet they can never afford principles dictated by reason, which must have their source wholly *a priori,* and thence their commanding authority, expecting everything from the supremacy of the law and the due respect for it, nothing from inclination or else condemning the man to self-contempt and inward abhorrence.

Thus every empirical element is not only quite incapable of being an aid to the principle of morality, but is even highly prejudicial to the purity of morals, for the proper and inestimable worth of an absolutely good will consists just in this, that the principle of action is free from all influence of contingent grounds, which alone experience can furnish. We cannot too much or too often repeat our warning against this lax and even mean habit of thought which seeks for its principle amongst empirical motives and laws; for human reason in its weariness is glad to rest on this pillow, and in a dream of sweet illusions (in which, instead of Juno, it embraces a cloud) it substitutes for morality a bastard patched up from limbs of various derivation, which looks like anything one chooses to see in it; only not like virtue to one who has once beheld her in her true form.[11] To behold virtue in her proper form is nothing else but to contemplate morality stripped of all admixture of sensible things and of every spurious ornament of reward or self-love. How much she then eclipses everything else that appears charming to the affections, every one may readily perceive with the least exertion of his reason, if it be not wholly spoiled for abstraction.

It should now be obvious that Kant is not primarily concerned with the consequences of a moral act; that is, he does not consider an act good because it promotes human welfare or increases happiness. He tells us, indeed, that the consequences of any action are virtually impossible to forecast, that human happiness is most difficult to define and its causes are most difficult to determine. Kant

[11] The reader should compare the sentiment of this quotation with the attitude of the poet Wordsworth in his famous "Ode to Duty":

> Stern Lawgiver! yet thou dost wear
> The Godhead's most benignant grace;
> Nor know we anything so fair
> As is the smile upon thy face:
> Flowers laugh before thee on their beds
> And fragrance in thy footing treads;
> Thou dost preserve the stars from wrong:
> And the most ancient heavens, through
>   Thee, are fresh and strong.

insists that if we are to look in this direction, we shall never succeed in determining the moral quality of any action. He looks
rather to the logical consistency of the agent's intention, which is a
very different thing.

But even so, all activity, thinks Kant, must have an end for the
sake of which it is performed. This the first formulation of the imperative does not supply. But since the purpose of nature seems to
be the production of rational life, the end of human activity should
be the preservation of rationality. Thus we should treat human
personality—that is, potential rationality—always as an end and
never as a means. This is perhaps Kant's most important ethical
conclusion.

Accordingly the practical imperative will be as follows: *So act as
to treat humanity, whether in thine own person or in that of any
other, in every case as an end withal, never as means only.*

Kant illustrates as follows: [12]

He who contemplates suicide should ask himself whether his
action can be consistent with the idea of humanity *as an end in itself.*
If he destroys himself in order to escape from painful circumstances,
he uses a person merely as a *means* to maintain a tolerable condition
up to the end of life. But a man is not a thing, that is to say, something which can be used merely as means, but must in all his actions
be always considered as an end in himself. I cannot, therefore,
dispose in any way of a man in my own person so as to mutilate
him, to damage or kill him....

...he who is thinking of making a lying promise to others will
see at once that he would be using another man *merely as a means,*
without the latter containing at the same time the end in himself.
For he whom I propose by such a promise to use for my own purposes cannot possibly assent to my mode of acting towards him, and
therefore cannot himself contain the end of this action. This viola-
tion of the principle of humanity in other men is more obvious if
we take in examples of attacks on the freedom and property of
others. For then it is clear that he who transgresses the rights of
men, intends to use the person of others merely as means, without
considering that as rational beings they ought always to be esteemed
also as ends, that is, as beings who must be capable of containing in
themselves the end of the very same action.

[12] *Ibid.*, pp. 56-57.

We should live, says Kant, *as if* we were members of a Kingdom of Ends in which everyone's personality is respected. The fact that in this life we are not in such a state matters little; for the value of our actions lies not in the actual results, but in the will that prompts us to try our utmost for the good. In this Kingdom of Ends there are two types of wills. A will whose activity necessarily coincides with the moral law—that is, the will of a personality that of its own desire seeks the good—is a sovereign will, and good absolutely. A will not absolutely good experiences obligation. The moral necessity which this obligation imposes upon the personality is called *duty,* which occurs only when reason strives to guide a wayward personality. Without duty the will moves in confusion, drawn hither and yon at the call of impulse. Recognizing duty, the will approaches autonomy, or stable and even serene self-control. Without duty the will is, to use the Kantian term, heteronomous.

The problem of free will and determinism troubled Kant persistently, for, as we have seen, he believed that the possibility of experience in space and time demanded absolute determination of effect by cause. Kant had accordingly to admit that moral values are not apparent in the phenomenal world, and that ethical judgments presuppose a field of action in which final causation is firmly established. Kant describes this field of action as an "intelligible" world in which activity is guided by reason and takes place for the sake of intelligible ends. In this field of action, teleology replaces mechanical cause and effect. Kant tentatively identifies this intelligible world with the noumenal world of the *Critique of Pure Reason.* The central difficulty of such a conception lies in that Kant is inclined to describe the intelligible world as being without a spatiotemporal framework. Still, in the detail of our moral decisions we certainly seem to recognize both space and time as relevant factors. And according to the *Critique of Pure Reason,* such recognition commits us to a causal determinism.

Whatever the difficulties of his position, Kant argues that man, as a metaphysical amphibian, belongs to both these worlds. He is autonomous when he acts rationally, for then he is claiming his right as a member of the intelligible world, and his action is a logical one determined by ground and consequent. When he fails to use his reason, when he follows impulse, man belongs solely to the sensible world and is determined in his action by the laws of cause and effect.

As regards a future life in which the righteous man is recompensed for the evils and oppression he has suffered on earth, Kant denies the possibility of any conclusive proof. For Kant, human certainty is limited to a narrow sphere, the natural sphere, and when we endeavor to climb beyond, we must limit ourselves to tentative judgments. Thus immortality is like the existence of the intelligible world, a matter for faith to grasp but not for reason to determine, for reason can offer no final judgment here. However, the man of good will does actually assume that the universe is ordered by a wise and a good God who rules from his seat in the intelligible world, caring for the survival of his creatures after death. Otherwise the highest and fairest ideal of all human activity, a life that is at once rationally moral and materially happy, is but a fiction; for in this life happiness and morality are often incompatible, and the former should always be subordinated to the latter.[13]

To choose between the moral philosophies of Spinoza and Kant is a difficult task, too difficult to be undertaken here. Let us say only, in passing, that people whose sense of obligation is a very lively one will prefer Kant, and those who see in moral life a cooperation on the part of human beings in the pursuit of their welfare will be inclined to prefer Spinoza. In this respect, the choice is very similar to that we must make if we are to choose between the ethics of Socrates and that of the Stoics. In any case, a person will be attracted to either of these philosophies only if he has confidence in the power of intelligence to mold human life.

---

[13] This last point is somewhat difficult to harmonize with Kant's earlier statement that happiness cannot be made an ethical ideal because it is too difficult to conceive of the causes and conditions that will make men truly happy. It is also interesting to notice that elsewhere Kant describes *our own* moral perfection and the happiness of *other people* as *ends* that are also our *duties*.

THE UTILITARIANS

It is important to note that both Kant and Spinoza are in agreement with Christian teaching insofar as they believe that motive and intention—in short, inner character—are the most important considerations in ethics. They are in this respect sharply to be contrasted with those thinkers who find the most significant factors in ethical discussion to be the social consequences of our actions. These thinkers tend to judge a man's excellence in terms of the social utility and influence of his opinions and actions. The extreme form of this doctrine requires that praise or blame be based wholly upon consequences without reference to the agent's attitude and intentions.

This might almost seem to be a return to the most primitive type of ethical belief (see above, page 49), and we are surprised to find that this view was, about the year 1800, advanced in an effort to render moral science as objective and impersonal as the study of nature. The motive behind this undertaking was laudable: many thinkers had grown all too weary of arguing with opponents who assumed in the course of debate the existence of an innate idea of right and wrong, or found it helpful to define good conduct simply as that which is "pleasing to God." It was a period when in both Europe and the United States strong democratic feeling was contrasted with a frightened and an angry aristocratic and oligarchic sentiment. The democrats were struggling to found their theories upon an objective and a reliable basis. For them this was all the more important because these radical thinkers employed the concepts of their ethical system as a background when they argued for social reform. The philosophy they produced was in reality a justification of humanitarian and equalitarian endeavor.

It is one of the cruel ironies of the history of thought that the champions of such endeavor could not make terms with the then established doctrines of Christianity, and that it was under a banner borrowed not from Christian schools of thought nor even from Platonism, but from Epicurus, the least social-minded of all great philosophers, that the cause of social and political reform was advanced. Christian teaching was far too much concerned with the supernatural to satisfy the scientific-minded reformers, and the established ecclesiastical institutions were far too conservative, even too reactionary, in their economic and political views to offer the reformers any aid. In fact the latter were fortunate if they escaped clerical abuse and persecution. Despite this fact, there can be no doubt that the sense of social responsibility—which might almost be said to amount to an obsession—of the reformers has Christian origins.

The philosophy of social reform, known in England as the Utilitarian school, has the distinction of being the ideology under which democratic liberalism fought its greatest battles. This fact explains much. In the first place, it makes clear why Utilitarian thinkers were willing to pass over certain grave theoretical inconsistencies. They were, as a matter of fact, primarily interested in legislation, and less sensitive to philosophical subtleties than more thoughtful and less active theorists.

Again, it explains their concern for evaluation in terms of consequences rather than intentions. A practical reformer naturally thinks in terms of consequences. He is indeed likely to think in terms of human happiness, and he is apt to think of happiness in such terms as health, comfort, recreation, and economic security, which he wishes to see as widely spread as possible. Furthermore, he will grow very weary of being told by people in comfortable circumstances that such "creature comforts" are, after all, not essential to the moral life, and that a people can preserve their human dignity and moral integrity without them. And he will be thoroughly irritated if his opponent introduces the subject of supernatural reward and punishment and suggests that in heaven the "last shall be first."

As a result of this attitude, early Utilitarian thinking is a bold re-evaluation of the "higher" spiritual and moral values of human life. These tend to be considered as important only as they ensure and reinforce such things as health, comfort, and security. Honesty, patriotic devotion, brotherly love, and religious faith are seen as valuable only insofar as they contribute to the widespread enjoyment of the less spectacular values of human comfort and freedom from worry. This is, in a sense, an ethical materialism. But the

Utilitarian embraces it, or rather is driven to it, in an effort to protect the material interests of those who profit least from membership in an oligarchy where the powerful prefer to offer the weak spiritual consolation and moral exhortation rather than material assistance.

Happiness, then, expressed in materialistic terms will be the central concept of the reformers' ethical theory. Accordingly a piece of legislation is, in general, to be approved if it tends to increase the happiness of the people. *The greatest happiness of the greatest number* becomes the slogan of political and social reform. But for practical purposes, equally as important is the corollary that of several proposed measures the one that tends to produce the greatest happiness is to be preferred to the others. This implies the availability of a unit of measurement in terms of which quantity of happiness may be determined. Utilitarian theory is committed to the assumption that such a unit exists. This unit is thought to be a unit of *pleasure,* and in this way Utilitarianism employs hedonistic concepts borrowed from the ancient theories of the Epicureans. As Professor Fite has put it,[14]

Whether consciously or unconsciously, the hedonistic comparison of pleasures is always an attempt to realize the ideal represented by physical measurements. Pleasure, like heat, is assumed to be an experience common to the race. Like heat, it is assumed to have certain well-defined and universally recognized marks of identification; it is as clear that a good dinner is a pleasure as that boiling water is hot. And, like heat, pleasure is assumed to vary in intensity and duration, its *quantity* being the numerical product of the two factors.

The Utilitarians' interest in measurement and calculation leads them to assume that all "feelings considered merely as feelings can be arranged in a certain scale of desirability, so that the desirability or pleasantness of each bears a definite ratio to that of all the others." (Sidgwick) The great historian of Utilitarianism, Leslie Stephen, writes to much the same effect.[15]

[14] Warner Fite, *An Introductory Study of Ethics,* p. 43. Longmans, Green & Co., New York, 1903. This and the next quotation are reprinted by permission of the publishers.

[15] *Ibid.,* p. 44.

According to hedonism the only primitive property which can be attributed to man is the desire for happiness; and we must conceive of happiness as a kind of emotional currency, capable of being calculated and distributed in "lots", which have a certain definite value independent of any special taste of the individual. Conduct, then, is moral or immoral according as it tends to swell or diminish the volume of this hypothetical currency. Pains and pleasures can be handed about like pieces of money, and we have simply to calculate how to gain a maximum of pleasure and a minimum of pain.

Professor Fite has pointed out that despite this ambitious program, the Utilitarians were never able to employ what they called their "hedonic calculus" so as to procure anything comparable to the quantitative precision of the natural sciences.

In order to simplify the concept of pleasure and to make possible the program of the calculus of pleasure, Jeremy Bentham outlined an elaborate system of psychology to stand as a background for Utilitarian morals. Here follow a series of "axioms" upon which Bentham undertook to establish his system: [16]

Happiness may be defined to be the presence of pleasures with the absence of pains, or the possession of a preponderant amount of pleasure over pain.

These pleasures and pains may be either negative or positive, growing out of the absence of the one, or the presence of the other.

The value of a pleasure, separately considered, depends on its intensity, duration, and extent. On those qualities its importance to society turns; or in other words, its power of adding to the sum of individual and of general happiness.

The magnitude of a pleasure depends upon its intensity and duration.

The extent of a pleasure depends upon the number of persons who enjoy it.

The magnitude of a pleasure or a pain, in any one of its qualities, may compensate or overbalance its deficiency on any other.

[16] Jeremy Bentham, *Deontology*, ed. by Sir John Bowring, 1834, Vol. II, p. 19.

Jeremy Bentham (1748-1832) has, as the historian Höffding says, his "place in the history of the theory of rights and of philanthropy rather than in the history of philosophy proper." He looked toward Hume as his teacher, and he borrowed many of his ideas from the British Empiricists who preceded him. A wealthy eccentric, perhaps something of a crank, Bentham's work is marred by his inability to appreciate any view at variance with his own.

The benevolence of a man must be measured by the number of beings out of whose pains and pleasures he draws his own pleasures and pains of sympathy.

The virtues of a man must be measured by the number of persons whose happiness he seeks to promote; that is, the greatest portion and happiness to each, taking into amount the sacrifice which he knowingly makes of his own happiness.

When the amounts of pleasures and pains are balanced, the balance of pleasure is the evidence of virtue, the balance of pain the evidence of vice.

In accordance with these presuppositions Bentham insisted that "quantity of pleasure [intensity and duration, and so on] remaining the same, push-pin [a game without subtlety of technique or intrinsic difficulty] is as good as poetry." This means that a moment of pleasure is a moment of pleasure, and that there is no distinction between higher and lower pleasures. As can easily be imagined, granted that no painful consequences arise, the few moments of contentment that pushpin or, say, playing a pinball machine may afford constitute an absolute good, a hedonistic profit. It is futile to consider study of the classics or of Italian painting as a more worthy pursuit than pushpin; for if they can offer us pleasure, they offer us no more than an agreeable absorption of attention, differing perhaps in kind but not in value from the interest aroused by pushpin.

On this point the earlier Utilitarians were insistent. But this position, being counter to such a mass of accepted opinion, was bound to be altered in time, and with the second generation of English Utilitarians we find John Stuart Mill ready and even eager to shift his ground.[17] According to Mill, pleasures differ not only in

[17] John Stuart Mill, 1806-1873, was educated largely by his father, James Mill, who was an intimate friend of Bentham. The younger Mill began to learn Greek at the age of three and Latin at the age of eight. During his early childhood he read widely in history and received instruction in logic. "Anything that could be found out by thinking, I never was told," writes Mill of his education, "until I had exhausted my efforts to find it out for myself." Like his father, Mill was employed by the East India Company in a position of responsibility. He took an active part in politics and sat in the House of Commons from 1865 to 1868. He was not reelected partly owing to his religious views. The scope of his writings is truly enormous. He presents his views upon logic, psychology, economics, political theory, religion, literary criticism,

quantity but, and this is more important, in quality. Some pleasures are intrinsically more valuable than others and this quite without the reference to their intensity or duration. Mill writes: [18]

> But there is no known Epicurean theory of life which does not assign to the pleasures of the intellect, of the feelings and imagination, and of the moral sentiments, a much higher value as pleasures than to those of mere sensation. It must be admitted, however, that utilitarian writers in general have placed the superiority of mental over bodily pleasures chiefly in the greater permanence, safety, uncostliness, &c., of the former—that is, in their circumstantial advantages rather than in their intrinsic nature. And on all points utilitarians have fully proved their case; but they might have taken the other and, as it may be called, higher ground, with entire consistency. It is quite compatible with the principle of utility to recognize the fact, that some *kinds* of pleasure are more desirable and more valuable than others. It would be absurd that while, in estimating all other things, quality is considered as well as quantity, the estimation of pleasure should be supposed to depend upon quantity alone.

The question, of course, arises how we are to distinguish higher and lower pleasures, and Mill answers in good Empiricist fashion by appeal to moral experience. This pushes the question a stage further: To whose experience shall we turn? And to this Mill replies: [19]

> Of two pleasures, if there be one to which all or almost all who have experience of both give a decided preference, irrespective of any feeling of moral obligation to prefer it, that is the more desirable pleasure. If one of the two is, by those who are competently

---

and current events, to say nothing of his work for the East India Company which involved the preparation of important reports. Mill's *Autobiography* is one of the great works of Victorian literature. In general, Mill's philosophical ideas constitute a careful and critical restatement of the earlier British empiricism. In social and political theory, Mill hesitates between the advantages of socialism and a laissez-faire economy, but in the end he favors the institution of private property. As Höffding says, Mill "sees no reason for abandoning the system of private property if only the law would do as much toward mitigating its inequalities as it now does to increase them."

[18] John Stuart Mill, *Utilitarianism*, pp. 11-12. Longmans, Green & Co., London, 1863.

[19] *Ibid.*, p. 12.

acquainted with both, placed so far above the other that they prefer it, even though knowing it to be attended with a greater amount of discontent, and would not resign it for any quantity of the other pleasure which their nature is capable of, we are justified in ascribing to the preferred enjoyment a superiority in quality, so far outweighing quantity as to render it, in comparison, of small account.

In describing the respect a good man will feel for the higher type of existence, Mill approaches Stoicism, and breaks almost completely with the narrower position of the early Utilitarians.

Mill's theory of happiness reflects his concept of the higher and lower pleasures: [20]

...the test of quality, and the rule for measuring it against quantity, being the preference felt by those who, in their opportunities of experience, to which must be added their habits of self-consciousness and self-observation, are best furnished with a means of comparison.

Now it is an unquestionable fact that those who are equally acquainted with, and equally capable of appreciating and enjoying both, do give a most marked preference to the manner of existence which employs their higher faculties. Few human creatures would consent to be changed into any of the lower animals, for a promise of the fullest allowance of a beast's pleasures; no intelligent human being would consent to be a fool, no instructed person would be an ignoramus, no person of feeling and conscience would be selfish and base, even though they should be persuaded that the fool, the dunce, or the rascal is better satisfied with his lot than they are with theirs. They would not resign what they possess more than he, for the most complete satisfaction of all the desires which they have in common with him. If they ever fancy they would, it is only in cases of unhappiness so extreme, that to escape from it they would exchange their lot for almost any other, however undesirable in their own eyes. A being of higher faculties requires more to make him happy, is capable probably of more acute suffering, and is certainly accessible to it at more points, than one of an inferior type; but in spite of these liabilities, he can never really wish to sink into what he feels to be a lower grade of existence. We may give what explanation we please of this unwillingness; we may attribute it to pride, a name which is given indiscriminately to some of the most and to some of the least estimable feelings of

20 *Ibid.*, pp. 17; 12-14.

which mankind are capable; we may refer it to the love of liberty and personal independence, an appeal to which was with the Stoics one of the most effective means for the inculcation of it; to the love of power, or to the love of excitement, both of which do really enter into and contribute to it: but its most appropriate appellation is a sense of dignity, which all human beings possess in one form or other, and in some, though by no means in exact, proportion to their higher faculties, and which is so essential a part of the happiness of those in whom it is strong, that nothing which conflicts with it could be, otherwise than momentarily, an object of desire to them. Whoever supposes that this preference takes place at a sacrifice of happiness—that the superior being, in anything like equal circumstances, is not happier than the inferior—confounds the two very different ideas, of happiness and content. It is indisputable that the being whose capacities of enjoyment are low, has the greatest chance of having them fully satisfied; and a highly-endowed being will always feel that any happiness which he can look for, as the world is constituted, is imperfect. But he can learn to bear its imperfections, if they are at all bearable; and they will not make him envy the being who is indeed unconscious of the imperfections, but only because he feels not at all the good which those imperfections qualify. It is better to be a human being dissatisfied than a pig satisfied; better to be Socrates dissatisfied than a fool satisfied. And if the fool, or the pig, is of a different opinion, it is because they only know their own side of the question. The other party to the comparison knows both sides.

In considering certain objections to this theory, Mill renders his view of the nature and origin of happiness much clearer: [21]

Against this doctrine, however, rises another class of objectors, who say that happiness, in any form, cannot be the rational purpose of human life and action; because, in the first place, it is unattainable: and they contemptuously ask, What right hast thou to be happy? a question which Mr. Carlyle clinches by the addition, What right, a short time ago, hadst thou even *to be*? Next, they say, that men can do *without* happiness; that all noble human beings have felt this, and could not have become noble but by learning the lesson of Entsagen, or renunciation; which lesson, thoroughly learned and submitted to, they affirm to be the beginning and necessary condition of all virtue.

[21] *Ibid.*, pp. 17-20.

The first of these objections would go to the root of the matter were it well founded; for if no happiness is to be had at all by human beings, the attainment of it cannot be the end of morality, or of any rational conduct. Though, even in that case, something might still be said for the utilitarian theory; since utility includes not solely the pursuit of happiness, but the prevention or mitigation of unhappiness; and if the former aim be chimerical, there will be all the greater scope and more imperative need for the latter, so long at least as mankind think fit to live, and do not take refuge in the simultaneous act of suicide recommended under certain conditions by Novalis. When, however, it is thus positively asserted to be impossible that human life should be happy, the assertion, if not something like a verbal quibble, is at least an exaggeration. If by happiness be meant a continuity of highly pleasurable excitement, it is evident enough that this is impossible. A state of exalted pleasure lasts only moments, or in some cases, and with some intermissions, hours or days, and is the occasional brilliant flash of enjoyment, not its permanent and steady flame. Of this the philosophers who have taught that happiness is the end of life were as fully aware as those who taunt them. The happiness which they meant was not a life of rapture; but moments of such, in an existence made up of few and transitory pains, many and various pleasures, with a decided predominance of the active over the passive, and having as the foundation of the whole, not to expect more from life than it is capable of bestowing. A life thus composed, to those who have been fortunate enough to obtain it, has always appeared worthy of the name of happiness. And such an existence is even now the lot of many, during some considerable portion of their lives. The present wretched education, and wretched social arrangements, are the only real hindrance to its being attainable by almost all.

The objectors perhaps may doubt whether human beings, if taught to consider happiness as the end of life, would be satisfied with such a moderate share of it. But great numbers of mankind have been satisfied with much less. The main constituents of a satisfied life appear to be two, either of which by itself is often found sufficient for the purpose: tranquillity and excitement. With much tranquillity, many find that they can be content with very little pleasure: with much excitement, many can reconcile themselves to a considerable quantity of pain. There is assuredly no inherent impossibility in enabling even the mass of mankind to unite both; since the two are so far from being incompatible that they are in natural alliance, the prolongation of either being a preparation for, and exciting a wish for, the other. It is only those in whom indolence amounts to a vice, that do not desire excitement after an interval of repose; it is only those in whom the need of excitement is a disease, that feel the tranquillity which follows excitement dull and insipid, instead of pleasurable in direct proportion to the excitement which preceded it. When people who are tolerably fortunate in their outward lot do not find in life sufficient enjoyment to make it valuable to them, the cause generally is, caring for nobody but themselves. To those who have neither public nor private affections, the excitements of life are much curtailed, and in any case dwindle in value as the time approaches when all selfish interests must be terminated by death; while those who leave after them objects of personal affection, and especially those who have also cultivated a fellow-feeling with the collective interests of mankind, retain as lively an interest in life on the eve of death as in the vigour of youth and health. Next to selfishness, the principal cause which makes life unsatisfactory, is want of mental cultivation. A cultivated mind—I do not mean that of a philosopher, but any mind to which the fountains of knowledge have been opened, and which has been taught, in any tolerable degree, to exercise its faculties—finds sources of inexhaustible interest in all that surrounds it; in the objects of nature, the achievements of art, the imaginations of poetry, the incidents of history, the ways of mankind past and present, and their prospects in the future. It is possible to become indifferent to all this, and that too without having exhausted a thousandth part of it; but only when one has had from the beginning no moral or human interest in these things, and has sought in them only the gratification of curiosity.

THE ETHICS OF SELF-REALIZATION

It should be clear from the above treatment of selfishness in its relation to happiness that Mill considers the life of the self-centered man an incomplete human life, one that is not fully developed in that it has failed to realize some of its fundamentally human capacities; and that for this reason the life of the self-centered man is an unhappy one. Just so, the life of the man who fails to develop his intellectual alertness is, because of this, incomplete and deficient in happiness. According to this view, happiness presents itself not so much as a sum total of pleasures as a realization or a fulfillment of the capacities of human nature. Mill begins with hedonism and ends in a position very close to Aristotle's.

In the writings of the English moralists following Mill this theory of happiness becomes more and more explicitly advanced, and the notion of pleasure ceases, as it does with Aristotle, to describe the ultimate aim or goal of life. The successful life is not thought of in terms of pleasure, as indeed Mill had himself almost ceased to think of it, but in terms of activity. Happiness or welfare consists, as Aristotle wrote, in the exercise of all powers and capacities, especially of the highest, let us say for example, of our practical aptitude, our social sympathy, and especially, since we are human beings, our intellectual and aesthetic powers.

T. H. Green, the outstanding advocate of self-realization among English philosophers, described the concept as follows: [22]

It must be a perfecting of *man*—not of any human faculty in abstraction, or of any imaginary individuals in that detachment from social relations in which they would not be men at all. We are therefore justified in holding that it could not be attained in a life of mere scientific and artistic activity, any more than in one of "practical" exertion from which those activities were absent; in holding further that the life in which it is attained must be a social life, in which all men freely and consciously co-operate.

But so full an exercise of human capacity is not an easy thing. It is no simple matter to harmonize the pursuit of many interests, as this ideal seems to require. To do so, one must possess some leisure and a certain amount of economic freedom, as well as a practical astuteness in directing one's activities. Even so, one can hardly be equally adept as an athlete, as an artist, and as a scientist, to say nothing of the performance of duties required by family relationships and so on. Each individual must make his decision, and must renounce much for the sake of development along a course of his

---

[22] T. H. Green, *Prolegomena to Ethics,* p. 311. Clarendon Press, Oxford, 1883. This and the next quotation are reprinted by permission of the publisher.

Thomas Hill Green (1836-1882) an Oxford philosopher, furthered the cause of Idealism, largely through criticism of the Empiricists. One of his chief writings is a critical study of Hume. He is perhaps the most typical exponent of the ethics of self-realization.

own deliberate choosing. But here the philosophy of self-realization will warn us to avoid, in making such a choice, the serious error of wholly neglecting a fundamental aspect of our personality, the physical, the social, the aesthetic, the intellectual, or the religious.

It is clear upon a little reflection that man cannot cultivate his several capacities in solitude, and that social life is quite essential to human development.[23]

The good has come to be conceived with increasing clearness, not as anything which one man or set of men can gain or enjoy to the exclusion of others, but as a spiritual activity in which all may partake, and in which all must partake, if it is to amount to a full realisation of the faculties of the human soul. And the progress of thought in individuals, by which the conception of the good has been thus freed from material limitations, has gone along with a progress in social unification which has made it possible for men practically to conceive a claim of all upon all for freedom and support in the pursuit of a common end.

Self-realization is a co-operative, social enterprise. Thus it often involves insistence upon the doctrine of the equality of opportunity. This is for two reasons. In the first place, the self-realizationists accept Spinoza's statement that an intelligent human being is of all things the most useful and helpful to other human beings, so that in general we all profit by the development of the capacities of our fellows, who as they develop are in a position to contribute more to social life. Again, the self-realizationist is inclined to admit that there is no ultimately valid reason why one human being should be singled out to become the recipient of opportunities of self-development, and another not. Thus the self-realizationist usually accepts Kant's teaching that all human beings should be treated never merely as means to an end, but as ends in themselves.

However, much criticism of the ethics of self-realization turns upon the rather narrow individualism that sometimes appears along with it. Such individualism at times appears in the thought of Ralph Waldo Emerson, who may be described as an early prophet of the philosophy of self-realization in the United States. Emerson

[23] *ibid.*, p. 309.

has written: "No law can be sacred to me but that of my nature. Good and bad are but names very readily transferable to that or this; the only right is after my constitution, the only wrong what is against it."[24] This attitude involves us in a false antimony between self-reliance and tradition. In the writings of the more individualistic self-realizationists, this unfortunate conflict is over-emphasized with an almost religious enthusiasm.

Sometimes, in order to avoid this pitfall, self-realizationists flee to the other extreme and identify the full realization of character with social conformity, insisting that the successful life can be achieved only by a loyal and almost docile citizen, one who "identifies" himself with a social group. Such a man is said to recognize that once removed from a social group, he would be physically and spiritually impoverished, and that accordingly he can realize himself only through complete harmony with the group. The logic of this reasoning we may leave to the reader.

The philosophy of self-realization, which is in many ways the most typical ethical theory of recent times, being the outcome of the best thought of the past century in Europe and the United States, faces the great problem that haunts modern life: Are individual freedom and social co-operation to be maintained in one and the same system? In other words, how is the individual's full realization of *all* his capacities, including his social sympathies and aptitudes, to be achieved? If we are to answer this question, we shall need a steady theoretical vision, and if we are to embody our vision in practical living, we shall need tolerance and a readiness to compromise. For where clarity of vision and willingness to accept practical compromise are both lacking, there is neither progress nor conservation.

Modern philosophical thought has reaffirmed and reworked the Aristotelian notion of the highest good and, going beyond Aristotle, has dreamed of a society in which that good might be within the reach of all. For many years, philosophers were inspired by the belief that the enjoyment of this ideal stood open to all modern civilizations, and that its realization was indeed likely to come to

[24] Emerson, "Self-reliance," paragraph 7.

pass. This belief was founded upon a faith in the progressive nature of modern life. The development of technology and the diffusion of education were thought surely to further this progress.

Such a belief, a product of late eighteenth-century speculation and of nineteenth-century observation, arouses more than occasional skepticism in the Europe and the United States of today. The last few years have taught us that human progress is by no means automatic. More nearly perfect social order does not evolve of itself, but is achieved only as the outcome of very unusual co-operation and intelligence. At the present time, such co-operation among men and nations seems to many people a very unlikely thing, and accordingly we find some philosophers, perhaps reluctantly, turning away from the Aristotelian ideal of the fully developed life. Such a movement reminds us of the beginnings of Hellenistic philosophy, when the Stoic and Epicurean schools were replacing the ethical teachings of Plato and Aristotle.

RECENT ETHICAL THOUGHT: EXISTENTIALISM

New ways of thought are already appearing, the significance of which it is difficult to interpret. Whether these will ultimately contribute a philosophy of individual self-defense, and isolation, or, through their appeal to the individual's power of choice and self-commitment, aid in reawakening the social conscience of the modern world, is still an open question. These new ways of thought appeal strongly to people, especially European people, who have lost faith in "modern progress" and who frankly expect the social and political conditions of modern life to deteriorate. For them, the philosophy of self-realization is too optimistic and too confident. The ideal of complete self-realization seems to them feasible only under comparatively favorable historical circumstances. Such circumstances are not apparent in the western Europe of today. Since World War II, even academic conservatism has occasionally yielded to these new ways of thought, and thus the discussion of moral philosophy has often been enlivened. The center of such innovation is, as so often it has been in the past, the academic and literary world of Paris, in whose lecture halls and cafés the new philosophy has been formulated.

This way of thinking might be said to constitute an intellectual resistance movement, rallying against the heavy-handed orthodoxies now prominent in European culture. Today the champions of the new philosophy, deeply influenced by the spirit of wartime resistance in France and elsewhere, see themselves as "resisting" both Thomism and Marxism, in which the original insights of Aristotle and of Hegel have been adjusted to fit the needs of self-perpetuating institutions, almost pathologically fearful of the free cultivation of ideas. No wonder that the new philosophy is so uncompromising an individualism, or that it is so sharply attacked at once by Right and Left. In spirit the movement is as opposed to the respectabilities and *snobisme* of the capitalistic middle class as to the propaganda of Rome and of Moscow. The less authoritarian pressures often exercised by advertising, by radio, and by motion picture are recognized to be as destructive of inner personal freedom as the more direct methods of other institutions.

For this new philosophy, freedom is the quality of man; free choice and individual responsibility constitute the characteristic marks of humanity. Freedom, so conceived, is not limited to social and political contacts. It involves a metaphysics of its own, and a theory of man. What we usually call "human nature" is the product, not the source, of human choice. Man, whether he will or no, is forever choosing his own life and constituting his own human nature.

The outward details and conditions of life are often forced upon us by circumstance. Its human or moral essence is always chosen. Herein lies the new stoicism of the Existentialists. Thus a man permanently crippled still may determine the attitude that he is to take toward his physical infirmity. He is free to decide whether he is to recognize his condition as "intolerable" or "humiliating," as "something to be ignored," as a topic for conversation, as a source of humorous anecdote, or as a justification for shortcomings. He may clarify his attitude and make it communicable by giving it vivid and powerful expression, thus concentrating attention upon it, as

Milton did in the sonnet on his blindness. Again, to choose another example, the exploited worker cannot by a sheer act of will escape his predicament, but he can fix his attitude as one of resignation, passive resistance, or revolution, thereby offering this attitude to his fellows; or he may refuse to think of himself as a worker at all, and look forward to the time when he can find some other way of supporting himself.

In every one of these cases an individual is formulating a decision that not only meets the needs of a present situation, but characterizes the individual in his own eyes and offers to himself and to his fellows an interpretation of human nature and the proper human attitude toward the world. Thus we are always "making" human nature. Viewed in this light, a human being is an idea incarnate in the world through the decisions of an individual. Nor can any individual escape the responsibility of contributing an idea of human nature. As human beings, we are "condemned to be free."

Recognition of our inalienable and inevitable freedom is not always a pleasant one, and many people would prefer to renounce it in order to escape the burden of responsibility. Hence comes man's morally self-destructive yearning for orthodoxy and respectability, with ready-made patterns of self-justification. But here, paradoxically enough, man's freedom is limited simply in that he cannot abdicate it. He cannot choose not to choose. Resignation, detachment, and conformism are themselves optional attitudes, even when we do not clearly recognize them as such. In assuming them we become responsible.

Freedom, with its complementary responsibility, is at once the cross and the crown of human life. The burden of our freedom in face of the dark complexities of contemporary social and political development is a source of anguish. We experience the forlornness of our finite autonomy. There is after all something desperate in the human situation. There results a conscientious uncertainty that characterizes the man of good will who refuses to ask shelter of the traditionally vested orthodoxies. Still, the man of good will must choose and act.

Human consciousness is problematic, a theater of self-questioning in both theory and practice. It centers precariously upon uncertainties. As some brilliant but long-neglected thinkers of the last century have insisted, our human situation is best epitomized in the religious faith of modern times, which is based upon a stubborn sense of values, and everywhere beset with paradox and contrariety. Our sense of actuality is one of varying perspectives, shifting horizons, and of possible catastrophe.

Metaphysically speaking, our sense of being is complemented by a feeling of the nonbeing that envelops and interpenetrates the world of our consciousness. This nonbeing appears in the distinction, familiar to everyone, between imagination and perception, and is present in any distinction, however imperfectly recognized, between appearance and reality. It is also involved in the feeling of the instability of all things, natural or human, and in our recognition of death as inevitable. But our uncertainty and our sense of nonbeing distinguish our consciousness from mere animal perception. They constitute what Miguel de Unamuno so aptly termed our "tragic sense of life." Allegorically speaking, man is a "fallen" creature. But he thinks and decides for himself, even if he does so in fear and trembling.

Human nature, considered as such, centers in acts of choice; it is a matter of self-commitment. Human life as such, insofar as it is distinct from plant and animal life, is not a process of realizing some given value or set of values. The ends toward which man strives are not assigned him along with his biological and psychological endowment. Ends are human entities. Hence they are themselves objects of choice and creatures of choice. Man by choosing creates or gives life to the very values he decides to pursue. The fact that ends or values thus appear as man-made is welcomed by the new thought.

As Simone de Beauvoir has put it, we are mistaken if we imagine that "our reasons for living fall from heaven ready-made: we must create them ourselves." [25] Here we often encounter an objection,

[25] Simone de Beauvoir, *Le Sang des autres*. Paris, Librarie Gallimard, 1945. Passage trans. by N. P. Stallknecht.

based upon the widespread longing for an orthodox security. "If we know that we have created these ideals, we can no longer believe in them. If we do, we are only fooling ourselves." The answer is characteristic. "We do not arbitrarily create these things out of nothing; we create them through the strength of our own love and our own longing; and thus our creatures stand before us, substantial and real."

Human life, like all things in our world, is in the making. The mystery lies in that human life is making itself, projecting its own ends and ideals before it. Human nature, the essence of human life, is the product of human living. Human life is not and cannot be the outcome or the realization of human nature. In man *existence* fashions *essence:* man makes himself. Hence the name Existentialism by which the new philosophy is known. Man's existence is his effective presence in the world, his active self-assertion in its full setting of mind, body, and environment. This self-assertion is, as we have seen, also self-interpretation. It commits each one of us either explicitly or by implication to an interpretation of the human individual in his relation to his fellows and to the world. This concept, varying as it does from man to man, is human nature, the outcome of man's own self-definition. Without such self-orientation, man is not truly human, being no more than a richly endowed animal. Once he possesses such a concept, man participates in his own humanization. Unlike a mere thing, he exists "for himself," transformed by his own self-consciousness.

Existentialism puts no limits upon the objectives at which human decision may aim. It does, however, describe the human situation, and makes clear the difference between an honest choice and one that glosses over the full implication which this human situation, or human *subjectivity,* involves. These implications take on, at any rate in the writings of Jean-Paul Sartre, a stoic or Kantian aspect. We are reminded, at least of the spirit, of the categorical imperative: [26]

[26] Jean-Paul Sartre, *Existentialism,* trans. by Bernard Frechtman, pp. 18-20. Philosophical Library, New York, 1947. This and later quotations are reprinted by permission of the publisher.

Man is nothing else but what he makes of himself. Such is the first principle of existentialism. It is also what is called subjectivity, the name we are labeled with when charges are brought against us. But what do we mean by this, if not that man has a greater dignity than a stone or table? For we mean that man first exists, that is, that man first of all is the being who hurls himself toward a future and who is conscious of imagining himself as being in the future. Man is at the start a plan which is aware of itself, rather than a patch of moss, a piece of garbage, or a cauliflower; nothing exists prior to this plan; there is nothing in heaven; man will be what he will have planned to be. Not what he will want to be. Because by the word "will" we generally mean a conscious decision, which is subsequent to what we have already made of ourselves. I may want to belong to a political party, write a book, get married; but all that is only a manifestation of an earlier, more spontaneous choice that is called "will." But if existence really does precede essence, man is responsible for what he is. Thus, existentialism's first move is to make every man aware of what he is and to make the full responsibility of his existence rest on him. And when we say that a man is responsible for himself, we do not only mean that he is responsible for his own individuality, but that he is responsible for all men.

Responsibility is universal. I am never responsible for myself only, considered in isolation, but for the concept of human nature in general to which my choice commits me. This concept is relevant to all human beings. Thus I am responsible for it to them all, insofar as I claim recognition and consideration as a human being. If I did not make this claim, I should not even recognize myself as human. To ignore this element of universality is to blur my choice and to seek blindly to avoid my human responsibility.

There is a negative concept of freedom viewed as detachment from all entangling commitments that, if pursued consistently, con-

Jean-Paul Sartre, French philosopher, psychologist, novelist, playwright, and critic, has appeared as a prominent figure in the thought and letters following World War II, in which he served as a soldier and later as a member of the "underground" resistance. Although a professed atheist, Sartre is greatly influenced by certain theological and religious writers, of whom the Danish thinker of a hundred years ago, Sören Kierkegaard, is the most prominent. He has also continued the work of certain recent German thinkers, the Phenomenologists, including Edmund Husserl and his pupil Martin Heidegger. Sartre's drama and fiction are deeply philosophical, reflecting the same ideas and the same experience that enter into his theoretical works.

demns us to an empty and self-defeating life. Our human existence has been "thrown into the world," and as we become conscious of ourselves we cannot escape this original entanglement: [27]

Historical situations vary; a man may be born a slave in a pagan society or a feudal lord or a proletarian. What does not vary is the necessity for him to exist in the world, to be at work there, to be there in the midst of other people, and to be mortal there.

The fact that we are involved in a world does not limit our responsibility; rather it gives our responsibility possible content. Our entrance into the world as conscious individuals presents us with the problems of free and responsible agents.

Sartre views all forms of deterministic belief, including theological providence, as seriously endangering the integrity of human choice: [28]

If existence really does precede essence, there is no explaining things away by reference to a fixed and given human nature. In other words, there is no determinism, man is free, man is freedom. On the other hand, if God does not exist, we find no values or commands to turn to which legitimize our conduct. So, in the bright realm of values, we have no excuse behind us, nor justification before us. We are alone, with no excuses.

Determinism, predestination, or fatalism tempts us to make excuses for ourselves and for others: [29]

Those who hide their complete freedom from themselves out of a spirit of seriousness or by means of deterministic excuses, I shall call *cowards;* those who try to show that their existence was necessary, when it is the very contingency of man's appearance on earth, I shall call *scoundrels.* But cowards or scoundrels can be judged only from a strictly unbiased point of view.

The coward blames his heredity or his early environment for his confusion; the scoundrel presents himself as an inevitable man of destiny. In either case, the human situation is gravely distorted by

[27] *Ibid.,* p. 45.
[28] *Ibid..* p. 27.
[29] *Ib.d.,* p. 55. We prefer "scoundrel" to the slang "stinker," which is picturesque but ambiguous.

people who seek to evade their personal responsibility. According to Sartre, even cowards and scoundrels are free; they choose their lives and must answer for them. They tacitly admit this, else they would not continually be attempting to justify themselves. But the answers they give are irrelevant, limited by determinist assumptions and interpolations that have no moral significance. This happens whenever we say "I could not help doing this," "Anyone would do this," instead of "I chose to do this." The determinist often remarks that, "human nature being what it is," we are limited in many ways. The Existentialist replies that, "the human situation being what it is," we are always free, but that we sometimes perversely deny our freedom and caricature our humanity.

We are responsible for the full content of our lives as human beings. Thus we are responsible even for the development of our emotions. I *choose* the fear that I do not effectively will to suppress or ignore. Existentialist choice is a deep-seated activity. Verbally formulated deliberation is often comparatively superficial. We often choose and commit ourselves without surveying detailed arguments. The decisions are nonetheless our own.

The Existentialists continue a central tradition of modern philosophy that is concerned with the notion of freedom, personal and political. But they differ from the followers of Spinoza and those of Kant in that they do not consider freedom itself as the arch-achievement of human life. They insist that human beings are inevitably free, so that freedom is primarily a condition of human life, not one of human virtue. The good man is one who recognizes his freedom and accepts in good faith the responsibilities that his action involves. What Spinoza and Kant would describe as "genuine freedom" appears to the Existentialist as freedom with responsibility honestly interpreted and accepted. For the Existentialist, the man who undertakes to argue himself out of responsibility, who denies his freedom, is deceiving himself and thus, by falsifying his humanity, falling into what Spinoza would describe as human bondage. But the Existentialist insists that however grossly our freedom misrepresents itself, we remain free and incur the full responsibility of human beings.

Existentialist ethics often reminds us of Socratic teaching. Self-knowledge purged of self-deception and rationalization is a primary condition not of freedom, but of moral life. Recognize the full scope of your freedom and your responsibility and in the light of this full self-consciousness do what you will. Only be sure that your decision is clear and that you are being honest with yourself, not confusing quite distinct things. Thus a young man may say to himself that he wants to write a certain book, whereas he may someday have to admit that what he really wanted at the time was to be known as a writer, which is quite a different thing. One cannot codify in advance the pattern that honest decisions will take Moral activity in this respect, like the work of the artist, is inventive even creative. But sincerely responsible invention is far from being arbitrary or capricious.

The human situation is manifest to us only as the setting of our decisions, so to speak, as the margin of choice. Through acts of choice we "come to ourselves" and achieve consciousness of ourselves and of others. But we can be aware of ourselves as human beings only insofar as we are aware of our actual relations with other people. The first and second personal pronouns, the *I* and the *you* are, so to speak, correlative: [30]

In order to get any truth about myself, I must have contact with another person. The other is indispensable to my own existence, as well as to my knowledge about myself. This being so, in discovering my inner being I discover the other person at the same time, like a freedom placed in front of me which thinks and wills only for or against me. Hence, let us at once announce the discovery of a world which we shall call inter-subjectivity; this is the world in which man decides what he is and what others are.

Full consciousness overshadows the detailed objectivity that it surveys—overshadows it with the recognition that these objects can be seen in other perspectives, that there can be other consciousness of the same thing. Again, the problematic nature of human consciousness involves recognition of points of view and centers of agency other than our own. It is by being aware of ourselves and

[30] *Ibid.*, p. 44.

of other people at one and the same time that we become conscious
of ourselves as taking a point of view that is but one of the many
points of view possible, but for which we make ourselves responsible. Thus we become aware of the breadth of our freedom. The
recognition of freedom is a social experience. To feel that I am
observed, that my behavior appears in another person's view of
things that does not coincide with my own, is the beginning of
freedom and self-consciousness.

Thus gradually we come to ourselves and participate in human
reality, the world of intersubjectivity. Our enjoyment of such reality
is, like Descartes's *Cogito,* at once a starting point and a justification of our interpretation of things. It is the central human certainty with reference to which all theories and hypotheses, all
categories of interpretation, derive their plausibility. Theories of
nature, of causation, and so on possess only a derived and relative
authority. Our enjoyment of the human situation in its unquestionable intersubjectivity is absolute. We share directly in the human
situation, we fashion hypotheses concerning nature.

As the Existentialist sees it, the primary function of the philosopher is to illuminate this human situation, largely by finding phrases
to objectify what we have always vaguely felt to be true. For such
a philosophy the world or the universe is an important topic of
investigation only insofar as it constitutes the horizon of the human
situation itself. In this, as in other points of doctrine, Existentialism
revives the skeptical humanism of Socrates.

CHAPTER XV

Contemporary Logic

Contemporary emphasis upon the concreteness of real, particular things, and upon the meaninglessness and emptiness of abstract form, has produced a new freedom and generality in the investigations of such "empty" formal structure. Both in mathematics and in logic, new abstract, possible structures have been discovered, defined, and investigated. This development has become possible because the stress on concreteness has made the student of such forms far less dependent than ever before on limitations imposed by the demand that form have an empirical content.

Our contemporary feeling that abstractions are entirely different in kind from concrete realities, and that they represent aspects of real events arbitrarily chosen and emphasized, underlies this greater sense of freedom in creating and studying new systems of abstraction.

The greatest impetus to the development of mathematical logic came from the publication in the first fifteen years of the twentieth century of the *Principia Mathematica* by Bertrand Russell and A. N. Whitehead. In this volume, beginning with a few undefined variables and logical postulates, the authors showed that the foundations of mathematics are the same as the axioms of logic. They demonstrated this by deducing certain selected theorems of the mathematical sciences from the logical principles that they had established. The new logic with which their formulation began consisted entirely of operations with symbols, in the manner of mathematical computation. Only, unlike those branches of mathematics in which the possible values of a variable are limited to quantitative values, variables of greater *range* were introduced.[1] Suppose for example that the letter p is a variable representing any proposition; a proposition is defined as a statement that is either true or false.

Suppose that we represent the conjunction of two propositions by a dot (.); then the expression

$$p.q$$

is a simple symbolic notation for "Any proposition conjoined to any other proposition"; and a property that holds true of

$$p.q$$

will hold true in any particular case when we substitute specific propositions for the variables in this general expression.

$$p.q$$

is itself a proposition, and therefore taken in its entirety must be either true or false. Its truth or falsity depends upon the separate truth and falsity of p and q. Just how it depends is determined by the definition given of "conjunction" or "joint assertion."

In practice, the definition used is that

$$p.q$$

is true when both p and q are true, false when either p or q is false. (Thus the proposition "I am wise and witty" is true only if both of its constituents are true; that is, only if it is true (1) that I am witty, and (2) that I am wise.)

"Truth tables" are diagrams showing the relation of the truth value of compound propositions, such as

$$p.q$$

to the truth of their simple constituents, in this case p and q. For example, we have said that

$$p.q$$

[1] The "range" of a variable is defined as the class of the particular values for which the variable may stand. Thus the variables x, y, etc. in high-school algebra may stand for any particular numbers, a, b, etc. So the range of x and y is the class of numbers. In symbolic logic, the variables x and y are interpreted as standing for any particular existing entity, such as a star, a wheelbarrow, or a cat; hence the range of these variables is said to include all particular entities. Whatever equations hold for the variable will also hold when it is replaced by one of its specific values.

is true if and only if both constituents are true. Since p and q may be either true or false, the possible combinations of the truth values of p and q are:

p	q
T	T
T	F
F	T
F	F

To show the relation of these combinations to the truth of $p.q$ we may then write:

p	q	$p.q$
T	T	T
T	F	F
F	T	F
F	F	F

That is, if p is T and q is T, then $p.q$ is T.

When we come to the "if...then" relation, symbolized by $\supset$, the definition seems less natural. For purposes of logic, the case that must be denied to have an "if...then" connection is that in which the first proposition of a pair is true and the second proposition is false. For example, the statement "If I go out in the rain, then my cloak will stay dry," is a compound proposition, the parts of which are not really in an "if...then" connection, since the first part ("I go out in the rain") will, when it is true, not be accompanied by the truth of the second part ("my cloak will stay dry") but by the very opposite.

"Implication" is defined in such a way that

$$p \supset q$$

is false only when p is true but q is not, the one case in which an "if...then" connection between p and q is patently impossible.

When p is false, the relations of truth conditions do not tell with certainty that the asserted connection does not hold (that is, if it is false that "it is raining," it does not follow that the proposition "If it were raining, I would get wet" is a false proposition). Consequently, we will allow

$$p \supset q$$

to be treated as a *true* assertion when p is false.

This makes for greater convenience in operations with the symbols, and also in their application to practical problems, where a more exclusive definition might lead us to discard actual connections whenever these were asserted with the first term untrue.

For example, if we symbolize "If it is raining, my cloak will get wet" as

$$p \supset q$$

p is false, since as I write it is not raining; but

$$p \supset q$$

is true, since if it were true to say "it is raining," it would be true also that "my cloak gets wet."

Thus this relation of "implication" has a truth table as follows:

p	q	$p \supset q$
T	T	T
T	F	F
F	T	T
F	F	T

—that is, $p \supset q$ is T except when p is T but q is F.

The opposite of a proposition is its negation. Thus the opposite of p is *"not-p"* (written $\sim p$). Whenever p is true, $\sim p$ is false; and whenever $\sim p$ is false, p is true. The truth table of negation is therefore simply:

p	$\sim p$
T	F
F	T

For example, if it is true that I am wealthy, then "I am not wealthy" is false; if "I am not wealthy" is false, then "I am wealthy" is true. (Assuming that there is no intermediate state between "wealthy" and "not wealthy" as I define them.) It is also possible, as earlier truth tables have shown, to state that a compound proposition such as $p.q.$ taken as a whole is false—this is written $\sim (p.q.)$. Since by our definition the negation of a proposition is always true when the negated proposition is false, false when the proposition itself is true, the truth table of $\sim (p.q)$ is as follows:

p	q	$(p.q)$	$\sim(p.q.)$
T	T	T	F
T	F	F	T
F	T	F	T
F	F	F	T

This table exhibits the property of $p.q$ mentioned above, that $p.q$ is false (hence $\sim(p.q)$ is true) only if either p or q is false.

In addition to negation, conjunction, and implication, there are other propositional connections for which it is convenient to have special symbols and clear-cut truth-condition definitions in a formal logic. One of these is "disjunction" or "alternation," an "either ... or" connection, where at least one of the disjoined alternatives is true. The truth value of p or q, written pvq, is therefore diagramed and defined in this way:

p	q	$p\,v\,q$
T	T	T
T	F	T
F	T	T
F	F	F

That is, an "either ... or" form of compound proposition is false only when all of its constituents are false.

For example, the proposition "Johnson is either a Democrat or a Socialist" is true only if (1) "Johnson is a Democrat" is true, or (2) "Johnson is a Socialist" is true. The "either ... or" disjunction is true whenever one or more of the disjoined alternatives is true.

Another relation, so frequently used that a special symbol is helpful, is that of "logical" or "formal" *equivalence*. Two propositions are *equivalent* when they have the same truth values, that is p is equivalent to q (written $p \equiv q$) if and only if q is always true when p is true, and when p is false, q is false also. We can show the truth conditions of "equivalence" as follows:

p	q	$p \equiv q$
T	T	T
T	F	F
F	T	F
F	F	T

For example, the proposition "If it is raining, my cloak will get wet" is equivalent to the proposition "Either it is not raining, or my cloak is getting wet." We can see this by constructing a truth table. Let p be the proposition "it is raining"; let q be "my cloak is getting wet." Then the first statement above, of an "if...then" connection, has the form

$$(1) \ p \supset q$$

The second statement, of the "either...or" connection, the first part of which ("it is not raining") is the negation of p, may be symbolized:

$$(2) \ \sim p \ v \ q$$

The equivalence of (1) and (2) may then be written:

$$(3) \ (p \supset q) \equiv (\sim p \ v \ q)$$

As before, we first construct a table to determine the truth values of (1) and (2), remembering that the truth value of $-p$ is always the opposite of that of p:

$\sim p$	p	q	$p \supset q$	$\sim p \ v \ q$
F	T	T	T	T
F	T	F	F	F
T	F	T	T	T
T	F	F	T	T

We can now compare these truth values to determine whether $(p \supset q) \equiv (- pvq)$ for every case of truth or falsity of q and p:

$(p \supset q)$	$(\sim pvq)$	$(p \supset q) \equiv (\sim pvq)$
T	T	T
F	F	T
T	T	T
T	T	T

Since in every case the truth values are the same, we see the correctness of our statement that $p \supset q$ is equivalent to $\sim pvq$.

Another symbol often used in formal logic is the sign of "identity by definition," written $= df$. This symbols indicates that the two expressions it connects are *defined* as having the same meaning. No truth table will be given, because the truth values of a definiendum and a definiens are always the same, and one can always be substituted for the other in a compound proposition without affecting the truth or falsity of the compound. Thus, if "man $= df$ rational animal," and "man $\supset$ mortal," the new proposition, "rational animal $\supset$ mortal," derived by substituting the definition for the term defined by it, is true whenever "man $\supset$ mortal" is true. The meaning of $= df$ differs from that of $\equiv$ in that "equivalent" expressions happen to have the same truth values, but "defined identities" necessarily have the same truth values, because they have been so created that the one part of the definition may be regarded as an abbreviation of the other, and both sides mean the same thing.

A peculiarity of the symbol $= df$ is that the statements made with it are statements *about* the language we are using, rather than statements *in* the language. In other words, a "definition" asserts something about the way in which the symbols are to be used; the expression on one side may be replaced at will by that on the other. Statements in the language we have been discussing refer to propositions; statements about the language refer to the logical symbols themselves. Logicians usually refer to the language in which statements about nonlinguistic things are made as the *object language,* and call the language in which we describe and discuss the symbols of this object language the *metalanguage.* Consistency requires that statements *about* the language be kept separate from statements about objects made *in* the language; otherwise, various fallacies and paradoxes arise.

Just as the Stoic logician found that there were certain combinations of his ideas that he could not doubt, so the symbolic logician finds certain compound propositions of his symbols true in every case, or "valid." An example, made from the symbols that have already been explained in this section, is:

$$[(p \supset q) \cdot p] \supset q$$

"If (if p then q) and p are true, then q is true." (The brackets operate as in algebra, to indicate the scope of the symbols of connection.)

A form of statement that is "valid" is necessarily so; it can never lead to a false conclusion from true starting points, so the cogency of any piece of reasoning can be checked by seeing whether it can be symbolized in a set of *valid* forms, or deduced from a valid form by operations so chosen that the deductions to which they lead will also be valid.

An example of the $[(p \supset q) \cdot p] \supset q$ form of proposition is: if "when it rains I get wet" is true, and "it is raining now" is true, it is also true that I am getting wet. Let p be "it is raining"; let q be "I am getting wet." The compound proposition above, if it is a valid form, must never lead to a false conclusion from true premises; in other words, the expression as a whole must be true whenever its first two constituents are true. (Thanks to the definition of $\supset$, discussed above, the expression as a whole will be true also when its constituents are false.)

As before, we first construct a truth table for the expressions $p \supset q$ and p; then from the truth values of these, we extend the table to include the expression $(p \supset q) \cdot p$:

p	q	$(p \supset q)$	p	$(p \supset q) \cdot p$
T	T	T	T	T
T	F	F	T	F
F	T	T	F	F
F	F	T	F	F

We can now use this table to construct the table for

$$[(p \supset q) \cdot p] \supset q:$$

p	q	(1) $(p \supset q) \cdot p$ (from table above)	(2) q	$[(p \supset q) \cdot p] \supset q$ (col. (1) $\supset$ col. (2))
T	T	T	T	T
T	F	F	F	T
F	T	F	T	T
F	F	F	F	T

Additional extensions of scope in the logical system are made by introducing variables that represent "any class" or "any relation" as well as the variables we have been using, which represent "any proposition." It appears that, with these extensions, from a few simple premises, such as

$$p \supset p,$$

one can deduce theorems about classes and relations that lead to all the theorems of mathematics.

With the aid of its new variables and connectives, logic has been given a greater flexibility and range than the traditional Aristotelian analysis had provided. As a result the newer logic has to point out the need for an additional rule of validity for the Aristotelian syllogism. Since modern logic is so extended in scope, it includes empty as well as full classes (an empty class has an abstract definition, but no actual individual members). We must safeguard the classical rules of inference by insisting that no class can be said to have some members if it is an empty class. For Aristotle, the user of logic is the scientist whose premises are always propositions about full classes, and the need of this rule does not arise. But if a class may be empty and still part of logic, we can no longer say that an A or E proposition always guarantees the truth of its corresponding I or O subaltern. For example, it is not true that "All unicorns have one horn" implies "some unicorns have one horn"; "unicorns" is an empty class, but the "some" proposition means "there are existing members of this class such that ..." Thus syllogistic inferences of such forms as AAI, which conventional logic admits, are reliable only if the universal propositions refer to classes that are not empty; that is, classes some members of which do actually exist.

One of the immediate needs of this extended symbolism is a way of differentiating "universal" and "particular" propositions, and defining the truth relations of each. Using the symbols P and Q to stand for classes, of which individual entities are members, we may write "All P is Q" in the form "If anything is a P, then it is also a Q."

(1) $$(x) \, [P \, (x) \supset Q \, (x)]$$

Here (x) is read "for every entity x ..." (In this case, "if x is a P, then it is a Q"). We may also write "something (that is, at least one thing) is a P and also a Q" as follows:

(2) $(\exists x)\ [P\ (x) \cdot Q\ (x)]$

Here '$(\exists x)$' is read "there exists an (that is, at least one) entity such that ..." (in this case, "such that x is a P and a Q"). The "for every" symbol, (x), is called the *universal operator*," '$(\exists x)$' the *particular* or more commonly the *existential operator*.

One must now define the conditions under which a given universal proposition is false. Evidently, a statement such as "For any entity, x, if it is a man, then it is generous" is false if there exists an ungenerous man. This suggests that we define the contradictory of $(x)\ [P\ (x) \supset Q\ (x)]$ as

$$(\exists x)\ [P\ (x) \cdot \sim Q\ (x)]$$

and say that "Every x that is a P is a Q" will be *false* if and only if "There exists at least one x which is a P and not a Q" is true. This is the usually accepted contemporary definition of *contradiction*.

In its application, this definition of falsity creates the need for the new rule of validity for the syllogism, which the Aristotelian logic did not provide. For suppose someone asserts the proposition "All unicorns drink milk." This is a proposition of the form:

$$(x)\ [U\ (x) \supset M\ (x)]$$

that is, "For every x, if x is a U(nicorn), then x is a M(ilk drinker)." But as falsity was defined above, this proposition can be shown to be false only by proving its contradictory, "There is at least one unicorn that does not drink milk,"

$$(\exists x)\ [U\ (x) \cdot \sim M\ (x)],$$

to be true. But since there are no unicorns, the case of the non-milk-drinking unicorn can never be discovered. Therefore evidence will never be available to prove $(\exists x)\ [U\ (x) \cdot \sim M\ (x)]$ true.

Accordingly, with consistency and simplicity as their goal, recent logicians have decided to call statements of the form (x) $[U(x)]$, where there are no existent members of the class $U(x)$, *true*. So long as universal propositions are recognized as not necessarily conveying information about existence, this decision can do no harm. But suppose we use "all unicorns drink milk" as the minor premise of an Aristotelian syllogism, and "All milk-drinking creatures are animals" as the major, the syllogism:

> All milk-drinkers are animals;
> all unicorns drink milk;
> hence some unicorns are animals.

would be accepted as valid. But with out modern interpretation of the respective existential import of (x) and $(\exists x)$ propositions, this would become:

$$(x) \ [M(x) \supset A(x)]$$
$$(x) \ [U(x) \supset M(x)]$$
$$\therefore (\exists x) \ [U(x) \supset A(x)]$$

and this conclusion now asserts "there exists at least one unicorn that is an animal." This should not really follow from the premises, if they are given their modern interpretation; therefore to protect syllogistic inference from errors of this type, if we give universal propositions this interpretation, we must add the following rule to the traditional set: "No particular conclusion (that makes a commitment as to existence) can be derived from universal premises which do not themselves make such commitments." Of course, if we have independent knowledge that the classes referred to in the universal premises do have existent members, a particular conclusion can legitimately be inferred from the premises plus this added knowledge of existent members.

Since the present discussion makes no pretensions to be a history of analytic technique, the discussion of the actual technical aspect of symbolic logic will stop here. The reader who intends to become something of a specialist in philosophy, however, would be well advised to master these techniques; preferably, since there is an element of art in their use, under the guidance of a competent logician. Some books cited in the Bibliography afford a good introduction to the field, and from these, with application, one may become a good logician self-taught.

The development of symbolic logic has met with a number of problems of wider speculative interest than the details of formal systems in themselves can possess. Such questions are of interest because they suggest either limitations in the analytic instrument itself, or problems that demand some speculative resolution in the relation of this formal analysis to other branches of science and philosophy. The reader who wishes to consult material in current technical logical journals will find that most of the contributions are aimed at the clarification and resolution of the speculative problems of the analyst, to be discussed below. The development of this analytic has met three main classes of problems: (1) ontological problems, particularly in the interpretation of elementary symbols; (2) technical problems, certain limitations on permitted forms that must be imposed to make sure that only valid forms will follow from valid premises by the permitted operations; and (3) empirical problems, which arise when the logician attempts to extend the system to take account of kinds of connection other than those of his formal language. (The Logical Positivists, discussed above in connection with the philosophy of Hume, had no such problems, since they denied that any statements not made in the form of logical implications had any "meaning" to them. As is often the case in the history of philosophy, the proprietors of a new theory or discovery begin by belligerently asserting everything outside the scope of their own position to be nonsense, as the Eleatics dismissed earlier analyses of change; and they end by a speculative elaboration of their own position that can incorporate and make sense of the previously rejected alternatives, as the great Greek speculative systems incorporated both Eleatic and Ionian theories as to the nature of change. We are now witnessing the extension of the notion of meaning and analysis by a comparable process of speculation. The purpose of the present discussion of problems is to sketch for the reader some of the more significant of these speculative lines of thought.)

Current discussions are centered around problems that would have been called "metaphysical" by a classical philosopher who thought of metaphysics as that branch of philosophy which establishes and distinguishes the principles of each science. These problems may be classified as the problem of ontology (how far commitments regarding symbolic manipulation are to be interpreted as commitments about the nature and existence of nonsymbolic things); [2] the problem of closure (what extrasystematic warrant the starting points of a logical system have, since an infinite regress results if one tries to prove every assertion from prior premises); and the problem of extension in scope (how formal symbolism can be revised and extended to incorporate a wider variety of linguistic usages and structures within its formalized system). Any discussion of these problems is conducted with the proviso that no system is acceptable that can be shown to contain an internal inconsistency or contradiction.

The ontological problem has been met by an increasingly rigorous nominalism—the idea that logic is a key to ontology is being more and more strenuously denied. Although the development of contemporary symbolic logic first took form at the hands of men who were realists in their acceptance of a close interconnection of logic, mathematics, and ontology, certain paradoxes that their investigations encountered led to a conviction that consistency can be maintained most easily by separating consideration of linguistic or symbolic systems from the consideration of the natures of thoughts or things.

With the conviction that logic was actually metaphysical or ontological in orientation, having as its subject matter real entities called "classes" and "relations," the early symbolic logicians elaborated formal systems. This was a frame of mind with which Leibniz, who thought that the laws of mathematics described the general

---

[2] The reader interested in this point will do well to read the clear statement of ontological commitments by an outstanding contemporary logician, "What There Is" by W. V. Quine (*Review of Metaphysics,* October 1948).

conditions of all possible worlds, would have sympathized. But this conviction was shaken by the discovery that some of the entities that could be "discovered" and "described" by their formal systems were internally self-contradictory in character, hence could not really exist. As long as the concepts of existence and nonexistence were to be differentiated, one could not believe that a system of symbols which contained antinomies could represent a system of entities corresponding to the symbols.

It must, of course, be one of the concerns of a logician to avoid talking nonsense. If from true premises, and by legitimate operations, he derives a nonsensical conclusion, it is time for him to find a new logic. Since, by definition, every proposition must be either true or false, a statement made up of defined symbols that has the same form as other permitted statements in the system, but which is neither true nor false, is *nonsense*. However, logicians have found that if they allow certain classes of statements to be interpreted as meaningful propositions, their logical systems will yield nonsensical conclusions. Such statements as "the class of red objects is not red," or "Goodness is good" are statements of this excluded sort.

To understand the problem they present, it is necessary to classify "classes." A group of individual objects having some common property, or represented by a common symbol, is what we commonly call a "class." But such classes themselves may be classified in terms of *their* properties. For example, the *number* of members that they contain is a *property of classes*. Such classes as "cardinal number" have members that are themselves classes, and these are said to differ in *type* from the classes whose members are individuals.[2] We will call the individual objects that are classified in various ways, and which are usually symbolized by small letters ($a, b, c \ldots x, y, z \ldots$) entities of *type o*. Then classes the *members* of which are type-o individuals, and which are usually symbolized by capital letters ($P, Q \ldots F \ldots H \ldots$) we will call entities of *type 1*. Analogously, such a class as number, the members of which

---

[2] This discussion disregards some of the elaborate cross-classification of entities which the original rule of types (the "branched theory") required. The criticisms made hold just as well, however, for the ontology corresponding to the simpler rule here given.

are all classes of type 1, we designate as classes of *type 2;* thus a class is always of a type one higher than the type of its members. These type relations may be diagramed:

Type N: Classes members of which are of type $(N-1)$; symbolized ^nP

Type 2: Numbers, etc., that are classes of type-1 members; symbolized $m, n, o, 1, 2, 3,$

Type 1: Classes of individual objects, red, white, etc.; symbolized $A, B, C \ldots P, Q, R \ldots$

Type 0: Individual objects; symbolized $a, b, c \ldots x, y, z \ldots$

The "theory of types" consists of this classification and the rule that "A class and its members must differ in type in any meaningful statement." For suppose that one admitted statements such as "Redness is not red" as meaningful. "Redness" and "red" are both classes of type 1, so we can symbolize this statement:

$$\sim [P\,(P)]\ (\text{read "not } [P \text{ is a } P]\text{"})$$

This expression suggests that we might classify classes into two groups, those which do include and those which do not include themselves as members. (This, of course, is just what the rule cited above is intended to prevent.) The class "red objects" is not itself a red object; hence "red" is a self-excluding class, since the class is not one of its own members. But the class of "large classes" is large, hence the class "large classes" is itself included among the other large classes that are its members; it is a self-including class. Perhaps the clearest illustration of a "self-including class" is "the class of all classes," which patently must be a member of itself. In making this classification, we have assumed that $\sim [P\,(P)]$, $Q\,(Q)$, and so on are meaningful propositions in the system. Notice what follows: I let the symbol H represent the class of self-excluding classes. Symbolically,

$$(1)\quad H\,(P) = df\ \sim [P\,(P)]$$

That is, "P is an H" means, by definition, that "It is false that P is a member of P." By substituting H for P in (1) (a legitimate substitution, since P is a variable for any class, H a specific class, hence one of the values of P), I get:

$$(2)\ H\,(H) = df\ \sim[H\,(H)]$$

That is, when one asks whether the class of self-excluding classes is or is not itself a self-excluding class, a forthright formal piece of nonsense results. For while $H\,(H)$ has the form of a proposition in the system, it can be neither false nor true. First, assume $H\,(H)$ to be true; then, since expressions equal by definition have the same truth values, $\sim[H\,(H)]$ is true; hence the assumption that $H\,(H)$ is true leads to the conclusion that $H\,(H)$ is false. On the opposite assumption that $H\,(H)$ is false—that is, that $\sim[H\,(H)]$ is true— it follows from (2) that $H\,(H)$ is true also—the same self-contradiction. Since it has led to nonsense, the only alternatives are to revise or reject this logic. The introduction of the rule given above, that the class must always be considered as a type one higher than its members, is the most satisfactory revision yet devised.

But this revision is not completely satisfactory. In the first place, it discards as meaningless a whole range of questions and statements that seem to have a perfectly clear meaning. In the second place, it spoils the generality of such expressions as $7 + 5 = 12$, which we usually think of as holding for all types simultaneously. That is, I am certain that if I add 7 classes to 5 others, the result will be a set of 12 classes, whether they are of type 1 or type N. But since 7 is itself a class, there really is a different *type* of 7 for each set of seven entities differing in type. Thus if the type is represented, as is sometimes done, by a superscript prefix, a class of individuals that has the property, as a class, of having 7 members can be written:

$$^{2}7\,(^{1}P)$$

That is, the class P, of type 1, is a member of the class 7, of type 2. Then if one has a class of seven *numbers,* and wants to assign a number to it, one must write this:

$$^{3}7\,(^{2}m)$$

That is, this class has members of type 2, hence it must by our rule be of type 3. One is tempted to write

$$\overset{3}{7} = df\ \overset{2}{7}$$

but the rule will not permit this either, since $= df$ holds only between classes with the same members, which cannot possibly be true of two classes of types 2 and 3. Hence $7 + 5 = 12$ refers to a *different* set of 7's, 5's and 12's, depending on the type involved. There is no way in this system of saying meaningfully that, for example,

$$\overset{2}{7} + \overset{2}{5} = \overset{2}{12} = \overset{3}{7} + \overset{3}{5} = \overset{3}{12},$$

which is a rather difficult limitation to accept, even for the sake of a consistent logic.[4] We might diagram these types of 7 as:

$\overset{\text{N}}{7}$ which refers to classes with seven type $\text{N} - 1$ classes as members

$\overset{3}{7}$ which refers to classes with seven type 2 classes as members

$\overset{2}{7}$ which refers to classes with seven individual objects as members, *i.e.,* classes of type 1 classes.

This system of types is strongly reminiscent of the Neo-Platonic levels of emanation. The Neo-Platonists also insisted that different number classes must be used, depending on whether objects, souls, or forms were being numbered. (Thus Proclus, in his *Commentaries on Plato,* is always anxious to differentiate the mathematical statements using "psychic" and "somatic" from those involving "paradigmatic" number.)

One of the standing problems of modern analysis is to find a way of evading the paradox of the self-excluding class by less drastic limitations on the generality and range of meaningful expressions

---

[4] To avoid the separation of levels, it is necessary to introduce an assumption of translatability or isomorphism between them, an assumption that cannot be demonstrated and which greatly reduces the elegance, simplicity, and intuitive evidence of the set of axioms and postulates underlying the logical system.

than the theory of types involves. The structural similarity of the type hierarchy to the Neo-Platonic hierarchy of emanation suggests that some solution may lie in the direction of more flexible, less abstract concepts than those of "unit class" and "class," as now defined, as elements of logical formulation.[5]

At first the resolution of this difficulty was interpreted as an ontological problem, and the rule "A class and its member must differ by one in type" was treated as though it described a real separation in being of the strata of the entities symbolized. However, the symbolic devices necessary to attain consistency on this basis were very complex, and, as we have seen, the entities themselves had to be multiplied in a way that was neither technically satisfactory nor intellectually convincing. For example, since a number is a class, the theory required an infinite number of series of cardinal numbers, and "a" number, such as 2, was fragmented into an infinite number of different 2's, one for each type level (above the second). Thus the laws of mathematics, originally advanced as "holding for all entities simply in virtue of the fact that they are entities," lost the generality which this theory had originally claimed for them.

It seemed to later logicians both more modest and more probable to believe that the problems presented by the possibility of constructing paradoxes in what had seemed intuitively the simplest and the most useful logical systems, was not a reflection of some idiosyncrasy of the nature of things, but was rather the product of some

[5] This criticism may simply reflect an oddity of the current vocabulary of the logicians. Symbolic logic still uses a terminology haunted by the ghosts of metaphysical language, which was originally intended to signify commitments of an ontological kind. These terms, such as "individual" and "existence," persist, although their meanings have been restated in a mode that cuts them off as sharply as possible from ontology. The result is, too often, that the logician, hearing a philosopher use familiar language, thinks that he understands the terms of the discussion, and finds the doctrine erroneous; and the philosopher, transferring his own notions of the meanings of terms to the statements of the logician, finds the latter's statements that seem to him to be about ontology ill-considered, unanalyzed, and trivial. Perhaps the criticism in the text (above) reflects this typical misunderstanding by the philosopher of the symbolic logician. The danger of this equivocalness of vocabulary lies in the fact that many logicians are deceived by it into thinking that they are resolving traditional problems of philosophy when they are in fact only resolving problems of syntactical construction.

defect in our concepts or in the rules of the logical symbolism itself.

The results of the attempted resolutions of the logical paradoxes that treated these as ontological problems were extremely disconcerting. If, on the other hand, these paradoxes were regarded as the result of having set up an unsatisfactory body of conventions governing the use of symbols, they presented no great cause for concern; since all that was needed was to devise new conventions that would determine a syntax within which such nonsense statements could not be formed meaningfully. Thus the paradox of the self-excluding class, which had at first been of great interest to philosophical circles generally, presently came to be regarded as a technical problem in the construction of symbolic systems, having no immediate philosophical implications for the philosopher who was not a specialist in symbolic logic.

Although at first the theory of types was widely regarded as a problem of ontology, since Whitehead in particular felt that the statements of mathematics were metaphysical—that is, descriptive of the nature of reality—subsequent logical discussion has tended to give these problems a different interpretation. Several of the paradoxes that the theory was invoked to avoid, such as the truth of the classical statement "Epimenides the Cretan says that all Cretans are liars," are now explained as "syntactical" or "epistemological"; that is, their contradictions are explained as resulting from "erroneous ideas about the nature of language or about the nature of thought" rather than as pointing out some idiosyncrasy in the nature of things. The remainder, including Russell's paradox of the "class of self-excluding classes," are referred to as defects in the syntax that our common sense accepts; and various technical grammatical conventions that will avoid cases of nonsense statement without making metaphysical commitments have been developed as alternatives to the original type theory.

Mathematics is not usually construed in such systems as speculative or informative, as it was by Plato and Whitehead, but as a separate analytic intellectual enterprise, a branch of syntax, much as it is separated from metaphysics and natural philosophy in speculative systems oriented as are those of Kant and Aristotle.[6] However, a reminiscence of the problems raised by the ontological type hierarchy is preserved in the more recent investigations of what might be called "syntactical system closure."

It appears that every syntactical system extensive enough to include arithmetic cannot make reflexive statements about itself as a whole; for example, the statement "This system, which I call language I, is logically consistent" cannot be meaningfully made within language I itself, but only in a second, more inclusive system, language II.[7]

---

[6] The likeness to Kant and Aristotle extends only to the use of literal distinctions, The modern logician does not, of course, as Aristotle and Kant did, apply this technique of differentiation to the point at which there is a literal difference between logic, syntax, arithmetic, and geometry, since in that case his formal systems would be reduced to collections of accidentally true analogies between different domains, and would no longer be "logic" at all.

[7] The proof that no system can prove its own consistency, which is given in the following note, is fairly technical and may be skipped by any but a specially interested reader.

An informal outline is here given of the proof of Goedel, which makes the strategy of the now famous *Goedelsatz* available to the reader whose normal idiom is English rather than formal symbolism. A "system" consists of a series of axioms and postulates from which certain sentences are demonstrated. The system also contains rules for combining symbols into "sentences" such that every correctly formed "sentence" makes an assertion that is either true or false. Those sentences which can be proved true from the axioms and postulates given are called "theorems." A "consistent" system is one in which a given sentence, S, and its contrary, $- S$, cannot both be theorems. In other words, to prove that a system is consistent, it is necessary to prove that certain sentences do not appear as theorems in that system. Suppose the sentences are listed and numbered; then there will be proofs of the form "$S\ x\colon S\ x$ is not a theorem in this system." $S\ x$ stands for "sentence number x" in my list of sentences. Now consider the case of such a sentence which refers to itself; *e.g.*, suppose the eighth sentence on my list is "S8: S8 is not a theorem." Since I have admitted "S8x is not a theorem" as a legitimate sentence, this assertion must be either true or false. *Case* 1. Suppose there is a proof for S8; S8 is then a theorem, and is true. But since S8 says that S8 is not a theorem, if this assertion is true, S8 is false. Thus there is a legitimately formed sentence in the system that is true and false at the same time, and the system is not consistent. *Case* 2. Since to prove consistency we must prove that either S8 or $- S8$ is not a theorem, and the proof that S8 is not a theorem leads to inconsistency, let us assume that there is in the system a proof of $- S8$; *i.e.*, a theorem proving $- (S8$ is not a theorem). Then on this hypothesis, the two negatives in "not" (S8 is not a theorem) will cancel out, and the theorem proving $-S8$ will be a proof that "it is false that S8 is not a theorem"; *i.e.*, it will have proved S8 to be a theorem after all. But since by hypothesis this proof was to show that S8 is not a theorem, S8 again comes out as a theorem and not a theorem, true and false, at the same time.

In the same way, "Language II is consistent" can be meaningfully stated only in a still further system, language III. This hierarchy of languages is oriented in such a way that there can be no reflexive evaluation of a syntactical system within its own resources. This inability to establish a reflexive closure, a certain starting point guaranteeing its own adequacy, of the sort called a "principle" by Plato and Aristotle, ultimately leads (though most logicians prefer to gloss over the fact) to the use of an *ethical* criterion as the basis of *logic*. Since the choice of logical *principles* cannot be evaluated from those principles themselves, logicians have often shocked and misinformed their fellow philosophers and iconoclastic stray listeners by asserting that the choice of the starting points or first assumptions of a logical system is a matter of arbitrary preference or personal caprice. They often say that the choice of first principles is purely arbitrary, like the choice of the rules by which we are going to play some new card game. But this asserted freedom seems a bit of bravado that the competent logician belies in practice.

Any logical system that is to have interest or importance must possess three properties: 1. It must, of course, be consistent. 2. It must be sufficiently complex to possess a kind of aesthetic interest. (Thus while one can easily imagine symbolic systems with only two symbols and one operation, it will be the exceptional one of these which has enough complexity to be of interest, though all are consistent.) 3. It must be usable; that is, capable of some interpreta-

---

The only way out of this dilemma that preserves the consistency of the system is to prohibit sentences of the form "Sentence number so-and-so is not a theorem," a form which, when the number assigned to the sentence and the number referred to in the sentence happens to be the same, leads us to the demonstrated inconsistency.

It is always possible to construct another system, broader in scope than the initial one, in which the consistency of the first system can be tested and proved. But since the consistency of system I can be demonstrated only in the richer system II, and, by the same argument, the consistency of system II can be demonstrated only in some third, more comprehensive system, system III, a logician is confronted with an infinite hierarchy of language systems if he tries to decide whether his logic is consistent after all. For if he builds that same logic into his system II, and uses it to prove the consistency of system I, what he has shown is only that system I is consistent *if* the consistency of system II can be trusted; and the same regression confronts him if he then seeks to prove the consistency of system II by incorporating the same logic into a broader system III.

tion that applies to entities other than the symbols themselves. The logical symbolism we have been studying is usable in this sense; it gains in interest because it works when we interpret p and q as variables standing for propositions, so that the manipulation of these symbols serves as a kind of useful shorthand for studying propositional relations and structure. Systems with all three of these characteristics are not easy to invent. It is not a matter of establishing arbitrary rules. On the contrary, the decisions involved are in some ways comparable to the most conscientious ethical choice. Sound moral decisions must also conform to three conditions, similar to those mentioned above: (1) they must be consistent, (2) must preserve an aesthetic harmony of ends and means, and (3) must issue in practical action, not simply remain as practically "uninterpreted" wishes. It is less of a paradox than it might seem, therefore, to say that the logician designing a system is constrained to act "responsibly" in this ethical sense, and the requirements are so stringent that his situation is the very opposite of that of a man choosing with no restrictions or responsibilities.

Some mathematicians have been equally shocked by the doctrine that mathematics consists solely of analytic propositions; that is, that the predicates of its statements make explicit only what was already contained in the definition of the subject, and thus really never give new information, but simply elaborate forms of restatement. There is an artistic creative and constructive aspect to the work of the mathematicians, which they feel is done scant justice by this doctrine. In the past, some efforts have been made to reconstitute mathematics on a wholly constructive foundation. At present, however, mathematicians and logicians seem to have agreed on something like the description given by Leibniz of the two methods of efficient and final causes. All new mathematical creations and discoveries can be exhibited as analytic consequences of the axioms of logic, but the methods of the discoverer and the constructor are recognized as closer to those of the artist than to those of the pure deductive analyst.

Another group of speculative problems confronts the contemporary exponent of analysis when he tries to extend his system to take account of the varied forms of statement and meaning that actually occur in our experience. To devise formal machinery that can efficiently symbolize and manipulate such connections of terms as "belief," "possibility," and "necessity," let alone "aesthetic appropriateness," in a calculus that is mechanical and rigid in character is one of the objectives of contemporary symbolic logic. Founded upon various theories of "semantics," [8] formalizations that incorporate "modal" and "belief" sentences are now appearing.

But this attempted extension of analysis has been subject to sharp critical attack. Fixed rules of definition and connection seem to offer very poor possibilities for representing the way in which words and concepts really work. A term the "meaning" of which is clear is here taken by the logician, as it was by Aristotle, as "signifying indifferently any member of a given class, and always in each use signifying the same set of members." However, in the absence of Aristotle's separation of kinds of linguistic classification (which may yet be developed as three qualitatively distinct types of symbolic system) this approach must somehow explain the meaningful behavior of terms that are, say, the constituents of poetry. But this it cannot do, for in metaphorical, compact, imaginative speech and writing, the individual word, like the monad in Leibniz's universe, reflects its whole context from its distinctive point of view, and its "meaning" is determined by this reflected context. This type of meaning can never be expressed by a set of literal statements of

---

[8] "Semantics," as the term is here used, refers to the study of the way in which words and other symbols derive their meanings. In current discussion, three components of the "meaning" of a symbol are usually differentiated. A word gains some of its meaning from its syntax—its relation to other words in context; some meaning is contributed by the thing the word designates, some by the subjective attitudes and emotional associations the word has. Evidently, different words vary in the relative importance of these components in their meanings. As examples of words the meanings of which emphasize components of each type, "plus" or "and" are meaningful primarily as indicators of syntactical connection, "stone" or "goat" primarily (except for the man who has an unusually strong affection or abhorrence for goats) as designating objects, while "ouch!" derives its meaning from the emotional state it expresses. A scientist or a logician will try to minimize as far as possible the emotional overtone component of the meanings of his vocabulary, while an orator or a poet will not. The student interested in further study of semantics is advised to read C. W. Morris' *Foundations of the Theory of Signs* (University of Chicago Press, 1938).

semantic rules of use or by logical class-inclusion relations. Nevertheless, this metaphorical use of language has characterized some of the greatest speculation in our tradition, so that it can hardly be dismissed as "merely poetic"—nor as "illogical" if "logic" is thought of as a tool for establishing speculative truth.

Thus in the recent refinements of logical analysis, there remain, to disrupt the self-contained status that formal logicians would like to establish for their field, problems involving a wider, not purely logical, aspect of philosophy. The first of these problems is the problem of choice, as it appears to determine the principles of a formal system. In the second place, it is impossible for an observer who has sufficient sympathy with Platonism to approve the attempt to present syntax mathematically not to be disquieted by the hierarchy of languages that logic in its present stage of development presents to him. This stratification of languages must seem to the observing Platonist a shadowing in the realm of symbols of some latent stratification of things; and thus the loss of generality which these revisions of type theory were designed to avoid reappears in the revised version after all. What in Whitehead's analysis was criticized as a loss of ontological generality is criticized by W. V Quine in its revised form as a loss of syntactical generality.[9] The

[9] Professor Quine sums up the dilemma as follows: "The contradictions which instigated this whole series of researches, from Russell and Zermelo onward, were implicit in the inferential methods of uncritical common sense; and the various reformulations of logic which have been proposed for avoiding the contradictions have been correspondingly artificial and foreign to common sense. The least artificial and at the same time the technically most convenient formulation would seem to be that which comes as close as it can to the over-liberal canons of common sense without restoring the contradictions. But the more closely we approach this ideal in point of liberality, the more risk we run of subtly reinstating a contradiction for posterity to discover. If we undertake to prove consistency, moreover, we find ourselves in this curious predicament: the proof would itself have to proceed by logic, and hence would be conclusive only in proportion to our prior confidence in the consistency of the logic used. The most we can hope for, in such a proof, is to show that one theory is consistent if another is, and this is interesting just in case the one theory was more suspect than the other. Intuitive obviousness thus becomes the last arbiter—and a fallible one, in view of the contradiction which Russell was able to draw from common-sense logic. But there are degrees of obviousness; future analysis may enable us to derive logic from a set of principles yet more obvious and natural than those which Russell discredited. Meanwhile we adopt a smooth-running technique which does not appear to be inconsistent."—*Mathematical Logic*, p. 165. Harvard University Press, Cambridge, 1947. Reprinted by permission of the publisher.

latent Neo-Platonism derivative from the formal character of the definitions of existence, individual, and class reasserts itself in a hierarchy of languages after the problems it seemed to present in its earlier appearance as a hierarchy of entities have been resolved.

The limitations of contemporary logical philosophy, some of which we have discussed in connection with the theory of types and the problems posed by modes of connection other than logical implication, seem to stem from inadequacies in the analysis of the concepts of "individual" and "entity" as a preliminary to elaborate systematic speculation.[10]

Just as early Greek philosophy was "stymied" in its treatment of the natures of things until the criticism of the Eleatics forced the need for an analysis of the nature of "being" on the attention of their contemporaries, so the paradoxes that have given rise to the syntactic hierarchy are a "stymie" for contemporary logic in its attempt to analyze the nature of syntactical systems. The "individual concrete thing" appears in this philosophy as the small-letter constant or variable, $a, b \ldots x, y \ldots$ It is a "something" that exists and has a set of properties in virtue of which it can be recognized and classified. Its "individuality" depends solely on the fact that no other collection of exactly the same properties exists. (That is, if for every property, P, when x has this property, y also has it, x is identical with y: $(P)(x)([P(x) \supset P(y)] \supset (x = y))$.) This conception does not seem to do justice to the difference, central in other contemporary speculation (such as that of A. N. Whitehead, himself a great logician) between *actuality* and *possibility*.

One may therefore hope, on the basis of past intellectual history, that the future of logical speculation will take the form of a further analysis of the concepts of "existence," "individual," and "class," an analysis that should ultimately serve to establish new foundations for a less limited system of formal logic, one that will be less sharply insulated from other currents of contemporary discussion and speculation.

[10] The affinities of contemporary logic to the Neo-Platonic philosophy, in which for the first time the individual was reduced to the status of a class, while something very like the hierarchy of types appeared in the levels of emanation, suggest this same point.

In a context of speculation in which time is felt to produce real novelty, the philosopher becomes an intuitive creator, and the central philosophical problems are analogous to those of artistic creation. The contemporary speculator recognizes the logician as a fellow worker; the creation of logical systems is after all a kind of aesthetic creation of new forms from the raw materials of the structural realm of possibility. The formal logician can thus be regarded as a fellow creator and poet in an age of creation and poetry.

On the other hand, the logician, although he cannot incorporate the nuances of poetic meaning into such a clear-cut, fixed, symbolic system as he finds most congenial, is coming more and more to recognize the affinity between the consistent, tightly knit, abstract relational structure that his work represents and the concrete embodiments of such consistent, tightly knit structures that appear in the work of the poet. Future speculation will probably involve new speculative combinations of the insights gained from the poet's exploration of the significant structures that emerge in the realm of concrete history and the logician's exploration of the nature of the structures that constitute the abstract realm of possibility.

Bibliography

Books suited for library reserve collection for use in elementary work in the history of philosophy are marked with an asterisk.

I. GENERAL WORKS ON ANCIENT PHILOSOPHY AND RELATED FIELDS

Nahm, M. C. *Selections from Early Greek Philosophy*. Appleton-Century-Crofts, 3rd edition, 1947. Selected translations.

Baldwin, Chas. S. *Ancient Rhetoric and Poetic*. Macmillan, 1924. A standard work.

Beare, John. *Greek Theories of Elementary Cognition from Alcmaeon to Aristotle*. Oxford, 1906. A scholarly study of theories of sensation and perception.

Bulfinch, Thomas. *The Age of Fable*. Various editions. A convenient reference book for the elementary student who needs a simple manual of Greek divinities and legends.

Burnet, John. *Early Greek Philosophy*. Macmillan, 4th edition, 1930. A standard, authoritative discussion of the development of philosophy and science before Socrates.

—— *Greek Philosophy. Part I, Thales to Plato*. Macmillan, 1914. A standard and scholarly work.

Bury, John B. *A History of Greece*. Modern Library, 1937. An excellent one-volume history, from Homer to Alexander.

Bury, J. B., and others (eds.) *Cambridge Ancient History*. Vols. V and VI. Cambridge, 1923-27. A standard, authoritative work.

*Cornford, Francis M. *Before and After Socrates*. Cambridge, 1932. A brilliant, brief treatment of the influence of Socrates on Greek speculation.

Diogenes Laertius. *Lives and Opinions of Eminent Philosophers*. Translated by R. D. Hicks; Loeb, 1925. A gossipy compendium of anecdotes from the history of philosophy. The sections on the Stoics and Epicureans, which were taken from contemporary materials, rank high as primary sources on those schools. The remainder is neither profound nor very reliable.

511

Duckworth, George E. (ed.). *Complete Roman Drama.* Random, 1942, 2 vols. Translations of the works of Plautus, Terence, and Seneca.

Empedocles. *Fragments of Empedocles.* Translated by William Ellery Leonard; Open Court, 1908. A fine translation into free verse of Empedocles' cosmological poem which, despite the unfavorable opinion of Aristotle, contains much excellent poetry.

Euclid. *The Thirteen Books of Euclid's Elements.* Translated by T. L. Heath; Macmillan, 1908, 3 vols. Definitive edition.

*Freeman, Kathleen. *Ancilla to the Pre-Socratic Philosophers.* Harvard, 1948. Translation of the Diels definitive collection of the accounts that have been preserved of the philosophers before Socrates. Possibly rather extensive and technical for the beginning student.

Fritz, Kurt von. *Pythagorean Politics in Southern Italy.* Columbia, 1940. A learned attempt to reconstruct and date the events of the anti-Pythagorean revolutions in southern Italy.

*Fuller, B. A. G. *History of Greek Philosophy, Thales to Democritus.* Holt, 1923. A detailed, objective history, with judicious presentation of the better-known alternative treatments of the many controversial problems.

Godolphin, F. R. B. (ed.). *The Greek Historians.* Random, 1942, 2 vols. Translations of the works of Herodotus and Thucydides; the latter's account of the social movements and conditions in Athens during the Peloponnesian War is of great value to students of the Sophists and of Socrates.

*Gomperz, Theodor. *Greek Thinkers.* Scribner, 1905, 4 vols. Eminently readable studies of the Greek philosophers and their relation to the social and cultural background of their times.

Guthrie, Kenneth S. *Pythagoras.* Platonist Press, 1919. Translations of many Neo-Pythagorean documents which were forged, pre-dated, and offered as proof that the ancient Pythagorean school had completely anticipated Plato and Aristotle. Many of these papers are simply abstracts of Platonic or Aristotelian works, signed with the names of early Pythagoreans. The translator accepts most of these forgeries at face value, but the student should remember that the actual dates of composition are second and third centuries after Christ rather than those suggested in the text.

Harrison, Jane. *Prolegomena to the Study of Greek Religion.* Cambridge, 1921. The origins of the Greek gods, their rituals, cults, and legends.

Head, Barclay V., and others. *Historia Numorum: A Manual of Greek Numismatics.* Oxford, 1911. A comprehensive, standard work on ancient Greek and Roman coins.

Heath, Thomas L. *History of Greek Mathematics*. Oxford, 1921, 2 vols. An authoritative work.

—— *Aristarchus of Samos, The Ancient Copernicus*. Oxford, 1913. An important and scholarly work on the history of astronomy; contains a translation of the Treatise on the Sizes and Distances of the Sun and the Moon.

*Homer. *The Iliad* and *The Odyssey*. Various translations. Homer was the ancient Greek bible; his poems were studied in every school, quoted on every occasion. The Homeric epics colored the culture and thinking of the Greek world.

Lovejoy, Arthur O. *The Great Chain of Being*. Harvard, 1936. A study of the "history of ideas," tracing the idea of the fullness and connectedness of being from Greek to modern times, giving valuable insights into the problems raised by this metaphysical doctrine in Greek and Roman philosophy.

Murray, Gilbert. *Euripides and His Age*. Oxford, 2nd edition, 1946. Valuable discussion of the rise of individualism in Greek culture, with the contributions of the Sophists and of Euripides.

—— *Five Stages of Greek Religion*. Columbia, 2nd edition, 1925. A brief, readable treatment of the evolutionary development of religion among the Greeks.

Northrop, F. S. C. "The Mathematical Background and Content of Greek Philosophy," in O. H. Lee (ed.): *Philosophical Essays for Alfred North Whitehead*, Longmans, 1936. A brilliant reconstruction of the mathematical analysis underlying the natural philosophy of Democritus and Plato.

Oates, W. J., and E. G. O'Neill (eds.). *Complete Greek Drama*. 2 vols. Random, 1938. Excellent material for the student interested in another facet of the culture from which the great speculative systems of the Greeks emerged.

Rohde, Erwin. *Psyche*. Translated by W. B. Hillis; Harcourt, 1925. A comprehensive study of the notion of the soul, the religious cults, and the forms taken by the belief in immortality among the ancient Greeks.

Sarton, George. *Introduction to the History of Science*. Vol. I. Williams & Wilkins, 1927. An unusual, chronological treatment of scientific discoverers, including oriental as well as occidental scientists.

*Shorey, Paul. *Platonism Ancient and Modern*. University of California Press, 1938. Lectures on Plato's influence, by a great humanistic Platonist.

Smith, David E., and Ginsburg, J. *Numbers and Numerals*. Teachers College, 1937. Brief, simple presentation of the development of number notations in the west and their effects on techniques of computation; many examples and illustrations.

Thomas, Ivor. *Selections Illustrating the History of Greek Mathematics.* 2 vols. Vol. I, Thales to Plato. Loeb, 1939. Primary source material, with translations and useful diagrams and notes.

Windelband, Wilhelm. *History of Philosophy.* Translated by J. H. Tufts; Macmillan, 2nd edition, 1901. A standard, judicious work. The current German edition contains extensive bibliographical notes in which the student, even if he reads no German, may find additional references on any period or topic of special interest.

*Zeller, Eduard. *Philosophy of the Greeks.* Longmans, 1876. A monumental history, still outstanding. Six volumes have been translated: *The Pre-Socratic Schools; Socrates and the Socratic Schools; Plato and the Older Academy; Aristotle and the Earlier Peripatetics; Stoics, Epicureans, and Sceptics* and *The History of Eclecticism in Greek Philosophy.*

II. ADDITIONAL WORKS ON SOCRATES AND THE SOPHISTS

Aristophanes. *Clouds.* Various editions in translation. A contemporary portrait of Socrates by an Athenian reactionary who distrusted the intellectual radicals of his time. Socrates, as one of the best known Athenian "intellectuals," is chosen as target for this attack on the Sophists, with whom Aristophanes confused him. Written in a day before libel laws, this is a scurrilous, lively, amusing, and historically inaccurate caricature.

Winspear, Alban D., and Thomas Silverberg. *Who Was Socrates?* Cordon, 1939. A study of Socrates, in many ways reminiscent of Aristophanes' *Clouds.*

III. PLATO

Plato. *Works.* Translated by H. N. Fowler; Loeb, 1914, 6 vols. Greek and English on facing pages, a surprising help once the student has learned the Greek alphabet and begins to make comparisons.

—— *Dialogues.* Translated by Benjamin Jowett; Oxford, 3rd edition, 1892, 5 vols.; Random, 1937, 2 vols. Regarded as the standard translation, although it is not as sharp as some of the other editions cited below in its rendering of scientific, mathematical, and logical passages.

—— *Five Dialogues Bearing on Poetic Inspiration.* Dutton, Everyman Edition, 1910. Contains translations of the *Ion* and the *Symposium* by the English poet Shelley.

Plato. *Epinomis*. Translated by J. A. Harward; Oxford, 1928. Not included in Jowett. Translation of an appendix to the *Laws,* outlining a program of higher education for the rulers of the "second-best" Platonic state. The prominence of astronomy in this curriculum has raised some doubt that Plato wrote it. Evidence bearing on the question is examined in the translator's introduction, and the conclusion is reached that it is Plato's own work.

—— *Thirteen Epistles*. Translated by L. A. Post; Oxford, 1925. Not included in Jowett. Invaluable autobiographical material by Plato, with embellishments by later forgers. The longest letters, VII and VIII, which seem designed as "open letters" for circulation in Athens, have excellent claims to being considered genuine. Most of the others, despite a strange recent vogue of scholarly acceptance, are patently not genuine.

—— *Republic*. Edited by James Adam; Cambridge, 1897, 2 vols. Text with critical notes. Although the text is in Greek, the notes in English will clarify some of the problems met by the reader.

—— *Republic*. Translated by F. M. Cornford; Oxford, 1942. A recent translation by a noted scholar, rendering Plato's ideas in clear, accurate, colloquial English; excellent brief summaries and analyses.

—— *Republic*. Translated by B. Jowett and L. Campbell; Oxford, 3rd edition, 1908, 3 vols. Two volumes of notes and essays give material on various specific questions and problems.

—— *Timaeus* and *Critias*. Translated by Thomas Taylor; Pantheon, 1945. Taylor was an enthusiastic British nineteenth-century Neo-Platonist; many notes from Proclus and Theon, the Neo-Platonic commentators, supplement the somewhat inaccurate text of his translation. Taylor's translation was widely used by English readers of Plato in the pre-Jowett period.

—— *Selections from Plato*. Edited by Raphael Demos. Scribner, 1929. Appreciative and interesting presentation of Plato's philosophy, by a student of A. N. Whitehead.

Anderson, F. C. A. *The Argument of Plato*. Dutton, 1934. A selection of Platonic passages that bring out significant dialectical connections in Plato's thought.

*Barker, Ernest. *Political Thought of Plato and Aristotle*. Putnam, 1906. A standard and erudite treatment.

Bjorkman, Edwin A. *The Search for Atlantis*. Knopf, 1927. Plausible conjecture on the raw material of the Atlantis legend which first appears in Plato's *Timaeus* and *Critias,* interestingly but somewhat disjointedly presented.

Cherniss, Harold F. *Aristotle's Criticism of Plato and the Academy.* Vol. I. Johns Hopkins, 1944. An exhaustive, erudite collection and analysis of passages in which Aristotle speaks critically of Plato's science and logic. Criticism of Plato's mathematics is to appear as a second volume.

―――*The Riddle of the Early Academy.* University of California Press, 1945. A profound student of Aristotle is baffled by the problem of what and how Plato must have taught the students in his Academy.

Cornford, Francis M. *Plato and Parmenides.* Harcourt, 1939. A translation, with running commentary, of what has always been regarded as one of the most difficult dialogues. Probably of value only to the student with special interest and background either in mathematical logic or in the history of logic.

―――*Plato's Cosmology.* Harcourt, 1937. A translation of the *Timaeus,* with running commentary. A detailed exposition of the scientific doctrines presented in the dialogue, which Cornford believes represent Plato's own views.

―――*Plato's Theory of Knowledge.* Harcourt, 1935. Translation, with running commentary, of Plato's *Theaetetus,* in which epistemological problems are central. Probably advisable only for the student with special interest or background in such problems.

England, Edwin B. *The Laws of Plato.* Manchester University Press, 1921. Standard English commentary on Plato's *Laws.*

Fite, Warner. *The Platonic Legend.* Scribner, 1934. A vindictive, not entirely serious, challenge to admirers of Plato, in which the author sets about to prove that Plato never had any of the merits that have since been attributed to him. Unfortunately the book suggests a preposterous line of interpretation which some other later writers have, of course, followed in solemn, pedantic earnest.

Isenberg, M. *The Order of Discourses in Plato's Symposium.* Chicago, privately printed, 1942. A Ph.D. thesis that suggests a brilliant and original interpretation of this dialogue.

Merejkowski, Dmitri S. *The Secret of the West.* Translated by John Cournos; Harcourt, 1931. Begins with a passionate, if unconvincing, defense of the historical accuracy and authenticity of Plato's Atlantis legend. Cited as representative of books embodying similar defenses.

Morrow, Glenn R. *Studies in the Platonic Epistles.* University of Illinois Press, 1935. Translations of the thirteen letters attributed to Plato; illustrates the present style of Plato scholarship of accepting many hitherto disputed works as genuinely Platonic.

Pater, Walter. *Plato and Platonism.* Macmillan, 1893. A nineteenth-century study of Plato, with special emphasis on the aesthetic aspect of Plato's philosophical system.

Stewart, John A. *The Myths of Plato.* Macmillan, 1905. Translation of and commentaries on all the Platonic myths, emphasizing their religious significance; contains a brilliant introduction.

―― *Plato's Doctrine of Ideas.* Oxford, 1909. An English presentation of recent Kantian interpretation of Platonism, developed particularly by the German scholar Natorp.

Taylor, Alfred E. *Commentary on Plato's Timaeus.* Oxford, 1928. A detailed and erudite exposition of Plato's dialogue on natural science. However, the basic thesis that these doctrines are those of an earlier period than Plato's own has spectacularly failed to convince other Plato scholars.

*―― *Plato: The Man and His Work.* Dial Press, 1927. An appreciative biography and analysis of Plato's individual works by an outstanding twentieth-century Platonist.

Winspear, Alban D. *The Genesis of Plato's Thought.* Dryden, 1940. A serious extension of the line of argument suggested by Fite's *The Platonic Legend,* cited above.

Xenopohon. *Memorabilia. Symposium.* Various translations. A portrait of Socrates, different from Plato's, by a famous Athenian soldier and writer who was his personal friend. Xenophon's Socrates has seemed to many readers too like a portrait of Xenophon himself to be historically convincing.

IV. ARISTOTLE

*Aristotle. *Works.* Edited by J. A. Smith and W. D. Ross; Oxford, 1910-31, 11 vols. The standard English translation. A briefer edition is also available: *Student's Oxford Aristotle,* edited by W. D. Ross, Oxford, 1942, 6 vols.

*―― *The Basic Works of Aristotle.* Edited by Richard P. McKeon; Random, 1941. A large selection of works, in the Oxford translation, with an excellent introduction by one of the few contemporary scholars who, while not identifying Aristotle's philosophy with the medieval scholastic interpretation, is an enthusiastic Aristotelian.

*―― *Introduction to Aristotle.* Edited by Richard P. McKeon; Modern Library, 1947. A brief selection from the Oxford translation, containing the entire texts of the *Posterior Analytics, De Anima,* and the *Nicomachean Ethics.* The introductory notes are brilliant and illuminating.

*Aristotle. *The Constitution of Athens.* Various translations. Not in the briefer editions cited. A recently discovered document, one of the collection of 158 constitutions in the library of Aristotle's Lyceum, treating of Athenian constitutional law and history; provides an excellent background for the student of such works as Aristotle's *Politics* and *Plato's Republic* and *Laws.*

———— *De Melisso, Xenophane, Gorgia.* In *Works,* Smith & Ross; Vol. VI; Oxford, 1913. Not in the briefer editions cited. Interesting picture of the way in which the Sophists adapted Eleatic dialectic to defend their intellectual scepticism. The author (probably not Aristotle) muddles the arguments by his tacit assumption that they were intended to be cast in strict syllogistic form.

———— *Metaphysics.* Edited by W. D. Ross; Oxford, 1924; 2 vols. Text in Greek, but the English notes are valuable for authoritative information on specific problems.

———— *Physics.* Edited by W. D. Ross; Oxford, 1936. Greek text with introduction and notes in English.

———— *Poetics.* Dutton, Everyman Edition, 1934. Also contains Horace's *Ars Poetica,* Demetrius' *On Style,* and Longinus' *On the Sublime.*

Butcher, Samuel H. *Aristotle's Theory of Poetry and Fine Art.* Macmillan, 1895. Long a standard translation and interpretation of the *Poetics.*

Cherniss, Harold F. *Aristotle's Criticism of Pre-Socratic Philosophy.* Johns Hopkins, 1935. An attempt to disentangle the pre-Socratic philosophies from the deflections intruded by Aristotle's dialectical use of history; an exhaustive collection of relevant information.

Cooper, Lane. *The Rhetoric of Aristotle, Expanded with Examples, for Teachers of Public Speaking.* Appleton, 1932. Despite its subtitle, of considerable value to students in other fields.

———— *An Aristotelian Theory of Comedy.* Harcourt, 1922. An attempt, aided by a later Peripatetic manuscript, to reconstruct the aesthetics of comedy which occupied the lost second book of Aristotle's *Poetics.*

———— and Alfred Gudeman. *A Bibliography of the Poetics of Aristotle.* Cornell University Press, 1928.

Jaeger, Werner. *Aristotle.* Oxford, 1934. A comprehensive and meticulous attempt to place Aristotle's work in a sequence that reflects his intellectual growth and philosophical development away from Platonism to his own mature system. Like all genetic studies, this has seemed to some readers to tend to hide the unity of Aristotle's works through overemphasis on the stages of their composition. This book will give information and insight but probably will not convince admirers of McKeon's introductions and prefaces.

McKeon, Richard P. "Philosophical Bases of Art and Criticism." *Modern Philology*, XLI, 2, 3 (November, 1943, and February, 1944). An excellent article on aesthetics.

Taylor, Alfred E. *Aristotle*. Nelson, 1943. A good exposition of Aristotle, by an outstanding modern Platonist. The conviction is latent throughout that the merits of Aristotle's system are really there because the system derives from that of Plato.

———— *Aristotle on His Predecessors*. Open Court, 1907. A translation of the first book of Aristotle's *Metaphysics,* summarizing the history of earlier speculation. Taylor's notes add considerably to the value of this translation.

Aristarchus. *On the Sizes and Distances of the Sun and the Moon*. In T. L. Heath: *Aristarchus of Samos, the Ancient Copernicus;* Oxford, 1913. A primary source of major importance in the history of astronomy.

Aristoxenus. *The Harmonics*. Edited by H. S. Macran; Oxford, 1902. An attempt, by an Aristotelian, to construct an aesthetics of Greek music. Without some technical background or a willingness to study the translator's notes carefully, the student will not be much enlightened by this treatment of the various Greek musical modes.

V. HELLENISTIC PHILOSOPHY

*Clark, Gordon H. *Readings in Hellenistic Philosophy*. Crofts, 1940. A representative selection and translation of primary source materials from writings that are more frequently disparaged than read.

*Oates, Whitney J. (ed.). *The Stoic and Epicurean Philosophers*. Random, 1940. An excellent one-volume anthology of translations, including Epicurus, Epictetus, Lucretius, and Marcus Aurelius.

Plutarch. *Lives of Noble Greeks and Romans*. Various editions. Some of these well-known biographies, such as the Life of Dion, contain much pertinent biographical and historical information useful to the student of philosophy.

Boethius. *Consolations of Philosophy*. Various editions. A sixth-century blend of Christianity and Stoicism which greatly influenced medieval letters. Translated by Alfred the Great, Chaucer, and Queen Elizabeth.

Cicero. *Academia, De Finibus, De Natura Deorum, De Officiis, The Republic,* and *Tusculan Disputations*. Various translations. Cicero's works constitute a polite Latin version of Greek philosophy for Roman consumption; they exerted a profound influence upon Renaissance and early modern speculation.

Iamblichus. *The Egyptian Mysteries*. Translated by Alexander Wilder; American School of Metaphysics, 1915. Gives a picture of the strong admixture of Oriental religion with Neo-Platonic philosophy. A sample of the sort of Hellenistic speculation that historians of philosophy rather uniformly find deprecable nonsense.

———*Life of Pythagoras*. Translated by Thomas Taylor; Theosophical Press, 3rd edition, 1918. Credulity and superstition mark this biography. The collection of legends associated with Pythagoras is interesting reading but without much claim to historical veracity.

Philostratus. *Life of Apollonius of Tyana*. Translated by E. C. Conybeare; Loeb, 1912. A presentation of the Hellenistic "ideal of the sage," from which many of our contemporary notions of "the philosophical man" derive. Apollonius appears to the modern reader far more sincere and admirable than he does profound.

Proclus. *The Elements of Theology*. Translated by E. R. Dodds; Oxford, 1933. A fair sample of Neo-Platonism as it had developed by the sixth century after Christ.

Sextus Empiricus. *Against the Mathematicians*. In *Works*, translated by R. G. Bury; Loeb, 1933-36, 3 vols. One of the most complete works of systematic scepticism we have. Sextus defends his position of "no intellectual commitment" by a wholesale criticism of all contemporary dogmatisms.

Theophrastus. *Metaphysics*. Translated by W. D. Ross and F. N. Forbes; Oxford, 1929. Some questions about Aristotle's *Metaphysics* that occurred to his successor as head of the Lyceum. In general, they seem to indicate there had been a blurring of Aristotle's sharp distinctions in transmission.

Bailey, Cyril. *The Greek Atomists and Epicurus*. Oxford, 1928. A standard, scholarly treatment.

Lucretius. *De Rerum Natura*. Translated by Cyril Bailey; Oxford, 1898. An authoritative, judicious edition of Lucretius.

Fuller, B. A. G. *The Problem of Evil in Plotinus*. Cambridge, 1912. A study of one of the most difficult problems—the doctrine that evil, being essentially privative, is unreal—raised and treated in Plotinus' speculative system.

Hicks, Robert D. *Stoic and Epicurean*. Scribner, 1910. A standard source.

Longinus. *On the Sublime*. Various translations; included in the Everyman Edition of Aristotle's *Poetics*. A primary source on classical aesthetics that has had a long and widespread influence on Western tradition.

Lucian. *Sale of Lives, The Fisher*, and *Peregrine*. In *Works*, translated by H. W. and F. G. Fowler; Oxford, 1905, 4 vols. How the philosophers looked to a Hellenistic satirist who had a lively wit and no great reverence for his more speculatively inclined contemporaries.

Nicomachus. *Introduction to Arithmetic.* Translated by M. L. D'Ooge; Macmillan, 1926. A manual of Neo-Pythagorean mathematics and number theory.

VI. MEDIEVAL PHILOSOPHY

*Anselm, Saint. *Proslogion, Monologium.* Translated by S. N. Deane; Open Court, 1903. The ontological argument and the explanation of the Incarnation by one of the most lucid and brilliant of the medieval Augustinians.

Augustine, Saint. *De Magistro* and *De Libero Arbitrio* (Concerning the Teacher, and On Freedom of the Will). Various translations. Good sources for tracing the ancestry of the proofs of the existence of God used by Anselm and Descartes.

Bonaventura, Saint. *On the Reduction of the Arts to Theology.* Translated by C. G. Wallis; St. John's College, 1938. Good brief example of the Augustinian-Platonic use of analogy as a technique of analysis, by one of the leaders of the opposition to the Aristotelianism of St. Thomas Aquinas.

Bacon, Roger. *The Opus Majus.* Translated by R. B. Burke; University of Pennsylvania Press, 1928; 2 vols. A comprehensive treatise on human knowledge and education by a controversial Franciscan defender and expounder of experimental science, giving a picture of the conception and scope of experimental science in the latter part of the Augustinian tradition.

Giles of Rome. *Errors of the Philosophers.* Translated by J. Koch and J. O. Riedl; Marquette University Press, 1944. An interesting picture of the medieval philosophical scene, through the eyes of a contemporary of St. Thomas Aquinas. Giles begins with an enumeration of the theological errors in the philosophy of Aristotle, and surveys critically the problems faced by medieval philosophers in their attempts to reconcile speculation with orthodoxy.

Justin Martyr, Saint. *Apologies.* Various translations. A primary source, valuable for the insight it gives into early Christian doctrine, faith, and thought.

Occam, William of. *The Sacrament of the Altar.* Edited by T. Bruce Birch; Lutheran Literary Board, 1930. A nominalistic analysis of the sacrament as commemorative, found apt enough to have been reprinted by the Lutheran Church.

Porphyry. *Introduction to the Predicaments of Aristotle.* Various trans-lations. The explanation of Aristotle's logic which gave rise to the controversy over universals in medieval philosophy.

Thomas Aquinas, Saint. *Summa Theologica.* Translated by the Fathers of the English Dominican Province; Benziger Bros., 1912-25; 21 vols. Now the official exposition of Roman Catholic philosophy.

———— *De Ente et Essentia* (Concerning Being and Essence). Trans-lated by George G. Leckie; Appleton-Century, 1937. Aquinas' sepa-rate treatment of one of the distinctions most difficult for a medieval Aristotelian to maintain against Augustinian pressure.

Pegis, Anton C. (ed.). *Basic Writings of Thomas Aquinas.* Random, 1945, 2 vols. Selections from the monumental *Summa* and other writings.

Abelson, Paul. *The Seven Liberal Arts: Studies in Medieval Culture.* Teachers College, 1906. A study of medieval education, distin-guished by its extensive use of primary source material.

De Wulf, Maurice. *History of Medieval Philosophy.* Translated by E. C. Messenger; Longmans, 3rd edition, 1935, 1938, 2 vols. A standard history.

Gilson, Étienne. *The Philosophy of St. Thomas Aquinas.* Translated by Edward Bullogh; Herder, 1925. A standard, scholarly work.

———— *The Spirit of Medieval Philosophy.* Translated by A. H. C. Downes; Scribner, 1936. An outstanding, scholarly interpretation.

Haskins, Charles H. *Studies in the History of Medieval Science.* Har-vard, 2nd edition, 1927. Pins down some of the elusive facts basic to establishing the history of medieval science; too specialized and technical for the beginner.

Hopkins, A. J. *Alchemy, Child of Greek Philosophy.* Columbia, 1934. An attempt to trace the real origins of medieval preoccupation with transmutation of metals. The author believes that reports of a lost Egyptian art of metal dyeing were the source of much of the stimu-lation of alchemical activity.

Kozminski, Isidore. *Numbers, Their Meaning and Magic.* Putnam, 1927. A specimen of the numerology that was a frequent Hellenistic and medieval diversion.

McKeon, Richard P. (ed.). *Selections from Medieval Philosophers.* Scrib-ner, 1929, 2 vols. Crucial passages illustrating the development of the problem of knowledge. A standard book of primary source ma-terial for the beginning student; brief but excellent introductory notes.

Maritain, Jacques, *Art and Scholasticism.* Translated by J. F. Scanlan; Scribner, 1930. A scholastic interpretation of aesthetics.

Moody, Ernest A. *The Logic of William of Ockham*. Sheed, 1936. A scholarly study, much less specialized than the title indicates; full of valuable insights into medieval Aristotelianism.

Morley, Henry (ed.). *Ideal Commonwealths*. Various editions. Contains translations of More's *Utopia*, Bacon's *The New Atlantis*, Harrington's *Oceana*, and Campanella's *The City of the Sun*.

Thorndike, Lynn. *A History of Magic and Experimental Science*. Columbia, 1934-43, 6 vols. Translations of documents from the Roman through the medieval period dealing with the occult sciences, from which in these times experimental science was indistinguishable.

Weinberg, Julius R. *Nicholas of Autrecourt, A Study in 14th Century Thought*. Princeton, 1948. An account of the life and writings of a noted natural scientist.

VII. MODERN PHILOSOPHY

*Cassirer, Ernst. *An Essay on Man*. Yale, 1944. Philosophy considered both as an expression and as a study of human nature; an excellent cross section of modern philosophy and its problems.

*—— *Substance and Function*. Open Court, 1923. A brilliant, historical orientation of modern science and philosophy, for the advanced student.

*Collingwood, R. G. *Speculum Mentis, or The Map of Knowledge*. Oxford, 1924. Considers art, religion, science, and history in their relation to philosophy. The point of view is close to that of Italian idealism, influenced by Vico and Croce.

Cunningham, Gustavus W. *Idealistic Argument in Recent British and American Philosophy*. Appleton-Century, 1933. An excellent supplement to Royce.

*Gilson, Étienne. *The Spirit of Medieval Philosophy*. Translated by A. H. C. Downes; Scribner, 1936.

*—— *The Unity of Philosophical Experience*. Scribner, 1937. In this and the book above, Gilson sketches the development of western thought from the time of St. Augustine to the nineteenth century. The evaluation is scholastic and the modern period is interpreted in an unsympathetic manner, although brilliantly and with great subtlety; nonetheless, very stimulating and enlightening.

Hart, Ivor B. *Makers of Science: Mathematics, Physics, Astronomy*. Oxford, 1923. A compact treatment of the history of science.

Hegel, G. W. F. *Lectures on the History of Philosophy*. Translated by E. S. Haldane and O. H. Simson; Kegan Paul, 1892-96; 3 vols. Although itself a historical item, it will repay study.

*Hoeffding, Harald. *History of Modern Philosophy*. Macmillan, 1924. Somewhat less thorough than Windelband and Ueberweg, but of real value to the ambitious beginner.

James, William. *Some Problems of Philosophy*. Longmans, 1940. An important statement of the revolt against absolutism.

Joad, C. E. M. *Introduction to Modern Philosophy*. Oxford, 1924. Excellent and compact treatment of early twentieth-century philosophy; discusses Bergson, James, Russell, and the Italian idealists.

*Langer, Susanne K. *Philosophy in a New Key: A Study in the Symbolism of Reason, Rite and Art*. Harvard, 1942. Philosophy and the theory of knowledge approached through the study of symbolism and the theory of meaning.

Levy-Bruhl, Lucien. *History of Modern Philosophy in France*. Open Court, 1899. A classical study.

*Randall, J. H., Jr. *The Making of the Modern Mind*. Houghton, 1926. Valuable as background; philosophical ideas appear in a broad, historical context of political, economic, scientific, religious, and literary developments. The point of view is that of modern liberalism.

*Royce, Josiah. *Lectures on Modern Idealism*. Yale, 1919.

*——— *The Spirit of Modern Philosophy*. Houghton, 1896. These readable and scholarly lectures present the developments of modern philosophy, interpreted by a post-Hegelian idealist.

Ruggiero, Guido. *Modern Philosophy*. Macmillan, 1921. Contains a fine treatment of post-Hegelian idealism, with emphasis on developments in Italy.

Runes, Dagobert. *Twentieth Century Philosophy*. Philosophical Library, 1943. A very useful collection of essays on recent philosophy, with major trends well represented.

*Schneider, Herbert W. *History of American Philosophy*. Columbia, 1946. A thorough study, rich in bibliography.

Sorley, Wm. R. *History of English Philosophy*. Cambridge, 1937. Especially thorough and sympathetic treatment of Locke.

Stallknecht, Newton P. *Studies in the Philosophy of Creation, with Especial Reference to Bergson and Whitehead*. Princeton, 1934. The idea of creation as an important theme in post-Kantian philosophy; besides Bergson and Whitehead, mention is also made of Schelling, Ravaisson, Boutroux, James, Alexander, Croce, and Gentile.

*Townsend, Harvey G. *Philosophical Ideas in the United States*. American Book, 1934. An admirable survey containing sympathetic studies of the major figures from colonial times.

Ueberweg, Friedrich. *History of Philosophy*. Translated by G. S. Morris, Scribner, 1903, 2 vols. Biographical, giving attention to each thinker in turn and considering his contribution as a whole.

Wahl, Jean André. *The Philosopher's Way*. Oxford, 1948. A penetrating study of certain persistent themes in ancient and modern philosophy; valuable for the advanced student.

——— *Pluralistic Philosophies of England and America*. Open Court, 1925. Historical treatment of this movement.

*Whitehead, Alfred North. *Religion in the Making*. Macmillan, 1926. The simplest available statement of Whitehead's position.

*——— *Science and the Modern World*. Macmillan, 1925. An outstanding interpretation of the philosophical background of modern science, historically presented; includes Whitehead's own philosophical position in outline.

Wild, John D. *Introduction to Realistic Philosophy*. Harper, 1948. Urges a return to Aristotelian concepts in facing problems of modern philosophy.

Windelband, Wilhelm. *History of Philosophy*. Translated by J. H. Tufts; Macmillan, 2nd edition, 1901. A study of the development of thought by tracing the growth of concepts from thinker to thinker.

Wolf, Abraham. *A History of Science, Technology and Philosophy in the Sixteenth and Seventeenth Centuries*. Macmillan, 1935. Very valuable for relation of philosophy to natural science and mathematics.

VIII. MODERN ETHICS

Broad, Charles D. *Five Types of Ethical Theory*. Harcourt, 1930. Difficult but rewarding.

Field, G. C. *Moral Theory, An Introduction to Ethics*. Methuen, 1932. A fine study in ethical contrasts: Aristotle, Kant, and Mill.

Grene, Marjorie. *Dreadful Freedom, A Critique of Existentialism*. University of Chicago Press, 1948. A provocative treatment.

Paton, Herbert J. *The Categorical Imperative, A Study of Kant's Moral Philosophy*. Hutchinson, 1947. For advanced students.

Rogers, Arthur K. *Morals in Review*. Macmillan, 1927. A series of critical essays on the work of the greater moralists.

Stephen, Leslie. *The English Utilitarians*. Various editions. A classical study.

Tsanoff, Radoslav A. *The Moral Ideals of Our Civilization*. Dutton, 1942. Comprehensive survey of the history of ethics, with emphasis on the modern period; very readable.

Wahl, Jean André. *A Short History of Existentialism.* Philosophical Library, 1949. A helpful orientation.

IX. DETAILED STUDIES OF MODERN PHILOSOPHERS

The following commentaries and studies of individual thinkers should be consulted by anyone especially interested in the philosophers listed.

Descartes

Fischer, Kuno. *Descartes and His School.* Translated by Noah Porter; Scribner, 1887.

Haldane, E. S. *Descartes, His Life and Times.* Murray, 1905.

Smith, Norman Kemp. *Studies in the Cartesian Philosophy.* Macmillan, 1902.

Spinoza

Alexander, Samuel. *Spinoza and Time.* G. Allen & Unwin, 1921.

Bidney, David. *The Psychology and Ethics of Spinoza.* Yale, 1940.

Joachim, Harold H. *A Study in the Ethics of Spinoza.* Oxford, 1901.

McKeon, Richard P. *The Philosophy of Spinoza.* Longmans, 1928.

Pollock, Sir Frederick. *Spinoza, His Life and Philosophy.* Duckworth, 1935.

Wolfson, Harry A. *The Philosophy of Spinoza.* Harvard, 1934.

Leibniz

Leibniz, G. W. *The Monadology and Other Philosophical Writings.* Translated by Robert Latta; Oxford, 1898. Contains fine notes and analyses.

Carr, Herbert W. *Leibniz.* Little, Brown, 1929.

Russell, Bertrand. *A Critical Exposition of the Philosophy of Leibniz.* Macmillan, 1937.

Locke

Aaron, R. I. *John Locke.* Oxford, 1937.

Gibson, James. *Locke's Theory of Knowledge and Its Historical Relations.* Cambridge, 1917.

Fraser, A. C. *Locke.* Blackwood, 1890.

Morris, Charles R. *Locke, Berkeley, and Hume.* Oxford, 1931.

Berkeley

Luce, Arthur A. *Berkeley and Malebranche, A Study in the Origins of Berkeley's Thought.* Oxford, 1934.

Wild, John D. *George Berkeley, A Study of His Life and Philosophy.* Harvard, 1936.

Hume

Hendel, C. W. *Studies in the Philosophy of David Hume.* Princeton, 1925.

Laird, John. *Hume's Philosophy of Human Nature.* Dutton, 1932.

Smith, Norman Kemp. *The Philosophy of David Hume.* Macmillan, 1941.

Kant

Caird, Edward. *Critical Account of the Philosophy of Kant.* Macmillan, 1877.

Ewing, Alfred C. *A Short Commentary on Kant's Critique of Pure Reason.* Methuen, 1938.

Lindsay, A. D. *Kant.* Peter Smith, 1934.

Paton, Herbert J. *Kant's Metaphysic of Experience.* Macmillan, 1936, 2 vols. For the advanced student.

Smith, Norman Kemp. *A Commentary on Kant's Critique of Pure Reason.* Macmillan, 2nd edition, 1929. For the advanced student.

Hegel

Caird, Edward. *Hegel.* Blackwood, 1896.

Stace, Walter T. *The Philosophy of Hegel.* Macmillan, 1924.

SUGGESTED TRANSLATIONS

Descartes

Descartes. *Discourse on Method.* Translated by John Veitch. Open Court, 1926.

—— *Philosophical Works.* Translated by E. S. Haldane and G. R. T. Ross; Cambridge, 1911-12, 2 vols.

Spinoza

Spinoza. *Ethics.* Translated by W. H. White. Various editions.

—— *Philosophy of Spinoza.* Translated by R. H. M. Elwes; Tudor, 1933.

—— *Short Treatise on God, Man and Human Welfare.* Translated by L. G. Robinson; Open Court, 1909.

—— *The Correspondence of Spinoza.* Translated by A. Wolf; MacVeagh, 1927.

Leibniz

Leibniz. *The Monadology and Other Philosophical Writings*. Translated by Robert Latta; Oxford, 1898.

—— *New Essays Concerning Human Understanding*. Translated by A. G. Langley; Open Court, 1916.

—— *Discourse on Metaphysics, Monadology, and Correspondence with Arnauld*. Translated by G. R. Montgomery; Open Court, 1902.

Kant

Kant. *Critique of Aesthetic Judgment*. Translated by J. C. Meredith; Oxford, 1911.

—— *Critique of Judgment*. Translated by J. H. Bernard; Macmillan, 2nd edition, 1914.

—— *Critique of Practical Reason*. Translated by L. W. Beck; University of Chicago Press, 1949.

—— *Critique of Pure Reason*. Translated by N. K. Smith; Macmillan, 1929. Also translated by Max Müller; Macmillan, 1881.

—— *Metaphysic of Ethics*. Translated by T. K. Abbott; Longmans, 3rd edition, 1901.

—— *Selections from the Philosophy of Kant*. Translated by John Watson; Macmillan, 1901.

Hegel

Hegel. *Lectures on the Philosophy of History*. Translated by J. Sibree; G. Bell, 1902.

—— *Logic, from the Encyclopaedia of the Philosophical Sciences*. Translated by W. Wallace; Oxford, 1892.

—— *Science of Logic*. Translated by W. H. Johnston and L. G. Struthers; Macmillan, 1929, 2 vols.

X. LOGIC AND MATHEMATICS

Ayer, A. J. *Language, Truth, and Logic*. Oxford, 1936. Lucid introduction to the theory of logical positivism.

Black, Max. *The Nature of Mathematics*. Harcourt, 1934. A modern Zeno scrutinizes the progress of recent speculators who have been trying to define the nature of the continuum.

Bloomfield, Leonard. *Language*. Holt, 1946. Clear exposition of the basic concepts of a science that has much to contribute to contemporary logic and semantics.

Buchanan, Scott. *Symbolic Distance in Relation to Analogy and Fiction.* Routledge, 1932. A short, suggestive work, in which a semantics and logic of matrices is suggested as an alternative to the formal apparatus of classes.

——— "Introduction to the *De Modis Significandi* of Thomas of Erfurt," In Otis H. Lee (ed.): *Philosophical Essays for Alfred North Whitehead;* Longmans, 1936. A suggestive treatment of the medieval realists' conception and the development of "speculative grammar."

*Carnap, Rudolf. *Foundations of Logic and Mathematics.* Chicago, 1939. Unusually clear, brief, and accurate exposition of the structure of modern mathematical logic.

——— *Meaning and Necessity, A Study of Semantics and Modal Logic.* Chicago, 1947. Modal symbolic logic.

——— *Philosophy and Logical Syntax.* Routledge, 1935. A clear, brief exposition of the "logical positivist" position. The position here defended is no longer advocated by Carnap himself with the same rigor in his later work.

Cooley, J. C. *A Primer of Formal Logic.* Macmillan, 1942.

Jevons, W. S. *Logic.* Macmillan, 1889. Long the standard text for courses in introductory formal logic; a manual for handling the apparatus of term, proposition, and syllogism.

Latta, Robert, and Alexander MacBeath. *Elements of Logic.* Macmillan, 1929. A fine modern exposition of the "Aristotelian" syllogistic logic.

Maritain, Jacques. *Introduction to Logic.* Sheed, 1937. A refurbishing of the medieval version of Aristotle's logic. The treatment of impositions, intentions, and suppositions shows how the medieval logicians went about making their logics more precise and flexible.

*Morris, Charles W. *Foundations of the Theory of Signs.* Chicago, 1938. Clear and interesting discussion of the basic problems and dimensions of modern semantics.

Quine, W. V. "Whitehead and Modern Logic," in Otis H. Lee (ed.): *Philosophical Essays for Alfred North Whitehead;* Longmans, 1936. Contains a summary and some cogent criticism of the uses of variables in the three volumes of *Principia Mathematica;* a good way of getting a survey of the contents of the relatively formidable, but important, volumes II and III of the *Principia.*

Whitehead, Alfred North. "Mathematics and the Good," in Otis H. Lee (ed.): *Philosophical Essays for Alfred North Whitehead.* Longmans, 1936. Among its other suggestive and speculative features, this paper contains a sharp and brilliant criticism of the "theory of types."

Whitehead and Bertrand Russell. *Principia Mathematica.* Cambridge, 1910-13, 3 vols. The classic statement of the modern analytic interpretation of mathematics. The elementary student will probably find the presentation too compact and rigorous; however, the earlier sections are still a standard presentation of the calculus of classes and of propositions, and reward the careful study of even the beginner.

*Young, J. W. *Lectures on the Fundamental Concepts of Algebra and Geometry.* Macmillan, 1911. Fine material for the student interested in foundations of mathematics or mathematical logic; elementary presentation.

XI. HISTORICAL FICTION

Beauvoir, Simone de. *The Blood of Others.* Knopf, 1948.

Deutsch, Babette. *The Mask of Silenus, A Novel about Socrates.* Simon & Schuster, 1933.

Fielding, Henry. *Tom Jones.* Various editions.

France, Anatole. *At the Sign of the Reine Pedauque.* Various editions.

———*Thaïs.* Various editions.

Kingsley, Charles. *Hypatia.* Various editions.

Merejkowski, Dmitri. *The Death of the Gods.* Modern Library, 1929.

——— *The Romance of Leonardo da Vinci.* Modern Library, 1928.

Mitchison, Naomi. *Cloud-Cuckoo Land.* Harcourt, 1926.

Pater, Walter. *Marius the Epicurean.* Various editions.

——— *Gaston de la Tour.* Various editions.

Petronius Arbiter. *Satyricon.* Various editions.

Radin, Max. *Epicurus, My Master.* University of North Carolina Press, 1949.

Rydberg, Viktor. *The Last Athenian.* T. B. Peterson. Philadelphia, 1869.

Santayana, George. *The Last Puritan.* Scribner, 1936.

Sartre, Jean-Paul. *Nausea.* New Directions, 1949.

——— *No Exit* and *The Flies.* Knopf, 1947.

Waddell, Helen. *Peter Abelard.* Holt, 1933.

Wilder, Thornton. *The Ides of March.* Harper, 1948.

Index of Names and Titles

531

Index of Topics

535